STUDENTS
IN REVOLT

THE DAEDALUS LIBRARY

Each of these volumes is available as a Beacon Paperback.

STUDENTS
IN REVOLT

EDITED BY SEYMOUR MARTIN LIPSET
AND PHILIP G. ALTBACH

BEACON PRESS   BOSTON

First published as a Beacon Paperback in 1970 by arrangement
with Houghton Mifflin Company

Published simultaneously in Canada by Saunders of Toronto, Ltd.

Beacon Press books are published under the auspices of the Unitarian
Universalist Association

International Standard Book Number: 0–8070–3185–2

With the exception of "The Possible Effects of
Student Activism on International Politics" by
Seymour Martin Lipset, "Dreams of Plenitude,
Nightmares of Scarcity" by Edward Shils, "The
Revolution Betrayed: The French Student Revolt of
May–June 1968" by A. Belden Fields, "The
Positive Marginality: Notes on Italian Students in
Periods of Political Mobilization" by Guido
Martinotti, and "Vanguard of Revolt: Students
and Politics in Central Europe, 1815–1848" by
Edith Altbach, which are published here for the
first time, the essays in the book appeared
in the Winter 1968 issue of *Dædalus*, the
Journal of the American Academy of Arts
and Sciences.

Printed in the United States of America

SEYMOUR MARTIN LIPSET
AND PHILIP ALTBACH

Foreword

The Universities have been to this nation, as the wooden horse was to the Trojans . . . . I despair of any lasting peace among ourselves, till the Universities here shall bend and direct their studies to the settling of it, that is, to the teaching of absolute obedience to the laws of the King . . . .

The core of the rebellion, as you have seen by this, and read of other rebellions, are the Universities; which nevertheless are not to be cast away, but to be better disciplined.

Thus wrote Thomas Hobbes of Oxford in his book *Behemoth: The History of the Causes of the Civil Wars, and of the counsels and artifices by which they were carried on from the year 1640 to the year 1660.* But even this description of the unsettling role of the universities is far from the beginning. Students in Bologna and Paris during the Middle Ages were a frequent source of tension. Riots were a common phenomenon in many university communities. And when student activities took on an ideological character, descriptions of student behavior and orientations have a contemporary ring. Martin Luther found his most immediate and intense support from the students of Wittenberg and other German universities. A description of their behavior and attitudes sounds almost contemporary both in their dedication to absolute ends and their anti-intellectualism.

[Luther] was forced to hold the students in check to prevent them from going too far in their protests against Pope and Emperor. Melanchthon also fought an inclination to primitivism among students. Some of them carried their opposition to Aristotle and scholasticism to the point of rejecting all scholarship, and advocated the innocent simplicity of the Apostles.[1]

[1] Herbert Moller, "Youth as a Force in the Modern World," *Comparative Studies in Society and History,* Vol. 10 (April, 1968), p. 238.

Moving forward in history to the Parisian left bank of the nineteenth century, we find descriptions of youthful and student protesters which could easily be mistaken for contemporary writings.

The French Revolution, for example, had, as one of its aftermaths, the appearance of youthful gangs and coteries dedicated to the cultivation of special passions and adventures. [T]he *Bousingots* [one translation is the "Hell-raisers"] of the Restoration Period were apparently recruited from among middle-class discontents and held radical-sounding, erratic political ideas which somehow were never followed by practical action. According to Balzac they could be recognized by their off-center cravats, greasy coats, long beards, and dirty finger nails. The Bohemians of the 1830's and 1840's were young, actually and ideologically; they claimed that youth itself was the collective expression of genius. It is exaggerating very little to say that Bohemians hoped to be seen as a band of intellectual raiders and freebooters, who routed convention everywhere and kept all contented souls in a state of dazzled alarm . . . . In all accounts of the Bohemia of the Orleanist years, the first impressions have always to do with its ingenious techniques of social outrage. When Thackeray first came on the Paris Bohemia, he was astonished enough to make a careful record of their appearance — their ringlets, straight locks, toupees, English, Greek and Spanish nets, and the variety of their beards and jackets.[2]

The unwillingness of student protesters to subject themselves to the discipline of adult groups, even to the leaders of a revolution, was noted by Friedrich Engels, Marx's closest collaborator, in his description of their activities in the Revolution of 1848 in Vienna.

[T]he students, about 4000 strong, well-armed, and far better disciplined than the national guard, formed the nucleus, the real strength, of the revolutionary force, and were noways willing to act as a mere instrument in the hands of the Committee of Safety [the governing organ of the revolution]. Though they recognized it, and were even its most enthusiastic supporters, they yet formed a sort of independent and rather turbulent body, deliberating for themselves in the "Aula" . . . preventing, by constant agitation, things from settling down to the old everyday tranquility, and very often forcing their resolutions upon the Committee of Safety.[3]

Two decades later, Engels in a letter to Marx bemoaned the possibility that Russia's revolutionary students might emigrate to Western Europe and corrupt the proletarian movement there.

[2] César Graña, *Modernity and Its Discontents* (New York, 1964), pp. 73-74.

[3] Henry M. Christman (ed.), *The American Journalism of Marx and Engels* (New York, 1966), p. 40.

How awful for the world . . . that there are 40,000 revolutionary students in Russia. . . . If there is anything which might ruin the Western European movement, then it would have been this import of 40,000 more or less educated, ambitious hungry Russian nihilists: all of them officer candidates without an army.[4]

Lenin, who himself first joined the revolutionary movement while a university student, complained of the infantile leftism of the post-World War I generation of pro-Communist youth in Europe. He was disturbed by their violating conventional customs and morality as a means of expressing their moral antagonism to the system. Lenin pointed out to them that even revolutionary politics required compromises and retreats. For Marxists, from Marx and Engels to Lenin and Trotsky, revolutionary dedication by youth required long hours of work and study. Each of them, in turn, was to condemn as irresponsible the expressive politics and personal style of students newly converted to the revolution. The desire of youth to make the revolution at once, without consideration of realistic possibilities, was seen by them as "putschism" or "left-wing adventurism," behavior which they related to the "bourgeois" origins and position of the students, as well as to their youth. Marx, Engels, and Trotsky denounced various groups of left-wing youth for their anti-intellectual attitudes and behavior — that is, an unwillingness to acknowledge that a commitment to Marxism or the revolution did not provide its devotees with an easy understanding of any given society or situation. Rather, the Marxist "fathers" found themselves forced to tell their youthful followers that such understanding required serious and prolonged scholarship. Engels reminded them that Marx had spent twenty years in the British Museum doing research for *Das Kapital.*

Clearly, much of what we see today in the expressive style of the radical student activist movements of the world is not new. There are components inherent in the situation of youth and students that have shown up in similar fashion through the ages. Unfortunately, as yet we have little in the way of detailed scholarly knowledge about these earlier periods. No one can argue that the present wave of student activism is simply a reemergence of traditional patterns of student protest against the adult world. In fact, though often similar in style and tactics, the contemporary student movements vary considerably in goals and functions.

[4] Engels to Marx, April 25, 1870, as quoted in Shlomo Avineri, "Feuer on Marx and the Intellectuals," *Survey,* No. 62 (January, 1967), p. 154.

But if student activism has ancient roots, the study of such behavior is relatively recent. Much of the significant literature on the subject is a product of contemporary events. This volume is an outgrowth of an effort to coordinate comparative studies of student politics in many countries. We first became interested in the subject as part of our concern with the processes of modernization and political development in the Third World. It seemed evident that student-based movements were playing a decisive role in many countries, and that the university was a major source of political leadership. Since our research interests were first aroused in the subject in the early 1960's, the phenomenon has reemerged in most of the developed world as well.

In March, 1967, we conducted a conference dealing with analyses of "Students and Politics," which was held at the University of Puerto Rico in San Juan. Many of the papers presented at that conference were subsequently published in *Dædalus* (Winter 1968). We then took the opportunity presented by the decision to publish the *Dædalus* issue in book form to have our various collaborators rewrite their original papers, as well as to secure a number of new contributions that had not appeared in the original issue of *Dædalus*. The results of this attempt to investigate the causes and consequences of varying types of student activism around the world are included in this volume. Unfortunately, reasons of space forced us to eliminate a number of articles that we had hoped to publish here. We confidently expect that the next few years will witness the production of a veritable library dealing with various countries and events. It is in the hopes of furthering more comprehensive research, much of which should be historical, that we submit this book.

Our obligations for assistance on the comparative study of students are many. The project itself is jointly sponsored by the Brookings Institution under a grant from the Hazen Foundation and the Center for International Affairs of Harvard University with the Ford Foundation funds. Funds allocated to Lipset for studies in political and social development by the Carnegie Corporation have helped support many of these researches. The San Juan Conference was made possible through financial assistance from the U.S. Office of Education, the University of Puerto Rico, the Inter-University Study of Labor Problems in Economic Development (with funds made available by the Ford Foundation and the Carnegie Corporation), and the Instituto Latinoamericano de Relaciones Internacionales.

A number of individuals have contributed to the conference and the book, among them President Jaime Benitez of the University of Puerto Rico and Mrs. Marina Finkelstein of the Center for International Affairs. Mrs. Meena Vohra, also of the Center, helped greatly in preparing the book for publication.

This book is one of a number of publications of the Comparative Students and Universities Project. Others include

Arthur Leibman, *The Children of Their Fathers: The Politics of Puerto Rican Students* (Austin, Texas, 1969).

S. M. Lipset and Aldo Solari (eds.), *Elites in Latin America* (New York, 1967);

S. M. Lipset (ed.), *Student Politics* (New York, 1967);

Philip Altbach, *Students and Politics in Bombay* (Bombay, 1968);

Philip Altbach, *A Select Bibliography on Students, Politics, and Higher Education* (Cambridge, 1967);

Philip Altbach, *Student Politics and Higher Education in the U.S.: A Select Bibliography* (St. Louis, 1968);

Philip Altbach (ed.), *Turmoil and Transition: Higher Education and Student Politics in India* (New York, 1969).

SEYMOUR MARTIN LIPSET
PHILIP ALTBACH

Cambridge, Massachusetts
Madison, Wisconsin

CONTENTS

V. Historical Perspectives

VI. Future Possibilities

SEYMOUR MARTIN LIPSET

Introduction: Students and Politics in Comparative Perspective

TEN YEARS AGO, hardly anyone devoted himself to research on students and politics. Today hundreds of scholars are analyzing student political movements, behavior, and attitudes. It is evident that student activism and the importance of students in politics long antedates the current interest. Students were a key element in the Revolutions of 1848 in Germany and Austria, and student activism stimulated the "Professors' Parliament," which almost succeeded in toppling several monarchs. In Czarist Russia, students spearheaded various revolutionary movements, and the university campus was a major center of revolutionary activity. In the East European countries, where education was limited to a small proportion of the population, students were often the carriers of modern ideas of liberty, socialism, industrialization, and equality of opportunity.

The important role of students in the movements for national independence in the developing areas also goes back a half century or more. In Imperial China, students were crucial to the Imperial effort at modernization, but at the same time spread republican and radical ideas throughout the society. Students helped overthrow the dynasty in 1911, and were thereafter one of the elements continually pushing China toward modernization and radical ideologies. In other Asian and African countries, students were often a central element in anticolonial struggles. Particularly important were the "returned students" — those individuals who had lived and studied abroad, mostly in Europe, and returned home with ideas of modernization and Marxism, socialism and struggle. International student meetings were held as early as the 1920's, and such men as Nehru of India and Hatta of Indonesia were profoundly influenced by these student organizations and movements.

Scholars in the past paid relatively little attention to the rather major role students played in reform and radical movements, in part because student movements are quite transitory in character and have left fewer records than adult organizations. Moreover, to stress the role of youth and students, rather than that of the social classes or religion, seemed in a sense to underemphasize the seriousness and significance of the happenings and to turn them into "children's crusades."

Then, too, from the Marxist perspective, intellectuals and students are not significant independent social forces. Rather, they have been viewed as vacillating, unreliable, *"petit-bourgeois* elements" who are inclined to shift with the prevailing ideological winds. Although students have played a rather major role in supporting various Communist movements at different times, the Party has tended to deprecate their role.

The greater willingness to recognize the political role of students stems, in part, from the awareness by many on the left that other social forces are not always available for support. The organized workers of the developed countries of Europe and America, for example, have become a conservative force, as C. Wright Mills pointed out. Trade unions and labor-based parties have been integrated into an institutional system of representation and collective bargaining. As such, they are not concerned with policies and programs that may upset the political pattern. The orthodox (pro-Russian) Communist Parties in many countries have also become part of the regular system of representation and no longer advocate use of extralegal and extraparliamentary tactics. In Latin America, they oppose the guerrilla tactics fostered by Castroites and Maoists.

Mills saw in the intellectuals and students a major potential mass base for new revolutionary movements. They have *remained* a source of new radical leadership and mass support, while other elements of society have not. Thus, more attention is being focused on the American student movement at present than occurred during the 1930's, even though the movement was larger in both absolute and proportionate terms in the thirties. But beyond the emergence of an intellectual concern with the politics of students, well-publicized events of the past decade have illustrated the significance of student politics. Student demonstrations and movements played a considerable role in the overthrow of Perón in Argentina in 1955; the downfall of Pérez Jiménez in Venezuela in 1958; the successful resistance to Diem in Vietnam in 1963; the massive riots against the

Japan-U.S. Security Treaty in Japan in 1960 which forced the resignation of the Kishi government; the anti-Sukarno movement in Indonesia in 1966; the downfall of Ayub Khan in Pakistan in 1969; the October demonstrations for greater freedom in Poland in 1956; the 1956 Hungarian Revolution; and the massive movement for liberalization in Czechoslovakia in 1968. It is important to note, however, that although students may be catalysts for political action, they can seldom bring a revolutionary movement to fruition. In Korea, students began the movement that succeeded in toppling the Rhee government in 1960, but they replied on popular pressure and the army to make their movement successful.

The university campus is an ideal place in which to be a radical activist. Many universities have tens of thousands of students concentrated in a small area. It takes only a small percentage of these massive student bodies to make a large demonstration. Hence, campus-based radicals may have great influence even though, as Herbert Marcuse has pointed out recently, the majority of the students in all countries are politically quiescent and moderate in their views. Opinion data for various countries assembled by Glaucio Soares indicate that the left-wing students are in a minority, often very small, even in countries where leftist demonstrations have made international headlines. Even though university campuses provide a significant proportion of the future radical leadership, as well as the mass base for antigovernment demonstrations, most students are not involved in such activities. In most countries, the vast majority of students are apolitical and tend to endorse the moderate or even conservative parties. According to national surveys of American student opinion taken by the Harris Poll in 1965 and the Gallup Poll in 1968, approximately one fifth of the students have participated in civil rights or political activities (17 per cent in 1964–65, the year of the Berkeley revolt, and 20 per cent in 1967–68, the year of the McCarthy and Kennedy campaigns). The radical activist groups generally have tiny memberships. Students for a Democratic Society (SDS) claims a total membership of about 30,000, out of a national student body of 7 million, of which about 6,000 pay national dues. A Harris Poll of American students taken in the spring of 1968 estimated that there are about 100,000 radical activists, or somewhere between 1 and 2 per cent of the college population. A Gallup survey also conducted in the spring of 1968 reported that 7 per cent of male students indicate that they will refuse to go, if drafted.

The Backgrounds of the Activists

Influences derivative from university experiences are, of course, not the sole or even primary determinants of student political beliefs. Family perspectives often influence students' orientations. The high correlation reported between the political stance of students and that of their parents would imply that the children of poorer families should be more leftist than those of the more well-to-do, since socio-economic class and political choice are generally related in this way. Although research in various countries tends to validate the generalization, it does not, for a number of reasons, apply this simply to student populations. Students from relatively poor families tend to come from that minority within the lower strata which is strongly oriented toward upward mobility and the values of the privileged. Hence, their parents are often among the more politically conservative of their class. Moreover, upwardly mobile students who represent the first generation of their family attending university tend to be vocationally oriented. They are more likely to be found in fields that lead to professions. This strong concentration on careerist professional objectives, plus the need to have a job during the school term, results in these students being less available for political or other extra-curricular activities than those from more privileged backgrounds.

In Scandinavia, a student of working-class origins is likely to shift from a Social Democratic family orientation to a conservative one. There is less probability that a student from a conservative middle-class background will shift to left-wing parties. Recent American data suggest the reverse finding. Attendance at university is stronger in pressing well-to-do students to a position to the left of their parents, than in moving those from less-privileged Democratic and liberal families to the right. Such findings should be subjected to more precise specification as to type of school attended and academic discipline studied. The greater shift to liberalism among the more well-to-do in the United States may reflect the high proportion attending the better universities, which characteristically have the most creative, intellectually oriented, and liberal faculties. Conservative students on such campuses experience a political atmosphere hostile to their family political beliefs.

Well-to-do parents are also among the better educated. Particularly this is so among professionals. Increased education is associated in most underdeveloped countries with approval of modern, as contrasted with traditional, values and in the developed societies with belief in "noneconomic liberalism" — support for civil liberties for unpopular minorities, internationalism, and so forth. These orientations are generally fostered by the more liberal or leftist campus groups. Matters related to economic class are less salient sources of campus politics than noneconomic ones. Students in the United States, for example, are much more concerned with civil rights for Negroes or political rights on campus and in the larger society, than with the power of trade unions or the consequences of different systems of taxation on economic growth.

Many of those who experience a tension between the political atmosphere of the university and their family tradition escape the choice by abstaining from politics, by accepting the doctrine that school and politics do not mix. Most students from conservative backgrounds remain in this tradition. In countries where there is a visible difference in the dominant political orientation of universities, continuity in family political orientations may be facilitated by the process of conscious selection of universities because of their political reputations. In Latin America, conservative privileged families will often send their children to schools with a conservative or apolitical reputation, such as the Catholic or other private universities. Unfortunately, there is little reliable information on this subject.

American research findings suggest that there is congruence between the characteristic political orientation of different disciplines and the political beliefs of entering students who plan to major in them. Conservatives are more likely to study engineering or business, and liberals the humanities or social sciences. Such selection reflects the extent to which varying political orientations influence students to opt for different career goals. Leftists, particularly those from well-to-do and well-educated families, are inclined to favor academic fields concerned with social and political issues or careers in the arts, social work, scholarship, and public service.

Academic ecology, the social environment in which a student happens to find himself by virtue of his choice of university or academic field, tends to be more important than his social class background in affecting his opinions. The faculty within which students are enrolled seems more predictive of their political stance than class origins. In various Latin American countries, the differences among universities in their modal political choice are greater than the social-class variation within them. Nevertheless, those who bring strong traditionalist values with them to the university are more likely to remain conservative and apolitical than others. This may be seen most strongly in the role of religion. In the Catholic countries of Latin America and Europe, practicing Catholic students are much more conservative than nonbelievers. Thus, reported differences in family religious practices are highly predictive in this respect. Similar findings have been reported for India. In the United States, Catholics and evangelical Protestants are also among the most conservative groups in the university.

Minority-majority social status also seems more important than economic class background in affecting student propensity for action. In Germany and Austria, for example, students from minority groups (Jews and Slavs) and from the lower-middle class spearheaded the Revolution of 1848. Students from minority ethnic backgrounds were also active in the pre-revolutionary Russian student movement as well. Today in the United States, Britain, and Argentina, Jews contribute heavily to the membership and support of activist left groups.

In many of the developing countries and in nations like Belgium and Canada, there are often deep cleavages that prevent a sense of community among the students. Religious divisions, regional, linguistic, caste, racial, and tribal differences often severely inhibit the growth of national student movements devoted to societal objectives, or even to university reform. In a number of countries, divergent student groupings based on such variations are locked in conflict. In India, students have taken to the streets because of religious or linguistic differences. In Indonesia, student groups are often organized on the basis of religious or regional affiliation.

University Pressures

The varying demands that universities make on students also affect the possibilities for political participation and the political climate on the campus. The examination system used is a key factor in determining student political activism. In the American system, for example, students are generally required to take examinations at regular intervals and to maintain at least minimal academic standards to stay in school. They may take part in extracurricular activities, political or other, but these are at the expense of their studies. In Latin America, where examinations are not so important or may be postponed, such sanctions do not exist.

In many countries, it is possible to predict accurately the cycle of student activism on the basis of examination schedules. In India, students do not generally study until a month before the annual examinations. Thus, most students have a very substantial amount of free time during the year. In Latin America, many student leaders are able to maintain their status within the university for years by postponing their examinations and devoting themselves full-time to political activity.

Entrance requirements to a university may also affect political reactions. The Japanese and American patterns place great emphasis on getting into the best universities and require high-school students to work long hours under considerable psychic pressure. These patterns clearly affect the way some students behave after they are admitted to the university. A great deal of Japanese and American student activism is concentrated in the freshmen and sophomore years, which may reflect the students' reaction to being released from the pressures of entrance anxiety. Upperclassmen tend to be more liberal in their attitudes than lower-division groups, but to give less time to politics. Presumably years of university attendance are associated both with greater liberalism and more concern with preparing for jobs or admission into good graduate schools.

The greater activism of lowerclassmen may also reflect the liberating influences of the university. Students often express their newly found freedom by engaging in various forms of "nonconformist" behavior. Regardless of class in school, students living away from home, either in dormitories or in private accommodations, are more likely to participate in activist politics than those commuting from home. Berkeley data suggest that "new" students — whether freshmen, juniors, or graduate students — are more likely to be activists than students who have been in residence for some time. In other words, recent transfer students contribute disproportionately to the activist core. This raises a general question about transferring from one campus to another. A campus is not always a community in which students remain for the entire period of their education and in which they are gradually socialized into the community norms. Frank Pinner suggests that young people, particularly students, join organizations or integrated collectivities because they have just left their families, their home town, or friends and are anxious, disoriented, and lonely. They find in organizational life — particularly in movements that have a sense of commitment, purpose, and high intimacy — a kind of replacement for the collectivity they have just left. This factor, which would apply more to the new than to older students, would also vary by country and university system. It would depend, in part, on what proportion of students live at home or close to home.

Types of Student Politics

Opinions as to the place of politics in the university are inherently related to feelings about the larger society. Those — whether of the extreme left or right — who believe that drastic changes are necessary, that major evils exist, or that the basic verities are under attack will feel that students and faculty ought to be deeply involved in politics. Conversely, moderate conservatives and liberals are more likely to accept President Benitez's formula that a university is a "house of study," rather than a "house of politics." Conservatives, as believers in the *status quo,* will generally be even less active politically than liberals or moderate leftists. Glaucio Soares's Brazilian data indicate that conservative students not only are not interested in politics, but often "perceive student politics as an undue interference with their studies." The leftists, on the other hand, feel that they have a duty to be politically engaged and that the university should be an agency of modernization and radical change. As Soares puts it, conservatives argue that the political and academic roles should be compartmentalized, while leftists seek to integrate the two. This means, of course, that under current conditions in most countries, the student left will mobilize a much greater proportion of its potential strength for politics than will the moderates or the rightists.

Most of the recent writing on student activism tends to ignore the phenomenon of rightist activism. Indeed, although many students are conservatives, there has been little rightist campus activism since the 1930's. As a result, little material has been published concerning the activities of the extreme rightist student groups of the 1920's and 1930's in much of Europe. German and Austrian students were on the left during the early-nineteenth century, but many turned to rightist nationalism in the late-nineteenth and early-twentieth centuries. Anti-Semitism and extreme nationalism were characteristic of many of the more politically sophisticated German fraternities, and Nazism had great appeal in the universities in the 1930's. French Fascism, strong during the interwar period, received considerable support from university students.

From a functional point of view, such "rightist" behavior is quite similar to contemporary left-wing styles of politics. Rightist students were nationalistic, anti-authority, and concerned with the seeming inferiority of their nation within the world community. The subtleties of ideology were not meaningful to the rightist student movements of the 1930's. There was often a mixture of rightist and Marxist rhetoric, which combined notions of racialism with ideas of "proletarian" and exploited nations.

As Frank Pinner suggests, student organizations may, for analytical purposes, be divided into two categories: *transgressive* groups, which are directed mainly against the authority structures of their societies, and *traditional* groups, which socialize their members into their role as conventional citizens of the society. A similar distinction can be made in the role of the university itself. On the one hand, universities are centers of innovation in which scholars are expected to challenge the traditional truths of their fields and receive the highest rewards for work which is sharply innovative. On the other, they are schools with faculties of teachers and, thereby, part of the socialization process of their society. Universities and the subdivisions within them vary in the extent to which they emphasize these functions. Many parts of the university, particularly the professional schools, are essentially concerned with a socialization function — training students in socially useful skills. The so-called liberal-arts subjects, on the other hand, tend to value scholarly innovation and competence in research more highly. Thus, transgressive student groups are more likely to be found among liberal-arts students than among those in professional schools, such as engineering, education, or business. In Latin America and other countries, universities that are affiliated to religious bodies tend to have little student activism. In Japan and the United States, the most important centers of scholarship tend also to be the strongholds of transgressive student movements.

It is possible to differentiate further among transgressive social movements: Some are concerned with changes in basic social *values* (ultimate ends or conceptions about basic social institutions) and others with affecting *norms* (means to attain agreed upon social values).

Movements concerned with value change are more prevalent and stronger in the underdeveloped countries than in the developed ones. Talcott Parsons and S. N. Eisenstadt have suggested the need to look at the magnitude of the differences between the values of the adult and youth generations in varying types of societies. They indicate that generational conflict is caused, at least in part, by sharp value differences among generations, and that such cleavages — particularly between the better educated (younger on the average) and the uneducated (older) — are great in modernizing societies, but relatively minor in the developed societies.

Similarly, the difference between the values of the university and those of society is considerable in backward societies and small in developed societies. Michio Nagai has argued, for example, that the university is basically universalistic and meritocratic, even in societies that are neither universalistic nor meritocratic. On the one hand, the university judges people, events, and research on the basis of objective achievement criteria, and, on the other, it values freedom of inquiry and discussion. Thus, when we speak of a university anywhere in the world, we have a similar model in mind, no matter how far reality may deviate from that model. The norm of academic freedom is basic to the idea of the university. The tension between the formal values of university and society will, therefore, be great in authoritarian societies, considerable in emerging and developing nations, which are normally quite particularistic, and relatively small in the developed democratic societies. Faculty and students will reflect the depth of these tensions in their behavior. One should expect *value* conflicts (differences about ends) between student movements and the society in emerging or authoritarian nations and more normative conflicts in developed societies. Education, particularly university education, is inherently a modernizing force, and hence in underdeveloped countries it will be in conflict with those elements seeking to maintain traditional values and institutions. In the democratic developed states, the society more generally accepts the values of universalism, achievement, and freedom.

These distinctions help to account for the varying emphases on ideology among student movements. In general, ideological concerns declined among student activists in advanced industrialized countries during the postwar period, as compared to the 1930's, but remained important in many of the developing countries. Nationalism, which involves a concern for modernizing and industrializing, is also particularly important in developing countries. Even such relatively non-leftist groupings as the Philippine student movement and the militant KAMI organization of Indonesia are extremely nationalistic. The ideological concerns of student groups in the emerging nations reflect their interest in value change in the larger society. They are at odds with any forces that support traditional values or stand in the way of rapid economic growth.

In the West, however, where the tension between social values and the political concerns of students is less manifest, even the relatively small, extremely radical student movements do not show a strong attachment to formal ideologies. Thus, pragmatism and a preoccupation with specific issues characterize its student politics. This obtains even in Eastern Europe, perhaps because ideologies would be difficult to voice. Students there have been a key element in demanding liberalization in the name of the manifest socialist values and have argued for a nondogmatic approach to society and politics. Even the French Communist students have been in the forefront of revolt against the ideological commitments of the parent Party. Scandinavian students have campaigned for individual freedom and an end to social regulations, particularly those related to sex.

Orientation Toward Youth

In many countries, one may find some version of the maxim: "He who is not radical [socialist, Communist, anarchist] at twenty does not have a heart; he who still is one at forty does not have a head." There is a notion that it is normal, appropriate, and morally correct for young people to be radicals or revolutionaries. Indeed, many societies treat radical youth, particularly students, as if they believed this maxim. They permit students a degree of political freedom, even license, to violate the norms and laws of society without being punished, or with less punishment than is generally meted out to others. Thus, Berkeley students who surrounded a police car and held it captive for thirty hours were neither arrested nor otherwise sanctioned. Even in authoritarian countries like Czarist Russia, Communist Poland, or Franco Spain, student oppositionists have been treated more lightly by the authorities than have other organized opponents. Sentences against student revolutionaries are usually mild compared to those given non-students.

This tolerance reflects, in part, the fact that university students are often the children of the "elite." The vast majority of the offspring of the privileged strata go to university. This elite finds it difficult to employ stringent measures against its own children. In Cuba, the Batista regime was undermined, in part, because some of the young people with Castro in the mountains were the children of Cuban upper-class families. Members of the Havana elite exerted tremendous pressure on Batista to quit because they wanted their children back from the mountains alive. In recent years, many of the trials of student activists in Spain have involved at least one son of an important family. In this context, the Spanish courts have been faced by two conflicting forces: the particularism of the society, which requires that an offender who belongs to a privileged family be treated lightly, and the universalism of the law, which implies that all those who commit similar offenses be treated in the same way. Most of the punishments of Spanish students have, therefore, been relatively mild.

Nations may also be differentiated by their varying conceptions of youth. Revolutionary ideologies are generally positive toward youth. Hence, the vitality of revolutionary ideologies may be measured by the extent to which they still identify virtue with youth. One of the best pieces of evidence that the American revolutionary tradition is still viable is the prevalent belief in youth, which interestingly the Russians no longer have. The United States is very much a youth culture; it stresses the truism that the young will inherit the world and are probably on the side of justice and progress, as opposed to adults. Many adults thus feel youth should be encouraged in their disdain for the old, in their advocacy of progress and change. Older people consequently lack assurance when debating with youth. It is significant that the Soviet Union has sharply modified the belief in youth that prevailed immediately after the Revolution. Stalin eliminated the notion that youth is right in its conflicts against the older elements, and his successors have not reinstated it. Mao Tse-tung, in his seventies, however, is attempting to emphasize the role of youth as the main source of support for a continuing revolutionary ideology in China.

Authoritarian systems like Fascist Italy or Communist Cuba have, however, been interested not in encouraging students to be critical of the system, but in using "youth" as a social base to support a supposedly "revolutionary" regime against conservative adults. They have hoped to inhibit adult opponents by impressing on them the idea that they represent a historic anachronism. A stress on the worth of youth politics in a democracy may bring to reform movements the support and encouragement of students and other youth. Conversely, it may inhibit some adults who disagree from strongly resisting the proposals of activist students.

It may also be argued that student activism is the most recent expression of the need of youth to have a separate culture of their own. The student stratum, as such, has always tended to create a whole array of age-group symbols, which set it apart from others in society, and from adults in particular. The changes in the political role of the university increasingly make politics a particularly critical source of self-expression. The institution, itself, may be nonpartisan, but its professors fulfill ever growing roles as party activists, commentators on events, advisers, consultants, and researchers on policy matters. Many students are thus in centers of great political significance, but have little or no share in the political status of the institution. In addition, even in countries where most of the faculty political involvement is generally on the left of the spectrum as in the United States, it occurs within the "establishment." Hence, if it is to express a sense of separate identity, student politics as part of the student culture must be outside, and in opposition to, the politics of most adults.

The Role of Universities

Michio Nagai has suggested that as societies "modernize," their universities necessarily move from a diffuse to a specific relationship with both the state and religion. The growth of the scholarly and research function has required universities to separate themselves from the clergy and the politicians. The university must be free to find and teach what is scientifically "true," without concern for the reactions of religious or political establishments. The norm of academic freedom assumes that these outside bodies will leave the university alone. Conversely, if the university insists on freedom from external interference, from being criticized or coerced by those not involved in scholarly pursuits, the norm implies that it must abstain as a university community from attacking others.

The extent to which universities have differentiated themselves from society will, of course, differ. The Confucian ethic stresses the linkages between scholarship and the state. Chinese, Japanese, and Korean scholars were civil servants and supporters of the state. They maintained a relationship with the state similar to that between the religious scholars and the church in the West. In more recent times, universities in the East, particularly state universities, have been expected to be agents of state purposes. Nagai concludes that the considerable involvement of students in the political life of these countries is to some extent linked to the continued strength of Confucian values.

Similarly, in many developing countries the national emphasis on economic development and modernization overrides the idea of the completely autonomous university. Various sections of the governing elite, as well as many faculty members and students, believe that the university should serve the national interest of fostering development. They do not think the nation can afford the "luxury" of supporting pure scholarship which is not related to development objectives, nor can students or faculty isolate themselves from active involvement in politics. These are, of course, highly debated issues in many of the countries, but insofar as the university is perceived as serving political objectives, it necessarily becomes a source of political stimulation.

The effort to separate the university from extramural influences has been most successful in the developed countries of Western Europe and the English-speaking world. The university gradually freed itself from political and religious interference in the late-nineteenth and twentieth centuries. In recent decades, however, the growing role of the university as the key center of research and development for the public sector has necessarily involved it in political controversy. Governments and scholars have broken down the barriers between politics and science by using academics as temporary government officials or as consultants. Scientists have not been able to escape taking responsibility for the social and political uses of their discoveries. Physicists have had to take a position on the various controversies concerning the military uses of atomic energy, academic economists have been called on to take part in the debates on national economic policy, and sociologists and psychologists are involved in issues concerning race relations, education, and the culture of poverty.

Seemingly, the process that brought about increased differentiation between the academy and other institutions has been reversed. The growing complexity of modern society has challenged the effort to segregate the university as an "ivory tower," seeking primarily to serve scholarly ends. As the university in the West becomes a "multiversity," to use Clark Kerr's term, it will continue to be a center of political agitation, as those who favor or disagree with specific endeavors seek to use or attack it. The growing involvement of the Western university as the research arm of the governing elite has, for example, led some critics to view it as a "tool" of the establishment. Universities have nevertheless generally remained as major sources of criticism, despite their growing ties to government. In France, where all universities are state controlled, faculty and students were in the forefront of the opposition to the Algerian war. In the United States many have been the principal centers of support for the Negro struggle for equality and an important source of protest against the Vietnam war.

Student politics is also affected to a considerable degree by the social position and political values of the country's intellectual community. The position of the English intellectuals vis-à-vis power in the political establishment differs from that of the French or the American intellectual. The English have been included in effective political life; the French are outside it. In the United States, intellectuals have great power as experts, but there is no intellectual political community comparable to that in Britain. In many ways, the "nonexpert" American intellectual, similar to the French, has high status but little power and views himself as alienated from the power structure, while the American academic "expert," like the English, has considerable status and power and is more likely to identify with the political-decision makers.

The attitudes of intellectuals and of students toward the national *status quo* are, moreover, not simply a function of their position within the society. More than any other group, intellectuals tend to have an international reference group. To use Merton's distinction between "cosmopolitans" (oriented to outside groups for standards of comparison) and "locals" (concerned with the evaluations of the community within which one resides), intellectuals are clearly more likely to be cosmopolitans. As such, they will be aware of the shortcomings of their nation compared with the standards of the leading countries. The intellectuals and academics of the underdeveloped countries generally realize that they are at the summits of nations or university systems that are considered "backward." This awareness heightens their desire to foster change within their own society and increases their resentment against local or foreign groups that inhibit modernization. The intellectuals in Central and Eastern Europe in the nineteenth century regarded their countries as backward compared to France and Britain, and many of them supported radical political movements.

Intellectuals who are resentful of their society often stimulate rebellious "apprentice intellectuals" — students. In many countries professors see themselves as a deprived stratum, one which is not given the rewards of working conditions appropriate to their role. This sense of resentment will vary, of course, both within nations and among them. Students, particularly in the better universities, are also prone to rebel when the faculty are relatively incompetent in their teaching and show authoritarian tendencies. Student indiscipline in India has been linked with the low salaries, long hours, and bad working conditions of the faculty. The historic pattern of the "part-time" professor in Latin America is a crucial factor in the lack of commitment to scholarly endeavors and values by many students. The very bad faculty-student ratio of French universities and the low salaries of Japanese professors, which require them to find other sources of remuneration, have been cited as factors lowering the educational level of the institutions of higher education and encouraging protest movements.

Student political patterns are also determined, in part, by variations in political institutions. As Robert Scott points out, the lack of political stability in much of Latin America has stimulated student activism, since the possibility of successful agitation has been substantial, and students have occasionally been able to exert political leverage on weak governments. And, as Edward Shils indicates, the great wave of protest in 1968 occurred in countries which had significant governmental crises. In Scandinavia, on the other hand, as Erik Allardt and Richard Tomasson indicate, the stability and legitimacy of the established political structures have discouraged student activism, and national politics is not generally seen as a legitimate domain of student concern. The same pattern can be seen in other politically stable nations.

Confrontation politics is characteristic of polities in which students, and other groups as well, lack legitimate channels of communication to authority. Clark Kerr has observed that political groups turn to activist demonstrations when they find themselves ignored by the adult power structure. Nevertheless, the existence of student militancy, in and of itself, does not necessarily indicate that such channels do not exist. Youth generally lack a long time-perspective; they tend to become quickly frustrated if their demands are not met immediately. Hence, even in countries with reasonably good channels of political communication, students may turn to confrontation politics if their political idealism has been activated by a major moral issue. For example, American students concerned with civil rights for Negroes or with ending the Vietnam war have not been satisfied with communicating with authority. Whether such alienation becomes pervasive and long-term will be related to the reality of the democratic institutions. In stable democracies, student unrest tends to be a temporary phenomenon.

The pressures on higher educational institutions to expand have been tremendous, but countries have responded to them differently.

Introduction: Students and Politics in Comparative Studies

The military government of Burma has used severe repressive measures to keep the university population limited. In other nations — notably, the Philippines, Korea, India, the United States, and Japan — rapid educational expansion has caused substantial strains on the educational system and may be a factor in student unrest.

There is no clear-cut simple relationship between size or rate of expansion of the student body and patterns of political behavior. The emergence of large student populations on one campus or within given cities, particularly national capitals, has facilitated student activism. It has become relatively easy to mobilize a visibly large protest demonstration. A small minority of the students in Buenos Aires, Mexico City, Berkeley, Calcutta, Tokyo, or Paris can constitute an impressive protest in absolute numbers. The creation of "University Cities" in places like Caracas or Paris has increased the potential for mass student action. On the other hand, in nations in which there are few universities and the student body is small and homogeneous, a small group of activists can have an impact on the ideological climate of the national student body and on political events. This was true in the Congo after independence in 1960. The growth of the student population increases the size of the minority available for activist protest and makes for a more heterogeneous student body, one which may sustain competing campus political groupings.

In many countries, the university system is completely state-financed; in others, both in the developed and underdeveloped world, the universities are divided among public, private, and religious schools. Such differences permit substantial variation in quality among institutions. Universities with religious affiliations not only tend to recruit from the most traditionalist sectors of society, but their administrations and faculties are more likely to ban politics than are those in secular universities. Nippon University, the largest private university in Japan, prohibits participation in the *Zengakuren*, the national student union. Other private universities like Waseda, which have a history of student activism, were originally established as a means of training opposition to the governmental elite educated in the University of Tokyo. In the Philippines, the extensive system of private colleges includes many "diploma mills" designed to get students, often from less-well-to-do families, through a nominal university education as quickly and easily as possible. As might be expected, there is little student politics in these institutions.

Internal Differences

"Statistically significant" relationships found in one country need not hold up in others. There are, for example, interesting variations concerning the effects of different disciplines on politics. Disciplines tend to be identified with student activism and leftist ideas in some countries, but not in others. Medicine has a leftist aura in various Latin countries in the Americas and Europe, but is traditionally quite conservative in most of northern Europe and the Anglophonic world. In the Catholic world, this orientation seems to stem from the historic conflict between science and the church, a tension relatively absent from the politics of most Protestant countries. Where economics is taught as an extremely technical, mathematically based subject, those who concentrate in the field are less radical than where it remains concerned with qualitative and historical institutional analysis. Similarly, in some countries "law" means a preprofessional discipline or a professional field as it does in the United States; in other places, it denotes a broad social-science or philosophical training. Consequently, the behavior of law students may vary considerably from country to country.

One may also differentiate between subjects that lead to explicit role models and those which involve diffuse objectives. (Pre-professional subjects have explicit role models, while some of the humanities and social-science subjects have diffuse postgraduate role expectations.) Glaucio Soares has distinguished between students whose role image is that of the intellectual as against those who conceive of themselves as scientists or professionals. These images are highly predictive of political orientations. Those with an intellectual role identity are much more leftist and activist than those who identify as scientists or professionals.

This difference is, of course, a subjective one. In every discipline, those who think of themselves as intellectuals rather than professionals are more politically activist. It also works out objectively, in terms of the types of disciplines. Those disciplines that are thought of as "intellectual" — the humanities and most of the social sciences — are more activist and leftist than those that are oriented toward the professional or scientific world. In Puerto Rico, almost all the supporters of the radical and nationalist FUPI (pro-independence) movement have come from the social sciences and have seen themselves primarily as intellectuals, with strong ambitions toward writing and journalism. Chile and Argentina have demonstrated similar patterns. Most of the activists in the Indian and Indonesian student movements, particularly during the nationalist periods, came from the liberal arts. In the United States, the activists in groups like the Students for a Democratic Society tend to be in the social sciences and humanities and to see themselves as intellectuals rather than as professionals.

Thus, differences in the political behavior of students in different universities or countries may be linked to variations in the fields in which they specialize. Certain schools deal primarily with liberal-arts subjects; others, like the University of Moscow, are essentially institutes for technology and science. Most underdeveloped countries, particularly in Latin America, tend to have proportionally fewer students enrolled in technical and vocational subjects. (In some, however, like Israel and Nigeria, the proportion is quite high.) The Communist countries rank highest in proportions of students engaged in vocational and professional training, which may contribute to the relative political passivity of their student bodies.

The political orientations of professors and their students do not necessarily vary in the same way. There is a congruence in some fields. In such professional schools as engineering, education, or business, faculty and students are both relatively conservative. In other areas, such as mathematics or molecular biology, they tend to be relatively leftist. In still others, particularly sociology or political science and especially in the better universities, the students tend to be to the left of the faculty. Where discrepancies between faculty and student orientations exist, the student and the faculty often differ in their conceptions of the subject. Thus, students view some of the social sciences as fields concerned with remedying "social problems." As scholarly disciplines, however, they are essentially concerned with the elaboration of knowledge within scientifically rigorous conceptual frameworks and methodology. Since social scientists see crucial political questions as having complex causes and difficult solutions, they tend to refrain from endorsing simple solutions. Thus, political concerns motivate many students to major in the social sciences, while the canons of scholarship press social scientists to refrain from taking public political positions. Natural scientists or humanists, on the other hand, may take political positions without reference to their special roles as scholars. Politically motivated students who hold to an "ethic of ultimate ends," which requires a total commitment to furthering politically desirable goals, will not understand nor sympathize with Max Weber's insistence that introducing one's personal values into scientific analysis undermines the ability to understand the facts. Accepting Weber's position often places social scientists in conflict with their best students, who see any faculty reluctance to link scholarly and political roles as cowardly.

These are some of the issues with which any analysis of the role of students in politics and higher education must deal. The university is premised on the belief that "knowledge will make man free" and will increase his ability to control and to better his environment. Those interested in the role of students in politics are obligated to avoid using their special competencies and knowledge as weapons in ongoing campus politics. To separate one's role as scholar and citizen is often difficult. In this case, it is almost impossible.

STUDENTS
IN REVOLT

EDWARD SHILS

Dreams of Plenitude, Nightmares of Scarcity

I

AT THE BEGINNING of the 1930's, there was no student movement to speak of in the United States. The young people's branches of the socialist and Communist parties — the Young Communist League (YCL), the League for Industrial Democracy, and the Young People's Socialist League (YPSL) — and tiny sects of anti-Stalinists existed as national organizations and as small isolated bodies at the major universities (at, for example, Harvard, Chicago, Berkeley). They were a little stronger in Wisconsin where they were attracted and supported by a strong local tradition; their main activity was at the City College of New York. Although the motives for their radicalism might have been personal and private or abstract and universal, all of them were attached to national organizations under the umbrella of which young persons — not students as such — stood.

In the United Kingdom, some students became Communists; pacifism and anti-fascism became moderately widespread at the London School of Economics and in Oxford by the mid-thirties. Despite the notoriety of the refusal, at the Oxford Union, to defend king and country, radical undergraduates at British universities were few, and those few were conventionally radical in their affiliation to the adult "left-wing" political parties.

In Germany, many students supported the National Socialists and the *Deutschnationale;* many fewer supported the Social Democrats or Communists. Many students expressed their hostility toward Jewish and socialist teachers by unruliness and rudeness in lectures; much more visible were their frequent altercations with socialist and Communist students, their disruption of the latter's meetings and their physical assaults on their members. Whatever they did, they did to express their affiliation with and to promote the progress

1

toward power of their non-university elders. With all their brutality, they were extremely submissive to their masters; they espoused the program of the NSDAP in all things; they denounced Jewish science and those teachers whom, by reason of their humanity, liberality and lack of xenophobia, they regarded as traitors to the German people; they stood by gleefully when their ringleaders realized the eternal dream of delinquent pupils and burned a pile of books; they marched in parades under the auspices of their adult patrons.

In Eastern Europe, nationalist student organizations created disturbances in lectures of Jewish and liberal teachers and assaulted physically Jewish and socialist students. There, too, youthful delinquency and brutality were coordinated into the movement of adults who carried on the tradition of Polish anti-Semitism. In France, students were members of the *Camelot du Roi,* which was not exclusively for students; steeped in an old tradition of the youthful upper-class brawler, they joined in the public disorders attendant on the Stavisky scandal. They were youthful ruffians at the disposal of their elders.

There were no university students in black Africa, except for the handful of pious, well-behaved students at the Fourah Bay College. In the Middle East, students were few and, their political activities being radically nationalist, anti-imperialist, and Arabophile, were kept in check by the political elites of that period who lived under French and British influence and who tried at least publicly to conciliate the foreigner. Such public manifestations as they made were a part of a larger nationalistic or ethnic movement of sentiment; students did not act on their own.

In India, at the beginning of the 1930's, the student movement was beginning to rise to the plateau of the decisive years of the independence movement. It had ostensibly one main aim: to bring about the departure of the British so that India could become independent. This entailed the organized truancy called strikes and boycotts; it involved processions and demonstrations and assorted "Jimmy Higgins" services. The political activities of students were practically always under the guidance of the Congress; when students began to become socialists, they did so under Congress patronage; when they became violent, they did so under the leadership of Congress socialists. In China, students were active politically, denouncing the Japanese invaders, the Kuomintang government and the European imperialists; there, too, students struck, boycotted classes, and demonstrated, but they always did so in close association with adult politicians. In Burma, the small number of students were beginning to be markedly anti-British. Later in the decade they conducted important strikes and published occasionally-appearing and short-lived periodicals. Since they were practically the first generation of nationalists, they had relatively little adult collaboration and guidance, but in this they were exceptional.

The varyingly small proportion of students who engaged in the demonstrative, expressive, and always aggressive actions of student politics were always against the existing regime — that is, where they were free to do so and could do so with impunity. (The situation was different in the Soviet Union and in Fascist Italy, where student activities were closely controlled by the government.) Where they were free to act, they always went beyond the existing regime. Where the regime was anti-Semitic, for example, they went further in their anti-Semitism. In most cases, they did not just go further, they actually went against the existing regime. Their beliefs made them oppositional; the urgency and passion of their espousal made them into extremists. They were not just against the incumbent party; they were against "the system as a whole" — either against the "Weimar system," against the entire secularist tolerant culture of the Third Republic, or against the "capitalist system." They were ideologically radical in that sense. Yet although their actions were usually directed against the prevailing system ruled by adults, they practically always had the support and encouragement, guidance and discipline brought by adults. Their organizations were almost always parts of or affiliated to oppositional organizations in which adults were in control. They were, of course, not simply creatures, instruments, and copies of the adults to whom they were affiliated; they added something of their own — resiliency, verve, dramatic actions, and an element of carnival. They were often violent, and they were sometimes courageous in their violent actions — and frequently they were only brutes and bullies. They usually enjoyed engagement in acts of violence, and they sometimes suffered injuries. They could act with more spontaneity than the adults; they had more enthusiasm than their elders; and they enjoyed the excitement of antagonistic encounters with the ruling authorities, who were usually restrained in their treatment of them,[1] and with their antagonists and victims who in Central and Eastern Europe were often weaker than themselves. They acted from a privileged position that radicals of the lower classes did not enjoy, and they had the great advantage of more freely adaptable time-schedules. Universities have always been freer than factories and offices, and they could absent themselves from their postponable university duties as the spirit moved them.

Actively and aggressively anti-authoritarian though the relatively small student movements of those days were, their activities were sponsored and legitimated by the authority of elders. They had a tradition that sustained them, but their tradition was not theirs alone; nor was it of their own finding. It was exemplified and embodied in the corporate organizations of their elders, to which their own were affiliated. They accepted the anti-authoritarian authority of adults in the wider movements of which the student movements formed a part. They also accepted in general the authorities of the university system. Although their rebellious activities were often planned and sometimes took place in university buildings or on university grounds, they were seldom concerned with university matters. The university was not the home of their heart; that lay outside. They aimed at the world outside the university although this sometimes involved action within the university, such as the beating of Jewish classmates or the disruption of the lectures of Jewish or socialist or expatriate teachers.

Student rebellions in the present decade are more comprehensively and more fundamentally hostile toward authority than they were three and four decades ago. They are hostile, in principle, toward authority whereas their predecessors were hostile only to particular authorities and submitted enthusiastically to others. They act now without the sponsorship of external adult organizations, and they feel little sympathy with most of them. The innovators in the present generation of student radicals are antinomian; the rejection of authority by their predecessors of more than a third of a century ago was sustained and limited by a legitimating authority. They did not venture so far or so daringly from authority as the most advanced student radicals do nowadays. The present-day student radicals act without the legitimating authority of older figures; their middle-aged courtiers who offer their legitimatory services are offering something that is neither wanted nor needed. Paul Goodman and Sartre provide agreeable but unsought applause. When the student radicals group themselves around an older figure he is of their own creation, as was the case of Senator Eugene McCarthy — who is not a charismatic person but was made into one by the student radicals' need for one. The adults most closely associated with the student radicals are usually young teachers little older than themselves, and they function more to affirm than to guide and legitimate. The "big names" of present day student radicalism — Mao Tse-tung, Fidel Castro, Ché Guevara, Frantz Fanon — are remote in space or dead; they have no commanding power over them, and they all share in the eyes of the student radicals a quasi-bohemian, free-floating, anti-institutional aroma. Even though they govern tyrannically, it is their anarchic element that appeals to the radical students. Castro's period in Oriente province, his conduct of the affairs of his high office in cafés at 3 A.M., and the generally impromptu air of his tyranny attract just as the image of Mao Tse-tung owes much to the period in the caves and the "long march." Neither of these two living amulets is in charge of an organization that the student radicals must obey.

How are these major differences to be accounted for?

II

The turbulence of student radicalism now has the appearance of being worldwide. Alongside the formal international federations of students that appear to be of scant significance for the more dramatic activities of the student radicals, there is a spontaneous and un-organized, or at best an informal, unity of sympathy of the student movement which forms a bridge across national boundaries. In 1968, student radical movements seemed to be synchronized among different countries and uniform in content and technique to an extent reminiscent of the monolithic phase of the Communist International and its subsidiary organizations.

Student radicalism is no longer the possession of small, relatively closed sects within larger student bodies; on the contrary, it can reach out toward the sympathy of a large minority, occasionally even the majority of students, at particular places and for limited times. Its organizations within each country, despite numerous ups and downs, are more persistent in their action and have a larger following than they used to have. They show a self-confidence reaching to arrogance in their dealings with hostile authority, and they are aware of the transnational scale of their undertaking. None-theless, the movement is not unified, either nationally or inter-nationally. Synchronization is a function of a generally identical mood, not of concerted organized action.

Nor is the movement uniform internationally. There are major differences between countries and continents. In India, for example, where until the outbursts in Western countries since 1964 the university student population was the most turbulent in the world, the student radicals do not as a rule make the structures of the larger society and of the university objects of a general critique. Indian student radicals declare no fundamental criticism of their society; they have no schemes for the reconstruction of their universities. They do take stands on public issues — for example, on behalf of the construction of a steel mill in Andhra Pradesh or on behalf of or in opposition to the use of English as the medium of instruction in higher education, the nearest they come to espousing a general policy for higher education. The Indian student agitation is "occasionalist"; it responds to particular stimuli, local, regional, or national, but grievances do not become generalized and are therefore not persistent. India, however, is exceptional in its relatively apolitical agitation.[2] In Indonesia, student radicalism is, contrarily to India's, wholly and over the past few years continuously, political. Internal university conditions, terrible though they are, scarcely engage its attention; its interest is in the public realm, where in collaboration with but not under the dominion of the army it was important in the ultimate undoing of former President Sukarno.

Elsewhere in Asia — omitting mainland China[3] — in North Africa,[4] and, to a lesser extent, in black Africa, Latin America, and Spain, student agitation follows the conventional nineteenth-century pattern of nationalist agitation against the repressive character of the incumbent government and its insufficient devotion to the national cause (even though the foreign rulers have departed, in some cases very long ago). Their actions are larger, more vehement, and more frequently recurrent than they were in the earlier period, but, except for the magnitude and intensity of the manifestations, they have not changed. They agitate against restrictions on freedom of organization and propaganda and against their government's moral corruption and its alleged subservience to foreign powers — in most cases nowadays the United States. The creed that declares "neo-colonialism" to be the chief enemy is to a large extent a student creed. It is a shoddier version of the Marxist-Leninist analysis of colonialism and imperialism which was a fairly common possession of the nationalistic student movements in Asia during the 1930's or of the African student movements in France and England during the 1940's and 1950's.

Nonetheless, despite these similarities with their earlier outlook, the student movements in most of the countries of the Third World, like those in the advanced Western countries, have broken away from the pattern of their antecedents by becoming independent of adult organizations. They have practically no significant older political figures to whom they look for guidance or inspiration. The leaders of an earlier generation are in power or apolitical, dead or in exile. They are, whether dead or alien, out of the question as the leaders of an effective opposition. Despite some exceptions, aggressive student radicalism is forced to stand alone, to the extent that it stands at all. In India where public opposition is still permitted, the Indian student agitation, too, has by and large lost its connection with a dominant organization of adult politicians. Although in many particular instances, party politicians are able to exploit some of the disruptive capacities of Indian students, the organizational links are loose or nonexistent. In India, too, there is no larger adult political movement of which the students regard their own movement as a part, and this is one of the main reasons why most Indian student agitation voices have no general political demands.[5]

In Eastern Europe, particularly in Poland and Czechoslovakia, courageous students have agitated against tyranny in the larger society and on behalf of the traditional freedoms of thought, expression, and assembly, and for the rule of law — with some of the same nationalist, anti-Russian accompaniment that was characteristic of their nineteenth-century antecedents. And they do these things alone, except for the patronage of a few literary men and professors. Even in the brief periods of liberalization in Poland and Czechoslovakia, the students acted independently with the "liberalizers," not under them. The administration and functions of the university do not worry them, except insofar as party tyranny and favoritism manifest themselves there.

In Western Europe and North America, the situation is both similar and different from the other parts of the world. In their relationship to adult oppositional organizations, Western student radicalism resembles that of the Third World. In Britain, the Labour Party is ingloriously in power; in Western Germany, the Social Democratic Party is part of the Grand Coalition. In France, the socialists are futile and the Communists in their odd way, and despite what General de Gaulle claimed, are pillars of the existing order in the face of student "provocation" and "adventurism." In Italy the socialists share government responsibility, and the Communist Party has no sympathy with the student radicals whom it regards as Maoist provocateurs. In the United States, the major parties are abhorrent

7

to the student radicals and the only adult opposition to the major parties is a racist know-nothingism. In North America, the bourgeois parties have never concerned themselves with student support, the socialist parties have always been negligible, and the Communist parties have dwindled in size and in moral standing. Official Marxism is unaccredited or discredited. There is no ideology ready to hand for student radicalism.

The student radicals have, therefore, no adult political masters; they act on their own. Those sections that maintain organizational relations with adult parties or groups are either in a state of conflict with their elders or are relegated to positions of despised insignificance by their radical contemporaries. The discrediting of the Communist parties, the moderation of the Social Democratic parties, and the eclipse or disappearance of Fascist and Nazi parties in Western Europe have left the students without either a parent organization of elders or an authoritatively promulgated doctrine to which they can give their loyalty or adherence. A "natural" Castroism, amorphous, passionately hostile to organization forms a powerful, profound undercurrent of sentiment and of vaguely formulated belief.

In most of the countries in which there is much radical student agitation, there has been nothing commensurate to it on the intellectual side. In Eastern Europe, liberalism, admirable and courageous though it has been, is no intellectual innovation. In India, *hic et nunc* protests against very particular features of university and college administration and against very particular deprivations represent a retreat from the variety of nationalist, Marxist, and Gandhian creeds and ideologies of the early depression decade. For the rest, the student movements in Africa, Japan, Indonesia, and Latin America have added nothing fundamentally new to the intellectual repertoire of the student movements.

Technologically, there are innovations; students commandeer lorries; they use "bull-roarers"; they confront the police armed in helmets and bearing shields; they have adopted Molotov cocktails from the Russians they despise and the "sit-in" from the American automobile workers' union with which their sympathies are minimal. Nor have they been original organizationally; even the spectre of a worldwide movement — which has been created for them and from which they profit through the heightening of their self-consciousness and confidence — is the work of the bourgeois press and television.

All this being said, the differences between student radicalism at the beginning of the 1930's and in 1968 are greater than the mere differences of organizational independence from adult parties or the criticism of the universities. Far more important are the differences in fundamental beliefs about the self, about authority, about institutions, and about what is "given" by the past and the present. These differences are of the greatest importance and merit close analysis since they refer to serious matters. I will begin from the outside and try to move inward.

<h1 style="text-align:center">III</h1>

University students were a far smaller proportion of the population at the beginning of the 1930's than they are now. They were less noticed by the public at large or by politicians, and they did not conceive of themselves as an independent estate of the realm. Even in Latin America where they were constitutionally incorporated into university governing bodies, they did not apparently conceive of themselves in their capacity as students as a "permanent interest." Being a student was thought to be a transient condition, subordinate or derivative from other statuses.

Most university students in most countries came from the relatively privileged classes of their societies. Even in the United States, with its open state universities, students formed a small proportion of their generation, and they came from the better-off sections of American society. They expected to enter into the better-paid occupations and professions. The radicals among them did not regard themselves as "representatives," even if unchosen, of all students, and they did not regard the "student class" as an entity central to their respective societies. Their parental social class, the social class to which they sought entry through their studies, the ethnic group of which they were part, or the political party under whose guidance they acted were the "powers" of their societies, and they drew their significance from those. These collectivities and aggregates are still very important in society, and they are still very important to most students, but they are not so important to student radicals as they used to be. Why?

Students in the late 1920's and early 1930's were at the university for a variety of reasons; some were ambitious to learn more; some wished to ascend in society, to earn more than their co-evals who did not go on to university. Some attended university because their parents had done so and because it was the "normal" thing to do for full membership in their stratum of society. Others attended uni-

9

versity for all or any of these reasons, and because it was pleasant and exciting to be there. The pleasures of friendship and discovery and the excitement of games were available there.

It was generally regarded at that time that to be able to go to university was a privilege, an advantage in itself and for the future. It was an experience and opportunity open to relatively few. It was to be exploited for the immediate pleasures of intellectual acquisition, convivial experience, and the prospective rewards that it rendered available. The privilege was of a special kind; it implied no present ascendancy over teachers, officials, politicians, or elders in general; it was a privilege in a subordinate role that adumbrated a more substantial and central privilege at a later stage of life. It was a privilege in an inegalitarian society and in an inegalitarian institution where those at a particular level in the hierarchy accepted the ascendancy of those at higher levels. The privilege of attendance at university was the privilege of entry into the middle classes and perhaps even into the upper class — either to enter it for the first time in the history of one's own family or to enter it as one became an adult at a level approximately similar to that of one's own family. In any case, to be at university was very much a middle- and upper-middle-class sort of thing. The life lived at university was of a pattern thought to be appropriate to the style of those classes, and the completion of a course of studies there was regarded as the qualification for subsequent membership in those classes. Even in India and Germany, where it had become difficult for university graduates to find suitable employment, this conception of the potentialities of university education still prevailed.

Society before the Great Depression and World War II was much less egalitarian than it has since become. Among the main criteria for distinguishing the strata from one another was their respectability, their diligence and dutifulness, their capacity and readiness to persist faithfully in a given task, and their willingness to submit their performance to the assessment of authorities they regarded as legitimate. Most university students, however idle or uproarious or rebellious, accepted this set of arrangements; they thought it just, insofar as they thought about it at all. They expected to enter society and to take superior places in it. Of course, the prospect, except for the minority of the "highly born," was a strenuous one, but the strain was accepted as "given" in the nature of things and as a precondition for the privileges to be enjoyed later.

There were among the students some rebels — nationalists,

fascists, socialists, Communists, aesthetes, and bohemians — who were not wholly reconciled to the university system. Variously, they thought the larger system unjust or they were appalled by the philistinism of their fellow countrymen or they disapproved of their moral conventions and, insofar as they perceived some of these qualities in the universities, they were against them. The fascists and nationalists usually disapproved of ethnically alien rule or of the presence in the middle classes of ethnically alien elements. They wished to expel the foreigners from their countries or at least from positions of high authority and reward; they therefore criticized the universities where they thought that the aliens were benefiting from them or controlling them. But all of these objectionable qualities did not raise any question concerning the ideal nature or function of universities. Their function as a preparatory stage to the professions and toward the superior occupations was accepted. Their role in the transmission and extension of knowledge and appreciation was accepted. Their methods of government, their use of the resources available to them, the substance of what they taught, the research they did were not regarded by students as "their business"; these matters were the universities' business, and the students were only there as transient, present, or prospective beneficiaries of what they offered. Particular teachers might be disliked, insulted, and in a few cases assaulted; some students might absent themselves from classes and try to prevent other students from attending them. Other students might have little interest in what was taught and would do the minimum of study, but they did not challenge the "system." The university system was unimpugned and its place in society un-questioned. This was so even in Germany and India, where the students were fervid with nationalistic political passions and where Jews and Englishmen held prominent positions in the universities. They wished them to go, but they accepted the structure of the university and its place in society and the modalities which flowed from its tasks. The rebellious students of this earlier period, thus, not only accepted the authoritative structures of their rebellious elders, but they also accepted the university as an institution.

Their beliefs about the nature of society and the rights and privileges of men also showed this same duality. The beliefs of student radicals were received beliefs, shared with those of their elders who led and spoke for the larger movement to which the student organizations were affiliated. They were beliefs that had an authoritative promulgation in the programs of parties and in the writings of doctrinaires. They stood generally in an alienated tradition that heightened the authority of the elders to whom the students looked for guidance. The rebellious students were ideologically disposed, and they had an ideology made available to them. Marxism in one or another of its variants, national socialism, fascism, monarchism, and Gandhism were in their diverse ways the accomplishment of sometimes learned and sometimes genius-like intelligences and of charismatic madmen. None of them was as systematic nor as elaborate as Marxism, but most of them had their literary or theoretical classics and all invoked an intellectual past.

The new generation of student radicalism is by contrast relatively unideological. They might be ideologically disposed, but they have no elaborately and systematically promulgated set of beliefs. They do not accept the ideological services that are offered to them, and they have constructed no ideology of their own. Their own anarchistic inclinations do not lead them to seek the guidance of the writings of Prince Kropotkin or Élisée Reclus. They have affinities with Fourier and Proudhon, but they do not look to them for an intellectual construction of the university. Lukacs is singularly not in demand.

Instead of ideology, they have a mood that a powerful systematizing mind might cast into an ideology. No one has thus far done so.

IV

The great innovation in student radicalism that has occurred in Northwestern Europe and the United States is a moral mood. In a certain sense, the radicals among the students of France, Western Germany, Great Britain, and the United States — and increasingly of Italy and Spain — testify to a moral revolution.

The moral revolution consists in a demand for a total transformation — a transformation from a totality of undifferentiated evil to a totality of undifferentiated perfection. Evil consists in the deadening of sentiment through institutions and more particularly through the exercise of and subordination to authority. Perfection consists in the freedom of feeling and the fulfillment of desires. "Participation" is a situation in which the individual's desires and "demands" are fully realized through complete self-determination of the individual and the institutions which such freely feeling, self-determining individuals form. A good community is like Rousseau's; the common will harmonizes individual wills.[6] But the contemporary proponents of participation do not think of the individual will as anything but the concrete empirical will of actual and immediate sentiments, impulses, and desires. The common will is not the resultant of the rationally arrived at assent of its members; it is not actually a *shared* decision-making; it is certainly not the outcome of consent to a compromise arrived at by bargaining and exchange. It is not acceptance of anything less than what one initially desired. It is the transformation of sentiment and desire into reality in a community in which all realize their wills simultaneously. Anything less is repressive.

This is why the advance guard of student radicalism is so resolute in its reaction against repression. It is resolute not just against the violent and often brutal repression by the police, but just as much against the moderate repression that is entailed by the application of the principle of *in loco parentis*. It is against the "repressiveness" of the rules of the game of parliamentary politics and of distributions of rewards in accordance with a criterion of merit. It is against "institutional repression" or "individual violence" by which is usually meant the discipline of a practicable consensus in a regime of scarcity. Whatever hampers the fulfillment of whatever happens to be desired at the moment — whether it is a student housing arrangement which stipulates the hours of visiting in halls of residence or an examination or a convention regarding dress or sexual behaviour in public places — is repressive. And, as such, it is part of an undifferentiatedly repressive system.[7]

V

The conception of a life in which desires cannot be completely realized at the moment they are experienced is part of a larger view of existence as a realm of scarcity. It is a tradition with the longest history in the moral repertoire of mankind. The acceptance of the fact of scarcity has been an essential element in the outlook of most of mankind over most of its history. Poverty and injustice, illness and the brevity of life, the limitations on the possibility of gratifying desires and impulses have been regarded as inexpungible elements of the situation of mankind, and ethical patterns and theodicies have been constructed to justify or to censure — and to integrate — this ostensibly inevitable condition. The opening of the self and its elevation was confined to festivities, carnivals and rites, but everyday life was marked by constriction imposed by nature, society, and the moral powers of the personality. It consisted in limits on experience, the suppression of experienced impulse, the "avoidance of temptation" to impulses not yet experienced to come forward into consciousness or conduct. Poverty, ignorance, oppression took care of most of the preconditions for the constriction of individuality. A few great personalities transcended these limitations and made their lives into "works of art."

Christianity, particularly in its dissenting Protestant form, the growth of wealth, the spread of literacy, and the gradual recession of the primordial categories and criteria of assessing the meaning and worth of a human being have in the course of centuries worn away some of these individuality-suppressing and -constricting conditions. A profound revolution was worked by romanticism, which spread more widely in intellectual circles the conception of genius that need not regard the laws of society and its authorities and that aimed only to be guided by the inner necessities of the expansion of the self — to embrace new experiences, to enrich itself by the opening of its sensibilities. World War I and the Great Depression were the watershed. The erosion of the bourgeois ethic and the puritanism of diligence, respectability, and self-restraint on behalf of results which rendered one respectable were greatly aided by the Great Depression. The vanity of self-restraint was made evident, saving and striving were discredited; sexual self-restraint had been undermined by psychoanalysis and its literary popularization in the period between the wars. More or less liberal, tolerant, and constitutional political elites had been shown to be incompetent by the prolonged slaughter of World War I and by their failures in dealing with unemployment during the Great Depression. The regime of scarcity with which they were associated was discredited when their own legitimacy diminished. The same happened to the virtues of abstinence and self-discipline preached from the pulpits. Ecclesiastical authority had been under a steady pressure of rational disbelief and indifference; its legitimacy was further undermined in intellectual circles because of the association of the churches with the earthly regimes of external constriction and internal restraint under assault from other sources.

World War II was followed by an efflorescence of material well-being in the advanced countries on a scale never previously experienced. Particularly for the educated classes, there seemed to exist a relatively unbounded vista of opportunity for interesting employment, for travel, and for freedom from the restraints of impecuniousness, boring toil, and confinement. Full employment, the welfare services, and inflation made unrealistic the conception of a rainy day for which to save. At the outermost reaches was the perpetual awful threat of extinction in a war fought with nuclear weapons. The anxiety about the latter accentuated the attachment to pleasures of the moment. The heir of these developments was the generation born after the end of World War II.

In a variety of ways, this was a uniquely indulged generation. Parents who were in a state of unprecedented prosperity were persuaded of the merits of hedonism and were capable of giving some reality to its precepts in the raising of their children. They were convinced of the beneficence of a life free of repression and inhibition, and they treated their offspring with a concern and affection which seemed to confirm the prediction made by Ellen Key at the beginning of the twentieth century that this was the "century of the child." Expanding incomes and unceasing freedom from the threat of unemployment — for the middle classes at least — made for a readiness to believe that scarcity had been expelled from human existence. A life beyond the dreams of avarice seemed to have become accessible to those whom the fortunes of birth — in time and status — had favored. They were an increasingly larger proportion of the population.

The postwar generation has grown up, too, in a society in which authority has lost its sacredness. As the center of society expanded, those in positions of authority acquired a new conception of their obligations. Democratic elections moreover — and a populistic outlook even where there were no democratic elections — have made rulers believe that they have to justify themselves to realizing the desires of their citizenry. The expansion of individuality and the appreciation of the self, intricately related to enhanced self-esteem throughout much of Western societies, have diminished to some extent the arrogance of authority. The range of dispersion between the highest and the quite low has narrowed. It is certainly true that all Western — and all other — societies are far from the fulfillment of an ideal of equality. Power is unequally distributed; wealth is unequally distributed; income is unequally distributed; but the deference-system of modern societies strains toward egalitarianism. Of course, this "moral equality" is far from being realized; the strength of inherited beliefs and the presence of such tremendous concentrations of authority in the state and in great economic organizations — public and private — stand in the way of its realization. Nonetheless, the younger generation — living in the midst of the culturally juvenocentric society which Johan Huizinga discerned already in the 1930's — is experiencing this moral egalitarianism to a far-reaching degree. New methods of pedagogy and exclusion from the labor market — as far as middle-class young persons are concerned — have reduced the amount of experience with severely hierarchical and repressive institutions. But as much as the arrogance of authority has diminished, it has still not disappeared. Its diminution, moreover, has been more than balanced by the increased intolerability of what it seeks to impose. Sensitivity to the impositions of authority has greatly increased, and almost every impingement on it from the outside — unless voluntarily chosen as part of the expansion of individuality — is painful to the point of unsupportability.

Basic in all this is the view that every human being simply by virtue of his humanity is an essence of unquestionable, undiscriminatable value with the fullest right to the realization of what is essential in him. What is essential is his sensibility, his experienced sensations, the contents of his imagination, and the gratification of his desires. Not only has man become the measure of all things; his sentiments have become the measure of man. The growth of the capacity for unconfined sensation is the measure of the value of an institution. The goodness of a life consists in its continuous enlargement of these sensations and of the experiences that give rise to them. Institutions — with their specialized and prescribed roles, their restrictions on individual willfulness, the crystallization of traditions and their commitments that bind the future by the past — are repugnant to this aspiration toward an individuality that creates its boundaries only in response to its internal needs. Authority is repugnant, too, and so is tradition and all that it brings down and imposes from the past.

All this is old stuff. This is what the romantics taught us. But romanticism was only a literary and more or less philosophical movement; it did not become a widely pervasive outlook and style of life for many persons. Writers, artists, and bohemians espoused and embodied it, but its consistent following was small. The desacralization of authority, the productivity of the economy, the growth of moral equality, and the spread of enlightenment and educational opportunity have resulted in the diffusion of a much more consequent romanticism throughout a much broader section of each Western society. The more prosperous classes are the recipients of its diffusion; the offspring of these classes are their purest products.

University students in Western countries, despite an increased recruitment from among the offspring of the working classes, still come largely from middle- and upper-middle-class families. Many of those who have not come from these classes live in a cultural atmosphere of hedonistic expectations for the present and the future as much as do those who have come from families in which such expectations are to some extent realized. Many are supported from the public treasury at the expense of taxpayers. The availability of opportunity to attend university is still interpreted by many students, as it was in the past, as a first step into a less constricted future. Attendance at university, which was once regarded as a stroke of the good fortune of birth or the result of exertion and which offered its beneficiaries a chance to diminish to some extent the rigors of the regime of scarcity, is now, however, regarded by student radicals as itself part of an actual realm of plenitude. Anyone should have it for the asking.

University students, in the view of forty years ago, appeared to be on a straight road into a future which, in the light of the standards of the Enlightenment and in view of the immemorial fate of human beings, seemed to be extraordinarily rich in the possibilities of a better life — at least for themselves, if not for all the other members of their own societies. The student radicals of today have a quite different view of the matter: They do not wish to live in a society in which "the danger of death by starvation is replaced by the danger of death by boredom." The denunciation of the "consumers' society" is the common slogan of the French and West German student radicals; less explicitly but no less pervasively, the same view obtains among the American and British student radicals. They do not wish to be part of a "repressively tolerant society" that seduces by its favors. They wish their universities to be "restructured" to become the microcosms of a total revolution from which, in moments of exhilaration, they think that the rest of the society can be no less totally transformed. The universities must become "participatory," and from there outward their "societies" must become "participatory." They criticize their universities for having become "integrated" into their respective societies, but it is only evil integration which they oppose. They do not believe in the possibility of dispassionately acquired knowledge; they insist that "objectivity" and "neutrality" are simply masks that conceal the intention to serve the "system." They do not wish their universities to become "ivory towers"; they refuse to acknowledge the differentiation of tasks, a division of labor among institutions. There is no task that they would not have their institutions undertake in the transformation of society; only the transmission of knowledge[8] and discovery are left unmentioned by them.

The slogans of "student power" (Great Britain and the United States), *cogestion* (France) and *Drittelparität* (Western Germany) disregard the particular tasks of universities and the functions that these tasks qualify them to perform. The idea that there is a measure of inequality which is constitutive in the university's transmission of knowledge from those who possess more of it in particular spheres to those who possess less of it in those spheres is alien to their conception of the right order of life. For the same reason, equally alien is the idea that different institutions have different functions to perform. The very notion of differentiation and specialization in a division of labor among individuals and among institutions is alien to them. They wish their universities to become the centers from which their societies can be forced to become "participatory."

They demand — at least in the United States, but also in France — that their universities cease to be connected with government, except to be supported financially by it. At the same time, in the United States and in France, they insist that the universities take the responsibility — financial primarily — for forming "participatory" communities in their own neighborhoods. They wish their universities to be open to everyone; they are resolutely opposed to *selection*, to *numerus clausus*, and to the restriction on the use of university facilities and amenities to those who are its inscribed members. The "openness" or boundarylessness of institutions for which they contend is paralleled by their insistence on the openness of individual existence to new experience and new sensations. Hence, within their universities, the rebellious minority wish to be rid of all remnants of the institutions that embody the principle of *in loco parentis*. No restraints on their conduct are to be tolerated; neither restraints on their living arrangements, on their sexual associations, nor on their consumption of narcotics. They insist on an expanding series of subsidies for whatever activities they wish to engage in.

These views of life, society, and the university are not shared by any means by the entire generation of students today in the Western countries. Most of the students in most universities still share in the older culture. Nonetheless, the new "communitarian," "participatory" culture — which is really the romantic hunger for *Gemeinschaft*[9] on a more grandiose scale — pervades a substantial minority of the intelligent, sensitive, and hyper-reactive students.

VI

Why should all this have come to such a clamorous outburst and in so many of the most advanced countries now? Certain causes were implicitly indicated in what I said earlier. It is now twenty-three years since the end of World War II. Most of today's undergraduates were born in the second half of the 1940's, most of the more advanced or graduate students were born during the war. They were raised during the prosperity of the 1950's; they came to such maturity as they possess after the thaw of the Cold War.

In most of the countries of Western Europe and in North America, a considerable state of consensus has been obtained between the ruling party and the bulk of the opposition. Socialist parties of aggressively radical bearing have been lacking; the Communist Parties, as in the United States and Great Britain, have nearly disappeared, or in countries where they are strong, they have gradually, as in Italy and France, become domesticated to bourgeois society. Therewith they have lost the attractive power which Communist parties had for young antinomians in the heroic period of the Communist International. The hypersensitive anti-authoritarian student radicals of the past few years came, as they left adolescence, face to face with a "reactionary mass." No adult party has been able to attract their enthusiasm or their loyalty; no adult party could as a result discipline and sophisticate their antinomian zeal. On the contrary, their political relations with sympathetic adults all run in the opposite direction; adults seek to affiliate to them. Abendroth, Enzensberger, Touraine, Mahler, Tynan, MacDonald, and countless others flatter them and assure them of how right they are in whatever they demand.[10] Middle-aged adults seek the ardors of their youth in the vicarious exhilaration of "sit-ins" and strikes. Old memories of revolutions dreamed of in cafés and salons are revived, and embittered disillusionments are dissipated by the thought of the new revolutionaries in the universities. They praise the "sincerity" of the radicals and find in it a vindication of their own benefits from the existing regime. All such elderly enthusiasts can do is to offer confirmation, but they cannot temper or qualify.[11] How could they when they are despised as all weak authorities are bound to be.

Weak authorities occupying the highest positions in authoritative institutions — which must, by their nature and task, exercise authority — do not arouse respect or instill fear. They only generate contempt and hostility, particularly when they themselves seem to believe so little in the authority that they exercise. Split, disunited, temporizing, halfhearted authority that repeats against itself the charges made by the student radicals serves only to encourage more hostility. Its halfheartedness on its own behalf and its readiness, even eagerness, to acknowledge the rightfulness of the charges laid against itself do not reconcile the radicals to a moderation of their demands. It must be said on behalf of the student radicals that they take with a large admixture of salt the flattery and self-abasement of their elderly admirers. But the feebleness of those whom they expect to be strong encourages their hostility. The absence of effective positive models and the faintheartedness of those who oppose them open a free field for their aggressive dispositions.

In all the advanced Western countries,[12] the governments are generally humanitarian in their sympathies and progressive in their domestic social and economic policies. In many particular instances, their conduct diverges from these norms but on the whole, as compared with the constitutional governments of earlier decades — to say nothing of the fascist and Communist governments — they are liberal; they respect the freedom of expression; they legislate for the extension of welfare benefits and educational opportunity and submit to the insults and abuse directed toward them. They seldom order security forces to shoot looters and depredators; they generally attempt to restrain their agents in the face of rioters, and they are usually successful in doing so. (Chicago, it is true, was a grave exception, but it would be as wrong to deny its exceptional character as it would be to deny its gravity.[13]) They are even more yielding and conciliatory in speech. They find it hard to refuse the claims to rightfulness of the students who are against them. At most, they denounce the malfactions as the work of a "tiny minority of extremists," while acknowledging in many respects the legitimacy of the demands of the student radicals. What is true of governments is even more true of university administrations.

Despite all this, the existing authorities do not abdicate their authority; they are only liberal in social policy and compliant before the denial of their own legitimacy. Despite their conciliatory statements that the students are right in this and right in that, despite their forebearance, they still go about the business of conducting their governments. They maintain and use their armed forces; they impose burdens of national military service; they administer regimes of scarcity that cannot provide enough for everyone.[14] The same is true in universities; the teachers continue to occupy their professorships (and associate and assistant professorships), to receive their salaries, to set, administer, and mark examinations, pass judgments on dissertations, and grant or withhold degrees and diplomas. Presidents and rectors of universities might make speeches and write articles explaining that much of the criticism which student radicals make of the ideal-less, faltering, contemporary liberal society is just, but they do not dissolve their universities and they do not resign. They continue to operate their universities which, despite permissiveness and flexibility and flattery, continue to be selective institutions in a world of scarcity.

The radical students are opposed to competition and the scarcity which necessitates it. Their ethos is the ethos of a regime of plenitude, but they know, too, that their societies are regimes of scarcity. They know, too, that if they do not accept the rules of the regime of scarcity, they will go to the wall. Dean Marc Zamansky said to the striking students of the faculty of sciences in Paris when they were debating the boycott of examinations that even "a socialist society must be selective." How much more so a bourgeois society! Honors are scarce, first places are scarce, research grants and stipends are scarce, professorships are scarce. They are, of course, all more available than they used to be, but the student rebels do not know the past any more than most other young persons, and they do not take seriously what little they do know of it. They are entranced by a vision of plenitude of which they disapprove when they conceive of it as the "affluent society" or *société des comsommateurs* or the *Konsumentengesellschaft*, but which has nonetheless become an essential part of their construction of reality. Nonetheless they also know that they live in a world of scarcity run by adults whose legitimacy they do not acknowledge and whose ascendancy they hate; they deny the inevitability of the realm of scarcity and at the same time they know that they will not be able to avoid it. The examination system is the focal point of the repugnance for the regime of scarcity, particularly in the European universities where they are so concentrated in comparison with the dispersion of the American examination system; but in the United States, as if to compensate for the attenuation of strain from the concentration of examinations, there is the other strain of having to obtain marks high enough to qualify for admission to an eminent graduate school — and the radicals among undergraduates are also those disposed to go on to graduate school for no other reason than that it is less obnoxious than the bourgeois world outside.

It is not for nothing that the French "revolutionaries," once they occupied the Sorbonne and distracted their minds from examinations by the exhilaration of action committee meetings and fighting on barricades, soon began to worry about their examinations. Nor is it for nothing that the German student radicals — sprung from a breed famous for putting off the dreaded examinations — should demand that students sit on examining bodies and that the examination system be "transformed."[15]

It is to those better universities with famous graduate schools, which are also more liberal and therefore more popular with student radicals, that admission is sought. Places in such universities are scarce, and their regime is severe for those who succeed in entering. For those who are successful, life turns out to be very hard. In American universities, postgraduate studies are densely organized; many of the students are married and feel the pressing proximity of philistine life — family, job, routine responsibilities, and assimilation into the great machine where ideals are only a fragrance and hard decisions in the allocation of scarce resources to alternative ends must be made. The long drawn out proceedings of acquiring a post-graduate degree — several sets of examinations and an elaborate research dissertation — and a real or imagined dependence on the good will and sponsorship of one's supervisor for financial support and then for appointment to a teaching or research post on completion, add to the strain. All this underscores the discrepancy between the ideal of a regime of plenitude and the "hard facts of life" so often and so rightly referred to by older critics of student radicalism. It all comes at the worst possible time — at the point of passage that separates the open life of the expanding individuality from the dreaded knuckling under to authority.

It does not, therefore, seem to me to be accidental that the outbursts all over Europe and the United States reached their height in the spring of 1968 just at the time when students normally begin to prepare themselves for examinations. It was fitting that within a short time after the occupation of the Sorbonne, examinations — whether they should be put off, abolished, transformed, or, in the last resort, taken — came to occupy the center of the revolutionaries' attention.

I do not contend that examinations and examinations alone are the causes of the present student unrest,[16] nor that they provide an exhaustive explanation of why the disorders occurred on such a grand scale in the first half of 1968. The examinations are causes; they do not often become issues. As far as Europe and America and other countries are concerned, some of the issues on which the radical students confront authority so aggressively are really — and sometimes justly and reasonably — felt by them as genuine grievances. Some of the issues have become more urgent in the past year. University facilities and amenities in France and Italy are extremely insufficient, and grievances about this have accumulated. The Spanish government has been unjustified in its obstinate insistence on a monopoly of all student activities by the official student organization, and the persistence of unyieldingness on both sides has led to intensification and politicization. The West German universities have been plagued by the haughty self-righteousness and rigidity of the professorial oligarchy, and the conflict between this and the "Berlin model" has become more patent during the past few years. The internal domestic regulations and disciplinary arrangements of British and American universities are certainly irksome to some students, as are the arrogation of power and its unthinking use by professional university administrators (for example, the withdrawal of the "speakers corner" at Berkeley a few years ago), and sensitivity to this has always become sharper and more reactive in the past few years. Above all, there is the war in Vietnam with all its cruelty and its unending ineffectiveness and the menace of conscription into the most individuality-constricting of environments. Finally, there is the Negro problem in the United States, more severe now than it was four or five years ago. (The preoccupation of white students with it is less now than it was while it was still the "civil rights movement.")

In addition to these issues that obtrude, there are the issues that an issue-seeking desire for confrontation discovers. For British radical students there are Rhodesia, the supply of arms to Nigeria, and the tacit, uncomfortable, and negligible support of the British government for American action in Vietnam. For German students, the Springer concern, the Shah of Iran, the alliance of the federal government with the United States, the recognition of the German Democratic Republic and the legalization of the German Communist Party. For French students, there has been little since the end of the war in Algeria, except for anti-Americanism and unlimited visiting between the sexes in university cities. From time to time specific issues like the free distribution of *cours polycopiés* arose but passed away. There were also fights with the extremist *Occident,* but these did not lead to large-scale demonstrations or strikes.

In Italy, there were many fights between antagonistic extremists

of various designations, but these did not precipitate a "confrontation" with the authorities on a broad front. In Spain, the conflict
between students, on the one hand, and the authorities in government and the university has been unremitting, and the original
domestic issue of "free student syndicates" has been increasingly
supplemented by anti-Americanism (Vietnam, American aid to
Spain) and overtures to the illegal workers' syndicates.

Now all these issues are very disparate and do not tell us why
they should have broken out with such an uproar this year. The
earth is a vale of tears, but it is certainly not much worse this year
than in other years in the past century and a half. Nor does the
general analysis which I have offered in this paper of the horrified
resistance of those attached to visions of the regime of plenitude in
contact with the oncoming pressure of the regime of scarcity explain
why the outburst occurred this year.

The only explanation I can give for the approximate simultaneity
of the outbursts of the present year is one that combines the general
distressfulness of the student situation with a number of accidental
coincidences and the working of the "demonstration effect."

VII

We are far from living in a single world community, but the
rudiments of a world society do exist. The international scientific
community is the most international of all the elements of this
rudimentary world society. Learned and scientific periodicals, international scientific societies, and the universities are the most elaborated and most internationally coherent parts of this rudimentary
worldwide network of institutions. They do, at least at their peaks,
have common standards, common heroes, and a unifying sense of
affinity. Students, through their membership in universities, share in
some of this, and their sense of sharing is accentuated among a fluc-
tuatingly small group by an acute sense of generational identity.
Although international student organizations are of little significance
in the concert of action of 1968, and although students have nothing
like a major scientific or scholarly press which creates a common
focus of attention and a common awareness of leading accomplishments and personalities, it has an effective surrogate in the mass
media — the newspaper press, wireless, and television. Information
flows rapidly without a student international, without the use of a
cumbersome system of couriers and coded messages such as inter-

national revolutionary organizations once had to use. The radical students have not created this organ of their movement, but they have been responsive to it and indeed, being aware of its value, direct their actions to it. They value television publicity as much as do the figures of the entertainment world or politics.

The international society is no more egalitarian in fact than are the various national societies. This is as true of scientific distinction as it is of wealth and political power. The scientific world has its centers and its peripheries just as any national society has and so does the sphere of student radicalism. What happens in the periphery does not radiate to the center; the movement is in the contrary direction. When the Indian students erupt as they have been doing quite continuously for about twenty years, student radicals do not attend to that. They attend to it even less than their teachers in biochemistry or sociology attend to what is being done in biochemistry or sociology by their colleagues in the Indian universities. Even a more powerful country like Japan produces little demonstration effect. When the *Zengakuren* went on a rampage to prevent President Eisenhower from visiting their country, the facts become known, but they did not become exemplary. When the Indonesian KAMI's helped to bring down the unspoken coalition of Sukarno and the PKI, what they did was admired, but not attended to. When the gallant students of the *Po Prostu* circle helped to bring about the short-lived and now dead Polish October, the students of Berkeley and London found no inspiration there. But when the Berkeley students and then after them students in many other American universities began their "revolution," the radiation from the center outward began. It was like the radiation of the revolution of February from Paris in 1848, when all of Europe felt the repercussions.

The Berkeley model was diffused to West Berlin. It was perhaps no accident that one of the original instigators of the events of West Berlin was Ekkehard Krippendorf who had been a graduate student in political science in the United States at the crucial time. From West Berlin, the movement spread later to the rest of Western Germany; from Berkeley, it spread to the London School of Economics and to a much smaller extent to other British universities. From Western Germany, it spread to Nanterre through the personal embassy of Daniel Cohn-Bendit and — with a reinforcement of inspiration from Columbia in April, 1968, and from the riots which followed the attempted assassination of Rudi Dutschke in the same month — from Nanterre to the Sorbonne. For a time, in a way not pleasing to General de Gaulle but in conformity with the main direction of his desires, Paris once more became the center of the world. (He would have been even less pleased than he was, however, had he reflected that the technique of those who made Paris momentarily into the center of the world of *chienlit* had been imported from the United States where it had first been used by working men and later by Negroes.) From Paris it spread to such peripheral academic backwaters as Brussels, Rome, Florence, Milan, and Dakar.

Was there a coincidence of issues in the various countries that would help to explain the speed and intensity with which the demonstration effect operated? I doubt this because most of the issues on which the radicals seek "confrontation" are factitious and not imperatively obtrusive in themselves. There are really and deeply felt issues among those I listed earlier. The Vietnam war and the draft overshadows all others in the United States, but on the whole this is a secondary matter in other countries. There are scarcely any other issues than those connected with the war in Vietnam that do not seem to be contrived by those who are bent on confrontation.

Most of the issues that arouse the passions of the radical students are not serious in the sense of being well grounded in fact or deeply cared about. The accusations of anti-Negro prejudice against the newly appointed director of the London School of Economics, for example, were baseless. The accusations of anti-Negro prejudice or of indifference to Negro needs on the part of the Columbia University administration were a little better based, but they were not quite as the SDS alleged. The insulting of M. Missoffe, the Minister of Sports and Youth, when he opened the swimming pool in the faculty of letters and human science at Nanterre was a confrontation pure and simple; it was not an issue. The protest against the visit of the Shah of Iran which was the occasion of the death of Benno Ohnesorg at the hands of the police was not a serious issue for the West Berlin students; it was the occasion for a confrontation. The striking thing about all of these precipitating issues is how soon they disappeared under the onrush of subsequent responses.

At the London School of Economics, the merits and demerits of Dr. Adams were forgotten in favor of resistance to the disciplinary actions threatened by the authorities of the School following the death of the porter; the long "sit-in" disregarded Dr. Adams. At Columbia, protests against the action of the university administration in summoning the police and against the police for their unnecessarily harsh action dwarfed protests against the university's policy to build a gymnasium in Morningside Park and even against its relationship to the Institute of Defense Analysis. At Wisconsin, protests against the university's use of police and against the conduct of the police placed the prior protests against the Dow Chemical Company in the shadows. In West Berlin, the agitation following the death of Benno Ohnesorg consigned the Shah of Iran far into the rear of the student radicals' memory. In Paris, even the issues of visiting rights of the two sexes in university cities and of the disciplinary proceedings against Cohn-Bendit and his colleagues were put aside in favor of amnesty of those arrested during the demonstrations and skirmishes of the nights of May.

VIII

This transience of initial issues does not testify to the forgetfulness of the student radicals and the unseriousness of their original complaints. The transience of many of the issues is a function of the more important fact that they are the occasions for confrontations with authority.

It is authority that the radical students wish to confront and affront — and almost any stick will do for the camel. This brings us back not only to the general predisposition with which we dealt earlier, but also to the immediate precipitation of this year's outbreaks. In Western Germany, Great Britain, and the United States, this has been a poor year for governments. In the United States, in particular, the image of the ineptitude of President Johnson — exemplified in the faltering and failing conduct of the war in Vietnam, the inability to bring the disturbances in Negro districts of the big cities to an end, the enfeeblement of urban public order in other respects, and the lack of spectacular results from the poverty program — has made government authority an easy target. The possibility that he could be succeeded by Senator McCarthy made for an even greater aggressiveness against incumbent authority. In Great Britain, the recurrence of the crisis of sterling and the devaluation, the failure to compel admission into the Common Market and powerlessness in the face of the Smith regime in Rhodesia, as well as the flagrant impropriety of the government's treatment of the East African Asians who held British passports have darkened the visage of the Labour government. For different reasons, the federal German government is in the same position. In France the mounting criticism of General de Gaulle from the ineffective opposition parties and the immobilism of the General's government as well as the small majority by which he was returned in the general election which preceded the crisis had similar consequences — which were aggravated, too, by the absence of the two most powerful figures in the government (General de Gaulle in Rumania and M. Pompidou in Afghanistan) when events were cascading — have all replaced the image of a strong and effective authority by one of feebleness and abdication. Where authority abdicates through failure, ineptitude, and weakened self-confidence, it invites aggression against itself. That is what happened this past spring.

If this complex of factors accounts for the concert of confrontations in the advanced Western countries, how do we account for the magnitude and especially for the speed with which movements of *groupuscules* became "mass movements"?

Wherever authority is confronted and takes aggressive but limited counteraction, there are victims. The repressive actions — police action and intra-university disciplinary proceedings — always enlarge the size of the student group drawn into the confrontation of the second stage. The students whose moral sensibilities are affronted by repressive action are much more numerous than the student radicals; they are drawn into confrontation on an issue which is quite different from those on which the smaller group of radical pioneers took the initial steps of challenging authority. The issues become quite different and the newly involved protesters are drawn from a different stratum of opinion among the students. This is when amnesty becomes the main issue.

Why is the second and usually much larger group drawn in? Originally they were more moderate and kept their distance from the extreme, particular, and often fairly specific demands of the pioneering nucleus of disturbance. Yet when the action changes its character, they become as involved, as adamant, and as daring as those whose initial confrontation was the prelude to their own involvement. It is also usually among these somewhat more responsible elements that demands for *cogestion* and *Drittelparität* obtain their strongest support.

The rapidity with which repressive measures by authority galvanize a larger support among previously inactive students seems to indicate that there is moral consensus within the student generation deeper than that about the particular issues the tiny minority of extremists invoke. In one form or another, this consensus centers on the value of the unconstricted expansive individuality, free in its movements, determinative of its own fate. The strength of the demand is not so great that it is continuously prominent, but constrictive and repressive activities by authorities shock it into prominence. This aspiration toward the romantic ideal of the ego is the bond that unites the extremist *groupuscules* and the larger circle around them. The difference between them is that in the former it is intense and continuous, while in the latter it is attenuated, only intermittently intense, and easily subsided.

Nonetheless, the expansive power of individuality and the dream of a regime of plenitude have opened up in the world. They cannot be conjured away, and they cannot be gratified by flattery by elders. In the United States, the war in Vietnam will be brought to a halt, the Negroes will be treated with a greater measure of indifference to their color. The universities will be somewhat reformed in France, Germany, and Italy, and the Spanish government might allow students to have their own unions — it is already moving haltingly in that direction, although perhaps the moment has passed when it could do it without cost to anything but its obstinate pride. If the parents who are still legally responsible for their offspring agree that university should not stand *in loco parentis,* then that feature of Anglo-American university life will be modified. Students everywhere outside the Communist countries are likely to be granted consultative powers in certain university decision-making bodies, and in some matters they will be given full responsibility. All these changes, desirable in themselves, will not, however, resolve the deeper tensions between a cultural tradition that fosters individuality and the vision of a realm of plenitude and a society the institutions of which require efficiency, competence, selection on the basis of past and prospective accomplishment, and differential rewards.

REFERENCES

1. The late Professor Tawney once told me that when in the late 1920's he was in China on a League of Nations educational mission, he and his colleagues were forced to wait at a railway station for several hours. On enquiring of the stationmaster as to the cause of the long delay, the stationmaster told them it was because students had squatted on the track several miles up the line. Professor Tawney asked why the students were not removed by the police; he was told the students would resist. But, he said, could not their resistance be overcome by the police. The answer was that it was inconceivable because some students might be hurt.

2. Commentators on the indiscipline of Indian students often explain the dissatisfactions of the Indian students by saying that the political leadership presents no acceptable ideal to the student generation, that it is corrupt and purposeless, and that it is therefore unable to inspire the students. The students themselves, however, seldom refer to the general features of contemporary Indian society.

3. Where the recent form of the student movement appears to be a more mob-like variant of the youth movements of the Soviet Union, Fascist Italy, and other countries where state authority dominates the student scene.

4. The countries of the Maghreb still, as in colonial times, have the seat of the most virulent oppositional student organizations located in the former metropolis.

5. This is true even for West Bengal where, considering the aggressive restlessness of the students, relatively few of them are willing to subordinate themselves to the Moscow or Peking Communists.

6. The SDS in the United States spoke about "participation" long before General de Gaulle's recent proposal of the participatory solution as an alternative to the solutions of "totalitarian communism" and "competitive capitalism." Lucien Lévy-Bruhl spoke about it before either, and he referred to the extension of the boundaries of the self — among other things — to include within it objects apparently alien to it. Contemporary student radicals base their criticism of modern society and its institutions, particularly the university, on an aspiration to an expanding individuality. Lévy-Bruhl's idea of participation entailed a transcendence of individuality. Yet the two apparently contrary conceptions converge in the seemless unity of the community of expanded individualities or egos.

7. Student radicals in France, Germany, and the United States do not know that their frequent denunciations of the "system" are evocative of the Nazi abuse of the Weimar "system." But why should they know it when all of the past and practically all of the present is "little more than the register of the crimes, follies and misfortunes of mankind." But the similarity is there, and it bespeaks an affinity of outlook.

8. They seem to think so poorly of the transmission of knowledge as a university task that they insist that all learning must be through "dialogue" and "contestation." They assume that the past has accomplished nothing and that those who are ready to transmit the fruit or record of its accomplishments are simply repressive of the essential individuality of each student.

9. I should like to take this opportunity to call attention to a forgotten book which deserves to be recalled and studied for its sober assessment of an earlier form of the present *Gemeinschaftsschwärmerei*. It is Professor Helmuth Plessner's *Grenzen der Gemeinschaft: Eine Kritik des sozialen Radikalismus* (Bonn, 1923).

10. The moral self-abasement of a large part of the French literary and academic intellectual class in May and June, 1968, expressed a disposition which is to be found in nearly every Western country. The students have for the time being replaced the "working classes" in the highest point of the pantheon of the "progressive" intelligentsia.

11. When one of the middle-aged sympathizers of the student radicals has the courage and good sense to attempt to qualify their views as Professor Habermas has done, the result is denunciation.

12. In October, 1968.

13. The roughness of American and French police is notorious, but in all of the student demonstrations in Paris last spring only one young man was fatally wounded during an altercation between demonstrators and police, and he was the victim of a knife wound which has not been attributed to the police. In the United States, the behavior of the police in Chicago in front of the Hilton Hotel in August was utterly incommensurate with the provocation, but the recollection of American police conduct in labor disputes and toward radicals over the past century would soon disclose the relative domestication of the police in the past few years in dealing with "dangers to public order." All I contend above is that the agents of public order are much less harsh and repressive than they were during the 1930's in Western Europe and North America — and in many other places in the world.

14. The ineffectiveness of authority is a stimulus to aggressiveness against it. A deprivational, scarcity-administering authority puts itself into a difficult position when it acts ineffectively. If the United States government had been able to fight the war in Vietnam successfully, even using the same technology it is now using in fighting without a positive outcome, I venture to say that it would not have aroused the animosity among student radicals which it has done in the past few years. I say this while agreeing with many criticisms which student radicals make of the war, and particularly about the need to bring it to a halt.

15. Examinations and their appurtenances are among the main occasions of student disorder in Indian higher education. The confrontation of a kinship-dominated culture of diffuse expectations such as that of the student in his familial *foyer* with the culture which demands specific performances as conditions for prospective rewards such as examination marks, appointments to particularly desirable positions, and so forth creates much tension.

16. I have dealt elsewhere with the whole range of causes in the Indian situation. Compare Philip G. Altbach (ed.), *Turmoil and Transition: Higher Education and Student Politics in India* (New York, 1969).

I

THE STUDENT REVOLUTION

IN THE WESTERN COUNTRIES

A. H. HALSEY AND STEPHEN MARKS

British Student Politics

The Significance of Activism

ON A LONG VIEW, there is nothing novel about student involvement in civil disturbance. Histories of the medieval universities in Europe abound with records of violence. Here, taken almost at random is an account of one such riot in Oxford — the battle of St. Scholastica's Day in 1354:

All night the citizens from surrounding towns and villages poured into Oxford, thirsting to crush the hated clerics once and for all. The students naturally received no access of reinforcements. The next day the battle was resumed, the townsmen again being the aggressors. They caught certain scholars walking after dinner in Beaumont, killing one and wounding others. Then on into the University quarter itself, where the scholars defended themselves desperately, fighting from street to street, pouring their bolts and arrows from the windows of beleaguered houses. But the army of townsmen was not to be denied. The students were overwhelmed; their ranks broke, and the fight developed into a total rout. Whoever could, fled the town; others attempted a last stand in their houses, and still others sought sanctuary in the churches and monasteries of the quarter.

For two days the mob rioted and pillaged and slew. There was no glutting their bloodlust and their hatred of all clergy. The poor scholars were dragged out of their hiding places and ruthlessly butchered; the houses were literally torn down and the schools were wrecked. Even the churches provided no sanctuary, nor did the appeals of the monks avail, even though the Regulars were held in far greater respect than the secular clergy. Trembling clerics were torn from the altars, and there is testimony to the effect that two chaplains were flayed alive, the mob having suddenly reverted to the practices of their barbarous ancestors. When the pillage was over, the University had vanished, seemingly never to return.[1]

What is described here is an example of traditional "town and gown" conflict. It serves as a reminder that there are many forms taken by conflict in which intellectual institutions are involved and several directions in which aggression may run, including violence by the laity against students. Recent student newsworthiness, however, is neither exclusively nor typically generated by conflict of this kind and far less is it akin to the licensed horseplay of a panty raid on a sorority at Wisconsin or of undergraduates at Oxford who would demonstrate their conformity to the traditional mores of

> . . . . the upper class
> to like the sound of broken glass.

What is at stake is the legitimacy of university authority and, behind this, the acceptability of the social system into which the university is an invitation to the young on terms which promise privilege in exchange for what, until recently, have been widely agreed to be minimal, reasonable, and undemanding conformities. For most students most of the time these terms are acceptable. But the attention of the newspapers is focused not on the majority, but on two minority cultures[2] — the hippy and the activist. Both are more or less radical rejections of what is pejoratively termed "the system." They stand together against the conformist majority which is oriented to join a career and a way of life from which the one would withdraw and which the other would change. Political scientists and this essay are concerned primarily with the activists but, though frequently left to be interpreted by sociologists of religion, the withdrawal type of phenomenon is also of basic political relevance as one of the modern movements based on a theory of the impotence of all political activity. If men seek realization of their interests on some kind of calculus as to likely opportunity cost, then it is of interest to political sociology to know how politics in the university setting can price itself out of the psychological market of this outlandish minority. How and why do its members differ from the activists who turn away from conventional politics, but set themselves the task of constructing other new forms of political activity?

The significance of activism is not one of simple arithmetic. It involves typically a "tip of the iceberg" conception of politics, and it centers on the legitimacy of the values presented and functions performed by universities on behalf of the larger society. Both have been changing in the present century, roughly along the lines of a widening basis of recruitment at one end and a more direct servicing of the professional and managerial requirements of the industrial work force at the other. A characteristic expression of this view is that "the prime function of higher education used to be the recruiting and cultural buttressing of the social élite. Nowadays it has an added dimension — the fundamental role it plays in the economy. For skilled manpower is the scarcest resource of industrial society."

In this sense, the university is a representative institution to the student. It represents "the system" as an opportunity structure and along with it the medley of conflicting values in politics, religion, and sex from which the young must somehow choose a way of life. However, the university not only represents, but also *is* the world for young people whose increasing proportionate attendance enhances the potential of the campus as a cockpit of intergenerational conflict. The responsiveness of universities to social pressures from without has led to increasing scale and therefore to bureaucratization, to increasing specialization and therefore to weakening community, and, what is less often noticed, to changes in the career interests of those who teach, research, and administer, and therefore to greater and more uncertain distances between teachers and taught. Conflict, in short, may be ritual, may be against the non-academic world, but may be in a distinctive modern form centered on the structure of relations within the university while at the same time reflecting larger struggles in a wider social context.

The more explosive of the recent disturbances seem to have occurred where internal friction allowed easy generalization to broader social discontents. It is for this reason that the British case is instructive: The twentieth-century history of student politics in this country has been a notably peaceable one. But the degree to which this internal friction allows such generalization relates to two variables: not only the internal structure of the institution and particular conjunctural conflicts within it, but also the national political perspective and mood of the activists. "Generalization" is thus subject to an external "pull" as well as to an internal "push." Thus conflicts can occur over incidents which have arisen before in the past without such consequences. When the "external" political situation and the current political attitudes among activists "internally" make this appropriate, "generalization" may be a conscious objective. Thus Cohn-Bendit's group at Nanterre openly proclaimed their objective as being the "provocation" of the authorities into showing their true faces.[3]

Our thesis is that the characteristic internal organization — the English idea of a university — and at least one external factor — the recognized existence of an organized political left — together account for a relatively low level of campus activism, but that both these "protections," internal and external, are weakening with consequent signs of an unfamiliar type of student movement.

The English Idea of a University

The English idea of a university has been examined in detail elsewhere.[4] It is rooted historically in a combination of medieval commensality (the college) and the humanistic education of the governing classes. This traditional form of educational institution provides for maximum solidarity between teachers and taught through the absence of a separate administration and an emphasis on close personal relations through tutorial teaching methods, high staff-student ratios, and shared domestic life. The ideal of university life embodied in this form of education precedes the rise of specialization in scholarship and the widened social recruitment to professions that are associated with industrial society. More recent adaptation to the demands of industrialism have accordingly modified the life of the English universities by trends toward larger scale, more specialization, more impersonal instruction, and less collegiate social life. At the same time, the older traditions have resisted modernity — most successfully in the ancient universities and least in the Colleges of Advanced Technology. The student role defined in terms of these traditional norms is such as to promote close identification with the college. More recent "meritocratic" tendencies in selection for the prestige universities have served to merge college identification with adherence to the intellectual purposes of the institution and, in this way, to make for heightened identification with the don.

The organizational changes associated with mass higher education, the "multiversity" described by Clark Kerr, are scarcely in evidence in England yet. Apart from London, which is in any case a federal structure of more or less autonomous colleges, there are no universities approaching the scale of the larger American campuses, the Sorbonne or the University of Moscow. Student alienation from "Berkeley" conditions, as described for example by Bryan Wilson, is not, or at least not yet, a feature of the English scene.[5] The traditional norms of staff-student relations seem to be threatened less by size and bureaucratic organization than by the changing career patterns of dons in relation to the expectations and mode of recruitment of the modern student.

But over and above these cohesive influences within the universities there is, as we shall see, a marked recent increase of political activism among students that is directed not so much against their teachers as against what are seen, correctly or incorrectly, as incipient tendencies in governmental policy toward reduction of the autonomy of higher education, its functional separation in the interests of "manpower" needs, and expansion of student numbers by dilution of established standards of amenity and financial support. The fullest statement of the position of these activists is to be found in a pamphlet recently published by the RSA.[6]

Student Politics Before 1956[7]

The principal British student organization is the National Union of Students (NUS) with 366,000 members. The three main political organizations in the late fifties and early sixties were connected with the major national political parties. They were the National Association of Labour Student Organisations (NALSO), a federative organization of Labour and Socialist clubs with a membership fluctuating between 7000 and 10,000 and until 1967 a bilateral agreement with the Labour Party; the Federation of Conservative and Unionist Organisations (FUCUO); and the Union of Liberal Students, claiming a membership of 10,000. These last two, unlike the first, are closely integrated with their parent parties both ideologically and structurally.

The way in which the NUS has carried out its task of representing the interests of its student membership and the views which its more political organizations have held on the relevance of their political positions to students have all been affected by the distinctively English idea of the nature of a university. Contrast between the norm, to which the practice in the older universities has approximated, and the relatively vocational realities of the "redbrick" universities is in fact the background from which the NUS emerged after World War I, and in which it developed its combination of moderate methods and a purely university-limited orientation. This pattern of activity has lasted almost unchallenged until the recent emergence of advocates of student unionism on the European model with their demand that NUS adopt similar methods to those of professional associations and white-collar and industrial trade unions.

The work situation of the student can, of course, be described in the terms used to analyze other work situations and forms of collective activity — that is, by reference to common location, ease of communication, and common economic situation. But the weight of these factors is modified not only by the transient nature of student status, but also by the special features of the student role in the British universities. By contrast with the American or continental counterpart, entry to student status is formally selective; the role is sponsored in the sense that maintenance and graduation are almost universally guaranteed by the national system of scholarships and the low "drop-out" rate from a short (three years) full-time and closely supervised program of studies. The scope for "perpetual" or "professional" students as a "continuity staff" of student organizations is therefore highly restricted.

The early history of the NUS clearly reflects these conditions.[8] Before 1914 a body called the British Universities Congress had met annually in different universities and was replaced after the war by the Inter-University Association. Both were entirely confined to "redbrick" universities and were not attended by any representatives from Oxford, Cambridge, or London. The NUS was formed in 1922 from the IUA under the influence of individuals who came back from the first Prague conference in 1921 of the *Confederation International des Etudiants* (CIE) with the intention of forming an English union so as to bring more pressure to bear among students against the intransigent anti-German feelings of the French Union. The NUS differed from the IUA in that it was "formed to include the student unions of every university and every university college in the country. Such an organization is novel to England only because the great majority of the universities are almost equally novel."[9]

Concern with concessions and reduced fares for foreign travel — which were the staples of NUS activity and which even today are the only purposes for which most British students have any contact with their union — was present from the outset. The English Union took responsibility within the international organization for all travel arrangements and apart from this confined itself to fostering various welfare services, a sanatorium, and a vacation employment scheme.[10]

In this early period students as an organized body developed little or nothing in the way of a coherent theory of the role of the university or of the student. At their 1927–28 session, it is true, the Council and Executive of NUS did discuss "the formidable question of the purpose and value of a university education, and indeed of all education as practised in England at the present time,"[11] but the somewhat prim and hesitant turn of phrase seems to indicate that this was considered an exceptional innovation for the Union. No previous discussion of this topic was mentioned at any time in the previous five years of existence of the Union, and this occasion seems to have been an opportunity for an exchange of views rather than an attempt to formulate any general position on the part of the Union. No decisions were recorded. Mention was made, however, of the fact that, among the Union presidents attending, "there was a general complaint of prevailing apathy among undergraduates toward anything not strictly relevant to the acquisition of a degree; a too concentrated attention to the letter of the syllabus and an almost complete lack of imaginative purposeful enterprise in fields of inquiry not falling within the orbit of the final examination." The reasons for this were thought to be "the desire to obtain a final qualification that raises social status and probably remuneration; the necessity for reaching or maintaining scholarship standard; the need to have done as quickly as possible with preliminary training and become self-sufficient."

Some change in the narrowness of British student unionism appears to have taken place in the 1930's, partly as a reflection within the universities of the heightened political consciousness of the period, and more specifically as a reaction to the effect of the economic depression on unemployment prospects. The minority of activists were almost certainly proportionately greater in the thirties than at any time since, with the possible exception of the climax of the CND campaign in 1960. Activism of the Left, led by the Communist Party, included attempts to define the student role as a vital element in the "class struggle": Activism of the social democratic center was closely linked to support and criticism of the Labour Party platform, and there was a complex series of splits, popular front combinations, and realignments. Nevertheless, although students certainly participated in politics, they did not do so distinctively as students or for students.

In the General Strike of 1926, for example, many volunteered as strike breakers. But there is evidence that this was seen by those involved not as a distinctively student intervention, but rather as a response to "national emergency" by young citizens. Participants, moreover, were supported by university authorities. Thus in Oxford, which together with Cambridge was the main source of volunteers, university examinations were postponed to assist student strike breakers.[12] While the university authorities forbade student involvement in the dispute in Oxford, as the local strike committee had requested them to do, they did not prevent nearly 2000 students from volunteering to work as dockers, busmen, or special constables in London and the provincial cities. There was also, it should be noted, a nucleus of university support for the strike, organized by G. D. H.

Cole and his University Strike Committee. One undergraduate, Hugh Gaitskell, volunteered as a chauffeur between the Oxford Council of Action and the T.U.C. (Trades Union Congress) in London.

In the thirties, left-wing passions frequently reached a high pitch. The Oxford Union resolution of 1934 that "this house would in no circumstances fight for its King and Country" is well known. What is less often remembered is that this debating society also later passed the motion that "this house recognises no flag but the Red Flag."

NUS affairs did not escape some influence from this general background of a politically "heroic" period. Insistence on the need to join the NUS was, for example, a standard issue for the activist Left in the Oxford and Cambridge colleges. Nonetheless, there were no fundamental changes in the aims, methods, or activities of the NUS. The nearest approach to a new formulation was the work of Brian Simon, a former president of the Union and a member of the Communist Party, which though written on the invitation of the NUS was not officially adopted as a policy statement.[13] Simon emphasized the dichotomy within the traditional system of higher education between the narrow vocationalism of the "redbrick" universities, especially in their science departments, and the older universities' ethic of "pure scholarship" in non-vocational academic subjects, which in these fields was also shared by the newer universities. Student apathy was again decried and the 1939 NUS Congress report was quoted: "In a university of about 2000 students only about 300 could be said to take a real interest and an active part in student activities."

The reasons Simon gave for apathy were partly derived from the situation of the student in the university (the allegedly deadening nature of the curriculum and the effects of a non-residential system on student social life) and partly from factors which can be grouped as the origins or the destination of the student (the class-biased nature of the selection system, and the importance of university performance for future job prospects). In this situation, and given the attitudes to the proper role of students implicit in the "English idea," participation by students in organized political activity tended to come only with the irruptions into the university of external issues of national or international politics, or in the form of developments which directly affect the students themselves, but not in their capacity as students; it is to factors in this second category that Simon attributed the decline in apathy at the time at which he was writing, namely, concern with the academic situation of the student in the university. It was not till much later that any student movement was to claim to be so based; and by that time far-reaching changes had begun to take place in English higher education.

After World War II

The immediate postwar period saw a considerable increase in the numbers of students, due chiefly to an unexpected volume of applications for places by ex-servicemen. In October, 1945, a joint Congress of the NUS and the Association of University Teachers demanded more, and more adequate, maintenance grants for students, a demand largely met by 1947 except for a parental means test which the NUS continued to oppose. Periodic negotiations with the government about the financial value of state scholarships and discussions of them at NUS Councils now became a regular feature in the activity of the Union.

By 1953, which represented the trough of the postwar ex-servicemen "bulge" in university applications, the total number of full-time students at UGC-aided institutions had settled down to some 80,000, a considerable increase over the 1938–39 figure of 50,000.[14] The postwar period was one of right-wing trends in the universities, in reaction against the 1945 Labour Government and the egalitarianism associated with it.[15] This may have been linked with the recrudescence of a perennial strand of hostility among some British undergraduates toward student representative organizations, which are seen as providing an opportunity for bureaucratic careerists to bury themselves in a form of activity associated more with industrial disputes than with the cloistered calm of the traditional English university.[16] These attitudes are found more frequently in universities than in other institutions of higher education. Thus there was a spate of disaffiliations from the NUS in the early fifties, when Manchester and Southampton Unions disaffiliated specifically in protest against the presence in the NUS of unions from colleges other than university colleges.[17] In the case of Manchester the expense of affiliation was also mentioned.

The New Left

The postwar decade, then, saw no political movement among students that was based on the situation of the student in the university or was other than the activity within the university of national political organizations; nor was there any motive to action in

the economic climate outside the university and its effects on graduate prospects, such as there was in the 1930's. But after 1956, "the
watershed year of British politics,"[18] new trends emerged on the national political left in which young people, and students in particular, played an important part — the Campaign for Nuclear Disarmament and the trends known collectively as the New Left.[19] Both of
these had declined before the emergence of the current wave of student radicalism. But the organizations and attitudes which they left
behind were to have a considerable influence on the precise form
taken by student reactions to changes in the nature and role of the
universities in the early 1960's.

The British New Left movement as it existed between 1957 and
1961–62 had its origins in the political events of 1956 and grew in the
atmosphere created by the Campaign for Nuclear Disarmament in
the years after 1958.[20] The Hungarian Revolution and its suppression led to the foundation of the *New Reasoner* by a group of dissi-
dent Communists in Northern universities who left the Party in
protest while the Suez war generated considerable radical feeling
among students from which emerged *Universities & Left Review*
based in Oxford; the two magazines merged in 1960 to form the
New Left Review.

At its height the movement associated with the *New Left Review*
numbered some thirty or forty Left clubs in centers outside London,
and a variety of lecture, discussion, and study groups in London —
including *Education, History of Socialism,* and *Literature* groups,
and a *London Schools Left Club,* which was made up of secondary
school sixth formers. The main orientation of the movement was
theoretical rather than practical. Politically, a running battle was
waged with the chief theoreticians of Gaitskellism on such questions
as the nature of modern capitalism and the workings of the Labour
Party and the theoretical perspective it should adopt. Culturally, the
movement concerned itself with a critical analysis of the workings of
the mass media which was most fully developed in the work of
Raymond Williams and in the report of the Government's Pilkington
Committee on radio and television which appeared in 1962 and was
strongly influenced by the New Left.

The subsequent development of the movement can perhaps be
clarified by comparison with the American New Left. This latter
movement, springing partly from the Negro struggle which was seen,
after Civil Rights legislation, as a symptom of structural features in
American society, has been influenced deeply both by the con-
current student reaction to the "multiversity" and by the absence of

any independent political tradition in the labor movement and, in particular, of traditional socialism. These can be seen as causally related to the American New Left's alienation from established political institutions and also to its lack of any clear theoretical perspective. The British New Left, by contrast, generated and reinforced by a single-issue nuclear campaign which ultimately lost impetus, was confronted by the enigma of the Labour Party. The failure to follow up the momentary capture of the Party conference in 1960 and the decline of CND after 1962 led to a crisis in the movement. The absence of any mass base outside intellectual circles other than the single issue of CND forced the different elements within the movement to come to terms with the Labour Party in one way or another, especially after the election in early 1963 of a reputedly left-wing leader of the Labour Party. The network of Left Clubs was disbanded, or fell apart.[21] The magazine fell under the direction of a small group of intensely theoretical Marxist intellectuals, most originating from Oxford where some of them had been associated with a New Left student journal called *New University*. Modeling itself to some extent on Sartre's *Temps Modernes*, the magazine now consists almost exclusively of theoretical essays in neo-Marxist sociology and philosophy, together with detailed historical and sociological analyses of particular countries. Its immediate political influence is thus not what it was in 1962, though as the chief English contact with West European Marxism it may have a more diffuse and intangible influence.

Thus the existence of a politically independent Labour movement is one of the crucial factors in the differences between student activism in Britain. Concern among student radicals about what is seen as subordination of higher education to the requirements of modern industrialization and a dissociation from the conventional channels of political action (both features of the American New Left) did not become important in Britain until 1966–67 under the joint impact of the post-Robbins expansion in higher education and disillusion with the performance of the Labour Government. And by this time the influence of the New Left had been dissipated.

NALSO and the Labour Party

Among the consequences was a shift in the role of NALSO, which was taken over by the Left in 1958[22] and lost its former role as a recruiting ground for future members of the Labour Party elite.[23] The New Left period saw a growth in NALSO strength from 1500 in

1956, mostly concentrated in Oxford and Cambridge, to 4760 in 1960 and some 6–7000 in the mid-sixties.[24] Unlike the other two party organizations, NALSO was not formally integrated into the constitutional structure of the party, but was an independent organization with a bilateral agreement with the Labour Party and a financial grant which was subject to certain conditions. Because the organization is a loose federation of constituent clubs, its strength at the center is a function of, on the one hand, the external provision of financial and administrative assistance and, on the other, of the felt need by college activists for a national organization to coordinate radical student action. With the decline of CND and the concentration of the Left on securing the return of a Labour Government, the need grew for increased assistance from the Labour Party if the organization was to consolidate the expansion that had taken place in the New Left period.

Here NALSO ran up against the Labour Party's perennial suspicions of all its youth organizations, a suspicion reinforced by contemporary experience in the newly founded Young Socialist movement. This organization was also influenced by the leftward mood promoted by CND, but the mainly middle-class New Left played no part in it. Instead, the traditional Left and various Marxist tendencies were the sources of the groupings that formed in the Party's new youth section, and their brand of radical politics were a source of embarrassment to the Party's leaders.[25] This was, no doubt, a contributory factor in the failure of the Party to respond to NALSO's demands for assistance in reorganization that were first put forward in a memorandum presented to the National executive of the Party in November, 1963. Small clubs cannot survive without outside help, while the large ones have little need of NALSO as they are almost self-sufficient. Yet the interests of the national organization encourage recruitment of members from larger clubs where they can easily get assistance as well as political and administrative experience. The answer was seen to lie in a greatly improved system of regional organization for which extra grants were requested from the Party. An appeal was made to the Party to give a new status to its student section:

The universities are expanding both in numbers and in student population *now;* when Robbins recommendations are enacted, expansion will of course proceed much faster. Nor are the new generation of university students the socially selective bunch they were as recently as 1939. The field for Labour Party proselytization is no longer just the colourful and eccentric revolt of a few upper class scions; university students represent a growing class, and a class whose votes are of great importance to the Party. They are now, or will be, the professional, managerial and scientific middle class; they represent the new middle class in the affluent society where votes were so significant in Orpington and Luton.[26]

These demands were not met. In the period between 1963 and the General Election of 1966 only such extra assistance was given as was necessary to improve NALSO's contribution to the Labour Party's election work. After that, the Labour Party became increasingly unwilling to help. Consequently attempts by NALSO to call meetings in London on the future of the Left, with Labour MP's and trade unionists on the platform, could not be publicized effectively and led merely to empty halls while posters, circulars, and campaigns on any issue opposed to party policy could not be sent out through the official administrative and secretarial facilities in Transport House. There was, thus, no nationally effective student socialist movement in the crucial period after the return of a Labour Government — a period in which there was not only a general disorientation among left-wing students, but also a quickening of the pace of expansion in higher education and, consequently, a new wave of political activity in an organization that had recently changed beyond recognition and had previously been ignored by all but a handful of radical students: the NUS.

NUS and the Radical Student Alliance

While the attention of the Left in the universities shifted from CND to the return of a Labour Government and thence to directionless disillusion, the consequences of the Robbins Report began to be worked out as a fundamental reappraisal of the scope and size of higher education. Expansion of the system as a whole and the redefinition of status for Colleges of Education (for teacher training) and Colleges of Advanced Technology (as technological universities) led to a phenomenal increase in the membership of NUS, from 150,000 members in 250 colleges and universities in 1962 to a total of 366,000 members in 700 colleges and universities in 1966.[27] This compares with a total university population that had increased from 80,602 in 1953–54 to 138,711 in 1964–65 and a total, including CAT's, of 168,607 in 1965–66.[28] At the Exeter Council of NUS in April, 1966, there were delegates, in addition to 58 universities and university colleges, 4 universities designate,[29] from 8 colleges of agriculture, architecture, art, music, or drama, 2 colleges of occupational therapy, 47 colleges of technology, 106 colleges of education, 4 colleges of physical education, and 2 theological colleges.[30]

This increase in numbers had also been accompanied by an increase in the scale of NUS activities. In 1962 the clause in the Union's constitution limiting discussion to student issues was altered to permit a general consideration of the whole area of education, while still preventing the introduction of politics. The *Times* reported a considerable feeling at that Conference against the decision of the Government of the day to cut back the rate of expansion of education as a part of the current economic freeze.[31] In the following period, the Union acquired or confirmed an expansionist and radical set of policies, including demands for the abolition of the means test on student grants, the crediting of students with national insurance, and expansion of student accommodation, of health services, and of extracurricular and recreational facilities. As new charters were prepared for Colleges of Advanced Technology to be transmuted into universities, the NUS prepared revised draft charters providing for student representation on disciplinary boards. This led to similar demands from older institutions, and the NUS adopted representation as a demand, issuing a pamphlet on "Student Participation in College Government." The 1966 NUS Executive Report refers ten times in different places to the question of participation, and the NUS delegation prepared a paper on this question for an International Conference of European Student Unions in 1966.[32]

Thus a future Treasurer of NUS was able to write in one of the irregularly appearing issues of NALSO's journal under the headline "The NUS Is Our Trade Union" that:

The NUS is clearly changing its role from that of a club arranging cheap travel and varied concessions for its members to that of a union organised to defend and advance the interests of its members in all fields. Such a transformation sucessfully followed through could make a decisive difference to the British student movement, which has traditionally been one of the most apathetic and conservative in the world.[33]

This expansion of the scope of NUS policy, however, did not represent a "shift to the Left" so much as a response to the expanded scale of education. The methods of action on which the Union relied remained unchanged, still emphasizing personal contacts with Ministers and "respectability." Indeed, it was over methods rather than objectives that the newly founded Radical Student Alliance clashed with the NUS executive.

The first issue over which radical opposition made itself apparent to the executive was, however, the untypical question of the Union's international affiliations. Since the IUS (International Union of Students) had come under Communist control in 1948 and the NUS had left it in 1950, the Union had taken an active part in the pro-Western International Student Conference. This was a loose federation of independent unions rather than a membership organization, and the question of the NUS joining it did not formally arise until it became one in 1965. The opposition to ISC came not merely from the small minority of Communists who had at various periods in the 1950's advocated a return to the IUS, but from a much broader spectrum of neutralist opinion as well as from those who felt that the political objectives of ISC (a general condemnation of "imperialism, colonialism, neo-colonialism, militarism and totalitarianism") were, however laudable, incompatible with NUS' ban on political commitment. Dispute also centered on the question of whether the ISC was not so firmly committed to the Americans as the IUS to the Communists — a point which owed its force to, among other things, the influence of the neutralist attitudes of CND on a large section of active students. It was pointed out by ISC defenders that a large majority of ISC affiliates were from developing or uncommitted countries; opponents replied that most of these were members of IUS as well, a compromise course of action that was one of the widely canvassed alternatives to the executive's policy.[34]

More significantly, a feature of this controversy that was soon to recur was the attention drawn to the connection of past officers of NUS with the ISC and the Labour Party's administrative machinery. Both Transport House, especially its international department, and the ISC were alleged to provide jobs for retiring officers of the Union, and it was inevitably claimed that this affected the attitudes of NUS officials both to ISC and to the Government.

The international issue marked the beginning of an *ad hoc* "popular front" of Labour, Liberal, and Communist students that led early in 1967 to the foundation of the Radical Student Alliance. On such issues as Vietnam and Rhodesia (both the subjects of joint campaigns by the three organizations during 1966), all radical students found themselves acting together and against the Labour Government. The initiative for these joint campaigns came from the now thriving Union of Liberal Students, which had benefited greatly from disillusion with the government among left-wing students and from the periodic crises and general ineffectiveness of NALSO. Like the Conservative and unlike the Labour students, the Liberals are well integrated into the structure of their parent party. But the weakness and heterogeneity of that party enable the students in alliance with the Young Liberals, both of them much to the left of their elders, to have a much bigger effect on the policies of that party than either of the other two have on theirs. At the Brighton Conference of the Liberal Party in September, 1966, this youthful influence succeeded, with the help of some adroit manipulation in the selection of delegates, in pushing the parent party into more left-wing positions on a number of issues, especially workers' participation in industry, which was central to the semi-syndicalist inclinations of what are called the Liberal "Red Guards."

The week of February 3, 1967, saw three events: the founding conference of the Radical Student Alliance, a demonstration at the London School of Economics against a decision by the principal to ban a meeting to consider means of direct action against the appointment of Dr. Walter Adams as the new principal (in the course of which a porter died of a heart attack), and a lobby of Parliament by 4000 students in protest against a Government decision to raise the fees charged to overseas students in universities and colleges. In subsequent press comment, the first of these events was widely linked with either or both of the other two.

The events at the LSE were at least partly due to factors peculiar to that institution. The LSE is unique in England — perhaps the only significantly "new" university of the post-Victorian period. It has always attracted a minority of left-wing students with serious political and intellectual preoccupations, anxious to translate political ideas into immediate action and therefore peculiarly vulnerable to disappointment with their environment and with their seniors. These young men are, for example, especially proud of the multiracial traditions of "the School." Whatever the facts, the appointment of anyone but the most extreme and militant opponent of racial discrimination to be Director of the School was liable to be interpreted by them as a betrayal of their conception of LSE's values. At the same time, however, the LSE is a college that approaches more nearly to the anonymity of the American "multiversity" than most other English institutions and suffers from a breakdown of student-staff relations of a kind not merely absent but actively countered by the wide range of support for protests against the overseas fees decision. As one observer wrote:

To counterpose those *in loco parentis* and *in statu pupillari* is outdated in the same way as, but rather more than, the simple model of the "two sides of industry." If students are the academic proletariat, one can distinguish a salariat in the form of lecturers, technicians, research workers, and other "staff" — and a managerial class distinct from the ultimate employers. With students lobbying (as they did last year) to demand more pay for lecturers, and with vice-chancellors now opposing Mr. Crosland on the issues of overseas students' fees, the lines are less clearly drawn than they might seem to those who think in terms of "authorities" and "rebels." If the idea of the academic community is valid, this is how it should be.[35]

The connection between the issue of overseas students' fees and the central "student syndicalist"[36] concerns of RSA is closer than may appear at first. Many senior members of universities were concerned by the method of implementing the increase, which they saw as an interference with the independence of the universities, while many students saw it as a dress rehearsal for the introduction of loans as a partial substitute for, or alternative to, grants. The justification of the increase in terms of the necessity to give priority to British students was objected to not only because more British students were studying in foreign universities than foreign in British, not only on international principle, and not only as a concealed cut in overseas aid, but also as a sign of increasingly vocationalist spirit in the Government's rationalization and expansion of higher education.

The binary system of non-university as well as university institutions of higher education was attacked as if Mr. Crosland had invented it to replace those invidious distinctions between types of secondary school that the progressive supporter of expansion had determined to eradicate. All these developments were seen as symptoms of the trend toward subjection of traditional university freedoms to the needs of a more complex, more technological, and increasingly planned and integrated society, in terms very similar to American criticisms of the integration of the "multiversity" into the industrial system and UNEF's (Union Nationale des Etudiants Français) criticism of the "technocratic" Fouchet plan.

The definition of this conflict takes the extreme form expressed by one RSA supporter as resistance to a conversion of institutions of higher education into "battery farms for broiler technicians." But even in the official NUS newspaper the sense of crisis is conveyed:

British students have always been remarkably unpolitical. . . . This tradition will end; universities and colleges are having to account for themselves to the public, to answer the nation's needs. . . . There is a very great choice to be made. Are the people we produce to answer the public need going to be technicians, executives with enough "liberal culture" to talk with their bosses' wives or to "understand" how the workers feel? . . . Or are we to make full use of a new opportunity . . . with students in a more public setting able to attain a broad accomplishment, a political and cultural awareness and activity?[37]

Broad aims are agreed upon. The issue between RSA and NUS is one of method — with the former concerned more with the "grass-roots" and the mobilization of mass student support through demonstrations and petitions. The NUS executive, however, prefers personal approaches to policy-makers. This difference was well brought out in an exchange at the April, 1966, NUS Council:

There might have been more publicity from NUS about the binary system because members of his college did not know what it was, nor did the public, confessed *Mr. D. Adelstein*, LSE. As NUS policy categorically condemned the system in higher education, it might have done more to make it public. "There were two sides to any campaign against the binary system; one was to try and get the public on their side," said Mr. Fisk (vice president). The brief statement against it circulated at this council would afterwards be published in a form suitable for the public.

Or as a member of the RSA Council put it:

One of the fundamental weaknesses of the Executive (and RSA's corresponding strength) is its refusal to think in terms of mass political action. The NUS leaders have an elitist and very unidimensional picture of the student's little slot in society. . . . There is an indefinably middle-aged quality about the NUS leadership which alienates the young student.[38]

CONCLUSION

The rise in the number of students reflects also a profound change in their social situation. Before the second world war students engaged in higher education only constituted 2.7% of their age group. By 1967, however, this had risen to 11%. Students are still an elite group, but their social destination has shifted. The university no longer provides the almost automatic entrance into an elite professional class. Now a much larger and less exclusive social strata demands degree qualification. The pre-war university pre-eminently prepared its members for law, medicine, church or civil service. In the modern university the predominant goals of students are bifurcated between industry and further academic research. This changing social function of the university is partly reflected in the growth of new subjects — in particular sociology, a discipline still socially unmoored from professional needs. It is significant that much of the leadership in the LSE revolt came from students in the sociology faculty.[39]

These changes in the origin and destination of the student would by themselves be sufficient to pose a profound challenge to the traditional "English idea" of a university. They have been interpreted by radical students as symptoms of a subordination of higher education to the manpower needs of a changing industrialism and have provoked conflict both locally and nationally through their impact on the immediate situation of students.

An examination of the most widely publicized of these local conflicts, that at the London School of Economics, shows a generalization from original demands and grievances of a limited and "liberal" kind (in this case the alleged undesirability of a proposed principal, the question of student freedom of speech, and the victimization of elected representatives). A widespread feeling grew among the students involved that what was at stake was the whole structure of the administration of the School, the composition of their syllabuses, and the relationship between both of these and wider political and social trends.[40] The exact mode of this generalization was affected by a number of factors highly specific to the LSE, which may seem to suggest that the events, however spectacular, will remain unique. These factors, some of which were seized on by contemporary press comment on the "causes" of the events, include the specific features of the LSE's student body; the peculiarities of the administrative structure of the LSE which placed full power in a board of governors, none of whom were fully engaged in the work of the School and large numbers of whom had outside contacts in industry and commerce, which lent particular force to the view of the social function of the School put forward by the radicals; the physical layout of the School, overcrowding, and lack of student-staff contact; and various tactical mistakes of the authorities.

But while all these factors are peculiar to the LSE, they do not restrict the relevance of the events there. Radical students both at LSE and at other colleges and universities interpret these special factors not as "causes" but as common conditions clearly visible within LSE, though less immediately perceived elsewhere. Thus, generalization from the LSE example is a possibility. A noticeable feature of the LSE sit-in was the participation by delegations from other universities and colleges, which also sent larger contingents to a protest march. Definitions of the situation "imported" by foreign students, especially Americans, were only acceptable because of their congruence with existing fears as to the future development of policy toward higher education in Britain, and with the immediate needs of the conflict in LSE. For example, the project for a "free university" in the LSE buildings during the vacation was organized and advocated particularly by a group of American postgraduates. But it was taken up at a particular stage in policy discussions in the Union meetings because it was useful to counter the extreme demand for continuation of the sit-in through the vacation without advocating what seemed like a retreat.[41] It also continued a previous student concern with control over the content of the syllabus. In the term before the Adams question was first raised, the Union had questioned the dismissal of an economics lecturer in circumstances that were seen to be connected with conflicting views on what was to be taught.[42]

The precise forms taken by such generalizations from the experience of distinct or unique campus situations by student radicals on other campuses, as well as the response to such national issues as the possible introduction of student loans as a partial alternative to grants, will be determined in large part by the "political culture" shared by student radicals in institutions of differing kinds and by the organizational links between them. There is no sign as yet of any tendency for the attitudes of student radical activities in any of the constituent groupings of RSA to be differentiated by the type of institution.[43] This may to some extent be attributed to a common political background shared by many activists before arriving in their respective institutions, in CND, Young Socialists, or Young Liberals. As one member of the RSA Council said at the founding convention: "We all cut our political teeth in the New Left." There is so far no research on this aspect, though this interpretation is quite widely accepted. Nor is it clear what the future consequences might be of the decline of CND and the New Left, the Labour Party's purging of the Young Socialists and the apparent spread of the apolitical "hippy" culture among teenagers at the possible expense of the active political concerns of their immediate predecessors.

Of some importance in this connection is the further decline of NALSO. As the performance of the Government deviated still further from the expectations of its erstwhile student supporters, so the gap between the resources needed by NALSO to conduct a campaign against it and the willingness of the Labour Party to provide them widened. As a result, the perceived relevance of NALSO to its members declined and an ill-attended and ill-publicized emergency conference in January, 1967, led to the election of a new committee dominated by the same *Keep Left* faction of the sectarian

Trotskyists who had previously taken over the Young Socialists. As a result, all Labour Party assistance was withdrawn. Although a subsequent conference in April saw the defeat of *Keep Left* by a coalition of all other tendencies, the new committee was no more capable than its predecessors of finding a role for the organization which was relevant and useful to the activists in the constituent clubs. These had turned, in the period of disillusion with the Labour Party after the 1966 election, either to national political campaigns, such as RSA, or else to work outside the campus in the various Marxist groupings, to local student issues, or to various combinations of these. Thus, there was no single strategy round which the activists in NALSO at national level could mobilize the clubs, and for this reason as well as those mentioned above, the organization finally fell apart, the rump falling into the hands of the SLL (Socialist Labour League).

Recent changes in higher education have begun to undermine the traditional English notion of the university and its normative hold over student conduct, but no clearly stated alternative concept of the status and purpose of higher education has taken its place. The ability of the British Radical Student movement to be anything more than a spasmodic reaction to the period of transition is connected with its ability to elaborate its own alternative concept of a university: It has not yet done so.[44] Meanwhile there is a tendency for the traditional idea to be defended along left-elitist lines against the impact of "technocratic" reform.[45]

Even were such a critique to be elaborated, its political and organizational consequences could vary between the "American model" and the "French model" of an "official" students' union captured by the Left, based on a more or less explicit Marxism and seeing itself as a Trade Union.[46] Trends are present in both directions, and the future is indeterminate. What is certain is that since student radicals define their conflicts with university authority as being of a piece with the question of the legitimacy of the total social system, the development of the British radical student movement is ultimately bound up with both the future shape and organization of higher education and the future of the British Left.

REFERENCES

1. N. Schachner, *The Medieval Universities* (New York, 1962), pp. 204–5.

2. It is necessary to use the term "culture" here. Conformists, hippies, and

activists are styles of personhood available to the young at and around the university. He or she may adopt each in turn, wholly or in part, or may vacillate between them.

3. This is not to say that the quantity, as opposed to the quality, of activism is now markedly different from formerly. On the contrary, such imprecise evidence as is available suggests that a greater proportion of students were politically active in the thirties than now.

4. A. H. Halsey, "British Universities," *European Journal of Sociology*, Vol. 3, No. 1 (1962), pp. 85–102; "University Expansion and the Collegiate Ideal," *Universities Quarterly* (December, 1961); "A Pyramid of Prestige," *Universities Quarterly*, Vol. 15, No. 4 (September, 1961); "The Academic Hierarchy," *Universities Quarterly*, Vol. 18, No. 2 (March, 1964).

5. Bryan Wilson, "Freedom Under Clark Kerr," the *Spectator* (February 3, 1967). It may be, however, that such definitions of the situation have been imported by some American students at the London School of Economics.

6. "Teach Yourself Student Power," ed. David Adelstein, *RSA* (1968), especially the first article, "Crisis in Higher Education," by David Adelstein.

7. An adequate history of British student politics has yet to be written. The notes in this article are no more than the minimal background necessary for understanding of developments in the fifties and sixties.

8. See *NUS: A Survey of Seven Years of Development* (London, 1930). *Passim* for all references.

9. *Ibid.*, p. 4.

10. *Ibid.*, pp. 18–21.

11. *Ibid.*, p. 22.

12. Richard Hyman, "Oxford Workers in the Great Strike," *Oxford Centre for Socialist Education*, pamphlet, (1966).

13. Brian Simon, *A Student's View of the Universities* (London: Longmans & Co., 1943), p. 142.

14. UGC Returns, 1964–65.

15. See W. T. Rodgers, "Politics in the Universities," *Political Quarterly*, 1959, for trends in the relative memberships of three political clubs in Oxford during this period.

16. See, for instance, Peter Marris' findings (P. Marris, *The Experience of Higher Education*, p. 98, and *passim*), especially that Union officials were thought of as much more radical than they in fact were.

17. NUS Council Report 1953–54. See also the *Times*, March 20, 1954, p. 3, for a report of the Manchester University decision. The *Times* correspondent was told that the intention of the movers of the motion for disaffiliation was to set up a new organization restricted to universities and

university colleges, and "on a less formal basis than that represented by the NUS" — presumably a return to the old Inter-Universities Federation which preceded the NUS.

18. "News of NALSO," No. 1 (November, 1961).

19. Though Left activism, as always, was particularly conspicuous among the minority of students involved in politics it may also be noted that Tory radicalism was also vigorous and influential at the end of the fifties and remains very much alive in such Conservative organisations as PEST.

20. Satisfactory sources on the history of the New Left movement are scarce, as opposed to contemporary polemics against it in the established periodicals. The most satisfactory is an article, "The Two New Lefts," by Peter Sedwick in *International Socialism* 17, Summer, 1964, a critical account from a political position close to that of the Independent Socialist Club at Berkeley. An article in *Survey*, January, 1967, "The British New Left," by James D. Young has much useful material but seems patchy and confused in its account. It is the former article on which we have mainly drawn for this account.

21. The last appearance of the list of Left Clubs was in *New Left Review* for December, 1963.

22. This is of course a short perspective. NALSO was originally founded as a breakaway from the Communist controlled SLF and has a history of oscillation in relation to the leadership of the Labour Party.

23. Several of its chairmen in the early and middle fifties entered Parliament as Labour MP's in the 1964 and 1966 elections.

24. "News of NALSO," No. 1 (November, 1961), for the first two figures and Conference reports for the last.

25. The three main tendencies among the Young Socialists in the early sixties were known by the names of their respective journals. *Keep Left*, a Trotskyist group, was the medium of an ultimately successful takeover by the Socialist Labour League. *Young Guard* was the youth paper produced by those sympathetic to the views of the magazine *International Socialism* referred to earlier and later the main left-wing group after the expulsion of *Keep Left*. *New Advance* was the name of the official Young Socialist journal and supported the leadership. The second of these two groups also became strong in NALSO as those who had been active in CND and the Young Socialists came up to university, and most NALSO Executive Committees from 1961–67 were made up about equally of supporters of this group, independents still using the New Left label, and adherents of the traditional Labour Left.

26. "Memorandum on the State of NALSO for the December meeting of the Youth Sub-Committee," Angus Calder. Document in NALSO secretary's files.

27. NUS Executive Report, 1966.

28. UGC Annual Survey 1965–66, UGC Returns 1964–65, and Review of University Development 1962–63 to 1965–66.

29. Counting London colleges separately, but counting Oxford and Cambridge as one each.

30. NUS "April Council Meeting held at Exeter University, April 13–17, 1966. Minutes and Proceedings," August, 1966.

31. The *Times*, April 17, 1962, p. 6.

32. See NUS Executive Committee Report (1966), pp. 35, 127.

33. Roger Lyons, "The NUS Is Our Trade Union," *Labour Student* (Winter, 1964–65).

34. For a debate between the two sides of the controversy in Oxford, see articles and letters by Peter Wilenski and Hannan Rose in *Isis* (February and March, 1966). The issue of NUS' international affiliations may yet revive in view of recent disclosures as to the influence of the CIA; the financial dependence of ISC on various American foundations was, in any case, a chief plank in its opponents' platform.

35. Mervyn Jones, "What's Worrying the Students?" *New Statesman* (February 7, 1967).

36. Some of the leading activists in RSA object to the phrase "student syndicalism" as an overly literal translation from the French and prefer the more accurate "student unionism."

37. That these sentiments were expressed in the official journal of the NUS was the result of some intensive lobbying of the editor by two officers of CUCND (Cambridge University Campaign for Nuclear Disarmament) who wrote the article quoted above, and one of whom has since become press officer of RSA.

38. NUS April Council Meeting 1966, Minutes and Summary of Proceedings.

39. "Student Power: What Is to Be Done?" G. Stedman-Jones, A. Barnett, T. Wengraf in *New Left Review*, Vol. 43 (May-June 1967). No exact analysis exists as yet of the composition of political activists by social, ethnic, or religious background, or by disciplinary attachment, year and type of course, and so forth. That activism is centered in the social studies faculties needs no special explanation. It is partly a matter of self-selection among schoolchildren and is reinforced by the political outlook of the typical university teacher in the social sciences. Sociology is, however, particularly interesting in Britain as the most recent vehicle of political awareness for the young. Another possible source of radical recruits is from experience of marginalism and mobility. But the patterns are undoubtedly complex and await systematic investigation.

40. The most detailed single sources for the events at LSE so far available are both published by students, though from slightly different positions. The first is a pamphlet, "LSE: What It Is and How We Fought It," produced

by *Agitator*, the journal of the LSE Socialist Society. The second is an article by Alexander Cockburn and Ben Brewster, "Revolt at the LSE," in *New Left Review*, Vol. 43. Brewster was a member of the Graduate Committee headed by Marshall Bloom, one of the two suspended leaders. The description of events in the two articles and the theoretical analyses are broadly similar, though there are interesting differences in the conclusions for future student action.

41. See LSE pamphlet, p. 13.

42. The case is referred to in *New Left Review*.

43. The one apparent exception to this is in the teacher training colleges which are known to be staunch supporters of the executive at NUS conferences. This absence of political activism may be connected with the ban on political clubs in many of these institutions.

44. A possible first step in the direction of such an elaboration is the pamphlet edited by David Adelstein referred to above.

45. For one attempt at this from a left-wing position, see Alasdair MacIntyre, "On Bureaucratising a University," the *Oxford Magazine*, No. 3.

46. This difference in approach seems to underly the difference in interpretation of the LSE experience between the pamphlet referred to above, which is continually suspicious of the official Union hierarchy and emphasizes grass-roots initiatives, and the two articles in *New Left Review*, Vol. 43, which stress the role played by the Union in crystallizing student opinion, praise the role of the student leaders and outline a strategy for RSA based on capturing the NUS. Disagreement within RSA on whether to aim at taking control of NUS is similarly based.

FRANK A. PINNER

Western European Student Movements
Through Changing Times

Recent Radicalization of Student Movements

THE LAST TWO academic years have seen a marked aggravation of conflicts at universities of the Western world with the rise or renewal of student protest movements in countries of the Soviet bloc and in developing countries.[1] (The movements of the Chinese Red Guards — even though endorsed and, indeed, set in motion by the Maoist leadership — must be included among such movements.) The phenomenon of student discontent and rebellion is worldwide; it respects neither national boundaries nor differences among economic systems and political regimes.

In the Western world (but also in many non-Western countries) the most pervasive symptoms of the radicalization process are

Greater frequency and severity of incidents (demonstrations, strikes, building occupations, violent clashes with the police and so forth);

Participation of large numbers of students in these incidents;

Intensification of interest, particularly among organized student leaders and activists, in ideological questions, together with the revival of socialist and anarchist doctrines of the past;

The use of new forms of action, particularly occupations of university buildings (which, in their intent, go well beyond that of sit-ins), and the "happening," first used as a political device by the Dutch Provos.

The sudden emergence during crises of previously unknown student leaders — for example, Daniel Cohn-Bendit, who prior to the French May rebellion was virtually unknown outside Nanterre, or Rudi Dutschke, who had occupied no central position in the German SDS (*Sozialistischer Deutscher Studentenbund*) and had done no writing in the organization's main organ "*Neue Kritik*."

These five symptoms reflect two underlying conditions: a greater availability of the student masses for overt action and a stronger commitment of the leadership to a policy of total opposition to the regime, an opposition based on elaborate analyses using the intellectual tools of Marxism, anarchism, and their modern off-shoots. The two conditions are not related to each other in a simple cause-and-effect fashion. The large-scale student revolts in Paris in May 1967 had clearly not been planned by any of the left-wing groups. Indeed, the emergence of charismatic leaders at moments of crisis indicates that the masses of students, set in motion by some event, do not necessarily accept the organizational leadership of the politically committed groups.

The similarities in the political behavior of students in different countries can be explained only in part by the speed and thoroughness of modern communications. Exposure alone does not mean adoption of ideas. Nor is there any evidence that the student movements in different countries have any effective central international direction; on the contrary, it is rather astonishing how few formal and persistent contacts have been established among the student protest movements.

Thus, hypotheses which seek to ascribe the worldwide student revolt either to the efficiency of modern communications or to some central direction seem implausible. The only remaining alternative is that students, irrespective of the political regimes and the economic systems of their countries, undergo similar experiences which predispose them to similar forms of action.

But do students everywhere constitute a special group subject to similar experiences? In a recent study of the Dutch student trade union movement, C. J. Lammers has proposed that students in modern society should be regarded as a social class.[2] Lammers uses the term "class" advisedly, because he believes that there are telling parallels between the development of working-class movements and those of students. The growth of large-scale industry resulted in the concentration of large masses of workers in plants and factory towns and the increased dependence of these masses upon one or a very few employers. The structures of vertical integration — for example, the guilds — first loosened and then disappeared, while the vertical relationships, those between master and worker, became depersonalized. As a result, horizontal associations emerged among workers through which they fought for common interests. Similarly, students were transformed into a conflict group (or "class") as vertical ties weakened and an increasing number of students came to depend upon the same impersonal authority.

To show this, Lammers describes the circumstances which have led to the partial supersession of the traditional guild-like structures of Dutch fraternities by the *studentenvakbeweging* (SVB, Student Trade Union Movement). In the past, the fraternities provided a link between age groups and served as means of social mobility. These structures became irrelevant as the number of students enrolled in the universities increased and as an even larger proportion among them came to depend on government subsidies. In the years 1950–51 to 1965–66, the proportion of students receiving direct government stipends grew from eight to thirty-seven per cent — and this leaves out the even larger proportion of those who obtain subventions in the form of housing, meals and other benefits. Survey results indicate that students financially dependent on the government are more likely than are other students to vote for the SVB in student elections and to support the student trade union's view.[3] Since the trend toward government support of higher education through individual stipends is worldwide, students may increasingly see themselves as a clientele confronting the official bureaucracy.

To be sure, the mere emergence of students as a conflict group is not enough to explain the specific forms of organizations and action, of beliefs and mass behavior; it cannot account for the strikingly parallel patterns of change. In order to understand these changes, it will be necessary to examine the types of student organizations and the social mechanisms which account for the obsolescence of some of them and the rise of others.

Typology of Student Organizations

For the student leader or activist, the student organization is for a time at least a way of life, and the movement has significance that goes far beyond specific issues featured for public consumption and arousal — a significance that reflects the transitory and precarious status of the student. A student trade union, for example, cannot have the same meaning for its active members as an industrial union has for workers. The worker normally expects to spend a life in his occupation or trade, and his union exists to make that life as rewarding as possible. But no student expects to remain a student forever, and no matter how he looks upon his organization, it must in some way permit him to pass from his current status to a different one, and from his present role to another. Thus, the forms and ideologies of student organizations are likely to reflect different ways of coping with the problem of transition that faces all students.

Two broad possibilities are open to the student: He can either prepare himself to occupy a position in society such as he knows it, or he can commit himself to a restructuring of society that would make new roles and new positions available. The two major forms of student organizations correspond to this dichotomy: "socializing" organizations that see their main task in educating their members so as to prepare them for their future roles in society, and "transgressive" organizations that aim to bring about social and political change.

Some socializing organizations prepare the student mainly for his future occupation, while others — the traditional organizations — prepare him for status positions in society by inculcating traditional values. Thus, all socializing organizations, but particularly the traditional ones, are structures of vertical integration. Accordingly, former members, acting as sponsors, always have considerable influence upon the decisions of these organizations. Moreover, the old members serve as living role images, exhibiting to the student the position to which he aspires and the behavior that goes with that position.

Where vertical structures of integration have become irrelevant or inoperative and such socialization cannot take place, "transgressive" organizations tend to develop. If the student cannot prepare himself for a more or less clearly glimpsed role or status in society, and student organizations are unable to help him in this striving, the student has two alternatives: He can either oppose the "system," hoping for its destruction and a more livable world thereafter, or he can work for a transformation of the social role structure that will satisfy his need for the social definition of his role and status.

These two forms of reaction will be labeled "ideological protest" and "role seeking" in this paper. The term "transgressive" is intended to cover both of these variants. To every role and status system corresponds a topological map of human groupings and action systems — a map which defines the boundaries within each system. Thus, there are boundaries between classes, status groups, occupational, religious, geographical and other groupings. There are also boundaries between forms of human activity, e.g., work and play. The topological map can thus be taken to describe either social reality as seen by an objective observer, or else as the image of society in an individual's mind. In its second meaning, the term is analogous to Kurt Lewin's concept of the "life space."

Rejection of the existing system of roles and social strata almost necessarily leads to transgression of social boundaries. A few examples may illustrate this. The West-German SDS has repeatedly organized conferences or seminars with the East-German FDJ (*Frele Deutsche Jugend*), whose university groups consist of students sympathizing with SED (*Sozialistische Einheitspartei*), the leading East-German party.[4] Given the strength of the border traversing Germany and the feelings that accompany its existence, this is a case of transgression by physical act. The French student trade union UNEF introduces its programmatic Charter of Grenoble with the statement: "The student is a young intellectual worker." The juxtaposition of the terms "intellectual" and "worker" constitutes a conscious ideological transgression of social boundaries. And when the Dutch Provos, a quasi-anarchist group, organized "happenings" in the streets of Amsterdam, they were transgressing the boundaries between art and politics, between actors and audience, between play and reality.[5]

Transgressive organizations tend to be engaged more deeply in politics than are socializing ones, while traditional or vocational organizations usually regard their "educational" activities as their primary purpose, with political engagement understood as a secondary aim resulting from these activities.

A type of organization between the socializing and the transgressive forms is the interest organization. Its major concern is the physical and economic well-being of students within the existing university structure. From 1950 to 1956, this was the chief orientation of the French UNEF, earning its leaders the uncomplimentary label of "corporatists." Until recently, the ASVA (*Algemeene Studenten Vereniging Amsterdam*) was also of this type, as are, in principle, the representative student organs established by law in all German universities.

Traditional Organizations

The German *Korporationen* and the Dutch *Gezelligheidsverenigingen* (social associations) constitute social hierarchies in microcosm, with the oldest and richest groups, called *Corps* in both countries, considered the most prestigious. The organizations differ from one another in the elaborateness of their ritual, the rigidity of age groupings within the groups, their emphasis on formal codes of behavior, and the content of these codes. They are intensely selective. In the leading groups, students preparing themselves for the liberal professions — law and medicine — predominate, while the next layer of organizations draws a greater variety of students, many of whom are aiming for jobs in business and industry. As one moves down the organizational pyramid, the membership becomes even more heterogeneous.

In the German *Korporationen*, the *Alte Herren* (alumni) play a decisive role, and the composition of these sponsoring groups is of great importance. Bernard Oudin has found that 41 per cent of the *Alte Herren* of the major Catholic federation of *Korporationen* were physicians and lawyers.[6] The lists of *Alte Herren* in six *Burschenschaften*, considered to be reasonably representative of this type of *Korporation*, show that in 1966 nearly 40 per cent were physicians, over 22 per cent were lawyers, and over 16 per cent were owners and managers of business and industry.[7] Thus, the views of the liberal professions frequently prevail in the councils of *Alte Herren*, reflecting traditionalist attitudes more characteristic of pre-industrial societies than of the modern world.

The role of the *Alte Herren* has given rise to much public controversy. Since the *Korporationen* consider themselves *Lebensgemeinschaften* (communities entered into for life), in principle all *Alte Herren* remain members of their *Korporationen* and thus have the right to attend their official meetings. In some groups, *Alte Herren* have limited voting rights (on questions "of principle," or through a representative who can cast one or two votes in the meeting of the *Aktivitas*); in others, they are said not to vote at all. Without the intense effort and considerable financial sacrifices of their *Alte Herren*, most *Korporationen* probably would never have been reconstituted after the war. Their continued financial support gives the *Alte Herren* a certain weight in the affairs of the *Korporationen*. Adversaries consider this influence a danger, since they believe that many of the *Alte Herren* were either pro-Nazi during the Hitler period or at least right-wingers not hostile to the regime. The *Korporationen* tend to deny this charge or to minimize the importance of the issue.

Telling differences exist between the Dutch and the German fraternal organizations. The Germanic *Korporation* is typically a fairly small group of up to fifty active members; conflict between fraternity brothers is minimized and considered undesirable, while conflict with outsiders — members of other *Korporationen* — is ritually encouraged. In Holland, the *Gezelligheidsverenigingen* are generally larger structures with several hundred active members, and all challenges of the younger members originate *within* the organization.

The archetypical form of conflict in German student fraternities is the *Mensur*, a modified and relatively harmless form of the duel in which the goal is not victory over the opponent, but testing of the contestants' *Haltung* ("attitude," in the military sense of the term). In the Dutch fraternity, the challenge consists primarily in a matching of wits. The difference in role images is evident. The German image of a worthy member of the elite still retains some of the attributes of the military aristocracy whose standards were eagerly adopted, often in their most corrupt form, by the middle classes in the second half of the last century. The Dutch role image is that of the *academicus*, a respected member of an urban society in which economic success rests upon cleverness in business and the ability to maintain a certain decorum.

Still, all traditional organizations share particular objectives and techniques. They create a certain *esprit de corps*, a conception of social hierarchy, and an attitude toward conflict in society. Communality is fostered by selectivity in recruitment, preemption of the student's time (particularly during his early years of study), and elaborate rituals emphasizing the uniqueness of the group and the distinctiveness of the social stratum to which it belongs. Conceptions of hierarchy are reinforced by sharp social distinctions separating the older and the younger students in the organization, and the "older" and "better" fraternities from less prestigious ones. Specific orientations toward conflict are generated through institutionalized behavior designed to challenge the young student's wit or courage.

Traditional organizations are conservative in social outlook and behavior. The accusation invariably leveled against them is that of elitism. Coupled with this social conservatism is often a strong sympathy for, if not alignment with, reactionary political parties and movements. Yet, the strength of such political bonds varies considerably with differences in social structure and political tradition, as the cases of Germany and Holland will illustrate.

The *Korporationen* stood in vigorous opposition to the Weimar Republic throughout its existence, defending their assumed right to impose their values upon the entire student body and to indulge in the most virulent forms of anti-Semitism. The absorption of the *Korporationen* into the Nazi movement thus met with little resistance from within the *Korporationen;* where opposition existed, it reflected an elitist disdain for the Nazi plebeians rather than an adherence to democratic principles.[8] Under these circumstances, the revival of the German *Korporationen* after the war was surprising. The Allies prohibited the reconstitution of the *Korporationen* because of their pro-Nazi positions, and the Conference of German rectors declared in 1949 and several times thereafter that the *Korporationen* could not be regarded as legitimate student organizations deserving public support. The battle for the reestablishment of the organizations was eventually won in the courts where many *Alte Herren* no doubt sat on the bench. In a 1954 survey of four universities, Hans Anger found only about half of the instructors opposed to the *Korporationen*, although opposition was considerably stronger among the occupants of regular chairs.[9] The proponents were strongest in the Faculties of Science and Medicine, while the opponents were strongest in the Faculties of Philosophy and Economic and Social Sciences.

Nearly all traditional German student organizations consider themselves patriotic. They favor reunification and insist that the Oder-Neisse line should not be recognized as the permanent boundary of Germany. Thus they espouse the rigid positions adopted by the West German government. Some also insist on the right of the refugees from the lost Eastern areas to settle in these areas.[10] Official statements of the *Deutsche Burschenschaft* and its subdivisions often insist on the continued significance of their motto: "Honor, Freedom, Fatherland." Among the *Burschenschaften*, the Austrian federation is doubtless most nationalistic. Thus a volume, the Austrian *Burschenschaft*, published to celebrate its one-hundredth anniversary, contains the following passages:

When in the year 1933 Adolf Hitler took over the government in Germany, and, during the first five years of his government, proved successful beyond anyone's boldest expectations, then it became clear that his movement was the only one able of conquering Austrian Germanism's (*Deutschtum*) right of self-determination. . . .

The Great-German Reich has collapsed. The sole bulwark that protected Europe against the powers of the East, Central-European Germanism, is broken. Bolshevism stands in the middle of Europe.

The *Burschenschaften* of Austria, reconstituted since 1950, see the struggle against Bolshevism as a task which can be accomplished only through the cooperation of all states and peoples in Europe that are still free.[11]

The official statements of organizations cannot be taken to express the positions and attitudes of all their members, but it is difficult to argue that the politics of *Korporation* members represent the full range of political views.

Dutch traditional organizations, on the other hand, have shown much greater political flexibility, a matter-of-fact acceptance of democratic processes, and a certain tolerance for the ideas of opponents.[12] The Amsterdam student weekly *Propria Cures*, for instance, was in the hands of socialist editors several years before World War I. During World War II, the Dutch *Corps* chose to dissolve themselves rather than comply with the orders of the German occupation forces to expel their Jewish members, and many members of traditional organizations joined the resistance movement. Together with their "nihilist" (unorganized) comrades, they planned a single student association that would obliterate all social distinctions among students; these proposals were published in the illegal student paper *De Geus* in September 1943.[13] Such an association was indeed founded soon after the war under the name of *Algemene Studenten Vereniging Amsterdam* (ASVA). But the old traditional groups, while promising ASVA their support, also reconstituted themselves, the social pressures evidently operating in favor of the *status quo ante*.

Until 1963, the Dutch traditional organizations have dominated both the ASVA and the national association of Dutch Students, the *Netherlands Studenten Raad* (NSR). They were able to maintain this control through complicated systems of representation that gave them built-in advantages. When the Student Trade-Union Movement suddenly emerged in 1963 and showed unsuspected strength, the traditional organizations immediately responded by agreeing to a more democratic system of electing student representatives. Members of traditional groups then organized a student party, the *Netherlands Studenten Akkoord* (NSA), which managed to rally a considerable electoral following.

Certain bridges seem to have been built between the traditional Dutch organizations and their trade unionist opponents. In the ASVA elections of 1966, the leading candidate on the trade union list was a member of the *Corps*, and other *Corps* members appeared in favorable positions on the list. At the same time, the NSA list, which is commonly believed to represent the traditional groups, contained only two *Corps* members. This should not be interpreted as a case of "infiltration," for the *Corps* candidates on the trade union list belonged, for the most part, to the less prestigious *disputen* (subgroups within the *Corps*). It does reveal, however, a certain flexibility on the part of the members of traditional organizations and a certain pluralism on the part of the *Corps*.

In Germany, a sample of the representatives in the student "parliaments" showed that 41 per cent belonged to *Korporationen*, while 32 per cent came out of political and other groups. [14] In these assemblies, the *Korporationen* representatives seem to have played a moderate role and are said to lack interest in the problems debated. (Often they have run for office at the urging of their *Korporation* brothers and without great personal motivation.) The traditional groups are strongly represented in the *Verband Deutscher Studentenschaften* (VDS), the head organization of all student governments. The main activity of this group has been to argue for a type of university reform that would profoundly change the authority structure of the university by reducing the exclusive power of the *ordinarii* (occupants of chairs) and by giving students and other groups a measure of co-determination in university affairs. These proposals are based, in large part, on a programmatic study published by the left-wing *Sozialistische Deutsche Studentenbund*, but adopted by the traditionalist members of the VDS as well. Today's *Korporation* representatives are considerably more flexible than their forebears were under the Weimar regime.

There have been no traditional student organizations in France since the end of the Middle Ages. Prior to the rise of political and trade-union organizations, the only signs of some feeling of community among French students were humorous public parades accompanied frequently by pranks intended to frighten mildly the average citizen. French informants, when questioned about the lack of traditional organizations in France, simply insist that such groups would be totally out of keeping with the French student's traditions and his image of himself as a young intellectual. Moreover, French students do not display the need for affiliation evident in other societies.

Pierre Bourdieu and Jean-Claude Passeron explain the atomism of French student life in the following terms:

If the behavior patterns whereby the observer commonly recognizes a student are above all symbolic behaviors, i.e., actions by means of which the student proves to others and to himself his ability to produce an original image of the student, this must occur because the student is condemned by his transitory and preparatory state to be only what he projects to be, or even only a project of being.

This project does not unequivocally predetermine the symbolic conduct of which it consists. The often eager and studied desire of self-realization as students does not presuppose the unanimous recognition of an ideal image of the student, since the image of what one wishes to accomplish may reduce itself to the imperative of producing an image. The will to be and the will to choose one's own being means that one must first of all reject what he has not chosen to be. Among the rejected or transmuted necessities, there is above all the rootedness in a social *milieu*. Students are alike in that, most often, they deliberately avoid mentioning their parents' occupation, no matter what it may be. These are all devices for exorcizing the unbearable notion that a determinant which is in no degree a matter of one's own choice might determine a person who is entirely occupied by the task of choosing his own existence.[15]

This need for a unique self-image also explains the feeble success of student groups. French students meet in the university or at a café, but no group larger than the small cluster surrounding the café table tends to emerge.

This basic attitude has intellectual and political consequences, particularly in Paris, and explains the constantly changing spectrum of philosophical, aesthetic, or political opinions. There is a constant need to invent new labels — such as "constructive anarchism," "renovated trotskism," "revolutionary neo-communism" — for many new tendencies that emerge and disappear. That these labels and the varying ideologies tend to have an *avant-garde* and radical tinge may be explained by the student's need to dissociate himself from social givens of his existence — his bourgeois background, for instance — in order to forge an independent image.

Many scholars have remarked on the relative absence in French society of organizational structures intermediate between the family and the organs of central administration.[16] This absence is usually ascribed to the success of the liberal revolution under a highly centralized political regime. This same liberal success has resulted in the creation of a university structure devoted primarily to the selection of the most gifted students as recruits for the central administration.[17] This system makes of the student a *bête à examen*. Since virtually all examinations are competitive with frequently only one third or fewer of the candidates passing, student life has a tendency to degenerate into a fight of all against all. Moreover, since success seems, superficially at least, to be entirely dependent on achievement, there appears to be no obvious need for vertical structures of integration. Also, in France more than elsewhere, the intellectual has great social visibility, partly because of the concentration of the intellectual elite in Paris and the role that intellectuals, particularly left-wing intellectuals, have played in French history.[18] The psychological processes described by Bourdieu and Passeron in the passage just quoted reflect this social orientation of students in the humanities and social sciences (who constituted the bulk of the interviewees in their study).

Interest Organizations

Interest organizations are usually not membership groups in any real sense. In Germany, for instance, all students must by law belong to the student association at their university and pay dues to it, but 95 per cent of the students are not even aware that they are members. Participation in elections of student parliaments or boards (ASTA, *Allgemeiner Studentenausschuss*) is usually low, around 40 per cent on the average.[19] The federal association of all West German student associations, VDS (*Verband Deutscher Studentenschaften*), has very low visibility among students.

In countries where membership in interest organizations is not compulsory, as in Holland and France, the organizations must offer the students special benefits, such as mimeographed course notes, discount prices in stores, travel opportunities, and the like in order to make membership attractive. In such cases, the student behaves more like a customer or client than a member. The UNEF controls, in effect, the *Mutuelle Nationale des Étudiants de France*, the system of social security for students, established after UNEF's determined lobbying in Parlement in 1949. Even so, elections of UNEF and MNEF officers attract only between 5 and 15 per cent of the eligible student voters. In Holland and Austria, however, where candidates are chosen from lists representing student parties, participation is higher, fluctuating around two thirds of the eligible voters. In Frankfurt, where a similar list system was tried in 1967, the anticipated increase in participation did not occur. The Frankfurt student body is rather atomized, and the electoral lists did not represent any strong groupings.

In general, students do not exhibit a strong desire to organize for the defense of their material interests, although they are willing to pay to have these interests protected. For this reason, the analogy that C. J. Lammers draws between working-class and student trade unionism appears somewhat questionable. Students may well emerge as a conflict group in modern societies, but not necessarily as a group devoted to the defense of its material interests. Indeed, the Dutch SVB, which Lammers regards as a student interest group, has probably devoted as much time and energy to political battles (for example, anti-Vietnam demonstrations) as to bread-and-butter issues. When the SVB was initially formed, it borrowed its slogans and ideas directly from the UNEF — the definition of the student as a young intellectual worker, the demand for a student salary, the demand for co-determination in university administration, and so forth. A survey that I conducted in Holland early in 1963, prior to the emergence of SVB and to the spread of its ideas among Dutch students, showed that the majority of Dutch students supported these demands and ideas.

The weakness of interest organizations makes them a convenient target for those who have a stake in influencing students or academic institutions. Inside the organizations' councils, the battle is frequently joined over the issue of political participation or, as the West Germans put it, the "political mandate" of the student associations. Traditionalists insist on the essentially apolitical nature of these associations, while the transgressive groups claim that student interest and politics cannot be separated.[20]

Although the extent of the political involvement of interest organizations has fluctuated over time, the long-run trend has been toward politicization. The UNEF — whose original program formulated in the Charter of Grenoble was clearly transgressive — remained under left-wing leadership for only the first four postwar years and in the atmosphere of the Cold War years became "apolitical" under moderate "corporatist" guidance. But it reached the height of its influence among students after 1956, when its left-wing Catholic leaders, supported by the Communist students, were able to mount a successful campaign of strikes and demonstrations against the Algerian war.[21] From then on, the political involvements of UNEF and its basic opposition to the Gaullist state have steadily increased, even at the expense of membership strength.[22] The head organization of Dutch student associations, the *Nederlands Studenten Raad*, has been forced increasingly by SVB pressure to take political positions. And its German counterpart, the VDS, after laboring for years over issues of university reform and student welfare, reacted to the violent incidents of last year by declaring itself a member of Germany's "extra-parliamentary opposition" — a loose coalition of left-wing student organizations, anti-war groups, opponents of the emergency laws recently adopted by the West-German parliament, and critics of the current coalition government.[23]

Approval of Student Trade Unionism

Percentages of Students, in Three Dutch Universities, Approving of Eight Items

	AMSTERDAM Municipal		AMSTERDAM Calvinist		NIJMEGEN	
	Leaders	Sample	Leaders	Sample	Leaders	Sample
A. In order to give access to higher education to all whose intellectual abilities may benefit society, the student must be given a salary.	75	77	61	77	33	73
B. A salary would give the student material independence and would preserve his personal dignity, both of which are necessary for his intellectual development.	87	71	48	62	25	65
C. Society must recognize the student's role as a young intellectual worker.	85	78	65	74	33	71
D. Since the university is an organic community, it would be better for students to cooperate with the academic authority instead of taking the path of student trade unionism.	51	50	44	62	92	57
E. It is only normal for students to organize themselves in trade unions.	75	65	74	71	50	61
F. Student organizations should deal with political problems as well as with cultural questions, social service, and leisure.	90	81	91	89	100	78
G. Student representatives should participate in university administration as well as in the financial decision affecting student life.	96	87	96	87	83	86
H. Student groups which speak for groups with various political tendencies must exist, even if this produces tensions.	87	60	58	56	42	35
Sample size	47	217	23	82	12	94

Transgressive Organizations

Students for whom role models are either unavailable or unacceptable tend toward transgressive movements. The *syndicaliste* wing of the UNEF as well as the various socialist, Communist, and anarchist organizations have their main strength in the fields of social science and the humanities for which there exist no clear occupational goals.[24] The growth of transgressivism may be directly related to the critical conditions at the French universities whose student populations have increased at a rapid rate, *particularly* in the social sciences and the humanities, which offer the fewest occupational outlets. During the last ten years, the number of students in French universities has risen from 170,000 to 602,000; and the number of entering students is expected to rise from 133,500 last year to 172,000 this fall. At the same time, the proportion of students going into science and technology is falling (25 per cent of the entering students last year to 15 per cent this year). For every mathematics student, there are two philosophy students.[25]

Particularly striking is the large number of sociology and psychology students in transgressive organizations.[26] In the German SDS and the Dutch SVB, their proportion of the membership is totally out of keeping with their still relatively small number in the universities. In these instances, the student's choice of major clearly reflects his general concern with social questions or human affairs. The exposure to other students with similar concerns and to some of the leading left-wing intellectuals who teach in these fields may help to transform personal or academic interests into active participation. Thus, the student of the social sciences is doubly predisposed to transgressive organizations. The role he might occupy in the social world after his studies is only dimly perceived, if perceived at all, and ideological influences may make him question the appropriateness of the existing system of roles.

To some degree, a social role system always reflects the division of the society into groups constituted on the basis of social class, religion, ethnicity, and so forth.[27] During certain periods, young people may come to reject not only those roles, but also the group structure that corresponds to them. Clearly, such transgressive tendencies are less likely so long as social boundaries effectively delimit the social horizon. Transgression usually occurs when the members of a movement perceive the future — their own or that of their group — as either particularly barren or particularly promising. To the young Russian intellectuals of the late-nineteenth and early-twentieth centuries, for example, all avenues toward a rewarding future appeared blocked. Thus, they felt the need to ally themselves with other groups of the population in order to achieve the downfall of a regime that frustrated all legitimate ambition.

The second condition of transgression, the perception of an expanding social universe, is often associated with the end of a war or with prerevolutionary gains in economic well-being and political freedom. The end of the Napoleonic wars and again the period preceding 1848 are the two rare instances in which sizable groups in the German universities attempted to ally themselves with other groups in the population. At the end of the Second World War, French students who had shared the experience of the resistance movement with young people from all walks of life resolved to remain actively engaged in a common effort of all young people to rebuild and reshape their country: the Charter of Grenoble expresses this aspiration to play a role in a process of social transformation made possible by the common experience of a catastrophic past and the common hope for a brighter, more humane future. Toward the end of the last decade, the thaw following Stalin's death and the growth of modern trends in Roman Catholicism once again encouraged optimism concerning the possibility of productive cooperation among groups previously separated by social and ideological barriers. Herbert Marcuse, to whom many student leaders have looked for intellectual guidance, has repeatedly expressed this philosophy of hope by pointing to the tremendous technological potential of our society and to the need for a new social structure capable of realizing that potential. Such rising expectations have made for dissidence of youth groups from their parent organizations and furnished the impetus for the spread of the trade union movement from France into Belgium and Holland. Thus, historical conditions have powerful effects upon the types of transgressive movements likely to gain a following.

If frustration and despair preside at the birth of a transgressive movement, its members are apt to adopt ideological orientations that help them to interpret or to render psychologically tolerable their marginal and precarious situation. Unable to hope for success in the present or the immediate future, such a movement will look forward to a total destruction of the social fabric. It may adopt conspiratorial attitudes and practices, thus accentuating its separateness from society.

A transgressive movement born of optimism will, on the other hand, tend to de-emphasize ideological divisions and stress the values that unite its members and followers. Such a movement seeks achievements in the present rather than in the distant future. Thus, the UNEF set in opposition to the individualistic liberalism that had dominated the Third Republic the value of social obligation, an element common to the philosophies of Marxism and Catholicism. Most of the UNEF leaders, particularly during the period when the so-called *syndicaliste* wing was in command, were profoundly critical of the socio-economic and political order; they thought, however, that the system could be transformed radically if young intellectuals, allied with other progressive groups in the population, actively participated in the process of policy-formation. Indeed, a central point in the internal debates of the UNEF has been the search for an adequate definition of the student's role.

Role-Seeking and Dissidence

Role-seeking movements are frequently alliances of dissidents from established parent organizations. If young Communists and Catholics worked together in their student trade union, they rarely did so with the approval of their parent organizations. Both the Catholic and Communist hierarchy (indeed all party and religious leaderships) tended to regard their student groups as auxiliaries whose main tasks were to spread the organizations' beliefs, attract young supporters, and prepare them for their future role as full-fledged members. The youth organizations, however, tend to insist on autonomy in their beliefs, actions, and alliances. The last of these demands regularly meets determined resistance; the parent hierarchy usually feels that it would lose young supporters to an opponent were such alliances tolerated.

Both the French Catholic students, organized in the *Jeunesse Étudiante Chrétienne* (JEC), and the *Union des Étudiants Communistes* (UEC) have gone through repeated crises due to attempts by the adult organizations to regain control of student groups that they felt had gone too far afield. The JEC experienced its first major crisis in 1956, when the Catholic hierarchy forced the dissolution of the *Association Catholique de la Jeunesse Française* (ACJF), and the second in 1965, when the officers of the JEC were forcibly removed from their positions.[28] In both cases, the point at issue was the role of the so-called "lay apostolate." The hierarchy insisted that the sole task of young people in Catholic Action was to evangelize their *milieu* — to combat godlessness by spreading the teachings of the gospel. The JEC leaders countered these demands by saying that Christian charity means helping others better understand their own situation and that the success of evangelism depends on the lay apostle's ability to participate in the struggles of his social group and generation. They further contended that such participation necessarily required close cooperation with non-Catholics, particularly Protestants and Communists.

The crisis of the UEC dragged on from 1962 to 1966.[29] The UEC, contrary to the wishes of the party, had written a programmatic statement of its own that described students as a progressive force in society. Party theoreticians pointed out that most students belong to the bourgeoisie or petite-bourgeoisie and therefore cannot be considered natural allies of the working class. To these doctrinal objections, the president of UEC had a rather unorthodox answer: He affirmed that a person's class membership is determined not by what he is, but by what he does. Since most students act as progressives, he argued, they belong to the progressive forces in society. This debate with the party leadership, published verbatim, enabled the young Communists to increase their prestige greatly among the students and, as a result, to play a greater role within the UNEF. But continued efforts of the party's Central Committee to recapture control of the Communist student organization were eventually successful. The party was aided in its efforts by a general resurgence, in the mid-sixties, of political sectarianism. The UEC soon became prey to intensive internal squabbles between "Italians" (followers of the line of Palmiro Togliatti), neo-Stalinists, neo-Trotskyists, Maoists, and a variety of opposition groups within each of these major denominations. By 1965, the party had regained control of the organization, and most of its talented leaders withdrew.

Similar phenomena of dissidence and transgression are clearly observable among the student groups of German political parties. The SDS, currently the most influential left-wing student organization, was originally the official student group of the Social-Democratic Party. Because of continuing disagreements over the issues of German rearmament and of contacts with East Germany, the party created, in 1960, a second organization consisting of students faithful to the party and its official policies. In 1961, the party declared that membership in the SDS was incompatible with party membership, thus effectively excluding the entire SDS membership and withdrawing all subsidies. This separation from the party eventually re-dounded to the political benefit of SDS, which could then ally itself with any other left-wing groups and thus become the most vocal and effective member of the "extra-parliamentary opposition." The *Sozialistische Hochschulbund* (SHB), successor to SDS as the official Social-Democratic student organization, has traveled approximately the same path as SDS. The organization now opposes the party on nearly all important issues, such as support of NATO, projected emergency legislation (which would suspend basic rights whenever the government declared a national emergency to exist), and the current policy of coalition with the Christian-Democratic Party.

Nearly everywhere, the student organizations of political parties are to the left of the officialdom, often considerably so. The Dutch socialist students, organized in a club called *Politeia*, are far to the left of the Labor Party and tend to associate with elements much further to left; the student trade union movement has given them increased opportunity to do this. A recent revolt in the socialist student organization of Austria has given control to a group that rejects the establishmentarianism of the socialist party, takes a self-consciously "Marxist" stand, and tends to embarrass the party leader-ship by exposing its bureaucratic tendencies.

Once rebellious leaders of a youth group have been disciplined or removed by the parent organization, the group usually loses mem-bers, vitality, and influence. But when the crisis is over and new members have begun to join the youth club, the process of dissidence is apt to begin again. Organizational memories are short, in any event, where "generations" span but a few years.

Ideological Protest Movements

While role-seeking movements tend to be ecumenical, ideological protest movements are sectarian. The most obvious examples of such organizations are the many small groups that are currently re-viving past trends in socialist thought. Numerous Trotskyist, sparta-cist, or anarchist groups combine the thoughts and style of historic socialist doctrines with ideological elements taken from Mao or Castro. Their mood is invariably one of total aversion toward the society of today, and their style is often esoteric. The least esoteric among the protest groups are the Dutch Provos, who have had con-siderable influence upon the tactics of protest groups by introducing new and imaginative techniques.

The movement's ideology shows particularly well the relationship between exasperation and protest. The following passages from the first issue of the review *PROVO* make this point clear:

Provo has something against capitalism, communism, fascism, bureaucracy, militarism, snobbism, professionalism, dogmatism, and authoritarianism.
Provo feels that it is faced with a choice: desperate resistance or painful disaster.
Provo calls for resistance whenever it can.
Provo sees that it will lose in the end, but it does not wish to pass up the chance thoroughly to provoke this society at least once more.[30]

The Provos provoke the authorities mainly by creating commotions. Their movement became internationally known when, on March 10, 1966, it disrupted the marriage of Princess Beatrix and the German diplomat Claus von Amsberg. But their favorite means of provocation has been the "happening," a modern dramatic form that relies on improvisations in which the spectators become participants. The Provos made it a practice to organize such happenings every Saturday night in a small square off one of Amsterdam's main thoroughfares. Their themes tended to be more or less political — that is, protests against Claus von Amsberg or the police. When the police considered that these events got out of hand, they would intercede, often with more vigor and severity than was justifiable.

Professor Buikhuisen, a criminologist and the inventor of the term "provo,"[31] believes that a considerable number of young people suffer from feelings of powerlessness. The Claus affair, he states, heightened such feelings since no amount of public disapproval could prevent the marriage of the crown princess to a former Nazi.[32] If his diagnosis is correct, the conditions of modern bureaucratic society should bring about increasing instances of ideological protest. In actual fact, the Dutch Provo movement was able to achieve a measure of success. The chief of police, whose brutal response to the provocations was widely criticized, was forced to resign. And three months after the Claus affair, one of the Provo leaders was elected a member of Amsterdam's City Council. And although the Provos were spending some of their days in jail, they managed to play roles that society recognized. A pamphlet describing "what the Provos want" was taken by many as a sign of change in the direction toward greater responsibility, or, in the terminology of this paper, toward role-seeking.

Provo is not quite typical of ideological protest movements because its theory is weak, and it is radical in rhetoric and feeling tone
only; its program does not really break with Dutch society, and its
actions are not nearly so shocking as the Provo leaders like to believe. The typical ideological protest movement is more deeply
involved in questions of social analysis and doctrine. The mode of
thought is often quite complex, and the writing (particularly that of
the German authors) exceedingly obscure. Following is the beginning of a speech that Rudi Dutschke wrote on the occasion of a
congress held in Hanover by various left-wing groups to assess the
political consequences of the killing of a student during the June 2,
1967, demonstrations against the Shah of Iran.

Given the reduction of the possibilities of overcoming the barriers to ac-
cumulation [of capital] through expansion of the field of capitalism — the
world is divided up, the Third World has begun its struggle — given the
resulting extent of destruction of capital through armaments, artificial
inflation of a gigantic apparatus of bureaucracy and administration, structural unemployment, unused productive capacity, advertising, and so
forth — that is given the growth of social dead costs, given that advances
in production increasingly fall short of possibilities, new tendencies appear in the dynamics of the class struggle [and thus] changes occur in the
traditional relationship between theory and practice in Marxism.[33]

Like many of the younger socialists, and indeed his teacher Marcuse, Dutschke considers the materialistic determinism of classical
Marxism excessive. Another issue, closely connected to this, concerns
the role of students and intellectuals in society. Marxists and neo-
Marxists tend to assign a secondary role to students; they cling to
the classical teachings according to which the proletariat is the only
revolutionary class, while members of the New Left, including Marcuse, argue that the working class in modern capitalism has been
integrated into the system, and that the intellectuals alone can be
regarded as a potentially revolutionary force.[34] This debate —
whatever may be the merits of the arguments on either side — reveals rather clearly the main psychological source of ideological protest: concern over the likelihood of one's own political effectiveness.

Role-seeking movements consider society malleable enough to
be transformed by vigorous action, whereas the protest movement is
forever concerned with the question of the potential (revolutionary)
effectiveness of various social groups. This concern betrays an anxiety over the likelihood of change, a feeling that one's own action
may be blocked and therefore ineffective. When people feel that

they cannot act effectively, they tend to search for intellectually satisfying explanations and guides to behavior: hence, the strong emphasis of protest movements upon detailed ideological explanations and
the critical importance of being "correct." Unfortunately, the protest
movement's analyses are rarely based on careful examination of
empirical evidence; rather, arguments proceed by chains of declara-
tive statements which, although unsupported by evidence, sound
like so many assertions about the nature of reality.

This intellectual style takes assertions for realities and can easily
lead to confusion. Jürgen Habermas, a teacher of many members of
the German New Left, has recently pointed to certain dangers flow-
ing from the intellectual style now current in the protest movement.[35]
Widely accepted interpretations of the contemporary world, he
states, are either false or unproven and provide no reliable guide to
action. Such doubtful interpretations, he continues, lead to the erroneous belief that the opportunities for effective action are determined by the conditions of an increasingly revolutionary situation
and by the international unity of anti-capitalist protest. Symbol and
reality are often confused, as when the occupation of university
buildings is interpreted as an actual seizure of power.[36] The ideological protest movement clearly builds for its members a hermetic world
in which reality-testing becomes increasingly difficult. By overesti-
mating the revolutionary potential in today's world as well as the
extent and intent of official repression, it tends to fall into the trap of
self-fulfilling prophecies.

Changing Hegemonies

During given periods of historical time, specific types of organizations tend to predominate. Traditional organizations "belong"
most clearly to the nineteenth century, but despite the gradual decline of their memberships and ethos, they have been able to exercise
considerable influence in this century. The first short blooming of
role-seeking movements occurred after World War II when the
French UNEF was transformed into a student trade union and the
Free University of Berlin was founded. But as the Cold War divided
the world into armed camps, role-seeking movements gave way to
traditional and interest organizations. Rigidities were introduced
into all political systems by international tensions, by the painful
dissolution of colonial empires, by the crushing of libertarian movements in East Germany, Hungary, and elsewhere, and by the disci-

pline the Catholic and Communist hierarchies imposed on their followers.

The hopes for a more equitable social order that spring up anew at the end of each war found little nourishment in the world of the early and middle fifties. UNEF became an interest organization, and the *Korporationen* reestablished themselves in Germany. The resurgence of role-seeking transgressivism and its spread into new territories coincided with the end of Stalinism, the liberalization of the Catholic Church, and the thaw on both sides of the Iron Curtain. Yet the movement soon encountered new obstacles as academic and political leaderships everywhere attempted to set limits to a movement that interfered with the structure of authority. The forced withdrawal of the transgressive forces has tended to drive them into the positions of ideological protest.

So long as authority is divided and authorities are in conflict with one another, role-seeking movements can assert themselves. When authority congeals and forms a solid bloc, the stage is set for ideological protest. Thus, the consolidation of the Gaullist regime thrust the transgressive student leadership into uncompromising opposition to the government. And the coalition government in Germany has led German student leaders to feel that the walls of a social and political prison have been closing in on them, and that freedom can be gained only by breaking down this rather formidable structure. Since July, 1960, when the Social-Democratic Party decided that membership in SDS was irreconcilable with membership in the party, an increasing number of student organizations have come to the conviction that nothing can be gained by attempting to work within the parliamentary system.

The blockage of political energies due to the consolidation of authority structures has its counterpart in the university itself. Here, efforts toward the reform of obsolete structures have been consistently frustrated. The inadequacies of existing systems of higher education are directly felt by many students and most directly experienced by the student leadership involved in the task of changing the system. While official resistance to changes in academic structures and inertia of the university authorities varies but little over time, student resentment against the university becomes heightened in periods of political stagnation. Energies which cannot usefully exert themselves in the political arena then become directed upon more proximal targets: the academic authorities.

In both France and Germany, the authority structure of the university and the methods of teaching and doing research are clearly superannuated. Since the end of the war, university reform has been under discussion by academic administrations, faculties, and students, but there have been no appreciable results from these talks. The conceptions that underly academic organization and practice in both Germany and France date back to the beginning of the nineteenth century; yet in many respects they are direct opposites. Originally the primary objective of the German university was *Erziehung durch Wissenschaft*, the "formation of a morally independent and cognitively integrated individual through scholarship."[37] The French university, developed under the auspices of the Napoleonic reforms, was intended chiefly to select and train a ruling elite. Thus, the image of the German professor was that of an intellectual leader who, surrounded by a small and intimate circle of students, pursued knowledge for its own sake; the French professor, to the contrary, was an agent of the state entrusted with the task of "forming" the cadres of the regime. The German ideas called for the insulation of the university from society, while in the Napoleonic conception the university was enmeshed in the society, particularly the apparatus of government.

Accordingly, the German professor was and still is conceived to be sovereign. Once he has attained the coveted position of *Ordinarius*, he alone has the right to determine what scientific work is to be done in his institute and by whom, what courses and seminars are to be offered and by whom, how students are to be examined and by whom, as well as a great variety of other matters. The French professor, on the other hand, is essentially a lecturer; such matters as curricula and examination systems are, in principle, left to the Ministry of Education to decide. This picture is deliberately overdrawn, however; in both systems, actual practice does not completely coincide with legal norms, and legislation as well as formal and informal regulations have come to soften somewhat the absolute authority of professors and government.[38]

As a further consequence of diverging ideological and sociopolitical origins, the two academic systems assign quite different functions to their examination systems. Originally, the German system was oriented entirely to the eventual production of a major scientific contribution. In this endeavor, each individual was supposed to progress according to his own needs and predispositions, and examinations, which might have provided common standards for the evaluation of each student's progress, were regarded with suspicion. In France, on the other hand, the student's progress was paced almost entirely by frequent examinations, many of them competitive.

Both German and French students object to their respective examination systems. The German students feel a lack of guidance and think that they often waste time in misdirected efforts; the French students feel excessively restricted in their freedom to explore their field of study. Again, the picture is overdrawn. The needs of an industrial society have led to increasingly specialized courses and curricula in Germany against which students have protested in the name of the freedom whose wasteful nondirection they resent.[39] In France, on the other hand, the scholarly predilections of individual professors have gradually led to the introduction of courses remote from social reality and current intellectual problems.

The obsolescence of both of these systems of academic organization is obvious. To provide only a single full professor in each field of academic study — as is still the rule in Germany — is clearly out of keeping with both the number of students and the growth of knowledge and literature in each discipline.[40]

The French system, geared as it is to the training of a social and technological elite, becomes a paradox when it enrolls large masses of students. Often lecture halls are not large enough to accommodate the students enrolled in a course, the library is unable to provide the books whose reading is required of those who wish to pass the all-important examinations, and course notes mimeographed either commercially or by student organizations become the students' main intellectual fare.

In actuality, the French academic system, while still pretending to form a single national system of higher education, has undergone a process of stratification. The young members of the elite are actually formed in a few small institutions (for example, the *École Normale Supérieure*, the *École Polytechnique*, and the *Institut National d'Administration*). But the elitist myths persisting in French higher education create unnecessary strains and study programs that have little to do with the objectives that the student could realistically set for himself.

All of these facts and many more document the maladaptation of the French and German academic institutions to social needs, yet all efforts to reform these systems or to develop some generally acceptable programs of reform have thus far borne little fruit. The main obstacle to reform in Germany is clearly the determined resistance of the *Ordinarii*. Despite the crying need for more professors and the willingness of the *Länder* ministries to make funds available for new positions, the number of full-fledged faculty members has not increased significantly. Rather, there has been a large increase in the number of *Assistenten* and other members of the "intermediate structure," which, by extending the span of control of the *Ordinarii*, has contributed to the further bureaucratization of the system. The *Wissenschaftstrat*, an advisory body consisting of representatives of the academic profession and the ministries of education of the several *Länder*, recommended in 1966, after twenty years of deliberation, a more coherently designed curriculum and a curtailment of some of the professors' freedoms in determining the content of their teaching. Since these modest recommendations require the consent of the faculty, they have thus far had few practical consequences.[41] The only suggestion that has been implemented in some instances is the reduction in the number of semesters that a student may spend pursuing his degree. The reaction of the students to such a "reform" was understandably emotional. The average student felt that delay in the pursuit of his studies might result in his losing the entire time he had devoted to his academic career; and student leaders believed, with some justification, that the measure was directed particularly against them, since participation in student government or political activities frequently slows academic progress.[42]

German student organizations see the main remedy to the crisis of the German university in "democratization" — particularly, the participation of the "intermediate structure" and the students in academic decision-making. The limited experience with student representation at the Free University of Berlin has not been encouraging, however. The one or two students sitting in the senate and on academic committees have found themselves regularly outvoted by unanimous faculty groups. An exception is the *Otto-Suhr-Institut* (of political science) at the Free University of Berlin, whose members and students worked out an institute constitution that was endorsed by conservative professors as well as radical students. But the university's senate, which must approve such arrangements, refused to ratify the new constitution. Professor Sontheimer, a co-director of the *Otto-Suhr-Institut,* made the following comment on this decision:

As the Academic Senate of the FU has indicated unmistakably, only those reforms shall be approved that do not change the substance of the traditional structure of the *Ordinarienuniversität* (university controlled by the Ordinarii).

Ergo: Reform is all right, but change is not.[43]

While the unyielding authority structure of German universities resides in the professorial guild, the corresponding French structure is the Gaullist regime itself. Since the power to make decisions on university reform rests almost entirely with the Ministry of Education, official plans for reform are most heavily affected by budgetary considerations. A further consideration is France's need for academically trained technicians and other specialists at the intermediate levels. Finally, social pressures, particularly within the petite-bourgeoisie, call for general cultural curricula.[44]

The Fouchet plan of reform published by the Ministry of Education in 1965 attempted to deal with these issues by introducing curricula of general education, creating technical institutes that would be a part of the university system without requiring a stringent scientific education, and making curricula more consistent with the needs of the economy. The student Left saw in this plan the nefarious influence of the technocrats who were attempting to make the university subservient to the purposes of neo-capitalism; the student masses, intent upon the culturally prized diplomas in disciplines which would make them part of the "intellectual" strata, reacted with indifference. A strike that UNEF launched against the Fouchet plan in March, 1966, ended in a Pyrrhic victory that came close to destroying the organization.

The basic realities of French university life are overcrowding and aimlessness. The government responded to the critical overcrowding by establishing new campuses, such as Nanterre where the May revolt began. Nanterre can hardly be regarded as an intellectual home. It is situated in a bleak semi-industrial suburb, has insufficient library facilities, and its teaching staff lives in Paris and often spends no more time at the university than is needed to deliver a lecture.

French university reform generates confrontations between students and government over issues that neither side has been able to define clearly. The proposals of the student leadership — to make university work productive and to pay the student a salary as compensation for his productive labor — fall on the deaf ears of a government whose major concerns are financial.

The UNEF leadership has tended to treat the crisis of the French university as a social and pedagogic problem. It has vigorously opposed the *cours magistral*, the lecture course which gives the student no opportunity for active participation. UNEF's demand for seminars to take the place of lectures did not elicit much enthusiasm among the faculty. In the absence of any centrally directed pedagogic reform, UNEF attempted in 1962 to institute a system of educational self-help. The organization floundered after the end of the Algerian affair and was unable to define an effective program of action. A new Secretary for Academic Affairs — the first Communist to enter the *Bureau National* — then developed the theory that a student trade union must clearly be concerned with university *work*, and the organization then began to organize the so-called "University Work Groups." These groups were established to combine — with or without the help of faculty members — the activities of teaching and research and thus transform the student into a productive member of society. After a short initial success, and despite the cooperation of some faculty members, the work group program disintegrated when the time for examination drew close. It had not been possible, in the course of one year, to change the basic values and premises of a student culture in which the passing of examinations counts among the highest priorities.

In both France and Germany, the failure to achieve university reform has resulted in the predominance of ideological protest. After the collapse of the *politique universitaire,* symbolized by the Work Groups, various socialist, Communist, and Maoist groups engaged in ideological battles and complex maneuvers for control of UNEF. In Germany, the left-wing student organizations have also become more embroiled in doctrinal debates.

Dynamics of Conflict

The question raised at the beginning of this paper has now been partially answered: Acute and often violent conflict situations arise when student activists espouse a posture of ideological protest and when, at the same time, large masses of students become available for action. Both the ideological posture and the despair of the student masses are generated by the belief that the structures of authority have become increasingly congealed and thus unresponsive to demands for change.

These conclusions deal only with the conditions which predispose students to conflict. They do not consider the proximate causes — the types of situations and developments — which make for the outbreak, the escalation, and the eventual settlement of conflict. While it is obvious that these causes vary considerably from country to country and from university to university, the following propositions represent an attempt to capture some of the most generally observable characteristics of conflict processes in universities.[45]

Proposition 1: *Since authorities are charged with the preservation of social and political boundaries, they will be particularly vulnerable at points where the boundary system is weak. Conflicts tend to originate at such points of weakness because authorities usually overreact to any act of transgression.*

It is not accidental that Berlin is a center of the student protest movement in Germany. The boundary surrounding West Berlin is weak, and not for military reasons alone. The economy of West Berlin is not self-sustaining and depends to a large extent on West German subventions of various types.[46] West Berlin's political leadership, moreover, considers it particularly important to remain in the good graces of the Western Allies. Neither the university authorities nor the Berlin government ever objected to student demonstrations or collections in favor of the Hungarian freedom fighters, but it did object to similar collections in support of Algerian refugees. For similar reasons, demonstrations against the war in Vietnam produce more official resentment in Berlin than anywhere else in Germany.

Another kind of boundary weakness occurs when the political fronts are not clearly defined — for example, when the public representative of a rigidified authority structure is considered a possible ally of the students. It is noteworthy that most of the incidents in Germany start in universities with a liberal rector and in cities with a socialist government. This is the case of Berlin, Frankfurt, and Hamburg.

The May revolt in France also started at one of the weakest points in the French educational system. It was triggered by the unprecedented decision of the dean of letters to bring the police into the inner court of the Sorbonne after the arrival in Paris of a group of students exiled from Nanterre (their campus had been closed because of disturbances over a free-speech issue) and a counter-demonstration was threatened by right-wing elements.[47]

Proposition 2: *A defeat of student protest leads to scattered protest activities of varying types.*

Following the violent protests against the Shah of Iran in Berlin on June 2, 1967, there were demonstrations and spoofs on the occasion of the yearly official ceremonies during which the outgoing rector passes his authority on to his successor. Other incidents involved interruptions of lectures by professors with a Nazi past. Most of these actions were locally organized and did not involve any central coordination. Indeed, both the left-wing student leaders and their opponents tend to ascribe more effectiveness to their own planning and decisions than is likely to be warranted.

Clearly, the incidents were spontaneous that occurred throughout Germany in April, 1968, after a drifter shot Rudi Dutschke. The offices of the Springer publishing house were obvious targets for demonstrations and acts of vandalism. Virtually the entire student press agrees that Springer's newspapers (which account for 40 per cent of the entire circulation in Germany and for 70 per cent in Berlin) have systematically fostered public hostility against the students.[48]

Proposition 3: *The magnitude and the protractedness of a conflict depends on the isolation of the students.*

The magnitude of the May events in France resulted from alliances formed more or less spontaneously as a response to the government's use of force. The *Syndicat National de l'Enseignement Supérieur* (a trade union in which most of the professors are organized) immediately called a strike. At first there was some cooperation between the workers' trade unions and UNEF. But the movement lost the support of these other social groups. Workers, for example, proved more interested in bread-and-butter issues than in social revolution. It remains to be seen whether the outburst of passion has been entirely futile. In virtually all French universities, student-faculty groups have been working on reform projects that provide for student participation in academic administration.[49] Government reaction to these proposals is still a matter of conjecture, although the government has promised university reform.

In Germany, students are pitted against the faculty, the government, most of the press, and most of the population. Indeed, the students' political beliefs diverge radically from those of the average citizen. A survey conducted recently by Professor Wildenmann among three thousand German students, one thousand young people in the age group seventeen to twenty-four years, and two thousand adults shows striking differences.[50] Forty-three per cent of the young people and 50 per cent of the adults believed that Hitlerism was basically "a good idea that was badly carried out," while 93 per cent of the students reject this view. Twenty-five per cent of the young people and 30 per cent of the adults believe in a "single, strong party," whereas 95 per cent of the students object to one-party rule. Fourteen per cent of the young people and 25 per cent of the adults are in favor of a "strong leader personality," but only 4 per cent of the students are.

The students' fear of "restorative forces" at work in Germany are not without foundation. It is also clear that the students' campaigns engender little sympathy or understanding among the population. The common reaction against the unwarranted or excessive use of force that precipitated the May events in France has no parallel in Germany. In the absence of any appreciable support, the students cannot count on the solution of their problems, and their conflict with the authorities is likely to be a protracted one. Indeed, the German student protest movement threatens to degenerate into a bitter contest with prevailing public opinion. At the same time, attacks upon the Springer press — the most vocal exponent and, in the students' view, the main source of this public opinion — lead to further consolidations of the forces of authority.

Proposition 4: *Students exhibit a special sensitivity and tendency toward conflict when issues of justice and truth are involved. This sensitivity sets students increasingly at odds with prevailing social values.*

Heribert Adam has noted that the German student does not participate in day-to-day political affairs, but becomes aroused when large moral issues are involved.[51] The students reacted as vigorously against the repression of the East German and Hungarian uprisings as they now do against the Vietnam war. Similarly, the Springer press, which indulges in sensationalist distortions and demagogic attacks upon nonconformists, clearly arouses passionate antagonisms among students.[52]

Conclusion

Students in Western Europe increasingly find themselves at odds with academic and civil authorities. The transitory status of students makes it doubtful that they themselves can exert consistent pressures within the social system. At most, they can serve as catalysts, precipitating events that are in the making and forging alliances to accelerate social change.

Student "interests" appear to be quite different in character from the interests of, say, organized labor. Indeed, they are basically the interests of intellectuals concerned with the destinies of society as a whole. It is rather significant that the French students saw their movement as the beginning of a social revolution, while the workers did not. Despite the economic pressures that affect many students, they evince no sustained concern with furthering their material well-being; their current poverty is taken to be either transitory or part of the student's life style. It is difficult, therefore, to define student "interests" apart from a commitment to their own intellectual growth and, in some instances, to the betterment of society.

Whether we see the emergence of an intellectual class in which the students occupy an avant-garde position is a different matter. Intellectual labor now constitutes one of the major factors of production, and the producer of intellectual commodities is often "alienated" when the fruits of individual intelligence enter the market. But this raises once more the perennial and thus far unsolved problems of "correct" and "false" class consciousness. It raises the question further of whether intellectuals are any more capable of emancipating themselves than have the social strata been that have gone before them.

REFERENCES

1. This is a thorough revision in the light of recent events, of the article published in *DÆDALUS* under the title "Tradition and Transgression." Much of the material appears here for the first time.

2. C. J. Lammers, *Studentenvakbeweging en universitaire democratie* (Amsterdam, 1968), p. 8. Lammers follows the usage of Dahrendorf here, who defines social class not with reference to property relations, but rather as a conflict group consisting of people with common interests. See Ralf Dahrendorf, *Class and Class Conflict in Industrial Society* (Stanford, 1959), pp. 179–205. Note that Dahrendorf regards the use of the term "class" to designate conflict groups as a purely definitional matter. Lammers, in a footnote (p. 53, ftn. 9) indicates his own reservations about the term "class," but uses it for the sake of simplicity.

3. Lammers, *op. cit.*, p. 13 and pp. 22–25.

4. See, for instance, Helmut Schauer, "Rechenschaftsbericht des Bundesvorstandes" in *Beiträge zur 20. Ordentlichen Delegiertenkonferenz des Sozialistischen Deutschen Studentenbundes* (SDS), Vol. 14, No. 17 (October, 1965) in Frankfurt/M (multilith), p. 8.

5. See Aad de Jongh, *PROVO* (Rotterdam, 1966), pp. 108–133; Duco van Weerlee, *Wat de PROVO's willen* (Amsterdam, 1966), pp. 13–17.

6. Bernard Oudin, *Les corporations allemandes d'étudiants* (Paris, 1962), p. 105.

7. The lists were put at my disposal by the *Archiv und Bücherei der Deutschen Burschenschaft*. I wish to express my thanks to Mr. Wilhelm Wreden, director of the archives, for permission to tally the lists.

8. Virtually the entire literature on German fraternities is strongly partisan and argumentative. See Friedrich Schulze and Paul Szymank, *Das deutsche Studententum von den ältesten Zeiten bis zur Gegenwart* (Leipzig, 1910; Bernard Oudin, *Les corporations allemandes d'étudiants*; Ernst Wilhelm Wreden, "Die Entwicklung der Burschenschaft," in *Handbuch der Deutschen Burschenschaft* (Bad Nauheim, 1964), as well as other chapters of this volume; Lutz E. Fink, *Gestatte mir Hochachtungsschluck* (Hamburg, 1963). Somewhat less biased and more recent accounts may be found in Werner Klose, *Freiheit schreibt auf eure Fahnen: 800 Jahre Deutsche Studenten* (Hamburg, 1967). For the transition to nationalsocialism, see Hans Peter Bleuel and Ernst Klinnert, *Deutsche Studenten auf dem Weg ins Dritte Reich* (Gütersloh, 1967).

9. Hans Anger, *Probleme der deutschen Universität* (Tübingen, 1960), pp. 108ff.

10. A number of statements by federations of *Korporationen*, including some of their views on the "German question," can be found in Rolf Neuhaus (ed.), *Dokumente zur Hochschulreform, 1945–1959* (Wiesbaden, 1961), pp. 537–621.

11. Günther Berka (ed.), *100 Jahre Deutsche Burschenschaft in Österreich* (Graz, 1959), pp. 32, 34.

12. A. J. C. Vrankrijker, *Vier Eeuwen Nederlandsch Studentenleven* (Voorburg, n.d. [probably 1938 or 1939]); Amsterdamsch Studenten Corps, *Geschiedenis van het Amsterdams Studentenleven, 1932–1962* (Amsterdam, 1962).

13. *Geschiedenis van het Amsterdams Studentenleven, 1932–1962*, pp. 153ff.

14. Heribert Adam, *Studentenschaft and Hochschule, Möglichkeiten und Grenzen der Studentischen Politik*, Vol. 17 of *Frankfurter Beiträge zur Soziologie* (Frankfurt, 1965), pp. 12–13.

15. Pierre Bourdieu and Jean-Claude Passeron, *Les héritiers: Les étudiants et la culture* (Paris, 1964), p. 63.

16. See William Kornhauser, *The Politics of Mass Society* (Glencoe, Ill., 1959), pp. 84–89. Cf. Duncan MacRae, Jr., *Parliament, Parties and Society in France, 1946–1958* (New York, 1967), pp. 28–32.

17. See Alain Girard, *La réussite sociale en France* (Paris, 1961), particularly Part 2.

18. Possibly, the French intellectuals, conscious of their role in society, have written more about themselves than intellectuals anywhere else in the world. Julien Benda's phillipic *The Betrayal of the Intellectuals* (orig-

inally published in 1928; English translation: Boston, 1955) is by now a classic. See Louis Boudin, *Les intellectuels* (Paris, 1964). Also see an analysis of change in the intellectual strata by Frédéric Bon and Michel-Antoine Burnier, *Les Nouveaux Intellectuels* (Paris, n.d. [1966]).

19. Adam, *Studentenschaft and Hochschule*, pp. 5–6.

20. The process of politicization of the UNEF is described in great detail in Pierre Gaudez, *Les étudiants* (Paris, 1961).

21. Chiffre, *Les sources du syndicalisme étudiant depuis 1945*, mimeographed thesis, n.d. (1963), p. 199. Michel de la Fournière and François Borella, *Le syndicalisme étudiant* (Paris, 1957).

22. See A. Belden Fields' article, "The Revolution Betrayed: The French Student Revolt of May-June 1968," in this collection.

23. Rolf Seeliger, *Die ausserparlamentarische Opposition* (Munich, 1967), discusses the organizations that belong to this loose alliance.

24. This discussion is based on the works cited above (references 19 and 21), on proceedings of the UNEF annual congresses and personal interviews.

25. *L'Express*, No. 882 (May 13–19, 1968), p. 6, and No. 889 (July 22–29, 1968), pp. 34–35.

26. The data on the social composition of fraternities are estimates solicited by the author from the officers of the organizations.

27. A series of pamphlets published in Munich under the title *Braune Universität*, can be regarded as a symptom of the profound doubts which many German students must feel about the preceding academic generation. The editor of the series, Rolf Seeliger has culled lengthy quotations from the writings, published during the Nazi period, of professors now occupying chairs in German universities. The editor has asked each of these professors to express his current views concerning the writings quoted. The object of the exercise, according to Seeliger, is not to expose or unmask, but to help the current generation understand the past. Few professors have refused to answer this request. The published replies, which range from self-castigations to tortured interpretations, are painful to read. They are bound to raise questions in the reader's mind not only about the persons involved, but about the roles of academicians and the functions of universities.

28. The historical developments are described in A. C. J. F., *Association Catholique de la Jeunesse Française, Signification d'une crise* (Paris, 1964); and Pierre Dansette, *Destin du Catholisme Français* (Paris, 1957).

29. For the debates between the Central Committee of the Communist Party and the UEC leadership, see: Comité Central du Parti Communiste Français, *Les étudiants face aux grands problèmes de notre époque*, Paris: Editions Sociales, 1963. The dramatic sequence of subsequent events is described in an anonymous article, "Les étudiants communistes affrontent le parti," written by one of the participants for *Citoyens "60,"* No. 2 (April, 1965), pp. 14–20. For the subsequent discussions within UEC, see *Clarté*, Nos.

59 and 60 (1965), which include documents stating the positions of the various factions.

30. Translated from Aad de Jongh, *PROVO*, p. 168.

31. He employed it in a sociological study of certain juvenile gangs who resorted to provocations as a pasttime. Roel van Duyn adopted the term for the movement he initiated; he felt that the wasted energies of the young might be used for more goal-directed and more effective protests.

32. W. Buikhuisen, "Provo en provo," in Frenkel (ed.), p. 91.

33. *Bedingungen und Organisation des Widerstandes. Der Kongress in Hannover* (Berlin, n.d. [1967]). Dutschke's address (p. 78) has been translated as closely as possible to retain the flavor of the original text.

34. Herbert Marcuse, *One-Dimensional Man* (Boston, 1964).

35. Jürgen Habermas, "Die Scheinrevolution und ihre Kinder," reprinted from *Frankfurter Rundschau* (June 5, 1968).

36. Very similar developments are, of course, evident in the American organizations belonging to the student New Left.

37. Helmut Schelsky, *Einsamkeit und Freiheit* (Hamburg, 1963).

38. The literature on French university organization is quite sparse. A recent volume entitled *Les universités françaises, Education et gestion,* published at 4, rue Danton, Paris 6, has not been available to the author.

39. In 1967, an unsigned leaflet dealing with university reform and distributed during a university assembly in Berlin coined the term *"Fachidioten"* (idiot specialists) which offended the professors and thus gained great currency.

40. Most professors believed that the power of the *Ordinarii* is necessary, but that its abuses and generally negative social effects have been grossly exaggerated. Outside observers, however, tend to be critical of the system. The following is a passage from an article written by a British professor for the consumption of German students (my translation): "When visiting Germany, I am struck again and again by what we would consider a definitely servile attitude of many assistants, lecturers, and even associate professors, many of whom are older than I am, and many of whom have proved themselves through important studies (which I would be glad to have written) — and this for the only reason that I am an *Ordinarius* (and therefore something of a little God). Each time I am embarrassed and don't know what to say. I am all the more surprised by my German colleagues (even the most decent ones), who evidently consider this perfectly natural, who regard it as a sort of respect due to them, something they are entitled to." Leonard Forster, "Die deutsche Universität von aussen gesehen" in Petra Kipphoff, et al. (eds.), *Hochschulführer,* Hamburg, Nannen, 1964.

41. Jürgen Habermas, "Zwangsjacke für die Studienreform — Die befristete Immatrikulation und der falsche Pragmatismus des Wissenschaftsrates,"

in Stephan Leibfried (ed.), *Wider die Untertanenfabrik* (Cologne, 1967).

42. The problem is discussed in several issues of the *FU-Spiegel*, official organ of the Berlin student government, 1966.

43. Kurt Sontheimer, "Freiheit, die die Ordinarien meinen," *Die Zeit*, No. 29 (July 23, 1968), p. 2. It is generally acknowledged that perhaps the best scholarly discussion of the issue of university reform is a book written originally as an SDS memorandum and then expanded into a full-fledged study: Wolfgang Nitsch, Uta Gerhard, Claus Offe and Ulrich K. Preuss, *Hochschule in der Demokratie* (Berlin-Spandau, 1965). An excellent short discussion of the major issues is Eduard Baumgarten, *Zustand und Zukunft der deutschen Universität* (Tübingen, 1963).

44. See *Faire l'Université*, special number of *Esprit* (May-June, 1964).

45. The following discussions are based on reports in German weeklies, e.g. *Die Zeit* and *Der Spiegel*, as well as a number of accounts in book or pamphlet form. The best historical account is Kai Hermann, *Die Revolte der Studenten*, Hamburg: Christian Wegner, 1967. A sociological analysis by three Christian-Democratic writers recommends itself because of its lack of bias: Wulf Schönbohm, Jürgen Bernd Runge and Peter Radunski, *Die herausgeforderte Demokratie — Deutschlands Studenten zwischen Reform und Revolution*, Mainz: v. Hase und Köhler, 1968. See also: Hans Julius Schoeps and Christopher Dannenmann, *Die rebellischen Studenten — Elite der Demokratie or Vorhut eines linken Fschismus*, Munich: Bechtle, 1968; and Uwe Bergmann, Rudi Dutschke, Wolfgang Lefèvre and Bernd Rabehl, *Rebellion der Studenten oder Die neue Opposition*, Hamburg: Rowohlt, 1968.

46. On the economic situation of Berlin see: Sven Thomas Frank, "Was wird aus Berlin?" in *Der Monat*, No. 234 (March 1968), pp. 7–18.

47. The references to the recent French events are based, for the most part, on reports in *The New York Times, L'Express, Le Nouvel Observateur*, and the weekly airmail edition of *Le Monde*.

48. Kai Hermann, "Der Aufstand nach dem Attentat," *Die Zeit*, No. 16 (April 23, 1968), p. 3.

49. A summary of these plans appears in *Le Monde*, weekly airmail edition, No. 1028 (July 4–10, 1968), pp. 6–7.

50. The only data from Prof. Wildenmann's study that were available to the author were published in the *Süddeutsche Zeitung* (February 12, 1968).

51. Adam, *Studentenschaft und Hochschule*.

52. The rather strong language in the text will be understandable to anyone who has read the Springer concern's best-selling paper *Das Bild*. The sensationalism, inaccuracy, and bad taste of the paper are in the worst traditions of the yellow press. When Rudi Dutschke recovered from nearly fatal wounds in the hospital, *Bild am Sonntag* entitled its story "Dutschke is back cussing."

RICHARD F. TOMASSON AND ERIK ALLARDT

Scandinavian Students and the Politics of Organized Radicalism

STUDENT POLITICAL organization has reached a higher level of organization, differentiation, and interest articulation in the Scandinavian countries than anywhere else in the world.[1] This is true both of organizations with political viewpoints and of the local and national student unions with essentially trade union aims. Nevertheless, student politics has less national political importance in Scandinavia than is the case, for example, in Japan or in France, or in most of the developing nations of the world. But, on the other hand, its significance is greater than in any of the Anglo-American countries. Scandinavian student politics and political organization are microcosms of the advanced level of political and occupational organization so characteristic of the Scandinavian societies.

In early 1967 we wrote: "Compared with other societies, developed and developing, student politics in Scandinavia have been characterized by an extraordinary tranquility and a virtual absence of mass activism or of what Clark Kerr has called 'confrontation politics'." After the tumultuous worldwide student rebellions of 1967 and 1968, we need to modify this statement, but only slightly. New Left demands for greater student power and the use of direct action to obtain it became apparent in Scandinavia in 1968. Mass demonstrations and the seizure of university buildings occurred at the Universities of Stockholm and Copenhagen during the spring of 1968. At the University of Copenhagen five thousand of the twenty thousand students demonstrated in April for more student power, against professorial domination, and in support of students who were occupying some psychology laboratories. In May several hundred students took over the student union building at the University of Stockholm to protest a proposal to establish thirty-five different lines of study in the philosophy (Liberal Arts) faculties which, they argue, lessened the traditional freedom of Swedish students to choose their courses.[2] Some departments have experienced confrontations between students and staff, but these incidents have been isolated to the departments concerned.

From a cross-national perspective, this student activism has been rather amicable, has not involved violence, and has not led to extended battles between students and police as in the United States, France, Germany, Italy, Belgium, Poland, Mexico, and other places. As recently as March, 1968, Thomas Adlercreutz, the Vice Chairman of the Radical Democratic Party at Uppsala University (New Left in ideology, supporting the Vietcong position) told a *New York Times* reporter that Uppsala students have "no real grievances."[3] This view was the main theme of an article on student politics at Uppsala; the article, based on a number of interviews, was entitled, with some exaggeration, "School in Sweden Is Grievance-less." Of fundamental importance here is that established channels for protest and grievances existed before the current activization of the students in the advanced countries.

Yet the spring of 1968 saw great concern on the part of the government and the press in Sweden over the use of violence by protesting groups of which there has been an almost total absence in Scandinavia during the past several decades. The most publicized incident was the demonstration of May 3, 1968, in the south coast resort town of Båstad which resulted in the cancellation of the Davis Cup tennis match between Sweden and Rhodesia. There were altercations between the protestors and charges of police brutality, but there were no serious injuries.

Students in Finland and Norway have displayed much the same general pattern. There has been a growing activization of Finnish and Norwegian students in university affairs; there have been some small and peaceful demonstrations in support of greater student power; and the debates in the student newspapers and at meetings have been lively. The largest number of participants are generally drawn by demonstrations and rallies supporting the Third World. Several minor political demonstrations in all four countries, mostly over Vietnam, have involved encounters with the police, but none of these can be regarded as specifically student demonstrations.

The relative tranquility of Scandinavian students, which has been interrupted only recently, does not mean, however, that there are not strains and discontents in student life. Most important are those stresses growing out of the radical egalitarian and humanitarian values of the students and the traditional social forces represented by the university authorities and the political and economic establishment.

Characteristics of Scandinavian Higher Education Pertinent to Student Politics.[4]

Students in Scandinavian universities[5] are at least a year older than their counterparts on the Continent and about three years older than those in Anglo-American universities. In all the Scandinavian countries, formal schooling does not begin until age seven. After a preuniversity education of twelve or thirteen years the student is nineteen or twenty years old. Add to this another year for compulsory military training or the common practice of a year of foreign travel, and it is clear why in all Scandinavian higher education only a small percentage of students are under twenty.[6] For example, the mean age for getting the first degree in the philosophy faculties of Swedish universities in the late 1950's was between 25.5 and 26.5[7]; this is three to four years later than in the Anglo-American countries. The older age of Scandinavian students is an important consideration that should not be overlooked, for a few years difference in age, say between nineteen and twenty-two, signifies major differences in maturity and kind of activities and interests that will occupy students.[8] In terms of age, Scandinavian undergraduate students approximate American college seniors and graduate students.

Scandinavian students are about as free of university control in nonacademic matters as it is possible to be. As Torgny Segerstedt, rector of Uppsala University, put it: "If they [the students] are drunk or disorderly or seducing women, it is not the business of the university. They're on their own."[9] This is in striking contrast to the *in loco parentis* traditions of the Anglo-American universities. A study of the adjustment of Scandinavian students at the University of Wisconsin in 1952–54, showed that "no other aspect of university life here was as frequently objected to as the regulation of social and moral behavior."[10] A similar study of the American experience of fifty Swedes who had studied at American universities reports the same kind of objections.[11] This also contrasts with German and Swiss universities where the university rector and certain faculty committees can discipline or dismiss a student from the university for political, sexual, or criminal offenses.[12] Whether Scandinavian universities even have the authority to dismiss a student for committing a crime or for "moral turpitude" — except for cheating in examinations — is not at all clear. It never seems to happen.

A large proportion of Scandinavian students live in student housing, but none is under any university surveillance; most is owned by local student unions or by other student groups. There is no discrimination by sex in assignment of rooms; unmarried couples frequently live together in the dormitories. Most housing consists of single rooms with common facilities for preparing meals (and usually in Sweden with private bathrooms). As far as we can determine, only in the Scandinavian countries and Russia is there no sexual differentiation in the housing of students.

Perhaps nowhere in Western Europe, not even Germany, has the prestige of professors and students been traditionally higher than in the Scandinavian countries. A number of occupational studies show the professor to have a very high order of prestige.[13] This reflects the scarcity of the title "Professor" as well as the traditional role of universities in training the official elites.

Other characteristics of higher education in the Scandinavian countries pertinent to student politics are the following:

(1) Most of the universities have added few faculties outside of the traditional ones of theology, medicine, law, and philosophy (arts and sciences). Parallel and equal to these institutions are a large number of specialized university level schools of dentistry, forestry, veterinary medicine, engineering, business administration, and so forth. It is mainly in the universities, and particularly the faculties of philosophy and law, however, that most student activism is to be found. There is rather little political activity in the technical and professional schools or in the teacher training institutions.

(2) Most higher education is publicly owned and governed. Where institutions are "private" (particularly in Finland), it is primarily a technical distinction without social relevance. (They receive substantial state support and do not charge tuition.)

(3) Students are free to move between universities in their own countries and even to have all their credits accepted at a university in another Scandinavian country. Nevertheless, there is little movement between institutions, unlike in Germany and Switzerland. This is true even between degrees. This is, perhaps, best explained by the relative lack of prestige variation among institutions. The result is an enormous year-to-year stability of personnel, both faculty and students.

(4) Studies, particularly in the philosophy faculties (where most

student politics are to be found), are little structured. Students present themselves for examinations when they feel ready. (This is, however, becoming less and less the case as lecture-discussion classes and seminars increase.) Students have many fewer class and test obligations than in the United States and are much freer to work at their own speed. They can do the work of two semesters in one, or — much more likely — the work of one semester in two. Scandinavian students who have attended an undergraduate school in the United States report that they worked harder in the U.S., although gymnasium students who have spent a year in an American high school have just the opposite opinion.[14]

(5) There is a great stress on professional training in the universities and little emphasis on liberal education. The faculties are the important decision-making bodies, and students are enrolled in specific faculties. Students tend to identify with their faculty and to associate with students from their own faculty. Scandinavian students do not form a large diffuse mass, but are tied to the university through their faculties and through all kinds of associations. There are both student political associations and professional student associations. In Sweden and Finland, students also belong to "nations," which correspond to the geographical divisions of the country. All this makes for a vast amount of crisscrossing cleavage within Scandinavian student life. The structure of Scandinavian universities thus prevents easy mobilization of students for mass action.

Recruitment Into Higher Education

In all the Scandinavian countries, selection of those who will go on to universities or university-level institutions occurs largely with entrance into academic secondary school. In Sweden and Norway, the first selection *by the schools* does not occur until the competition to enter the gymnasium at about age sixteen. In Finland the separation comes at age eleven or thirteen. But Finland passed legislation in 1965 according to which this country, too, will follow in the egalitarian direction of her two neighbors. Denmark continues its school system with separation beginning at age thirteen and has shown no signs of moving in the more egalitarian paths of her northern neighbors; even compulsory schooling ends at age fourteen.

The overwhelming majority of those who successfully complete academic secondary school then go on to the universities. For example, over 95 per cent of the 1961–62 graduates of the Swedish general gymnasia matriculated at a university.[15] The percentage is lowest in Norway — probably not more than two thirds.

Higher education everywhere tends to select the children of professionals and businessmen, of the upper and middle classes, but there are marked variations among countries in the proportions of the children of the lower social classes who get to the universities. Patterns of recruitment to the universities are strikingly different among the developed societies. While the children of workers and farmers are clearly underrepresented in Scandinavian higher education, they are less so than in most of the other developed societies.

In the Scandinavian countries in the last third of the nineteenth century, there was a great increase in the proportion of children of farmers entering the universities. This was undoubtedly a consequence of the growing availability of academic secondary education to the rural population. At this time 15 to 20 per cent of the students at the Universities of Oslo, Uppsala, and Lund were the sons of farmers; such a large representation of farm youth was probably not to be found anywhere else in Europe at this time.[16] From the 1920's there were marked increases in the proportions of two new categories of university students: women and the children of the industrial working class. Sweden and Finland, in addition to having the highest proportion of youth in higher education in Western Europe also have high proportions of female students.[17] Finland, with 48.6 per cent in 1963, probably has the highest percentage of women in higher education in the world.

Norway, Sweden, and Finland, together with Great Britain, seem to have the highest proportion of working-class youth in higher education in Western Europe. About 25 per cent of all male youth who entered Norwegian universities in 1961–62 had fathers classified as working class.[18] Sweden drew 14.1 per cent of all first-year students in 1961–62 from the working class,[19] while Finland drew 17.6 per cent of all students from the working class that year.[20] Denmark, however, had only 9 per cent in 1959–60.[21] The only country in Western Europe with comparable percentages of students from the working class appears to be Great Britain where, according to the Robbins Report, 25 per cent of all students in 1961–62 had fathers classified as workers.[22] Only 13 per cent of those at Oxford and 9 per cent of those at Cambridge, however, had fathers so classified, compared with 31 per cent at the civic universities.[23]

Data for a number of continental European countries indicate substantially lower proportions of university students from the working class. In French universities in 1962–63, 5.5 per cent of all students had fathers who were workers.[24] Until recently only 5 per cent of German university students came from the working class; by the middle 1960's the percentage had risen to just over 6 per cent.[25] In the fall of 1959, 9 per cent of the male and 3 per cent of the female students in Dutch universities came from the working class.[26] In Austrian universities in the fall of 1958, 8 per cent of all students came from a working-class background.[27] A highly detailed study at the University of Bern in Switzerland in 1959–60, found only 4 per cent of students' fathers classified as workers.[28]

Both Canada and the United States and the countries of Eastern Europe, on the other hand, have more representative student bodies than the Scandinavian countries. In Canada in 1956–57, 26.2 per cent of all university students had fathers classified as workers.[29] In the United States, the over-all percentage is in the 25 to 30 per cent range, although the inclusiveness of the American concept of higher education leads to enormous variations in level.[30] The selective private universities have a very low representation of the sons of the working class, whereas, at the other extreme, working-class youth predominate at some public junior colleges. Eastern European countries — such as the Soviet Union, Poland, and East Germany — give youth from working-class and peasant background preferential treatment.[31] One estimate is that half of the students at East German universities have a working-class background.[32] A third of Polish students are the sons of workers.[33]

Another way of looking at the "democratization" of the composition of the student bodies of the Scandinavian countries is the observation that only about a quarter of the students in Finland, Norway, and Sweden have fathers who were university graduates. Not much more than a third can be considered to have come from an upper- or upper-middle-class milieu. One pattern that persists in Scandinavia, and probably elsewhere, is the higher status backgrounds of students in the faculties of medicine and law compared with those in theology and philosophy.[34]

Admission to the faculties of philosophy, law, and theology is traditionally open to all who pass the university matriculation examination. Entrance to the so-called "blocked" faculties and professional schools is wholly on the basis of objective criteria: grades and results of the university matriculation examination. This is in marked contrast to much of American and English higher education. Personality, "moral capacity," well-roundedness, participation in extracurricular activities, and the like have importance in gaining admission to the more prestigious colleges at Oxford and Cambridge or to the aggressively elitist American universities.[35] What Carlsson and Geeser have said about Swedish universities applies to all the Scandinavian countries: "It should . . . be kept in mind that the Swedish university system, and educational system in general, abhors all informal and discretionary methods of selection, when selection is necessary."[36] There is no personal interviewing or reliance on letters of recommendation (not even for the medical faculty). Professor Bror Rexed of the Uppsala University Medical faculty has stated the Scandinavian attitude succinctly: "This method of selecting medical students [using only objective academic criteria] is based on the view that medicine is a wide and varied field, in which there is scope for many different types of personality."[37] The desire for a university education has become almost universal in Sweden in recent years. In July, 1955, a national sample of mothers were asked whether they would be pleased if their son or daughter took the *studentexam* (university matriculation examination); 65 per cent answered that they would be.[38] A similar question was asked of all parents in August, 1963, and the percentage had increased to 82 per cent for sons and 84 per cent for daughters. There was little difference in the answers for sons and daughters, as well as little difference between urban and rural parents. Among working-class respondents in 1963, the percentages were almost as high as the over-all percentages. Anthony Kerr comments in his *Universities of Europe* that "having a son or daughter at a university carries in Sweden the same sort of prestige as running a respectable-looking car in England."[39]

Student Politics and Modernization: The Case of Sweden

While Sweden is the most industrialized Scandinavian country, it began the process of modernization later than either Denmark or Norway, though before Finland. The decade of the 1880's is the great watershed of modern Swedish history. Before that decade Sweden was an agricultural society with over two thirds of the population living on farms.[40] At the end of the 1880's, it was launched on the path to a mature industrial economy. This was a generation after Germany and at least a decade after Denmark. Even Norway at this time had a more developed lumber industry than Sweden, relatively more university graduates, was more urbanized, and had a more developed political party system.[41] This was the decade when socialist and radical liberal ideas, rationalist and anticlerical thought swept over isolated Sweden with irreversible effects on urban intellectuals and students in the universities.

The major pillars of the "official society" of this time were the national bureaucracy, the church, and the universities. The civil servants, the clergy, and the professors were the dominant elements of the upper class in traditional bureaucratic Sweden. The clergy and professors were the most energetic articulators and apologists of the values of the old agrarian society. Accounts of university life at this time characterize it as "stuffy and reactionary in spirit, with the average student seeking relief from his ennui in drink and song and dubious escapades preferably of a sexual kind. Not even the serious student is interested in formal university studies, for he can see no relation between his liberal social and cultural interests and the stale varieties of intellectual fare dispensed by a complacent corps of conservative university professors."[42] In this context, a number of young radicals formed the Verdandi Student Society at Uppsala in 1882 and De Unga Gubbarne (The Young Old Men) at Lund in 1887, radical discussion clubs which dealt with the burning issues of the day.[43]

Verdandi has probably been the most influential student organization in Sweden since it was founded. Its influence has been attested to by many generations of Uppsala students.[44] The society was formed to promote "freedom of thought and expression," and it was devoted to rationalist criticism of the Swedish State Church, conventional morality, and the paternalistic and hierarchical values of the Swedish establishment.[45] Among the twenty-five young men who came together to found the organization were a number who gained the greatest distinction in the Sweden of the next century: the most notable were the brilliant advocate of birth control and companionate marriage, and later world famous economist, Knut Wiksell, and Sweden's first (1905) Liberal prime minister Karl Staaff. During its early years, it was looked on with great disfavor by the academic establishment, but traditions of academic freedom in the university and a heritage of civil liberties in the society prevented any attempts at suppression.

Cultural radicalism, the term the Swedes use for critical rationalism such as that represented by Verdandi, is an element in both the Liberal and Social Democratic traditions, but it has been relatively more important among the Liberals, even though "cultural radicals" are a numerical minority among them. A number of the major Swedish newspapers specifically identify themselves with this tradition, including *Dagens Nyheter,* the most influential newspaper in Sweden. During the brilliant editorship of Herbert Tingsten (1946–1959), the editorial page of *Dagens Nyheter* became the single most important influence on Verdandi and the Liberal Student Clubs.[46] The paper "aims to be an organ for opinion formation in a liberal and radical spirit, a newspaper which takes up the burning problems, pushing aside the fetters of catchwords and thought clichés, and prepares the way for a better society, without unreflective respect for established opinions and institutions."[47] A number of *Dagens Nyheter* journalists were formally active Verdandists.[48]

John Stuart Mill was clearly the patron saint of the early cultural radicals. Annie Besant, Charles Bradlaugh, and the National Secular Society, together with the republican clubs in England in the 1870's, represented the English version of cultural radicalism, but the tradition declined in England.[49] The influence of this radically rationalist liberalism has been subsequently much greater in Scandinavia, and particularly Sweden, than in England. The tradition continues in a number of Liberal and Social Democratic papers, a tradition which has little counterpart in the American or English press. The strongest and purest manifestation of this tradition is to be found in Verdandi and the liberal and socialist student organizations in the universities.

Verdandi has had an extraordinarily continuous history. The concerns of the 1880's are in many ways similar to those of the 1950's and 1960's: criticism of Christianity and the State Church, equality between the sexes, opposition to conventional sexual attitudes, egalitarian issues, and international relations.[50] The most recent descriptive statement of the organization states:

The Verdandi Student Organization, which is not bound to any political party, aims to stimulate intellectual debate in social, international, and cultural matters and to maintaining the common thought tradition of liberalism and the labor movement, which can be characterized in brief as *radical humanism,* and whose principal endeavors are:

1. to give greater place to *critical reflection,* especially in questions of life conceptions, in opposition to emotional thinking and belief in authorities;

2. to uphold the formation of opinion and *cultural freedom* in intellectual matters in opposition to official and other conformist tendencies;

3. to stand in defense of *social justice* and to endeavor to insure that human needs are not disregarded for the believed or real interests of society;

4. to work for the elimination of economic and social class distinctions;

5. to defend an *active internationalism* in opposition to an emphasis on national interest.[51]

New Left ideology with its vague ideological commitment to socialism is manifest in the current campaign to revise the first paragraph in the above statement to specifically link the organization to the "socialist tradition" and to delete all references to liberalism.[52]

In recent years Verdandi has held a number of special and much publicized symposia. In 1961 they had an "Atheist Week" to which "no Christian apologists" were invited. Later some of these lectures and other "atheist" writings were published in a volume *The Atheist's Handbook*.[53] The book contains articles by a number of the most distinguished Swedish intellectuals and academics. In 1964 they held a four-day symposium on sex roles devoted to criticism of traditional sex roles and to the inequalities still existing between the sexes. This conference also resulted in a book.[54] Other areas of particular concern at their meetings have been the developing nations, the future directions of higher education, and abortion. Since about 1965, however, Verdandi has tended to emphasize questions of foreign policy and egalitarian issues.[55] This has resulted in a lessened concern with questions of God and religion, sex and sex roles. Verdandi has moved from a rather positive position toward American foreign policy to an extremely negative attitude resulting from intense opposition to America's role in the war in Vietnam.

There has also been a reassertion of a concern with class differences in Swedish society. In 1966 Verdandi organized a teach-in on "The Swedish Class Society" and "waged a war" against the Swedish Confederation of Professional Associations (SACO), a union of associations of professionals (doctors, engineers, academics, civil servants, and so forth) who require a university education. Verdandi argued vehemently against the attempts of SACO to raise salaries of those in the professions, including university and upper-level teachers, urging their members to resign from the organization. SACO argued that increases in income among their membership had not kept pace with general income increases. The egalitarian argument against SACO is that if there is to be an over-all policy of income solidarity, the highest paid categories in society cannot expect their salaries to increase to the same extent as lower-income categories.[56]

Verdandi, however, is more than a lecture and debating society. It has also been concerned with popular education and publishing paperback "debate" books on controversial subjects. In addition to the books on atheism and sex roles, volumes on republicanism, abortion, Sweden's military role, and class distinctions in Swedish society have recently been published.[57] The society has also actively protested the authoritarian regimes of Spain, Portugal, and — with particular concern — South Africa. More recently there has been much concern with the nondemocratic regimes in Rhodesia and Greece. In addition, it has also sent statements supporting the radically liberal positions on immigration legislation, abortion, and the role of the State Church to the specific governmental departments concerned.

In the 1966–67 school year, Verdandi had a dues-paying membership of between 700 and 800 students out of the more than 18,000 enrolled students at Uppsala.[58] It is one of the largest student organizations in Sweden, apart from the student unions. The appeal of Verdandi has been predominantly to those of middle- and upper-class background. Its tradition has been clearly liberal, not socialist, yet many Verdandists end up as active Social Democrats and later join Laboremus — the Uppsala University Social Democratic organization. It is probably quite unusual to find an organization so committed to radical causes and having such high prestige in the upper classes. On the governing board of Verdandi are a number of the sons of the nobility — a Wachtmeister, an Adlercreutz, and a Fogelcou — and of long-standing upper-class families like Boethius and Murray. In recent years, the cultural radicalism espoused by Verdandi has come to be characteristic of all the Liberal, Social Democratic, and socialist organizations in the universities.

The most publicized recent manifestation of cultural radicalism was the 1964 "Sex and Society" conference arranged by the Liberal Student Club of Stockholm University.[59] Included in the program, held in the Stockholm Town Hall, was a six-minute "pornographic" film of a couple having intercourse followed by a roundtable discussion on the uses of pornography by a housewife, a doctor, a professor, and a newspaper editor.

In 1891, nine years after the founding of Verdandi, a group of conservative students at Uppsala (including the later liberal Archbishop of Sweden, Nathan Söderblom) came together to form a society called Heimdal to promote and defend the values of patriotism, the State Church and Christianity, the monarchy, and traditional values in general.[60] Heimdal and Verdandi were formed at a time of intense conflict between the values of the official classes and the democratic and egalitarian, rationalist and scientific ideas of the young radicals. Down to the present they continue to debate many of the same topics: republicanism, the relation of the church to the state, traditional moral and religious values. But even though there are basic differences on these rather intellectual and not very pressing issues, there is a high degree of consensus on absolute acceptance of the democratic method, the essentials of the social-service state, an international point of view, and so forth. Heimdal specifically regards itself as having a "reformist conservative attitude toward politics."[61]

The decline of ideology and growth of consensus in Swedish politics has probably proceeded as far as in any of the developed societies and is very much reflected in student politics. The extent of this is indicated in the introduction to the program adopted by the Liberal Student Association (SLS) in 1959 in which it is maintained that it is no longer tenable to use terms such as:

socialism, liberalism, and conservatism in regard to the democratic parties [a phrase used to exclude the Communists]. They have influenced each other so that there is more that unites them than separates them. In spite of this there is an ideological continuity in the development of the parties; the conflicts of opinion have declined, but have not disappeared. The differences which still remain SLS regards as attitudinal differences.[62]

Precisely because of this broad consensus on fundamentals and the extraordinary efficiency of Swedish society, student politics can be so centered on issues of unrestricted abortion, republicanism, sex roles, sex issues, class distinctions, the developing countries, the regimes in South Africa and Greece, and the role of the United States in Vietnam. These were the principal issues in all the student political journals in the middle 1960's.[63]

There are national federations of the student political organizations. The largest is the National Union of Conservative Students to which Heimdal is affiliated, followed in size by the National Union of Social Democratic Students. The Liberal Student Association of Sweden is third. The Center Student Association is the smallest, representing students who support the Center (Agrarian) party. There is no student association in Sweden specifically for Communists, but many Communist students, along with left-wing Social Democrats, belong to Clarté chapters affiliated with the Swedish Clarté Association.[64] Like all of the other student political associations, except Laboremus, Clarté is unaffiliated with any political party. It is directed to "intellectuals and others interested in socialist study and enlightenment" and "takes no position in controversies between different socialist organizations."[65] Like other radical student political associations, it is not limited to students or academics. For example, Laboremus has always been an association of "mental and physical workers," and Verdandi has recently manifested its concern with egalitarian issues by dropping "student" from the organization's formal name. At Uppsala (where student politics are particularly active) not more than 15 per cent of the students are members of any political association (including Verdandi). Membership in Heimdal and Laboremus has been running around 3 per cent of the student population in recent years.

All of these national student organizations publish lively journals of opinion which sometimes contain articles by or interviews with leading Swedish intellectuals or political figures. Articles and editorials in these journals are frequently reported or excerpted in the press, and they are sometimes the subject of editorials. *Clarté* (radical socialist), *Liberal debatt* (Liberal), and *Libertas* (Social Democratic), in particular, can be regarded as important contributors of radical ideas in the intense Swedish cultural debate over issues of religion, morals, social problems, education, art, and international questions.[66] *Tidskrift Heimdal* is the most important student conservative journal.

Of all the student political groups, the Social Democrats are the most active in working for the party and in election campaigns, and they are the only student political group in which members are collectively enrolled in the party. All of the political groups, however, do attempt to influence the parent parties, and from the early 1950's, the Liberal, Social Democratic, Conservative, and Center groups have written detailed political programs, generally longer than the official programs of the parent parties. There is constant conflict between the student political organizations and the parent parties, particularly among the Liberals and Social Democrats, whose students are much more overtly radical than the parent parties. But this is true even of the Conservatives, whose student group criticized the presence of orthodox Christian items in the party program. In the Liberal Student Association, the strong cultural radical orientation is strongly at variance with the parent party which contains cultural conservatives, many of whom adhere to the nonconformist churches and to a philosophy of temperance. Liberal students of these persuasions have taken little role in the Liberal Student Clubs, choosing instead to belong to nonconformist religious groups or to temperance groups.[67] The Social Democratic Student groups also follow a consistently more radical line than the parent party (which has been the government party for over a third of a century), but the disparity is probably not so great as with the Liberals. The Social Democratic students are more "political" than the Liberals, and they are generally more concerned with economic than with libertarian issues. Not many Liberal students come from a working-class background compared with Social Democratic students.

The changes that have occurred since 1965 in student attitudes and in general public opinion toward the United States as a result of the Vietnam War are striking. In 1963 Gunnar Myrdal wrote (accurately, we think) "that the only two countries in Europe without a trace of anti-Americanism, either in the post-war era or today, are Sweden and Switzerland."[68] But since then anti-Americanism growing out of the American role in Vietnam has become endemic, particularly so among students and in the press (including some of the Conservative press). In a public opinion poll taken in February, 1967, a majority of respondents of all ages in all parties — with the exception of older Conservatives — opposed American policy in Vietnam.[69] In fact, only 8 per cent of the entire sample supported the American position. All of the major student political organizations, except the Conservatives, have come out in support of the NLF. The generally conservative Center Student Association has been particularly strong in their opposition to America ("they bomb farmers") and their support of the NLF. Yet this opposition to the war and support for the NLF is not "radical" in Sweden nor a cause for student alienation from the government. In February, 1968, Olaf Palme, the heir apparent to the prime minister and with his support, marched in an anti-Vietnam war parade with the North Vietnamese ambassador to the Soviet Union. In January, 1969, Sweden established full diplomatic relations with North Vietnam, the first Western European nation to do so.

The other Scandinavian countries resemble Sweden in student political organization, but without such complex development. The extent of radical concern over sexual, religious, and republican issues has been less, though they share the other radical concerns. The standard of living is substantially higher in Sweden than elsewhere in Scandinavia; there is a high level of consensus even compared with the other Scandinavian countries; and Sweden has no external model to look to for invidious comparison in most areas. This is, perhaps, why issues that would appear to be of a low order of importance in other societies can be of so much concern to Swedish students. In addition, the tradition of cultural radicalism is stronger in Sweden, particularly in the press, than elsewhere.[70] The battle against the values of the old class society has been won, but the cultural radicalism adopted at the end of the nineteenth century has continued. The student political groups of the Left manifest these antitraditional positions in high degree. Regard for the legitimacy of the state and the social and political system itself is, however, always apparent.

Student Politics and Modernization: The Case of Finland

The historical role of students in national politics has been greater in Finland than in the other Scandinavian countries. The reasons for this are not hard to find. Finland did not gain her independence until 1917. In addition, Finland's upper class was traditionally Swedish-speaking, and the upper and middle classes were small. Finland's dependent status and the absence of a well-developed Finnish-speaking upper class provided opportunities for Finnish students somewhat analogous to Norwegian students vis-à-vis Sweden. Swedish and Danish students were never presented with such nationalistic opportunities. The Finnish historian Eino Jutikkala has observed that students have "played an important role in the history of Finland."[71]

The role of student movements and politics can be documented on a number of counts. Students were an important element in the rise of the nationalist movement and national feelings in the 1840's, and the nationalist movement in turn gave students a sense of common purpose. At this time, the students were "in fact beginning to participate in the nationalist movement in a manner that gave it a force it had previously lacked."[72] Norwegian students had a similar role in the development of national identity and patriotism.[73]

Students also played an important part in Finland's struggle for political independence during the first two decades of this century. For the most part, the older generation spoke of passive resistance against the increasing violation of Finnish prerogatives by Russia, while the students were becoming increasingly activist. "Not a few of the students and younger instructors believed that the war [the First World War] offered a solution for the problems of the preceding half-dozen years. The solution was political independence."[74] The idea of complete national independence was a relatively novel idea for Finland, which had never been a separate nation. This idea was transformed into action by the students. They formed an important element in the secret organizing activities for a war of liberation against Russia. Norwegian students played a similar, though less dangerous, role in the independence activities of the Left party in the years prior to 1905.[75]

During the 1920's and 1930's, after Finland had become independent, nationalist activities, particularly on the part of the Finnish-speaking students continued. The course of student activities and their successes have been summarized by Jutikkala as follows:

Finnish students returning from East Karelia, where they had fought as volunteers against the Red Army side by side with the native East Karelians founded the Academic Karelia Society (AKS), whose primary purpose was the support of the nationalistic aspirations of kindred peoples. But when this sort of activity became increasingly fruitless, as time passed, and more and more dangerous to Finland, the society began to work with all its youthful zeal toward promoting national defense. . . . Simultaneously, the society (AKS) adhered to the ultra-Finnish line and thereby aggravated internal tension. The AKS held practically undisputed sway over the Finnish-speaking student world up to the collapse of the Lapua movement. . . .[76]

Up to this time, the activity of the students was centered on the search for national identity. This has very much changed in the years since the close of World War II.

In this period, particularly since the late 1950's, student organizations have moved toward a cultural radicalism similar to that of Sweden. It was not until after World War II that this movement gained strength in Finland. The nationalist movement among the Finnish students in the 1930's was only socially radical. It was directed against many forms of ascription in Finnish society, but its nationalism had clearly particularistic tendencies.

The weekly organ of the National Union of Students, *Ylioppilasiehti* is a journal of the student unions throughout the entire nation and has become of great importance in the general cultural debate. It is opposed to authoritarianism in all its forms, strongly promotes egalitarian and internationalist values, and takes an avant-garde position in questions of literature, the arts, and sex. It is frequently a source of consternation in conservative circles and is continuously the focus of vigorous debate. It is open to all students, but most contributors are radical students, who are much more activist than the conservatives. But the organ has no affiliation to any political party. This journal has become the principal organ of cultural radicalism in Finland, achieving a status comparable to the traditional cultural journals; its writings are taken with the same seriousness as those in the cultural pages of the major newspapers. In recent years *Yiloppilasiehti* has devoted increasing attention to the problems of student welfare, making welfare provisions for students a national issue.

While the students of the 1930's staged a few marches and demonstrations in support of their claims, the students now press them mainly through the mass media and through mediation and committee work as elsewhere in Scandinavia. A number of legitimate channels exist for the voices of both organized and unorganized student opinion to be heard. Despite a different kind of history and external problems not shared by the other Scandinavian countries, the role of student political organization in Finland has become similar to that of the other Scandinavian countries.

The Trade Union Organization of Scandinavian Students

In the trade union aspect of student organization, the Scandinavian countries have made much progress since the 1940's.[77] Student unions have become important in representing student interests before the government, the universities, and other segments of society. At an international student conference held in 1965, one of the principal speakers concluded that "there are still relatively few countries in Europe that allow student participation in governing bodies. The countries most advanced in this field seem to be the Scandinavian countries."[78] This can be seen as a continuation of traditions of university students in the Scandinavian countries being left to themselves to handle their own affairs and to organize to promote their interests.

Membership in the student unions of all the Scandinavian countries is compulsory. A similar compulsory membership is found in West Germany, but is not true of the national student organizations of France, Belgium, or the Netherlands. Each semester all students pay a modest fee that enrolls them either directly or indirectly in the student union of the university which they attend. The various unions in each of the countries are then affiliated into a national union of students. The student unions are not bound to any political party, nor are they committed to any ideology other than that of democracy and internationalism. A predominantly two-party political system has, however, developed in recent years in the student union-elections organized around more-or-less conservative-radical lines.

At the University of Oslo students elect one member to the eleven-member senate of the university, three out of five members of the Oslo Student Welfare Organization (the other two members are representatives of the Ministry of Church Affairs and Education and of the university), and two of the eight members of the National Union of Norwegian Students.[79] The two-party system in these elections involves a conservative and a left-wing party. The Conservatives are made up largely of the members of the Conservative Student Association; the Left runs from Liberals to Communists. But from time to time the Liberals run their own candidates. Most active in these elections are students from the faculties of law and philosophy; the former are predominantly on the conservative side, the latter on the left. Recent elections have been clear victories for the Left.

The Student Union of the University of Helsinki is run by a sixty-member senate elected by the students. The Helsinki Student Union owns valuable properties and oversees all student housing. The biennial elections attract nationwide attention. In the 1965 election a remarkable 57.5 per cent of all students voted. The two main parties are the Academic Coalition, made up of the nations (provincial associations) and the Coalition of Professional Associations (for example, chemistry, law, sociology students). In the past, the nations completely dominated student life, and they determined the allocation of the Student Union's huge budget. The specifically political organizations have, for the most part, remained outside the politics of the Student Union, although the most activist of the socialist students participate in the elections with their own coalition. In general, the Academic Coalition holds to a more conservative position, the Coalition of Professional Associations — whose strength is increasing — to a more radical position.

At Uppsala University a political-party system in student-union elections began in 1963. One party, Uppsala University Students

(UUS), was founded to support candidates who adhered to a moderate position. They have obtained most of the seats. The party claims to be "a moderate association for progressive union politics and dedicated to an effective student union with an emphasis on adequate student service and active trade union activity."[80] The minority radical students then came together and formed a party called the Uppsala Radical Democrats (URD) to "work as a party in the Uppsala Student Union for a radical union politics based on openly proclaimed values and free of trade union mindedness."[81] The party clearly adheres to New Left ideology. Such a position is in direct contrast to the essentially non-ideological role of the Swedish student unions. In contrast to the high turnout in Helsinki elections, only 8 per cent of the Uppsala students voted in the Student Union election of 1965, but this increased to 22.3 per cent in 1966 and to 24.7 per cent in 1967.[82] Party politics of a similar sort are to be found at Stockholm University. Here the political situation is more complex; two major parties and six minor parties obtained seats in the 1966 elections. Election participation was around 20 per cent in 1962–1964, only 15 per cent in 1965, and 24 per cent in 1966.[83]

The general aims of the student trade union organization in all of the countries are the same even though the organizational structure is peculiar to each country. The aims of the student unions and similar associations include the following:

1. to act as the unified voice of the interests of students toward the government, the university authorities, and society in general;
2. to influence the curricula;
3. to represent students in international organizations;
4. to improve the general welfare and living conditions of students, particularly as regards increasing the amount of student housing;
5. to obtain more generous loan funds and salaries for students;
6. to gain special rates in national and international travel;
7. to obtain discounts on books and to conduct special student stores with a wide variety of goods at discount prices;
8. to publish periodicals for the expression of student opinion;
9. to provide innumerable other services such as the maintenance of nursery schools for students with children and medical and psychiatric services.

A brief description of the organization and accomplishments of the Swedish National Union of Students (*Sveriges forenade studentkårer*, SFS) can be used to exemplify student organization in all the Scandinavian countries.[84] The national organization was formed in 1921, though local student organization has a history of several centuries in Sweden and Scandinavia. It came into being as a result of appeals from abroad for student cooperation in Europe. For the first twenty years of its existence, into the 1940's, SFS dealt primarily with international issues. The formal goals of the organization are as follows:

The purposes of the SFS are to safeguard the common interests of the affiliated unions as regards study conditions and social welfare, to discuss — after request of a single member union — such questions which concern this union alone as to study conditions and social welfare, to represent the member unions in the Scandinavian and international student work, and when special circumstances render this desirable discuss other questions within the scope of activity of the member unions.[85]

It was not until the late 1940's that the organization made what has been called the trade union breakthrough. Pinner has claimed that the student trade union movement in the Western European countries first developed in France as an outgrowth of student resistance against Nazism.[86] He has called their Grenoble Charter of 1946 the Declaration of Independence of the student movement in that it proclaims the "general principles of student rights and responsibilities."[87] The nonpolitical aims of the French student movement, particularly under the Fourth Republic, were essentially the same as those of the Swedish and other Scandinavian movements. The difference is the greater degree of organization of the Scandinavian movements, their institutionalized and orderly communication with government, and consequently their greater success in realizing the trade union aims of the movement. Another factor is the greater age of the Scandinavian students; student union leaders in Sweden are generally over twenty-five.[88]

The SFS is a confederation of thirty-five local student unions ranging in size from the Uppsala Student Union with about nineteen thousand members down to the Dairy Farming Institute in Alnarp with only about a half dozen. The total membership is always equivalent to the total number of students enrolled in higher education. In 1967–68 this was around ninety thousand. The National Assembly, highest administrative body of the organization, is made up of delegates from all of the local unions with four hundred or more members. For every eight hundred members in excess of four hundred, each union obtains an additional mandate. Unions with fewer than four hundred members pool their membership with other small unions to get a delegate. The chairman of SFS is employed full-time and occupies a prestigious post which is, in most cases, indicative of future success in Swedish politics or management. Olof Palme, probably the next Social Democratic Prime Minister, was a past chairman of SFS.

SFS, like all professional and trade-union organizations in Sweden, places great emphasis on operating by its regulations, tries hard to represent the opinions of its membership, and is in fact very much subject to the views of the locals. The result of the highly democratic organization of SFS, according to Lars Tobisson, chairman of SFS in 1964, is that "discussion is often long-winded and slow but, on the other hand, everyone knows that the attitude adopted by the SFS has been preceded by thorough and expert consideration and that the views presented are representative of the country's students."[89] Even if there is some exaggeration in these remarks, they reflect the high order of discussion, planning, and organization characteristic of Swedish organizations. It is important to note, however, that only a minority of students have any active interest in the local unions or in SFS. One of the increasing criticisms of living in the organized society *par excellence* that is Sweden is that organizations do their jobs so well that most people become apathetic and give up active participation.

SFS never resorts to pressures other than their arguments and using open channels to the government and parliamentary committees. They have never called a strike or demonstration of any kind. Tobisson has described how SFS operates as follows:

Contacts with different government bodies play a decisive part in the daily work of the SFS . . . and if the SFS is to influence matters in favour of the students, its best plan is to present its views to the administrative authorities concerned. We therefore attempt to speak with these authorities at as early a stage as possible in the discussion of a problem. The problem is then followed throughout the whole decision-making process and all opportunities are taken to influence the form of the decision. This work is facilitated by the fact that the SFS is accorded representation on government committees appointed to investigate matters of interest to the organization. The SFS is in some cases also represented on the government bodies whose work affects the students' interests.[90]

This is only a specific manifestation of the general practice of consulting all groups affected by proposed legislation. Even the national trade union organization of secondary-school students, SECO, is consulted in the process of writing legislation involving secondary education. It is indeed remarkable to see seventeen- and eighteen-year-old "leaders" influencing government decisions. They showed their strength during the 1966 teachers strike when secondary-school students were able to run the schools in the absence of teachers.

SFS can take some or all of the credit for a number of accomplishments since the late 1940's. The organization claims major credit for the formation of the 1955 University Committee which laid the basis for the enormous expansion of higher education. They are continuing to pressure for increased expansion. Some student unions have developed detailed proposals pertaining to revisions in the university curricula, but they always channel these proposals through SFS. The organization also claims credit for increasing the amount and conditions of loans available to students, and for the student allowance of 1750 *kroner* ($350) which *all* students began to receive in the 1965–66 school year. They have succeeded in getting favorable government loans for the building of student housing. By 1965 rooms were available in student housing for a third of all Swedish students. The organization has also negotiated with the National Railways to provide students with round trip tickets during the school year at one-way prices. In the 1950's SFS entered into agreements with the Swedish Booksellers Association providing discounts on Swedish and foreign textbooks. One present concern of SFS is to bring a credit system into the universities aimed at shortening the length of time students need to spend in the university and at bringing more organization and predictability into the process of higher education.

Conclusion: Sources of Stability and Strain[91]

Student politics in the Scandinavian countries are characterized by a high degree of organization, differentiation, and interest articulation, and, until 1968, by a virtual absence of confrontation politics. Prior to 1968 there was almost no student demonstrating or agitating aside from general anti-Vietnam war activities and such idealistic protests as the picketing of South African ships.

The jurisdiction of Scandinavian universities over students is limited to the narrowly academic. There are no issues arising out of university authority over students. The great bulk of the responsibility for the general welfare of the students is carried out by student organizations. Students have been granted representation in policy-making bodies of the universities in all the Scandinavian countries. In higher education, as in other areas, the leadership strata has gracefully absorbed new elements into the decision-making process to preserve stability and tranquility. The university authorities and the government are responsive, by and large, to organized student demands, and established channels of communication exist. Fundamental in all the Scandinavian countries is the legitimacy of special interest groups to organize for the promotion of their own interests. Even the national organization of secondary-school students in Sweden has achieved official recognition by the government and is consulted in the framing of legislation pertinent to secondary education.

To this must be added the traditionally high status of the university, the professors, and the students as well as the high status of formal education and specialized knowledge. There is little difference between "intellectuals" and academic experts in Scandinavia. Indeed, an intellectual is considered to be one who possesses expert knowledge and skill. There has been a notable absence in Scandinavia of any important group of free, unattached intellectuals who could rally students for mass activism. The intellectual and academic establishment in Scandinavia is highly competent, provided with a high degree of functional deference, and is without competition from alienated intellectuals. The degree to which these societies have solved their domestic problems, together with the enormous respect for specialized knowledge and orderly procedure in solving problems, also lessens the opportunities for mass activism. The recent incidents at the Universities of Copenhagen and Stockholm were indeed minimal compared with student rebellions elsewhere in recent years.

The structure of Scandinavian higher education further inhibits an easy mobilization of students. Even in the universities, to say nothing of the specialized institutions of higher learning, there is little emphasis on liberal education. The emphasis is predominantly on vocational preparation. The students are very much tied to their faculties, and in the philosophy faculties to their departments. Another form of institutionalized divisiveness of students is that of regional isolation. In Sweden and Finland, university students are still organized on a territorial basis in "nations." These nations are the centers of traditional student activities. Yet they must compete for the involvement of students with student political associations, on the one hand, and with student professional associations, on the other. Internal student politics are divided on conservative-radical lines, so it is difficult to imagine that all students could be mobilized to support any particular political cause. The existence of various kinds of involvements results in a vast amount of criss-crossing cleavages within Scandinavian student life. The consequence is a high degree of stability. This developed organizational life, most of which is related to the society outside the universities rather than solely to internal affairs, is as pervasive a characteristic of Scandinavian universities as it is of the greater societies.

The comparative calmness and smooth operation of student politics in Scandinavia should not disguise strains and the existence of discontent and frustration among students. There are clear signs of strain between students and the traditional social forces represented by the university authorities and the political and economic establishment. There is a sharp discrepancy between the comparatively strong democratic freedom and egalitarianism of the students and the hierarchial organization of the universities. Interaction between faculty and students is more deferential, distant, and restrained than in the Anglo-American countries, though probably substantially less so than in, for example, France.

There are certainly also strains stemming from the rapid rise in enrollments and the resultant overcrowding and acute shortage of housing, together with a rate of faculty increase which has not kept pace with enrollments. More significant, however, are the discrepancies between the expectations of new knowledge and the ability to provide it within the framework of university teaching. There is also the chronic discrepancy between the expectation of teaching efficiency and actual teaching efficiency.

A refined and increasingly significant source of strain is the discrepancy between expectations regarding the ability of science and humanitarianism to contribute to social improvements and the actual state of the world. The Scandinavian countries, probably more than any other group of nations in the world, have come closer to solving their basic social and economic problems through an advanced system of welfare legislation. Consequently, this disillusionment does not focus on welfare goals at home. Rather, it is manifested in a strong concern with the problems of the developing nations, peace — above all, Vietnam — and opposition to authoritarianism in all its forms. At home an increasing concern with egalitarianism has developed into a new emphasis on ideology in the socio-political debate among the students. The New Left has emerged with great strength around all of these issues and criticizes Scandinavian society from the standpoint of radical egalitarianism. This has, to some extent, called forth activity on the part of moderate and conservative students. Yet in spite of the increasing ideological content given to political issues by the radicals, student politics continues to rely on discussion, meetings, writing, and debate. Probably nowhere in the world is student politics so radical in its discussion, yet so orderly in its behavior as in Scandinavia.[92]

Scandinavian Students and the Politics of Organized Radicalism

REFERENCES

1. See comments by T. Mailand Christensen in "The Participation of Students in Governing Bodies — Myth or Reality," *Social Problems of Students: Report on the Council of Europe Seminar*, Oslo, July 25–31, 1965 (Oslo, 1966), p. 40. What Christensen says here is also true of other aspects of student organization.

2. Actually, a new form of cleavage has developed in recent years. The students and the professors support a greater emphasis on liberal education, whereas educational planners in the Ministry of Education favor training geared to specific occupations.

3. The *New York Times*, March 29, 1968, p. 15.

4. Discussions of the structure of higher education in the Scandinavian countries can be found in UNESCO, *World Survey of Education*, Vol. 4, (New York, 1966): Denmark, pp. 396–409; Finland, pp. 451–64; Iceland, pp. 597–602; Norway, pp. 869–80; and Sweden, pp. 1041–57. For a more superficial overview, see Anthony Kerr, *The Universities of Europe* (London; 1962), pp. 31–51. On Sweden, see Richard F. Tomasson, "Some Observations on Higher Education in Sweden," *Journal of Higher Education*, Vol. 37, No. 9 (December 1966), pp. 493–501. No attempt will be made in this paper to touch on student politics in Iceland, the smallest nation in the world (about two hundred thousand population) to have a university.

5. Unless otherwise implied, we use the term "universities" in the American sense to apply to the whole complex of higher education. The specialized institutions of higher learning in the Scandinavian countries, as in most of Europe, are not commonly called universities.

6. For example, at the University of Copenhagen in 1959 only 12 per cent of all male students were under twenty, in 1947 only 4 per cent. See Torben Agersnap, *Studenterundersøgelsen 1959* (Copenhagen, 1961), p. 20.

7. *Statens Offentliga Utredningar*, Vol. 44 (1963), p. 25.

8. See comments and citations of Seymour M. Lipset and Philip G. Altbach on propensities of younger students to be involved in protests and demonstrations in "Student Politics and Higher Education in the United States," *Student Politics*, ed. S. M. Lipset (New York, 1967), pp. 199–252.

9. The *New York Times*, March 29, 1968, p. 15.

10. William H. Sewell and Oluf M. Davidson, *Scandinavian Students on an American Campus* (Minneapolis, 1961), p. 19.

11. Franklin D. Scott, *The American Experience of Swedish Students* (Minneapolis, 1956), pp. 67–88.

12. See *World Survey of Education*, pp. 514–15. This point has also been discussed with the German sociologist Günther Luschen now at the University of Illinois.

13. See, for example, Edward C. McDonagh, Sven Wermlund, and John Crowther, "Relative Professional Status as Perceived by American and Swedish University Students," *Social Forces*, Vol. 38, No. 1 (October, 1959), pp. 65–69; Kaare Svalastoga, *Presige, Class and Mobility* (Copenhagen, 1959), pp. 74–78, 145; and Urho Rauhala, *Suomalaisen yhtelskunnan sesiaalinen kerrostuneisuus* (The Social Stratification of Finnish Society, with an English Summary; Helsinki, 1966).

14. This is an opinion of Tomasson based on perhaps a dozen cases.

15. Gösta Carlsson and Bengt Geeser, "Universities as Selecting and Socializing Agents: Some Recent Swedish Data," *Acta Sociologica*, Vol. 9, Fasc. 1–2 (1966), pp. 25–37, 28.

16. See Vilheim Aubert, Ulf Torgersen, Karl Tangen, Tore Lindbekk and Sonja Pollan, "Akademikare i norsk samfunnsstruktur, 1800–1950," *Tidskrift for samfunnsforkning*, Vol. 1, No. 4 (December 1960), pp. 185–204, esp. 196–199; and Sten Carlsson, *Bonde-präst-ambetsman* (Stockholm, 1962), pp. 81, 100.

17. Elina Haavio-Mannila, "Aktivitet och passivitet bland kvinnor i Finland," *Kynne eller kön* (Stockholm, 1966), pp. 103–144, esp. 122.

18. Tore Lindbekk, "Den sosiale rekruttering til de akademiske profesjoner i vår tid," *Tidsskrift for samfuunsforkning*, Vol. 3, No. 4 (December 1962), p. 240.

19. Sveriges Officiella Statistik, *Högre Studier 1961–62* (Stockholm, 1964), p. 5.

20. Päivi Elovainio, *Korkeakolu-uran ja opintoalan valinta*, Research Reports from the Institute of Sociology, University of Helsinki, No. 58 (1966), mimeo, pp. 123, 130–132.

21. *Higher Education: Report of the Committee Appointed by the Prime Minister under the Chairmanship of Lord Robbins*, Cmnd. 2154, London: Her Majesty's Stationery Office, 1963: Appendix Two (B), *Students and Their Education*, p. 5.

22. *Ibid.*, p. 428–429. These figures are for entering students in 1955. The assumption is that they were about the same in 1961. The original source is P. K. Kelsall, *Applications for Admissions to Universities*, Association of Universities of the British Commonwealth, 1957.

23. *Ibid.*, p. 428–429. The discussion on p. 428 gives an over-all figure for Wales of 46 per cent, but the table on p. 429 gives a total of 40 per cent — 46 per cent among men and 31 per cent among women.

24. *Annuaire statistique de la France, résultats de 1962* (Paris, 1963), p. 57.

25. Ralf Dahrendorf, "The Crisis in German Education," *Journal of Contemporary History*, Vol. 6 (1967), pp. 139–147.

26. Frederick van Heek, "Soziale Faktoren in den Niederlanden, die einer Optimalen Nachwuchsausiese für Akademische Berufe im Wege Stehen,"

p. 245. In David V. Glass and Rene König (eds.), *Soziale Schichtung und Soziale Mobilitat* (Köln and Opladen, 1961).

27. Leopold Rosenmayr, "Soziale Schichtung, Bildungsweg und Bildungsziel im Jugendalter," *Ibid.*, p. 274.

28. R. F. Behrendt, *Die Schweizerischen Studierenden an der Universität Bern* (Bern/Stuttgart, 1960), p. 63.

29. Dominican Bureau of Statistics, *University Student Expenditure and Income in Canada, 1956–57* (Ottawa, 1959), Chapter 19, Table II. Quoted in John Porter, *The Vertical Mosaic* (Toronto, 1965), p. 184.

30. See discussion and citations in Richard F. Tomasson, "From Elitism to Egalitarianism in Swedish Education," *Sociology of Education*, Vol. 38, No. 3 (Spring 1965), pp. 203–223.

31. See Kerr, *The Universities of Europe*, pp. 55, 76–77, and Nigel Grant, *Soviet Education* (Middlesex, 1964), pp. 118–119.

32. The source of this estimate is the Swedish journalist Gunnar Fredriksson.

33. The source of these figures is the Polish sociologist Adam Sarapata, Spring 1967.

34. See sources in footnotes 17, 18, and 19 for data on occupational backgrounds of students by university faculty.

35. For example, Kingman Brewster, Jr., President of Yale, said in 1964 that "moral capacity" was a factor in the admission of freshmen; see *Time*, October 2, 1964, p. 87. The use of any such nonacademic criteria would be looked on with disdain in Scandinavia.

36. Carlsson and Geeser, "Universities as Selecting and Socializing Agents: Some Recent Swedish Data," p. 27.

37. "Medical Education and Research," in *The Intellectual Face of Sweden* (Uppsala, 1964), pp. 97–98.

38. SIFO (Svenska Institutet för Opinionsundersökningar), Stockholm, 1955 and 1963.

39. Kerr, *The Universities of Europe*, p. 38.

40. For an English account of the economic transformation of Sweden, see Chapter 6 of Eli F. Heckscher, *An Economic History of Sweden*, trans. by Göran Ohlin (Cambridge, 1954).

41. See Herbert Tingsten, *Den svenska socialdemokratiens idéutveckling*, Vol. 1 (Stockholm, 1941), pp. 18–24.

42. Alrik Gustafson, *A History of Swedish Literature* (Minneapolis, 1961), pp. 249–250.

43. *Ibid.*, p. 250.

44. See the various accounts of the influence of Verdandi in the special volume published on the occasion of the fiftieth anniversary of the organization: *Verdandi: genom femtio år* (Stockholm, 1932).

45. See the original statutes of Verdandi, *Ibid.*, pp. 13–15.

46. Jorgen Ullenhag, *Studentliberal utveckling: Liberala studentförbundet åren 1947–1962* (Stockholm, 1963), pp. 50–51. What Ullenhag says here of the Liberal Student Association can be said of Verdandi as well.

47. This statement of purpose was printed in large letters in the center of page 3 in *Dagens Nyheter* for December 23, 1964.

48. From a conversation with a recent chairman of Verdandi.

49. See David Thomson, *England in the Nineteenth Century* (Middlesex, 1950), pp. 177, 227. There were fifty republican clubs in England around 1870–71. For an account of one of the most well known of the English cultural radicals, see Arthur H. Nethercot, *The First Five Lives of Annie Besant* (Chicago, 1960).

50. See pp. 280–292 of *Verdandi: genom femtio år*, for a listing of all lectures, discussions, and publications in the period 1882–1932.

51. Translated from a recent statement of purpose of Verdandi.

52. *Dagens Nyheter*, December 12, 1967, p. 2.

53. C. A. Wachtmeister (ed.), *Ateistens handbok* (Verdandi, 1964). The quotation in the previous sentence is from the introduction by Ingemar Hedenius, a well-known professor of philosophy at Uppsala.

54. Ingrid Fredriksson (ed.), *Könsroller* (Verdandi, 1964).

55. The information on the activities of Verdandi since 1965 has been supplied by Sten Johansson, an Uppsala sociologist and past chairman of Verdandi.

56. This was also the point of view in an editorial in *Libertas*, the journal of the Social Democratic Student Association, see "SACO och solidariteten," No. 5 (1965), p. 4.

57. The following "Verdandi debate" books — in addition to *Ateistens handbok* and *Könsroller* — have been published by Bokforlaget Prisma in recent years: Jacob Palme, *Fri abort;* Per-Erik Back and Gunnar Fredriksson, *Republiken Sverige;* Vilhelm Moberg, *Därfor är jag republikan;* Bengt Abrahamsson and Dieter Strand, *Svensk militar tänker;* and Andreas Murray (ed.), *Det svenska klassämhället.*

58. Sten Johansson's estimate.

59. The Conference was held on October 10–11. The proceedings have been published: Maj-Briht Bergström-Walan, *et al., Sex och samhället,* (Stockholm, 1965).

60. For a history of the first forty years of the organization, see *Föreningen Heimdal, 1891–1931* (Uppsala, 1931). In a very moderate way, *Heimdal* continues to support these same value orientations.

61. A phrase from the most recent *Heimdal* pamphlet inviting membership.

62. Quoted in Ullenhag, *Studentliberal utveckling,* p. 48.

63. However, there is much in all these journals that is not narrowly political.

64. Clarté was founded in France in the 1920's by Henri Barbusse to promote international socialism.

65. Clarté constitution, revised 1966.

66. For a discussion in English of the Swedish culture debate, see Lars Gustafsson, *The Public Dialogue in Sweden: Current Issues of Social, Esthetic and Moral Debate* (Stockholm, 1964). For a discussion in English of the New Left in Sweden, see Göran Therborn, "The Swedish Left," *Studies on the Left,* Vol. 7, No. 2 (March-April 1967), pp. 69–81.

67. Ullenhag, *Studentliberal utveckling,* p. 66.

68. *Challenge to Affluence* (New York, 1965), p. 126.

69. See Gunnar Myrdal, "The Vietnam War and the Political and Moral Isolation of America," *New University Thought,* Vol. 5, No. 3 (May-June 1967), pp. 3–12, p. 4.

70. In 1962, 44.7 per cent of the daily press circulation was Liberal, 21.9 per cent was Social Democratic, and only 19.9 per cent was Conservative. See Lars Furhoff and Hans Hederberg, *Dagspressen i Sverige* (Stockholm, 1965), p. 14.

71. Eino Jutikkala, *A History of Finland* (London, 1958), p. 271.

72. John H. Wuorinen, *Nationalism in Modern Finland* (New York, 1931), p. 100.

73. Knut Gjerset, *History of the Norwegian People* (New York, 1915), pp. 462, 471.

74. Wuorinen, *Nationalism in Modern Finland,* p. 216.

75. Karen Larsen, *A History of Norway* (Princeton, 1948), pp. 458f.; and Yngvar Nielsen, *Norge i 1905* (Horton, 1906), pp. 215–217.

76. Jutikkala, *A History of Finland,* p. 272.

77. See a discussion of analogous developments elsewhere: Frank A. Pinner, "Student Trade-Unionism in France, Belgium, and Holland," *Sociology of Education,* Vol. 37, No. 3 (Spring, 1964), pp. 177–199.

78. T. Mailand Christensen, "The Participation of Students in Governing Bodies — Myth or Reality," *Social Problems of Students: Report on the Council of Europe Seminar,* p. 40.

79. See Kristian Ottosen, "Important Tasks for a Student Welfare Organization — Their Nature and Relative Importance," *Ibid.,* pp. 24–35; and the discussion of Norwegian student welfare in UNESCO, *World Survey of Education,* pp. 869–880.

80. *Uppsala universitets katalog*, Vol. 2 (Fall term, 1966), p. 470.

81. *Ibid.*, p. 467.

82. *Tidskriften Heimdal*, No. 1 (1966), p. 4. Percentages for 1966 and 1967 supplied by Anne Chaabane, information secretary, Swedish National Union of Students (SFS).

83. Anne Chaabane.

84. See Lars Tobisson, "The Swedish National Union of Students (SFS)," *The Intellectual Face of Sweden*, pp. 38–39; and Lars Tobisson, "SFS i farten. . . ," *Ergo*, No. 14 (September 25, 1964), pp. 6–8. See also *Introducing SFS* (Stockholm, 1966), mimeo.

85. Anne Chaabane.

86. Pinner, "Student Trade-Unionism in France, Belgium, and Holland," p. 178.

87. *Ibid.*, p. 179.

88. For example, the editors of the *Ergo* international staff pictured on p. 5 of *The Intellectual Face of Sweden* were twenty-eight, twenty-nine, twenty-nine, twenty-three and thirty-two. This is perhaps exceptional, but the average age of leaders in the SFS is probably twenty-six. The average age of leaders in the local unions is one or two years younger.

89. Tobisson, "The Swedish National Union of Students (SFS)," p. 38.

90. *Ibid.*, p. 39.

91. For a summary account of Scandinavian student politics, based to some extent on material in this paper, see Erik Allardt and Richard F. Tomasson, "Stability and Strains in Scandinavian Student Politics," *Dædalus* (Winter, 1968), pp. 156–165.

92. We want to thank, above all, Sten Johansson, Department of Sociology, Uppsala University, who supplied an important part of the material on which this paper is based and who commented on an earlier version of this paper. We also wish to express our appreciation to Päivi Elovainio, Department of Sociology, University of Helsinki; Erik Høgh, Department of Sociology, University of Copenhagen; and Ulf Torgersen and Henry Valen, Institute for Social Research, Oslo, for providing material and comments used in writing this paper. Anne Chaabane, information secretary, Swedish National Union of Students, commented on the section on the Swedish Union.

We acknowledge that this paper deals disproportionately with the Swedish and Finnish cases and tends to slight the Danish and Norwegian. The explanation is only that we have more intimate experience with and knowledge about student politics and higher education in the former two countries.

A. BELDEN FIELDS

The Revolution Betrayed:
The French Student Revolt of May-June 1968*

DURING THE LAST two weeks of May, 1968, it looked as though the Gaullist regime stood little chance of survival. An incredible phenomenon seemed to be occurring. For the first time in history, students appeared to be well on the way to spearheading a revolution to change both the political regime and the basic socioeconomic relations and structures of a highly industrialized Western nation. And even more intriguing for social theorists, the confrontations seemed to be verifying the hypotheses proposed by the French syndicalist, Georges Sorel, a half century earlier.

Most Frenchmen and foreign observers looked on in awe and with not an inconsiderable degree of anxiety. Politicians jockeyed for position. Civil servants gambled over whether or not to desert the ship. And de Gaulle once again displayed his political genius. The nearly successful revolution was parlayed into an election issue

*The author would like to express his appreciation to the Center for International Comparative Studies and the Department of Political Science at the University of Illinois, the Comparative Student Project of the Center for International Affairs at Harvard University, and the Brookings Institution for grants which enabled him to conduct field research in France in June and July 1968. Initial research in the area of French student activism in 1963 and 1964 was made possible by a grant from the Council on International Relations at Yale University. The author would also like to thank the many people in France who were so generous with their cooperation and assistance. Deserving of special expressions of appreciation are the national officers of the *Union Nationale des Etudiants de France* and the *Union des Grandes Ecoles*, M. Frédéric Bon of the *Foundation Nationale des Sciences Politiques*, M. Hassane Karkar of the Faculty of Science in Paris, and Professor Jean Touchard, Secretary General of the *Foundation Nationale des Sciences Politiques*. Marvin Weinbaum and Kathryn Fields offered very helpful and much appreciated editorial criticism.

which resulted in a disastrous defeat for the French Left and gave the Gaullists an absolute majority in the National Assembly.

What actually happened in France in May and June, 1968? What kinds of structures and personalities were involved? Why did it happen? What did it accomplish? These are the questions with which this essay will deal.

I

What Happened?:

The Chronology of Events[1]

The student revolt had its immediate origins at Nanterre, a working class industrial suburb of Paris. What makes Nanterre different from most other French towns is that it embraces two very special categories of people. First, there are the slum dwellers. Mainly Arabs and Iberians, these people live in what is undoubtedly one of the worst *bidonvilles* in an industrialized country. Second, there are the 16,000 students who attend the faculties of letters and law at the newly opened and still unfinished university campus. The two populations coexist in relative proximity.

The confrontations between students and the administration at Nanterre began during the school year 1966–67. Students reacted against the rule forbidding visits of members of the opposite sex in dormitory rooms by holding lectures and debates on the question, distributing tracts, and finally occupying the women's dormitory. The administration reacted by expelling twenty-nine students. The question of files kept on student activists was raised and remained a pressing one throughout the next academic year. One of the facts which kept alive the suspicion that files were being compiled on activists was the receipt of a letter by an activist informing him that in 1967–68 he should take his courses at the Sorbonne in Paris rather than at Nanterre. Other students and professors protested and the student managed to enroll at Nanterre. His name was Daniel Cohn-Bendit.[2]

During the academic year 1967–68 the campus was in constant turmoil. In November the students conducted a ten-day strike. Their grievances were the value of the *license* (first degree) under the new degree system introduced by the Fouchet educational reforms, overcrowding of classrooms and ineffective teaching, and compulsory quiz sections. Strike committees were formed to negotiate with professors and administrators.

Nothing was gained by the strikers, except perhaps some faculty sympathy. The administration's refusal to take action on the demands became an issue around which there was an attempt to mobilize the mass of the students. In early January the Secretary of State of Youth and Sports went to Nanterre to dedicate the new swimming pool. Daniel Cohn-Bendit was there to challenge him. Cohn-Bendit maintained that a publication of the Ministry on the problems of youth avoided the basic problems. There was an exchange of words and Cohn-Bendit was threatened with expulsion and ordered to go before a disciplinary committee. At the end of the month, January 29, there was a demonstration against the banning of political expression and activity and against the presence of police officers in civilian clothes on the campus.

The next step in the confrontation took place on March 22. Two days earlier some members of the *Comité Vietnam National*, which opposes American policy in Vietnam, broke windows and wrote on the walls of the Chase Manhattan Bank and the offices of American Express and T.W.A. in Paris. Several high school and university students were arrested. One was a student at Nanterre.

On the afternoon of the 22nd, Cohn-Bendit led a small group of militants into classrooms where they interrupted courses and announced that there would be a meeting at 5 P.M. to discuss what the students could do faced with ". . . such menacing repressive machinations."[3] Militants claim that from 600 to 700 students attended the meeting.[4]

The decision was made to occupy the Administration Building. This target was especially attractive for several reasons. The administration was the *bête noire* of the students. The chamber of the *Conseil de la Faculté*, the faculty governing group, was located in the Administration Building. And, control over the Administration Building meant control over the central microphone with which one could issue announcements over the entire campus. One hundred and forty-two militants actually occupied the building. This group came to be known as the *Mouvement du 22 Mars*.

The occupiers did not remain idle. They decided to plan a day of discussions and debates on such subjects as the struggle against imperialism, the relationship between the struggles of the students and the workers, the struggle of students in Communist countries, and the "critical" university. The day selected was Friday, March 29.

On the night of the 28th, Dean Grappin, with the approval of the faculty assembly, announced that he was closing the campus until Monday. The Dean blamed a group of irresponsible students who, for several months, have disrupted courses and examinations and practiced guerrilla methods on the campus. These students belong to no known political organization. They constitute an explosive element in a very sensitive milieu. The campus has grown very quickly, too quickly. It has received too many students too soon. It constitutes a fertile terrain for the most unexpected movements.[5]

The Minister of Education did not agree to a formal closing of the campus. Thus, the Administration Building was kept open but no courses were offered and the classroom buildings were locked. Approximately 500 students came for the discussions of the 29th. It was decided to put the day of discussion off until April 2 when the university would be operating normally and access could be had to the classrooms. The idea was to split up into small discussion groups of not over 25 students. At any rate, a political discussion on the grass of a deserted campus would not serve to make the point of the activists that open political discussion would hereafter be the norm at Nanterre.

On April 2, the day before Easter vacation, the students had their way. Approximately 1200 students met for a day of political discussions without any interference by the authorities. During the vacation, some of the militants of the *Mouvement du 22 Mars* participated in the April 13th demonstration before the German Embassy in Paris. This protest against the attempted assassination of Rudi Dutschke resulted in some minor acts of violence between students and police officers, the first of the academic year.

The days immediately following the return from Easter vacation were characterized by violent confrontations between students of the Right and the Left. On April 21, a special assembly of the *Union Nationale des Etudiants de France*, the large French student union, was broken up by members of the right-wing group *Occident*. On April 25, the Rector of the University of Toulouse called in the police to put an end to the violence at that university. On April 27, Cohn-Bendit was arrested on a battery complaint filed by a right-wing student. Cohn-Bendit maintained that he had attempted to break up the fight and was released from custody.[6]

Sunday, the 28th, approximately 200 students who opposed American intervention in Vietnam raided an exposition of a group which supported American policy, the *Front Uni de Soutien au Sud Viêt-nam*. The *Occident*, which supported the *Front*, swore that it would "smash the Bolshevik vermin."[7] On Thursday a fire destroyed the office of the student union at the Sorbonne. The arsonists left the insignia of the *Occident*.

At Nanterre there had been constant political meetings, demonstrations, and discussions since the students returned from Easter vacation on the 19th. It was decided to hold two "Days of Anti-Imperialism." The *Occident* threatened to break them up and a defense of the campus was organized by the pro-Chinese students of the *Union des Jeunesses Communistes Marxiste-Léniniste* (UJCML). The imitation of the combat tactics of the students at the University of Pekin struck most of the militants of the *Mouvement du 22 Mars* as nonsense. They accused the pro-Chinese students of creating an atmosphere in which it would be impossible to hold discussions. This led to a falling out between the two groups and even some fighting in the corridors.

Given this state of affairs on the campus, a threat of the students to boycott their examinations, and the *Occident's* threats and arson at the Sorbonne, the Dean decided to close the campus and suspend courses on the 2nd. Cohn-Bendit and five other students were ordered to appear before a disciplinary hearing on May 6. By this time the faculty members at Nanterre were deeply split between those more or less sympathetic with the students and those who called for strong action to put an end to the agitation.

The next day, May 3, the situation completely exploded and the student revolt began in earnest. The militants of the *Mouvement du 22 Mars* went into Paris to join leaders and militants of the student union and all of the other left-wing student groups in a meeting to protest the closing of the Nanterre campus and the disciplinary hearings. The meeting was to be held in the courtyard of the Sorbonne, seat of the Parisian Faculty of Letters.

However, at 2 P.M., when many students were congregated there, the Rector of the University of Paris, Jean Roche, ordered the Sorbonne closed and called in the police to evacuate the students. The police not only evacuated the building but arrested between 500 and 600 students, including most of the prominent student leaders. In an operation which lasted several hours, the students were placed in police vans and led off to jail in groups of 25.

All of this took place before the eyes of the thousands of students who inhabit the Latin Quarter. Students in the streets began to cry, "Free our camarades!" and "The Sorbonne belongs to the students!" At 7:30 P.M., after the last arrests had been made, the police charged the protesting students and the Latin Quarter erupted into violent confrontations which lasted six hours.

Both the national student union (the *Union Nationale des Etudiants de France* — UNEF) and the university teachers' affiliate of the large National Education Federation (the *Syndicat National de l'Enseignement Supérieur* — SNESup) protested the closing of the Sorbonne and the police action. The SNESup called for a strike in all faculties and UNEF called for a strike, demonstrations, and a meeting in the courtyard of the Sorbonne on Monday, May 6.

Over the weekend the situation worsened. Daniel Cohn-Bendit of the *Mouvement du 22 Mars* and Jacques Sauvageot, Vice-President but actual leader of UNEF, were questioned by police for approximately twenty hours. Special judicial proceedings were instituted against some of the demonstrators. On Saturday, seven or eight received suspended sentences for violence against police officers. On Sunday, four received prison sentences of two months.

On May 6 Paris saw its first barricades since the Algerian War. The SNESup became a joint sponsor of the demonstration called by UNEF. Approximately 20,000 demonstrators — university and high school students, teachers, and nonstudents and nonteachers — assembled at Denfert-Rochereau. As they made their way north, toward the university area, the police attempted to block them. The barricades were erected as protection against police charges. The fighting was intense. Three hundred and forty-five police officers and several hundred students were hurt. There were 422 arrests. UNEF first condemned the more extreme action of the demonstrators but, later in the night, withdrew its condemnation.

Two other interesting events occurred on the 6th. First, students in at least 15 *lycées* or secondary schools began what was to become a national strike and a considerable number of them joined in the demonstrations. Second, the Secretary General of the Ministry of Education resigned after a disagreement with the Minister over how to handle the situation.

On the 7th, students in Paris and the provinces responded to a call for a demonstration issued by UNEF. In Paris alone, somewhere between 30,000 and 50,000 demonstrators marched up the Champs-Elysée to the Arc de Triomphe where they sang the "International." There was no attempt by the police to interfere. The student union laid down three conditions which the government would have to meet before the strike and the demonstrations would end. First, the students sentenced to jail had to be freed and all pending charges and judicial proceedings had to be dropped. Second, the police had to evacuate all university buildings and the large police forces had to leave the university area. And, third, the campus at Nanterre and the Sorbonne had to be opened.

On the following day, both UNEF and the SNESup declared their willingness to negotiate with the government if the three conditions were met. They also called another demonstration. Approximately 20,000 people in the Latin Quarter and over 40,000 in the provinces responded to the call. After taking a hard line before the Council of Ministers, the Minister of Education told the National Assembly that he hoped the Sorbonne could be reopened the next day. And several Nobel prize winners called for an amnesty for the students and the opening of the faculties.

It looked as though there might be a deescalation on the morning of the 9th. The Rector and the deans of the University of Paris announced that instruction would begin again at the Sorbonne and Nanterre. And the Rector announced the cancellation of the disciplinary hearings against the militants from Nanterre.[8] However, the problem of the imprisoned students was still unresolved. Louis Joxe, the Minister of Justice, refused to intervene in any way on behalf of these students. Outside of the Sorbonne there was a spontaneous sit-in in which students talked about occupying the university facilities until the release of the students. Cohn-Bendit called for the occupation of the Sorbonne and the campus at Nanterre should they be opened. At 8 P.M. the Minister of Education, Mr. Peyrefitte, announced that the Sorbonne would remain closed until calm was restored.

This was the situation on the 10th. UNEF and the SNESup called for a demonstration at Denfert-Rochereau at 6:30 P.M. The university students were joined by about 5000 *lycée* students who had held their own demonstration earlier. The total group of from 20,000 to 30,000 marched to Boulevard Saint-Michel via the prison of the *Santé* where they mistakenly believed the convicted students were being held. The police met the demonstrators at the intersection of Boulevard Saint-Germain and Boulevard Saint-Michel, blocking their access to the Place Saint-Michel. The demonstration thus made its way south to the Luxembourg gardens where it was blocked again.

The time was approximately 9 P.M. It was at this point that the demonstrators decided to resist any attempts of the police to disperse them. Approximately 60 barricades were erected. Trees on the Boulevard Saint-Michel were chopped down, parked cars were moved into place, and anything which could be yanked from its position was used as material for the barricades. Bricks (*pavés*) were dug out of the streets to be used as weapons to repel the anticipated police charges.

At 10:15 P.M. the demonstrators learned from radio broadcasts that the Rector was willing to receive a delegation of students to discuss the possibility of reopening the Sorbonne. UNEF's Jacques Sauvageot and Alain Geismar, the Secretary General of the SNESup, immediately responded that no discussion was possible until the incarcerated students were granted an amnesty. Their response was also made via the radio. At 12:15 A.M. Daniel Cohn-Bendit and several other students and professors went to the office of the Rector. The Rector was in telephone contact with the Minister of Education who, in turn, was in contact with the Ministers of Justice, Interior, Finance, and the Secretary General of the President's office. After an hour and a half (1:45 A.M.), Cohn-Bendit and the delegation rejoined the demonstrators. Cohn-Bendit announced that there were no negotiations as the government refused to grant the demands of UNEF. He said that he had informed the Rector that the students would remain behind the barricades until all three demands were met.

At 2:15 A.M. the Minister of Interior, Christian Fouchet, issued the order to the police and the paramilitary *Compagnies Républicaines de Sécurité* (CRS) to destroy the barricades. The ensuing battle marked the apex of violence and destruction. The forces of order used concussion, smoke, tear gas grenades, rifle butts, and clubs to subdue the students. The students used bricks and anything else which would serve as a missile to defend their positions. In some cases, molotov cocktails were hurled.

The last barricade on the now famous rue Gay-Lussac did not fall until 6:00 A.M. By the time the battle was over almost 400 people had been injured, about 460 arrested, and, what made perhaps the greatest impression upon the French population, 188 automobiles had been either damaged or thoroughly destroyed. There were also demonstrations and confrontations of a less dramatic nature in the provinces.

The question of police brutality had already been raised after the battles of the 3rd. The Minister of Interior had dismissed the issue by stating that if it is impossible to have perfectly measured action during a game of rugby, it is certainly impossible during an uprising.[9] But the behavior of the police on the night of the 10th and 11th had a profound effect upon the Parisian population. At issue was not so much the storming of the barricades but the beating of students after they had been isolated in the street, the pursuit of students into apartments of Parisians who attempted to offer them sanctuary and the mistreatment of all concerned, the beating of spectators or anyone who happened to be near the combat zone, the firing of tear gas into enclosed areas where the police suspected that students were seeking refuge, and the reported brutalities and indignities committed at the Beaujon police station in Paris. The cry "CRS — SS!," equating the CRS with the Nazi elite corps, was taken up by the students.

The intransigence of the government and the tactics of the police resulted in a very strong prostudent sentiment in Paris. There was another march from Denfert-Rochereau on the 11th. While the *Confédération Générale du Travail* (CGT — the Communist-dominated labor union) and the *Confédération Générale du Travail — Force Ouvrière* (CGT-FO, a moderate socialist labor union) had expressed concern over the students going too far after the barricades of the 6th, UNEF and the SNESup were now able to enlist the support of all three of the major labor unions to the extent of their agreeing to call a twenty-four hour general strike on Monday the 13th.[10] The demands of UNEF and the SNESup were supported by the *Parti Socialiste Unifié* (PSU) and the Communist Party, although the latter continued to oppose what it considered to be adventurism on the part of the students.

From the point of view of the government, the situation was deteriorating rapidly. Premier Pompidou, who was on a diplomatic mission in Afghanistan, returned to take the situation out of the hands of Peyrefitte, Fouchet, and Joxe, Minister of Justice. On the night of the 11th, the Premier went on television in an attempt to restore calm. He declared that on Monday the Sorbonne would be opened and the case of the four imprisoned students reviewed by an appeals court. He also announced that students would not suffer a delay in their academic progress because of the events. By Monday afternoon the four imprisoned students and the 24 other people who had been in custody were either freed unconditionally or released on a provisional basis. While the consideration of a general amnesty was already under way in government circles, it was not until the 22nd that the National Assembly was presented with and accepted a law granting an amnesty to all participants in the demonstrations and clashes with the police.

Monday, the 13th, was the day of the general strike. Joining the UNEF, the SNESup, and the labor unions were the *Fédération de l'Education Nationale* (the huge teachers' union of which the SNESup is one of the smaller affiliates) and the *Confédération Generale des Cadres.* This put the entire union movement behind the students and their professors. It also put between 500,000 and one million demonstrators in the streets of Paris, not to mention the provinces in which there was serious violence.

The responsibility for preventing violence was assumed by the CGT, the largest of the labor unions and the one with the most effective *service d'ordre*.[11] The CGT was terribly afraid of the more radical student groups, especially the *Mouvement du 22 Mars,* which participated in the demonstration. During the march from the Place de la République to Denfert-Rochereau, it attempted to keep the workers isolated from the students. A group of students around Cohn-Bendit managed to take the lead of the procession and, once at Denfert-Rochereau, the CGT gave the order to disperse.

At this point most, but not all, of the workers did leave the demonstration. Approximately 10,000 students, teachers, and workers, however, marched to the Champ de Mars, red and black flags flying in the breeze. UNEF and the SNESup announced that all university buildings would be occupied by students and teachers. Cohn-Bendit called for the demonstrators to organize *"comités d'action"* in neighborhoods and factories. At 9:30 P.M. the demonstrators arrived at the Sorbonne and the occupation of almost all university facilities in France by students and sympathetic professors was begun. The deans of the faculties of letters announced that they were favorably disposed toward giving the students some say in the running of their faculties. But it was a little late since the deans no longer had any say. That evening President de Gaulle announced that he would address the nation on the 24th.

On the 14th, the fortunes of the Gaullists seemed to decline even further. The Federation of the Left and the Communist Party placed a motion of censure against the government before the National Assembly. And, more seriously, the workers at the factory of Sud-Aviation in Nantes took their cue from the students and occupied the factory while the Renault workers at Cléon held the factory director prisoner and instituted a partial work stoppage. On the 15th, while Pompidou was making concessions before the National Assembly regarding the autonomy of the universities and student participation in educational reform, students went out to Nantes to spend a night of solidarity with the strikers while others occupied the National Theater approximately three blocks from the Sorbonne. The only union leaders to return expressions of solidarity were those of the second largest union, the *Confédération Française et Demo-*

cratique du Travail (CFDT). They met with the students at the Sorbonne on the 16th.

The extra-syndical strike wave spread with incredible speed. By 11 P.M. of the 16th all Renault factories were occupied by striking workers defiantly flying the red flag. On the same day, Rhodiaceta at Lyon was occupied and a newspaper and magazine strike hit Paris. On the 17th railroad workers, employees of Air France, and all transportation workers in the Parisian area went out on strike. The journalists of the government-controlled radio and television network declared their independence from the Gaullist Ministry of Information. Students marched out to the Renault factory at Billancourt where they asked the workers to assume the leadership of the battle against the regime. The leaders of the CGT, whose control over the workers was nonexistent at this point, desperately tried to keep the workers from communicating with the students. They joined with the leaders of the Communist Party in warning their militants against the "adventurism" of the students.

On the 19th de Gaulle, who had returned from Rumania the day before, issued his famous statement before the Council of Ministers: "*La réforme oui! La chien-lit non!*"[12] In the face of a possible civil war, the Gaullists began to build their defense. The Gaullist *Comités de Défense de la République* were organized and tracts denouncing the "anarchy and disorder" were distributed.

Despite this counteroffensive, the Gaullists continued to suffer reverses. On the 20th, all truck transport and mail deliveries ceased. The movement to occupy *lycées* throughout the country demonstrated a new spurt of activity. And the *Fédération de l'Education Nationale*, which groups approximately 90 per cent of the primary school teachers and two thirds of the secondary school teachers, called a national strike to begin on the 22nd. On the 21st the strike spread to textile workers, department store employees, and bank employees. The country was paralyzed by the strikers who numbered between six and seven million. And farmers, whose organizations had already called for demonstrative action to begin on the 24th, began to demonstrate their solidarity with the strikers in the West of France. In the face of this, two Gaullist deputies, Pisani and Capitant, resigned their seats in protest against the government's handling of the situation.

The government's decision to forbid Cohn-Bendit's return from a short trip to Berlin, announced on the 22nd, set off a new wave of demonstrations and violence. The most serious violence took place on the day that de Gaulle informed the nation that a referendum would be held, the 24th. The CGT held a demonstration for its own bargaining objectives which comprised approximately 150,000 people. There was no attempt on the part of the police to interfere. But the *Mouvement du 22 Mars* also called a demonstration which was supported by UNEF, the CFDT, and the CGT-FO. The demonstration was huge, some estimates running as high as 100,000. The police and CRS attempted to prevent the passage of the demonstrators toward the Bastille and the Hotel de Ville. Both banks of Paris were turned into a battlefield and a small fire was set on the steps of the stock exchange. One person was killed, hundreds wounded, and approximately 650 arrested. In the provinces fighting was especially serious in Nantes, Strasbourg, Bordeaux, and Lyon where a high police official was killed.

On the 25th, leaders of the labor unions and the business community met with members of the government in an effort to get the strikers, who by now totaled about 10 million, back to work. A proposal was agreed upon on the 26th and submitted to the workers on Monday, the 27th. It was rejected by the workers in all of the major industries (including Renault, Citroen, Berliet, and Rhodiaceta) who showed their determination to continue the strike and the occupations and who called for the downfall of the regime and the installation of a *"gouvernement populaire."* The Secretary General of the CGT, Georges Séguy, did a hasty double step in an attempt to keep pace with the membership. He insisted that he had signed nothing and called for demonstrations in Paris.

On the same day, UNEF and the SNESup called a rally at the Charlety Stadium. Between 50,000 and 60,000 people packed the Stadium. Leaders of the PSU, the CFDT, and the CGT-FO extended their support as did former Premier Pierre Mendès-France. The speakers and the crowd called for the resignation of de Gaulle and the institution of a *"gouvernement populaire."*

In what could only be regarded as a disavowal of his handling of the situation, Minister of Education Peyrefitte was forced to resign on the 28th. Premier Pompidou personally assumed control of the Ministry. Cohn-Bendit, who swore that he would return to Paris when border police stopped him at Forbach on the 24th, sneaked across the border and called reporters in for a news conference at the Sorbonne. The government announced that the *baccalauréat* examinations, which are roughly equivalent to university entrance examinations, were being postponed. And, just to make matters a little worse for the government, the *Conseil d'Etat* informed de Gaulle that his proposed referendum was unconstitutional.

It seemed to most observers that the Gaullists were finished. François Mitterand, the candidate of the Federation of the Left who had opposed de Gaulle in the last presidential election, announced that he was in the running for the presidency. He suggested that Mendès-France form a provisional government which would include members of all parties on the Left. On the 29th Mendès-France gave his assent to the proposal. Both Lecanuet, leader of the center Catholics, and Descamps, leader of the CFDT, came out in support of the idea.

While neither the Communist Party nor the CGT gave public backing to a provisional government headed by Mendès-France — in fact both were bitter over the anti-Communist tone of the rally at Charlety Stadium at which he had spoken — they did harden their attitude toward the Gaullists. They called for the replacement of the Gaullist regime by a *"gouvernement populaire"* and held a massive demonstration of several hundred thousand people. While UNEF did not officially participate in the demonstration, several other left-wing student groups did and student participation was heavy. The cry was *"Adieu de Gaulle."*

In effect, de Gaulle did go away — to his estate at Colombey where most observers thought that he was writing his statement of resignation. But from Colombey de Gaulle flew to Germany where he negotiated the support of the army with General Massu, commander of French troops in Germany. It later became evident that the *quid pro quo* was the release from prison of Massu's old friends in the OAS during the Algerian War and the readmission of Georges Bidault into France.

With the support of the army assured, de Gaulle returned to Paris and went before the public on television (May 30). He announced that he was dissolving the National Assembly and calling new legislative elections. He stated that the choice was between him and totalitarian Communism. Other Gaullists had not been idle either. That evening close to a million demonstrators, led by Gaullist ministers, marched from the Concord to the Etiole shouting their support for de Gaulle. Some of the demonstrators reflected the increasing anti-Semitism among those opposed to the revolt and cried "Cohn-Bendit to Dachau."

The next day, May 31, there were important changes in the government. Peyrefitte was already out of the Ministry of Education.

Now Fouchet (Interior), Joxe (Justice), and Gorse (Information) were removed from their posts. And Debré (Finance) and Couve de Murville (Foreign Affairs) exchanged ministries.

On June 1, UNEF called a demonstration to show the solidarity of the students with the striking workers. Some 40,000 students and workers marched from the railroad station at Montparnasse to Austerlitz. The demonstrators called upon the workers to continue their strikes and occupations and denounced participation in the elections as a betrayal.

By the 6th of June, most of the workers were back on the job. The major holdouts were in the automobile industry, the building trades, chemical works, and the radio and television network. The situation at two factories, Renault at Flins and Peugeot at Sochaux, was especially serious. On the 6th, the CRS drove the workers from the factory at Flins and there was serious fighting between police and strikers. Students had gone to Flins to demonstrate their support of the workers. On the 10th, Gilles Tautin, an eighteen-year-old *lycée* student and member of the pro-Chinese student organization was drowned in the Seine near Flins during a charge by the CRS.[13]

This set off another wave of student demonstrations in Paris. Late in the evening of the 10th there was a demonstration on Boulevard Saint-Michel. Bonfires for which electoral posters served as fuel were set and the barricades went up once again. At the police station across from the Panthéon molotov cocktails destroyed three empty police wagons. The fighting lasted well into the next morning.

On the 11th it was announced that a young striker had been killed by the CRS near the Peugeot factory at Sochaux. UNEF, the *Mouvement du 22 Mars*, the *Comités d'Action Lycéens*, and the *Comité de Coordination des Comités d'Action* called a demonstration at the Gare de l'Est to protest the deaths and the "repression." The demonstration enjoyed the support of the PSU and the CFDT. The police and the CRS blocked the route. Once again the Latin Quarter was the scene of barricades and violence during the entire night.

The government began its concerted offensive against the students on the 12th. All demonstrations were forbidden for the duration of the electoral campaign and most of the student and non-student organizations on the extreme Left were outlawed. While leaders of the PSU and the SFIO (the large Socialist Party) protested the ban, not a word was heard from the Communist Party. Several of the student organizations organized "long marches" out to the factories to indicate their continued support for the strikers.

On the 14th the government recaptured the National Theater from the students. It also began a roundup of known leaders and militants of the outlawed organizations. There were seventeen arrests of such individuals. The government announced that the *baccalauréat* examinations would begin on June 27 and would be entirely oral. The next day de Gaulle kept his apparent promise to Massu and released General Salan and ten other former members of the OAS from prison. In the light of this alliance with the army and the political Right it is interesting to note that none of the right-wing groups which had been engaging in violent activity, such as the *Occident* and the student affiliate of the *Action Française,* were declared illegal. Nor did their activities cease.

The police occupied the Sorbonne on the rainy Sunday morning of June 16th. The occupation itself was peaceful but it set off more demonstrations and fighting which lasted until 8 P.M. The center of activity was moved to the Faculty of Science. On the 17th, the day on which the CGT-supported proposal for a resumption of work was presented to the strikers in the automobile industry, Sauvageot announced that UNEF would not organize or support any further demonstrations. He warned students against attempting to go it alone in clashes with the police. And he urged them to devote their energies to reinforcing the occupations of university facilities and developing new structures within the university. The next day Renault workers at three factories voted to go back to work.

By the 23rd, when the Gaullists won the first round of elections, all of the automobile workers were back on the job. The only important holdouts were the students, the university teachers, and the journalists of the radio and television network. From then on it was a mopping-up operation for the Gaullists. On the 27th, the police occupied the *Ecole des Beaux Arts,* the source of most of the imaginative posters which adorned Paris during the revolt. One week after the smashing electoral victory at the second round of elections (June 30), every faculty in Paris was back under the control of the government. But if taking the universities was a victory of sorts for the Gaullists it was not a victory over which anyone could be jubilant. For the government controlled the shell of the French university, its buildings. The vital substance of the university, its students, professors, and researchers, was missing.

II

Who Was Involved?:

The Structures and Personalities of the Revolt

In general, the press reports which appeared on the events of May and June have left the public confused as to the structures and personalities which were involved. Here we shall very briefly indicate the position of the more important organizations which had existed before the month of May, discuss the new structures which were developed during the confrontations of May and June, and make several general points on the nature of the uprising.

Student Organizations. The catalyst for the student revolt was provided by the response to the initiatives taken by the *Mouvement du 22 Mars*. With the exception of a few sympathizers in Parisian faculties, the *22 Mars* was confined to the campus at Nanterre.

It is difficult to speak of the *22 Mars* as an organization. The name was first applied to the 142 militants who occupied the Administration Building at Nanterre on March 22. The most prominent of these people was Daniel Cohn-Bendit, a 23-year-old sociology student whose conception it was to create a movement almost entirely without structure which would overcome the divisions which fragmented the student extreme Left. Among the 142 militants were members of the Trotskyist *Jeunesse Communiste Révolutionaire,* of the student affiliate of the *Parti Socialiste Unifié* (PSU), and of the *Comité Vietnam National.* Also included were students who associated with no other political organization and anarchists. Cohn-Bendit himself was a member of a very small anarchist group, *Noire et Rouge.* The pro-Chinese students at first denounced the *22 Mars* as being reactionary, came in *en masse* after Easter vacation, and quit on May 2 claiming that the *22 Mars* was made up of adventuristic anarchists.

The *22 Mars* was, indeed, highly unstructured. At Nanterre it attracted between 1000 and 1500 people to its debates and discussions. Issues and problems on which there would be general agreement were sought. No votes were taken and there was no established structure to implement decisions. Tracts were issued and the major spokesman for the group became, *de facto,* Cohn-Bendit. While the militants of the *22 Mars* became less and less visible after the middle of May, its charismatic leader had a remarkably pervasive and lasting effect upon the student milieu. He was unquestionably the most profound theorist of the revolt.[14]

Once the site of the confrontations was moved to Paris, the national leadership of the *Union Nationale des Etudiants de France* (UNEF), after an initial hesitation, attempted to direct the confrontations with the regime and broadened them to a national scale. In fact, UNEF has been in a virtual state of war with the Gaullists ever since it opposed the war in Algeria. Since that time the organization has been the object of punitive measures by the government. In recent years it has experienced a serious decline in membership — from approximately 46 per cent of the student body in 1957 to approximately 15 per cent in 1967 — and a deterioration in organizational cohesiveness.[15] Despite this fact, it was UNEF which formulated the specific demands of the students and UNEF which issued the calls to demonstrate responded to by swarms of students all over France. Its leader, Jacques Sauvageot, a 25-year-old student of art history, became one of the student heroes of the revolt and shared the spotlight of publicity with Cohn-Bendit.

Two other student organizations worked closely with the leadership of UNEF. They were the *Etudiants Socialistes Unifiés* (ESU), the student affiliate of the *Parti Socialiste Unifié,* and the *Jeunesse Communiste Révolutionnaire* (JCR). For the prior sixteen months, the national offices of UNEF had been controlled by students of the ESU. The ESU, which has between 1000 and 1200 members, thus gave its unqualified support to the initiatives of UNEF.

The JCR, while enjoying almost no influence within UNEF before the events of May, worked in close cooperation with the leadership of the student union during the events. Of the two Trotskyist student organizations in France, it is viewed by the students as being the less rigid, dogmatic, and hierarchical. The JCR was created in March, 1967, under the leadership of students at the Sorbonne who had been purged from the *Union des Etudiants Communistes* (UEC) in 1965. Its membership, which is heavily concentrated in Paris, probably runs between 1000 and 1500. It claims that half of its membership in Paris is composed of young workers and half of students. Along with the *Mouvement du 22 Mars*, it was outlawed by the government on June 12. Its most prominent leader at the Sorbonne, Alain Krivine, announced that the organization would not disband and he was hunted by the police. The leaders of the JCR, UNEF, and ESU were often at odds with Cohn-Bendit over the degree of organization which should be imposed upon the "student movement."

Also present at all of the demonstrations, barricades, and occupations were the anarchists who proudly displayed their black flags. Their numbers are small and they are extremely fragmented. The *Fédération Anarchiste* serves as a kind of clearinghouse and information center for the multitudes of groups and individuals. It estimates that it serves perhaps 1000 individuals in all of France.

Also of importance were the people from the *Comités Vietnam National* (CVN). While they did not carry the standard of the CVN during the events of May and June, their attacks on American offices in Paris were an important part of the catalytic stage and most of them switched their attention from the issue of Vietnam to the general confrontation.

One of the more interesting aspects of the events of May and June was the participation of *lycée* or secondary school students. The politization of these students was something very new in France. Its origin can be traced to February, 1967, and the creation of the first *Comités Vietnam Lycéens* in several Parisian *lycées*. The movement spread very quickly.

Once the concept of organization for activist purposes had penetrated the *lycées*, it was not long before the students turned to direct action techniques to manifest their discontent with the educational system. On December 13, 1967, a large majority of students at eight Parisian *lycées* decided to join the CGT and the CFDT in a twenty-four hour strike. The leaders of the strike movement were activists in Vietnam committees. Taking note of the successful mobilization of the students for the strike, they called for the creation of structures for a general confrontation. Thus were created the *Comités d'Action Lycéens* (CAL). The approximately twelve leaders who had proposed the idea constituted themselves into a national committee of coordination.[16]

Several incidents contributed to the growth of the CAL. First, there was the January strike at the *Lycée Condorcet* in Paris. One of the militants was expelled. This led to a demonstration by approximately 2000 students from several Parisian *lycées* to protest the lack of freedom of expression in their schools and to call into question the entire educational policy of the government. Second there was the secondary school teachers' strike on February 26. The national leadership of the CAL called their own strike on the same day.[17] Finally, there were the events of May and June themselves. Students in the *lycées*, led by the militants of the CAL, struck, demonstrated, and occupied their schools. The CAL was a joint sponsor of many of the major demonstrations and its militants were on the barricades.

UNEF, the ESU, the *Mouvement du 22 Mars*, the JCR, the CAL, and several anarchist groups formed the hard core of preexisting student organizations which supported and attempted to give direction to the student uprising. However not all student organizations, not even all student organizations on the Left, sympathized with the barricades and the revolutionary aims which the uprising adopted.

A most determined opposition to the barricades came from three of the four Communist student organizations: the *Union des Etudiants Communistes* (UEC), the *Fédération des Etudiants Révolutionnaires* (FER), and the *Union des Jeunesses Communistes (Marxiste-Léniniste)* (UJCML). These three groups supported the three specific demands of UNEF posed on May 7 but were strongly opposed to the violent confrontations.

The largest of these organizations is the UEC, the student affiliate of the French Communist Party.[18] It adopted the line of the parent organization and attacked the students who participated for "leftism" and "adventurism." Its special targets were the national leadership of UNEF and the PSU. It maintained that those who thought that change could only be brought about by violence were wrong, that UNEF provoked the government and invited people out to the barricades to get their skulls cracked without even specifying the goals. The charges of irresponsibility and provocation earned the UEC a very deep resentment among the supporters of the revolt.

The FER is a Trotskyist organization which claims a membership of 1100 students. While the Trotskyist *Jeunesse Communiste Révolutionnaire* is independent of nonstudent organizations, the FER is the student affiliate of the *Parti Communiste Internationaliste* (PCI). As such it represents the "hard" brand of Trotskyism (Lambertism) in France. As opposed to the JCR which represents the "soft" (Frankist) tendency, the FER demonstrates a higher degree of political exclusiveness, a more rigid doctrinal line, and a tighter and more disciplined organizational structure. It is viewed by many of its opponents on the Left as a kind of left-wing fascism. Both the PCI and the FER were declared to be illegal in June.

The FER earned the animosity of the students on the barricades by attempting to encourage them to disperse on the night of May 10 and 11 and by ordering its own militants not to participate. Its position was that the revolution would have to come at the initiative of the workers, not of the students. It issued calls to the workers to demonstrate and felt that until the workers responded, the job of the students was to continue to agitate near factories and in workers' neighborhoods. It was extremely hostile toward the *Mouvement du 22 Mars* and the JCR. The FER had no faith that workers would respond to the confrontations between students and the government. And it had a great fear that the *22 Mars* and the JCR were out either to destroy UNEF or to take it over — comparable things in the FER's estimation. After the government banned the FER its militants adopted the name *Comité pour la Defense de l'UNEF.* An organization with a similar perspective but with less involvement of and with students was the group which produced the Trotskyist newspaper, *Voix Ouvrière.* This group was also declared to be illegal.

The third Communist student organization to have opposed the barricades was the pro-Chinese UJCML. The organization was created after the expulsion of pro-Chinese students from the *Union des Etudiants Communistes* in early 1966. And it has maintained a total independence from the pro-Chinese *Parti Communiste Révolutionnaire (Marxiste-Léniniste).* Like the JCR, its strength was centered in Paris where it had something on the order of 2000 members and sympathizers before it was declared to be illegal.

Of all of the student groups discussed here, the UJCML is the least interested in student politics. As we have seen, the organization was erratic in its attitude toward the initiatives of the *22 Mars* at Nanterre. Its attitude toward the barricades was similar to that of the FER. The revolution must be made by the workers and confrontations without workers were meaningless. Once the workers did go out on strike, however, the UJCML, through its *Comités d'Action pour le Soutien des Luttes du Peuple,* joined forces with the broader movement in attempting to mobilize student support for the strikers. It maintained that the proper mode for showing such support was not to demonstrate in the Latin Quarter but to go out to the factories and join the workers on their home territory. It therefore supported the idea of "long marches" to factories in the Parisian area. It was on one of these marches that Gilles Tautin, a member of the UJCML, lost his life.

While the FER maintains that the battle against the regime must be carried on by the workers, it remains very much involved in student affairs and is an extremely aggressive, if not very successful, participant in the internal life of UNEF. Such is not the case with the UJCML. Following good Maoist doctrine, it views the students as being a group of bourgeois intellectuals who are isolated from the life of the working class. The student, like all intellectuals, must therefore break out of his isolation by working with the proletariat. True to this code, a good number of the members of the UJCML left their studies at the beginning of the school year and went to work in factories where they lived the life of workers and attempted to spread their ideology. Those who remained in school were expected to work on projects in working-class neighborhoods and suburbs.

Agitation in the factories was an activity in which the Trotskyist organization, *Voix Ouvrière,* had been engaged for a long time. It is impossible to judge with any degree of certainty the effect of this kind of agitation upon the workers and upon their decision to strike, to seize the factories, and to reject the proposals of the union leadership. What can be said, however, is that the UJCML had been active in some of the factories where the workers were most militant and that the union leadership, especially that of the CGT, was almost pathologically afraid of them. This was demonstrated on numerous occasions, for example when the leaders of the CGT attempted to prohibit the workers at the Renault factory in Billancourt from even talking with the students who had marched out there to demonstrate their solidarity.

As one might expect, opposition to the revolutionary goals of the student demonstrators was not limited to the left wing of the student milieu. One source of opposition was the smaller student union created with the assistance of the Gaullists as part of their campaign to destroy UNEF during the Algerian War. This union is the *Fédération Nationale des Etudiants de France* (FNEF).

The FNEF had always proclaimed itself to be apolitical. Nevertheless, the organization attracted an important segment of the student activists in the center and right wing of the political spectrum. It had thus been militantly anti-Marxist. And, despite the fact that the Gaullists aided in its founding and have consistently extended it preferential treatment, the FNEF has been strongly opposed to the education policy of the government.

During the events of May and June, the FNEF was caught in a bind. It shared the alienation from the government's education policy of those who manned the barricades and it was outraged by the action of the police. But it was also concerned about the participation of groups on the extreme Left and the active role played by its rival, UNEF. The national organization therefore adopted a policy which included nonendorsement of the demonstrations, condemnation of the violence and brutality of the police, and the issuance of a warning to the students that certain antilibertarian groups were attempting to use the demonstrations for their own purposes and that this would only serve the purposes of the government. But it did not denounce the barricades as such. The national office was also embarrassed by what it considered to be the overly reactionary and proadministration position of its chapter at Nanterre, the president of which subsequently resigned and joined a Gaullist action group.[19] The FNEF was so shaken by the widespread politization which occurred in May and June that it jumped on the bandwagon at its national meetings in July and repudiated what its leaders now called the "sterile policy of apoliticism." This signifies a shift to a much more generalized and intense antiregimist position.

The two most important student organizations on the extreme Right were the *Occident* and the *Etudiants de la Restauration Nationale*. The *Occident* is by far the most violent nonregimist political organization in France. Its propaganda output is limited to scribbling on the walls of buildings and *métro* stations. It is intensely anti-Marxist. But if the *Occident* has any positive political line it is as carefully guarded a secret as is its organizational structure. It recruits both students and nonstudents. The chief of the organization is reputed to be a nonstudent about thirty-five years old.

It was the *Occident* which broke up UNEF's national meetings in April, thus preventing Sauvageot's certain election as president of the organization. It was also the *Occident* which set fire to the headquarters of the student association affiliated with UNEF at the Sorbonne and which threatened to attack the campus at Nanterre. During the occupations the *Occident* led raids upon several of the provincial faculties.

The students involved in the revolt felt that Dean Grappin and Rector Roche had either bowed before the tactics of the *Occident* or simply used them as an excuse to close the Nanterre campus and the Sorbonne. Moreover, there was a widespread suspicion that the *Occident* included some right-wing Gaullists and that the government was lending it either active or passive encouragement. This suspicion was intensified when left-wing organizations were banned under a law forbidding the formation of civilian fighting forces while the *Occident* was permitted to continue to operate in its usual fashion.

Another right-wing group which opposed the student revolt was the student affiliate of the *Action Française,* the *Etudiants de la Restauration Nationale* (ERN). This organization, which claims to have anywhere between 1000 and 3000 members, differs from the *Occident* in several important respects. It is not a secret organization. It has a highly structured political ideology which is characterized by a desire to return to a monarchial form of government and by an intense anti-Marxism, antibourgeois liberalism, and anti-Semitism. And it is even more anti-Gaullist than it was antibarricade. While it was proud of its violent attacks against the occupied faculties in the provinces, its violence in Paris was exclusively directed against Gaullist campaigners. Another organization opposing the revolt, *Jeune Révolution,* contained a good number of students who had split with the ERN over the question of the monarchy. But it was much less visible during the affair than the ERN.

Nonstudent Organizations. Thus far we have considered the role of student organizations in the events of May and June. We shall now turn to a consideration of the role of teachers' organizations, labor unions, and the left-wing political parties.

Four organizations of some importance attempt to represent the interests and desires of university teachers in France. They are the *Fédération des Syndicats Autonomes de l'Enseignement Supérieur,* the *Société des Agrégés,* the *Syndicat National de l'Enseignement Supérieur* (SNESup), and the *Syndicat Général de l'Education Nationale* (SGEN). The first two of these organizations restrict their interest to problems of education and the material interests of their members. They are extremely conservative and disapproved of the occupations and the reforms demanded by the activist students and professors.

It was quite otherwise in the case of the SNESup, the university teachers' affiliate of the large *Fédération de l'Education Nationale* (FEN). The SNESup claims a membership of approximately 7000 university teachers or approximately one third of the total number of academics in France. Its national leaders tend to be quite young, many of them having recently passed through a stage of militancy in UNEF or other activist student organizations.

The SNESup worked so closely with UNEF that the student revolt would be more properly referred to as the student and teacher revolt. It served as a sponsor of most of the more important demonstrations. Its members were on the barricades. And it assumed a leadership position in the occupation of the universities. Its former Secretary General, Alain Geismar, a 29-year-old teacher at the Faculty of Science in Paris, was one of the three major leaders of the uprising along with Sauvageot and Cohn-Bendit. During the events of May, Geismar engaged himself on political issues further than the membership was prepared to go. He therefore resigned as Secretary General on May 27 in order to play a purely political role. But even after Geismar's resignation, the SNESup maintained its close alliance with UNEF.

The SGEN is an affiliate of the *Conféderation Française et Démocratique du Travail* (CFDT), a labor union of progressive Catholic inspiration. Unlike the SNESup, the SGEN represents teachers at all three levels of education. It claims to speak for 1000 university teachers. On both political and educational issues, the SGEN is more conservative than the SNESup. The organization supported the three specific demands of UNEF. It also participated in the general strike and demonstration of May 13 in protest against the action of the government and the police on the night of the 10th and 11th.

But as early as May 4 the SGEN condemned the resort to violence on the part of the students by refusing "any kind of solidarity with those groups whose incoherent action is compromising any true [educational] reform."[20] On the 6th, it called upon students, professors, and the unions to put an end to the "absurd violence."[21] And it took strong exception to the tactics employed by the SNESup, including the calling of the teachers' strike on May 3 and the threat to refuse to administer the *baccalauréat* examinations.

Ironically, the strongest support from organized labor which the students received came from the labor union with which the SGEN is affiliated, the CFDT. While the leaders of UNEF had almost no contact with the SGEN, they had extensive contact with, and support from, the leadership of France's second largest labor union. The leaders of the CFDT visited the faculties and held at least one joint press conference with UNEF's leaders (May 20). They also supported several of the later student demonstrations and the rally at the Charlety Stadium (May 27), all of which the SGEN refused to support.

The leadership of the social democratic *Confédération Générale du Travail — Force Ouvrière* (CGT-FO), the smallest of the major labor confederations, occupied a position somewhere between the very open and sympathetic leadership of the CFDT and the extremely hostile leadership of the Communist-controlled *Conféra-*

tion Générale du Travail (CGT). Like the SGEN, the CGT — FO denounced the violence of the students very early. But it also joined with the CFTD in supporting the student demonstration of May 24 and the Charlety rally.

By far the most hostile union was the CGT, the largest of the three confederations. The sole support of the CGT for the students was its participation in the strike and demonstration of the 13th. And even during this demonstration, the CGT insisted upon a physical separation between the students and the workers. As we have seen, the leaders of the CGT had a great fear of losing control over their membership, particularly their younger members, because of the example and the exhortations of the students. They were constantly denouncing the students' "excesses." The leadership of all of the unions participated in negotiations with the government and the employers. But it was upon the shoulders of the CGT's leaders that the students placed the major responsibility for betraying the workers and the entire revolution by selling out for minimal concessions.

Sharing the label of traitor was the Communist Party itself. We have already discussed the attitude of the party in our discussion of the *Union des Etudiants Communistes.* The party did support the three specific demands of UNEF and, like the CGT, it participated in the demonstration of the 13th. But, the Gaullists aside, it was the harshest critic of the barricades and the revolutionary goals of the students. It denounced the leaders of the student revolt for their "adventurism" and "incredible pretensions" before the elections. And after the crushing losses of the Left at the polls, it accused the students of playing into the hands of the Gaullists.

The only political party to completely support the student revolt was the *Parti Socialiste Unifié* (PSU). It attempted to justify its participation in the elections to the student activists by maintaining that it was not attempting to seek power the way the other parties were. It was only attempting to show the electorate that there were other options than those in the party platforms of the Communist Party and the Federation of the Left with whom it had refused electoral alliances. One of its two national secretaries, Marc Heurgon, assumes responsibility for youth affairs and has a very close relationship with the student members of his party who control the national apparatus of UNEF. While the leadership of the Communist Party was silent after the banning of the groups on the extreme Left and while Guy Mollet of the Federation of the Left issued a verbal protest, Heurgon announced that the PSU would place all of its facilities at the disposal of the groups should they wish to continue to operate. It is interesting to note that while it did not elect any deputies, the PSU was the only party of the Left to gain votes over the last election. Its appeal to the electorate doubled.

New Structures Resulting from the Uprising. As we have seen, the core of organizational support for the revolt came from the *Mouvement du 22 Mars*, the *Jeunesse Communiste Révolutionnaire*, the *Etudiants Socialistes Unifié*, UNEF, and the SNESup. While the catalytic role of the *22 Mars* and the attempts of the other organizations to supply some degree of coordination and direction were very important, these contributions must be placed within the context of a tremendous politization and desire for participation among a large segment of the student body which had not been oriented toward activism before the revolt.

The preexisting organizations were simply unprepared for the response to UNEF's leaders' call to action and were engulfed by a sea of activism. It must be remembered that the combined *national* membership of the *22 Mars*, the JCR, and the ESU is only between 2200 and 2900. Even UNEF's local organizations were completely incapable of channeling the activity of the participating students and in many cases were shattered by it. The national leaders operated in almost total isolation from the local organizations. The impact was so brutal that in many cases the national leaders did not even know whether or not some of the local organizations were still in existence. The revolt thus gave rise to the creation of its own structures.

The most proliferous of these were the *Comités d'Action* (CA). The first CAs were created on May 8. By the end of the month, there were 460 in the Parisian region.[22] There were neighborhood CAs, faculty CAs,[23] and CAs in factories, business establishments, hospitals, and even among actors. Some CAs were dominated by a given ideological tendency and some were not.

Since the purpose of the CA was to provide some kind of structure and coordination for those who wished to participate in the struggle, it was obviously necessary to coordinate the CAs. Theoretically, a center on rue Serpente in the 6th Arrondisement coordinated the neighborhood and faculty CAs while another at a branch of the Sorbonne (Censier) in the 5th Arrondisement coordinated the others. In practice, a third center was created at the *Ecole des*

Beaux Arts. There was thus the problem of coordinating the centers of coordination.

Since all policy-making powers were lodged in General Assemblies of the CAs to which each CA sent representatives, and since the personnel of the centers of coordination were changed each week, the role of the coordination centers was limited to the dissemination of propaganda. *ACTION*, the quasi-official newspaper of the revolt supported by UNEF and the SNESup, was produced at rue Serpente. It was not the elected members of the center which did this, however, but a permanent editorial staff working under the direction of J-P Vigier. Vigier, a researcher at the National Research Center, was a former Communist who had been expelled from the party for his participation in the *Comité Vietnam National.* He was extremely prominent during the crisis and managed to produce about twenty issues of the newspaper. The center at the *Ecole des Beaux Arts* issued the imaginative posters of the revolt and the center at Censier issued tracts.

Within the universities themselves, several interesting kinds of structures were created. The first were the strike (*comités de grève*) or occupation (*comités d'occupation*) committees. These committees were responsible for setting the ground rules which governed in the occupied faculties and for organizing the defense of the faculties. They were created immediately after the faculties were seized by the students and the professors.

Once the faculties were under occupation, the students set about creating model structures which would satisfy their demands for participation in the regular decision-making process and for the veto power over unfavorable decisions. Students in the various sections and disciplines of the faculties, who constituted the *comités de base,* elected representatives to all-faculty general assemblies. These assemblies, in some cases in conjunction with parallel assemblies elected by sympathetic professors, created structures which replaced the traditional centers of power in the university — the professors' *Conseils de l'Université,* the deans, the rectors, and the Minister of Education.

These structures were called the *Commissions Paritaires.* Generally the students asked for equal representation with the professors plus a veto power. The SNESup was on record as favoring this formula. But in some faculties, such as the Faculty of Science in Paris, the professors balked and attempted to receive greater representation for themselves. Where agreements were reached between students and professors, elections were held for the *Commissions*. The earliest and most successful experiences took place in the provinces, particularly in the Faculties of Medicine at Lille, Poitiers, Limoges, Toulouse, Rennes, and Nantes.[24] But before the occupations were terminated such *Commissions* had also been elected in at least three Parisian faculties — Law, Science, and Political Science.

The results of the elections at the Parisian Faculties of Law and Science reflected the radicalization of the student body which had occurred during the revolt. The Faculty of Law had traditionally been the stronghold of conservative and right-wing student activists. The local chapter of the *Fédération Nationale des Etudiants de France* had been stronger than that of UNEF. Yet the most extreme ticket of candidates, the one submitted by the strike committee, won an overwhelming victory by receiving approximately 57 per cent of the votes. The most conservative ticket, which enjoyed the backing of the FNEF, received only approximately 21 per cent of the votes. A third reform ticket which was ideologically between the two received approximately 23 per cent. What makes the victory of the strike committee so impressive is that the election had been well publicized and 12,500 students, about 60 per cent of those regularly enrolled, came to the Faculty to vote.[25]

Since 1956, the Faculty of Science has been the stronghold of students who have fought against the politization of UNEF. Once again, however, the radical ticket submitted by the strike committee won. But here it received only a plurality of 38 per cent because it was opposed by a second extreme ticket. This ticket received 28 per cent, giving the two extreme tickets a majority of 66 per cent. Two more moderate tickets received 18 per cent and 14 per cent. This victory was less impressive than that at the Faculty of Law because only 6211 students or something inferior to 20 per cent of the regularly enrolled voted. Voting was much higher among the two lowest ranks of teachers at the Faculty, the *assistants* and the *maîtres-assistants,* where 1313 or an incredible 79 per cent participated in the voting for their representatives. Again, the most extreme ticket which supported the positions of the national office of the SNESup received a plurality of approximately 37 per cent.[26]

Before leaving the structures within the universities, something should be said about the substantive nature of the activities within the occupied faculties. To be sure, political organizations had their literature tables, showed movies, and held meetings to which all were invited. But the academic work did not cease. Sympathetic teachers were encouraged to work in very small groups with their students and extend the individual attention which was unknown under the normal operating conditions of the faculties. And seminars and discussions were held on problems of educational reform, on subjects relating to areas of study which the students therein felt were important but which were not treated in the formal programs which heretofore existed, and on general social, political, and economic problems. It was this kind of learning experience, in which everything was open to question, that the students were referring to when they called for the establishment of *l'université critique*.

A major project which the students and the professors were preparing was the *université d'été* (summer university). This would have served two purposes. First, it would have been an attempt to invite workers and farmers into the university to give them both practical training and a political education. Second, it was designed to permit pedagogical experimentation. Approximately two weeks of sessions were held at the Faculty of Science in Paris before it was taken by the police.

Three other extra-university structures are worthy of brief mention. *Comités de Liaison Etudiant-Ouvrier* and *Comités de Liaison Etudiant-Ouvrier-Paysan* were created to facilitate and encourage communication and joint action between students, workers, and farmers. At the National Theater of France, *le Théâtre de l'Odéon*, the students held a Free Tribune to which workers and the general citizenry were invited to come to discuss the revolt and general political problems. In fact, such discussions were held daily and nightly on the streets of the Latin Quarter. The discussions in the Theater, but especially the spontaneous discussions in the streets, proved to be one of the most fascinating aspects of the revolt. The traditional aloofness of the Parisians seemed to have disappeared during the months of May and June. Lastly, there was some attempt to create a loosely structured Revolutionary Movement which would provide a completely new and broadly aggregative political structure for the recently politicized and for those older political activists who found the pre-existing political organizations unattractive or insufficient.

In conclusion, two points should be stressed. First, there was no clear agreement or idea among the participants on the specifics of the political regime which would replace the present one. As should be obvious by now, the contention that the revolt was the work of the

Communist Party in a violent bid for power is very far from the reality of the situation.

Four general lines of agreement among the participants can be delineated. First, there was a general indignation over the behavior of the government and the university administration and a unanimous acceptance of the three specific demands of UNEF: the release of the jailed students and the dropping of all criminal proceedings against other students, the removal of the police from university premises, and the opening of the faculties. Second, there was general agreement that the Gaullists had to go and that the only effective way of bringing this about was the confrontations in the streets in which the regime would clearly demonstrate its brutish nature. Third, there was a general agreement that French society was in need of basic changes. French social institutions were viewed as inequalitarian, extremely hierarchical and authoritarian, and completely ill-adapted to the modern world. What was needed was the construction of a society in which egoistic and exploitative social relationships would be replaced by cooperative and humanistic ones, inequality by equality, and extreme hierarchy and authoritarianism by decentralization and participation. Fourth, there was a widespread disenchantment with parliamentary democracy because of its unresponsiveness and toleration of social injustice. Many of the students viewed the major parties of the Left in much the same way that Sorel viewed the "parliamentary socialists" of his day. It didn't really matter to them who won the elections since they were convinced that nothing would be changed anyway.[27] Participation in the elections, in which most of the activists were not entitled to vote, was viewed as a betrayal of the revolution.[28]

The second major point is that the magnitude of student participation and the participation of the workers took almost everyone by surprise. The exception was perhaps Cohn-Bendit and the extremely small group of students around him who shared his Sorelian theories. But all of the other pre-existing organizations unexpectedly found themselves riding the tiger of a spontaneous wave of political and social consciousness which extended itself to workers and young people in almost all endeavors. The revolt thus generated a mass of overlapping and uncoordinated or ill-coordinated structures which served as experiments in the search for new modes of participation in a society and a university which heretofore had offered precious few.

III

Why Did it Happen?:

The Causes and Accomplishments of the Revolt

Before the night of the 10th and the 11th, a night now referred to as the "Night of the Barricades," it is doubtful that many of the student demonstrators thought that the students stood a chance of reversing the regime or even thought in terms of such a reversal. Before the battle actually began, Sauvageot, Cohn-Bendit, and Geismar implied that they would be willing to discuss grievances with responsible decision-makers if incarcerated students were granted an amnesty. After that night, after the huge manifestation of disapproval of the governments' action by the unions on the 13th, and most particularly after the workers began to strike and to seize the factories, there was no longer any thought of negotiating. What began as a massive angry protest became an attempt to bring down the regime. Why?

In a study of UNEF and French student activism which was completed before these events, this author indicated that there are three general reasons for the high degree of student unrest in France.[29] First, there is the authoritarianism of the social institution to which the young person is subjected before he enters the university — the family, the church, and the schools. By the time he enters university, the desire for independence and self-assertion is extremely strong. He is ready to cast off the yoke. Second, there is the traditional role of the French intellectual as the social critic and the fighter for social justice. Coupled with the strength of political ideals in France (ideology far from dead in this *industrialized* society), this tradition has had a heavy impact upon the student milieu. Third, the system of higher education itself has provided most important stimuli. As we have given extensive treatment to the causes of student activism in France in our previous work, we shall limit our discussion here to a brief enumeration of some of the difficulties in the educational system.

Since the Second World War, UNEF has not ceased to be critical of the educational system and to make proposals for its reform. These criticisms and proposals have received the support of the vast majority of students. Five general lines of criticism have been of supreme importance.

1. *The French university is an inequalitarian institution.* French society, which pays lip service to the value of equality is, in fact, highly stratified and inequalitarian with very limited opportunity for upward mobility. This is reflected in, and reinforced by, recruitment into the system of higher education. In 1961–62, children from working class families made up only 6 per cent of the university student population.[30] UNEF has called for a "democratization" of the educational system. It has supported the Langevin-Wallon proposals for equalitarian reforms at the primary and secondary levels and has called for more adequate systems of financial assistance and student housing and benefits at the university level.

2. *The French university is deprived of sufficient resources.* The budget of the French university is determined by the government in Paris. Education has ranked low on the priorities of the government and students and teachers have been made the victims of governmental austerity. There are not enough classrooms and the existing ones are hopelessly overcrowded. Library facilities are inadequate. There are not enough teachers. In 1961–62, the student-teacher ratio was an incredible 27:1. By 1965–66, it had been reduced to 22:1 but this is still extremely high.[31] University housing facilities are inadequate. In 1965–66, they accommodated only about 17 per cent of the student body.[32] Students who are not fortunate enough to obtain such housing are obliged either to live with their families and continue in a dependency relationship or rent private rooms. And any kind of decent private room goes for an exhorbitant rent, especially in Paris. Financial assistance is inadequate. Approximately 20 per cent of the students receive scholarships. In 1964–65, UNEF reported that only 45 per cent of the students from working class families received scholarships. And a study conducted at the University of Lille revealed that in no socioeconomic category do scholarships cover even 25 per cent of the aggregated expenses of students.[33]

UNEF has called for greater expenditures from the government for the construction of more physical facilities and the hiring of more teachers. It has also called for the implementation of a system of sustaining scholarships for all students regardless of the financial situation of their families. This would both assure students from lower class families of the financial means of obtaining an education and render possible a higher degree of independence from parents for students coming from wealthier families. UNEF has attacked the government for investing so much of the resources of the country in a nuclear strike force while depriving its universities of sufficient resources.

3. *The structure and pedagogy of the university are not conducive to either effective teaching or effective research in modern disciplines.* The high student-teacher ratio in French universities is not so much the cause as the reflection of an impersonal and authoritarian pedagogical tradition. The almost exclusive teaching technique, at least in the humanities and social sciences, is the large lecture course. At the undergraduate level, almost no importance is attached to communication between the students and the professor. The professor is there to dispense knowledge and the students are there to absorb it and to regurgitate it on examinations at the end of the year. Students are judged solely on the basis of these one-shot examinations. UNEF has made concrete proposals for the kind of learning experience it feels would be more valuable.[34] In the process it has called into question the entire structure of the university, substantially unchanged since the Napoleonic reforms. It has called for the elimination of the traditional system of faculties and grafted-on technical schools (*grandes écoles*) and institutes and the institution of divisions and departments conforming to modern conceptions of academic disciplines. It has called for the elimination of the degree process known as the *agrégation* for the preparation of French academics and the substitution of a program which would place greater emphasis upon pedagogical formation. And it has called for smaller classes, more individual attention, and a more positive role for the student in the educational process.

It has, moreover, firmly opposed the recent Fouchet Reforms as an attempt to substitute inexpensive partial solutions for real renovation. In fact, in its modification of the degree system, the Fouchet Plan has caused a great deal of unrest among people who have taken or are working toward the traditional first degree, the *licence*. They simply do not know what it will be worth. This was one of the issues raised in November at Nanterre. Another measure announced by the government on April 3, limitation of access to the university even among those students who pass the *baccalauréat* examination, has been viewed in the same light. It is easier to cut the number of students who will have access to a university education than to reform the university and invest in it.

4. *The French system of higher education is too highly centralized and too authoritarian.* All important decisions made in the French

university system are either made by the Minister of Education or require his approval. The participation of professors is very limited. And the participation of students is nonexistent except in the area of student insurance. At one time students played an important role in decision-making in the area of student benefits. They were deprived of this by the Gaullists. And while student representatives help to gather evidence for disciplinary proceedings, they have no voice in the judgments.

As we have seen, the situation in the classroom is perceived as being oppressively authoritarian. The same perception exists when it comes to the campuses and the housing complexes (*cités universitaires*). The rules are made at the top without any student participation. For a long time UNEF has demanded a role in the decision-making processes both in the faculties and at the *cités*. In February, 1968, UNEF called upon students to disregard the rules against visits between the sexes and political and student union activity at the *cités* and the campuses. The campaign was followed throughout France and in some cases minor concessions were made. But no real attention was ever paid to UNEF's demand that students be allowed to participate in decisions at the faculties, a demand which encountered strong opposition within the academic community as well as in the Ministry.

During the occupations of May and June the students attempted to establish four principles: a) local autonomy for the faculties and the *cités* with no strings attached to funding by the government, b) student control over the administration of the *cités* and housing complexes of the campuses, c) student and professorial control over decisions taken at the faculties with the students possessing the right of veto, and d) the right of free political and student union activity in all university areas.

5. *Job opportunities for university graduates are inadequate.* There is an extremely serious lack of coordination between the output of the universities and the recruitment demands of both the private and public sectors in France. The situation is especially acute for students who take degrees in humanities and social sciences at the faculties of letters. A notorious case is that of the sociologists. While the discipline is becoming extremely popular there are very few research and teaching posts open to the graduates. But the problem exists even for the students in science. A teacher in the mathematics program at the Faculty of Science in Paris reported to this writer that of the approximately 1600 students who anticipated taking

a degree in his program in 1968 only approximately 200 had found jobs as of June.

In sum, French students have been severely alienated by their educational system. They resent its inequalitarianism and point out that it is inconsistent with the espoused values of French democracy. They resent its deprivation of sufficient resources and point out what they deem to be the distortion of values in a society which is willing to make a great investment in the development of nuclear weaponry and delivery system while rigorously holding the line on investment in education. They resent what they view to be a shortchanging in terms of the content of their education and professional formation when compared with that in certain other countries — particularly the United States. They resent what they interpret to be the excessive centralization and authoritarianism of the system and their exclusion from active participation in the learning and decision-making processes. And they resent the waste of human resources which is entailed in the present system. For it is a fact that, despite the rigorous preselection processes at the primary and secondary levels and the rigor of the *baccalauréat* examinations, only one out of three students who enter a French university even takes the first degree. And many of those who do take degrees find that their academic training is of little value in the marketplace.

Since the system is under the centralized control of the government, the students have placed the blame for this situation upon the government. UNEF, as the most highly representative student organization in the country, has attempted to convince the government of the gravity of the problems and of the need for reform and heavier investment. Despite the fact that the Gaullist Minister of Education admitted that the university system was in a state of crisis as early as Ocober, 1964, the government has consistently rejected the proposals of the students.

But the Gaullists have not contented themselves with simply rejecting the proposals. Because UNEF took a position against the war in Algeria and continues to take positions on political and social issues, the government has taken measures to attempt to destroy the organization. Since the spring semester of 1964, it has blocked all access to decision-makers. And when the students took to the streets to demonstrate for their demands in 1963 and 1964, the government banned the demonstrations and sent in the police and the CRS to beat them off of the streets.

As this author wrote before the events of May and June, the government had the resources to weaken UNEF seriously, to continue to reject its demands, and to drive the students from the streets through the use of violence. But we also pointed out that the combined policy of rejection of demands which were widely supported in the student milieu, of blockage of all the normal points of access for the articulation of these demands, and of the physical and often brutal suppression of attempts to publicize these demands in the streets was having consequences which no rational government could accept with equanimity. The most important consequences were the radicalization of UNEF and the spread of an extremely strong antiregimist sentiment throughout the entire student milieu.[35]

To be sure, the activist tradition of the intellectual in France and the authoritarian nature of French socializing institutions have contributed to a high degree of student activism for some time. And the increasing militancy of students in other countries, particularly in Germany, did not pass unnoticed. But the impact of these factors was not sufficient to lead to a revolt on the scale of that of May and June, 1968. It was this smoldering antiregimist sentiment, ignited by the spark of Nanterre and fed by the chain of reaction and counterreaction, which blew up in the face of the Gaullists. And because they had severed lines of communication with the students, the Gaullists were caught completely unaware and attempted to explain the revolt as the work of "an international conspiracy," "totalitarian Communists," "anarchists," "small groups" (*groupuscules*), or just "criminals."

Indeed, the governmental actors who attempted to deal with the situation in early and mid-May were also the major architects of the hard-line policy toward the students. Louis Joxe, the Minister of Justice who refused to grant any kind of amnesty to the emprisoned students or in any way intervene in the proceedings against arrested students, was the Minister of Education who first applied sanctions against UNEF for its position on Algeria in 1960. Christian Fouchet, the Minister of Interior who denounced the students as criminals (*la pègre*) and ordered the police and the CRS to disperse the demonstrators and destroy the barricades in May, was the Minister of Education from 1962 to 1967 who reduced student participation in decision-making regarding student benefits to meaningless proportions and who cut off all channels of communication with UNEF. Alain Peyrefitte, the Minister of Education who followed Fouchet and who refused to reopen the Sorbonne or to negotiate with the students before the battle of the "Night of the Barricades," was the Minister of Information who imposed news censorship on student demonstrations and attempted to use the mass media as a weapon against the students during the confrontations of 1963 and 1964.

Both the students and the SNESup vow that they will renew the confrontations when the government attempts to reconvene the universities for the academic year 1968–69. While they will undoubtedly be true to their word, it is possible to assess the failures and the accomplishments of the revolt as of this month of August, 1968.

The most obvious failure of the student revolt was its inability to give rise to a successful revolution. The fatal blow was delivered by the workers when they accepted settlements negotiated by the union leadership. Moreover, the worst fears of the Communist Party were realized. While the revolt generated a great deal of sympathy in its early stages, the prolongation of the violent confrontations frightened the French electorate into a backlash vote which left the Gaullists stronger than ever and seriously weakened the parties of the Left. Secure in their election victory, the government drove the students and professors from the occupied universities.

But the revolt did accomplish two important things. First, old scores were settled with the hard-line Gaullists. The chickens came home to roost for Joxe, Fouchet, and Peyrefitte. All three were relieved of their positions before the end of the crisis.[36] René Capitant, one of the two Gaullist deputies who resigned his seat in the Assembly to protest the hard-liners' handling of the situation, has replaced Joxe in the Ministry of Justice. And more importantly, Edgar Faure, a non-Gaullist who twice served as a Radical Socialist premier during the Fourth Republic, has assumed control of the Ministry of Education. In his first appearance before the newly elected National Assembly, Faure said what most observers knew all along. The grievances of the students were legitimate and basic educational reforms along the lines which they have been calling for are necessary. Moreover, he promised to carry them out.[37]

Even more fundamental than the removal of unfavorable decision-makers has been the impact of the revolt upon the entire society. For too long French society has wallowed in a kind of apathetic and self-satisfied stagnation. The French call it *"je-m'en-foûtisme."* The price paid has been the perpetuation of social injustice and retardation in most areas of social and economic endeavor, of which education is only one example.

The student revolt has shaken that complacency profoundly. The workers have made it clear to the employers, the government, and the union leadership that they cannot be counted upon to accept passively whatever working conditions and material benefits French industry decides to bestow and French union leaders decide to accept. And young French people engaged in a multitude of professions were very responsive to the student revolt. Young doctors, young businessmen, young engineers were constantly talking about the confrontations and the possible and probable direction of reforms in their own places of work. Many of them participated in some kind of reform or action committee. Indeed, even President de Gaulle adopted the language of the revolt in his emphasis upon "participation." During the revolt, the traditional *"je-m'enfoûtisme"* and resignation of the French gave way to an extraordinary social and political consciousness which, if sustained, could lead to a profound transformation of a wide range of French institutions.

REFERENCES

1. Three sources have been invaluable in the construction of this chronology, the daily newsreporting of *Le Monde* and the chronologies appearing in *L'Evénement*, No. 29, Juin 1968 and *Partisans*, No. 42, Mai-Juin 1968.

2. Mouvement du 22 Mars, *Ce n'est qu'un Début, continuons le combat* (Paris: Francois Maspero, 1968), pp. 11–12. On the events at Nanterre and the Mouvement du 22 Mars see also "Daniel Cohn-Bendit et Jean-Pierre Duteuil" and "Le Mouvement du 22 Mars se définit" in *La Révolte Etudiante* (Paris: Editions du Seuil, 1968), pp. 60–72 and 118–123. This writer would like to thank the militants of the 22 *Mars* and the JCR at Nanterre who were kind enough to talk at length with him about the situation on their campus.

3. *Mouvement du 22 Mars*, p. 15.

4. *Ibid.*, p. 16.

5. *Le Monde*, 30 Mars 1968, p. 3 (translation mine).

6. The student was an officer of the *Fédération Nationale des Etudiants de France*. See the discussion of this organization in Part II.

7. Cited in *L'Evénement*, p. 26

8. The campus at Nanterre is under the jurisdiction of the Rector of the University of Paris.

9. Cited in *L'Evénement*, p. 27. On the question of police brutality see l'Union Nationale des Etudiants de France et le Syndicat National de l'Enseignement Supérieur, *Le livre noir des journées de mai* (Paris: Editions du Seuil, 1968). For an account somewhat more sympathetic toward the police see J-M Theolleyre, "Des accusations profondément ressenties par la police," *Le Monde, Selection Hebdomadaire*, du 1er au 7 Août 1968, p. 6.

10. The third major labor confederation is the *Confédération Française et Démocratique du Travail.* See Part II.

11. A *service d'ordre,* for which there is no exact English translation, is a group of people charged with preventing violence.

12. The familiar expression *chien-lit,* which became very popular in France after de Gaulle used it, has several meanings. It can mean a shirt-tail which is not tucked in a man's trousers, someone whose shirt-tail is exposed, a carnival mask, a masquerader, a piece of paper surreptitiously attached to someone's back as a gag, and, in its most literal sense, someone who defecates in his bed. No one dared ask de Gaulle to specify which he meant. The students responded to de Gaulle's remark by printing up posters with a sketch of the General's head and the words *"La chien-lit c'est lui"* (He is the *chien-lit*).

13. There are conflicting stories in the case of Gilles Tautin's death. The "official" story was that he jumped into the Seine in an attempt to escape the CRS. The students generally believe that he was forced into the river since he did not know how to swim and was carrying an expensive camera. They claim to have gathered eye-witness testimony to the effect that the CRS forced him into the water and did nothing to save him despite the fact that he was obviously drowning. They also claim that they sent this testimony to *Le Monde* and that the newspaper did not print it.

14. On the thought of Cohn-Bendit see "Daniel Cohn-Bendit s'entretient avec Jean-Paul Sartre: 'notre action a prouvé que la spontanéité populaire gardait sa place dans le mouvement social' " in *La Révolte étudiante, op. cit.,* pp. 86–97 (reprinted from *Le Nouvel Observateur,* 20 Mai 1968). Sartre publicly engaged the students in discussions at least twice during the revolt, once at the Sorbonne and once at the *Cité Universitaire Internationale.* His philosophy has had an important influence in the student milieu where he is accorded more reverence than perhaps any other living personage. Contrary to what many of the press reports would have one believe, almost none of the major figures in the revolt had read the works of Herbert Marcuse.

15. For a comprehensive treatment of UNEF consult the author's Ph.D. dissertation, *Students in Politics: l'Union Nationale des Etudiants de France* (Yale University, 1968) and forthcoming book (Basic Books, 1969).

16. See "Que Sont les Comités d'Action Lycéens?", *Partisans,* No. 42, Mai-Juin 1968, pp. 219–236.

17. *Ibid.*

18. The exact size of the UEC before the events of May and June is unknown and estimates vary widely. A reliable source reports that in 1965 it had between 2500 and 3500 members. But there were numerous expulsions and defections in 1965 and 1966. What is certain is that the UEC has not improved its recruitment possibilities by its actions during the student revolt.

19. We wish to thank the individuals at the national offices of the FNEF for their very kind cooperation.

20. From a *communiqué* reprinted in the SGEN's *Syndicalisme Universitaire,* No. 462, 9 Mai 1968, p. 5.

21. "Le SGEN dans le crise," *Syndicalisme Universitaire,* No. 463, 16 Mai 1968, p. 4.

22. "Les Comités d'Action," *Partisans,* No. 42, Mai-Juin 1968, p. 237.

23. The word "faculty" here as throughout this essay refers to institutions, such as the faculty of law or of science, and not to the teaching corps as it generally does in English.

24. *Le Monde,* 15 Juin 1968, p. 8. At Lille, Limoges, and Poitiers the Commissions enjoyed the strong support of the deans.

25. *Le Monde,* 20 Juin 1968, pp. 6–8.

26. *Le monde,* 30 Juin–1 Juillet 1968, p. 6.

27. On the images of the left-wing political parties among the student activists see A. Belden Fields, *Students and Politics: l'Union Nationale des Etudiants de France, op. cit.*

28. The voting age in France is 21. Since students enter the university when they are 18 or 19, a good number of them were under the voting age. But even some who were 21 were disenfranchised by the application of a provision whereby one had to have been 21 by January 1968 in order to vote. As one might have anticipated, the highest rate of abstention among registered voters was in the Latin Quarter.

29. For a much fuller treatment of the subject consult Fields, *op. cit.*

30. *Annuaire statistique de la France 1963 (résultats de 1962),* (Paris: Institut National de la Statistique et des Etudes Economiques, 1963), p. 57.

31. The ratio for 1961–62 was computed by the author from data in *L'Année politique, économique, sociale, et diplomatique en France 1965,* p. 398. The ratio for 1965–66 is from Bertrand Girod de l'Ain, "L'Enseignement dans neuf pays 'développés,' " *Le Monde Sélection Hebdomadaire,* du 10 au 16 Mars 1966, p. 7. The ratio in the United States in 1965–66 was 13:1.

32. Computed by the author from data in *L'Année politique, économique, sociale, et diplomatique en France 1965,* p. 400.

33. L'Union Nationale des Etudiants de France, *L'Allocation d'études* (Paris, 1965), p. 4.

34. See L'Union Nationale des Etudiants de France, *Manifeste pour une réforme démocratique de l'enseignement supérieur* (Paris, 1964).

35. See Fields, *op. cit.*

36. Also relieved of his functions was the Minister of Information, Mr. Gorse, who assured the nation on May 18th that " 'The *enragés* are being listened to and followed less and less. From now on the students will be preoccupied with their examinations.' " Cited in *L'Evénement,* No. 29, Juin 1968, p. 30 (translation mine).

37. See *Le Monde Sélection Hebdomadaire,* du 25 au 31 Juillet 1968, p. 6.

GUIDO MARTINOTTI

The Positive Marginality:
Notes on Italian Students
in Periods of Political Mobilization[*]

In 1968, bitter student riots in major Italian universities focused world attention on the discontent that had erupted to the surface. Numerous questions were raised about the roots and significance of the university students' movement; none of them have been easy to answer. For one thing, accounts of student unrest are widely scattered, indeed often unavailable. Furthermore, protests and agitation have taken such different forms and focused on such diverse issues that it is difficult to explain them in any consistent manner. Nevertheless, it is the author's belief that an explanation may be possible if one looks at the university students' activities as the result of conflict and inconsistency between the *transient* role of the student and his more *permanent* social status.

Medieval Origins

The Italian university traces its origins back to the medieval universities, such as the University of Bologna, established in the thirteenth century. Because the students came from many different areas, they were aliens in their place of study. They did not, according to the theory of the personality of the law, come under local jurisdiction and so formed guilds for their own protection as outsiders. Town-and-gown riots were not uncommon, ranging from scuffles to open battles in which citizens and students were killed. Occasionally these conflicts reached such proportions that the students fled the town (as they did in Bologna in the early days), threatening to open a new university elsewhere. From the start, therefore, the university students formed a separate community and were sharply differentiated from other elements of society.

[*] Written autumn, 1968.

At the same time, students were accustomed to privilege. Coming generally from well-to-do families, they were able to rely on the goodwill and protection of the higher political authorities. As independent gentlemen, they dominated their lecturers, whom they hired,[1] and they were able to afford expensive festivities.[2] Students were an economic asset to the town; their conflicts were mostly with the lower-class urban population. It should also be pointed out, however, that a substantial minority of pupils held scholarships, and that the university attracted a true intellectual proletariat consisting of brigands, traveling poets, and minstrels.[3]

To sum up, there were four characteristics of early university life in Italy that are significant even today:

1. The students had a marginal position vis-à-vis the population of the town in that they were aliens occupying a temporary role;
2. The higher authorities gave the students support in view of their family backgrounds and probable future roles;
3. The conflicts with the community resulted from the privileged position of students; and
4. There were two groups of students: those from the higher strata of society and the "intellectual proletarians." The change in the relative proportions from these two groups has in recent years been a cause of unrest in the universities.

The Risorgimento

To Italy, the Napoleonic period offered a model of a unitary state that might be created in Italy on the overthrow of the incumbent rulers. The Napoleonic years led to the wars of independence that marked the period between the Restoration in 1815 and the unification of the Italian states in 1861.

This period of the *Risorgimento* was a romantic era, stressing the heroic individualism of youth. The universities were troubled by political outbreaks, which occurred at ten-to twenty-year intervals. Thus, the first uprisings were in 1820–21, then again in the early thirties, again in 1848–49, and finally in 1858–61. The students who were active in one period often became the leaders of successive coups and eventually outstanding statesmen in the unified Kingdom of Italy: They included Misley, Carcano, de Cristoforis, Correnti, and Zanardelli. The young radicals from the Lombard universities, who had in the early twenties troubled the Austrian government, became the moderates who opposed the irregular bands of Garibaldi that challenged the Italian government for a long time after the unification.[4]

Notes on Italian Students in Periods of Political Mobilization

According to some authors, such as Michels, the independence movement was an expression of the rising urban bourgeoisie.[5] Others, among them Rota, argue otherwise, pointing to popular participation in voluntary militias and to the urban insurrections of the period. Two things are certain, however. *Popular* support for the independence struggle was urban, probably coming mostly from the lower-middle class. The peasants opposed independence, especially at first. This popular participation increased with the growth of the industrial working class. At the end of the struggle, the first workers' association supported Mazzini and especially Garibaldi, who was something of a socialist. There is also little doubt that the *leading* forces of the *Risorgimento* were the urban bourgeoisie, the aristocracy, and the intellectuals, from which strata the students were largely drawn. Thus contemporary accounts of "troubles" in the universities tell that students were included among the political suspects listed from the central government in Vienna.

After the Restoration, the Austrian authorities adopted a restrictive policy toward the universities, intended to produce civil servants loyal to the Emperor. Student admissions were screened and the politics of professors scrutinized. Even subject matter was controlled; for example, at Pavia the appointment of a professor of German idealist philosophy was vetoed in 1825 while in 1821 Austrian positivism had been imposed on the teaching of civil law in Padua.

At Pavia, however, the results were not what the government had intended. The Collegio Ghislieri[6] admitted only "sons of those who served the state well in the army, or in the civil service,"[7] and was run on the pattern of Austrian military schools. Nevertheless, at the first insurrection in Piedmont in 1821, seven of its sixty students crossed the border to join the voluntary brigades of patriots. Eighty-four students from other parts of the university also crossed over to join the Piedmontese army, kissing the ground on the other bank of the river when they got there.[8] From then on the students at Pavia — both in and out of Collegio Ghislieri — became more "political" and took to harassing the police. Increasingly, faculty and college administrators sided with them until in 1834, the Reverend Tomaso Bianchi, the radical vice-rector of Ghislieri, was arrested and committed suicide in jail. More and more students prepared for the insurrections until the study of foreign revolutionary literature at night came to replace the official curricula.

Although the students took an active role in political agitation, the police remained remarkably permissive. The Collegio Ghislieri was never closed, and the university remained a haven for the diffusion of ideas, even when they were disliked by the administration. Apparently the authorities were loath to interfere, and this observation is indicative of the three-way relationship that existed between the students, their families, and the central authorities of the state. The students came from families of privilege who were no doubt able to exercise a restraining influence on the authorities, even in the case of radical student activities.

Despite their conservative connections, students in 1848 supported the nationalist revolution led by the rising Italian bourgeoisie under the auspices of the Pope and the House of Savoy. One student battalion marched across the northern lands abandoned by the retreating Austrian armies and participated in the battle of Curtatone and Montanara with high losses.[9] Though there were some exceptions — such as that of the university battalion in Pisa which helped in "repressing disorder"[10] — they were very rare. These episodes suggest certain hypotheses about the political involvement of the students during the *Risorgimento*. First, students became politically active only in a crisis; routine politics did not involve them. Second, the political orientation of students was consistent with their family status: They were the sons of the bourgeoisie and behaved accordingly. Students were more concerned with the question of national unification than with the social issues raised by the *Risorgimento*. From this perspective, political participation by students during the *Risorgimento* was essentially a matter of formation of a new ruling class through a national revolution. As such, it merits comparison with situations in the new nations of the contemporary Third World.

After National Unification: From Socialism to Fascism

The unification of the Italian state was achieved in 1861 when the regular armies of the House of Savoy, coming from the north, joined the irregular troops of the popular hero, Garibaldi, who had conquered the southern regions. Withstanding the pressures to form a democratic republic in the south, Garibaldi submitted to the King, and the *Risorgimento* ended with the final victory of the "war of the king" over the "war of the people."

Some parts of Italy remained, however, under foreign domination, notably Rome and Trieste, and many problems were unresolved. In particular, the end of the national war of liberation led to the formation of groups of agitators, "social outcasts who are always in the front lines of every revolution and counterrevolution, who capitalize on disorder and who . . . as capitani, carbonari or fascist squadristi, have always been one of the most dangerous and explosive components of Italian society."[11] How many students were among the dissidents is difficult to say. If I am correct in concluding that the students who fought in the *Risorgimento* were an important part of the new elite, the great majority of students must have been integrated easily into the new state. They do not appear to have played a major part in the endemic uprisings of the first years after the unification.

As the economy developed rapidly, and with industrialization and the first stirrings of socialism, the issue of national liberation yielded to social questions. University youth increasingly came to realize that, though the nationalist ideal had been achieved, the national state was unable to solve the social questions which followed. This was a blow to students' idealism, and it led the new generation to concentrate more and more on the possible participation of the progressive bourgeoisie (especially the intelligentsia) in workers' and socialist organizations. As Michels put it: "The university youth in Italy . . . seems a living disproof of all the economic laws, and especially of historical materialism."[12]

Our analysis of student participation in the socialist movements will focus on three main issues: (a) "bourgeois socialism," namely the participation of middle-class individuals in Italian socialist organizations; (b) the question of the "intellectual proletariat," namely the role of students and other intellectuals in the Italian social structure; and (c) the reliability of students, and of other bourgeois groups, as revolutionary forces allied to working-class movements.

As early as 1869 Bakunin, back in Geneva from Italy, gave the Italian university students the leading role in the social revolution. Aware of the inconsistency between the class determinism of his ideology and his call on the students, he instructed them not to patronize the working class, but to help it find its class consciousness.[13] Actually, as Michels remarks, Bakunin was forced to appeal to the students, for he had to operate in the social environment of southern Italy where the proletariat was passive or hostile and where an educated bourgeoisie was favorably inclined and active.

The students' participation in socialist movements was indeed remarkable. According to Michels, students were one of three major groups represented in the First International in Italy. (The other two were urban proletarian and artisan groups and the landless rural population.)[14] The first political club founded by Bakunin in Naples in 1865 was composed mainly of young students. Some of the leaders of the movement were either students, such as Enrico Bignami, Enrico Malatesta, or Andrea Costa, or young graduates, such as Cafiero, Covelli, or Turati. A disproportionate number of students were to be found in the socialist party. Many Italian intellectuals of the period had similar leanings: in 1903, academic men formed 85 per cent of the socialist group in Parliament. That so many of the leading intellectuals and academic men of the time were socialists could not fail to have an effect on the students themselves. Economic factors can help explain student involvement in socialism. At this time, there was a dearth of suitable jobs for educated persons, and students belonged to what Michels called the intellectual proletariat.[15] Thus, without jobs and without attachments to organizations, students constituted a rather fluid urban group highly concerned with politics.

It is interesting to note that the socialist leanings of the student groups were a challenge to Marxist revolutionary theory and had to be explained or assimilated into it. On the one hand, the students supported socialist movements at a time when the proletariat was either absent or apathetic; on the other hand, from a classic theoretical point of view, the reliability of students in "hard times" was considered doubtful. Bakunin tried to resolve this dilemma on a voluntaristic and idealistic basis. To him, the middle-class sympathizer could become a real revolutionary only if he personally renounced, "once and for all, all the habits and vanities of the bourgeois way of life. [Then he could] enter unconditionally into the ranks of the workers and swear eternal hatred of the bourgeoisie."[16] Without such an act of renunciation, Bakunin felt, a member might support the workers, but in a pinch would inevitably betray the party. Marx was even less optimistic. He called the Italian socialist movement "a group of uprooted, the garbage of the bourgeoisie. All the so-called sections of the International in Italy," he stated, "are directed by lawyers with no clientele, by ignorant physicians with no patients, by students addicted to playing billiards."[17]

It was soon to become all too clear that the problem was more than ideological; as "hard times" came — first with the nationalistic outbursts that accompanied Italy's intervention in World War I, and later with the advent of fascism — the good relations between students and the working class quickly deteriorated. This is not to say that all students became fascist or that all had been socialist before. It is impossible to quantify the degree of change; in each case, only minorities switched allegiances, but these minorities called the tune. Thus in 1921 Roberto Mondolfo could write that "student youth, today in large measure composed of enthusiastic followers of fascism and supporters of its antisocialist action, in the previous generation made a large contribution of intellect and fervor to the socialist movement."[18]

In the years immediately preceding World War I students were active in private squads of nationalistic strike-breakers. They were among the most vocal supporters of Italy's intervention in the great war. At one point, demonstrating students invaded the Parliament to press for a declaration of war. Notwithstanding the democratic experience fostered by contact with soldiers and the expectations of a new society, the theme of nationalism remained dominant in the ideals of the youth. After the war, "the students, who were raised in an atmosphere of passionate and exasperated patriotism, and fed for years and years with the accounts of battles and heroic deaths, [saw in] fascism the way to make their homeland powerful in the world. Fascism most easily found its recruits among students."[19]

During the 1920–21 civil war that brought fascism to power, students led the vigilante groups and squads which sided with Mussolini. The Avanguardia Universitaria and the Gruppi Universitari Fascisti (GUF) were formed, and the universities became a stronghold from which fascist commandos attacked the workers' institutions. As one fascist historian put it, the students were the most reliable of fascist supporters. When fascists gained control, the GUF became an arm of the Fascist Party.

The students who supported fascism were not the same people who had earlier supported socialism. We are here dealing with two different generations, one socialist and the other fascist. But they shared one thing in common. Both generations were revolutionary, opposed to the *status quo* in the late nineteenth century and in the second decade of the twentieth century. But we should ask why the politics of students changed from the far left to the far right.

Some of the causes of this change were cultural. Early twentieth century Italy was in ferment, with idealism reacting against the predominantly positivist culture of the preceding periods. This transformation took place at the expense of the socialist movement, which had supported the positivist orientation. A second crucial factor was the change in relative political position of the socialists.

In becoming integrated into the political system, the socialist party had increasingly accepted the "rules of the game," while the national fascist groups came to represent themselves as a genuine revolutionary force, the only force against the system. Thus, the different generations of students were consistent: They were always "disposed to risk life for a great cause," as Bakunin said. The national ideals of the *Risorgimento,* the social issues of the positivist era, the war, the fascism were all, in turn, "great causes" to the students of succeeding generations. Thus, the fears expressed by Bakunin, Kautsky, and other socialist theoreticians — that the progressivism of the students might be short-lived — were justified. They were justified because an important factor in explaining the political activity of the students is their peculiar status. Students can base their political beliefs on either of two inconsistent status positions, the one they occupy temporarily as intellectuals and quasi-proletarians and the middle-class status of their parents which most of them will achieve. This status inconsistency is one constant characteristic of the student group.

Students and Fascism

In his analysis of fascism, Treves emphasized that Mussolini's generation differed from the preceding war generation in that it had been born not in opposition to, but in agreement with the previous generation; thus it had not been obliged to oppose the elders' regime but had had simply to integrate youth into it.[20] The fascist ideologist Bottai supported this view when he noted that "the predominance of the elders and of the aged, continued until the advent of fascism. The *ex post facto* justifications were for years and years a strong dike against any . . . waves of juvenile enthusiasm. Mussolini overthrew the dike. Being young, he trusted those who were younger than himself."[21] One antifascist author has characterized the shift of youth toward fascism as a revolt against a "generation characterized by a homely politics, dedicated to increasing the national welfare."[22] All these explanations have in common a heavy emphasis on youth.

As it became increasingly clear that promises to the young generation could not be kept, fascism became more aligned with the conservative forces of the country. Thus "with the constitution of the first fascist government and the assumption of command by forty-year-old war veterans, the generations became clearly divided. On one side was the generation that could be included in the new conservative institutions, and on the other, the very young who had actively provoked a political upheaval, from which they were then excluded."[23] It is particularly among the latter groups that antifascism developed later on.

At first the fascist regime created a series of party organizations for youth, structured in terms of age groups. The Gruppi Universitari Fascisti (GUF), created in 1920, became a revolutionary organization. Later it was transformed into a nationwide student association with the task of "educating youth according to fascist doctrine."[24] One could rise in Fascist Party organizations through the GUF. Together with the opportunists and the careerists, some very dynamic students were active in GUF. They worked on newspapers, were interested in theater and the arts, and therefore had occasion to reflect on both cultural and political matters. Gradually, during the second decade of the fascist regime, a nonconformism developed inside the GUF that later turned into outright antifascism.

Actually, the regime left a certain leeway for nonconformist students to judge what was dangerous in the cultural realm, partly because of a half-recognized need to breed a dynamic new ruling class, and partly because of its (mostly verbal) antibourgeois ideology. This "leftist fascism" led some students to grasp the contradictions of the regime and, by a tortuous process, to develop an awareness of the real nature of fascism. This was later turned into active resistance against the regime.

Documentation of this process is found in a controversial book by Ruggero Zangrandi, *Il Lungo Viaggio Attraverso Il Fascismo* (*The Long Journey Through Fascism*). Zangrandi had been part of a group of *lyceum* students who published a student literary magazine edited by Mussolini's son, Vittorio. Obviously granted considerable latitude, this group started to develop a kind of leftist fascism critical of the conservative regime. They saw the discrepancy between the principles in which they believed and its reality. Little by little, Zangrandi and other friends (having left the university and no longer in direct contact with Vittorio Mussolini) enlarged their contacts all over Italy and developed their critique. In time, they formed a movement propounding a doctrine called "universal-fascism," a fascism with strong internationalist and socialist tendencies, which later became an outright *Partito Socialista Rivoluzionario*. Zangrandi, who had become an official in the Ministry of Popular Culture and directed a press agency, chose a tactic of "double standard." Openly the group appeared to advocate fascism, but underground it worked to create an opposition movement. In 1942 Zangrandi was arrested and deported to a German concentration camp, as were many others of his group.

Other documents also indicate the process by which the younger generation came to fight against fascism. The Littoriali, which were annual public contests established by the regime to foster fascist culture,[25] by 1937 had become occasions for outstanding students to come into contact with the politically active youth of the country, in a climate that was usually nonconformist or even revolutionary. Many participants in the Littoriali later became prominent in antifascist ranks. This has been often cited by neofascists as evidence of their opportunism. But the meaning is quite different: Zangrandi shows very clearly that an intellectual opposition emerged inside a dictatorial regime. And some of the Littoriali participants learned antifascism unconsciously. They discovered democracy rationally during a search for an ideal fascism.

Zangrandi's book has been criticized for his criticism of the old antifascist groups, the "true antifascists," whom he accused of remaining "too much at the window" during the last years of the fascist regime. His motives were ambiguous, and it is now difficult to distinguish the opportunism in his behavior from truly Machiavellian tactics against the fascist regime. His very ambiguity was typical of his generation; indeed, some of the young fascists, unable to solve the contradictions in their ideology, went voluntarily to war, a near-suicidal gesture. The position of Zangrandi and the groups he describes is a consequence of the anomalous situation of students in a dictatorial regime. The immediate condition of the student is bound to promote criticism and opposition to the regime, while at the same time his integration into the ruling class is actually increasing.

In any case, the student generation of the late thirties and the early forties developed a new political orientation. The social characteristics of students had not changed much from that of previous generations who had supported fascism. Nonetheless, in the new cultural and political context, students once more embraced the ideals of democracy and socialism.

The Period After World War II:

From Political System to Social Revolution

Since World War II, student activism has passed through two distinctive stages: The first extends from 1943 to approximately 1964–65; the second is limited to recent years.

In the first stage, a system of student political representation developed within the university structure. There was a temporary political equilibrium, followed by a crisis in this balance and eventual breakdown of the students' institutions. The second period is marked by a massive student revolt, particularly in 1967–68, and by new forms of political participation outside and against the institutional structures.

In the forty-five days between Mussolini's fall and the German takeover, a number of student associations were formed. Student groups participated in resistance against the Germans and the fascist republic hastily reconstituted in the northern regions.[26] After the war, in the enthusiasm that followed the end of twenty years of dictatorship, student associations sprouted everywhere. "The New Democracy must not be left wintering outside the academic citadel," wrote Paolo Ungari. "This was the battle cry of various student groups that had begun to form during the *Resistenza*. The ancient Masonic *Corda Fratres* was revived, along with the picturesque Goliardic 'orders,' which in the south of Italy often took the form of clubs of 'students and graduates,' much like typical 'gentlemen's clubs'."[27]

Two factors increased instability in the universities. First, a large number of students enrolled in the postwar period, the bulk of them war veterans, and former partisans. Second, the fascist prohibitions on traditional student feasts and ceremonies were dropped, and the festivities were revived with great enthusiasm and a somewhat naïve overestimation of their traditional value. This "Goliardic myth" played a strong role in shaping the political forces that were to develop. In the changed political and cultural climate, the popular image of the university student as a fun-loving son of the bourgeoisie, half-vacationing through the romantic years of study, became tinged with seriousness and political engagement.

At the beginning there were no formal parties through which university students c uld channel political activity, but only associations, clubs, faculty [8] or interfaculty committees, and other groups. Yet the demand for political a·tion was strong and could not be ignored. The first university natiᵓ ıal convention was held in Rome in 1946 and attended by "that u· ˌque generation of veterans, former partisans, and old students" re urning to studies interrupted by the war, and discovering, in community student life, "a passionate, collective and brotherly dimension of democracy."[29] Three major political forces were soon distinguishable: the *Federazione Universitaria Cattolica Italiana* (FUCI), representing the Catholic students; the *Liberi Goliardi*, which included the democratic center and the traditional Goliardic associations; and the so-called *Studenti Democratici,* composed of leftist groups.

The Forces in Play

Among these, FUCI was the only group that had a continuity with the prefascist era, having been founded at the end of the nineteenth century. Its aim was to deal with religious problems in a nondogmatic way that could compete favorably with the scientific and philosophical sophistication of the milieu. The Federation was probably more dependent on the Catholic church than on the political Catholic organization of the Christian Democratic Party. Later on, it yielded in the university arena to the *Intesa Universitaria,* an alliance of various Catholic groups, including the FUCI, and the CUD (*Centri Universitari Democristiani,* more directly dependent on the party organization), and the GIAC (*Gioventù Italiana di Azione Cattolica*), representing the Catholic Action.

Although born in an old tradition, the postwar Goliards were a new force; this group has been the most dynamic, controversial, and unstable of the three major forces. It originated through the incorporation of the local *Associazioni Goliardiche,* which had originally represented the gay student traditions. At the beginning, the Goliards (later organized into the *Unione Goliardica Italiana,* UGI) ranged from the moderate-conservative *Partito Liberale Italiano* (PLI), to the non-Marxist left, including the *Partito Repubblicano Italiano* (PRI), the later-dissolved *Partito d'Azione,* and the *Partito Socialista-Democratico Italiano* (PSDI). For a long period, the mythological Goliardic tradition weighed on the new group, keeping alive certain ludicrous elements within the movement. Politically, the Goliardi at first demanded a unitarian associative structure, refusing to recognize the legitimacy of partisan political divisions in the university.

The third group was radically new. Representing the Marxist students of the *Partito Comunista Italiano* (PCI) and the *Partito Socialista Italiano* (PSI), it was largely dominated by the former. This group had the advantage of underground resistance experience and was the most ideological and the best organized. Incorporated in 1948 as the *Centri Universitari Democratici Italiani* (CUDI), it was strong at the beginning, but lost power until, in 1955, it was dissolved after a poor showing in the election. CUDI was tied to the Community Party and to "syndicalism" — that is, a policy of opposing the administration and importing to the university the dialectic between workers and owners. In tactics, CUDI joined a united front with the other groups on such issues as antifascism and peace. In university politics, however, the communists were unable to formulate an original policy and spent much of their effort trying to steer larger political groups. They were rather ineffective and eventually found themselves attacked by the "New Leftists" of the present.

A fourth force came to play in the universities later — namely, the rightists or, as they like to call themselves, the "national students." At the beginning, they were rather marginal and took pride in illegal acts such as stealing Mussolini's corpse from the cemetery of Milan or occupying the broadcasting premises in Rome. Temporary movements like the *Fasci di Azione Rivolutionaria* (FAR) were formed, until in 1946 the so-called "neofascists" united in the *Movimento Sociale Italiano* (MSI). Significantly, the youth section of the party was called *Raggruppamento Giovanile Studenti e Lavoratori* (Young Students' and Workers' Group). In 1950 the *Fronte Universitario di Azione Nazionale* (FUAN) began. This organization was to gain a sizable portion of the university electorate, especially in the southern universities. It pressed for more assistance to students and opposed private Catholic universities. Since the FUAN remained at the margin of university politics, however, its action was limited to disturbing other groups, often through violence or collusion with reactionary professors and administrators.

At the first national convention in Rome in 1946, the relative strength of the groups was as follows: Left, 8 seats; FUCI, 7; Goliardi, 6. As we shall see, this was the last time the left group had a plurality.

The Issues

In the first congress after the war, two problems were particularly important: the role of university and students in the new Italian society, and the specific political structure needed for student representation. Of the two the second was the more prominent.

The Italian university is an old institution — with authoritarian relations between masters and students, with perpetual shortages of research means and of teachers, and assistants in relation to the rising number of students. The student is left entirely to himself and must merely pass a number of examinations, almost without time limit. The system is totally inefficient for teaching. It is satisfactory for a few very good (or very zealous) students who gain the inner circle of some master and also for the "collegiate" student, often of well-to-do middle-class origin, who wants social contacts and some kind of professional degree with a minimal amount of study. It is highly unsatisfactory for the great bulk of students.

All the flaws of the Italian university were apparent when the universities reopened after the war. On one hand, a crowd of enthusiastic students was eager to learn and to change everything; on the other hand, the academic institutions were traditional, though battered and as authoritarian as ever.

In the confrontation that ensued, the reform of the university became the central issue in the students' fight. There were divergent models, however, one of which was the inappropriate notion of reviving the ancient communities of students and scholars. Clearly the quest was for more contact with teachers and for a heightened sense of community in the university. The students requested a share of administrative power, as well as material help.

The traditional role of the student was also questioned. Was he (as proposed by the Marxist left) part of an exploited group, dialectically opposed to the teachers and similar to workers in a factory? Or was he an individual in a peculiar position, in which cultural elements were paramount? Should he take action only inside the universities or should he extend his activity outside the university? The great majority of the politically active students rejected the "syndicalistic tendency," repudiating identification with the working class. The debate then moved to the other alternative that emphasized the special position of students and stressed cultural elements and the similarity of the students with the intellectuals. A debate developed between those who favored some kind of student corporatism and others who felt the dangers of such a position. Behind all this lay the dilemma of the students' unique role, a temporary one affected at once by the status of his family and by his expectations of his future role in society.

Political System: Formation and Breakdown

All this reflected the second great issue of that period — that is, the political structure to be adopted by the students. The debate soon focused on two alternatives, a unitary association open to all students and a representative structure of a parliamentary type in which various groups could confront one another. At the beginning, the latter solution was favored by the Left and the FUCI, and opposed by the Goliardi. Both the FUCI and the Marxists had political training and a national organization that was effective in a parliamentary system. The Goliardi, on the other hand, were accustomed to the traditional student associations, and viewed this development as a break of the consensus in the student community and as an unwarranted intrusion of party politics in the student's life.

Eventually the parliamentary model prevailed, and received the support of the Goliardi. In 1948, during their third national convention, representatives of the students established the *Unione Nazionale Universitaria Rappresentativa Italiana* (UNURI), which has subsequently represented the student body in the universities. Briefly, UNURI was a national federation of local student unions, with one representative for each university or campus. By and large, each university conformed to the following model. The students — on a campus or faculty basis — elected a legislative assembly from political slates. The legislative body (representing groups in proportion to their strength among the students) elected in turn an executive body representing the majority group or groups, plus various other officers, including the national delegates, in numbers proportionate to the number of students on campus. The executive managed the various cultural activities (movie or theater clubs, music, sports, exchange programs, university books and so on) and decided the political line of the local student union. All students were entitled to vote in the election, their university enrollment cards being the only registration needed.

This system never received an explicit recognition by university administrations or by the government and was in many ways discouraged by the authorities. Little by little, however, it became the sole legitimate representative student organization and gained official, even if indirect, recognition. For example, the compulsory student contribution was collected by university administrations together with other enrollment fees. The system was workable because a political equilibrium existed between two groups, the *Intesa* (Catholic) and the Goliardi, which shared power at the national level for many years and exercised rather balanced and imaginative political judgment. This equilibrium, in turn, was possible only because student politics underwent rather marked changes, which mainly concerned the Goliardi and the Left. The latter progressively lost strength as its constituency shifted to the Goliardi. First, the "left socialists" abandoned the CUDI to join the Goliardi; eventually the communists, finding themselves isolated, decided to dissolve their association and join the Goliardi on an individual basis.

For this to happen, the Goliardi in turn had to move rather a long way from their original positions. First, they had to abandon the idea of a unitary association including all students and become a "closed" association, open only to individuals who accepted a certain

National Conventions: Number of Seats and Presidents Appointed

Convention and Year	Group						Presidents	
	FUCI INTESA	UGI	FUAN	AGI	CUDI	Other	Name	Group
1946 ROMA	7	6	—	—	8	—	—	—
1947 TORINO	9	6	—	—	6	—	—	—
1948 PERUGIA	9	8	1	—	3	—	Greggi	INTESA
1951 VIAREGGIO	9	8	2	—	2	—	Delladio	INTESA
							Costa	UGI
							Stanzani	UGI
1953 MONTECATINI	9	7	3	—	2	—	Kluzer	INTESA
1955 GRADO	9	9	2	—	1	—	Boni	INTESA
							Ungari	UGI
							Lo Savio	UGI
							Pannella	UGI
1957 RIMINI	9	6	2	—	—	4	Piombino	INTESA
							Faustini	INTESA
1959 CATTOLICA	9	6	2	3	—	1	Morezzi	INTESA
							Motibelli	UGI
1961 MIRAMARE	9	7	2	3	—	—	Brondoni	INTESA
							Fava	INTESA
1966 VIAREGGIO	(+)							

(−) Indicates that the list was lacking.
(+) Data lacking for this congress.

political platform. Then, little by little, they shifted from the "democratic center" to the left, drawing first the socialists and then the communists. The entrance of the latter required a change in bylaws and caused secessions from the right. The liberal students left first, then the Social Democrats, and eventually, though somewhat later, the socialists themselves. These groups formed a new association of Independent Goliards, the *Associazione Goliardi Indipendenti* (AGI). Eventually this process brought about an entirely new situation that destroyed the traditional equilibrium between the Goliardi and the Catholic Intesa, leaving the original association almost entirely dominated by the Marxist left, the communists in particular.[30]

The Students' Political Orientation

The shifts of strength in the various university groups is indicated by the summary of the electoral results at the national conventions on page 182.

As can be seen, the communist CUDI decreased in strength as the UGI increased, until all the votes of the former were absorbed by the latter. The result is not equivalent to the sum of the two original votes, because in the same period the UGI suffered losses on the right. When the UGI and its right secessionists (AGI) split, the equilibrium of the system broke down, and as long as the present situation continues, it will not be recovered.

The strength of the rightist groups remained constant over time. The fascist students in the university have retained a greater relative strength than the extreme right groups have in the country as a whole, as can be seen from the following table.[31] This strength comes predominantly from the southern universities.

A comparison of student and national politics is not easy, because the group coalitions within the university do not fit the group alignments outside it.

The large majority of students are somewhere between the Catholic group and the Goliardi. The former has always been rather stable and is the only group that has maintained a large membership. This is understandable because the national Catholic party is well organized, with a common point of reference, and appeals to a rather wide range of social groups, which are not conditioned by the kind of class politics that influence the other parties. The Goliardi constituency, as we have seen, has shifted greatly over time. Although the political center of gravity among the students is to the right of the country, the dominant coalition was led by the Christian-Demo-

Electoral Behavior During the Years 1951–1965°

Academic Year	INTESA	UGI	CUDI	FUAN	Monarchists	AGI	Other
1951–52	31.27	33.12	7.67	17.24	1.42	—	9.26
1952–53	33.80	35.67	7.28	15.78	1.23	—	6.24
1953–54	31.22	39.71	7.23	14.88	2.46	—	4.50
1955–56	38.29	32.67	3.78	13.22	2.06	—	9.98
1956–57	42.17	29.90	2.27	16.32	2.97	—	6.37
1957–58	35.90	26.31	1.92	14.64	3.38	—	17.85
1958–59	36.00	24.71	2.20	13.86	4.92	12.91	5.40
1959–60	35.22	20.32	0.80	13.83	2.28	20.47	7.08
1961–62	35.87	21.02	—	14.57	3.78	19.53	5.23
1962–63	31.97	21.33	—	14.39	2.33	22.10	7.98
1963–64	28.25	20.44	—	11.65	1.20	25.30	13.16
1964–65	30.68	16.77	—	14.17	1.37	23.93	13.08

° The years 1954–55 and 1960–61 are missing from the original source.

crats and the leftist groups. This difference is simply a reflection of the social status of the students, who in Italy represent a small percentage of the population of their age and come from the upper strata of the population. It is, therefore, no surprise that they should represent a more conservative group, in terms of party politics, than the population as a whole. Indeed, in relative terms they are comparatively more to the left than one might predict on the basis of the political orientation of their families of origin. Thus the large proportion of fascist and, more generally, rightist students is the direct consequence of overrepresentation of the petty bourgeoisie in the university student population of the south.

We have repeatedly noticed that students share a very specific social status and are subject to the interplay of two factors on their political participation: their status as students, and the status of their families. This condition, defined as *positive marginality, allows a great deal of freedom in their political choices and the possibility of shifting allegiance, even abruptly,* as has happened in Italy in recent years.

Student Political Participation

For the large mass of the students, how representative is their political system? The development that I have been describing was the outcome of the action of an elite, but to what degree was this elite not also an oligarchy? This issue has been central in the debate concerning the system of student representation. One indicator of the degree of participation is the percentage of students who voted in the annual elections. Electoral participation has remained at the level of about 30 per cent of the enrolled students. Voting in national elections is compulsory in Italy, so 30 per cent participation is considered a low turnout. One should note, however, that only a fraction of the students enrolled are regular students and an even smaller number actually attend the university. Therefore, the level of participation is not unusually low, as can be judged from the following table.[32]

Electoral Participation, Year 1958–1959

Campus	Voters	Enrollment	Per Cent Voting
Turin	2,918	8,500	34.32
Milan	2,414	10,000	24.14
Pavia	1,050	4,000	26.25
Genoa	3,310	9,800	33.77
Padua	3,144	8,500	36.98
Bologna	5,741	13,400	42.84
Modena	1,102	2,500	44.08
Florence	2,591	8,000	32.38
Pisa	2,520	8,000	31.50
Perugia	1,101	3,500	31.45
Naples	8,204	31,000	26.46
Bari	4,350	13,200	32.95
Messina	3,911	8,000	48.88
Catania	3,026	8,700	34.78
Cagliari	1,157	3,300	35.06
All Campuses	46,539	139,400	33.4

At the beginning, the thrust for a student representative system came from the left as had the support for democratic institutions in the country. The system was identified with the regime, in that the left and the Catholics were in the government and the critique was in part instrumental. That the rightist groups always represented themselves as the opponents of the entire system, coupled with their abundant use of extraparliamentary forms of activism, accounted in large measure for their strength in the elections. On the other side, the more politicized students from the left often gave occasion to justify these criticisms by being overly ideological. In time, a class of semiprofessional politicians developed in the student body. The issues debated and the language employed were often remote from the interests and comprehension of the great majority of students. Student democracy turned into a bureaucracy.

Criticism of this situation took two forms. From the right came a quest for depoliticzation and for greater attention to the daily problems of students. From the left came a quest for "direct democracy," meant as a change in the representative parliamentary system toward a system that would allow greater occasion for contacts between the electorate and the elected officials. Moving in this direction the students of the University of Milan substituted for their former system one supposed to allow more direct democracy. The regular ballot was replaced by an assembly or convention, in which all interested students took part. The system was rather complicated and based on the idea that an assembly is more democratic than a regular ballot. In fact, this structure reduced the constituency to those interested enough to spend time in an assembly, and excluded those who would only be interested to the point of giving a vote. This mechanism was hardly sufficient to stimulate participation; it returned power to the "assembly of all the students."

This change in the political structure marked the beginning of the crisis of 1967–68. It coincided with the crisis in UNURI. UNURI had established representation at the national center, though it had failed to promote participation in the peripheral groups. In fact, the UNURI in Rome had much more influence with the central government than the individual unions had with the local administrations. Toward the end of the 1950's, UNURI activity focused on university reform. The Italian government had started to prepare a reform plan that became the famous project 2314 which was turned down in 1968. The UNURI supported the idea of reform, but opposed project 2314. Many of the strikes and fights of the later years were either against the project or for its modification. The UNURI failed to mobilize much support, however, because the crisis of the representative bodies had started.

During this period, the attitudes of the various political groups toward representative student institutions changed completely. The rightist groups and the conservatives began to support them and often to use them as instruments of compromise with the administration. But the leftist groups attacked the degeneration of the representative bodies and called for more active, extraparliamentary action against the administration. Thus, with the breakdown of the electoral equilibrium maintained by the Catholic groups and the left-of-the-center democrats, a crisis began that resulted in the near-revolutionary situation of 1967–68.

How much the representative institutions had become separated from their constituents is illustrated by some survey data collected from students of the University of Milan. In the spring of 1966, students of the Law faculty were asked to give the name of the president in charge of the student representative body and to explain the meaning of the abbreviation UNURI. Only 3.5 per cent knew what the UNURI was. Another survey, conducted in 1967 in four faculties of the same university, indicated that a higher percentage — 20 per cent — knew the political orientation of the majority group. But only 9 per cent of the sample knew exactly how the representative bodies were supported financially, and 68 per cent had not the slightest idea — a surprisingly high percentage since each student paid his contribution at registration, a requirement which had in the past been the cause of a hot debate. It is clear that the political system was no longer supported by its constituency. In the last few years, the great increase in the number of university students had not been balanced by a similar increase in the number of teachers, nor by improvements in the curriculum. (The ratio of students to professors increased from 77 to 1 in 1953–54 to 105 to 1 in 1964–65. The number of students increased from 137,783 in 1953–54 to 332,100 in 1966–67.) The entire academic structure was centralized and rigidly bound by rules that, for the most part, may be changed only through national laws.

In relative terms the increase in the number of students is large, but in absolute terms it is small. This observation indicates another important aspect of the situation: The Italian university is still an institution to which only a small proportion of the population has access. In fact, out of 100 individuals who enter primary schools, hardly 6.4 reach the university and only 2.2 graduate.[33]

Official data (about the social status of university students) are lacking or scarcely significant, but an approximate idea can be drawn from survey data collected in Milan and other universities.[34]

Little doubt exists as to the marked class selectivity of the Italian university; yet, in certain areas and for certain branches, it has ceased to be strictly an elite institution, including an ever-growing group of students coming from the lower-middle classes.

In this same period, the university organization did not adapt to the increase in students or to the necessity for changes in teaching methods. Professors resisted change, and this recalcitrance had a

Social Background of University Students
(*in percentages*)

Father's Occupation	Five Campuses (1966)	(1967)	Milan Law School (1966)	University Strikers (1968)
Manual Worker	14.4	3.6	0.7	2.5
Craftsman-Shopkeeper	15.6	10.4	8.7	14.0
White Collar	25.7	16.6	14.0	22.0
Upper Levels	27.9	65.3	66.5	56.7
No Indication	16.5	5.2	10.1	4.7
N =	(7565)	(392)	(286)	(400)
Father's Education				
Primary	21.7	7.9	5.2	8.2
Secondary	40.2	43.2	31.8	41.7
University	22.4	46.9	51.8	48.0
No Indication	15.7	2.3	11.2	2.0
N =	(7565)	(392)	(286)	(400)

remarkable effect on their behavior during the ensuing crisis. The privileges and power granted to the Italian academic man are considerable. Almost all decisions rest in the hands of the *Consiglio di Facoltà* (Faculty Councils), which include all full professors. Lower-level members of the teaching body, who depend in large part on the *Consiglio di Facolta* for yearly reappointment are excluded from its deliberations. In many respects, professors are more powerful than local university administrations — certainly in all matters related to teaching and to student-professor relations. Among the most resented privileges of professors is their freedom from any control over their activity. For many professors, teaching is secondary to their other activities.

As the demands for change went unanswered, the conflict grew acute. The original demands of the students increased considerably as the protest became a form of collective behavior.

The first significant outburst took place in 1963 at the Faculty of Architecture in Milan. In the Italian academic system, the Faculty of Architecture is likely to be more sensitive than other departments to a general crisis situation. It is not a technical faculty, but humanistically and politically oriented. In the Italian tradition, the architect and particularly the "urbanista" is supposed to be more than a builder. Ideally he is a social reformer who, by creating a new environment, deeply affects man and society. The Faculty of Architecture attracts many students who elsewhere would go into sociology — particularly those oriented toward social reform. The curriculum of the Faculty is old and outdated. Especially in architectural subjects, teaching is done mostly through practical demonstration, with little textual analysis. This has the double consequence of requiring almost continuous attendance and allowing a greater permissiveness of behavior than in other departments.[35]

The Faculty of Architecture is characterized by a high degree of cultural eclecticism, by insecurity about future professional roles, and by a student population much more mobile than those in other departments. The lack of codified knowledge in Architecture made the inadequacy of curricula and of professors more apparent. At the end of 1963, the students demanded a thorough review of curriculum and, receiving little or no answer from faculty and administration, occupied the building at the beginning of 1964 and kept it for several weeks. In the enthusiasm, the original demands soon widened to encompass the meaning of the professional role, methods of teaching and of appointing professors, and power relations between students and faculty. The occupation ended with a compromise by which the administration agreed to replace some old-timers in the Faculty with new members, and to form joint committees with the students. Although these are now regarded as token concessions, they were meaningful at the time.

The episode is important for a number of reasons. First, the absolute power of professors was questioned. Students showed that they could ask for and obtain changes in the faculty. Second, and more important, it broke the traditional pattern of student political action by employing direct tactics that bypassed the institutional representative bodies. For this reason, the occupation marks the beginning of the breakdown of the student political system described above. Finally, it set a model of direct democracy with a high degree of militancy and personal involvement that has since become the main political tool of the student movement.

This first victory and the peculiarities of the Faculty of Architecture set this department on a course somewhat apart from the rest of the university. For a time the reforms seemed sufficient. Later, however, in 1966–67 further occupations occurred in Milan, Venice, and other universities. In 1967–68, the students of architecture in

Milan occupied the Faculty for the entire academic year and, with the support of some of the professors, obtained complete power to manage the department.

The second relevant episode took place in Rome, the largest campus in Italy and one beset by all the imbalances of a large urban university which attracts students from a wide, mostly unindustrialized area. Even during the heyday of representative student democracy, the political climate in Rome was very radical, due to the presence of a large and active group of fascist students who often obtained support from the administration. In 1965 during the election of student representatives, a riot started, and a student was beaten by fascists and killed. His death occasioned a large demonstration that toppled the rector. The episode of Rome is not directly connected with the more recent student riots, because it arose out of a conflict between groups of traditionally opposed students — the leftists and the fascists. Its extreme violence, however, was entirely new, and the fight against the administration, which ended with the dismissal of the rector, encouraged student militancy.

The student revolts that developed in 1965 at the Instituto Universitario di Scienze Sociali in Trento began the new student movement. The University of Trento was founded by Catholic groups in 1962 as a private institute. It has the only Faculty of Sociology in Italy. For this reason, it attracted a large number of students, the great majority of whom came from out of town. They soon became actively radical, in contrast to the conservative population and university administration. As the first class of students approached graduation, a law for the official recognition of the university was successfully pressed through the Parliament. In support of this law, the students at Trento organized and occupied the university for eighteen days. The students, however, did not stop here, but soon pressed the administration for a new statute for the university, a completely new curriculum, and a dramatic change in the composition of the faculty. This phase of the movement in Trento, although still expressed in corporative terms — to use the students' language — enlarged the students' goals. They first asked that faculty members train them more adequately for their professions. They then called for limited sharing of power with the faculty and administration through joint student-faculty committees called *"co-gestione."* Soon the student critique was extended to the entire structure of the sociological profession and even to the role of the university itself. What is the function of the university? The answer of the sociology students of Trento has since been adopted by the entire Italian movement: "The university is one of the productive institutions of this social system, which is a mercantile system (i.e., a system of dealing in commodities). As such it produces *man* as a commodity, that is, as skilled [graduate] or semi-skilled [non-graduate] members of the labor force. The goal of this productive institution — the university — is to supply the labor market with such a commodity. There it will be sold and thereafter consumed in the cycle of social reproduction."[36]

As the original goals of the students widened to a critique of the existing social system, even the forms of co-management initially proposed became inadequate. The student movement came to demand complete control of the university by the students, who would administer it through direct democracy.

As these developments took place in Trento, other universities also simmered throughout 1966–67. But it was only in 1968 — "the year of the students" as it has been called[37] — that a widespread revolt developed. As the academic year opened, students in Trento and at the Faculty of Architecture in Milan quietly started a series of political and cultural activities that prevented the regular meetings of courses. These were not just sit-ins, but were also discussions of university reforms in which a number of professors participated. Other universities joined in rapid succession, and the gravity of the situation was revealed a few days later when the staid Catholic University of Milan was occupied by its students. This phase culminated at the end of the year with the police intervention in Turin.

After the Christmas holidays, the revolt spread to all the universities, which were paralyzed by February, 1968. Administrators, professors, government, political parties, the general public, and regular representatives of the students were completely overtaken by events. The impending elections made the actions of the government unpredictable and the police alternated between periods of relative restraint with episodes of brutal repression. Serious clashes took place in Rome during a bloody one-day riot. Many other places experienced police "over-reaction," with mass arrest and trials climaxing the revolt. The student leaders unsuccessfully attempted to extend the revolt outside the university.

As the leadership sought a unifying aim that could win the spontaneous support of large masses of students, participation decreased. Government and academic authorities cooled as the national elections approached. When these ended on May 19, the examination period was so close that the student leadership decided not to jeopardize the remaining support.

Although the revolt was widespread, some departments were definitely more active than others, among these the Department of Sociology in Trento and almost all the faculties of architecture. Here, however, the revolt was somewhat channeled due to the events of the preceding years and did not turn into violent conflict. The faculties of architecture remained strongholds of the student movements until the end. At the same time, they were set somewhat apart from the rest of the movement. Among the other departments, the most active have been philosophy and letters, physics, and political science. The physics departments had the highest degree of cooperation between students and faculty, but were not immune from the general hostility against the professors. Law had mixed situations, but generally was the stronghold of rightist students who counter-occupied or seceded from the general movement. Engineering and medicine were almost everywhere less active, and in many universities, as in Milan, engineering at one point was the only department not on strike.

The foci of the revolt were in different periods Trento, Turin, Pisa, Rome, and later Milan. By and large, the northern universities were more militant and contributed a large number of outstanding national student leaders. At the beginning, the revolt had been completely spontaneous; the leaders first met only at an advanced stage of the situation. Thus, the occupations and the issues debated varied considerably from place to place. Nevertheless, the movement was generally consistent as to methods, goals, and relations with other forces.

The professors, in general, did not cooperate with the students. Indeed, they became the main target of students' attack. At first, the relatively large group of progressive professors saw the student movement as an ally in pressing through long-expected reforms. They soon found that the students attacked them as much as the other professors. This first occurred during the occupation in Turin; lecturers were suddenly confronted with vast assemblies of booing and enraged students, and very few had the courage to repeat the experience. Nor were the progressive or leftist professors spared; on the contrary, they often provoked the most violent outbursts. The reason for this situation, particular to the Italian movement, lies in the great power and in the privilege possessed by the academic class.

The fight against authoritarianism and for student power found the professors on the other side of the fence. The administration and the government are by nature enemies of the students, but they are remote; the face-to-face contacts were with the professors, and they were seen as the first obstacle to be removed. By and large, moreover, the professors accepted this negative role. The majority literally disappeared, withdrawing to the quieter arena of extrauniversity activities. Others sided with the administration, a few tried to talk students into compromise, while a minority decidedly supported the students. On the whole, the professoriat did not renounce an inch of its privileges.

The administrations and the government, except in rare cases, tried to be as careful as possible. This did not mean that the immunity of the university was respected as it had always been, even by German troops. The main concern of the authorities was to avoid incidents that could have been "nasty" in an election year. The police, however, at times over-reacted brutally; much of their behavior must be attributed to their class differences with the students and to the provocative tactics of the latter. The violence, however, never reached the level of the French situation, although many newsmen and bystanders were beaten.

A most interesting relationship developed between students and the political parties, especially on the left, and the working class. In general, the student leadership was hostile to political parties, the communists receiving the largest and most violent share of criticism and being accused of being "part of the system." But the Communist Party and, even more, the PSIUP (Partito Socialista Italiano di Unita Proletaria [Italian Socialist Party for Proletarian Unity], a splinter leftist socialist party) managed to keep some ties with the movement. The other parties in various degree praised the "good intentions" of the students, but disapproved of their revolutionary methods. At a certain point, the leadership of the movement tried to convince students to vote a blank ballot, but the drive failed. It is likely that the great bulk of the students voted communist, and especially PSIUP. There is some doubt, however, that the violently antiparty position of the leadership, as it appears in the official documents, was shared by even the most active followers. The pattern of political orientations of students who took part in the Milan sit-in was more complex:

Compared to a sample of the student population of the previous year, the sit-in population is more leftist. But compared to the

Political Party	Four Faculties (1967)	Sit-in (1968)
PCI	6.4	13.7
PSIUP	2.0	12.0
PSU	9.9	15.7
PRI	1.5	2.7
DC	7.9	4.0
PLI	21.2	6.0
MSI	1.3	1.0
Other	—	1.5
Does not apply	49.8	43.0
	N = (392)	(400)

national population, the Communist Party is chosen only half as often, and the modal choice was given to the Nenni Socialist Party (PSU), which was considered by the students as a moderate left-of-center party. Thus, in reality, the largest portion of the leftist votes went to the tiny leftist Socialist Party (PSIUP), which was named two and a half times more often among students than among the voting public.

The student leadership tried a difficult gambit, by aiming to mobilize the working class in a revolutionary outbreak against the party organizations. This effort failed almost completely even though in certain situations the students, especially those in Trento and Turin, managed to stir up considerable unrest on the local level. The theoretical debate on the role of the students vis-à-vis the working class was particularly complex and reminiscent of the debate in the late nineteenth century. Most leaders rejected paternalistic ideas of teaching revolution to the working class, but the problem remained one of the unsolved issues of the revolt. The working class remained rather apathetic to the movement. The general public was also rather indifferent if not actually hostile, especially the middle class. A national poll taken at the climax of the revolt gave the following results:

It is clear that reaction to the students was overwhelmingly negative. Students are still seen as a privileged minority, and the lower classes react accordingly. The mass media, with few exceptions, gave a very unfavorable coverage to the student movement. This reaction is reflected clearly in the high percentage of disapproval in the upper-status stratum.

Notes on Italian Students in Periods of Political Mobilization

Public Attitudes Toward Students[38]

Attitude	Status				
	High	Middle	Lower Middle	Lower	All
Approve	25.0	27.6	16.0	9.2	19.5
Disapprove	51.5	36.8	25.5	16.2	31.1
Indifferent or no answer	22.1	35.7	58.5	74.6	50.9
N =	(68)	(370)	(431)	(185)	(1054)

Finally, a word should be added on the cleavages inside the student bloc. Obviously not all students took part in the sit-ins. In Milan, 25 to 30 per cent of enrolled students took part in the assemblies. Those who did not participate were not necessarily opposed, and among the participants, some opposed at least certain aspects of the occupation. Among the respondents in the sit-in sample, only 15 per cent unconditionally supported the occupation, 59 per cent were favorable but criticized some aspects, and 13.5 per cent were entirely opposed, while 11.7 per cent did not answer. (Data are lacking for those who used the occupation to take extra vacations.) On the whole the leadership received wide support, and most of the student body backed at least some of its claims. In many universities, however, there was a fascist opposition, with daily fights between the besieged occupants and the incoming fascist squads. In Rome, nonstudent "toughs," headed by a fascist member of Parliament, attacked the university and sacked an entire building. But for the most part the fascists remained marginal to the student movement.

In every university, the old forms of parliamentary representation were replaced by general assemblies of all students, in the name of "direct democracy." This new form of participation was intended to prevent the formation of "bureaucratic leadership" of the kind that developed during the previous period. Obviously not all the members of the assembly participated in the same way, and soon a group of leaders came to be recognized in each university. But there is little doubt that this structure maintained a much more sustained and organized participation. The leaders who emerged during the revolt were charismatic; among the leadership so formed, the turnover has been relatively high. One important latent function of this form of direct democracy was its disruptive effect on the opposing groups of professors and administrators. The latter group especially preferred to deal with established representatives who could be easily integrated in joint committees. This could not be done when the leadership changed daily, according to the orientation of the assembly.

In the long run, however, direct democracy created obstacles to coordinated action by students on the national level. After the first spontaneous outbursts, the local leadership groups had to extend the movement in three directions: to the national level, to the secondary schools, and to the working class. The extension to the secondary schools was rather successful at one point, but it failed to organize the secondary students continuously. The creation of a national leadership was debated all year without resulting in a national leadership structure. Even now the national leadership remains a group of "natural" leaders with no formal qualifications. The need for national coordination is great and is recognized as such. Any extension of organization will, however, require the creation of some kind of stable leadership, thus infringing on one of the basic principles that, at least theoretically, the movement has not yet rejected.

Another important form of participation fostered inside the occupied universities was the "counter-courses." They were begun as a series of seminars treating subjects not included in the regular curriculum, such as the war in Vietnam, social psychiatry, and the problems of deviants. Their conduct shows certain political aims and the desire of the Italian student to overcome the lack of participation imposed by the university system, with its lectures ex cathedra. As the revolt spread, the counter-courses were abandoned for more straightforward forms of political action.

The student revolt also saw an explosion of literary production. Documents, statements, pamphlets, and other materials considered a number of questions. It is possible to identify three major themes that appeared in the student writings throughout the revolt: a fight against authoritarianism, an examination of the student's role, and an attempt to clarify the aims of the student movement.

The first issue received the most thorough elaboration. "The first goal of the assembly and of the demonstration we were setting up," said the chronicler of the Turin occupation, "was to *organize a permanent fight against the power of the academic authorities,* capable of challenging such a power. A challenge does not consist of removing the power, nor of a simple protest. It means *creating continuous difficulties in the exercise of this power."*[39] In this sense, the students occupying the University of Turin accomplished unimagined progress against professorial authority. Almost without exception, the professors reacted negatively. Their reactions showed how deeply this kind of personal challenge touched them. The vision of the magnificent rector of the University of Turin lecturing, surrounded by policemen while six officers tried to convince one student to take his hat off, is almost farcical. The Turin movement was successful largely because it focused almost entirely on the question of academic authority and rejected more traditional "political" issues. After the example of Turin, few professors in Italy dared to confront a student assembly.

The second great issue — that of the student's role — was elaborated primarily by the sociology students of Trento, who saw the student as a commodity in a larger capitalist system of production. In their view, the problem was to justify the revolutionary potential of the students in largely Marxist terms. As university students were a privileged elite, it was difficult to set their action in a scheme of class politics. Indeed, the students at Turin flatly rejected any class identification with the workers, stating that "on the basis of past experience, it is perhaps better that the 'bourgeois' stay with the 'bourgeois' and the workers with the workers."[40] But as the revolt widened, so did the desire to extend it outside the universities to achieve a closer theoretical and practical identification with the working class. Actually, this issue remained unresolved and was dealt with on a personal or local basis. The students throughout the revolt remained much more a class *für sich* than a class *an sich*, to use a definition employed by an Italian sociologist closely involved in the student movement.[41]

The third issue was closely connected with the preceding one: What should the movement do, and what organizational form should its leadership adopt? Even on this issue there was a rather clear-cut difference as to goals inside the university and outside of it. Inside the university, the main theme was obviously the conflict with the academic powers. The demands for increased student power ranged from a simple request of co-management to a more drastic claim of "self-management." A theory of so-called "structural space," a sort of student *Lebensraum* was developed. This approach was first adopted by the architecture students in their long fight; it consisted of achieving a certain degree of power within the university and on its basis continuing student political activity and developing new lines of action. The architecture students in particular were able to secure wide areas of power. "Structural space" has probably been the most effective of the students' political proposals. When it has been achieved, a certain amount of faculty cooperation has usually proved necessary.

For a sizable portion of the movement, "structural space" was a final aim, but for other groups it was only an instrument to create new militancy. The students from Trento in particular theorized in favor of this second position, claiming university unrest to be a false target, useful mainly because it can be easily created. The ensuing conflict they claimed was more important because it helped select new active members to be socialized and then put to work with the working class. Thus one part of the student leadership made clear its effort to orient action mainly outside the university.

In a way, this was the more militant position. At the crucial moment of the revolt, the student leadership tried to take the conflict outside the university much in the same way as the French students did a few weeks later, but with far less success. The reason for this failure remains among the unresolved issues of the Italian student movement.

Summary and Conclusions

From this historical study of Italian students, certain facts emerge as constant. First of all, the degree of political participation has been consistently high among the university students. They have emerged as an important group particularly during periods of political mobilization. They have been highly active in extra parliamentary politics.

Looking back on the different periods, however, one notes much variation in students' political orientations. It is almost possible to perceive a cyclical pattern of politics in successive generations of students. Starting from nationalism during the *Risorgimento*, students leaned toward socialism in the following period, and toward nationalism and fascism later on. Later one observes an opposite swing, and now there is a predominantly leftist orientation.

On the other hand, the social status of students has not varied greatly until the last few years. They have constituted a privileged minority, in large measure from the middle and upper classes. One might argue that the students' family status has little or no effect on their political orientation, rejecting therefore any explanation of their behavior in terms of class politics. In effect, it seems reasonable to accept that the political orientation of students is at times inconsistent with what might be expected on the basis of their class standing. No doubt, much of their political behavior can be explained in terms of their specific role as students.

I am inclined to believe, however, that an explanation in terms of class should not be rejected entirely. The question hinges on the problem of the social nature of students, an issue debated by Marxist theorists at the end of nineteenth century and raised again during the recent revolt by students themselves. In my opinion, the particular position of the student — that is, his marginality vis-à-vis the adult roles of society — mainly determines the forms and degree of his political involvement. Thus his political orientation is affected both by the student's role, as such, and by his family status. In this sense it might be worth reconsidering Kautsky's interpretation — that leftist tendencies will prevail among students only in periods in which the larger society is *not characterized by a strong class conflict*. In a period in which class conflict is strong, and consequently when the inconsistency between students' political and social positions becomes more apparent, students tend to direct their political activism in another direction. Should this hypothesis be correct, the future political orientation of students could be quite different from their current outlook. Actually, the student's role and his importance in society have changed greatly. It is likely that his new situation could radically change the factors that we have examined and that have influenced his behavior in the past. The current revolutionary orientation of Italian students may in the future undergo yet another dramatic change.

REFERENCES

1. Hastings Rashdall, *The Universities of Europe in the Middle-Ages* (London, 1935), p. 150. Italics ours. As to age, there appears to be a difference between universities. In Paris a minimum age of twenty was required to get the M.A. In Italy, on the contrary, doctors could be seventeen years old, but of legitimate birth.

2. The rector was then the highest office of the students' guild and not, as the term now implies, a professor.

3. Stephen d'Irsay, *Histoire des Universités* (Paris, 1935), p. 159.

4. The *Risorgimento* could provide a unique setting for the study of political generations. As far as I am able to verify, however, no attempt has been made in that direction in current literature.

5. Roberto Michels, "Quelques aperçus sur l'histoire de la bourgeoisie italienne au XIX siècle," *Revue Historique,* Vol. 170 (1932), p. 401.

6. I use the word "college," although in Italy "collegio" has a different meaning and refers to the house where students reside.

7. *Collegio Universitario Ghislieri di Pavia* (Milan, 1966), p. 155.

8. This was almost one third of the students enrolled.

9. Although this was the most famous university battalion that took part in the 1848 campaign, it was not the only one; fifty-odd students from Siena fought in the same battle and in the correspondence of one of the Pisan students there is reference to two university battalions from Lombard universities.

10. Ersilio Michel, "Maestri e scolari dell' Università di Pisa negli avvenimenti del 1848," *Bollettino Storico Pisano,* Vol. 17 (1948), pp. 10ff.

11. Denis Mack Smith, *Storia d'Italia* (Bari, 1964), p. 32.

12. Roberto Michels, *Proletariato e Borghesia nel Movimento Socialista Italiano* (Turin, 1908), pp. 33–34.

13. *Ibid.,* p. 20.

14. *Ibid.,* p. 79 and *passim.*

15. *Ibid.,* p. 117.

16. *Ibid.,* p. 20.

17. *Ibid.,* p. 63.

18. Renzo de Felice (ed.), *Il Fascismo e i Partiti Politici Italiani* (Bologna, 1966), p. 37.

19. *Ibid.,* p. 70.

20. Renato Treves, "Il Fascismo e il problema delle generazioni," *Quaderni di Sociologia,* Vol. 14 (1964), p. 121.

21. *Ibid.,* p. 121.

22. *Ibid.,* p. 125

23. *Ibid.,* p. 129.

24. From the institutional point of view, the GUF's were an organ of the Fascist Party and constituted the highest level achievable in the youth organizations of the party. They were formed in every university town, in every provincial capital, and everywhere there were at least twenty-five students.

25. Ruggero Zangrandi, *Il Lungo Viaggio Attraverso Il Fascismo* (Milan, 1962; 2d edition), pp. 101ff.

26. A certain number of youths sided also with the fascists, enlisting in the various militia corps. It is difficult to say how many were the students among them.

27. *Il Veltro,* special issue on the Italian youth, 1943–1963 (1964), p. 167.

28. Faculty in the Italian sense, as department.

29. *Il Veltro,* p. 169.

30. Giuliano Urbani, *Politica e Universitari* (Florence, 1966), pp. 53–54. See also *Il Veltro,* p. 179.

31. *Ibid.,* p. 74. The data refer only to a sample of fifteen campuses comprising about 70 per cent of the entire population.

32. *Ibid.,* p. 94.

33. Alberto Valentini, *Scuola e Promozione Sociale* (Formazione e Lavoro, 1966), p. 4.

34. The Italian census has much too wide a breakdown for this population, as it includes in the same bracket all the white-collar workers up to the executive level.

35. On the situation of architecture, see Giancarlo de Carlo, *La Piramide Rovesciata* (Bari, 1968).

36. *Università: Ipotesi Rivoluzionaria* (Padua, 1968), p. 42.

37. Rossana Rossanda, *L'Anno degli Studenti* (Bari, 1968).

38. Doxa, Poll 6837.

39. *Quaderni Piacentini,* Vol. 33 (1968), pp. 29–30.

40. *Ibid.,* p. 39.

41. Carlo Donolo, "La politica ridefinita," *Quaderni Piacentini,* Vol. 35 (1968), p. 94.

RICHARD E. PETERSON

The Student Left in American Higher Education

As A RESULT of a remarkable series of events — some loosely planned, most worked out as the sequence of actions and counteractions unfolded — undergraduate academic life at Columbia University came to a standstill in late April, 1968. In some ways the situation at Columbia was like that at Berkeley in the fall of 1964: On both campuses certain of the responses of authorities were similar (use of police, for example). Students and faculty became polarized, and instruction-as-usual ceased as many students struck. Various committees were eventually constituted to deliberate on how to remake the university. The ostensive issues propelling the two outbreaks were, of course, different. Different also was the nature of the student leadership. While the leaders of the Berkeley rebellion came out of diverse radical organizations and experiences, the Columbia disruption was carried out almost entirely by a single group — the local chapter of Students for a Democratic Society (SDS). Most of the Berkeley leaders were already Movement veterans (especially in civil rights work; Mario Savio, then twenty-two-years old, had participated in the 1964 Mississippi Summer); the Columbia militants, led by sophomore Mark Rudd, were relative novices on the new New Left.

The Columbia SDS'ers, nonetheless, have shown students and others in the American radical sector that it can be done, that an old, wealthy, highly prestigious pillar of American higher education can be brought to a halt and made to plan for a whole new *modus operandi.* For the rebellion to achieve its longer range goals, there obviously had to be a broad base of support on the campus. Student and faculty at Columbia had to be "politicized," to be "radicalized," as the rhetoric has it. And they were — by the hundreds. Initially, for many, it was the proclaimed issues — the gym, Institute for Defense Analyses (IDA), previous disciplinary actions against students; a week later, for many more, it was the decision to bring in the police to remove the students from the occupied buildings. Busy with their academic and social affairs, the vast majority of students and faculty had previously had little interest in the governance and goals of their university except as their own activities might be directly affected. With the demonstrations, the abortive negotiation attempts, and the battles with police, the apathy was transformed either to sympathy for the striking students or to opposition to them. The campus, in short, was polarized, and some sort of restructuring of the university became a necessity if it was to survive as a viable institution. The SDS feat at Columbia, then, was a formidable one, and likely to be viewed by student left groups on other campuses as a model worth emulating.

The revolt at Columbia was perhaps the high point in a year that saw student militancy on an unprecedented scale across the country. Members of student Left groups were not responsible for all the incidents, probably not even a majority of them. The fall of 1967 was marked particularly by harassment of recruiters from the military services, the CIA, and most notably the Dow Chemical Company. Many of these demonstrations, as well as agitation at universities associated with the Institute for Defense Analyses, however, *were* sparked by SDS chapters, in pursuance of a decision approved at the SDS National Convention the previous July to act to end military involvement on the campus. The many disorders in the following spring were marked by new and generally more violent tactics. There was apparent arson at Stanford (the NROTC building) and at Catholic University of America, and a bomb explosion at Southern Illinois University. Seeking to make Howard University more responsive to the needs of an emerging black consciousness, students took over the administration building, after which authorities shut down the school for a week and eventually made a variety of concessions. Sit-ins, boycott of classes, and other forms of protest over local grievances — compulsory ROTC, disciplinary actions, poor condition of campus facilities — spread to other Negro colleges in the South and East. On an even larger number of white campuses, black students demonstrated for admission of more of their race and for incorporation of black studies into the curriculum. At other institutions, there was increasing militancy — with tactics ranging from sit-ins to seizing buildings to locking up trustees — over such old issues as parietal hours to such new ones as student participation in selection of a new president for the institution (University of Oregon).

Varieties of Contemporary Student Discontent

It may be useful to try to distinguish the student Left from at least three other varieties of contemporary student dissent — student rightists, campus-issue protesters, and hippies. The student Left is here understood as the student component of what is variously referred to as the New Left, the radical movement, or simply the "Movement." The New Left is indeed a "movement" in the sense that that word may mean an informal mass of individuals holding vague beliefs in common, rather than an organized, disciplined party or institution. The New Left has emerged in the past eight or nine years on the basis of shared rejection of social institutions in America that "exploit" and "dehumanize," outrage at social inequities at home and "imperialism" abroad, faith in participatory democracy, and a general commitment to some form of social action. While the New Left has grown out of an amalgam of shifting civil rights, peace, and anti-poverty sentiments and activities, its ultimate goal is radical reform of American society and the characteristic nature of human roles and relationships on which it rests. Relatively unconcerned about the specifics of their utopia, students on the Left are simply convinced that much in American life, including life in the university, is not good now, and that somehow drastic changes must be made.

The programmatic thrust for the student Left has come chiefly from two organizations — the now exclusively black, loosely structured Student Nonviolent Coordinating Committee (SNCC) and the almost totally white, nationally organized Students for a Democratic Society. Esteemed as the original and prototype Movement group, SNCC is no longer student oriented and appears for the time to be greatly weakened as an effective force for radical change. SDS, on the other hand, is now the predominant group within the New Left, continually forming new chapters and striving, against internal conflicts, to sort out priorities and tactics toward maintaining the viability of the radical movement.

The student Right, by comparison, directs its protest not so much at the *status quo*, but rather at what it perceives to be a rising tide of leftist influence ("liberal orthodoxy") on the campus and in the broader society. The educationally oriented tactics of the student conservatives are aimed chiefly at counteracting the efforts of both the student leftists and the campus-issue protesters.

Easily the most important conservative student organization is the Young Americans for Freedom (YAF), which claims a membership of twenty to thirty thousand spread across some two hundred campuses. From its founding in 1960, YAF grew to a peak in grassroots support during the Goldwater-Johnson campaign of 1964. Since then, YAF has probably been best known for its efforts on behalf of the Administration's Vietnam policy — demonstrations of support for various escalations toward a military victory, blood donations, Christmas packages for the troops, and so forth.

Parents of conservative students are disproportionately Republican and Protestant, and they tend to be authoritarian and achievement-oriented in their child-rearing practices. Student rightists, heavily concentrated in business curricula, appear to be active not only at the large, prestigious, and visible institutions, but also at many smaller colleges — especially church-related ones, southern universities, and technical and other career-oriented institutions.[1] As S. M. Lipset and Philip Altbach have observed, despite impressive financial and organizational backing, student conservatives "have not been successful in building a movement which has much commitment from its membership," nor has it "made any real impact on the campus."[2]

Quite the contrary is true of campus-issue protesters. In the years "since Berkeley" (fall, 1964), college campuses in many parts of the country have witnessed an unprecedented level of organized student protest over campus conditions, and the impact has been substantial. During the academic year 1964–65, there were more demonstrations about dormitory and other living-group regulations and campus food service than about U.S. actions in Vietnam. Moreover, larger numbers of students, most likely representing wider cross-sections of student bodies, were generally involved in protesting internal campus issues.[3]

While many of the trouble spots are old and somewhat trivial, there is an increasing urgency and stridency. Often led by legitimate (elected) student leaders, the campus-issue activists have borrowed some of the tactics of the student leftists — the marches, sit-ins, and confrontation strategies of the civil rights movement, for example. Certainly the strategies of the FSM (Free Speech Movement) activists at Berkeley have not gone unnoticed by students on other campuses who generally seek more limited objectives. With the emergence of new models of higher learning — the experimental colleges and free universities for example — as well as the appeal of a politics of "student power," concern for *real* educational reform is unmistakably on the rise among these more conventional students.

For the confirmed hippie, whose preferred response is to "be" (rather than to "do"), collegiate life in its usual form is anathema. The hippy-student exists mainly on the periphery of large urban institutions, in a sense dropping in and out. In contrast to the left-activist's commitment to work for change, real hippies have withdrawn from American culture and despair of any hopes that they, the "New Lefties," or anyone else can alter the prevailing patterns of that culture.

The Organized Student Left: SNCC and SDS

The "New" Left is not to be confused with the "Old" Left or, in Jack Newfield's words, the "hereditary" Left — the student wing which is now chiefly represented by the Progressive Labor Party.[4] Relatively weak numerically, the Old Left, with its doctrinaire adherence to Marxist economic analyses, contrasts sharply with the New Left's emphasis on "human" or "psychological" variables ("human freedom," "human liberation"). The Maoist-oriented PLP, whose members frequently also belong to SDS and attempt to influence its directions, is proving to be a particular thorn for the New Left.[5]

In further defining the New (student) Left, it may be asserted that its adherents share the belief that American society is so grossly defective that nothing short of fundamental reconstruction of basic institutions will provide an adequate remedy, and they are willing to act on behalf of this belief. This definition would distinguish the leftists from the hippies, who are disinclined to act, as well as from the liberal groups whose goals are less extreme. Among the latter would be the campus affiliates of ADA (Americans for Democratic Action), SANE (National Committee for Sane Nuclear Policy), ACLU (American Civil Liberties Union), the College Young Democrats, and probably also the recently established (fall, 1966) University Christian Movement.[6] By our definition, there would, of course, be many student leftists who are not dues-paying members of or active workers for leftist organizations. The student Left, as defined, includes perhaps something on the order of 1 to 2 per cent of the total student population. The *organized* Student Left — formal affiliates of SDS, Southern Student Organizing Committee (SSOC), SNCC — numbers fewer than twenty thousand.

SNCC came into being at an October, 1960, meeting in Atlanta, the result of efforts by Southern Christian Leadership Conference (SCLC) worker Ella Baker to bring together leaders of the various sit-ins that had occurred throughout the South since the original Greensboro and Nashville demonstrations earlier that year. Almost all of the early SNCC activists, both Negroes and whites, were of Southern middle-class background. They shared a religious devotion to the ideals of nonviolence, love, and peace, along with a suspicion of formal organization and leadership. Early tactics emphasized direct confrontation — sit-ins, freedom rides, and the like.

Late in 1961, SNCC embarked on a new course and began sending full-time workers into rural communities in the South to help Negroes register to vote. The incredible heroism of individual SNCC organizers in Mississippi and Alabama has been movingly described by Newfield: "They were shot, beaten, gassed, whipped, jailed." The summer of 1964 saw the failure of the SNCC-inspired Mississippi Freedom Democratic Party and the tragedies of the SNCC-conceived Mississippi Summer Project (notably the murder of Goodman, Chaney, and Schwerner).

After a period of black-white populism, SNCC organizers began to lose faith in white liberals and federal civil rights measures. The belief emerged within SNCC that it was best for blacks to make their own destiny rather than to integrate with a "sick" white society. In May of 1966, Stokely Carmichael replaced John Lewis, and a new SNCC was born out of a legacy of frustration and despair. Financially broken, its less than eighty paid workers have concentrated on stirring the younger Negro generation toward open militancy and eventual black self-determination.[7] Yet another phase of SNCC may be in the offing: Phil Hutchings, who replaced the jailed Rap Brown, is speaking (summer, 1968) about renewed emphasis on political activity — most importantly, about working to create a national political party of black people.

SDS also took shape soon after the original sit-ins. A small group of student intellectuals, mainly at the University of Michigan, established ties with the League for Industrial Democracy (LID) which was seeking to reconstruct its moribund student sector. Groups organized on eleven campuses, and Tom Hayden drafted SDS's manifesto, the *Port Huron Statement*. In June, 1962, fifty-nine people gathered for a founding convention at the F.D.R. Labor Center at Port Huron, Michigan.

After a year of organizing campus chapters and minor local polemicizing, SDS turned to community organization in northern urban ghettos, both black and white. ERAP (Economic Research and Action Projects) were under way in ten cities by 1965. "Community organization" has meant many things: fostering indigenous leadership, building a capacity to make decisions, initiating direct action, giving hope.

In 1965, SDS's focus was again on students, and the issues of Vietnam, the draft, and student power. In April, 1965, twentythousand people came to Washington for an SDS-organized march to protest the war. SDS helped set up the first teach-in at Ann Arbor and soon after initiated projects for draft resistance. SDS'ers in Cambridge helped guide the 1967 Vietnam Summer project. As noted earlier, most of the demonstrations against campus recruiters during the fall of 1967 were organized by SDS chapters. Open to any and all students, SDS grew from 1200 members and 30 chapters in 1965 to more than 6000 members and 227 chapters in 1967.[8] Various reports put the number of chapters at "over 300" in the spring of 1968.

In order to stimulate and coordinate intellectual activity within the Movement, SDS established the Radical Education Project (REP) as an arm for publication, theorizing, and "radical research." REP distributes a host of original and reprinted articles, several regular newsletters, and a book critique series; publishes a "Movement Speakers Guide"; and has sponsored a number of conferences, most of which have dealt with ways post-student radicals can continue radical work after graduation.

How ex-student radicals can remain active in "Movement work" as they fan out into the occupational world, mainly into the professions, is a topic increasingly discussed by SDS leaders. REP has sponsored conferences on "Radicals in the Professions" and publishes a "Radicals in the Professions Newsletter." Several projects involving efforts to organize professional groups (for example, welfare workers in New York City) have not been notably successful. Possibly the best current prospect for continued radical involvement is represented by the New Universities Conference. With the groundwork laid by a group of SDS alumni who are now members of university faculty as well as several REP staff, NUC was launched formally in March, 1968, as a base from which radical faculty and graduate students could criticize the role of the university in American society, press for educational reforms, and promote their own job security. Finally, it may be noted that the notion of SDS broadening into a larger organization that would embrace older people (workers, professionals, and so forth), as well as students, is regularly deliberated, although the idea was voted down at the most recent (1968) national meeting.

While SDS has long been criticized for its relative inattention to the details of its envisioned "Democratic Society," the question of what tactics to use to bring about the new society has generated fervent and quite disparate attitudes. At least four general "tactical positions" can be identified. The one perhaps currently dominant, held by most of the National Office leadership as well as other older veterans (old New Leftists), is that SDS should again move off the campus with renewed efforts to "build the movement" by organizing middle-class professionals (regarded by some SDS theorists as the new working class), blue-collar workers, G.I.'s, high-school students, hippies, and other potentially radical constituencies around a variety of local issues and grievances. In contrast to this digging-in-for-the-long-haul tactic, there are proponents of a strategy of single-issue-demonstrations — parades, confrontations, draft-card burnings, and other sorts of "flashy" protest, usually campus-based, designed to induce small or large reforms as well as some measure of attitude change in the local community. Then there would be two clearly minority positions: One, roundly condemned by Movement leaders and intellectuals, has stressed operating within "the system," relying on electoral politics, working for Senator Eugene McCarthy and various local Peace and Freedom Party (PFP) candidates; the other, an insurrectionist wing, is convinced that the establishment is entirely immune to nonviolent persuasion and must be violently overthrown if the goals of the Left are to be realized.

Finally, note may be taken of the continuing tension between the principle of local chapter autonomy (rejection of a "top-down" organization), on the one hand, and the need for a unifying ideology and nationwide programs, on the other. No new national "thrusts" for SDS were approved at national meetings in 1968. Thus, while a few chapters may be expected to pay some heed to national office admonitions (and, for example, try to engage in organizing among blue-collar workers), most local units will be doing their own thing, using whatever tactics the members decide upon. For the most part, this will mean staying alert to weaknesses, hypocrisies, the "right" issues — on campus and nearby — that may be exploited toward institutional reform and radicalization of people. At the same time, however, a growing number of SDS'ers *are* attempting to create intellectual perspectives to inform their activism. James Jacobs, late of the REP staff, has written of a rise of "theoretical activists" (alongside "plain activists")[9] whose thinking tends to stress socialist-like alternatives to capitalism, as well as psychological concepts of the sort advanced by the early Marx, Erich Fromm, and Herbert Marcuse. Whether or not SDS will be able to develop an ideological consensus out of which truly national programs may be developed and implemented remains to be seen.

The Spectrum of American Higher Education

Since the end of World War II, the proportion of the college-age population (eighteen to twenty-one) attending college has doubled — from 22 per cent in 1946 to 45 per cent in 1965.[10] In the fall of 1967, approximately six million students were attending about 2300 colleges and universities. Something over one third of these are public tax-supported institutions; given their typically large size and egalitarian admissions policies, however, the public institutions presently enroll two thirds of the total student population.

American higher education, in short, has undergone a remarkable democratization. Perhaps its most contemporary expression is the local community-supported and controlled "open door" two-year junior college. In 1945–46, there were 242 public junior colleges enrolling 110,000 students, while in 1965–66, there were 392 with enrollments totaling almost 700,000.

A second major theme in American higher education is its decentralization and consequent diversity. In 1965, there were 154 universities, 89 of which were public; 815 liberal-arts colleges, with six times as many private as public; 186 teachers' colleges, with all but 28 under public control; 57 technical institutions equally divided between public and private; 622 public and private junior colleges; 207 church-operated theological schools; with the balance of the 2230 made up mostly of private professional and technical schools. In the private sector, 490 Protestant-controlled colleges enrolled 8 per cent of the total student population, 376 Roman Catholic-controlled institutions slightly over 7 per cent, and 490 independent institutions 18 per cent. In size, institutions range from over thirty thousand students on one campus, as at several midwestern universities, to the several hundred schools with enrollments of less than five hundred.

There are also huge differences in affluence, preparation of faculty, admissions selectivity, and other indices of institutional quality. Almost half of the colleges and universities are *not* accredited by an official accrediting organization. In California, the seventy-two generally well-financed and competently staffed JC's are open to all citizens of that state. (Not even a high-school diploma is needed if the applicant is over age eighteen.) On the other hand, some thirty or so institutions (rated as "most selective" by Cass and Birnbaum)[11] comprise the "Paradise" of Kenneth Eble's cosmos;[12] old, independently controlled, well-endowed, and concentrated mainly in the Northeast, they receive three or four applications for admission for every freshman admitted. In intellectual sophistication, their student bodies stand well apart from the rest of the field.

With the exception of youths who live in states with poorly developed systems of higher education and lack the financial means to leave the state or the academic ability to obtain a scholarship, some form of higher education is available to all. Because of the many forms, prospective freshmen are often able, in Martin Meyerson's words, to "sort themselves according to their images of themselves and of the colleges to which they apply."[13]

A Typology of American College
Students for the Early 1970's

Given an open, mass educational system, the diversity in student characteristics is extremely great. As a summarizing and expository convenience, recourse to some sort of typology is unavoidable. One typology that has proved to be particularly meaningful was proposed by Berkeley sociologists Burton Clark and Martin Trow in the form of four "sub-cultures" — the vocational, the academic, the collegiate, and the nonconformist.[14] The model to be outlined clearly has roots in the Clark-Trow paradigm. It also draws on recent empirical studies, mainly the work of Harry Schumer and Robert Stanfield at the University of Massachusetts, the investigation by Jonathan Warren based on students from four southern California colleges,[15] as well as data gathered with the College Student Questionnaires

(CSQ), which contain a method for classifying students according to the Clark-Trow typology. In the past four years, the CSQ has been administered to over 120,000 students at some 250 colleges and universities.[16]

The model posited here consists of eight student types distinguishable in terms of their dominant value commitment. It is useful to consider how the types might be arranged on a continuum of degree of acceptance-rejection of prevailing American institutions. Lacking pertinent data, this venture — summed up in the diagram below — is largely inferential and speculative.

Stance vis-à-vis American Institutions

Acceptance	Neutral	Rejection

←——————————————————————————————→

Vocationalists Collegiates Ritualists Academics Intellectuals Left-
Activists

Professionalists

Hippies

It hardly needs to be said that the names refer to analytic, ideal types; they are oversimplified abstractions that mask the huge variability on many dimensions that unquestionably exists within each type.

Vocationalists. The basic commitment of the vocationally-oriented college student is to the training he is receiving for a specific occupational career. He views his college education chiefly in instrumental terms — as a means of acquiring a skill that will ensure the occupational security and social prestige that his family lacked. Vocationalists are predominantly from working-class backgrounds, and they differ from what we will refer to as professionalists mainly in terms of socio-economic origin. In college, they specialize in engineering, education, business, or other technical specialties. On various items in the CSQ, they evidenced a relatively firm and long-standing commitment to their vocational fields of choice, as well as a decidedly passive, dependent attitude toward learning. Students classified as vocationalists consistently score relatively low on the CSQ measures of cultural sophistication, social conscience, and liberalism (Figure 1). The vocationalist, in sum, is preparing himself to "make it" within the American system, which he accepts uncritically.

Figure 1
CSQ Profiles for Undergraduates Divided According to a Typology of
Student Subcultures Proposed by Burton Clark and Martin Trow

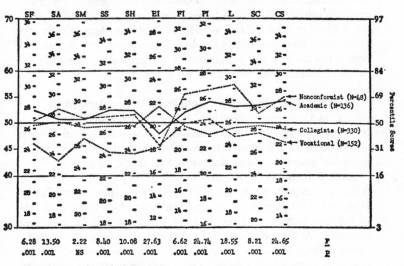

SF: Satisfaction with Faculty
SA: Satisfaction with Administration
SM: Satisfaction with Major Field
SS: Satisfaction with Students
SH: Study Habits
EI: Extracurricular Involvement

FI: Family Independence
PI: Peer Independence
L: Liberalism
SC: Social Conscience
CS: Cultural Sophistication

Description of the sample of students as well as definitions of the eleven scales are included in the *Technical Manual* for the *College Student Questionnaires*.

Professionalists. This type, the name borrowed from Kenneth Keniston, differs from the vocationalists in a number of important ways, but not, it is argued, in terms of the hypothetical dimension of acceptance-rejection of American institutions. Born of upper-middle class and professional parents, he (this category is practically all male) aspires to much the same life pattern as his highly successful father — achievement, expertise, *noblesse oblige*.[17]

Well-endowed intellectually, the professionalist was strongly motivated to succeed in secondary school (often one of the best), and in college he is bent on continuing his record of outstanding academic achievement toward early enrollment in a postgraduate

213

professional school (law, medicine, business, government, and so forth). Professionalists would be disproportionately found in the best undergraduate colleges, a necessary springboard to the right graduate school and first job. Characteristically "staying cool," they are seldom excited by issues and ideas. While there clearly are attitudinal differences within this hypothetical category, the general political outlook of the professionalist is conservative to middle-of-the-road, and oriented toward the *status quo*.[18]

Collegiates. The collegiate commitment is to popularity, play, and dating, as these proclivities may be realized through the various formalized extracurricular activities as well as informal off-campus events, such as spring-vacation congregations at beach resorts or fraternity weekends in the mountains, that define "college life."

Collegiates are from the middle classes. They are attracted to the relatively unselective public colleges and universities, especially the large and old ones in the South and Midwest, which are strongholds of big-time football and the national Greek-letter fraternities and sororities. Anti-intellectual, the collegiate's course work tends to center in fields that make relatively few intellectual demands. While particular subtypes of collegiates may exist on particular campuses, the common denominator seems to be an orientation toward the extracurriculum, broadly defined.[19] Collegiates scored significantly higher on the extracurricular involvement scale in the CSQ than the other three Clark-Trow types (Figure 1), and they tend to be conformist and other-directed (low peer independence). Although the self-reported political attitudes of collegiates gravitate toward the conservative, politics — in the sense of adult partisanship and real issues — are simply not relevant.

Ritualists. The distinguishing attribute of the ritualist (the name suggested by Harry Schumer and Robert Stanfield) is his lack of commitment to anything. Possibly of less than average academic aptitude and usually from lower socio-economic strata, he has in a sense been swept into college by forces beyond his control — parental prodding, friends going on to college, a college within easy driving distance with admissions standards that can be met.

Schumer and Stanfield describe the ritualistic type as more strongly oriented toward home than the university, as preferring solitary rather than social activity, and as uninterested in either the academic or the collegiate environment. For the ritualist (as an ideal type), lack of commitment is total. He is apolitical, having no beliefs one way or another about the efficacy of American institutions.

Academics. The fundamental commitment of the academic type is to scholarly achievement within a specific subject field or academic discipline. Academics are concentrated in the selective and prestigious colleges and universities. They plan to go on to graduate school, a Ph.D., and a career of research and scholarship.

As identified in the CSQ, academics are broadly middle class in background and have relatively well-educated parents. In high school, by self-report, they studied extensively, received recognition for academic achievement, and found particular satisfaction from course work in the natural sciences. As a type, they are not critical of their college (mean scores on the four CSQ-2 satisfaction measures fall about at the norm) and are serious and organized in their study routines (study habits mean is the highest of the four types).

On the attitude scales in the CSQ, the academic type tends to score above the norm. We would infer that as an analytic type, the academic is slightly left of center in his politics. By nature and because of the pressure of other commitments, he is not an activist; he would, however, be a sympathizer and possibly even a participant in some future, broadly-based radical student movement.

Intellectuals. Whereas the academic pursues knowledge within the confines of a specific academic discipline, the intellectual, as a type, is oriented toward ideas and networks of ideas irrespective of the curriculum. In distinguishing the intellectual from the academic, Christopher Jencks and David Riesman have characterized the intellectual as being concerned with "questions of interest . . . to intelligent men everywhere."[20] The prototype academic is a scientist, the prototype intellectual a philosopher or historian; the former seeks truth through the scientific method, the latter through an interplay of human insights.[21]

These students tend to come from middle- and upper-class families, to be highly individualistic, liberal in their political outlook (but rather cool or unemotional about it), and aesthetically sensitive. Motivation for grades, a mark of the academic type, is not noticeable in the intellectual.

In view of the illustrious history of the alienation of intellectuals, we infer that the intellectual college student of the 1960's stands well over on our hypothetical acceptance-rejection of American institutions dimension.

Left-activists. The basic commitment of the left-activist, dues-paying and otherwise, is to personal involvement in action directed at reforming some facet of American life — be it political, economic, or cultural. His parents are prosperous and liberal in outlook. Highly intelligent, activists are found for the most part in the most selective and best-known colleges and universities, where their noncareer-oriented academic interests center in the social sciences and humanities. Activists share many of the personality traits of the intellectual, although the radical activists are characterized by a more passionate sense of outrage at perceived hypocrisy, injustice, and wrong-doing; and they have the courage to act — to make their behavior consistent with their beliefs.

Hippies. Of the eight student types, the hippie's estrangement from American values and institutions is the most thoroughgoing. Unlike the left-activist who hopes for radical reform through direct action, the hippie is pessimistically apolitical. Immersed in a culture based on hallucinogens, hedonism, and anti-middle-class personal styles, hippies who are enrolled in college would reject most of the conventional student roles. On their respective campuses, they constitute, as Keniston has put it, "a kind of hidden underground, disorganized and shifting in membership, in which students can temporarily or permanently withdraw from the ordinary pressures of college life."[22]

Personal Characteristics of Student Radicals

The ten or so data-based studies of radical activists that have been published yield a remarkably consistent profile of the personal and background characteristics of these students.[23]

In terms of the usual criteria, student leftists are upper-middle-class in their social origins. Their parents are politically liberal or radical, and many have been involved in radical politics. Both the students and their parents consider themselves to be either non-religious, or liberal and non-formalistic in their religious orientation. Parents of activists are permissive and democratic in their child-rearing practices, and their children are both highly intelligent and intellectually rather than career oriented. They are disproportionately concentrated in the social sciences and humanities and underrepresented in preprofessional programs. They perceive themselves as independent from most sources of social influence and authority, and are interested in and sensitive to various forms of artistic expression. Radical activists perceive in themselves an altruistic sense of responsibility in relation to almost all people, and their intense interpersonal relationships stress empathy, openness, and honesty.

Student Activists at Michigan State University. As part of his doctoral work at Michigan State University, George Paulus gathered data during 1966 on three groups of students on that campus: 25 activist leaders, 25 student-government leaders, and a control group of 25 students carefully matched to the activist sample.[24] The activist group consisted of leaders of the local SDS and SNCC organizations, as well as the leaders of a campus group called Committee for Student Rights (CSR). The student government leaders were elected ASMSU officials. These 75 students completed CSQ Parts 1 and 2. Mean scores for the three groups on the 11 CSQ-2 scales are profiled in Figure 2.

Many commentators have spoken of the alienation and depersonalization of individual students at the multiversity. They often go

Figure 2
CSQ Profiles for Three Michigan State University Student Groups*

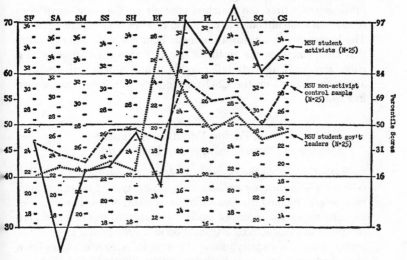

* Data made available by George Paulus of MSU

on to reason that because of frustration many students seek identity and fulfillment through involvement in radical politics and larger political issues. Judging from the pattern of mean scores on the four CSQ satisfaction scales in Paulus's data, the relationship between dissatisfaction with college and radical politics is not a simple one. Taking SF (satisfaction with faculty and student-faculty relations) and SM (satisfaction with major field work) as indicators of *academic* satisfaction, and SA (satisfaction with administrative rules and practices) as a crude index of satisfaction with the *non-academic* side of college life, it appears that the MSU activists were generally *not* displeased by their academic experiences, but were highly provoked by the university's posture regarding student life outside the classroom. Specifically, SF and SM (and SH) differences between the activist and matched control groups were not statistically significant; the gap on the SA scale, however, was fully two standard deviations.[25] The activists, furthermore, roundly rejected the usual "collegiate" brand of extracurricular activities (low EI).

The pattern of mean scores on the other scales, as shown in Figure 2, tends to agree with results of other studies in other settings. Judging from their high FI and PI scores, the MSU activists generally operate relatively independently of influence from parents or peers. The liberalism scale mean is the highest heretofore obtained with any student group. A standard deviation separated the MSU activists from the matched controls on the social-conscience measure, a scale intended to tap moral concern over human injustice. The high cultural sophistication mean is in line with other research that has pointed to the aesthetic interests of activist students. Finally, the MSU activists fell roughly a half a standard deviation above the "norm" on the CSQ-1 socio-economic index (not shown in Figure 2).

The Institutional Factor: Variation in Student Activism at Diverse Colleges and Universities

Earlier we noted the diversity in American institutions of higher education — in purpose and curriculum, size, type of control, admissions selectivity, and the like. Additional institutional characteristics are also important in understanding the current status and future prospects of the student Left: location of a college in a large urban center where the country's social ills tend to be focused; a tradition of student radicalism, as at Berkeley and the Universities of Michigan and Wisconsin; the degree to which a college — in both its explicit or informal policies — is closed and rigid or open and libertarian with regard to its students' personal and political lives. Many colleges and universities are known to prospective entrants in such terms. Institutions, in short, have reputations or images. The reasonably affluent student applies to or preselects three or four colleges whose images he thinks are compatible with his own interests, values, and aspirations.

This preselection mechanism is critical in understanding the variation in student activism from one college student body to another. In view of what is known about the personality and background of student leftists, the disposition to become involved in radical politics exists prior to entry into college.[26] Such students select colleges where their disposition may find fruition. The activist-inclined student, it is suggested, is particularly mindful of the rigid-libertarian dimension of a college's image in his preselection deliberations.

Institutional Variation in the Climate of Freedom

Edmund Williamson and John Cowan's *The American Student's Freedom of Expression* will surely stand as a milestone in research on higher education.[27] This study set out to describe the extent to which colleges allow their students freedom to express their beliefs on controversial issues. Questionnaires covering a host of policy manifestations were sent in the spring of 1964 to five officials at all the accredited four-year institutions in the country. Respondents included presidents, deans of students, chairmen of faculty committees on student affairs, student-body presidents, and editors of student newspapers. Eighty-five per cent of the colleges returned one or more of the five questionnaires, and almost 70 per cent returned all five.

The authors described private universities as being relatively permissive in regard to student freedom to discuss controversial topics, invite off-campus speakers, demonstrate actively, and engage in civil rights activity. Student-newspaper editors were exceptionally independent on these campuses, and there were many social- and political-action groups. Students clearly practice freedom more widely at private universities than they do at most other colleges.

Although students at private liberal-arts colleges enjoy freedom comparable to that in private universities, these colleges tend to be more in the "ivory tower" tradition, and students are less inclined to exercise their freedom or to engage in controversy about freedoms. Results for large public universities generally parallel those for private universities, except that administrators expressed only an "average" commitment to the principle of student freedom; student participation on policy-making committees was relatively greater, however.

Student freedom to discuss or demonstrate at small public universities was not significantly above the average for all schools in the study. Student leaders, however, were independent and active in policy-making. The number of administrators committed to a philosophy of freedom was not unusually large, and respondents disagreed about the extent of freedom on respective campuses. The pattern of results for Protestant universities and liberal-arts colleges also did not differ substantially from the responses of all the schools as a group. There was, however, greater than average independence for the student editor. There was also exceptional disagreement between deans and student presidents concerning prohibition of liberal student organizations. Technical institutions were essentially at the national mean with respect to practice of academic freedom; administrators disagreed about whether freedom for students to address themselves to controversial social problems was essential to education. Students were seen as seeking competence in specialized fields, rather than interesting themselves in social issues.

An "average" amount of freedom for student groups to take controversial stands was thought to exist at Catholic universities. Student freedom to invite controversial speakers was significantly below the national mean. There was a great deal of supervision of student editors, and few student political organizations existed on these campuses. Administrators showed relatively little commitment to the concept of academic freedom. This pattern was much the same for the Catholic liberal-arts colleges, except that students were significantly restricted in freedom of expression.

There was less than average freedom to discuss topics, invite speakers, or demonstrate at teachers' colleges. Student newspaper editors were unusually dependent on the administration. There were few student political organizations. Student participation in policy-making, however, was about "average," but freedom seemed to be more preached than practiced.

Institutional Variation in Incidence of Student Protest

Planning for our survey of organized student protest got under way in the late spring of 1965, in the wake of the Berkeley crisis and reports of widespread student unrest.[28] The general purpose of the study was to assemble some reasonably trustworthy information about the dimensions of discontent among America's college students.

In September, 1965, questionnaires were sent to deans of students at all the accredited four-year colleges in the country; the population of institutions, thus, was the same as that used by Williamson and Cowan. The deans were asked to indicate in relation to each of twenty-seven issues — class size, speakers regulations, dormitory rules, Vietnam, and so forth — whether there had been any occurrence of organized student protest during the preceding academic year (1964–65). They were requested to limit their judgments to planned, public expressions of disapproval on the part of groups and not to consider the usual complaints of individual students. Student personnel deans were surveyed on the assumption that among campus officials they are generally in closest touch with student protest activities. Based on an 85 per cent return, then, the survey results provide a picture of student activism as it is drawn by deans of students for the academic year 1964–65. The discussion that follows will be limited to the off-campus issues — civil rights and U.S. military policies — which, in contrast to the internal on-campus problems, most directly engage campus leftists.

Before turning to institutional variation in student activism, some mention of the over-all, national picture may be of interest. Of the twenty-seven issues considered, civil rights was the focus of student activism on the largest number of campuses. The year 1964, especially the summer, marked the heroic period in the civil rights struggle, at least insofar as the involvement of college students was concerned. Vietnam protests were reported at about one in five colleges (21 per cent), about the same as the number reporting protests about dress regulations (20 per cent). Agitation concerning food service and dormitory regulations was reported on 29 per cent and 28 per cent of the campuses respectively. While there was little geographical variation for the campus issues (dress regulations and so forth), proportionately fewer colleges in the South reported student activism in relation to the off-campus issues.

Percentages of nine different types of institutions indicating protest on the six off-campus issue-statements in the survey are given in Table 1. One can readily see the general parallel with the Williamson-Cowan results.

Civil rights involvement was most frequently reported by the independent universities. The deans at over half of these institutions reported that some of their students participated in civil rights ac-

Table 1
Percentages of Different Types of Institutions Reporting
Student Protest Over Six Off-Campus Issues

	All	Indep. Univ.	Indep. L.A. Coll.	Public Univ.	Public L.A. Coll.	Prot. Inst.	Cath. Inst.	Tech. Inst.	T.C.
	N=849	N=51	N=144	N=133	N=89	N=160	N=147	N=28	N=63
Civil rights: local area (off-campus) — protest and/or work	38	53	46	44	30	30	45	36	13
Civil rights: in the South during the summer of 1964 — protest and/or work	28	51	35	37	22	25	23	14	11
Other civil rights protest or work	24	33	33	29	16	13	30	11	14
Disarmament, "ban-the-bomb," peace, etc.	12	26	18	20	14	5	5	7	2
U.S. policies regarding Vietnam	21	61	27	36	17	8	8	25	6
U.S. policies regarding the Dominican Republic	5	6	6	11	6	1	1	7	3

tivities locally or in the South during the summer of 1964. At the other extreme, about one in eight teachers' colleges reported student involvement in civil rights. A crude ranking of the eight types of student bodies in terms of civil rights activism would be: independent universities, independent liberal-arts colleges, public universities, and Catholic institutions — all standing above the "national norm"; ranged below the norm would be the public liberal-arts colleges, Protestant institutions, technical institutions, and teachers' colleges.

Variation by institutional type was more pronounced for the U.S. foreign-policy issues than for civil rights. On the Vietnam issue, the incidence of organized student protest ranged from a high of 61 per cent in the independent universities to 8 per cent in both the Protestant and Catholic institutions and 6 per cent at the teachers' colleges.

The deans were also asked (multiple-choice questions) to give the following information about their colleges: proportion of faculty doctorates, proportion of student body living on campus, proportion of student body belonging to leftist groups, and total enrollment (institutional size). Relationships between each of these variables, as well as the response to the question on civil rights activity in the South during the summer of 1964 and each of the protest issues were studied by means of product-moment correlation analysis.

Correlations involving the faculty-doctorates dimension (a crude index of institutional quality) and the six off-campus issues ranged from .18 on the Dominican Republic situation to .43 for the Vietnam issue; this last finding may be of some significance if the Vietnam war continues, since graduates from the "good" colleges will tend to be the opinion leaders of the coming generation. All six correlations with the commuter-residential dimension were negligible, which suggests that, in general, this factor is not related to campus activism. The range of correlations between estimated proportion of student body belonging to the organized left was from .22 (other civil rights) to .47 for Vietnam.[29] Correlations for the response to the question concerning civil rights activities in the South ranged from .33 for the Dominican Republic situation, through .47 for Vietnam, to .54 for civil rights locally. The hypothesis here, of course, was that the presence on campus of highly committed civil rights activists would be associated with student militancy in behalf of other issues and problems.

Size of student body proved to be unrelated linearly to organized student protest to any meaningful degree. Reasoning that the relationship may be curvilinear — that is, that student protest would occur most frequently at the *very* large institutions — a separate tabulation was made for the fifty largest public universities in the sample. (All have graduate and undergraduate student bodies exceeding ten thousand.) The figures for this subsample turned out to be considerably higher than those for any of the institutional types included in Table 1 (specifically: civil rights locally, 56 per cent; civil rights in the South, 54 per cent; other civil rights, 40 per cent; disarmament-peace, 44 per cent; Vietnam, 68 per cent [34 out of 50 universities]; and the Dominican Republic issue, 26 per cent).

As we have argued elsewhere, the relative prevalence of organized student activism concerning off-campus political and social issues in the large institutions is probably less the result of multiversity-induced alienation than it is a reflection of the gross numbers of diverse individuals brought together at one time and place.[30] The larger the student body is, the greater is the likelihood of there being some student who wishes to start something — an SDS chapter, a speech walk-out, a student strike — and of his being able to find others who will sympathize.

"Discovery" of the subjection of Negroes in democratic, enlightened America gives rise to the radical student movement. It took heart, until his assassination, in a young idealistic President. It was intensified by the discovery of grinding poverty in the world's wealthiest nation and by the thought of the world's greatest power being engaged in a war of attrition in a tiny, undeveloped country. It is sustained by the view that students themselves are being degraded in the university and, indeed, that citizens everywhere are leading "lives of quiet desperation." And it is supported by the belief that the social system that permits these hypocrisies cannot be tolerated and must be altered.

Only a small fragment of college students shares this powerful sense of outrage — no more than about 2 per cent. Intelligent, independent, noncareerist offspring of affluent parents, the student leftists tend to be enrolled in the "best" and most libertarian colleges and universities. In the general student population, student radicals would be greatly outnumbered by almost every "type" of student, probably including even the hippies who share the activists' moral revulsion, but not their willingness to act on behalf of a vision that goes beyond the self. The overwhelming majority of American college students are politically apathetic — caught up in their vocational, academic, or hedonistic pursuits.

The Student Left in American Higher Education

Student leftists, working in league with various temporarily activated campus-issue protesters, have already had a significant impact on university life, especially its nonacademic aspects. New freedoms have been granted students on many campuses — probably more often out of fear of the boat being rocked, however, than on the basis of some model linking personal freedom with intellectual and personality development. Professors, with little at stake in the nonacademic issues, have generally stood aside, often relishing the sight of administrators being manipulated by students.

By contrast, the impact of student radicals on the academic side of college life has been less noticeable. Here the professors do have a stake, and their conservatism on matters of instruction, curriculum development, and the like is well known. Such student-initiated "parallel institutions" as the free universities and experimental colleges, while they currently exist on upwards of forty or fifty campuses, enroll relatively small segments of the respective student bodies — mainly intellectuals, activists, and hippies (and perhaps serve to sidetrack many activists from larger reform efforts). In response to student demands in the past two to three years, many colleges have indeed made a variety of changes that presumably bear on the manner of student learning: students have been seated on curriculum committees; course and teacher evaluations are being published by students; new grading practices are being tried out; and so forth. The reforms, however, are generally of a token nature. The essentials of student learning at most colleges have not yet been altered.

What do the student radicals want? In general, they want students to have power to share meaningfully in setting the conditions under which they learn. For themselves, most of the radicals look forward to "humanized" learning experiences: freely chosen experiences that are free of ritualistic requirements (such as mandatory attendance and periodic exams), rather than lockstep curricula and the same old teaching methods; experiences based on intense human relationships (by which student leftists live), rather than information impersonally dispensed; individualized, "helping" teaching rather than dog-eat-dog competition; integration rather than fragmentation of knowledge. They also want complete freedom in their personal lives. And they want their institution to be free of certain "obvious" immoralities — racism, cooperation with the military, complicity in exploiting the Third World.

"Student power," then, is neither an empty slogan nor a demand for power for its own sake. It symbolizes the demand that students be taken seriously; that they be given the opportunity to assume real responsibilities for governance of the total institution. It is a plea that their beliefs about the purpose and nature of the institution be heard, and that they have a meaningful role in charting institutional reforms. As events of the past years have shown, when student activists feel their verbal urgings are not taken seriously, they resort to physical disruption. Or worse, if the insurrectionists have their way, while somewhat unbelievable in view of the American past, one can nonetheless conceive of bands of student militants mounting guerrilla-type attacks on campus facilities (such as the job-placement office, ROTC facilities, the radiation lab, the dean's office) and perhaps other establishment outposts as well (selective service offices, "exploitive" merchants, socially or racially exclusive clubs, and so forth).

By and large white and black radicals no longer work together. Their goals are different, and all parties now agree that the major short-term goal of the blacks — development of racial consciousness and pride — must be accomplished by blacks, without help from whites. Black students on white campuses all across the country have organized themselves in the past three years, and their militancy has led rapidly to plans for larger numbers of Negro students and faculty and for programs of study in Negro history, literature, art, and so forth. These "Afro" student groups as well as militants on black campuses who are agitating not just for black studies but for lifting their colleges out of second-class status, however, should not be regarded as part of the Left. The black student groups are concerned almost totally with their own situation on campus, pretty much to the exclusion of the "immoral war," "institutionalized corruption," "one-dimensional man," and other New Left shibboleths.

So far, the impact of the student Left on life in America outside the university seems to have been rather small. While lunch counters, bus terminals, and some numbers of schools have been integrated, the lives of very few Negroes have been genuinely improved (Watts may be an exception). The war in Vietnam goes on, despite the dramatic shift in public opinion during 1967 which must, in part, be attributed to student activism. The gap between the have's and have-not's in America is not becoming smaller. Many relationships between people continue, seemingly of necessity, to be essentially bureaucratic in nature. Critical social institutions — political and governmental, business, labor, law enforcement — continue to harbor corruption. In short, meaningful achievements have been few;

all the conditions that spawned and nourished the radical movement still exist.

The future of the student Left is contingent on many things: a massive, repressive backlash spurred by forces opposed to social change; the capacity of the liberal establishment (assuming its continuation) to co-opt radical ideas[31]; the Left's ability, in the face of anarchic localism, to create a unifying ideology and then to mount coordinated national programs; the students' practical intelligence to deal with political, social, and educational complexities; the temptations of "straight" life — careerism, materialism, familyism, social acceptance, and all the rest. On this last, however, those who explain student radicalism as merely a generational revolt may be deceiving themselves, at least judging from the desire of many ex-SDS'ers to stay active in radical work.

In contrast to its seemingly minor influence outside the university, the impact of the student Left within higher education is proving to be substantial. Indeed one may argue, as Edgar Friedenberg for one has, that the *real* revolution in higher education is only just now under way, begun by the student radicals of the 1960's.[32] (And reform of the university, an increasingly pivotal institution in American society, is viewed by some New Left theorists as the first step in reconstructing the total social order.) At the present time, however, there are few signs that the student-propelled revolution in higher education will soon become a coordinated, concerted putsch. Humane men, both old and young, will trust that the revolution can go forward resolutely, creatively, and nonviolently without resort to "two, three, many Columbias."

REFERENCES

1. The half-dozen or so empirical studies of student conservatives have been summarized by Jeanne H. Block, Norma Haan, and M. Brewster Smith, "Activism and Apathy in Contemporary Adolescents," *Contributions to the Understanding of Adolescence*, ed. James F. Adams (New York, 1968).

2. S. M. Lipset and Philip G. Altbach, "Student Politics and Higher Education in the United States," *Student Politics*, ed. S. M. Lipset (New York, 1967), pp. 199–252. See especially pp. 206–207.

3. Richard E. Peterson, *The Scope of Organized Student Protest in 1964–1965* (Princeton, 1966), pp. 36–39.

4. Jack Newfield, *A Prophetic Minority* (New York, 1966), pp. 149–174.

5. In addition to SDS-PLP people, whose obstructing and diverting tactics were much in evidence at the June 1968 SDS National Convention, there are also SDS-CP'ers. According to some observers, the American Communist Party is presently experiencing something of a rebirth. See Michael Miles, "New Left, Red Left," *The New Republic* (February 3, 1968), pp. 21–25.

6. With the demise this year of its national structure, it remains to be seen whether local campus UCM groups, doing their own thing, will prove to be a viable element in the larger student movement. The "organizing principle" of UCM "is to bring about social change through reformulation of the university."

7. "The New SNCC: Weaker, Fierier," the *New York Times* (August 20, 1967).

8. Richard Blumenthal, "SDS: Protest Is Not Enough," *Nation* (May 22, 1967).

9. James Jacobs, "SDS: Between Reform and Revolution," *Nation* (June 10, 1968).

10. Statistics are primarily from the U.S. Office of Education's Digest of Educational Statistics, 1966, and also from Martin Meyerson's paper, "The Ethos of the American College Student: Beyond the Protests," *The Contemporary University: U.S.A.*, ed. Robert Morison (Boston, 1966).

11. James Cass and Max Birnbaum, *Comparative Guide to American Colleges* (New York, 1964).

12. Kenneth E. Eble, *The Profane Comedy* (New York, 1962).

13. Meyerson, "The Ethos of the American College Student," p. 269.

14. Burton R. Clark and Martin Trow, "The Organizational Context," *College Peer Groups,* eds. Theodore Newcomb and Everett Wilson (Chicago, 1966).

15. Harry Schumer and Robert Stanfield, "Assessment of Student Role Orientations in College," *Proceedings of the 74th Annual Convention of the American Psychological Association, 1966* (Washington, D.C., 1966). Jonathan R. Warren, *Patterns of College Experiences* (Claremont, Calif., 1966).

16. Richard E. Peterson, *Technical Manual: College Student Questionnaires* (Princeton, 1965). There are two questionnaires: CSQ Part 1 is designed for entering freshmen; Part 2, which contains 11 Likert-type scales (see Figure 1), may be completed by any undergraduates who have been in college for a term or longer. A study of thirteen thousand entering freshmen classified according to the Clark-Trow model is reported in Richard E. Peterson, *On a Typology of College Students* (Research Bulletin 65–9, ETS, 1965). A comparable analysis of seven hundred undergraduate respondents to CSQ-2 (Figure 1) is contained in the *CSQ Manual.*

17. For a more comprehensive description of the professionalist, see Kenneth Keniston, "The Faces in the Lecture Room," *The Contemporary University: U.S.A.*, ed. Robert Morison (Boston, 1966).

18. In a study with the CSQ, undergraduates planning to attend law school (N = 178) scored significantly higher than a group headed toward graduate schools of business (N = 175) on the measures of liberalism, social conscience, cultural sophistication, and extracurricular involvement (as in student government). R. E. Peterson, "Some Notes on the Prospective Graduate Business Student," *Proceedings of 1966 Graduate Business School Admissions Symposium* (Princeton, 1966).

19. At the University of Massachusetts, Harry Schumer and Robert Stanfield identified three collegiate types: (1) the "instrumental collegiate," involving "active participation in extracurricular activities as a leader, an organizer, or a worker"; (2) the "consummatory collegiate," involving dissipation of students' energies "in activity and inactivity that is experienced as intrinsically pleasurable"; and (3) a "Greek" factor centering on participation "in the Greek system on campus."

20. Christopher Jencks and David Riesman, "Patterns of Residential Education: A Case Study of Harvard," *The American College*, ed. Nevitt Sanford (New York, 1962).

21. Empirically distinct academic and intellectual patterns emerged from both Harry Schumer and Robert Stanfield's and Jonathan Warren's factor analyses. Both studies drew attention to the intellectual's intrinsic satisfaction from ideas as against satisfying course requirements. Schumer and Stanfield's intellectual factor was characterized also by a humanities content orientation.

22. Kenneth Keniston, "The Sources of Student Dissent," *The Journal of Social Issues*, Vol. 23 (1967), pp. 108–37.

23. Five of the studies deal with activists at Berkeley: Glenn Lyons, "The Police Car Demonstration: A Survey of Participants," and Robert H. Somers, "The Mainsprings of the Rebellion: A Survey of Berkeley Students in November 1964," both in *The Berkeley Student Revolt: Facts and Interpretations*, eds. S. M. Lipset and S. S. Wolin (New York, 1965). Paul Heist, "Intellect and Commitment: The Faces of Discontent," *Order and Freedom on Campus: The Rights and Responsibilities of Faculty and Students*, eds. O. W. Knorr and W. J. Minter (Boulder 1965). Block, Haan, and Smith, "Activism and Apathy in Contemporary Adolescents," W. A. Watts and D. N. E. Whittaker "Free Speech Advocates at Berkeley," *Journal of Applied Behavioral Science*, No. 2 (1966), pp. 41–62. In the other five studies, the samples were students from Chicago-area homes who belonged to several different "movement organizations": Richard Flacks, "The Liberated Generation: An Exploration of the Roots of Student Protest," *The Journal of Social Issues*, Vol. 23 (1967), pp. 52–75; peace activists at Pennsylvania State University: David L. Westby and Richard G. Braungart, "Class and Politics in the Family Backgrounds of Student

Political Activists," *American Sociological Review*, Vol. 31 (1966), pp. 690–92; SDS National Convention delegates: Westby and Braungart, "The Alienation of Generations and Status Politics: Alternative Explanations of Student Political Activism," *Political Socialization*, ed. Roberta S. Sigel (New York, 1968); a group of participants in the 1962 Peace March on Washington: Frederic Solomon and Jacob R. Fishman, "Youth and Peace: A Psychosocial Study of Student Peace Demonstrators in Washington, D.C.," *The Journal of Social Issues*, Vol. 20 (1964), pp. 54–73; and the leadership of the 1967 Vietnam Summer project: Kenneth Keniston, *Young Radicals* (New York, 1968). General reviews of this literature are available in Lipset and Altbach, "Student Politics and Higher Education in the United States"; Joseph Katz, *The Student Activists: Rights, Needs and Powers of Undergraduates* (Washington, D.C., 1967); Keniston, *Young Radicals;* and Block Haan, and Smith, "Activism and Apathy in Contemporary Adolescents." See also "Students USA," *Intercom*, Vol. 9 (July-August, 1967).

24. This section is based on George Paulus, *A Multivariate Analysis Study of Student Activist Leaders, Student Government Leaders, and Nonactivists* (unpublished Ph.D. dissertation, Michigan State University).

25. All three MSU groups stood below the multicollege "norm" on each of the satisfaction measures. This is a usual finding. Large-versus-small-college differences on the CSQ satisfaction scales are reported and discussed in the *CSQ Technical Manual.*

26. See especially Keniston, *Young Radicals.*

27. Edmund Williamson and John Cowan, *The American Student's Freedom of Expression* (Minneapolis, 1966).

28. Peterson, *The Scope of Organized Student Protest in 1964–1965.*

29. The magnitude of the organized student Left in the eyes of deans of students in 1965 is reflected by the facts that one in four deans (26 per cent) reported members of leftist student groups on their campuses, and only six out of 849 colleges reported that student radicals amounted to more than 5 per cent of the student body. Data from a follow-up survey at the end of the academic year 1967–1968 indicate a substantial increase in student Left groups on campuses around the country: from 26 per cent in 1965 to about 46 per cent in 1968 (based on returns from 859 colleges). By type of institution (in 1965), presence of student leftists was reported at 63 per cent of the independent universities and 48 per cent of the public universities, but at only 13 per cent of the teachers' colleges and 9 per cent of the Catholic institutions. Note again the parallel to the Williamson-Cowan conclusions.

30. Peterson, *The Scope of Organized Student Protest in 1964–1965.* This point was previously made by Somers ("The Mainsprings of the Rebellion: A Survey of Berkeley Students in November, 1964," p. 549).

31. Election of a liberal president in 1968 would probably not have generated much change in the pattern of student politics, with the only real activists

situated on the Left. A conservative win will probably lead to an increased polarization of campus political sentiment. The ranks of the student Left would swell with the new availability of issues and human targets. The student Right would also prosper under a more conservative national political climate; the many *status quo*-oriented vocationalists, professionalists, and collegiates on most every campus, who look with disdain on the activist "wierdos," can be expected to make a Republican year nationally a Republican year on the campus as well. Possibly YAF and the Intercollegiate Society of Individualists (Ayn Rand devotees) would be supplemented by a new student conservative organization with a more moderate image.

In view of the impressive student involvement in Eugene McCarthy's candidacy, observers are wondering what the effect will be of McCarthy's failure to survive the Democratic convention. Undoubtedly quite a few of the students, out of dismay at electoral politics and the debacle of Chicago, will move into the ranks of the hard-core Left. Most of the others — academics, intellectuals, hippies who made themselves "clean for Gene" — will revert back to their customary non-activist roles. (Very few from the organized student Left went out of their way to work for McCarthy.) The notion that the student supporters of McCarthy were critically responsible for changing the whole political picture in 1968 (McCarthy's New Hampshire win, Robert Kennedy's entry, Johnson's exit, onset of the Paris negotiations) is a fascinating one and should receive close historical analysis.

32. Edgar Friedenberg, "Toward Higher Higher Education" (review of Christopher Jencks and David Riesman, *The Academic Revolution*), the *New York Times Book Review* (May 19, 1968).

II

ASIA

PHILIP G. ALTBACH

Student Politics and
Higher Education in India

FOR OVER a century, student unrest has been one of India's most serious educational and political problems.[1] Student agitation has caused state governments to fall and has forced the central government to change its language policies. In recent national elections, student participation contributed to the weakening of the Congress Party. Students played an important part in the struggle for independence and traditions of student participation in national politics were developed. In the post-independence period, the motivations for student activism have been more difficult to understand, and agitation has centered primarily on local, non-ideological issues. While there has been much discussion of the problem of student unrest and activism in India, there has been little analysis of the underlying problems students face in a society strained by severe economic and educational crises. Indian students function in a "society of scarcity," a consideration central to any discussion of Indian higher education.[2]

Indian Higher Education —
The Context for Student Activism

Western-style higher education in India has a history of one hundred and fifty years; the university system itself is more than a century old. India's long struggle for freedom, ideologically centered in the universities and coupled with strong educational traditions, stimulated the growth of political awareness on the campus. Macaulay's famous "Minute" on education, approved in 1835, advocated a strong European bias in the educational system, a bias that still exists. Indian influences on higher education were also strong, and men like Ram Mohan Roy in Bengal and Dadabhai Naoroji in Bombay helped to stimulate the rapid growth of higher education in the nineteenth century.

Until the establishment of universities at Bombay, Calcutta, and Madras in 1857, higher education in India did not have a firm foundation. These institutions, begun as "affiliating" universities patterned after the University of London, set uniform educational standards for the growing number of colleges in India by regulating courses and examinations. The number of colleges in British-administered India increased from twenty-seven to seventy-two between 1857 and 1882.[3] During this period, higher education was almost exclusively limited to the sons of the very small Westernized middle and upper class and was largely confined to the cities. The student population remained numerically small and relatively homogeneous both in social class and caste. Most students hoped for careers in the civil service or the professions, particularly law and medicine.

The system of higher education developed by the British in India was designed to provide Indians with facility in English and with the skills necessary to fill the lower ranks of the civil service. As an Indian middle class developed, many realized that success depended upon a Western-style higher education, and growing numbers of Indians competed for the limited number of openings in the colleges. Indian higher education expanded to meet the demands placed upon it; in the first three decades of the twentieth century, the student population increased fivefold, while the number of universities doubled. In 1921, there were almost sixty thousand students in Indian colleges and universities, but by 1936 this number had doubled.[4]

As the educational system grew and the number of politically aware and articulate Indians increased, the small Indian nationalist movement changed into a militant mass movement, and students actively participated in the struggle for independence.[5] Since independence, however, student attempts to intervene in political affairs have been sporadic. Lacking the ideological fervor that characterized the nationalist period, the mass student movements have collapsed. The strong support given by the leaders of the Congress Party to the student movement has been withdrawn, and both political figures and educators now urge students to avoid politics and to concentrate on acquiring the skills necessary for national development.

The Student Movement and the Struggle for Independence

Several student organizations had been founded by 1900, although educational and social matters and not politics were their main preoccupations. Only a relatively small minority, perhaps numbering a few thousand throughout the country, took any interest in politics, and most of them were engaged in moderate discussion groups. As one British observer noted: "It was not till after the political and racial excitement [of the nationalist movement] that the youth attending schools and colleges showed signs of turbulence and insubordination."[6]

The period prior to 1920 was a time of establishing higher education in India, and political consciousness developed slowly among students. While the militant activism of later decades was missing, students were exposed to ideological currents from Europe, and the growing political tensions within India added to this ferment.

By 1905, students in Bengal were awakening to political issues. Members of a Bengali student terrorist organization made an attempt on the life of the British governor general to express their opposition to the British-sponsored partition of Bengal. Student agitation was partially responsible for forcing the British to abandon this plan, and Bengal remained temporarily united. According to a report of the government's Sedition Committee issued in 1918, 68 out of 186 arrested in Bengal between 1907 and 1917 for "revolutionary crimes" were students; another 16 were teachers in schools and colleges.[7] Maharashtrian students were active in the nationalist movement organized by the militant and strongly Hindu-oriented B. G. Tilak; they found his activist program more appealing than the moderation of the Congress Party at the time.

A number of organizations were formed during the early years of the twentieth century which provided some of the basis for the political activism that developed later. Discussion and debating groups were founded at many colleges, and elocution competitions provided training in public speaking. Cultural and literary societies were more concerned with Western knowledge than with traditional Indian scholarship, but these groups gave students a feeling of self-identification while supplementing their academic programs. Groups such as the Students' Brotherhood in Bombay, which was founded in the 1890's, provided a meeting place for students and soon became propagators of "modern" attitudes toward a number of social issues, like caste and the status of women. The Brotherhood was, for example, one of the few organizations in India at the time that opened its membership to women.

The 1920's brought both educational and political changes to India. Continued growth in the educational system created increasing problems for the students. The establishment of new colleges, many without stable financial arrangements or adequate staff, lowered the standards of higher education and intensified the competition for jobs. Politically, the twenties saw the growth of the Indian National Congress as a mass movement under Gandhi's leadership. During its early years, the Congress was a moderate organization recruited primarily from the Western-educated middle class and not given to political agitation. As the Congress grew more militant in the early years of the twentieth century, the student community also took a more active interest in politics. The articulate and militant nationalism of the Congress appealed to the students because it provided the opportunity for dramatic political action and promised speedy independence for India. The Congress leadership was based in the college-trained intelligentsia, but the influence of radical thought on the growing working class gave it added strength.

Gandhi's Non-Cooperation Movement of 1920 was the first major mass agitation initiated by the Congress. It was also the first political struggle that involved large numbers of students. Youth Leagues were formed in major educational centers to coordinate student efforts, and the discussion and debating societies of earlier periods became the nuclei of political organizations.[8] Students helped with Congress campaigns and provided much of the manpower for the almost daily street demonstrations in the cities. In some areas, students assumed the movement's leadership when Congress leaders were arrested. National (anti-British) colleges were established in the major cities, but they were only temporarily successful, for many students returned to their regular classes when the heat of the movement abated. Although the Non-Cooperation Movement failed to expel the British from India, it did establish the Congress as a militant mass organization and gave the students and the growing trade-union movement their first experience of mass political struggle.

The Non-Cooperation Movement stimulated the foundation of a national student federation in India. The first annual All-India College Student Conference was held in Nagpur in 1920 to provide coordination for the growing student political movements. Similar student movements took place throughout the 1920's, and these annual gatherings helped to keep the political spark of the student movement alive in a period of general political quiet.

Regional student federations were founded in the Punjab, in Bengal, and in other areas. The All-Bengal Students' Association claimed a membership of twenty thousand in 1929. The Bombay Presidency (provincial) Students' Federation, formed in 1936, helped to bring ideological politics to the local and provincial levels. The All-India Student Conferences, which normally attracted more than three thousand students from all parts of the subcontinent, provided left-wing Congressmen with a platform and support for their views. These conferences were characterized by militant nationalism, and the ideas of socialism and Marxism found support among the students.[9] The student movement was probably the most radical element in Indian political life during this period. The study groups organized by left-wing students brought to the Indian campus the ideologies of European Marxism and the Russian Revolution — both of which had a marked influence on the thinking of politically minded students. Although only a minority of the student community was politically active in the 1920's, the movement established itself during this period and gained both organizational experience and ideological sophistication. One of the main campaigns of this period was a series of demonstrations against the Simon Commission, a British committee that visited India in 1928 to investigate the problems of Indian self-government. Students spearheaded demonstrations in most cities and demanded that the Commission recommend independence for India — the first time Indian students had organized a series of demonstrations on a national scale on their own initiative.

The 1930's brought an intensification of the political struggle in India. The influence of radical nationalist and socialist ideas spread by left-wing leaders, both in the Congress and in the student movement, prepared the students for a more active phase of the nationalist struggle. Gandhi's Civil Disobedience Movement of 1930 involved students on an unprecedented scale, and many of the more militant activities, such as the boycotting of shops and the cutting of telephone lines, were carried out by students. The Gandhian concept of nonviolence was never fully taken up by the students, some of whom participated in terrorist activities.

One of the results of the agitation of the early 1930's was the creation of the All-India Students' Federation in 1936. From the beginning, the AISF was strongly nationalist and radical in its approach. Within two years, the new organization was able to claim one thousand affiliated organizations and fifty thousand members.[10] The AISF journal, *Students' Federation,* was circulated throughout

India and provided a radical viewpoint on both educational and national issues. The AISF effectively united the student movement for several years while Gandhians, socialists, and Communists worked harmoniously within the organization. Provincial student federations carried on the regional work of the AISF, and the annual meetings of the organization usually attracted more than three thousand delegates, as well as many of the top Congress leaders.

In addition to the "mainstream" nationalist student movement, a number of other important trends existed within the student community. Many Muslim students, previously apathetic or pro-Congress, were influenced by Mohammad Ali Jinnah's call for a separate Muslim state on the Indian subcontinent and joined the Muslim League's All-India Muslim Students' Federation, founded in 1937. This organization, which had substantial support among Muslim students, did not participate in the independence movement, but pressed instead for Muslim rights. While the importance of the Muslim student groups diminished after the formation of Pakistan, the Muslim student movement helped to shape the political ideologies of a whole generation of Muslim leaders.

The Hindu right wing also gained strength, in part as a reaction to Muslim separatist sentiment. The Rashtriya Swayamsevak Sangh (RSS), founded in the late 1920's, appealed to militant Hindu nationalism and to anti-Muslim and anti-Christian feelings among Hindus.[11] By upholding traditional Hindu values, then under attack from Westernized elements in India, the RSS was able to attract many students, particularly in smaller colleges. The Hindu Student Federation, founded in the 1930's and similar in ideology to the RSS, had a more sophisticated approach and greater appeal for college students. Its influence was limited to north India, however, and it never constituted a threat to the nationalist student movement.

The Civil Disobedience Movement of 1930 ushered in the most active period of political agitation undertaken by Indian students. By 1938, Indian colleges were highly politicized, and students were involved in a variety of protest activities. Strikes against college authorities occurred almost weekly in many parts of India, instigated as often to further nationalist purposes as to correct a particular educational grievance. Students not normally concerned with political issues were attracted to the dramatic nationalist struggle. Thousands served short jail sentences for their part in the struggle, and many left college to work in the nationalist and labor movements or the Gandhian educational and social-service projects.

The split within the All-India Students' Federation in 1940 indicated some of the problems of the growing ideological sophistication of the student movement. After a period of harmony, differences between the Communists, on one side, and the socialists and the Gandhians, on the other, came into the open in 1940, making the breakup of the organization inevitable. The Communist-dominated All-India Students' Federation lost a large part of its support when the Communist Party supported the British war effort after the Soviet Union entered World War II in 1940. The nationalists organized the All-India Students' Congress in 1945. This group continued the struggle against the British, but at the same time it opposed the Communists. The Students' Congress, which stressed both social revolution and patriotism, was by far the most important national student organization in India at this time.

The most militant and highly organized period of the Indian student movement came during the 1942 "Quit India" struggle. When the Congress leadership called for an all-out, although nonviolent, effort to drive the British from India, the student movement succeeded in closing most of India's colleges for extended periods and brought masses of students into the struggle. About 10 per cent of the student population of India (or fifteen thousand students) was involved in the day-to-day organizational work of the nationalist movement. Students not previously involved in politics participated in almost daily demonstrations. Student cadres took part in sabotage campaigns and tried, with some success, to disrupt the British administration.[12] When the adult Congress leadership was arrested, students often assumed leadership responsibilities and provided a key liaison between the underground leaders and the movement. Student groups published illegal newspapers and even operated a clandestine radio station. Although the 1942 effort failed to expel the British from India, it was the first time that the Indian nationalists became a kind of "national liberation movement." The militancy of the students' involvement in the 1942 movement was retained, although on a reduced scale, until the end of the independence struggle.

The growth of a militant student movement in the pre-1947 period can be attributed to a number of factors — the main one being the highly politicized character of Indian cities and towns during the 1930's and 1940's. Many members of the student generation were attracted to the movement in these urban centers. The pre-independence student community, being small and compact, was relatively easy to organize. Because young people from rural areas and from the lower castes and classes were virtually excluded from the secondary and higher educational systems, the large majority of the students came from upper-middle- or upper-class and caste backgrounds.

The emphasis in the universities at this time was on the liberal arts, and students in this area have traditionally been more concerned with intellectual and political issues.[13] As in the post-independence period, students in the liberal arts were most active in political affairs during the nationalist struggle. Law students, who were destined for an independent professional career and had little chance for a government post, were particularly active.

The Transformation of the Student Movement

By 1947, the student movement had lost much of its momentum. The Students' Congress and other major student organizations were unsuccessful in shifting their efforts from an emphasis on political struggle to a program of Gandhian constructive service. Many radical student leaders were disillusioned by the compromises that the Congress leadership made in order to achieve independence without further bloodshed. The 1946 mutiny of the Indian Navy was an additional shock to the student movement, for the Congress leadership ordered the militant sailors to surrender to the British in the interest of a political compromise. Radical student leaders felt that they had been betrayed by the nationalist movement, and many left the student movement.[14]

With a few isolated exceptions, the student movement in India has been unable to regain its sense of militant unity and ideological purpose. Students have not ceased to participate in politics, but there has been a dramatic transformation of their movement. The nationalist fervor of the pre-independence period has been replaced by generally unorganized and sporadic agitation usually aimed at specific grievances.

The most important cause for the transformation of the student movement was the end of the independence struggle. Prior to 1947, political issues were clear and dramatic — the British had to be driven from the subcontinent, and radical social change had to be instituted in Indian society. The caste system, communal animosities, food shortages, and other social ills would be eliminated when India achieved independence and could guide her own affairs. Respected nationalist leaders encouraged students to take an active role in the political struggle. Following independence, the issues were no longer so clear. The Congress leadership was divided on how best to deal with India's many social and economic problems, and the departure of the British solved very little. Conservative elements in the nationalist movement achieved substantial power after 1947, and many radicals were forced into the opposition. Moreover, following independence, the Congress leaders reversed their former position and urged students to stay out of politics.

The spirit of individual self-sacrifice that had marked the independence struggle almost disappeared, and many political leaders became more concerned with their own careers than with ideology or national development. Regional, linguistic, and caste loyalties, temporarily put aside for the nationalist cause, resumed their old hold. For the post-independence student leader, a political career still depended on dedication to the Congress cause, as had been the case before 1947, but it also involved such undramatic details as winning elections and placating various economic and ideological tendencies.

Indian higher education was also undergoing changes. The expansion in enrollments, begun in earnest during the mid-1930's, continued after independence at an accelerated rate. Between 1950 and 1960, the number of college students increased from 263,000 to 645,000. In 1966, more than 1,094,000 students were enrolled in about 2,565 colleges.[15] The traditional base of Indian higher education, the liberal-arts college, was also waning in prestige and importance because the standards of instruction at these colleges declined seriously, as the student population expanded at an unprecedented rate. The value of a science education, on the other hand, increased substantially, as India's industrial production rose, and the standards of admission into the scientific fields tightened in order to protect standards of instruction. Technological institutions were created and given sufficient financial resources, while the liberal-arts colleges were allowed to expand almost without limit and were not adequately financed. As the number of graduates of the liberal arts exceeded the number of jobs available, educated unemployment became an increasing problem, and holders of B.A. degrees could consider themselves fortunate in finding clerical employment. Many employers began to demand a college degree for positions previously filled by literate, but academically unqualified individuals.

As the educational system grew, higher education became available to broader segments of the population, thereby destroying the homogeneity of the student population. Members of the student community had little in common since students were drawn from diverse class and caste backgrounds. Students from the lower-middle- and working-class families were often unwilling to risk their college careers to participate in political activity, and, in any case, they lacked a tradition of political activism.

A kind of "dual culture" has evolved on the campus as a result of the changes in higher education. Students from lower castes and classes often constitute a rather isolated, although growing, segment of the college population and seldom take part in extracurricular activities. Such students suffer most from the disadvantages of Indian higher education — poor conditions and falling standards of instruction, crowded institutions and fear of unemployment — and enjoy few of its advantages. Thus, they are frustrated and willing to participate in sporadic and disorganized student unrest and demonstrations. Working-class students or those from rural areas have generally gone into liberal-arts subjects, while upper- and middle-class students, who have received adequate secondary training and who have facility in English, have tended to go into the sciences, when they have been able to meet the rigorous admissions requirements.

The fact that the most able and qualified students have gone into the natural sciences and technical fields has had important implications for Indian higher education and for student political involvement. Students in the natural sciences have traditionally been less concerned with politics and more professionally oriented than liberal-arts students, and recent shifts have meant that many of the best students are no longer interested in political affairs.[16] Students in the sciences often do not have time for political activity, since their academic programs are both time-consuming and demanding. These changing conditions have reduced the numbers of students available for continuing political activity and have lowered the quality of student leadership.

The Indian University in the Post-Independence Period — Higher Education and Student Politics

The transformation of the political student movement in India has altered campus life. The Indian campus probably has as many student groups and organizations today as at any time in its history, but the nature of these groups has changed with the decline of ideological politics. Student unions are, perhaps, the most ubiquitous organizations in Indian universities, and their functions often include responsibility for cultural and social programs. While the unions are intended to provide a link between administrator and student, in many cases their functioning is less than democratic, due, in part, to administrative regulations. In most colleges, student union representatives are elected by the students, although seldom on the basis of political views.

Student unions in a number of colleges have taken on political importance. In some of the more volatile of the north Indian universities, such as Aligarh and Benares, student unions have spearheaded protest campaigns. Agitations undertaken by student unions usually stem from local issues, such as university examination policies, increases in college fees, living conditions, and the like, but in some cases student unions are controlled by ideological factions attempting to use the union as a base of operations against an opposition political group within or outside the university.[17] Communists, socialists, and factions within the Congress Party have not hesitated to use student unions for their own purposes, all the while formally decrying political interference on the campus. As a general rule, however, student unions have not been involved in politics and have been limited to their social and educational functions.

It is useful to distinguish between the kinds of student leadership found in Indian universities. The "respectable," nonpolitical, cultural and social student organizations are led by students from upper-class families for the most part, and these students can be called the "academic" leadership of the Indian student community. Students active in direct-action campaigns have come more frequently from the lower social classes. This leadership constitutes a relatively new and dynamic force on the Indian campus. Students from social groups without a long tradition of education, often from illiterate families, have frequently led strikes and demonstrations. The continuing leadership of leftist student groups, however, is generally drawn from middle-class students, who have a political tradition and sufficient free time to devote to political matters. This dichotomy in student leadership is a peculiar characteristic in Indian student life.

Despite the changes in student political activity, a number of national student organizations have retained some influence. After the largest of the pre-independence student movements, the Students' Congress, was disbanded in 1948, Congress leaders expressed interest in the formation of a nonpolitical student organization, and the socialists agreed to unite with them in the formation of the National Union of Students (NUS) in 1950. The NUS proved unable to rid itself of the heritage of outside political manipulation and soon foundered, never becoming the representative nonpolitical student organization that its founders had envisaged. Inadequate financing, student apathy, and the difficulty of communication in a rapidly expanding educational system proved to be insurmountable obstacles. Factional disputes caused several splits in the organization, and by 1958 the NUS was, for all purposes, dead.

The National Council of University Students of India (NCUSI) was subsequently formed to fill the vacuum created by the disappearance of the National Union of Students. This organization has faced many of the same problems that plagued its predecessor — opposition from educators and political leaders, student apathy, and personal ambition among its own leaders. The Cold War has created the problem of foreign financial support. The Soviet Union has financially supported the Communist-sponsored All-India Students' Federation, while the NCUSI has received funds from Western sources. It is unlikely that the NCUSI will become the representative student association in India, although it has tried to keep aloof from partisan Indian politics and has occasionally been a moderating influence on the Indian student community by encouraging students to work with administrators rather than resort to immediate agitation.

The political parties in India have adopted an ambivalent attitude toward students in recent years. The Youth Congress was formed in 1949 by the All-India Congress Committee. Despite its claim that it was India's largest youth organization, it did not attract much attention and served mainly as a "front group" for aspiring Congress politicians. Because the leadership did not encourage open political discussion, the organization failed to draw able, politically oriented youth, and the Youth Congress had few active chapters before its dissolution in 1965 because of internal political conflicts.

The oldest national student organization in India is the All-India Students' Federation (AISF), which has existed without interruption since 1936. The AISF, under Communist control since 1940, has lost much of its support and a large proportion of its membership. In 1955, the AISF claimed a membership of one hundred thousand, with major concentration in West Bengal, Andhra, and

Kerala, all centers of Communist political support.[18] The AISF is, however, weak in areas without Communist strength.

Despite the considerable efforts the Communist Party has made to cultivate the students, the general decline in student organizations has also affected the AISF. The changing tactics of the Communist movement have also hurt its student allies. Although Communist support during World War II permitted the AISF to function legally while the nationalist student movement was forced underground, many students felt that the Communists were traitors to Indian nationalism. Immediately after Indian independence, the Communists violently opposed the Nehru government, thus alienating a large proportion of the student population. More recently, the split in the Communist movement caused by the Sino-Soviet dispute has disillusioned many leftist Indian students and complicated the functioning of Communist organizations. In many areas, the AISF's identity as a Communist student organization has been purposely obscured or de-emphasized. Despite this non-ideological policy, AISF students in Calcutta, many of whom support the (pro-Maoist) Communist Party Marxist, recently took a leading part in student demonstrations. Nevertheless, even these Calcutta demonstrations, led by ideologically committed students, erupted over purely local campus issues and spread only when the original student demands were not met by the university authorities.

Other left-wing student organizations claim national stature, although all are smaller than either the AISF or the Youth Congress. One of these groups, the Samajwadi Yuvak Sabha (Socialist Youth Organization) was founded in 1953 by the Socialist Party when the National Union of Students failed and socialist student leaders felt the need to have their own organization. The SYS has suffered from the many splits within the Indian socialist movement in the past decade, although in the very recent past it has regained some of its leadership in northern India by advocating a very militant, although largely non-ideological program that has appealed to many students. The SYS acts as a political arm of the Samyukta Socialist Party and participates in its various campaigns, as well as stressing campus issues. The success of the SYS indicates the popularity of militant tactics among Indian students.

In the recent past, right-wing student political organizational efforts have been quite successful in some regions. One of the most important student organizations in India today is the *Akhil Bharatiya Vidyarthi Parishad* (All-India Students' Organization). This group, commonly called the *Vidyarthi Parishad*, has claimed to be non-political despite strong evidence suggesting that it is the youth wing of the rightist Hindu communalist parties, and particularly of the *Jan Sangh* (Peoples' Party). The *Vidyarthi Parishad* has concentrated on a culturally oriented program, avoiding broader political issues as much as possible. It has appealed for patriotism and was active in the nationalist upsurge following the Indo-Chinese conflict of 1962.

It is difficult to generalize about post-independence student political participation in India. There is no longer a unified student movement, and only a tiny fraction of the Indian student population is involved in the day-to-day operation of student political groups. Nevertheless, the annual number of demonstrations in the past years has been quite high. In general, the emphasis of the student movement has shifted from societal concerns to campus ones. Even organizations that have a basic ideological commitment, such as the All-India Students' Federation, have appealed to students on the basis of single issues, usually directly related to campus conditions. Student political involvement continues in India, stimulated in large part by the severe stresses evident in Indian social and economic life, and student activism will continue as long as India suffers from social, economic, and educational tensions and inadequacies.

Student Indiscipline — Causes and Effects

No other issue in Indian educational life has received more publicity than the problem of "student indiscipline." Violence is a distinctive characteristic of student indiscipline in India. In the Hindi-speaking areas of northern India, student agitation has often involved destruction of private and university property. Even local agitations, such as protests against an increase in tram fares in Calcutta, are often accompanied by violent student outbursts. This tendency toward violence is perhaps related to the lack of channels through which the deeply frustrated Indian students can voice dissent. The widespread publicity given to student indiscipline may, however, obscure the statistical fact that most Indian colleges have not been plagued by student unrest.[19]

Student indiscipline is not a new problem in India. Even before the nationalist movement mobilized large numbers of students for political action, Indian students had engaged in sporadic outbursts of direct action, usually spontaneous and aimed at local campus issues, such as difficult examinations or poor living conditions. Shortly after the establishment of universities in India, students in Calcutta demonstrated when over 70 per cent of the candidates failed the annual university examinations, and forced the authorities to revise the grading scales.

The causes of the student unrest that swept northern India in 1966 are typical of the factors that have stimulated such agitation since 1947. It is difficult to discern one key cause for the 1966 agitation, for in most instances local grievances stimulated a demonstration or protest. An analysis of some 280 student strikes and demonstrations during 1964 gives some indication of the causes for student unrest. About one hundred strikes were stimulated by demands relating to examinations and the administration of educational institutions. Another sixty had their origins in protests against the police or other government functionaries; miscellaneous causes accounted for the rest. In most of the cases, there was no overt political motive. The Communists associated themselves with strikes on thirty occasions, the *Jan Sangh* twice, and other parties seventeen times. In 1964, 3 per cent of the agitations were due to nonacademic issues; in 1965, the figure rose to 5 per cent, and in 1966 to 17.4 per cent. In 1966, there were 2206 demonstrations, of which 480 were violent. Only two years before, there had been 700 demonstrations and 113 violent outbursts.[20]

Regional differences, so vital to Indian life, have been mirrored in patterns of student political activism. There are wide variations in the intensity and nature of student unrest and activism in the Indian states. According to a government report, students in Andhra Pradesh, Madhya Pradesh, Uttar Pradesh, and West Bengal have been very involved in unrest and political activity in recent years. Bihar was added to this list in 1966. Students in Maharashtra have been passive, as they have in most of south India, with the exception of the language agitations of 1964 in Madras. West Bengal, with its strong tradition of militant political activism, has been a center of agitation, yet Kerala, which also has a strong Communist movement and a large and fairly concentrated student population, has seen little unrest. The Hindi "heartland" of Bihar and Uttar Pradesh have been very much involved in student activism, yet the Punjab and Rajastan, which are also in the Hindi belt, have been fairly quiet.

It is difficult to generalize about the reasons for these strong regional differences. The political complexion of the student unrest differs from area to area. The right-wing *Vidyarthi Parishad,* for example, is strong in Madhya Pradesh and Maharashtra, but is practically nonexistent in Bengal and in the South, due in part to the language question. Socialists are strong in Uttar Pradesh, but not in Maharashtra. The Communists have strength in West Bengal and Kerala, with only pockets of support elsewhere. Conditions of study also differ from region to region, and from university to university. Clearly Calcutta students study under particularly adverse conditions; this situation no doubt contributes to their activism. Some universities have traditions of administrative factionalism and internal infighting, while others have been administratively stable. Where the university administration is in firm control, and there is little faculty discontent, student indiscipline is less likely to occur.

Student action aimed at political issues directly related to broader social issues is most significant, as it is the most widespread and often the most destructive. This type of agitation is triggered by a specific local issue, either within the university or in the vicinity of the institution. The real cause, however, lies beyond the specific incident and is related to the more general problems that Indian students must face, both in their day-to-day lives and in their vision of the future. The continuing pressure of inadequate facilities, obviously substandard educational preparation, and the fear of unemployment after graduation make students more open to indiscipline. The surprising characteristic of student indiscipline is not the large number of demonstrations, but the lack of more widespread violence and destruction.

In Orissa, a co-ordinated series of student demonstrations throughout the state forced the resignation of the government in 1964. Student leaders charged that the state chief minister, a Congress politician, was guilty of corruption and demanded his resignation. The chief minister was forced to resign, and the students won a major victory in the state. The Orissa agitations were carried out by a well-organized student committee with representatives from many of the colleges in the state, thus proving that it is possible for *ad hoc* student agitation in an area relatively free of student unrest to be successfully organized.

In 1965, students sparked rioting in south India against the imposition of Hindi as India's national language. The anti-Hindi agitation, in which more than fifty people were killed and much damage was done, caused a national crisis and forced the central government to postpone the implementation of its language policies. A Students' Action Committee from colleges throughout the Tamil-speaking areas co-ordinated demonstrations and strikes, which often became violent.[21] Opposition political groups in the south, particularly the anti-Hindi DMK Party, strongly supported the students.

In late 1966, Calcutta was convulsed by student demonstrations in favor of a United Left Front anti-government campaign. When violence broke out, university authorities shut all educational institutions — an action affecting one hundred thousand students. Local campus issues were combined with broader ideological concerns in the agitation, which spread for the first time to students from the prestigious Presidency College in Calcutta. Militant leftist leaders in Calcutta saw their movement as a first step toward an Indian revolution on the model of the Chinese "proletarian cultural revolution." Left-Communist Calcutta students are not so much pro-Chinese as super-militant in their political views.

Perhaps the most graphic demonstration of the importance of students in Indian politics was the role played by students in the 1967 general elections. Students throughout the country sided with the opposition parties against the Congress, and succeeded in a number of states in defeating the Congress. In Madras, an unknown student leader unseated the powerful president of the Congress and the student-supported DMK party was victorious in the state. Observers have said that student support for the opposition groups was largely responsible for the defeat of the Congress in Bihar. Yet, despite their apparent political importance, Indian students have not yet organized a national organization to press their demands; since the elections, the students have retreated to their campuses and have concerned themselves largely with local non-ideological issues. Student agitation continues despite the lack of a coherent student movement, and India is in the midst of a major educational crisis, due in part to the continued violence of students. Although exact figures are not yet available, the number of incidents of student agitation has clearly increased in the last two years, and there is no sign that it is leveling off.

There are important institutional variations in Indian student unrest. Indiscipline is not a problem in most of the prestigious and well-financed technological institutions. While it is generally agreed that most student unrest has originated in the liberal-arts colleges, there are some key differences among these institutions as well. In general, older colleges that have been able to maintain relatively high standards of instruction and a spirit of corporate identity have been less plagued by student indiscipline than have the newer institutions.[22] Missionary-administered colleges have had less difficulty than other institutions, perhaps because there is often a tradition of academic excellence and a more satisfactory teacher-student relationship at these institutions.

The Indian university is closely tied to its society and shares many of the characteristics and contradictions of modern Indian life. In no society are "academic" values completely separated from the norms of the broader society, but in India these distinctions are even less evident than they are in many countries.[23] Caste and regional affiliations are seen as normal criteria for academic appointments, and factional politics within the universities bear a marked resemblance to political infighting in national life. Students attempt to use family influence in order to gain admittance to the university, or they resort to agitational politics to change an examination result. Thus, while some critics attack the universities for being an "ivory tower," higher education is very much in the mainstream of Indian social and political life.

The underlying causes for student unrest are not difficult to perceive, and there seems to be a general agreement among educators and other officials concerning at least some of them. A recent report on student unrest stated that the four main causes for student unrest are "1) lack of proper academic atmosphere, 2) absence of respect for authority — parental, educational, and governmental, 3) ideological frustration, and 4) political interference."[24] The status of university teaching has also declined since independence, and the traditional respect for the *guru* has virtually disappeared on the campus. Students seldom have an opportunity to talk to their professors, since classes are large and the teaching loads are heavy. At the lower ranks, college teachers are poorly paid, and many instructors must hold more than one job.[25]

Indian universities annually administer externally prepared examinations to college students, and consequently the individual professor cannot control either the curriculum or the evaluation of his students. Examinations have been one of the main causes of student indiscipline throughout the history of Indian higher education. Since the late-nineteenth century, students have rioted against difficult examinations, often forcing authorities to lower standards or to reschedule tests. Even with these agitations, the examination failure rate at some universities reaches 70 or 80 per cent in some subjects.[26]

Many students begin their collegiate careers at the age of fifteen or sixteen and lack the maturity that a few extra years would give. Furthermore, students living in hostels and away from their families for the first time are probably affected by their unprecedented freedom, particularly in view of India's strict family system. The generational problem, present in almost every society, lies somewhat below the surface in India, although it probably influences the students by causing resentment against constituted adult authorities.

The economic uncertainty of many Indian students is clearly a cause for ambivalence and indiscipline. Many students hold part-time jobs in order to pay for their educational expenses and must therefore divide their attention between job and university career. It has become increasingly more difficult for graduates, especially in the liberal arts, to obtain suitable employment. Students who cannot obtain jobs frequently return to the universities to do graduate work even though they are often not interested in the academic preparation involved. The number of students who do not finish their college educations is also quite high, and many of these former students remain on the campus, since employment is not always obtainable. Well over half of those who enter college in India do not obtain a degree.

Related directly to the economic problem are the difficult conditions under which many Indian students must study. In addition to inadequate university facilities, many students are unable to provide the minimum necessities of life for themselves. A survey of students in Calcutta pointed out that a substantial number were undernourished. In urban institutions particularly, students often must live in crowded and unsanitary conditions.[27] These factors cannot but increase the frustration and alienation of a large part of the student population.

Political, social, psychological, economic, and educational issues are intertwined in India, and all have contributed to student unrest. Present educational trends are likely to continue. Despite the warnings of educators, unplanned expansion of the educational system continues unabated. The government is unwilling to restrict educational expansion even though it is unable to allocate sufficient funds to maintain educational standards. As higher education becomes available to increasing segments of the population, the value of the bachelor's degree decreases. Centralized standards have become even more difficult to enforce, since several new universities are established each year, and higher education remains a joint responsibility of the central and state governments.

The unprecedented expansion of the student population (India has the third largest number of college students in the world, after the United States and the Soviet Union) and its growing heterogeneity have made the mobilization of the entire student community difficult, if not impossible, and have obscured the role of national student organizations. The prognosis for student politics in India is unclear. Student political activism is clearly not dead in India. Statistics indicate that the rate of unrest is increasing, and there is no reason to expect a reversal of this trend. The frustrations of the educational system, increasingly difficult conditions for the educated urban segment of the population generally, and a remnant of the nationalist tradition of student political involvement — all combine to insure the continuation of sporadic and often violent student unrest and "indiscipline." A major factor mitigating against a rebirth of the student movement is, however, the educational system itself. Few students can jeopardize their degrees by becoming politically involved, for an academic degree is a necessity in an increasingly difficult employment situation. The risks of student involvement make ideological student politics unattractive for most students. Yet, if conditions in India continue to worsen, and students lose whatever hope they now have for employment and status, it is entirely possible that the potentially revolutionary Indian student population will turn to militant politics, as it did during the nationalist struggle. This development can have major implications for India's political system.

REFERENCES

1. Some of the material in this essay is also discussed in Philip G. Altbach (ed.), *Turmoil and Transition: Student Politics and Higher Education in India* (New York, 1969), and Philip G. Altbach, "The Transformation of the Indian Student Movement," *Asian Survey*, Vol. 6 (August, 1966), pp. 448–460.

2. See Myron Weiner, *The Politics of Scarcity* (Chicago, 1962).

3. Syed Nurullah and J. P. Naik, *A Students' History of Education in India* (Bombay, 1962), p. 158.

4. *Ibid.*, p. 282.

5. For an excellent account of the impact of English education on Indian intellectuals and its relation to the rise of the nationalist movement, see Bruce McCully, *English Education and the Origins of Indian Nationalism* (New York, 1940).

6. Dinkar Sakrikar, "A History of the Student Movement in India" (type-written manuscript, 1946), p. 33.

7. Weiner, *The Politics of Scarcity*, p. 161.

8. Prabadh Chandra, *The Student Movement in India* (Lahore, 1938).

9. M. Muni Reddy, *The Student Movement in India* (Lucknow, 1947), p. 30.

10. Weiner, *The Politics of Scarcity*, p. 163.

11. For a study of the Hindu nationalist movement, see Joseph Curran, *Militant Hinduism in Indian Politics: A Study of the RSS* (New York, 1951).

12. Darbara Singh, *The Indian Struggle, 1942* (Lahore, 1946), p. 278.

13. For a discussion of academic discipline and student political involvement, see Glaucio Soares, "The Active Few: Student Ideology and Participation in Developing Countries," *Student Politics*, ed. S. M. Lipset (New York, 1967), pp. 124–47, and Metta Spencer, "Professional, Scientific, and Intellectual Students in India," *Student Politics*, pp. 357–371.

14. Philip G. Altbach, "The Bombay Naval Mutiny," *Opinion*, Vol. 6 (August 31, 1965), p. 35.

15. Ministry of Education, *Report of the Education Commission, 1964–66* (New Delhi, 1966), p. 300.

16. Metta Spencer, "Professional, Scientific, and Intellectual Students in India," p. 367.

17. For a description of the role of the student unions in university politics, see Joseph DiBona, "Indiscipline and Student Leadership in an Indian University," *Student Politics*, pp. 372–393.

18. Weiner, *The Politics of Scarcity*, p. 168.

19. The literature on student indiscipline is quite extensive, although much of it is limited to platitudes and exhortations, with relatively little emphasis on the roots of student unrest. The following materials are among the most adequate in the field. University Grants Commission, *Report on the Problem of Student Indiscipline in Indian Universities* (New Delhi, 1960); Humanyun Kabir, *Student Unrest: Causes and Cure* (Calcutta, 1958); Chancal Sarkar, *The Unquiet Campus* (New Delhi, 1960); "Students in Turmoil," *Seminar*, No. 88 (December, 1966), pp. 10–46; "Crisis on the Campus," *Seminar*, No. 44 (April, 1963), pp. 10–41; and M. K. Haldar, "Education for Frustration," *Thought*, Vol. 17 (October 22 and 29, 1966), pp. 4–5 and 21–22. See also P. G. Altbach (ed.), *Turmoil and Transition: Higher Education and Student Politics in India* (New York, 1969).

20. A Correspondent, "Student Indiscipline Under Study," *Thought*, Vol. 17 (October 1, 1966), p. 11. See also *Statesmen* (December 19, 1966).

21. See "The English-Hindi Controversy," *Minerva*, Vol. 3 (Summer, 1965), pp. 560–585.

22. Margaret Cormack, *She Who Rides a Peacock: Indian Students and Social Change* (New York, 1961), p. 204.

23. For an account of general aspects of university life and administration in India, see Robert Gaudino, *The Indian University* (Bombay, 1965).

24. A Correspondent, "Student Indiscipline Under Study," p. 11.

25. For a sensitive discussion of the problems of intellectuals in India, see Edward Shils, *The Intellectual Between Tradition and Modernity: The Indian Situation* (The Hague, 1961). See also Nirad C. Chaudhuri, *The Intellectual in India* (Delhi, 1967).

26. University Grants Commission, *Report on Standards of University Education* (New Delhi, 1965), p. 255.

27. Ministry of Education, *Survey of Living Conditions of University Students* (New Delhi, 1961).

LESLIE L. ROOS, JR.,

NORALOU P. ROOS, AND

GARY R. FIELD

Students and Politics in
Contemporary Turkey

To UNDERSTAND student political activity in contemporary Turkey, it
is helpful to consider both historical and attitudinal data. A historical discussion of the factors underlying contemporary student
politics in Turkey aids in putting survey data into perspective, while
the survey material helps to point out differences in political attitudes and activities among individuals, schools, and academic
majors.

Since the beginning of the multi-party period, Turkish students
have become an active force in the political life of the Republic.
Their most dramatic involvement was an important stimulus to the
1960 revolution, and Atatürk's proclamation that youth is "the owner
and guardian of the revolution" is taken seriously by many elements
in the student population. The 1946 decision by the Republican
People's Party leadership to allow another party to compete for the
support of the rural masses brought a quick end to the period of
single-party dominance. In the first free election in 1950, Menderes
— supported by an apparently unbeatable combination of peasants,
businessmen, and professional people — led his Democratic Party
to an overwhelming victory.

Over the next several years, Menderes' uncoordinated free-
spending policies precipitated a spiraling inflation which especially
hurt such salaried groups as the bureaucrats and military men. Their
alienation was particularly intolerable because the Democratic Party
was accused of winning the support of the rural peasantry by sacri-
ficing many of Atatürk's religious reforms. Since bureaucrats and
military men had long formed the backbone of the Republic's elite,[1]
their frustration was understandable.

Menderes' repression of political opposition had grown increasingly strict and onerous during the late 1950's, while tension in the

major cities continued to rise. In 1960 he granted sweeping powers to an investigating committee that would have acted to destroy all open opposition, whether from other parties, newspapers, or other organizations. This act touched off a general student protest. Students gathered at the Law Faculty in Istanbul and at the Political Science Faculty in Ankara. When police were sent to break up the demonstrations, serious clashes occurred and one student was killed. Following these clashes, the universities were closed for a month, but almost every night students helped to incite riots on the main boulevard of Ankara. While these riots were not major affairs, the students continued to provide the significant overt opposition to the Menderes regime. This was dramatically underlined by the spontaneous march of a thousand Military College cadets on the presidential residence. Although they were dissuaded from completing the march by their commanders, the Turkish student had proved himself to be heroic in his battle against a repressive political regime.

While the student demonstrations aroused public opinion against the regime and created an intolerably tense political atmosphere, they were not directly related to the May 27 coup that toppled the regime just one month later. Most accounts indicate that the coup was the result of long planning and deliberation by a group of military men.[2] If anything, the student demonstrations were unwelcomed by the coup planners, since they served to warn Menderes and persuaded him to take countermeasures that he might not otherwise have taken. But the coup was successful, and the students' interpretation of their own role gave them a heady sense of power and righteousness. This experience appears to have altered the pattern of student political participation.

Before the coup, most student statements were meant only to be informative, but after the coup they became "much more dynamic, requesting quick action [and] containing warnings, . . . sometimes even threats."[3] Student actions in the period immediately after the coup also demonstrated this new-found power. In 1960–1961 they walked out to protest unpopular teachers, shortages of books, and poor food in university canteens. In almost every case (even when it was a protest over defining acceptable academic performance), the students prevailed.[4] Explicitly political demonstrations were held by students in 1962 when they wrecked two newspaper offices in Istanbul and the Justice Party headquarters. (The Justice Party is the most direct successor to Menderes' outlawed Democratic Party.) In 1963, about fifteen hundred students demonstrated in

Istanbul against the release of ex-President Bayar for medical treatment.

A period of normalization set in after the burst of student political activism in the early 1960's,[5] but recent disturbances indicate that a new activism has emerged. Up until 1968 student views were expressed largely through press statements, various meetings, and occasional demonstrations; the sit-ins and boycotts in the summer of 1968 and the anti-Americanism shown in the winter of 1968–1969 indicate that this phase has passed. Government statements of the intent to better conditions at the universities helped end the widespread occupation of buildings in June of 1968, but anti-Americanism could not be handled so easily. Turkish students have been upset by the American position in the Cyprus crisis, the Vietnam war, the appointment of Ambassador Komer in the fall of 1968, and the Turkish visits of American ships on NATO exercises. Violent demonstrations have become the order of the day.

Two of the main vehicles for the expression of student opinion have been the large student organizations that recruit from various universities. Since 1960, the two major organizations — the National Turkish Students' Federation (TMTF) and the National Turkish Students' Union (MTTB) — have been supported by funds from the national budget.[6] Both are legally obligated to remain politically neutral, although TMTF has long sympathized with the leftist parties — first with the People's Party and increasingly with the outspokenly Marxist Turkish Labor Party. MTTB has sometimes taken a much more pro-government position, roundly criticizing its rivals for dabbling in politics. Finally, the recent organization of students as members of extremist political parties has led to a different kind of political action. Opposing groups of students have battled each other over a number of political issues.

There appears to be some relationship between the level of student involvement and other significant dimensions of the political environment. The political atmosphere in Turkey was extremely tense and uncertain both before and immediately after the 1960 coup. Journalists were jailed, elections were thought to be rigged, and the two chief parties were almost incapable of civil communication. Although the political climate was generally considered intolerable, no clear solution was in sight. Students, by openly demonstrating their protest, had an obvious impact on so fluid a situation. Students were encouraged to take matters into their own hands because none of the acknowledged political leaders was able to provide the direction that could assure them about their own personal future and about the future of the nation.

The political climate changed, however, when the Justice Party was elected to office with a large majority in 1965. Prime Minister Süleyman Demirel won a personal triumph over the reactionary extremist elements within his own Justice Party and thus gained the support of many moderates of various political sympathies. He has neutralized the potential opposition of the military by choosing the former General Chief of Staff (another acceptable moderate) to serve as President, and has also proved to be surprisingly successful in the economic field. The Justice Party obtains its strength from a coalition of businessmen, professionals, and peasants similar to that which supported Menderes' Democratic Party; the Justice Party has continued its strong showing in 1968 senatorial elections. The capable leadership provided by Prime Minister Demirel has tended to reduce the political impact of students, but they have not been silenced. The open climate for political discussion encourages them to make their voices heard, and both left and right have turned to disruptive tactics.

Political Socialization in the Turkish Educational System

Any attempt to understand the role of students in Turkish politics since the founding of the Republic in 1922 must deal with the Kemalist legacy. Atatürk explicitly created the secular-nationalist system of education to win support for his ideological revolution, and his political successors have continued to use the schools as a means for inculcating a national identification into the traditionally privatistic rural populace.[7] All political parties have made this a central goal of education. Atatürk's bust occupies a prominent place in every school, while history courses emphasize both Republican accomplishments and the achievements of the Turkish "race."[8]

The effectiveness of such an educational system is clearly shown in the answers to a question asked on a 1963 national sample survey: "Who is the person in all the world, living or dead, whom you admire most — and why?"[9] With each increase in the level of education, the respondents were more likely to identify Atatürk as the person they most admired and less inclined to choose a religious figure. Only 15 per cent of the respondents who had never attended school named Atatürk as the person most admired, while 53 per cent of those with a university education chose him. The proportion of those saying they most admired a religious figure declined from 16 per cent of those with no education to 1 per cent of the respondents with a university education. Similarly, as one moved up the educational levels, people tended increasingly to admire a specific person because of his "usefulness to the nation," rather than his religious beliefs.

As one might suspect from the above data, one of the most nationalistic groups in Turkish society is the schoolteacher. The nineteen male school teachers sampled in the 1963 survey were characterized by their extremely high admiration for Atatürk. All of them noted Atatürk as one of the two people they admired most, but only 65 per cent of the other males with a similar level of education mentioned Atatürk. Teachers were also much more likely to cite "usefulness to the nation" as their reason for admiring him than were their counterparts.

In Turkish politics, this connection between education, nationalism, and admiration for Atatürk has important implications. As Robert Bellah has suggested,[10] in some sections of the Turkish population, the Atatürk cult has become almost a religious commitment to his tenets. The most committed Kemalists are likely to be found among the most educated members of society — including schoolteachers and university students. This helps to explain why the military junta sent teachers and students out to the villages to interpret the May 27 revolution for the peasants.[11] The revolution had been justified by the military as an attempt to return the Republic to the way of Atatürk, and the students and teachers were particularly sympathetic to such an interpretation.

The data also support the idea that nationalistic values are instilled early in the educational process. The proportion of the people who chose Atatürk as the person they most admired rose from 15 per cent among those with no schooling and to 48 per cent among those with a middle school education. After middle school (middle school consists of three years following five years of primary education), the increase was slight, with only 5 per cent more respondents with some university education mentioning Atatürk. Additional evidence supporting the hypothesis that Turkish students acquire national allegiance during their first eight years of education, before they reach the *lycée*-level schools, is provided from a study by Frey.[12] He compares the attitudes of students in their first year of *lycée* study with those of students in their last year and finds that no consistent changes in the politically relevant items can be observed.

Such a finding indicates that relatively little political socialization takes place after a student enters the *lycée*.[13]

Since political socialization in Turkey occurs so early in the educational process, all students seem to acquire similar political loyalties no matter what type of secondary education they receive. This is important, since an individual proceeds from middle school into various types of secondary schools that train students for the different career paths. Although one might expect that students in the less privileged schools would be less committed to the values that define the modern Turkish elite, this is apparently not the case. No matter what type of school they are from, secondary-school students are almost equally likely to say they would be willing to make a great personal sacrifice for national goals, that it is important to teach one's children loyalty to the nation, and that one should definitely vote in national elections.

Although attitudes toward the political system differ little among students in the various kinds of secondary schools, students in the elite regular *lycées* are more inclined to take an active role in politics. They tend to feel that "participation in activities directed toward national improvement" would afford them more satisfaction in the future than their career or family life. They expect to be most interested in national affairs, and the subject they most frequently discuss with their families is national problems.[14]

Since much of the research on students and politics has found that students in the humanities and the social sciences tend to be both more participant and more radical than students in commerce, the natural sciences, and technical fields, different sorts of *lycée* students might be recruited to the various faculties. These generalizations are relevant to Turkey, since the Law and Political Science Faculties have furnished the greatest number of politically active students. The differential recruitment of political activists does not, however, seem to be responsible for these inter-faculty differences. There are no obvious differences between the political attitudes and behavior of those students attracted to the politically activist faculties (Law and Political Science) and those attracted to other faculties. The *lycée* students who plan to attend the Law and Political Science Faculties are no more interested in national affairs, political careers, or political discussion than are students planning to enter other faculties.

The lack of a relationship between a student's political attitudes and his choice of faculty should not lead one to discount the political involvement of *lycée* students. In Turkey, such students have been quite effective as a political pressure group. In 1962 when the government introduced university entrance exams, those *lycée* students who failed marched through the main streets of Ankara carrying placards protesting such procedures and insisting that it was their right to be admitted to a university. Subsequently places were found for all students.[15]

The students involved in these demonstrations were those at the end of their *lycée* education, which is in line with our findings that students become more politically involved over the course of their three-year *lycée* career. Third-year *lycée* students, for example, are more likely to discuss politics with their friends than are first- and second-year students; 20 per cent of the third-year students, as compared with 10 per cent of the combined first- and second-year students, report such discussions. By the time Turkish *lycée* students are ready to enter a university, there appears to be a definite group interested in politics. Although such awareness does not seem related to their choice of faculty, it is related to other significant political attitudes. Students at the *lycée* who discuss politics frequently are also more likely to expect to obtain greater satisfaction from national affairs (40 per cent as against 29 per cent), to report discussing politics at home (39 per cent versus 20 per cent), to be interested in a national political career (62 per cent versus 56 per cent), and to devote their leisure time to intellectual pursuits (15 per cent versus 7 per cent).

Political Socialization at the University

By the time a *lycée* student has entered a Turkish university, he has been socialized to a high degree of national identification. While this nationalism remains strong and might even increase during his first year at the university, there seems to be some value reorientation during the following years. Privatism increases, as does an emphasis on international rather than strictly national interests, while political activity decreases. The longer a student remains at the university, the more likely he is to assume the role of a political spectator — interested in politics, but taking no active part.

These generalizations are drawn from studies of two of the most activist faculties — the Political Science Faculty (in 1958)[16] and the Law Faculty (in 1960).[17] The significance of the findings is magnified, since the studies documented the attitudinal and behavioral trends at two different points in time. Since the Law Faculty study was conducted just six months after the student activism that accompanied the 1960 military coup, it is important to note that this tendency for first-year students to be more active and interested than fourth-year students held even at a time of increased student involvement in politics.

The following table presents data pertaining to the students' changing value orientations. Where available, comparative data on *lycée* students who planned to enter the Political Science Faculty have also been included.

Table 1:

Progressive Socialization Covering Male Lycée Students
Wanting to Enter the Political Science Faculty
and Male Students Over the Four Years at the Faculty[18]

		Political Science Faculty Students			
National Orientations	Lycée Students	Fresh.	Soph.	Junior	Senior
Most important to teach children: usefulness to nation	12%	20%	10%	6%	9%
Expect future interests will be: national	69%	73%	65%	63%	60%
Would make greatest sacrifice for: nation	nd.	49%	46%	43%	41%
Most important thing in life: national-international affairs	nd.	25%	15%	11%	10%
Would be most proud of accomplishing in lifetime: service to nation	nd.	30%	27%	27%	13%
Number of respondents	42	154	114	73	58

Political interest also seems to lessen over the course of a student's university career. In his survey of Ankara University students, Özer Ozankaya asked respondents in different classes about their future political interest.[19] Fifty-seven per cent of the students in their first year replied that they would be more interested in politics in the future than at present, but this percentage diminished with increasing university experience. Fifty-one per cent of those in their second or third year anticipated more future interest, while only 37 per cent of the respondents who had been at the university for four or more years expected their future interest in politics to be greater than at present.

Matching the consistent decline in nationalism and political interest is a decline in a politically activist orientation among students at the Faculty of Law. From their responses to questionnaire items, the students have been divided into four categories according to political involvement. The "activists" (38 per cent of the respondents) are interested in politics, currently active in politics, and plan to enter politics after their graduation. The "Potentials" (15 per cent) are interested in politics, plan to enter politics after graduation, but were not active in politics at the time the survey was taken. "Spectators" (27 per cent) expressed an interest in politics, but were not currently involved and did not plan to enter politics after the university. Those who expressed no interest in politics, were not currently active in politics, and had no intention of becoming so after graduation made up 20 per cent of the respondents and were labeled "apoliticals." An analysis of the data by class indicated that personal political involvement is greatest among the first-year students and least among the graduating fourth-year respondents. Forty-one per cent of the freshmen as compared with only 29 per cent of the seniors were categorized as activists. On the other hand, 44 per cent of the seniors and only 23 per cent of the freshmen fit into the spectator category. There was a slight decline in the number of potentials from the first to the fourth year, but little regular change in the number of apolitical students.

The number of activist students in their third and fourth years is still great enough to permit the more advanced students to be disproportionately represented in student leadership positions; a 1965 survey noted that 64 per cent of the leaders of student organizations were in at least their third year.[20] Thus, the data on political activism may be most relevant for the average students, rather than for those in leadership positions.

The over-all figures on activism may be partially dependent on the first-year students' awareness of their elite status. An extreme sense of nationalistic zeal and a dedication to national service would seem to accompany this awareness. The first-year class may also be under less academic pressure or may at least be less conscious of the academic pressure than are students in the later classes. Under the Turkish educational system, at the end of each academic year students are examined in various fields to determine whether they will be allowed to pass on to the next year. While the yearly exam can be repeated, there is a rigorous selection process.[21] Some of those who survive the filtering process may develop a more professional orientation and feel that they must decide between devoting their time to political activities or to studies.

On the other hand, the 1960–61 survey data also indicated that it was the older students within each class who were the most politicized. The older students may be more active politically because yearly exams can be repeated. Activists — regardless of their class at the Law Faculty — may take longer to finish their studies than their less politicized counterparts. A high proportion of activists (55 per cent) in the first-year class were in the age group of twenty-five or older. This may be a result of the 1960 military coup; after the revolution, there were rather widespread dismissals within the lower and middle range of the officer corps. Some of those dismissed may have entered the Law Faculty, bringing with them a commitment to political activism.

Another attitude affected by the Turkish university environment relates to populism versus paternalism. If one compares the attitudes of *lycée* students with those of university students along this dimension, a striking change seems to have taken place. While only 14 per cent of those *lycée* students wanting to enter the Political Science Faculty preferred to define democracy as "government *for* the people" (rather than government *by* the people), fully 46 per cent of those students at the Faculty preferred the more paternalistic definition. Moreover, the Political Science Faculty does not seem to be unique in this socialization toward paternalism, since data from several studies of Turkish university students at various faculties in Ankara and Istanbul showed a similar pattern of change (from 19 per cent of the total sample of *lycée* students to 47 per cent of the university sample in one survey).[22] The major change among Political Science Faculty students seems to take place during the first year, since there is little consistent change in the amount of paternalism expressed by students in the later years.[23]

Additionally, Turkish students' feelings about religion are profoundly affected by their university education. The longer a student remains in the university, the less likely he is to feel the need for religion. None of the *lycée* students planning to enter the Political Science Faculty felt they could do without religion. Among freshmen at the Faculty, 12 per cent felt they had no need for religion, and by the time students were ready to leave the Faculty, fully one fourth had renounced the need for religion. Another study conducted in 1966 among a slightly different sample of students confirmed this secularizing tendency in the Turkish university system. When asked "how important is religion in your life?" the proportions of each class giving one of the negative responses "of little importance" or "not at all" were as follows: 20 per cent of the freshmen, 35 per cent of the sophomores, 42 per cent of the juniors, and 49 per cent of the seniors.[24]

The political relevance of the Turkish student's attitudes on religion should be particularly stressed, since one of the main issues in Turkish politics since the beginning of the multi-party era has been the disputed role of religion. The parties that have won the popular support of the country (first the Democrats and now the Justice Party) have the reputation for liberalizing the stringent religious reforms introduced by Atatürk.

Table 2:
The Relationship Between Students' Attitudes Toward Religion and Various Politically Relevant Attitudes[25]

	Importance of Religion		
	High	Moderate	Low
"Very much interested in politics:	18%	16%	29%
Describing selves as leftists of moderate leftists	36%	51%	80%
Defining government as government *for* the people	38%	42%	55%
Number of respondents	269	184	214

Secular students are more likely to be interested in politics, to be "leftist," and to support an elitist view of the governmental process.

Social Class and Political Orientations

Although the university experience helps shape the political attitudes of students, the students' opinions continue to reflect their own social backgrounds. The following data from a 1965 sample of male Ankara University students illustrate some of these relationships. Social class — as defined by father's salary and educational level —

is closely related to an individual's politically relevant attitudes. Across a whole series of questions, those from the higher social classes (members of the old elite groups) are much more elitist, secularist, and socialist.

Table 3:

Variations in Male University Students' Political
Attitudes According to Their Social Class[26]

	Social Class			
	Upper	Middle	Lower	Lowest
Elitism				
Not in favor of the equal vote	65%	50%	40%	42%
Would support a single party system (yes or maybe)	28%	26%	27%	13%
Feel that neighborhood elections are worth the trouble they take	55%	63%	84%	74%
Secularism				
Religious belief not necessary for full and mature understanding of life	48%	24%	25%	16%
Etatism-Socialism				
Attitude toward statement — socialism will bring a more just social order				
agree	72%	67%	64%	39%
completely disagree	3%	11%	13%	32%
Do not agree that etatism opens the way to low productivity and laziness ..	55%	46%	49%	39%
Number of respondents	29	54	45	31

These 1965 findings are also supported by data from the 1960 survey of Ankara Law Faculty students. Male respondents from upper-class backgrounds were more likely than the other students to score toward the etatist and elitist ends of two multi-item scales constructed to measure personal ideological orientation.[27]

During the single-party period before 1946, the upper class in Turkey tended to be an intellectual and governing class — not the usual economic upper class that is typical of the American class structure. Thus, support for socialism-etatism with its authoritarian elitist overtones is quite compatible with the self-interest of the Turkish upper class.

Just as social class is related to ideological differences, it is also related to political party preferences.[28] Students from upper-class families that were members of the older elite give no support to the Justice Party — the party of the new Turkish elites. Support for this party is found among the upwardly mobile.

Table 4:

Social Class and Students' Political Party Preference

Party Choice	Social Class			
	Upper	*Middle*	*Lower*	*Lowest*
Justice Party	0%	15%	24%	26%
Republican Peoples Party	41	50	38	29
Turkish Labor Party	17	4	7	10
Other parties	0	0	4	3
No party	28	15	20	13
Don't know & no answer	14	17	7	19
Number of respondents ..	29	54	45	31

A relatively high percentage of each group is unwilling to commit itself to any of Turkey's political parties. Whether this indicates alienation or unwillingness to respond to the questionnaire item is difficult to say. But the pattern is clear. Over half of the upper-class group chose the "old guard" RPP or the new socialist labor party compared to 39 per cent of the students in the lowest social-class group.

On the basis of American findings, it was expected that both social class and political involvement would be related to perceived political efficacy and to a sense of civic duty. But, none of the predicted relationships were found. Being politically active or coming from an upper-class background neither predisposes a Turkish student to feel that an individual can have an impact on the political process nor increases his felt obligation to participate. It should be noted, however, that students as a whole were characterized by at least a moderate feeling of political efficacy and a high sense of civic duty.

In over-all perspective, the social-class data are significant. Attitudinal differences linked to social class persist, even though the university educational process tends to socialize an individual toward more secularist and elitist values. But the data also indicate that there are no class differences among university students with regard to perceived efficacy or sense of civic duty. Such beliefs point toward participation by all sectors of the society, rather than toward alienation on the part of the university students from lower-class backgrounds. (Such a proposition is borne out by the limited data. When one compares social classes according to year at the Law Faculty, the regular differences in political involvement among various social classes are not present among students in their last two years. If anything, the lower-class students are more active than the upper-class students during their last year at the Law Faculty.)

Family Characteristics and Political Orientations

Social class is one indicator of family background that may be responsible for the development of various political attitudes and activities. Another family characteristic — having a relative in politics or government — provides a measure of political contact that is associated with a student's political interest. Law students who had relatives in politics or government were more likely to be activists than were those who did not have similarly-placed relatives; 44 per cent of the male law students with relatives in official positions were categorized as activists as compared with 34 per cent of the others. Political contact is associated with social class, but within each social class the respondents from the involved families were more activist than the students from the non-involved families.[29]

In an effort to assess the degree to which Turkish university students conform to or rebel against family political orientations, respondents were asked: "If political positions could be placed on a continuum ranging from the far left to the far right, where would you locate yourself? Where would you locate your father?" A five-position scale with the extremes labeled "left" and "right" was used for these items. Results from two university-level schools in Ankara can be contrasted with material from students at a business academy located in Eskisehir, a provincial city; in this analysis, the Ankara students will be described as cosmopolitans, while the Eskisehir students will be labeled provincials.

Table 5:

Political Views and Perceived Paternal Views of Turkish University Students

| | Cosmopolitans | | | | Provincials | | | |
| | Males | | Females | | Males | | Females | |
Political Views	Own Views	Perceived Paternal Views	Own Views	Perceived Paternal Views	Own Views	Perceived Paternal Views	Own Views	Perceived Paternal Views
Left and moderate left ..	70%	22%	50%	26%	40%	23%	40%	47%
Center	20	43	40	40	36	36	38	21
Moderate right and right	11	35	10	35	25	41	23	31
Number of respondents ..	302		102		278		61	

As might be expected, a majority of the Turkish university students polled perceived themselves as moderate leftists, the left-of-center students outnumbering those of the right-of-center by a proportion of more than three to one (53 versus 17 per cent). Both male and female Ankara respondents were substantially to the left of their provincial counterparts; about one quarter of the provincial students categorized themselves as rightists. These data on political positions of Ankara students are thus in general accord with Ozankaya's findings that the majority of the students preferred the leftist and left-of-center political parties.

The students' perceptions of their fathers' political positions reflects the so-called generation gap. A plurality of all fathers are seen as being in the middle of the political spectrum, while rightists are perceived as outnumbering leftists. Cosmopolitan men and women exhibit no real difference in their perception of fathers' political views, but nearly half of the female provincials (as compared with less than a quarter of the male provincials) perceived their fathers to be leftists. These differences among the provincial students may reflect the greater social mobility of males. The female provincials tend to come from less religious, better educated, and higher income families than do the males.

When the political positions of the Turkish students are compared with their father's political orientation, more than 70 per cent of the respondents are found to disagree with their fathers. As a whole, the students are more than three times as likely to move to the left of their fathers than to the right. The level of conformity with their father's political orientations is about the same for both cosmopolitan and provincial male respondents, but about four times as many provincials move to the right as do the cosmopolitan males. The most conformity was found among cosmopolitan female students, while the provincial females tended to move to the right of their relatively leftist fathers.

A number of hypotheses from American socialization research were tested using this sample of Turkish university students. When place of enrollment and sex were controlled, such variables as year in school, family income, level of religious interest, family political involvement, and place of birth were not consistently associated with the degree of conformity with the father's perceived political orientation. There was no relationship between, on the one hand, several retrospective items dealing with political socialization in the family and the school and, on the other, student agreement with paternal political attitudes. Two variables associated with deviation from the father's perceived political position were level of political interest and residence in a dormitory (as opposed to living at home); the students who were greatly interested in politics and those who lived in the peer-group atmosphere of a dormitory were particularly likely to adopt views to the left of their fathers.

The interaction between where the students are attending school and their social class is a particularly important determinant of student political orientation. As the following table shows, the Ankara male students from upper-class backgrounds are less likely to move to the left of their father's views than are their upwardly-mobile counterparts. But the upper-class provincial males appear more likely to move to the left than do the lower-class students. The concept of "relative deprivation" may help to explain these data. Lower-class students constitute the great majority of those attending provincial schools; these students may be less likely to resent individuals with more advantages than are the lower-class students in the metropolitan environment. Finally, it should be noted that the lower-class cosmopolitan students are still more conservative than their upper-class counterparts. They have moved to the left of their fathers, but the fathers of these lower-class students were much more likely to be to the right of center than the fathers of the upper-class students.

Table 6:

The Relationship Between Male Students' Social Class and Political Ideas, Controlling for School Location

	Cosmopolitans			Provincials		
	Upper Class	Middle Class	Lower Class	Upper Class	Middle Class	Lower Class
Own ideas compared with perceived paternal political views:						
Own ideas to left	61%	66%	77%	60%	55%	50%
Own ideas to right	11	6	1	25	24	24
Own ideas conform	29	28	22	15	21	27
Number of respondents..	94	104	104	20	66	190

LESLIE L. ROOS, JR., NORALOU P. ROOS, AND GARY R. FIELD

Differences Among Universities

Additional insight into the role of Turkish students in politics can be had by comparing students at different types of university-level institutions — at, for example, the Political Science Faculty and Robert College, a private institution founded under American auspices about one hundred years ago. Political Science Faculty students have traditionally entered high-level political and governmental positions, while the Robert College students, going to a foreign school located in a suburb of Istanbul, come from a more cosmopolitan background and are more likely to make their careers in the private sector.[30] The Political Science Faculty students were more likely to have had fathers in governmental or military positions and less likely to have had fathers in commercial occupations or in the professions.

The values of students at the two institutions are also quite different. The Robert College students demonstrate a higher commitment to internationalism, as opposed to nationalism, than do the Political Science Faculty students. These differences appear to be reflected in the type of political activities in which the two schools have been involved. At the height of political tension just preceding the 1960 coup, there were bloody student riots at the Political Science Faculty. A few days later, the government closed Robert College after one hundred and fifty students took part in an orderly and peaceful demonstration.[31]

Other differences among Faculties have important implications for political behavior. In 1965 data gathered by Ozankaya indicate that the Political Science Faculty and Law Faculty students differ from the other Ankara University students along several dimensions. The Political Science and Law students were characterized by greater political knowledge and higher levels of political interest than their counterparts majoring in other subjects.[32] The Political Science students seem both somewhat more knowledgeable and more interested than the Law students. These data are significant because it is generally agreed that students at the Ankara Law Faculty and particularly the Political Science Faculty were by far the most politically active during the disturbances leading up to the 1960 military coup. These differences in political involvement are also reflected in a 1959 survey contrasting the leisure-time activities of students at these two Faculties with those of students in the Administrative Sciences, division of Middle East Technical University.[33] Middle East Technical University, a new institution founded with

United Nations aid, is characterized by its modern curriculum, smaller classes, and emphasis on technical subjects, as well as by the fact that English, rather than Turkish, is the language of instruction.

There were regular differences in political interest among the three groups of students. Generally speaking, Political Science Faculty students, followed by students at the Law Faculty and Middle East Technical University, were the most interested in political news. Another difference among the Faculties, and one which has important political implications, concerns the students who spend their free time strolling on the streets. Such students are a common sight in downtown Ankara and can be readily mobilized for political demonstrations. Here again the 1959 survey showed the same rank order among Faculties as was discussed above. Sixty-one per cent of the Political Science students said they spent some of their free time strolling; the corresponding figures for the Law Faculty and Middle East Technical University students were 47 and 30 per cent respectively.

Student political culture in Turkey is predominately leftist and etatist. Not only are the attitudes of the leaders and the campus activists leftist, but university students prefer to read the more radical press.[34] Fully three fourths of the students said that they regularly read newspapers classed as leftist, while less than 10 per cent mentioned rightist papers. Similarly, leftist magazines were much more frequently read than were rightist ones.

While the students are important as an efficacious pressure group and as self-conscious members of the educated elite, it is difficult to say how politically "active" they are relative to other student populations. An impressionistic observation would be that Turkish student political activity (during normal times) takes place within the general bounds of the legitimized political system and uses both what Bakke calls "conservative measures"[35] and mass demonstrations. Student groups make their positions known through press conferences, letters, declarations, and by direct involvement in activities such as labor disputes. Mass demonstrations have become more frequent, and in the past year opposing student groups have clashed violently.

To some degree, Turkish students have been less involved and less revolutionary than students in some of the other developing countries. Although completely adequate data are lacking, several features of Turkish society and the Turkish educational system might be expected to dampen student political activism. Two of these are the persistent elitist bias in the educational system and the low level of unemployment among the educated classes.

Frederick Frey suggests that there has been an elitist dynamic to the Turkish educational system during the Republic because there has been a more rapid expansion of the upper levels of the system (particularly *lycée* and university) than of the lower, primary levels.[36] Such an educational investment policy results in a higher number of university graduates relative to other developing countries that choose to invest their money differently. But this aspect of the educational system would not make it elitist according to one aspect of Seymour Martin Lipset's classification system.[37] Lipset suggests that a distinction be drawn between elitist system where admission to the universities is difficult and mass systems where "almost anyone who wants to enter a university may do so." He goes on to say that, as a result of such mass admissions policies in Egypt, Japan, and India, attendance at the university has "skyrocketed" and far surpasses the rise in suitable job opportunities. In order to see how Turkey ranks relative to other systems which Lipset has termed "mass" or "elitist," comparative figures on the size of the system of higher education in various other countries are presented below.

Table 7:

Classification of Countries According to Proportion
of Students Enrolled in Higher Education[38]

	Higher Education Enrollment per 100,000
Mass Education Systems	
United States	1983
Puerto Rico	1192
Philippines	976
Argentina	827
Japan	750
Egypt	399
India	220
TURKEY	225
Elitist Education Systems	
Britain	460
Sierra Leone	19
Nigeria	4

On this indicator, Turkey would seem to rank closer to the mass systems of India and Egypt than to the elitist systems of Nigeria and Sierra Leone. But Turkey possesses many other attributes common to elitist educational systems. A relatively high degree of selectivity through examinations ensures that only a small proportion of the populace gains access to the university preparatory *lycées*. Only 3 per cent of all students entering primary school can hope to enter one of these *lycées*, although once this hurdle has been overcome, approximately 55 per cent of them will go on to the university.[39] It has been reported that about 40 per cent of Turkish students entering the university eventually graduate,[40] but other sources indicate that this figure may be somewhat inflated.[41] If a figure between 30 and 40 per cent is correct, this would compare reasonably well with the records of many developed countries. For example, in Sweden 32 per cent of those entering get degrees; in France, 38 per cent; in the United States, 45 per cent; and in Britain, 65 per cent.[42] Comparable data from developing countries are generally lacking, but Philip Altbach notes that "well over half of those who enter college in India do not finish their degree programs."[43]

One indicator of the relatively healthy nature of the Turkish economy is particularly important to the university system — the low level of unemployment among its graduates and the satisfaction that its graduates find in their work. According to the 1960 census, out of Turkey's more than 47,000 university graduates only 157 report that they were unemployed.[44] If Turkish university graduates have little difficulty in finding a job, they also seem to be relatively happy with the jobs they do find. A recent sample survey of people who had graduated from the Political Science Faculty between 1946 and 1961 found that 65 per cent of the respondents were satisfied with their jobs.[45]

On the other hand, Turkish universities are certainly not without major problems, and the students' behavior has been becoming less and less restrained over the past several years. High student-faculty ratios, an archaic examination system, and generally inadequate budgets cause continual complaints. In June, 1968 these factors helped spark nationwide disturbances centered at Ankara and Istanbul Universities. Furthermore, both the leaders of Turkish students organizations and the most politically active students tend to be considerably more leftist than the student body. These leftist students are motivated to lead the others toward more radical participation.

LESLIE L. ROOS, JR., NORALOU P. ROOS, AND GARY R. FIELD

Optimistic judgments are partially based on an assessment of the long-term effects of such newer universities as Middle East Technical University and Hacettepe Science Center; the curricular innovations and more professional atmosphere of these newer institutions seem to have had some feedback to the more established universities. The rate of change inside and outside the university system should be rapid enough to keep student disturbances from exerting a pervasive influence upon national political life. Moreover, continuing economic progress means that comparatively good opportunities for university graduates will remain to moderate the level of student protest.

Overall levels of student political activity in Turkey are probably affected by the strength of the national political leadership, the degree of student agreement with this leadership, the conditions of university life, and — most recently — the example of widespread student protest in other countries. Economic growth and sustained political responsibility on the part of Prime Minister Demirel's Justice Party government will make it difficult for leftist leaders to gain a mass following on other than university-related issues. Even though there is not widespread student support for the Justice Party, student discontent would have to be magnified and linked with support among other social groups in order to present a real threat to the government. Such developments seem rather improbable, but continued student protest over various issues is almost a certainty.[46]

REFERENCES

1. See Frederick W. Frey, *The Turkish Political Elite* (Cambridge, 1965), for further discussion of the social backgrounds of political elites.

2. George S. Harris, "The Role of the Military in Turkish Politics," *Middle East Journal*, Vol. 19 (Spring, 1965), p. 175.

3. Nermin Abadan, "Values and Political Behavior of Turkish Youth," in *Turkish Yearbook of International Relations, 1963* (Ankara, 1965), p. 90.

4. Walter F. Weiker, *The Turkish Revolution 1960–1961* (Washington, 1963), p. 58.

5. The authors have examined the daily publication *The Pulse* between May, 1966, and February, 1967. (This is a summary of the Turkish Press published by a Turkish news service in Ankara. While it is difficult to determine how representative and complete the coverage is, major papers are included and each issue runs from four to eight pages.) Our general impression is that many of the major student statements are at least men-

tioned, and most of the more overt demonstrations and speeches are covered.

6. TMTF received about 180,000 TL and MTTB 120,000 TL (respectively, about $20,000 and $13,300) annually as of the early 1960's. Abadan, "Values and Political Behavior of Turkish Youth," p. 88.

7. Andreas M. Kazamias, *Education and the Quest for Modernity in Turkey* (Chicago, 1966), pp. 220–221.

8. *Ibid.*

9. These data are taken from a re-analysis of a national sample survey conducted in 1963. For a description of this study, see J. Mayone Stycos, "The Potential Role of Turkish Village Opinion Leaders in a Program of Family Planning," *Public Opinion Quarterly,* Vol. 29 (Spring, 1965), pp. 120–130. Professor G. W. Angell, Jr., field director of the study, kindly helped us to obtain these data.

10. Robert N. Bellah, "Religious Aspects of Modernization in Turkey and Japan," *American Journal of Sociology,* Vol. 64 (July, 1958), pp. 1–5.

11. Weiker, *The Turkish Revolution 1960–61,* p. 145.

12. The findings presented in this section were obtained from a secondary analysis of the Turkish *lycée* study conducted by F. W. Frey, G. W. Angell, Jr., and A. Ş. Sanay in 1958. Some of the preliminary results of this analysis are presented in Frederick W. Frey, "Education," *Political Modernization in Japan and Turkey,* eds. Robert E. Ward and Dankwart A. Rustow (Princeton, 1964), pp. 224–229. We would like to thank Professor Frey for making the study available.

13. Data supporting the conclusion that American youths acquire many of their basic political beliefs relatively early in life is provided by several studies. See for example David Easton and Jack Dennis, "The Child's Image of Government," *The Annals,* Vol. 361 (September, 1965), pp. 40–57, and Fred Greenstein, *Children and Politics* (New Haven, 1965).

14. One notable exception to this trend should be mentioned. There was no difference between the various schools in the response to the question "Would you be personally interested in a political career?" The affirmative response to this question was high — approximately 55 per cent of each group.

15. Kazamias, *Education and the Quest for Modernity in Turkey,* p. 134.

16. The basic data on Political Science Faculty students was obtained from a secondary analysis of survey data collected by Herbert H. Hyman, Arif Payaslïoğlu, and Frederick W. Frey in 1958. Their original analysis is described in Herbert H. Hyman, Arif Payaslïoğlu, and Frederick W. Frey, "The Values of Turkish College Youth," *Public Opinion Quarterly,* Vol. 22 (Fall, 1958), pp. 275–291

17. This study was conducted by Gary R. Field. In 1960, 760 male students at the Faculty of Law were given the fifteen-page questionnaire in a classroom situation. Because of nonexistent student lists and other peculiarities of the Turkish university system, the study's sample was one of availability. According to the estimates of the several law school professors who assisted in the project, the number of respondents was approximately the average daily attendance at the Faculty of Law. The number of students according to class was: first year, 347; second, 268; third, 86; and fourth, 59.

18. Unfortunately, comparable data are not available for the *lycée* students on all of the above questions. While most of the questions were asked on both surveys, different coding schemes make direct comparisons hazardous at best. Where such comparisons were made, they supported the trend apparent in the first two questions: There seems to be a slight rise in nationalism among first-year students at the Political Science Faculty (compared with *lycée* student attitudes), but this is followed by a steady decline in nationalistic responses over the four-year period at the Faculty.

19. Özer Ozankaya, *Üniversite Öğrencilerinin Siyasal Yönelimleri* (Political Attitudes of University Students; Ankara, 1966), p. 21. The author of this study obtained a sample of 2.7 per cent of all Ankara University students and 82 per cent of the university leaders. There were 317 regular respondents and 109 student leaders surveyed.

20. *Ibid.*, p. 176.

21. The figures in Table 1 and the data cited in reference 17 provide a rough idea of the diminishing numbers of students in the higher years.

22. Abadan, "Values and Political Behavior of Turkish Youth," p. 87.

23. This attitude change in the university environment seems to remain after graduation. A 1965 resurvey of the Political Science Faculty classes originally studied by Hyman, Payaslıoğlu, and Frey found the same percentage of graduates emphasizing government "for the people" as was noted for the university students (47 per cent). Thus, the shift from a populistic toward a paternalistic orientation appears to take place at the university; the percentage saying government "for the people" seems to remain more or less constant thereafter. An additional analysis comparing Faculty graduates from the 1946–55 period with their counterparts who graduated in 1958–61 found few differences between younger and older graduates in the percentage choosing "for the people." The 1965 survey is described at some length in Leslie L. Roos, Jr. and Noralou P. Roos, "Secondary Analysis in the Developing Areas," *Public Opinion Quarterly*, Vol. 31 (Summer, 1967), pp. 272–278.

24. These are preliminary results from a study conducted by Gary R. Field in 1966. The sample includes interviews from three university-level institutions: the Faculty of Political Science; the Economics and Business Sciences Academy of Eskişehir; and the School of Social Welfare in Ankara. A total of 673 men were interviewed.

25. Based on the 1966 Field study described above, which includes students from three university-level institutions. "Importance of Religion" is derived from responses to the question: "How important is religion in your life?" People who answered "extremely important" or "quite important" are listed as high; people who answered "of little importance" or "not important at all" are listed as low.

26. Ozankaya, *Üniversite Öğrencilerinin Siyasal Yönelimleri,* pp. 158–64. Although the author bases his social background measure on father's salary and educational level, this is closely related to both occupational and urban-rural distinctions. Those students classified as belonging to the upper and middle classes do so by virtue of their families having been members of the older elite — the highly educated, largely urban, and official classes that were prominent during the early days of the Republic. Students classified as lower class come from the groups which have experienced upward mobility during the postwar period. The empirical data on these classifications appear in Ozankaya, pp. 140–141.

27. The upper-class respondents (31 per cent) are those whose fathers are high government and military officials, or members of professions such as law, medicine, and engineering. The middle-class category (32 per cent) is composed of children of proprietors, salespeople, public and private clerical workers, and the like. This middle-class group is basically an urbanized, salaried, white-collar group. The lower-class respondents (36 per cent) are those whose fathers are agriculturalists, service workers, craftsmen, and laborers.

28. Ozankaya, *Üniversite Öğrencilerinin Siyasal Yönelimleri,* p. 157.

29. This is from the 1960 Field survey.

30. These findings were available from a secondary analysis of the survey reported in Hyman, Payaslioğlu, and Frey, "The Values of Turkish College Youth."

31. "Chronology," *Middle East Journal,* Vol. 14 (Spring, 1960), p. 315.

32. Ozankaya, *Üniversite Öğrencilerinin Siyasal Yönelimleri,* p. 182–183.

33. The results are reported in Nermin Abadan, *Üniversite Öğrencilerinin Serbest Zaman Faaliyetleri* (Free Time Activities of University Students; Ankara, 1961).

34. Ozankaya, *Üniversite Öğrencilerinin Siyasal Yönelimleri,* pp. 154–56. Classified as Leftist papers were: *Cumhuriyet, Milliyet, Akşam, Vatan, Yeni Tanin;* as rightist were *Adalet, Yeni İstanbul, Son Havadis, Zafer, Tercüman,* and *Ege Expres;* the other category included *Ulus, Dünya, Hürriyet, Yeni Gazete,* and *Yeni Sabah.*

35. E. W. Bakke, "Mass Demonstrations," Paper presented at Conference on Students and Politics in San Juan, Puerto Rico, March 27–31, 1967.

36. Frey, "Education," p. 219.

37. Seymour Martin Lipset, "University Students and Politics in Under-developed Countries," *Student Politics*, ed. S. M. Lipset (New York, 1967), p. 140.

38. Data for this table are taken from Bruce M. Russett, *World Handbook of Political and Social Indicators* (New Haven, 1964), pp. 214–16: higher education universities and post-secondary professional schools, including higher teacher-training.

39. Kazamias, *Education and the Quest for Modernity in Turkey*, p. 171.

40. *The Mediterranean Regional Project — Turkey* (Paris, 1965), p. 118.

41. This evidence is summarized by Joseph S. Szyliowicz, "Students and Politics: The Turkish Case" (unpublished manuscript; Denver, 1967), p. 48.

42. Russett, *World Handbook of Political and Social Indicators*, p. 214. Similar data for several other countries are included in his tabulations.

43. See Philip G. Altbach, "Student Politics and Higher Education in India," in this volume.

44. Turkey, Bureau of Statistics, *23 Ekim 1960 Genel Nüfus Sayïmï, 1960* (General Population Census of October 23, 1960: Ankara, 1963), pp. 219–220, 488–489. The figures are based only on the "Faculties," not on the other higher schools that are also listed.

45. See Roos and Roos, "Secondary Analysis in the Developing Areas," pp. 272–278. Data taken from a survey by the authors. There were 310 Political Science Faculty graduates who responded to this survey.

46. The authors wish to thank the American Research Institute in Turkey for its help in providing funds to support the 1965–66 survey research reported here.

MICHIYA SHIMBORI

The Sociology of a Student Movement —

A Japanese Case Study

WASEDA UNIVERSITY — a private institution founded in 1882 in Tokyo as Tokyo Semmon Gakko (Professional School) — is one of Japan's Ivy League universities. The University of Tokyo, the first national university, was established in 1869, and Keio University, a private institution, opened in the preceding year. Since the beginning of the Meiji era (1868–1911), these colleges have been among the major higher educational institutions in Japan. In contrast with the public universities, Waseda and Keio were founded by private individuals according to a clear ideal (Keio by Yukichi Fukuzawa, a leading democrat, and Waseda by Shigenobu Okuma, a liberal politician). Enlightened and inspired by Western ideas of democracy and liberalism in their study abroad, they took a lead in the movements for civil rights and liberty and called for constitutional government in the early Meiji period, when a substantial number of feudal elements remained, both in and out of the government. They founded their schools in opposition to the University of Tokyo, which was mainly aimed at educating high government officials and stressed technology and science. Keio had a utilitarian slant and trained leaders in business, while Waseda was intended to be superior in political economics, journalism, and literature. Before Japan's rapid industrialization, the most prestigious positions available to university graduates were in the government and army. Thus, the divided market — training for government available primarily at Tokyo, business at Keio, and representative politics and journalism at Waseda — produced little conflict among the graduates of the three schools, although the Tokyo graduates had an advantage in the Japanese society as a whole. The government did not like the liberal, and therefore somewhat antigovernment, spirit of the private universities. Indeed, the government did not designate private colleges as formally equal to public universities until 1918. Waseda was suspected of being a training center for revolutionaries and from time to time was suppressed by the government. Among Waseda graduates there have been many liberal politicians, writers, and journalists who criticized the political elite and orthodox policies. Okuma, its founder, resigned his post as cabinet minister and became a leader of the Kaishinto (Progressive) Party.

During the prewar years, Waseda was the main center for student movements and within the past several years has again become the scene of student militancy. On December 20, 1965, the Board of Trustees decided to raise substantially the entrance fees and tuition. The student government opposed this increase and resorted to a strike, during which students refused to attend classes and to take examinations. After unsuccessful negotiations between the university authorities and the leaders of the student body, the students occupied the administration building on February 10, 1966. Alumni groups were unsuccessful in their attempts to mediate the dispute. Finally, at the request of the university, twenty-five hundred armed policemen invaded the campus on February 21, removing barricades the students had set up around the buildings. As soon as the policemen withdrew, the students reconstructed the barricades. In the meantime, the annual entrance examination, one of the main sources of income for private universities, approached, and the Waseda authorities were anxious to settle the dispute. Negotiations failed, but the arrest of 203 student leaders made it possible to hold the entrance examinations in a regular hall guarded by policemen. The struggle reopened after the examination, however, and the commencement and term examinations had to be postponed. The president resigned his office on April 23, to be followed by the members of the Board of Trustees. The new authorities made many concessions and showed a willingness to communicate with students. The students, in turn, voted to stop the strike, thus ending the six-month struggle.

Factors other than the traditional anti-establishment sentiment at Waseda were responsible for the general support this dispute evoked among the students. Private universities in Japan — supported neither by donations from corporate wealth and alumni, as in the United States, nor by the national budget, as in England — must depend almost completely upon student tuition. Fees and other expenses at private universities are, therefore, much higher than the standard expenses at national universities. According to a nationwide survey by the Ministry of Education in 1961, 46.3 per cent of the total income of private universities came from tuition and entrance fees, 17.8 per cent from loans, and 21.7 per cent from university-owned enterprises, such as hospitals; subsidies from national budget contributed only 3.2 per cent and donations from outside agencies 5 per cent. As a result, tuition at a private university is about four times higher than at public institutions. In addition, there are other expenses, such as entrance fees and parents' donations, that do not exist in national universities.[1]

Concomitantly, the private universities must enroll the maximum number of students in order to survive. To attract more students, they have to provide such amenities as modern buildings and make examinations easier by eliminating certain required subjects (like the natural sciences) that are disliked by high-school graduates. Some private universities often enroll students who are rich, but not necessarily able, and emphasize the humanities and social sciences which require less elaborate facilities than the natural sciences and medicine.[2] In this manner, many "mass" and "mammoth" private universities have developed — Waseda among them with its 36,000 students, in comparison to the 15,000 enrolled at the University of Tokyo, the largest national university. Nippon University, the largest school in terms of enrollment, has 68,000 students and is called the "Department Store University" or "University Industry."

Private universities also tend to employ fewer teachers per student in order to meet their budget requirements. There are twenty-six students per professor in the private schools, in contrast to eight per professor in the public ones. In most private universities, the professors have little right to participate in administration and, thus, often have a negative attitude toward it. Like the students, they are, in a sense, the victims of poor financial conditions. They are poorly paid, have inadequate facilities, and suffer from heavy teaching loads. They give their lectures through microphones to a large audience, and there is little opportunity for teacher-student interaction.

Moreover, expenditure per student in private universities is less than one third of that in the United States, where — in contrast to Japan — the state universities, like Berkeley, Michigan, and Wisconsin, are mammoth, and the private institutions, like Harvard, Chicago, and Stanford, are small.

Greater financial burdens, poorer educational facilities, impersonal relations between students and faculty, the sentiment that students are treated as a source of income — all lead to resentment and antagonism against the university authorities as well as the governmental policies concerning higher education. This subconscious resentment can easily be brought into the open whenever there is an overt incident. Moreover, "professional" student leaders who are experts in agitation and organization co-operate in the search for issues around which to agitate.

At Waseda, the former president and the trustees underestimated both the students' resentment and their ability to organize a strong mass movement. They thought the student movement involved only outside "nonstudents" and a small group of campus radicals. Nor had the administration maintained good communication with the faculty, which generally has a more adequate understanding of the campus atmosphere. The professors had not even been informed of the plan to increase fees.

Before the beginning of the Waseda struggle, there was little communication among students, professors, and administrators. This evil may be inherent in the bureaucratization of the "mass" university, but the Waseda authorities had done little to improve communication or to know the general feeling among students and faculty. Because the campus is the traditional sanctuary of academic freedom, the administration's request for police intervention outraged many who had not previously been involved in the struggle over tuition. Once this occurred, the number of students supporting the strike and taking part in the demonstrations increased substantially. Given their initial point of view, the behavior of the Waseda authorities is understandable. They assumed that the opposition movement was run by a handful of politicized leaders, many of whom were "nonstudents," and that it was not supported by many students. Consequently, they felt that the only effective way to end the disturbances was to suppress this small minority decidedly and forcefully.

Since the so-called *Ampo-Toso* (Struggle Against the Revision of U.S.-Japan Security Treaty) in 1960, *Zengakuren* (All Japan Federation of Student Governments) had, in fact, been seriously weakened. It had split into a vast variety of factions, each claiming hegemony, competing with the others, and remaining aloof from the general body of students. This factional strife blunted the effectiveness of the movement, even though all groups oppose the present political regime and university administrations.

The names and ideologies of the various factions confuse the general public as well as the ordinary student. In general, most of the factions are far more radical than the Communist Party (except *Heimin-Gakuren* [Student Federation for Peace and Democracy], which is under the control of the Party). They are against all the established, "bureaucratized" political parties and opposed to every kind of power elite and source of authority. It is impossible to negotiate with them, since they refuse any compromise.[3] Shortly before the Waseda struggle of 1965, the student leaders demanded that the student union building be administered directly by a student committee. The Waseda administration assumed that this was an attempt by the militant student leadership to use the fee issue to mobilize and agitate the student population for broader purposes, and that, as such, it was a preparatory exercise for a struggle for a "student governed university." On the one hand were militant student leaders opposed to everything and, on the other, hard-headed administrators accustomed to deciding everything according to their assumptions. In between were the majority of students and faculty, generally uninformed, yet vaguely dissatisfied with their life at the university.

One can see that many issues were involved in the Waseda struggle — the poor financial situation of private universities, the inherently bureaucratized character of mass universities, and the radical objectives of the leaders of the student movements. The Japanese universities must solve these key problems if they are to function adequately as centers of scholarship and education.

A Typology of Student Movements

Was the Waseda struggle a student political movement in the strict sense? Seemingly, it was an outgrowth of such academic issues as fee increases and the dysfunctions of impersonal mass education. Moreover, the agitation appears to have been confined to a particular campus, although some sympathizers and professional "nonstudent" leaders assisted the Waseda students. Nevertheless, the struggle must be called political, if radical leaders took up academic issues merely as a means to awaken a broader political consciousness and to unite the student body into an active anti-establishment organization.

Owing to the widespread system of higher education and the ideology of student leaders, a student movement can easily become political and national in scope in contemporary Japan. Any issue peculiar to a particular institution can be linked to broader political issues. Common in the national universities today are struggles for the right of student administration over dormitory and other facilities built with national funds. Students in private universities consider fee increases the result of governmental policy toward these institutions. Such university issues are thought to be products of the reactionary character of the capitalist system. A refusal of students' rights to control dormitories is a result of the desire of the imperialist elite to hinder and weaken student power; poor support for private universities reflects the government's policy of promoting industrial capitalism while ignoring the educational needs of the poorer classes. According to this logic, any trivial issue must be interpreted in a broader context — from the perspective of an evaluation of the social and political order, or even the state of international politics. Since this logic is unfamiliar to and cannot be accepted by the majority of students, the leaders must use every issue that is clearly relevant to the campus situation as a starting point in the process of "educating" the majority into an "enlightened and awakened" perspective. Accordingly, the student movement must continue to struggle until the present power structure comes to an end.

If one defines politics as a system or mechanism of power distribution, student political movements function along at least three dimensions: the intramural, national, and international. Student political movements or organizations can be classified into three categories as well: those, such as the Waseda struggle, that are confined to a particular university and within a campus; the national federations, like *Zengakuren;* and the international organizations, like the International Union of Students. In an age of organization and of close international interrelationships, intramural groups are easily absorbed by larger national or international federations. Thus, the ideology of local leaders tends to become influenced by national or international issues and ideas.

The impact of national and international ideologies on student movements was not great in their early history. The older universities of Europe were content to maintain their own freedom of inquiry. But the universities founded more recently in developed nations were established by secular powers, political or economic, in order to modernize the nation. Students at such institutions have been as concerned with secular matters as they have been with academic ones; they have been as much nationally-politically minded as intellectually-academically minded.

Whether student movements are intramural, national, or international in outlook is a function of the relationship of the academic community to the outside world. When universities are controlled largely by local boards of trustees with specific, particularistic educational orientations, the student struggles are often entirely intramural. When national issues — such as the unification of the country or constitutional and academic freedom — predominate, politically minded students do not show much interest in the struggles of students in other countries. The general concept of an international student movement did not arise much before World War II, except in a few cosmopolitan universities with students from many countries. Students, like workers, are more apt to respond to intramural sources of grievance, so that even where national and international organizations exist, student political leaders tend to seize upon local issues around which the less politicized students may be mobilized. Once students are drawn into the struggle against intramural "reactionaries," their horizons can be widened to include the nation, and even the world. Significantly, the largest continuous student movement, the University Reform of Latin America, began in Cordoba as a struggle over conditions in rooming houses.

In sum, student movements — whether intramural, national, or international — are essentially political in the sense that all the problems they tackle are, or are interpreted as, resulting from or related to the power structures of campus, nation, or world. At present, it is proper to say that international student movements do not exist — even though international student organizations have been formed, and many students are actually oriented to international politics — because a political movement must have a concrete object, and international issues have not yet provided such a clear focus. Thus, student movements can tentatively be classified into three categories — namely, intramural, intermural, and extramural — omitting the international aspect.[4]

The Waseda case was a typical intramural movement, although its leaders were professional and the ultimate concern of the leaders was political. As far as the form of the movement and the consciousness of the general participants were concerned, it was intramural. The movement was carried on within the campus, and it attacked the university administrators on the specific issues of raising fees and impersonal mass education. Although the Waseda struggle ended after six months of conflict, the problems inherent in the poor financial arrangements of private universities and in mass instruction cannot be said to have been settled. Thus, the Waseda solution may represent only a temporary armistice. As students have become aware of the similarity of their complaints, intramural or intermural movements have begun to appear. There are, however, enormous difficulties involved in building a national organization devoted to solving these problems.

National organizations are unlikely to retain the sympathy of the faculty and general public, who often tend to give stronger support to genuinely local intramural issues. Faculty grievances against administrators and the general support of adults for youthful idealism help to encourage intramural movements and thus to increase the possibility of their success. In contrast to an intramural movement, an intermural movement needs a bureaucratized organization like *Zengakuren*, with its liaison office and headquarters. Indirect democracy is a necessity, and representatives or delegates must be elected. Because these organizations are formed in order to solve the problems common to most universities, their dominant ideology tends to be political rather than academic. Thus, their leaders are professionals not only in organization and leadership, but also in political ideology. While an organization formed for the successful functioning of an intramural movement is easily dissolved once the initial objective is attained, an intermural organization, which is much more formal and bureaucratized, usually tries to survive the end of the given issue around which it was formed. It must create, invent, or discover, continuously and successively, new problems if it is to have a *raison d'être* and to attract the interest of ordinary students. Usually, "spontaneously formed" intramural movements precede intramural organizations. The reverse is true on the intermural level. In a national student organization in which political ideology is formed by professional leaders who are not always familiar with the sentiment of the wider student body, the more radical and more clear-cut ideologies are likely to be adopted. Principles that can guide movements on a nationwide scale must necessarily be more universal and general than those in a local movement.

The efforts to set up a national organization inevitably suffer because the distance grows between the leaders and their potential public as the ideology of the organization becomes more political, radical, and abstract and the leadership more professionalized and bureaucratized. In a circular process, the more unsuccessful the effort is at creating mass movements, the more radical and militant are the tactics adopted. When movements initiated by an intermural organization become purely political and not directly related to campus matters or to student life, the leaders tend to seek help from nonstudents, particularly the political parties and trade unions with ideologies similar to theirs. Since in most countries students are — not only in number, but also in organizability, mobilizability, and group identity — one of the largest politically conscious social groups, political parties and other organizations want to make full use of them. Hence, there is often close interdependence and co-operation between national student movements and other politically relevant organizations. Such joint efforts may be described as *extramural*.

Extramural movements have few standing organizations, because they are combinations of two independent groups, students and adults. They may be part of common federations and have common headquarters, but they do not have a unified organization. There always seem to be a struggle for hegemony and competition for power between students and their nonstudent allies. Sometimes a political party completely dominates a student organization; at other times, various party-linked factions in a student organization take over political movements. In many cases, the students become so much more radical, militant, and independent that the co-operating or sponsoring political parties cannot discipline them and are highly embarrassed by them.

In general, student movements in free societies are political and critical of the *status quo* and the present power structure, whether it be intramural or national. They are, therefore, against all university administrations, the ruling class, central government, and even leftist bureaucratic party organizations. Another type of movement is, however, not against the ruling powers, but allied with them. Pro-establishment movements or organizations are often seen in a totalitarian state (for example, Hitler *Jugend* in Nazi Germany and *Hokokudan* [Patriot Student Body] in wartime Japan). They are quite often organized artifically and intentionally by the government or the university authorities in order to counteract the oppositionist sentiments and illegal student groups. Since they are manufactured from above, they are supported by power and not by ideological principle. The majority of the students are indifferent or even antagonistic to such organizations or their sponsors even though they hold compulsory membership. Teachers or official leaders often have the role of supervisor or spy, and are suspected by the membership, so that the distance between them is greater and less intimate than in intermural organizations. Anti-establishment groups, although forced underground, get the greatest share of the spiritual and moral support of the student populations.

The nation of Japan consciously opened the door to outside influences during the imperialistic world situation of a century ago. At that time, the Western powers were struggling with one another for the world market. It is not difficult to understand why nationalism became important in Japan in this situation. The fall of the Tokugawa Shogunate regime in the 1860's meant the defeat of conservative isolationism. Progressives who held that Japan could survive only if it were modernized put through the Meiji Restoration in the name of the Emperor. Technology and material civilization could, however, not be assimilated independently of traditional Japanese ideology and philosophy. Soon after the new government was established, it founded Tokyo Imperial University (now the University of Tokyo), at which future leaders could assimilate Western technology and be trained. For some forty years after its establishment, this institution almost monopolized higher education. Because its graduates were relatively few in number, they could expect speedy upward mobility in government. Thus, as prospective national leaders, the majority of the students of Tokyo closely resembled the elite in their value system. They were politically minded, but did not question or oppose the ruling ideology. As indicated earlier, Waseda and other private institutions were established in opposition to the national university by leaders who were out of power and antagonistic to the government, or who wanted to expand the influence of Western ideology. An antagonism developed in this period between national and private universities, the latter becoming centers of an antigovernment movement, the so-called *Jiyuminken Undo* (Movement for Civil Rights and Liberty). *Aikokusha* (Patriot Party), the first national organization of this movement, was formed in 1875 with Fukuzawa and Okuma as its chief leaders. It prospered until 1890, the year of the first Diet. The government sought to suppress it by passing the Association Act (1880), the Meeting Act (1882), the Press Act (1883), and by prohibiting political discussions and gatherings of any kind. Many law schools, including that of Waseda, were founded during this period in order to train lawyers and journalists critical of the government. Under such circumstances, students, especially those in private schools, were ardently interested in politics and became proponents of the antigovernment movement. The first student strike occurred in 1879 at Keio University. Political lectures in schools and in the streets were in vogue, and many students were arrested for participating in political meetings.

The Sociology of a Student Movement — A Japanese Case Study

Even at the national University of Tokyo, built on the model of Western universities and thus the ideal of academic freedom, students opposed the suppression of the antigovernment movement. A political study group called *Oto-kai* was organized at Tokyo, and some of its members became active in the *Kaishin-to* (Reform Party) of Okuma. In protest against the government's supervision of discussions, students of the University of Tokyo boycotted commencement exercises in 1883.[5]

The first phase of Japanese student movements lasted until the end of World War I and was characterized by the social atmosphere of Meiji nationalism. There had previously been no national federations nor organized student movements. The majority of students, especially those at the University of Tokyo, viewed themselves as a prospective elite and did not participate in any opposition movements, although a few were involved in such groups as a counter-elite. Student activism did not last long and was rather spasmodic. The concerned minority of students were nationalists and humanitarians, regardless of ideological differences.

The second stage in the history of Japanese student movements took place in the Taisho democracy. During this period, the opposition between national and private universities and the manifest psychological distance between students and workers disappeared or at least diminished. Activist students attempted to establish a common front with the masses. They were attracted to international revolutionary ideology, particularly Communism. World War I brought about a rapid development of industrialism, the growth of big business and urbanization, as well as a strengthening of the world-wide democratic current. Shortly after the war, the great Tokyo earthquake (1923) and depression (1926) resulted in social disorders that the party-based parliamentary government of Japan could not solve. The impetus for improving the working conditions of the laborers and for universal suffrage became greater.

In this chaotic atmosphere, higher education expanded greatly. The University Act of 1918 provided an important stimulus to university expansion. Four new universities were founded in 1917, sixteen in 1920, and thirty-one in 1923. According to Michio Nagai, the functional distinction between the national and private universities broke down as a result of this expansion. Both became training centers for the needed growth of the salaried white-collar classes. The private universities, formerly the champions of academic autonomy and counter-elite ideology, began to suffer serious financial problems. The national universities, more secure financially, took over the leadership in the struggle for academic freedom.[6]

During the same period, the growth of the labor movement accompanied industrial expansion. To illustrate, in 1912 there were 49 strikes involving 5736 laborers, while in 1919 there were 497 strikes in which 63,137 workers participated. Shortly before the formation in 1918 of the first national association of students, *Shinjin Kai* (New Man Society), *Rogaku Kai* (Laborer-Student Society) was created through federation between the workers in *Yuai Kai*, the first national organization of workers, and the students of various universities in Tokyo and in Kyoto. *Shinjin Kai* was an offspring of *Rogaku Kai*, and it acted as the intellectual leader of *Rogaku Kai*, publishing the periodical entitled *Democracy* and organizing many branches in other schools. The Russian words *V Narod!* (To the Masses!) were adopted as its slogan. Students tried to co-operate with workers for their emancipation, although the latter did not identify themselves with the students. *Minjin Domei* (Union of Common Men), a similar leftist organization founded in 1918 in Waseda, attracted various students who supported the goal of democracy by working for universal suffrage and in trade-union movements. Under the growing influence of syndicalist doctrines, its activities grew more radical, and some of its members were dismissed from the university. Accordingly, some of those ex-students formed in 1920 a new organization, *Gyomin Kai* (Society of Pioneers), which was based near the campus. While most of these societies were oriented to off-campus leftist social movements, *Sodai Bunka Kai* (Waseda Culture Society), organized under the influence of *Gyomin Kai* in 1921 with more than two hundred members, was concerned only with the campus matters. It advocated dismissing incompetent professors, boycotting lectures of reactionary and militarist teachers, improving educational techniques, and decreasing tuition.[7]

Most of these organizations were limited to the students of a particular institution. In 1922, *Gakusei Rengokai*, a federation of these independent organizations, appeared under the leadership of *Shinjin Kai*. It had forty-six member institutions (including the high schools) and an individual membership of 1600 (in 1924).[8] The federation initiated a campaign against three proposed laws — the Act Prohibiting Radical Social Movements, the Labor Union Law, and the Conciliation Act for Tenancy Disputes.

Both the ruling elite and many of the student body feared the student political organizations and their consolidated federation, with its radical leftist orientation. The ruling elite, alarmed that the Communist Revolution might spread to Japan, soon suppressed these organizations. Freedom for student political activities lasted under the Taisho democracy until 1925, when the notorious Law for Maintaining the Social Order (*Chian Iji Ho*) was promulgated, and *Gaku Ren* was declared an illegal organization. At the end of 1925 and in 1926, the so-called *Kyoto Gakuren Jiken* (Kyoto Gaku Ren Affair) occurred. Thirty-seven members of the *Gaku Ren* in Kyoto were charged with violating the law and arrested. Soon afterwards, thirty-eight members in other cities were arrested. Some distinguished progressive professors at Kyoto and other universities were also taken into custody. After this affair, the oppressive actions by the government and the university authorities increased. Many other student organizations were prohibited. Some went underground or disguised themselves. Others pretended to be purely academic — that is, nonactivist groups for the study of social thought. Still others channeled their activities into more moderate and humanitarian areas — such as the Student Settlement House Movement and Student Cooperative Store Movement. Some students concentrated on intramural movements, instead of participating in off-campus political activities. Many students enthusiastically supported campus demonstrations against military training — the most famous of which occurred at Waseda University in 1923 and at Otaru Commercial College in 1925.

Intramural movements, called *Gakko Sodo* (school riots or school disturbances) and led by university student activists, took place in many institutions, including the high schools. Every potential source of discontent was used to organize students against the campus authorities. Authoritarian administrations, poor diet in the dormitories, incompetent professors, and increases in fees were some of the issues that led to student strikes and other agitations. Intramural movements increased rapidly after 1925, as is shown by the following table.[9]

Year	1925	1926	1927	1928	1929	1930	1931
Number of school riots	15	7	13	75	117	223	395
Number of students arrested	45	—	29	120	292	950	1,119

After the suppression of political groups in 1925, student activists found a refuge in intramural movements. The Student Cooperative Store Movement appeared first in the Waseda University in 1926. It attracted many students and expanded rapidly into other schools. The Student Settlement House Movement, begun in 1923 after the great earthquake, ran labor schools and medical clinics in slum areas. Activists often tried to turn these moderate and humanistic movements into *sub rosa* leftist ones. As a result, these movements, too, were suppressed around 1930. By the beginning of World War II, almost every kind of student movement had been dismissed from the campus. Except for the officially sponsored organizations that supported the government's militaristic and imperialistic effort, student movements had gone underground.

There were always struggles in terms of ideology, power, and direction within the student movements and organizations, especially after 1925. Study or activity, revolution or parliamentarianism, Bolshevism or anarchism, humanitarianism or Marxism, pragmatism or ideology, politicalism or academism were vigorously debated. In general, the more radical and thorough ideologies seem to have attracted the activist students. Faced with the increasingly radicalized and sophisticated movements, the government and school administrators made every effort to suppress them forcefully. By encouraging sports and establishing guidance offices, they hoped to involve the student body in more "healthy and safe" organizations. They also sponsored and supported proestablishment organizations. *Kokoku Doshi Kai* (Society of Patriotic Comrades) was formed at the University of Tokyo in 1919. Its members had a markedly militaristic and reactionary orientation, and it was led by conservative professors. In the 1930's, similar student groups were formed in many schools. These rightist organizations rarely had national federation or the support of many students. Shortly before World War II, all student governments and extracurricular organizations were dissolved in favor of a purely official organization called *Hokokudan* (Patriot Student Body). All students were formally made members of this organization.

Zengakuren

In the history of student movements, the period after 1925 is described as the dark ages. Bloody struggles went on between a small number of militant activists and the police. The majority of students may have been concerned about the fate of the nation, the growing militarism, and the decline of democracy, but they were voiceless and powerless. The military defeat in 1945 emancipated the nation from the repressive political order. Just as in the *Jiyu-minken Undo* (Movement for Civil Rights and Liberty) of the 1880's and the Taisho democracy of the decade after 1910, the new postwar age of social emancipation witnessed a nationwide spread of political concerns and movements, including student organizations. While *Shinjin-Kai*, or its offspring *Gakuren*, was the core of the prewar federated student organizations, the now famous *Zengakuren* took the lead in the postwar period.

In the early postwar period, there were many demonstrations in institutions, including the high schools. The first student demonstration after the war, in fact, took place in the Ueno Girls' Middle School at Tokyo, in October, 1945, demanding that the militarist principal retire. This affair proved to be the precursor of the demonstrations insisting on the "democratization of the campus." The student protest called for purges of the militarist, "war-criminal" teachers, demanded that the liberal or progressive professors who had previously been dismissed be brought back, encouraged the participation of students in school administration, advocated self-government of dormitories, recommended the abolition of official student-guidance systems, and the like. "Defend the students' life," another slogan of the time, implied a struggle for better conditions, decreased tuition, increased scholarships, more school buildings and dormitories, and a discount for student travel. In the broader polity, the Law for Maintaining the Social Order was repealed and its servant, the *tokko keisatsu* (special police for political thought), abolished. The Communist Party was openly recognized, and labor unions were encouraged. The inflation, the scarcity of food and shelter, the heavy destruction from the bombing, and the economic isolation of the nation — all contributed to the destruction of normal life. And it is not surprising that most students seem to be concerned with social and economic issues and participate enthusiastically in political movements.[10]

The most important of Japanese student movements, the *Zengakuren* (an abbreviation of *Zen Nihon Gekusei Jichikai So Rengo*, All Japan Federation of College Student Governments), was organized on September 18, 1948, with affiliated units in 168 national, 31 municipal, and 61 private universities. *Zengakuren* had 300,000 members in 1948, when the total enrollment in all the higher institutions was about 440,000. The first central committee was controlled by the Communist Party.[11] The agreement adopted at the foundation assembly of *Zengakuren* in Tokyo read as follows:

Zengakuren, with the objectives of realizing all justifiable demands of all students by democratic methods and of contributing to the foundation of a democratic Japan through movements for restoring education, shall emphasize the following programs: 1) security and improvement of student life, and equal opportunities for education; 2) defense of academic freedom and national culture; 3) thorough democratization of educational administration; 4) security of right of autonomy of faculties; 5) unification and enlargement of students' fronts; 6) defense of peace and democracy; and 7) support of all other kinds of movements necessary for realizing the federation's objectives.

In October, the Ministry of Education issued to each institution a circular entitled "On Student Political Movements." This circular declared that the study of politics and freedom of criticism should be encouraged on the campus, that individual students should be free to belong to a political association, but that educational institutions should be places for study and order and not centers of political struggle. Educational institutions should be politically neutral, and branch organizations of political parties and cooperation between workers and students should be discouraged. This statement reflected the government's attitude toward the student movement. The new plan for boards of trustees proposed, under the University Act, the introduction of outside powers into the academic administration. Students opposed this change with the slogan, "movement for defense of education," and progressive professors, schoolteachers, workers, and journalists assisted them in their efforts. Widespread political disorders linked to international tensions followed demonstrations around this university issue.

The opposition between the Occupation Forces and the government, on the one hand, and the workers, students, and "progressive intellectuals," on the other, became increasingly clear. The former pressed for a so-called "Red purge" in all spheres of the nation, especially education. The proposal to establish boards of trustees and to transform the national universities into local public institutions on the American model was interpreted as an attempt to weaken academic autonomy and freedom. In an order of July 15, 1950, the American General Headquarters prohibited a students' strike and demonstration. These actions stimulated the students' anger and led to more militant activities. Defense of freedom, democracy, and peace against "American imperialism" became the slogan of the movement. The outbreak of the Korean War in 1950, followed in 1951 by the signing of the Peace Treaty at San Francisco, which contained a U.S.-Japan Mutual Security Pact, could not but involve the nation in the Korean conflict. The international tensions of the period helped, therefore, to polarize Japanese politics inside as well as outside the university.

Except for the first postwar years, there has been a continuous history of student political movements both on and off the campus. The movements have seized on every possible issue. These range from purely institutional matters — for example, increased fees and the University Act — to purely political or international matters, such as the Vietnam war and the nuclear test ban. Each of these issues has led to general and enthusiastic movements. *Zengakuren* became well known because of its violent demonstrations in 1960 at Tokyo's Haneda Airport against the Mutual Security Treaty, an event which made it impossible for President Eisenhower to visit Japan. The slogans, "Down with Premier Kishi" and "Against *Ampo*" (the Pact) were heard everywhere. Almost every day, over ten thousand students demonstrated at the Diet, in the streets, or at the airport. Violent struggles went on, and many students were arrested or injured. About half of Japan's students participated in the general strike against *Ampo*. In spite of strong student opposition, the Security Treaty was finally renewed, although Premier Kishi was forced to resign his post.

Since 1960, the student movements have declined in strength, perhaps because of the economic prosperity or the more effective university administration, the factional conflicts in *Zengakuren* or the general sense of failure that followed the *Ampo* struggle. Students have recently resembled a politically apathetic mass concerned only with their individual lives.[12] The professional leaders have tried to awaken the students' political consciousness. Although they have had some success from time to time, no mass movements on the scale of those in 1960 have taken place since. The Waseda situation discussed earlier did not stimulate comparable movements at other schools. One would be rash, however, to see in the present situation more than a period of transitional armed peace. The strains caused by the Vietnam war and the tension between the U.S. and Red China are becoming more difficult for the Japanese to deal with. The explosive U.S.-Japan Security Treaty will come up for revision in 1970. Campus-based political struggles will necessarily reappear in the near future. The rapidly increasing numbers of students face economic uncertainty as to their future, and many will prove receptive to political radicalism.

It is difficult to compute the frequency of student unrest, but the following table demonstrates the three stages of postwar student movements up to 1960.[13] It can be readily noted that intermural and extramural movements increased relatively as well as absolutely over time.

	1st Period (1945–47)	2nd Period (1948–50)	3rd Period (1951–60)
Intramural Movements	117 (90%)	217 (59%)	137 (26%)
Intermural Movements	9 (7%)	119 (32%)	379 (51%)
Extramural Movements	4 (3%)	27 (9%)	124 (23%)

A high frequency of demonstration in a given period, however, does not necessarily indicate that there is more enthusiasm or more intensity in movements. It is also important to note that the number of universities and students increased radically during this period. Demonstrations may be small and may occur separately in many places on diverse issues. The attraction of a movement for the general student population can, however, be seen by the number of students participating. Since the main types of activity are meetings, demonstrations, and strikes, it is necessary to estimate how many students participate in various types of movements. There are little reliable data available, but I have tried to make some estimates based on various reports.

Name of Happening	Number of Student Participants		
	Meetings	Demon-strations	Strikes
I. Intramural movements			
A. Student Festival, Waseda (May, 1947)	3000		
B. Restoring Private Education, Waseda (April, 1946)		6000	
II. Intermural movements			
A. Restoring Education (June, 1948)	10,000 (100)		
B. Against Raising Fees (June, 1948)			200,000 (150)

Movement				
Against Raising Fees (Feb., 1956)		6000		
C. Defense of Education (Nov., 1948)	4000 (50)			
D. Against University Act (May, 1949)	35,000 (23)			200,000 (140)
E. Against Eells Speech (Sept., 1950)	5000			10,000 (40)
F. Against Students' Suffrage at Home (Oct., 1953)		3000		
III. *Extramural movements*				
A. For Overall Peace Treaty (Oct., 1951)	8000 (16)	7000		
B. Against Rearmament (Feb., 1952)		5000		
C. Against Law Prohibiting "Destructive Activities" (May, 1952)	8700	3000	8700	
D. Against U.S. Asama Base (June, 1953)		3000		
Against U.S. Sunagawa Base (Oct., 1956)		3000	26,000	
Against U.S. Okinawa Base (July, 1956)		2500		
E. Against Two Educational Acts (May, 1956)	10,000	10,000		250,000 (150)
F. Against Law Evaluating Teaching Efficiency (April, 1958)	4400			21,000 (60)
G. Against Institution for Moral Education, Nara (Sept., 1958)	1300			
H. Against Law of Police Activities (Oct., 1958)	3500	1000		29,280 (60)
I. Against Nuclear Testing (May, 1957)	1000 (30)	18,000		43,700 (168)
J. Against Revision of U.S.–Japan Security Pact (Oct., 1959)	20,000	5000		300,000 (90)
K. Down with Kishi (Oct., 1959)				350,000 (90)
Down with Kishi (April, 1960)		35,000		250,000 (90)*

( )* indicates number of schools that participated.

It is clear from these figures, which are far from complete, that students can be interested in and mobilized for various kinds of movements.

The number of students formally under the control of *Zengakuren*, when compared with the number of students engaged in activities and the total student population, constitutes some sort of index of the intensity of the various movements. The number of students under *Zengakuren* control is, however, difficult to estimate. The percentage of schools and students holding membership in *Zengakuren* is presented in the table below:

Year	A	B	%(A/B)	C	D	%(C/D)
1948	110	592	18.6%	220,000	453,917	48.5%
	or 272		or 45.9	or 300,000		or 66.1
1949 Feb.	312	769	40.6	300,000	398,340	75.3
May	394	769	51.2			
1950 May	200	884	22.6		405,310	
June	210	884	23.8			
1952	57	516	11.0	132,215	501,912	26.3
1953	57	454	12.6		511,124	
1956		496		190,000	624,397	30.4
				or 200,346		or 32.1
1957		500		250,000	637,591	39.2
1958 May	111	503	22.1	285,000	649,314	43.9
Sept.	110	503	21.9	300,000		46.2
1959	110	511	21.5	266,000	673,394	39.5
				or 300,000		or 44.6
1960		525		300,000	709,878	42.2

Note: A. Number of schools affiliated with *Zengakuren*
      B. Number of all institutions of higher education
      C. Number of students affiliated with *Zengakuren*
      D. Total number of students in universities

Roughly speaking, about a fifth of all higher institutions and about a third of all college students in Japan are at least formally or nominally affiliated with *Zengakuren*. This means that the colleges with larger enrollments are more likely to affiliate and that about half of all Japanese students may have participated in a *Zengakuren* movement, such as the struggles against the revision of U.S.–Japan Security Pact.

Factionalism is inevitable in most political movements, but it is perhaps most common in student movements, because students tend to be idealistic and puritanical and to cling to ideological principles. Strong national organizations require bureaucratization and an emphasis on formalism and professionalization of leaders. These, in turn, lead to a greater distance between the leader and the follower. The factional struggles for internal hegemony stimulate increased radicalization, dogmatization, and further factionalization. Each leftist political party seeks to exert control over the student movement, thereby increasing the sources of factionalism and internecine disputes within the movement.

Postwar Japanese student movements are not an exception. Various factions in *Zengakuren* depend, to a considerable extent, upon sponsoring political parties, which are in turn influenced by changes in the international political situations. This is especially the case with Communist-oriented students. The balance of power between the U.S.S.R. and Red China, between Stalinism and anti-Stalinism, has had considerable effect upon the factionalization within *Zengakuren*. In 1950, the theory of peaceful revolution was criticized by the Russian Party as contrary to Marxism-Leninism. The Communist Party split into two main factions, with the victory for the militant revolutionaries. After the death of Stalin in 1953, the Russian Party gradually became more moderate, while the Chinese Party began to insist upon armed revolution. At the general meeting of the Japanese Party in 1955, the principle of "beloved Communism" was adopted. These changes in world Communism had great impact on the direction of the student movement. In *Zengakuren*, the armed revolutionists defeated the peaceful ones, so that the conflict between the Japanese Communist Party and *Zengakuren* became clear cut. The leaders of *Zengakuren* were dismissed from the Party as Trotskyists.

This consideration of the Japanese student movement indicates that student movements are likely to arise during periods of rapid social and political change. In Japan, students were particularly active during the Meiji period, in the Taisho democracy, and after Japan's defeat in World War II. All these were periods of considerable social stress and change in Japan. Progressive intellectuals, workers, and students have cooperated with one another to resist the ruling elite. Students have been especially conscious of their own power either as prospective leaders or as a mass movement. They consider themselves an *avant-garde* social-reform movement. As their ideal or objective becomes broader and harder to attain, their movements are liable to become more radical. This can be seen typically in the history of the *Shinjin Kai* and the *Zengakuren*. The type of movement that attracts the greater number of students must be concerned directly with campus matters, such as fees, military training, or academic freedom.

Thus, there seems to be a cycle in Japanese and other student movements. Campus-based issues, particularly those involving threats to academic or political freedom, frequently stimulate widespread participation in student movements. The leaders of such groups are inevitably led to see wider, more radical national objectives. As they build a national movement, they lose contact with their local bases of support. Inevitably, therefore, the national movement declines and fractionates, and a period of relative weakness and passivity eventuates. This may in turn be followed by a new cycle involving new generations of students.

After a relatively long period of weakened intermural movement, the Japanese people have been struck by the revival of militant and violent activism since the middle of 1967. These outbursts are concerned mainly with the governmental policy toward the Vietnam war. Premier Sato left Haneda in October, 1967, in order to talk with President Johnson about the war. The Japanese people, especially the intellectuals and the progressives, were concerned that the Sato government was uncritically involved in the dangerous policy of the United States. In fact, Sato claimed at the White House that Japan agreed with the American policy in Vietnam in every aspect. As the bombing in North Vietnam escalated, as the struggles became more hopeless, and as the international public opinion became more unfavorable toward the United States, Sato's attitude toward world politics gave the Japanese people a feeling of uneasiness. This was expressed by journalists and politicians, but Sato seemed to pay it no attention. The militant students tried, in this context, to stop Sato's departure for America in October, 1967; to stop a U.S. atomic carrier, the *Enterprise*, from putting in at Sasebo in January, 1968; to hinder in February the development of the New Tokyo International Airport at Sanrizuka (which they said would serve as an American Air Force base); and to stop the opening of the American Army hospital at Ohji in March. More than a thousand students belonging to the so-called *Sanpakei Zengakuren* (*Zengakuren* of three factions) were involved. Armed with cudgel and helmet, they engaged in warlike actions against the police, and many were wounded and arrested. The public opinion toward their guerrilla tactics was not necessarily favorable, but the students are convinced that they are the only patriots who can keep the nation from the "corrupt imperialism" and that radical militancy is the only way to correct the dangerous direction of the government. The more force-ful the suppression, the stronger their conviction and their belief in violence. The public, although criticizing the violence, shared the students' resentment, dissatisfaction, uneasiness toward governmen-tal policy. Thus, the student movements are sometimes supported and justified in terms of their inner motives. In this manner, the intermural movements have been escalating and perhaps will con-tinue to do until 1970, when the U.S.–Japan Security Pact is to be revised.

The history of Japanese student movements suggests that a typology can be proposed to show the relation between the broader social and political context and student political activism. Let us assume that student political movement is determined by two main factors — namely, distance between government and people, on the one hand, and distance between university and people, on the other. Four types of status of university or student in the nation concerned can be deduced.

		Distance Between Government and People	
		Short	*Long*
Distance Between University and People	*Short*	I	II
	Long	III	IV

Distance between government and people is determined mainly by the degree of democratization of the polity and the degree of national consensus or integration of the people. The former refers to the development of parliamentarianism, the consideration of public opinion in decision-making of the government, the existence of legal and effective channels for expression of the wishes of the people, and so forth. The latter means that national objectives and interests are recognized by the overwhelming majority of the people, that there exist no fundamental opposition and polarization in the nation, and that the government — whether democratic or not — represents the integrated people. Take, for example, a colonized nation acting in union around the provisional government with independence as the supreme aim, and a wartime nation unifying around the government with victory as the sole goal. In both cases, there exists an identification of the people and the government, and the distance between them can be said to be short, even though the government is totalitarian or despotic. Conversely, even when parliamentary procedures are fully developed, at times the interests of two sectors are too far apart to make compromise likely, and the distance between the government which represents one sector and the remaining sector is great. In such cases, antigovernmental movements are likely.

The second dimension — namely the distance between university and people — has two main aspects. One is the gap or lag between the university culture and the national culture. For example, in a colonized country, where the master nation in Europe established a university to propagate and indoctrinate the Western ideology and technology to the natives, the distance is so great between the Western culture taught at the university and the tribe culture that students are keenly conscious of the backwardness of their own country and the necessity of its modernization as well as independence. They feel inferior to but also resentful toward the Western culture. Such attitudes can lead to a political movement for independence and a revolt against the *status quo*.

The other aspect of distance between the university and the people refers to the opportunity for access to university. When the door for higher education is equally open to the people of any social origin, or university enrollment expands greatly, the distance between the university and the people is necessarily shortened. In such cases, the gap in culture and value between the university and the larger society is generally small, and students are influenced by public opinion. Although apathy is often characteristic of a mass society, students sometimes initiate federated movements like trade unionism owing to an awareness of their power as a result of their increased numbers, to the growing sense of alienation in the bureaucratized university, and to economic interests of greater numbers of students from humble origins. When the distance between the university and the people is great, when the university is *for* and *of* the elite, students are generally conservative. Conservatives cannot be militant unless gravely threatened by the opponents, and they tend to be individualistic. In the aristocratic academy, the radical political movements are hardly developed, and social or traditional student organizations are likely, although a few sensitive lower-class students and a few humanitarian upper-class students may be admitted and devote themselves to political movements. In Japan, the distance between the university and the people is short, but the distance between the government and the people is long.[14]

REFERENCES

1. Mombusho (Ministry of Education), *Waga Kuni no Koto Kyoiku* (Tokyo, 1964), p. 141.

2. According to a national survey of annual income of the families of college students made by the Ministry of Education in 1963, the distribution of students among national, municipal, and private universities in terms of their economic level can be seen.

	less than 300,000 yen	*300,000– 900,000 yen*	*more than 900,000 yen*	*average income*	*total number of students*
national	13.0%	60.8%	26.2%	763,843 yen	192,290
municipal	6.5	58.3	35.2	912,486	29,980
private	5.2	44.1	55.9	1,329,485	434,210
total	7.5	49.7	42.8	1,000,480	656,480

Adapted from T. Kawaguchi, *Shin Elite Shiritsu Daigakusei* (Private University Students, The New Elite; Tokyo, 1966), p. 125.

It is one of the problems of Japanese higher education that students in so-called *Bunka-Kei* (humanities and social sciences) are more numerous than those in *Rika-Kei* (physical sciences and medicine), who are needed more in the age of industry and technology. The opposition between these two categories of science is discussed in C. P. Snow, *The Two Cultures: A Second Look* (Cambridge, 1964). The proportion of students in the two *Keis* is different in different kinds of colleges in Japan, as shown in the following table for 1958.

	Bunka-Kei	*Rika-Kei*	*Others*	*Total*
national	90,405	86,808	19,316	196,529
municipal	16,063	12,570	3,995	32,628
private	370,026	133,379	30,187	533,592
total	476,494	232,757	53,498	762,749

Adapted from Mombusho, *Higher Education in Japan*, pp. 34–35.

3. See "Ununderstandable Motives of Student Movements," *Asahi Journal* (July 19, 1964), pp. 12–17; also M. Nemoto, "Logic of Waseda Barricade," *Keizai Orai*, Vol. 18, pp. 172–79.

4. In my article, "*Zengakuren:* A Japanese Case Study of a Student Political Movement," *Sociology of Education*, Vol. 37, pp. 229–53, and also "Com-

parison Between Pre- and Post-war Student Movements in Japan," *Sociology of Education*, Vol. 37, pp. 59–70, I classified the types of student movement into three groups: in-campus, co-campus, and extra-campus, which are the same as those used here.

Type	Origin	Field of Activity
1. intramural	spontaneous and natural	within a particular campus
2. intermural	intentional and deliberate	with students in other universities
3. extramural	intentional and deliberate	with non-students off the campus

Type	Degree of Organization	Size	Relative Number of Participants in the Student Body
1.	least-organized	small	great
2.	most-organized	large	smaller
3.	less-organized	large	smallest

Type	Duration	Concern	Object of Ultimate Attack	Radicalness
1. short		immediate and academic	university authorities	moderate
2. longest		academic and political	government	most radical
3. longer		political and social	political regime	radical

Type	Leader	Distance Between Leaders and Followers	Chance of Success
1. amateur		small	great
2. professional		greater	smaller
3. professional		greatest	smallest

5. Some 1700 publications relevant to student movements in Japan were classified and listed in my article, "Bibliography of Student Movements in Japan," *Educational Studies of the Faculty of Education, Hiroshima University*, Vol. 11 (1963), pp. 97–143.

6. M. Nagai, *Nihon no Daigaku* (Higher Institutions in Japan; Tokyo, 1965), p. 47.

7. S. Inaoka and S. Itoya, *Nihon no Gakusei Undo* (Student Movements in Japan; Tokyo, 1961), p. 54.

8. Mombusho, *Gakusei Shiso Undo no Enkaku* (History of Student Ideological Movements, 1931), p. 35.

9. Adapted from S. Takakuwa, *Nihon Gakusei Undo Shi* (History of Student Movements in Japan; Tokyo, 1955), p. 156. A lot of surveys of the participant students by the Ministry of Education and other offices during the second stage are available. In general, the students involved in the move-

ments in the prewar period came from the middle class and had better achievement. See for example, T. Okada, *Shiso Sakei no Genin oyobi sono Keiro* (Causes and Processes of Getting the Leftist Ideology; Tokyo, 1935).

10. According to a survey done by the Ministry of Education in 1948 among 6801 samples of college students, 63.8 per cent said they found great difficulties in continuing their schooling mainly owing to economic reasons. T. Arai, *Kiki no Gakusei Undo* (Student Movements in Crises; Tokyo, 1952), p. 39.

11. Gakusei Mondai Kenkyusho (Institute for Student Problems), *Sengo Nihon Gakusei Undo Shi* (Postwar History of Student Movements in Japan; Tokyo, 1960), p. 15.

12. Professor Tsuyoshi Ishida of the Hiroshima Institute of Technology conducted research into the college students' attitude toward student movements in 1966. Some of the findings are cited below (unpublished data).

	Strongly agree	Slightly agree	Don't know	Slightly disagree	Strongly disagree	No answer
In general, student movements are run only by a few activists.	20.9%	31.1	29.1	10.5	4.2	4.2
Students should not have demonstration parades for political matters.	14.8%	27.4	24.9	21.1	8.5	3.3
Students should not strike for political matters. (Total — 1769)	18.5%	31.8	24.4	15.5	6.2	3.6

13. See Shimbori, "Zengakuren."

14. The author developes the above typology in "Why Are Student Movements Intensified?" *Chuo-Koron*, Vol. 83, No. 5 (in Japanese; May, 1968), pp. 242–255.

JOHN ISRAEL

Reflections on the Modern Chinese Student Movement

THE STUDENTS of the Sung dynasty (960–1279) would scarcely recognize their modern descendants. The former were seasoned scholars whose erudition secured their place in society. Through mastery of the prescribed classics, they aspired to the highest rungs of officialdom. Even degree-holders who failed to gain governmental positions became members of the "gentry" elite, entitled to special privileges and charged with numerous social responsibilities. Intellectuals were also expected to criticize officials — even emperors — who failed to live up to the standards of the Confucian ethos. For two thousand years, the scholar-official elite served the Chinese state well.

By the time of the Opium War (1839–42), however, the traditional scholar had become an anachronism. The classics failed to prepare China for the multifaceted challenge of the modern West. Beginning in the 1860's, the Manchu (Ch'ing) dynasty sought reinvigoration through a series of reforms, but none were equal to the need. By the end of the nineteenth century, the combination of external pressure and internal decay had proved too much for the rulers of the sprawling empire. In 1911 the dynasty collapsed, and a republic was established. Republican aspirations were quickly crushed, however, under the despotism of Yüan Shih-k'ai. From 1916 to 1949, national reunification eluded warlord rulers, the Kuomintang (KMT) government, and the Japanese. Throughout these years, reformers in various parts of the Chinese subcontinent followed in the footsteps of their Ch'ing forebears. In retrospect, even their boldest efforts were but preludes to the measures of Mao Tse-tung.

Youth and Revolution: 1895–1949

The Chinese student movement was both conditioned by and a condition of this historical transformation. Bridging traditional and modern movements was the Memorial of the Examination Candidates at the close of the First Sino-Japanese War (1894–95). More than twelve hundred scholars, who assembled in Peking for the triennial examinations, demanded a protracted war against Japan. In so doing, they played the historic role of heirs to their twelfth-century predecessors and forerunners of their twentieth-century successors. A truly modern student movement could, however, develop only with modern educational institutions. The first Western-style missionary college (St. John's) was founded in Shanghai in 1879, and the first modern public university (later to be called National Peking University, or "Peita") was officially established in Peking in 1898. But a certain ambivalence clouded educational reform: How could modern colleges prepare candidates for the traditional examinations? The contradiction was resolved in 1905, when the desperate dynasty abolished the thirteen-hundred-year-old examination system.

Thereafter no careerist incentive remained for memorizing the classics, nor was there assurance that alternative courses of study would bring success. The modern student thus felt an unprecedented degree of insecurity. His personal dilemmas were compounded by a pervasive sense of national shame stemming from China's backwardness and helplessness vis-à-vis the imperialist powers. Many resolved these problems by going abroad for study, hoping to return with the prestige of a foreign degree and a technological or philosophical understanding of the modern world. The Manchu dynasty, in its declining years, encouraged students to follow this path, assuming they would come home both skillful and grateful. By September, 1906, fifteen thousand Chinese were studying in Japan. From the government's point of view, the reform was a disaster; uprooted youths, free of Chinese controls and exposed to inflammatory ideas, provided an educated following for such radical reformers as Liang Ch'i-ch'ao and rebels like Sun Yat-sen. Students from all over China came together in Tokyo and returned to foment revolution. Recipients of government scholarships helped bring down the Manchus in 1911.

Deriving its energy from the unstable combination of China's historic grandeur and modern humiliation, the student movement developed an explosive potential. Its targets were oppression from abroad as well as inept government at home. It seemed increasingly obvious to young patriots that both would have to be eradicated if China were to become a strong modern state. The new education reinforced these sentiments. Reformers prescribed a stridently nationalistic course of study, conveyed to the younger generation through chauvinistic textbooks taught by patriotic teachers. Hence, the anti-imperialist theme of 1895 resounded with growing intensity in the twentieth century. In 1905 students joined merchants in an anti-U.S. boycott protesting discriminatory American immigration policies. When Japan presented Yüan Shih-k'ai with the infamous 21 Demands in 1915, Chinese students in Japan returned home by the thousands to join demonstrations against this threat to their nation's sovereignty.

The 1915 movement was a prologue to the Peking demonstration of May 4, 1919, which marked the emergence of students as a major force in national politics. The impetus for this historic demonstration was another manifestation of foreign imperialism, but its full significance can be understood only in the context of China's accelerating social and intellectual revolution. In the cities of China's eastern seaboard, where foreign-style institutions flourished under the protection of the unequal treaties, new social classes were emerging: bilingual merchants, financiers, and industrialists; an urban proletariat; a foreign-educated intelligentsia; and modern students. In the homes of the latter, a "family revolution" ensued as the experience, teachings, and institutions of the older generation became increasingly irrelevant to the needs and aspirations of the young. Revolutionary ideas were nationally disseminated through a multitude of popular magazines, newspapers, and political societies. The effects of these changes were felt both in cosmopolitan Shanghai, hub of economic modernization and refuge for China's political and intellectual rebels, and in Peking, which remained the nation's cultural capital.[1]

On December 26, 1916, National Peking University acquired a new chancellor, Ts'ai Yüan-p'ei. This remarkable man, who has been called "the moral leader of the new intelligentsia and one of the greatest educators and liberals in modern China,"[2] promoted the startling idea that a university should be a forum for the free development of diverse views. To the horror of traditionalists, he brought to the Peita faculty such men as Hu Shih, who advocated replacing the time-honored literary language with the vernacular, and Li Ta-chao, who shortly later eulogized the Bolshevik Revolution and helped found the Chinese Communist Party (CCP). Ts'ai's Dean of the School of Letters was Ch'en Tu-hsiu, later the CCP's first secretary-general, but even in 1917 a cultural radical who supported the slogan "Down with Confucius and sons!" and recommended science and democracy as panaceas for China's ills.

The iconoclastic doctrines of these teachers found a receptive audience. Peita's students had ample reason to feel rebellious: Their personal futures were uncertain; the republican revolution had ended in chaos; the country was at the mercy of corrupt militarists and foreign aggressors; and their own parents persisted in preaching obsolete notions of virtue and filial piety. The halls of Peita resounded with a cacophony of names and isms: Dostoevski and Kropotkin, Russell and Dewey, Shaw and Ibsen, Wilson and Lenin; democracy, equality, science, socialism, individualism, self-determination, nationalism, internationalism, and Bolshevism.

China's young rebels contrasted China's dreary present with a hopeful future. As war ended in 1918, they heard Woodrow Wilson promise equality to nations and dignity for mankind. They felt certain that the Versailles Conference would recognize the claims of their country, which had sent two hundred thousand coolies to aid the allies on the Western front. Principles of justice demanded that China regain her sovereign rights to the province of Shantung (birthplace of Confucius), seized by Japan in 1915. But youthful hopes proved illusory. By the end of January, 1919, reports reached Peking that Great Britain, France, and Italy had signed secret treaties agreeing to support Japan's claims to Shantung. On the heels of these tidings came even more foreboding news: The Japanese had used the $74 Nishihara "loans" to bribe China's warlord government into acquiescence. Outraged by these events, representatives of various student groups gathered at Peita and planned an orderly protest demonstration for May 4. The demonstration began peacefully, but ended in violence when a group stormed the home of a pro-Japanese official, beat alleged traitors discovered within, ransacked the house and set it afire. News of May 4 reached China's new social classes via her modern communications. Students demonstrated in Tientsin, Shanghai, Nanking, Wuhan, and other cities. Workers staged sympathy strikes. Merchants joined an anti-Japanese boycott. Professors demanded the release of arrested agitators. Local student groups proliferated, and on June 16, 1919, delegates gathered in Shanghai and formed the National Student Association.

The organization of a national body was a formidable accomplishment, for the unifying influence of a common written language and shared nationalistic sentiments were counterbalanced by powerful centrifugal forces: mutually incomprehensible dialects, regional loyalties, and the country's size. Considering these obstacles and in view of China's lack of experience with representative democracy, it is not surprising that the national body came to function in a highly elitist manner. City and provincial congresses were composed of delegates popularly elected at constituent schools, and these groups in turn sent delegates to meetings of the national union. The structure operated, however, in a Leninist fashion, more centralist than democratic. Even at the local level, professional and amateur agitators skilled in propaganda, oratory, and controlling mass meetings were generally able to dominate the majority of less interested and less adept schoolmates. The absence of democracy notwithstanding, the National Student Association had become by the mid-twenties one of the most influential voices of public opinion in China. It was less effective, however, as an organ of control, and even during nationwide movements, the nature and intensity of student political activity continued to vary according to local educational, political, geographical, and cultural conditions.

The May 4 Movement was the turning point in China's cultural upheaval. Just as the revolution of 1911 had constituted a definitive break with efforts at monarchial reform, the New Thought of the late teens marked a radical departure from attempts at halfway modernization in the world of ideas. For the first time, eminent teachers and men of letters advocated wholesale Westernization and total abandonment of China's Confucian heritage. The reaction of educated youth was highly favorable; henceforth, the more novel and shocking an idea, the more likely it was to win a receptive audience. The demonstration of May 4 also ushered in a decade of radical anti-imperialism. Vehement protests against the unequal treaties alarmed China's foreign community, and an anti-Christian movement jolted missionary schools. Disenchanted with the fruitless promises of Wilsonian liberalism and wooed by Soviet envoys, alienated intellectuals and students formed the Chinese Communist Party. Among them was Mao Tse-tung, a twenty-seven-year-old former Peita library assistant who had received his political baptism as a high-school student leader.

Sun Yat-sen, too, was carried along by the radical post-May 4 tide. Frustrated by twenty years of political failure, he welcomed the counsel of Comintern agents; he agreed to accept Russian aid, revamp the KMT along Leninist lines, form a united front with the Chinese Communists, and establish the apparatus for mass mobilization, including a Youth Bureau. During the mid-twenties, students under both KMT and CCP leadership organized workers and peasants for political action. In Canton, the KMT's newly-founded Whampoa Military Academy set out to mold an indoctrinated military elite under Commandant Chiang Kai-shek. Students from all over China flocked to this mecca on the Pearl River.

As Chiang consolidated his forces, a series of atrocities by warlords and foreigners stimulated student nationalism and boosted the fortunes of the KMT-CCP alliance. An incident on May 30, 1925, was the most famous of these. Like the May 4 demonstration, the immediate cause was an imperialist outrage: A Japanese foreman in a Japanese-owned Shanghai factory had shot and killed a Chinese worker. Protesting students in the foreign-controlled International Settlement had been jailed. When a crowd gathered in front of a police station to demand their release, a British officer impulsively ordered his men to fire. The slaughter of unarmed students by foreign police on Chinese soil evoked a nationwide storm of protest. Twenty-four days later, indignation reached a new peak when British and French machine-gunners mowed down Whampoa cadets and other youthful paraders in Canton. On March 16, 1926, more anti-imperialist student demonstrators were massacred by troops of the Peking warlord, Chang Tso-lin. When Chiang Kai-shek launched the Northern Expedition on July 9, 1926, China's educated elite responded with enthusiasm to the slogan, "Down with the Warlords and the Imperialists!"

Beneath the façade of unity, both KMT and CCP maneuvered for the inevitable showdown. Chiang struck first. On April 12, 1927, he began the Party Purification Movement. This anti-Communist campaign began in Shanghai and spread throughout the country. It resulted in the summary execution of many student radicals. The purge, rupturing as it did the bond between the KMT and a significant element of the younger generation, neutralized much of the enthusiasm that had been created by the success of the Northern Expedition and the establishment of a national government in Nanking. A further blow to student activists was the ruling party's decision to discontinue mass movements. Student unions were to be replaced by apolitical self-governing associations, and youngsters were to stick to their books.

Youth lost fervor for a government that wasted precious resources in fighting warlords and Communist remnants at the expense of social reforms, but they also recognized the Nanking regime as China's only hope. Indeed, they might well have set their sights on bureaucratic, technocratic careers had not Japan invaded Manchuria in September, 1931. The Chinese government's failure to resist prompted young war hawks to flock to Nanking. For three months in the fall of 1931, thousands of student zealots descended upon the capital, often lying on railway tracks to halt traffic until free transportation was provided. Foreign Minister Wang Cheng-t'ing (a former YMCA student leader) was nearly beaten to death by a student mob on September 28. But the protest was relatively peaceful until December, when a radical minority from Peiping steered the movement in a revolutionary direction. Violent demonstrators manhandled KMT officials and wrecked the offices of the party newspaper, thereby forcing the government to adopt suppressive measures.

Once leftists had been jailed or driven underground, youthful nationalism was dampened by increasing political, social, and economic stability and by a hiatus in Japanese aggression. Official exhortations to "save the nation by study" apparently were making an impression. New moves by the invader, however, brought students once more to the streets in December, 1935. The Japanese were demanding an "autonomous region" in North China, and Peiping students were alarmed by Chiang's ambivalent response: "We shall not forsake peace until there is no hope for peace; we shall not talk lightly of sacrifice until the last extremity." They feared they would become subjects of a North China Manchukuo.

Organized protest began at American-influenced Yenching and Tsinghua Universities rather than at National Peking University, the traditional center of student politics. Yenching was a liberal missionary institution, and Tsinghua had originally been established with American Boxer indemnity funds as a preparatory school for Chinese students planning to study in the United States. Yenching was partly protected by extraterritoriality, and both schools were located five miles outside the city walls, which gave them some freedom from Peiping police controls. Large demonstrations on December 9 and 16 provoked a nationwide response among students and intellectuals reminiscent of May 4 and spawned a National Salvation Movement, which pushed Chiang toward a united front with the Communists and resistance to Japan. In May, 1936, the pro-Communist National Student Association was founded. The contrast between this and the troublesome but still loyal NSA dissolved seven years earlier by the Ministry of Training symbolizes the leftward trend among student activists during a decade of KMT rule.

The majority of the student generation of the 1930's committed themselves to no political party. They offered their allegiance to whoever would lead the country against Japan. Because they realized that only Nanking had the power to fill this role, they applauded Mao Tse-tung's call for a national united front, but reserved their most enthusiastic support for Chiang Kai-shek when he indicated willingness to lead the nation into war. Though thousands of idealistic youth joined the Communists in the hills of Shensi between 1936 and 1939, tens of thousands retreated to the Nationalists' refuge in the southwest.

To the casual observer, the eight-year period of war witnessed an unprecedented unity of Chinese youth under the leadership of Chiang. Between the summer of 1938 and December, 1945, there was practically no discernible student movement — not even a solitary protest against their wretched diet and rat-infested dormitories. Indeed, during the early war years, as the government fought, students rallied to China's defense and risked their lives to aid her hard-pressed armies. But by November, 1938, a military stalemate had developed, and after December 8, 1941, it became apparent that the war would be won elsewhere than in China. Morale deteriorated behind the lines as the government diverted men and supplies to blockade the Communists, while inflation and black marketeering sapped China's economic and psychological reserves. In the colleges of Chungking, Chengtu, and Kunming, students pawned books and clothes to supplement meager government subsidies, prepared their lessons by kerosene lamps, suffered from malnutrition, and frequently contracted tuberculosis. Official policy dictated that these youths remain at their desks. Hoarded like the precious national resources they unquestionably were, the educated elite found no adequate outlet for their patriotic idealism. By late 1943, when students were finally encouraged to enlist in the army, cynicism had already begun to erode the foundations of academia.

The contrast with the Communist zones was striking. There students were trained and indoctrinated in special schools and sent to the countryside to mobilize the population for guerrilla warfare. The Communists emerged from the war with sufficient numbers of trained, dedicated young cadres to govern an area of a hundred million people. The nationalists had increased the number of students in institutions of higher learning from 41,609 in 1936, to 78,909 in 1945, and 155,036 in 1947. Aside from a loyal following in the Three People's Principles Youth Corps, however, these students were apathetic, if not hostile, toward the ruling party.

In the cities of East China that had been liberated from Japanese rule, the war's end reunited two groups — refugees returning from exile in the exterior and residents who had collaborated, actively or passively, with the Japanese and their Chinese puppets. For both of these groups, the psychological effect of eight years of war had been disruptive.[3] The refugees nursed sentiments of self-pity and resentment. They viewed themselves as unsung heroes who had endured nearly a decade of unrequited suffering for the nation. Further sacrifice seemed unjust, especially since those who had remained behind seemed to have prospered by cooperating with the invader. Many of the latter, on the other hand, felt a need to atone for the compromises they had made.

Sensitive youth from these two groups crowded onto postwar campuses and provided the material for a series of student rebellions that reached a crescendo in the antihunger, anti-civil-war movement of May, 1947. In the emporium atmosphere of Shanghai and other cities, wartime restraints had given way to an *enrichissez-vous* atmosphere. An inflationary economy hungry for consumer goods favored importers, speculators, and influential officials. But in the schools, shortages and inflation meant further sacrifices for teachers and students. To returning refugees, the ramshackle housing, substandard diets, shortages of books and laboratory equipment, and restraints on freedom that had been endured as necessary during the struggle against Japan now seemed not merely unnecessary, but intolerable. Students who had spent the war years in occupied China were inclined to sympathize with the Communists on practical and psychological grounds. Many felt that they had no future under the Kuomintang, which discriminated in favor of youngsters who had shared the bitterness of wartime "exile." The CCP, in contrast, presented itself as a forward-looking organization dedicated to universal ideals of youth. By enlisting in this noble cause, they might expiate feelings of guilt over the past and open up new possibilities for the future. In a contest that seemed to pit young idealists opposed to war and oppression against the old cynics responsible for these plagues, such students unhesitatingly cast their lots with the former.

Caught in a downward spiral typical of governments in the final stage of revolutionary overthrow, Chiang's regime vascillated between reform and force. Eleventh-hour moves to establish institutions of representative government failed to placate American and domestic critics and did nothing to halt political polarization, stem the devastating inflation, or prevent civil war. In this milieu, the Communists channeled youthful frustrations into demonstrations against civil war, malnutrition, American military misconduct, and Chinese police brutality. The government's response was "counterproductive"; bully boys beat demonstrators, and gunmen assassinated opponents, while official propagandists asserted that the highest priority of postwar reconstruction was the extermination of Communist rebels. Increasingly, the government became convinced that force was the answer in the cities as well as the rural areas. Police arrested thousands of students and intellectuals suspected of Communist sympathies and muzzled the left-wing press. Such action lent credence to Communist charges of Fascism and won additional recruits for the widening ranks of Mao's supporters. As the People's Liberation Army swept southward, student reaction ranged from stoic acceptance to jubilation.

This historical survey must conclude on a cautionary note. While Chinese students, individually and collectively, were important in their country's modern transformation and an essential ingredient in the victory of Chinese Communism, the student movement was not a sufficient cause for this victory. Mao's contribution to Communist practice was not his utilization of students (a universal phenomenon among Communist Parties), but his use of peasants in a political-military context. Students contributed heavily to the CCP's leadership and were a source of harassment to the KMT, but mass movements of urban intellectuals remained ancillary to the struggle in the villages and on the battlefield.

Students in Chinese Society

To understand the Chinese student movement, one must take a closer look at its participants. Who were the Chinese students? From what social strata did they come? Which of them played an active role in the events we have described? Unfortunately statistics are limited, and it is impossible to conduct thorough field studies. The answers of these questions must, therefore, be more in the nature of gross generalizations than of scientific findings.

China's students have always been members of an elite. The traditional scholar-gentry was, however, not primarily an economic class. The key to advancement was neither wealth nor social position, but education. Commoners often achieved gentry status, and gentry families lost their social standing over the course of several generations. Everything depended upon success in examinations that were open to poor and rich alike. Of course, the wealthy enjoyed obvious advantages: They could afford to give their sons years of leisure for education and to send them to school or to hire tutors. They could rear them in a world of scholars, a universe remote from the life of the poor peasant. Furthermore, the wealthy landowner or merchant might buy his son a degree, a procedure that supplemented the regular examination system. Hence, in premodern China, social mobility existed both in theory and in practice, though never to the extent suggested by the Chinese Horatio Alger tradition.

During the twentieth century, when college and even high-school attendance has involved living away from home, educational expenses have increased. Moreover, the prestige of a foreign degree made costly study abroad desirable for those aspiring to high government office. Hence, China's students were a highly urbanized, upper-middle- and upper-class group during the first half of the twentieth century. Available data do not answer the question: "Which elements of this elite were political activists?" As I have observed elsewhere, "disproportionate numbers of student radicals came from the lowest groups that could afford a post-grammar-school education — landlords and 'wealthy' peasants."[4] But how many of these radical thinkers expressed themselves in terms of political action is unclear. Communist recruitment in the schools was not necessarily from the most impoverished groups, nor were needy students averse to advancement via the KMT.

Regardless of which student sector may have been most active in politics, *all* students were members of a privileged elite. The cream of this elite were those who studied abroad, and it is noteworthy that these youths played a major role in the Chinese student movement from approximately 1905 to 1925. Personal confrontation with the modern world had a jarring effect on these students, as it so often does on young people from underdeveloped areas. Radical ideas and organizations in Japan, France, and (after 1917) the Soviet Union helped to turn these students toward revolutionary movements.[5]

By the mid-twenties, the importance of overseas student leadership had declined due to the increasing self-sufficiency and radicalization of the indigenous student movement, and the emergence of a KMT government supported by and largely staffed by returned students. Moreover, more and more students were going abroad for personal rather than patriotic reasons.[6] The gap between returned and native students widened during the Japanese invasion of the 1930's, when many Anglo-American-educated academicians (as well as those trained in Japan) supported the government, sought help from the League of Nations, opposed the radical nationalism of the younger generation, and rejected student arguments that the national emergency made it imperative to interrupt normal education. In the middle- and late-forties, when war had fused the academic community, foreign-trained professors became increasingly impoverished, disillusioned, and inclined to sympathize with student protests. A striking example of this metamorphosis was the American-educated poet, Wen I-to, whose criticism of the government and support of student radicalism led to his assassination in July, 1946.[7]

Both the economic position and the social outlook of China's students changed during the war. Previously, the average student was insulated from the stark reality of daily life among the four hundred million Chinese, even though groups of activists spread propaganda in factories and villages. Arduous journeys from occupied areas to Free China, however, made a lasting impression on these young people. Others gained still more unvarnished views of society after joining the regular army, guerrilla groups, or auxiliary military service organizations. After 1937, even the sons and daughters of the wealthy, cut off from their families, often found themselves living on the margin of starvation. To provide for these youths, the government introduced a system of scholarships, which soon supported tens of thousands of students. But wartime and postwar inflation virtually wiped out the Chinese middle class and lowered to a proletarian level the standard of living for scholarship holders, as well as teachers and other salaried officials. Though school food strikes had been common during the twenties and thirties, the "antihunger, anti-civil-war" movement of 1947 was the first nationwide student movement directed against substandard diets.

Sources of Youthful Rebellion

The postwar student movement marked a victory for Communist propagandists who, after three decades of experience, had reached a high level of sophistication in wielding weapons of mass persuasion.

But to assert that Chinese youth were duped by astute propagandists explains nothing. The question is *why* Communist slogans had such a wide appeal, *why* Leninism made so much sense to an educated elite, *why* Chiang Kai-shek was so easily cast in the villain's role, and *why* students helped to overthrow a lesser tyranny only to accept a greater one.

In the eyes of many observers, Chinese college students seem to have been driven to Communism by their relentless hostility to legitimate authority. The diversity of targets of school strikes and nationwide movements — England, Japan, and the United States, Manchus, warlords, and KMT, capitalists and landlords, principals and teachers, family and state — certainly suggests that there was an underlying impatience with established power. This, too, requires an explanation. Richard Walker has written that China's students and intellectuals were victims of "the mystique of 'the Revolution'" which "assumed an almost mystical and sacred quality in the language of the new literati."[8] As Walker observed, Kuomintang as well as Communist propagandists encouraged this semantic confusion. The students' profound commitment to the mystique was, however, based upon much more than confused semantics, as Robert A. Scalapino indicated in his trenchant analysis of Chinese students in Japan during the first decade of this century:

Many of the students, no doubt, became revolutionaries after a process of soul-searching and reflection that involved a consideration of alternatives, and used their intellectual facilities in reaching their decision. It cannot be denied, however, that the espousal of revolution was the most logical method of achieving an emotional release, a method with which reformism could not easily compete. To students discouraged and impatient, the commitment to revolution represented a concrete, dramatic personal act by which they could dedicate themselves to the cause wholeheartedly, unselfishly, and with finality. It did not involve them in any of the intricate compromises and potential corruption that reform efforts would inevitably evoke. It was a heroic, simplistic act so in tune with the psychological needs of the time.[9]

This statement is remarkably applicable to students of subsequent periods — especially 1923–27 and 1946–49. There was evidently nothing mysterious about the popularity of the revolutionary mystique, nor was the mystique ubiquitous. During the most dramatic periods of the movement, student activists chose the most radical of mentors, but this by no means implies that all students at all times were willing to sacrifice short-range goals of national unity, social order, and educational development to take the path of revolution.[10]

Reflections on the Modern Chinese Student Movement

The history of the modern Chinese student movement also demonstrates that rebellion against established authority did not necessarily imply rejection of all discipline. Anarchism did enjoy a vogue among Chinese students during the first two decades of the twentieth century, but its influence waned under the competition of Communism and nationalism in the early twenties. A similar fate befell romantic and liberal individualism. Students' submission to Leninist leadership in the CCP and KMT suggest that they welcomed discipline in the name of nationalistic and revolutionary causes.[11] Furthermore, every generation of students has upheld forces of unity and order when these appeared to be viable possibilities. Even in 1949 few students accepted the Communist revolution without reservations. Given a unified nation, unthreatened by enemies, many of them would have preferred the ideas of Hu Shih to those of either Chiang or Mao. Indeed, Hu's advocacy of literary reform, intellectual tolerance, political experimentalism, and the application of the scientific method to academic and social problems won a sympathetic hearing from students of the May 4 era and continued thereafter to find a sizable audience among nonactivists. Under conditions of imperialistic aggression and civil war, however, Hu's cosmopolitanism was unable to compete with strident nationalism. The rapid disintegration of the old social order called for something stronger than his prescription of "bit-by-bit, drop-by-drop" change.

The difficulties of the liberals were compounded by the social and mental chasm that separated Anglo-American-trained intellectuals from the realities of rural China. These men, who filled the majority of college positions, failed to win the support of socially-conscious students. Their analyses seemed shallow, their solutions inadequate, their frames of reference irrelevant. More enduring was the alliance between student radicals and liberal and leftist writers whose years abroad had been spent in Japan, rather than England or the United States. From the 1920's on, the writings of Lu Hsün, Kuo Mo-jo, and others profoundly influenced the younger generation, but these men were victims of political polarization and became identified with the Communist camp.

China failed to develop a social democratic tradition, in part because her introduction to foreign ideologies was telescoped — the ideas of Marx and Lenin following close on the heels of liberal constitutionalism. Moreover, her cliques of progressive, democratic intellectuals were poorly organized and unarmed. The National Salvation Association, formed in 1936 as an offshoot of the December 9

Movement, provided some organizational cohesiveness for student patriots and their nonpartisan allies, and the Democratic League had its student following in the forties. Flanked by the armed, highly organized KMT on the right and CCP on the left, however, the third forces were doomed. By 1949, the only choices left to the splinter parties and their student followers were to seek exile in Hong Kong or abroad, or to serve as window dressing on the mainland or in Taiwan. For most students, the cause of China seemed best served by remaining on the mainland and working with the new rulers.

Students and the Ruling Parties: KMT and CCP

Perennial student dissatisfaction with the *status quo* has created problems for both KMT and CCP rulers. By evaluating their divergent responses under varying conditions, one may consider whether the modernization process in China has made student rebellion inevitable.

The Kuomintang suffered from internal weaknesses as it entered the political-ideological arena. In retrospect, it seems clear that this ruling Party, badly divided as it was, had slim hopes of satisfying China's college students. Filled with the high expectations common among youth in modernizing societies, these radicals were inevitably disappointed when mortal men failed to solve unsolvable problems. In industrialized countries, such as the United States and postwar Japan, young idealists may be expected to mature into integrated units of the "establishment." Yet this is impossible unless the established order offers well-defined rewards — social, economic, and psychological. Considering the series of convulsions that have shaken Chinese society since the mid-nineteenth century, it is not surprising that many of the young intelligentsia eventually were drawn into the Communist camp. Nor is it surprising that the temporary loosening of authoritarian controls in 1957 produced a student rebellion and that the staging of a massive revolutionary movement under official auspices was necessary to forestall another outburst a decade later.

But the CCP, for all its blunders, has controlled the student movement far more skillfully than its rival had. The Kuomintang's short-lived success with the younger generation ended when the Party came to power, and the abolition of extramural student organizations betrayed the KMT's lack of confidence in its own ability to compete with the Communists and other dissidents. Moreover, this negative policy failed to gain support from two key factions — the

Ch'en Brothers' "Organization Clique" or "CC Clique" and the Whampoa Clique in the military. During the early- and mid-thirties, these groups competed, more or less clandestinely, with Communist organizers in the schools. After the outbreak of the Second Sino-Japanese War, the party reversed its negative policy by establishing the Three People's Principles Youth Corps under Whampoa leadership. The Corps' achievements, facilitated by wartime patriotism, were nullified after V-J Day. Under attack from jealous Party regulars, the Corps was amalgamated with the Party in 1947.

In recent years, the Communists have been plagued by competition between civilian and military factions in their Party for control of the youth movement. Since the failure of the Great Leap Forward, militant Maoists have criticized the CCP and its adjunct, the Youth League, for their policies of retrenchment. These ideological purists, led by Lin Piao and his adherents in the People's Liberation Army, circumvented the League and organized the Red Guards in the summer of 1966. The Guards' countrywide crusade was made possible by the army's organizational and logistic support.

The generation gap, which perplexes Communist leaders today, is accentuated by a cult of youth that has provided opportunities and problems for adult politicians ever since the May 4 Movement.[12] Students led both KMT and CCP through their formative years, but both the KMT (which had been in existence for more than two decades before 1927) and the CCP (which had operated for nearly three decades prior to 1949) inevitably lost touch with the younger generation. The KMT, as we have seen, responded negatively to the challenge. During the early fifties, the CCP promoted student political action in a series of mass movements controlled by the Party and the Youth League. But from the mid-fifties to the mid-sixties, functions of mass organizations were appropriated by the Party-League apparatus, League leadership became the preserve of middle-aged men, and its membership grew older. The generational crisis is not likely to be resolved by the Red Guards' attempt to reaffirm the values of the youth cult by glorifying a seventy-three-year-old patriarch.

The Red Guard imbroglio reminds us that the CCP's relationship with the students has not been free of contradictions. Since the twenties, the Party has realized the value of students in organizing workers, peasants, and intellectuals. By defining the class nature of students as wholly or partly *petit-bourgeois*, the Party has been able to use them both as allies in united fronts and as scapegoats for the

Party's failures. Communist ideologists have, however, found reliance upon such a privileged elite embarrassing to the Party of the proletariat. Thus, students have been expected to lose their sense of separate identity and to become one with the masses. Party ideologues repeatedly quote Mao Tse-tung's dictum:

The ultimate line of demarcation between the revolutionary intellectuals, on the one hand, and nonrevolutionary and counter-revolutionary intellectuals, on the other, lies in whether they are willing to, and actually do, become one with the masses of workers and peasants.[13]

Practical as well as ideological problems have compounded the Party's dilemma. By the Yenan period, the CCP was no longer a clique of intellectuals, but a rural-based political-military movement. This made it difficult for CCP to absorb the urban-intellectual youths who streamed in from Peiping, Tientsin, and other cities. From the viewpoint of the veterans of the Kiangsi Soviet and the Long March, these recruits were bookish and undisciplined. Thought reform was the Maoist cure for such ailments. The wartime movement labeled *cheng-feng* ("to correct unorthodox tendencies") was the first in a continuing series of attempts to remold students and intellectuals.[14]

Tensions underlying student-Party relations since the mid-1920's still exist. Students remain largely bourgeois in family origin, hence untrustworthy, though their skills are needed as much as ever. CCP leaders fear that nearly half a century of revolution may be negated by residual habits of traditional careerism and modern professionalism among the young. The very structure of Chinese education contains built-in contradictions. The Communists inherited a university system modeled on the West's, manned by a Western-trained faculty, and designed to produce graduates dedicated to the disinterested pursuit of truth via "scientific" disciplines. With their newly acquired skills, these youths have sought to enter careers that would both further their own interests and modernize their fatherland. The Communists regard such attitudes as unfortunate hangovers from China's feudal and semicolonial eras. The pursuit of individual self-interest is thought to be incompatible with the development of the state, and the disinterested quest for scientific truth is considered secondary to the development of a "correct" Maoist *Weltanschauung*. The attempt to reconcile the contradictory purposes of education is formulated in the slogan, "Both Red and Expert." Changes in emphasis between these two desiderata have produced a series of crises, the most recent of which is the Great Proletarian Cultural Revolution with its offshoot, the Red Guards.

Red Guard membership initially was granted only to politically active students of proletarian origin. Youngsters with these qualifications had been accepted in institutions of middle and higher education during the Great Leap Forward, when it was more important to be Red than expert. It was they who suffered when the pendulum swung back, and academic performance became more important than ideological orthodoxy. Hence, in the spring and summer of 1966 they became enthusiastic recruits in campaigns to expel "bourgeois" chancellors, to revamp the system of entrance examinations, and to close the schools so that students could devote all their time to politics. These youth have but one hope for advancement in the highly competitive educational and economic systems — that political activism will replace academic achievement as the principal criterion of success. If the Communist leadership fails to satisfy their expectations, its quest for a generation of revolutionary successors will be doomed to failure. On the other hand, if it ceases to reward academic and technological achievement, its vision of a modern industrialized China will be shattered, and the country will be forced to fall back on its overcrowded rural hinterland.

Thus the CCP, like the KMT, has been trapped by its own ideology, by its failure to satisfy the expectations of youth who have taken the Party's teachings too literally. The Nationalists lost their student following by not acting sufficiently nationalistic; the Communists are now threatened by rebellious youth who demand that they practice Communism. The challenge posed by the Red Guards is likely to plague the Party long after the current leadership struggle is concluded.

The course of the Chinese student movement follows logically from China's history. The nation entered the twentieth century stumbling in the shadow of her past brilliance. Unlike Russia, where centralized despotism made anarchism attractive, China was weak, divided, and exploited. Hence, the goals of the student movement were state-oriented, those of internal unity, solidarity against foreign foes, national power through modernization and national identity through social revolution. Nationalism was equally important in helping students retain their personal identity as Chinese even while they were discarding their traditional heritage in favor of foreign innovations.

The nationalism of the 1905–1911 movement was both racialistic and modern. Its assumption was that China would grow strong if the alien Manchus were dethroned and traditional governmental forms were replaced with republican institutions. Nationalism is the garb of anti-imperialism and anti-Christianity developed rapidly after the 21 Demands and reached its peak after the May 30 incident. Like anti-Manchu nationalism, it blamed foreigners for China's woes, and this enhanced its appeal. Students supported the goal of the Northern Expedition — national unification via military conquest — but failed to appreciate Chiang's continued obsession with this program during the Japanese invasion of the thirties. Civil war had less nationalistic appeal than anti-imperialistic war. Between 1937 and 1945, KMT and CCP vied for popular support, each arguing that it embodied the principle of national solidarity against the Japanese.

After the war, the KMT contended that its struggle against Communist rebels carried on the task of national unification begun in the fight against the Manchus and continued in the Northern Expedition and the anti-Japanese crusade. But instead of a decadent dynasty, venal warlords, or imperialistic Japanese, the KMT faced a resurgent Communist movement. Mao, who had also established his patriotic credentials during eight years of resistance, offered a "new democratic" China as an alternative to the discredited government of the postwar Kuomintang. Convinced that the KMT was the main obstacle to internal harmony and that continued attempts to extirpate the Communists could lead only to interminable civil war, the students became Chiang's harshest critics during this crucial period.

Even though successive generations of Chinese students may be characterized as nationalistic, this does not imply an absence of change. Political circumstances altered the quality of that nationalism from decade to decade. The most influential force for change was the intrusion of partisan politics into every sphere of student activity: hence, the enormous difference between the nonpartisan May 4 Movement of 1919 and the highly politicized May 30 Movement six years later, to say nothing of events in 1935 and 1947. This intrusion reached its logical conclusion after 1949, when the student movement became a tool of Party control. Partisan politics have similarly engulfed other areas of Chinese life — most notably in literature where the social consciousness of the twenties evolved into the revolutionary polemics of the thirties, the patriotic homilies of the war years, and then state indoctrination after 1949.

Student politics have also varied greatly in intensity. Movements have flourished in modern China when governments appeared weak and inept. Only those able to control the nation's territory, manage its educational system effectively, and carry out energetic programs in domestic and foreign policy have generally succeeded in avoiding massive student protest: hence, the frequency of student disorder during the late Ch'ing and warlord periods. The promise of unity and reform gave the Nanking government relative immunity from 1928 to September, 1931, and from 1932 to December, 1935. The December 9 Movement erupted in the least-controlled university (Yenching) of an insecure area (North China), endangered by vacillation in foreign policy. National resistance to Japan and tight KMT control of Southwest China's campuses dampened student protest during the war, but governmental weaknesses encouraged its reemergence in 1945.

There has been a tension in Chinese student thought between the desire for personal liberty and the quest for a strong state, but by and large liberty has been a secondary issue.[15] When the government has been strong, students have grumbled about suppression of civil liberties, but they have not rebelled. Only weak governments have had to answer for repressive policies. No rulers allowed greater academic freedom than the warlords who were more concerned with fighting battles than with running schools, but none elicited more bitter student opposition. KMT thought control failed because it was conceptually and operationally deficient, not because students valued freedom of thought above all else. CCP means of coercion have been more oppressive and more effective. The Communists mastered techniques of internal social control; the Kuomintang always seemed to approach students from the outside. Internal discipline, whether in a Peiping school or a Yenan thought-reform center, was more acceptable than external control by school administrators or military police. Pro-Kuomintang students were easily detected, labeled "running dogs," and isolated. Pro-CCP students were admired as self-sacrificing idealists.

Aside from its technical proficiency, the CCP was fortunate to arrive on the scene just in time to collect the fruits of revolutionary harvest. A century of national humiliation and a succession of thwarted reforms had imparted an irresistible allure to radical solutions. In the politics and literature of the students, as of the nation at large, unsuccessful fathers bequeathed a profounder radicalism to their sons. The generation of monarchial reform symbolized by K'ang Yu-wei (born 1858) was followed by one of republicanism epitomized by Sun Yat-sen (born 1866) and finally by the Communism of Mao Tse-tung (born 1893). In this context, the neo-Confucianism of Chiang Kai-shek (born 1888), modeled as it was upon the conservative reformer Tseng Kuo-fan (born 1811), seemed strangely out of place.

The intellectual, psychological, and moral vacuum left by the breakdown of the universal Confucian order was too vast to be filled by the relativistic pragmatism of John Dewey and Hu Shih. A new and totalistic world view was necessary — one that would explain China's failures without undermining national pride. Hence, the appeal evoked by a theory that blamed imperialists and reactionaries, but exculpated the Chinese people. Leninism did this. It analyzed a perplexing and oppressive environment in simple terms and plotted a corrective course of action. In its united-front version (incorporated into Mao's New Democracy), Leninist doctrine reserved an important role for the *petit-bourgeois* intellectuals. This was essential to an intellectual elite whose consciousness of its own political pre-eminence had survived the demise of Confucianism.

Mao offered China's students an attractive blend of the modern and the traditional, a combination by no means unique to Chinese Communism. Superficially, Chinese Communism appeared to be anything but modern. Under Mao's hegemony, life in the regions was technologically primitive compared with the urbanized sector under Chiang. In terms of social mobilization, however, Mao's efforts to bring the masses into politics were most modern even though they drew upon an indigenous tradition of peasant rebellions. Mao adopted a radically modern ideology, but he *adapted* it to Chinese conditions by finding the source of absolute virtue in the downtrodden rural masses. In the Communist countryside, students found assurance that they could be both pure and progressive, radical reformers and 100 per cent Chinese. On the other hand Chiang's attempt to foster Confucian values in a foreignized urban environment seemed to combine the least appealing features of past and present.

Similarities between the recent Red Guard phenomenon and student movements of the past can be found only at a high level of historical abstraction. For example, frustrated careerism and betrayed idealism continue to unsettle China's youths. Students still view themselves as incorruptible social critics, and the purity of their protests is, as before, compromised by adult intrigue. One can isolate features of the Red Guards reminiscent of the traditional censorate, the Boxer uprising, and the post-May 4 student movements, to say nothing of Hitler Youth.[16]

The historian, however, is more impressed by the discontinuities. The most striking of these is the change in scale. In December, 1931, the capital city of Nanking was deluged with an unprecedented 16,600 demonstrators. In the late months of 1966, Peking received eleven million. This is indicative of a second fundamental change: The present government is the first in modern Chinese history capable of disciplining and mobilizing students on all levels throughout the country. Even the Red Guards, a product of internal struggle, testify most eloquently to this development. Unlike pre-Communist student movements, they represent an induced rebellion of part of the system against the whole, not a more or less spontaneous attack by an extralegal revolutionary force. Finally, the nationalistic component of the Red Guards is relatively weaker than it was in pre-1949 student movements. To some extent, this is a tribute to the Communists' success in removing the two principal targets of student protest: internal disunity and foreign exploitation. But chaos, for which the Red Guards are partially responsible, has shattered national unity and invited outside interference. Thus, there is no reason to suppose that adulation of the Maoist cult has permanently superseded the tradition of nationalistic student protest.[17]

REFERENCES

1. Joseph Tao Chen draws a vivid comparison between Peking and Shanghai in "The May Fourth Movement in Shanghai" (unpublished Ph.D. dissertation, University of California, Berkeley), pp. 2–3. These two cities, containing the majority of China's college students until 1937, have been the major vortexes of twentieth-century student politics. In contrast with other countries, the political capital has not necessarily played a major role. It is difficult to generalize about the geographical and institutional determinants of Chinese student movements, but nationwide political activity has usually concentrated in the liberal-arts colleges of the larger universities in major cities that contained several centers of learning. National institutions have generally been more active than provincial ones in the public sector, secular institutions more so than Christian ones in the private. Colleges relatively inactive in countrywide movements are not always spared turmoil based upon local issues.

2. Chow Tse-tsung, *The May Fourth Movement* (Cambridge, 1960), p. 47n.

3. For some of the observations in this paragraph and the following one, I am indebted to the insights of Professor Lucian W. Pye, who served in Peking and Tientsin from September, 1945, to April, 1946, as an intelligence and Chinese-language officer in the United States Marines. Letter to the author, September 12, 1967.

4. John Israel, *Student Nationalism in China 1927–37* (Stanford, 1966) based upon Olga Lang, *Chinese Family and Society* (New Haven, 1946), pp. 317–318.

5. England and the United States produced fewer revolutionaries due both to the nature of society and education in those countries and to a natural selectivity of students going abroad: Those of radical proclivities went elsewhere by choice, and those of limited resources by necessity. Japan offered easy accessibility and inexpensive living, the USSR provided political subsidies, and France had a "work-study" program.

6. Y. C. Wang, *Chinese Intellectuals and the West, 1872–1949* (Chapel Hill, 1966), pp. 149–150.

7. See Hsü Kai-yü, "The Life and Poetry of Wen I-to," *Harvard Journal of Asiatic Studies*, Vol. 21 (December, 1958), pp. 175–178.

8. Richard Walker, "Students, Intellectuals, and 'The Chinese Revolution,'" *The Strategy of Deception*, ed. Jeanne J. Kirkpatrick (New York, 1963), p. 100ff.

9. Richard A. Scalapino, "Prelude to Marxism: The Chinese Student Movement in Japan, 1900–1910," *Approaches to Modern Chinese History*, eds. Albert Feuerwerker, Rhoads Murphey, and Mary C. Wright (Berkeley, 1967), p. 199.

10. We may assume that no more than 10 per cent of China's college students were perennial activists and that less than 1 per cent held positions of authority in local, provincial, and national organizations. Though an estimated three thousand marched in Peking on May 4, 1919, and nearly eight thousand on December 16, 1935, the inert majority could be mobilized only in times of crisis. The diversity of student political credos is emphasized in Olga Lang's study of college students in 1937. In interpreting her conclusions, summarized in the table below, one should bear in mind that (1) students are categorized on the basis of their answers to open-ended questions; (2) 85 per cent of China's college students were in non-Christian institutions; and (3), as Miss Lang notes, "whatever their political opinions may be, almost all students are nationalists."

Political Sympathies of College Students in 1937

(*percentages*)

Political Tendencies	382 Students of Christian Colleges	Male 305 Students of Non-Christian Colleges	Female 477 Students
Conservative	14	7	9
Fascist	19	14	11
Democratic	10	7	16
Christian	10	2	16
Radical	12	34	16
Nationalist	21	14	13
Not clear	14	22	19

See Olga Lang, *Chinese Family and Society*, p. 316

11. They shared this trait with students of other countries. See, for example, David Marr, "A Study of Political Attitudes and Activities Among Young Urban Intellectuals in South Viet-nam" (M.A. thesis, University of California, Berkeley), p. 79.

12. The writings of Pa Chin, portraying the breakdown of the traditional family, have been a mirror and a model for several generations of adolescent rebels. See Pa Chin, *The Family* (trans.; Peking, 1958), and Olga Lang, *Pa Chin and His Writings: Chinese Youth Between the Two Revolutions* (Cambridge, 1967).

13. Mao Tse-tung, *Selected Works*, Vol. 3 (New York, 1954), pp. 10–11.

14. For the *cheng-feng* movement, see Boyd Compton, *Mao's China: Party Reform Documents, 1942–44* (Seattle, 1952). For a study of "remolding" from a psychoanalytic point of view, see Robert J. Lifton, *Thought Reform and the Psychology of Totalism* (New York, 1961), especially Part 3, "Thought Reform of Chinese Intellectuals."

15. See Chow Tse-tsung, "The Anti-Confucian Movement in Early Republican China," *The Confucian Persuasion*, ed. Arthur W. Wright (Stanford, 1960), p. 309.

16. See John Israel, "The Red Guards in Historical Perspective," *The China Quarterly*, No. 30 (April-June, 1967), pp. 26–30.

17. I would like to thank the Committee on Contemporary China of the Social Science Research Council, whose grant made this research possible, and the East Asian Research Center at Harvard University, which provided facilities for my work.

JOSEF SILVERSTEIN

Burmese Student Politics in a Changing Society

AFTER SIX YEARS of military rule, Burmese political life has changed
both in style and content. This transformation did not take place
suddenly and without resistance. Its object went beyond limiting
political opposition to revolutionizing the values and ideas, the relationships and institutions of the people.

Among the more notable examples of change since 1962 are the
elimination of students from active political participation and the
redirection of their energies and interests into wholly educational
and socially constructive activities. For most of the students, both
high school and university, redirection began only after a series of
violent contests with the soldier-rulers in 1962 and 1963, during
which the universities were closed, and youth leaders who had persisted in resisting the new order were arrested. Since 1964, the
students have been separated from their political leaders, and they
have accepted the new roles assigned to them in a changing educational environment. A minority still persists in its opposition by
giving open or secret support to the outlawed political parties and by
participating in the guerrilla warfare conducted by rebel political
and ethnic groups against the government. The present role played
by the student differs vastly from that of the past, and in order to
understand the magnitude of the changes and assess their depth,
it is necessary to review the history of students and politics and to
look at the controlling variables that govern student behavior and
values.

The Burmese tradition of student involvement in politics began
during the first decade of the twentieth century as a response to
the growing influence of Westernization that accompanied colonial
rule and the development of commerce. In the port cities and centers

of trade, English and Anglo-vernacular schools gained an unequal advantage over traditional schools run by Buddhist monks because the content of the new education provided the training necessary for jobs in the government, law, and commerce and for acceptance in the universities and colleges in England and India. In addition to adopting Western language, dress, and technology, the students became acquainted with Western ideas and values that were, in most cases, in sharp contradiction to those of their own culture. In the face of this foreign challenge, many young people, both in and out of high schools and colleges, joined in a movement for the protection of the Buddhist faith — the core of Burmese traditions and values. The Young Men's Buddhist Association (YMBA) began as a nonpolitical movement with the object of looking after the people's religious, educational, and social needs. The topics discussed at the meetings, however, tended to be social or political rather than religious, and the movement became the training ground for Burma's future leaders. The movement took on an outright political function when it led a protest campaign against the wearing of shoes by Westerners in the precincts of pagodas and monasteries. The importance of this early manifestation of student political activity rests with its initial motivation — the protection of Burmese culture and traditions. This motivation continued for the next four decades and was one of the constant factors in student political activity in Burma.

Following World War I and the British promise to India of eventual self-government, the Burmese leaders moved actively to win the same concessions for their people. In 1921, the YMBA was succeeded by the General Council of Burmese Associations (GCBA). While students took an active interest in General Council, the leadership passed to older men who sought political power, as well as institutional changes.

This background produced the first purely student political movement. In 1920, the colonial government considered establishing a university in Burma to train a small number of highly qualified persons for eventual recruitment into the country's bureaucracy or leading commercial firms. At that time, the centers of higher training were Rangoon College, established in 1884 as an affiliate of Calcutta University, and Judson College, a small Baptist institution created a decade later. The colleges provided instruction, but the parent Indian university administered examinations and awarded degrees. This was not a satisfactory system for a growing province which needed a steady stream of highly trained indigenous people. The proposed University Act of 1920 called for the establishment of an independent residential university, on the model of Cambridge or Oxford, which would admit only the best qualified students. Those below the top might enter as probationary students. By setting high standards, it was thought that a small elite could be trained and later absorbed, thus assuring good personnel with a stake in the preservation of the system.

The university students rejected the Act and its limitations. They called a strike on December 4, 1920 — a tactic already in use by Indians in their disputes with the British. The strike won the immediate support of the national political leaders, the Burmese adults, and the younger students in the middle and high schools. The strikers objected to the idea of an elite school, the probationary period, and the proposed program's emphasis on the arts and humanities, rather than science and technology. From their headquarters on the grounds of Shwedagon Pagoda, the leaders demanded a system of national schools whose curricula would be devoted to teaching the Burmese language, literature, history, and technology. The students tried to establish such schools in the Buddhist monasteries and other buildings with themselves and Buddhist monks as teachers. The movement spread beyond Rangoon, and a hierarchy of student-founded schools, catering to the needs of all ages, sprang up. Despite the energy of the student-teachers and the support of the public and the political leaders, the national-school movement gradually collapsed because it lacked both sufficient funds and recognition by the Department of Education and failed to develop quality education. By 1922, most of the national schools had closed or had been taken over by the government.

The student strike ended nearly a year after it began with the students winning a few minor concessions, but not their major objectives — the creation of a popular university that would serve the masses and a national school system that emphasized Burmese culture and history. Nevertheless, the strike was important for several reasons: It marked the marriage of educational and national goals with political tactics and demonstrated the unity of students on matters that were vital to their interests. Moreover, it drew nationwide support from all classes and ethnic groups and laid the foundation for a new political coalition — student leaders, politically active Buddhist monks, and radical professional politicians. From 1920 onward, the students were a potential force in the emerging political process.

Nearly a decade elapsed before the students returned to the political scene. The 1930's saw several important changes in the politics and the economy of Burma that helped shape the student movement. Following the inconclusive visit of the Simon Commission, which was charged with assessing the constitutional system and making recommendations for change, and the London Round Table Conferences, the people became politically active over the question of whether to unite with or separate from India. Concomitant with the constitutional issue was the problem of the effect of the worldwide depression on the economy of Burma. Thousands of farmers were forced off their land and driven to the cities to find employment. Ethnic competition for the limited number of jobs available erupted into violence, and Burma witnessed anti-Chinese and anti-Indian riots. In the countryside, a peasant revolt against British rule broke out in 1930. Although it was easily crushed, it excited the people and stimulated their interest in the radical solutions offered by some political leaders.

Out of this environment came a new political movement that united the university students, the nation's youth, and the radicals on the fringe of national politics. Together they founded a new party called *Dobama* (We Burmans) and adopted the title *Thakin* (Master) as the prefix to their names. As both names suggest, their initial goals were the revival of national culture and freedom from foreign rule. The former goal dominated their thought and action at the outset, and it persisted throughout their campaigns for wider use of the Burmese language in all aspects of life. The students in the Party were concerned mainly with the development of a secular literature in the national language, a cause they furthered by publishing essays, short stories, and articles. The student *Thakins* were also active in organizing the All Burma Youth League, which recruited middle- and high-school students to the *Dobama*. The League sought to awaken the students' feelings of love of country and to involve them in the political campaigns of the day.

The *Dobama* differed with the earlier YMBA mainly in its emphasis upon secular nationalism and its interest in political action as a means for gaining its ends. The society had little or no formal organization and, in its early phase, did not seek political power either through elections or violence. Its members devoted themselves to study, and they read widely in an unsystematic fashion from the ideas of Sun Yat-sen, Marx, Engels, Stalin, Mussolini, the leaders of the Indian Congress Party, and the Irish Sinn Fein movement. The youthful *Thakins* found a friend in J. S. Furnivall, a retired British civil servant who ran a bookstore in Rangoon and permitted them to use his shop as a place to read and discuss politics.

In 1935, the *Dobama* became more involved in radical politics. It was reorganized as the *Dobama Asiayone* (We Burman Society), which united the older members with the All Burma Youth League. Its ideology still remained nationalistic with an emphasis upon land, literature, and language. Several of its members had, however, become committed to Marxism and other foreign ideologies, and they sought to unite nationalist goals with ideas borrowed from abroad. After the 1935 constitution came into effect, the *Thakins* formed a political party, *Komin Kochin* (one's own king, one's own kind), in order to contest the election and win seats in parliament for the express purpose of destroying the new system. The *Thakins*, especially the student leaders among them, played a major role in awakening urban workers to political participation. They were most successful in organizing the workers of the Burma Oil Company and later led them on an ill-fated march to Rangoon that drew national attention to the grievances of the workers and the leaders of the *Thakins*. After 1937, the *Dobama Asiayone* grew more radical and sought to present itself as the only alternative to the other parties whose leaders accepted the constitutional system and the gradualism it implied.

While these changes were beginning to take shape, the majority of university students lived in semi-isolation and busied themselves with social activity, passing examinations, and looking forward to gaining good jobs and making successful marriages. By 1936, however, they were aroused politically when the Rangoon University Students' Union was captured by students interested in making this debating forum the center of student politics on campus. The expulsion of RUSU President Thakin Nu[1] for making provocative speeches and the disciplinary action against other leaders for publishing an inflammatory article in the RUSU journal, *Oway*, provoked the student body to strike. Although the expulsion and disciplinary actions were the catalysts for the strike, they were not the beginning of student politicization. That had begun years before in the middle and high schools, under the direction of the All Burma Youth League. Although most students who aspired to a university education may not have been active during that period, they had acquired the ideas, tactics, and training they now put to use. The particular issues were aided, no doubt, by the imminence of final examinations since most of the students were not opposed to any action that might postpone them. Thus, the student body responded immediately to the RUSU leaders' call for a strike. The strike quickly spread to the high schools in the larger urban areas. The student leaders, like their predecessors in 1920, established the strike headquarters on the grounds of Shwedagon Pagoda. They called for popular support and the political co-operation of the *Dobama Asiayone,* which they received almost at once. In the face of the widespread sympathy given the students and the interest in the strike shown by both Burmese government officials and responsible political leaders, the university administration and the government made concessions that included student representation on the university council. Following their victory, the student leaders became national heroes in the struggles against foreign rule and for student rights.

This strike, like the earlier one, was effective because it was initially a response to a student issue — disciplinary action by university officials. By emphasizing the problems of the indigenous student under the rule of alien teachers and officials who exercised power arbitrarily, it also attracted national attention through its appeal to the people's antiforeign sentiments. It differed from the earlier strike because it became political almost immediately and sought the support of radical politicians, monks, and the people at large. By winning a political victory as well as a student one — the postponement of the final examinations both at the university and in the high schools — the strike established the students once again at the forefront of the nationalist movement and gave their leaders fame and prestige, both on and off the campus.

After the British government implemented the new constitution of 1937, the RUSU took the lead in organizing and controlling the high- and middle-school students in new organizations, the All Burma Student Union (ABSU) and the All Rangoon Student Union (ARSU). When student leaders, Maung Ba Hein and Maung Ba Swe[2] were arrested for their part in the oil workers' march on Rangoon, the students made a public protest outside the Secretariat Building. In the excitement, the police tried to block the procession; failing to do this peacefully, they used clubs to reinforce their words. In the struggle, a student was killed, an event which provoked further demonstrations and a government crisis. On December 21, 1938, the university students called a new strike — directed against the government's brutality. This strike won a double victory — no reprisals against the strikers and the postponement of final examinations until June, 1939. In Mandalay, on February 10, 1939, the students at the Intermediate College and the National High School, together with a large group of politically active monks, held a demonstration against the government. Again a clash ensued, but this time seventeen students and monks were killed. This conflict led to further demonstrations, both in Mandalay and Rangoon, and united the people behind the students, who charged the government with brutality and repression. Thus, in the short period between 1936 and 1939, the student population became full participants in the radical nationalist struggle and saw its causes intermingled with the nonstudent nationalist issues of the day.

As the decade drew to a close, the student leaders who earned fame in the strike of 1936 and the demonstrations thereafter gradually left the campus and became more fully involved in national politics. Thakin Nu and Thakin Aung San, along with several others, joined in forming the Freedom Bloc in 1939. This organization, which united a majority of the members of the *Dobama Asiayone* with Dr. Ba Maw's *Sinyetha* (Poor People's Party), called for independence, the holding of a constituent assembly, and the immediate grant of power to the cabinet, pending the establishment of a new political system. The move came just as Great Britain entered World War II and was not favorably received. The anti-British speeches of the Freedom Bloc's leaders led to their arrest or escape from the country. One of those who left Burma was Aung San; he eventually went to Japan where he met with Japanese military officials who promised aid and military training for the Burmese in their struggle for national independence. Aung San returned to Burma and recruited twenty-nine former students to leave Burma and receive military training. With Japanese help, they were to become the spearhead of a military revolt against the British. In 1941, the "Thirty Heroes," as they came to be known in Burma, were poised in Thailand and Indo-China awaiting an opportunity to re-enter Burma and open the revolutionary phase of their fight for freedom.

Thus, on the eve of World War II, the students were fully committed to the nationalist struggle. They and their leaders had become radical in both their tactics and demands. Although their ideology was couched in the language of Western radical thought, its content remained nationalist and made its strongest appeal by joining linguistic and cultural issues with the demand for political independence. The students' honesty, their unwillingness to compromise with the system by accepting good jobs, and their devotion to the cause earned them the respect of the nation and an immediate place in national politics. Finally, their link to the *Dobama Asiayone* and the Japanese placed their leaders at the forefront of the radical nationalist movement that gradually adopted violent tactics to win total independence.

The student political movement took a new turn following the outbreak of World War II and the Japanese occupation of Burma. One of the first casualties of the fighting was the university; the invaders confiscated the buildings and grounds and halted all higher learning. In this situation, many of the students joined the Burma Independence Army and turned for leadership to former students who had led the 1936 strike and the Freedom Bloc movement. Most, however, were bewildered by changing events, and either returned to their homes or remained in the urban areas without guidance and leadership.

To remedy this situation and to win the support of the students and the nation's youth, the Japanese created in June, 1942, a Burma branch of the East Asiatic Youth League (EAYL) under the leadership of ten former university students. They, in turn, recruited members from among their fellow students and trained them as organizers and leaders of the various branches of the EAYL. The League's formal tasks were nonpolitical and ranged from digging wells and canals to building structures, training people in public health and sanitation, and educating the very young. By 1944, it had more than seventy thousand members. As a mass organization, performing socially useful tasks, the EAYL was well received by the people of Burma. In the rural, somewhat isolated areas, it acted as a link between the officials and the people.

The strength and popularity of the EAYL brought it into competition with the authority and prestige of Dr. Ba Maw's puppet regime. Toward the end of 1944, the Burma government outlawed the League. By this time, however, its leaders had become involved in the resistance movement and had moved underground to participate in the final uprising against the Japanese. Following the war, the EAYL took a new name, the All Burma Youth League (ABYL), and as a member group of the Anti-Fascist People's Freedom League (AFPFL), it played a leadership role in the nationalist struggle for independence between 1945 and 1948.

The war's end, like its beginning, brought rapid changes and confusion to the nation as a whole, and to the students in particular. Many former students returned to the campus to resume and complete their interrupted education. They found the buildings partially destroyed, books and equipment damaged or stolen, and the faculty ill equipped to maintain prewar standards. These problems, however, were overshadowed by the nation's struggle for independence. As before, student and national issues became intermingled, and the students quickly found themselves involved in protests and demonstrations for educational and political goals.

The postwar period brought one other significant change in the student movement — the interlocking relationship between student political organizations and national political parties. Where in the past the students retained their separate political identity and cooperated with parties and leaders who were out of power and against the system, from 1945 onward the students and their organizations became part of the national political process and an object for control by the rival political parties. This was due, in part, to the times and political issues; in part, to the fact that the rivals for political power were products of the student movement and sought to continue their links, despite their graduation into the world of national politics.

On campus, the older student organizations reappeared. Both ABSU and RUSU were courted by the rival Communist and Socialist Parties in their competition to capture control of the independence movement. As long as the two parties co-operated inside the AFPFL (1945–46), their student counterparts followed suit. A division in the AFPFL, however, resulted in a split in the student movement. The students loyal to the AFPFL-Socialist coalition captured the RUSU, while those in favor of the Burma Communist Party (BCP) gained control of the ABSU. The BCP-controlled group sought to exploit student grievances as a means of capturing wider support, and the AFPFL-controlled group emphasized nationalist issues and appealed to the students on the grounds of patriotism. In effect, the two groups acted out in microcosm the larger drama in the nationalist movement. The ABSU returned to the control of the AFPFL in 1947 after RUSU successfully appealed to the ABSU rank-and-file to call a conference.

Aung San's assassination in July, 1947, precipitated a crisis in student politics, as well as among the political parties. With no leader in the government with the personal attraction of Aung San, the students drifted away from AFPFL and gave their allegiance to the BCP in support of student issues. Student problems soon gave way to national political concerns when the BCP went into open revolt against the independent AFPFL government in April, 1948. Students became involved almost immediately. Some went underground to aid the BCP, others joined more radical groups, and still others put their studies aside and joined the army in support of the government. Communist sympathizers maintained their hold on the student movements until 1949, when they tried to lead university and grade-school students in a strike in sympathy with the civil-servants union. The government arrested those it could capture and drove the rest underground. The socialists of the AFPFL moved quickly to take charge of the student organizations by backing a new student party, the Democratic Student Organization (DSO). The DSO then dominated student political life until 1952. Backed with both AFPFL funds and strength, the DSO leaders used their power arrogantly in support of the government and, consequently, alienated the students. Some became independents and took less interest in student political life, while others shifted their allegiance to groups that were not government-sponsored.

As resistance to the DSO grew, the BCP secretly supported a new student party, the Progressive Student Force — or Progressives — which appealed to the students on the basis of student issues and opposition to the government because of the poor conditions that existed at all levels of education. At this time, the AFPFL, in an effort to win voter support in the national election, opened new colleges and abolished tuition, thus permitting more students to enter the university. Students reacted negatively to these changes, which they thought could only worsen the present conditions and decrease the quality of their education.

The government, when faced with mass resistance to a decision to shorten the October, 1953, recess, used force to dislodge the protesters and jailed the Progressive leaders who led the boycott. The government's apparent victory turned to defeat as the "October Revolution" became the symbol of government interference and brutality. After this, government-sponsored groups (and DSO, in particular) supplied little leadership to the student political movement. From 1955 to the military seizure of power in 1962, the RUSU and the ABSU were in the hands of students who were sympathetic or allied with the BCP.

Student leaders continued to couch their antigovernment attacks in terms of student issues after the shift to the left. The students and government were both unwilling to face the dilemma they were in. Each wanted to see more students obtain higher education

343

and better instruction, but neither was willing to face the consequences of their desires. The government failed to supply real leadership on student and educational problems, and thus the leftist RUSU leaders were able to cloak political criticism in student issues and were assured of mass support. When they did not employ this strategy, they stood alone.

It is also necessary to note another aspect of student politics in Burma. Students from the indigenous minorities have, from time to time since independence, taken to violence in support of ethnic political issues. Many Karens left the universities in 1949 to fight with the Karen National Defense Organization (KNDO) for a Karen State in which their people would have political independence or autonomy, and in 1959 Shan and Kachin students left the universities to join with groups of their own people in revolt against the growing dominance of centralized government and the Burman people. Minority students at the universities and colleges tended to group according to their language or ethnic identity. While they did participate with the Burmans in many student causes and national issues, they did not hesitate to follow their own leaders and to take an independent direction on issues they considered basic to the survival of their culture and political identity. This is not to suggest that ethnic cleavage kept the student movement divided. Indeed, during the revolts in 1948–49, most of the students from the minority races remained loyal to the Union government, a major factor in preventing the destruction of the Union of Burma.

In comparing the student movement before and after independence, several significant differences stand out. National political parties competed for control of the student movement. National issues were no longer anticolonial, but antigovernment. Student issues came to be more important than national ones in uniting the students. Thus, in order to mobilize widespread student support, student leaders continually sought to join national and student concerns. After independence, and during the first years of the several rebellions, students turned away from politics and sought friendships and social activity in their ethnic, religious, or regional organizations. When the military seized power and displaced the constitution and the elected leaders, the students — like the citizenry at large — accepted the change with quiet resolution.

The coup of 1962 brought major changes to the political environment of Burma. With no hesitation in using force against any group or individual who opposed them, the soldiers-in-power eliminated all dissenting legal groups by arresting the leaders or silencing them through fear, by outlawing their activity, and by disposing of their property. By 1964, the military government controlled the population centers and most of the countryside, with only the border regions and the remote jungle areas in the hands of the rebels. Despite their power, the military cannot prevent an occasional attack on a government outpost or the other acts of violent protest that have become more frequent during the past two years.

The military rulers have sought to re-educate the people to the new socialist values they set forth in *The Burmese Way to Socialism*. According to the new ideology, the old educational system was wrong because it was not equated "with livelihood." In the new Burma, education was to be equated with livelihood, and it would be based on socialist moral values. Precedence would be given to science in the curriculum, and higher education would be open only to those "who have promise and enough potentialities and industriousness to benefit from it."[3] The military rulers began to implement these basic changes in the educational system in 1964. They have reorganized the university according to a plan for decentralization that separates arts and sciences from technical, professional, and vocational training. The new decentralized university makes no provision for student political activity and organization. A student is expected to devote himself fully to his studies in order to gain the knowledge and skills that can be used in building a new Burma; any who do not apply themselves are dropped. The military is conscious of the need to convince the nation that the change was necessary and long overdue, that education finally has been made relevant to the needs of the society, and that higher education is a reward reserved for those with both talent and the willingness to work.

It is too early to assess the strengths and weaknesses of the new educational programs. There has, however, been a forced tranquillity in the schoolyards and classrooms. With no demonstrations and strikes to distract them and with incentives to succeed, the students have produced better results on the national examinations. There is no shortage of students who seek admission to the university and employment in government service, and the government has been firm in restricting admission. If the educational system continues to receive the funds and equipment it needs, if it succeeds in training a core of teachers who can do their work with skill and imagination, and if the social system can absorb the talents of the youths when they complete their studies, the changes will be accepted, and education will at last have become relevant to the needs of the society.

The student movement no longer exists as it did before the coup. When the new school year began in June, 1962, the students found changes in the administration, a new set of stringent rules governing their behavior, and a requirement that they pledge to observe the regulations before they would be allowed to register. The RUSU organized a protest against this invasion of student freedom, and the demonstration degenerated into a riot. The government answered by sending troops who fired upon the students; more than fifteen students were killed. When order was restored, the university was closed, the students were sent home, the student leaders were arrested, and the RUSU building was destroyed. By the end of the rainy season, the government reopened the university to all who provided the authorities with letters from officials in their home areas guaranteeing their behavior. Despite this and other restrictions, the students continued to demonstrate and protest. The military tolerated these expressions of political opposition and even promised to rebuild the RUSU building. During the government's negotiations with the insurgents,[4] the student political organizations met with the rebel leaders, publicized their cause, and supported many of their demands. When the government finally broke off discussions in November, the students called for a mass demonstration. The government responded by arresting the student leaders, reclosing the university, and ending student politics.

The university reopened in 1964; this time real changes took place. The reorganization and decentralization program had been put into effect, and the students were carefully screened before readmission. Under stricter discipline and academic pressure, the students remained quiet and the university became nonpolitical.

Patriotism — response to riots caused by Chinese students wearing Mao badges in June, 1967 — brought the university students temporarily back into the streets. The local press reported that about 200 of them took to the streets in protest, despite initial efforts by their Rectors to dissuade them.[5] Apparently, such demonstrations will be tolerated as there is no indication that the government punished them in any way.

There are no indications of how the military leaders view the nonpolitical organizations of the university students. Because they tend to divide and isolate student groups from one another, they probably are not encouraged; on the other hand, because they fill an important social need, they probably exist. The soldier-rulers have pursued a campaign to demonstrate that Burma is rich in cultural diversity and social harmony. It is likely, therefore, that the groups are tolerated and will be until the other programs take deeper root. Thus far, the government, the newspapers, or other media of communication have not mentioned them.

It was clear before the coup that only student issues could unite the students and inspire them to demonstrate and take political action; after the coup, the student political leaders used student issues as a means for uniting campus opposition to the military government. For a long time, the students have sought a more meaningful experience at the university and a better education. The military leaders are attempting to satisfy these desires by isolating the students from outside distractions and by improving the quality of education. In the four years since the student movement was put down, there have been no signs of its revival on campus. Thus far, most of the university students have co-operated with the new rulers. Whether their co-operation reflects genuine tranquillity or a smoldering fire cannot be determined yet. The long tradition of the student movement is not totally erased from the memory of this generation. Many of the military leaders and high officials won fame and developed their political skills as student leaders during the 1930's. Perhaps when the military relaxes its hold on the government and the Burma Socialist Program Party replaces it at the helm of the emerging political system, the change-over may be the spark to ignite a new student political movement.

REFERENCES

1. After World War II and the assassination of Aung San, he became the head of the AFPFL and the first Prime Minister of the Union of Burma.

2. Maung Ba Hein became a Communist when the Party was formed in 1939; he died in 1946. Maung Ba Swe was a leader of the Socialist Party and became Prime Minister in 1956; he held the office until early 1957, when he gave it up in favor of U Nu.

3. Revolutionary Council, *The Burmese Way of Socialism* (Rangoon, 1962), p. 6.

4. In April, 1963, a general amnesty was proclaimed, student political leaders were released from jail, and the government offered to negotiate with all groups in open revolt.

5. Kyi Nyunt, "What Is Friendship and Amity?" *New Light of Burma* (in Burmese; August 6, 1967).

III

AFRICA

CLEMENT H. MOORE AND

ARLIE R. HOCHSCHILD

Student Unions in North African Politics

UNDER WHAT CONDITIONS do students constitute a social stratum that, in the words of C. Wright Mills, serves as an "immediate, radical agency of [social] change"? Paraphrasing Mills, we ask, under what conditions can a student union become a force for revolutionary political change and, reversing Mills, under what conditions can it reenforce political stability in a new nation by transmitting the political values of the generation in power to the new student generation?

North Africa is a fertile field for comparison not only because its student unions have been among the best organized and most active of the Third World since the mid-1950's, but because the societies share certain legacies. Each of the countries has experienced French colonial rule, the intrusions of substantial numbers of European settlers, the expropriation of rich farmlands, the rise of new cities, the decay of traditional strata, and the imposition of a French educational system. Moreover, the countries have a common precolonial Islamic and Arab cultural heritage. Many differences do, of course, underlie these broad similarities. The intensity and duration of the colonial experience was greatest in Algeria, least in Morocco. Their post-independence political systems are based on different elite strata, and they pursue radically different policies. Thus, some features can be held constant while differences among the three countries are compared for their possible effects on the roles played by the three student movements before and after independence.

I

The Political Role of Students Before Independence

In the Third World, the most effective agency of anticolonialism was usually the intelligentsia, those who had been most exposed to the culture of the colonizer.[1] In North Africa, where the French presence had obliterated indigenous military establishments, the intelligentsia consisted of students and graduates of French universities. The undisputed leaders of Tunisian nationalism by the mid-thirties, they appeared to be the core of any future Algerian Muslim political elite.

The colonial situation and the pattern of colonial emancipation differed, however, in the three North African countries. Before independence, Morocco, the least touched by colonial rule, produced too few French-educated students to be an agency of change. (Those it did produce tended to be sons of the traditional elite.) The class that took power after Morocco's independence was largely traditional, and radical social change has yet to take place. In Algeria, on the other hand, colonial influence was more profound, the economic stakes higher, and the nature of the colonial conflict more violent. While the French educational system in Algeria produced a larger student body of more diversified class origins, the student independence movement was largely overshadowed by a more radical guerrilla insurrection. In Tunisia, national political activity was tolerated by the French, and, as in Algeria, more French-educated students, largely of the rising lower-middle class, were able to join the student union, child of the modernist Neo-Destour Party. In retrospect, despite a spectacular development of student organization in the mid-fifties, students *as such* were not radical agencies of historical change even in Tunisia, where conditions were most favorable.

To be sure, individual students and former students were among the first nationalists in all three countries. Though Muslim students at the University of Algiers were prohibited from forming an autonomous student union, they founded their first "cultural" organization in 1920. More important for fostering nationalism was the *Association des Étudiants Musulmans Nord-Africains* (AEMNA), founded in 1927 for the fifty-odd North African university students in Paris.[2] Here aspirations for a united and independent North Africa were vaguely articulated, and a number of future leaders acquired radical ideas through AEMNA's contacts with the French Left and with Chekib Arslan, a Druze expatriot who expounded pan-Arab nationalism. During the thirties, AEMNA represented the Gallicized face of nationalist and pan-Maghrib sentiment. Occasionally it was even permitted to hold its annual congresses on North African soil. Apart from moral support, however, it could contribute very little to the active agencies of political change, the parties and clandestine political organizations at home that developed contrasting responses to three very different colonial situations.

Because most North African students were enrolled in French universities rather than those of their respective homelands, Paris remained the crossroads of organized Maghribi student activity until the late-fifties. The student community expanded rapidly after World War II. In 1955–56, for example, approximately eighteen hundred Algerian Muslims were pursuing higher studies, more than two thirds doing so in metropolitan France rather than at the University of Algiers. During the same academic year, 862 Tunisians and three or four hundred Moroccans were studying in French universities, although centers of higher studies existed in Tunis and Rabat.[3]

In 1950, AEMNA established a permanent secretariat to draw up plans for a unified North African student union, but political events hindered their realization. After January 18, 1952, the Tunisian nationalist movement was driven underground, most of its top leaders were arrested, and the country was virtually besieged by the colonial authorities. Meanwhile the escalation of colonial conflict was avoided in Morocco until August 20, 1953, the date of Mohammed V's deposition, and in Algeria until November 1, 1954, the day the Algerian insurrection was launched. The Tunisian nationalists were in immediate need of a national union of students, and accordingly, the *Union Générale des Étudiants Tunisiens* (UGET) was founded at a secret congress in Paris during July, 1953, with the backing of the Neo-Destour Party. Two years later, eight months after the outbreak of the Algerian revolution, the Algerians followed suit, founding the *Union Générale des Étudiants Musulmans Algériens* (UGEMA). The Moroccan students remained disorganized until after independence, when the *Union Nationale des Étudiants Marocains* (UNEM) was formed in the summer of 1956.

Morocco. Morocco came under French control only in 1912, thirty-one years after the French had established their protectorate in Tunisia and almost a century after the conquest of Algeria (1830–47). It was not fully "pacified" until 1934, when modern nationalism, reflecting the interests and outlook of traditional urban strata more than those of the tiny French-educated stratum, took organizational shape.

Morocco was, therefore, the last of the three countries to benefit from a modern French educational system and had far fewer French-educated students than Tunisia or Algeria. Within what was later to become the Istiqlal Party, there were a few young radical students and graduates, but products of the traditional University of Qara-ouiyine at Fez were more representative of the Party's conservative urban base. Students — especially radical modernizers, like Mehdi Ben Barka, who were of lower-class origins — could exercise their organizational skills in the Istiqlal before independence, but the cohesion of the nationalist elite obscured basic differences in outlook that became apparent with the scission of the Istiqlal in 1958-59. Before independence, neither students nor graduates could acquire sufficient prestige and authority to challenge the traditional Islamic values underlying Istiqlal nationalism. (Even traditional Party leaders failed to gain authority independent of their national symbol, the Moroccan monarch. After independence, King Mohammed V easily consolidated his power and neutralized the Istiqlal's bid to set up a one-party state.) Individual students did become leaders before independence, but any enumeration of these individuals must include Crown Prince Hassan, who succeeded his father in 1961, as well as Mehdi Ben Barka. Clearly, Moroccan students did not constitute a revolutionary stratum.

Tunisia. Tunisian students and graduates played a crucial role in the struggle for independence. They constituted the dominant stratum, the political class, the armature of the new Tunisian nation that developed in opposition to both the old society and the French presence. Virtually all of the Neo-Destour's top leadership were educated in French universities, and the Party's favorite recruiting grounds were Tunisia's modern French or Franco-Arab secondary schools. Though many of the Party's provincial cadres were educated in the traditional University of Zitouna, the Party took unequivocably "modern" stances against the "old turbans" (the religious elite) and other traditional urban strata long before independence.

The tension between the old elite and the new French-educated one led in Morocco to the split within the Istiqlal in 1958. In Tunisia, it was resolved in 1937 in favor of the modernizers with the Neo-Destour's decisive victory over the Destour Party, Tunisia's older equivalent to the Istiqlal. In this sense, Tunisia was at least one generation more "advanced" than Morocco, where even today traditional elites frustrate the radical intelligentsia. One obvious explanation is that Tunisia succumbed to French rule and thus received

French schools one generation earlier. Another explanation concerns the socio-economic status of Tunisian students. By the thirties, sons of the old urban elite were outnumbered in Tunisian *lycées* and French universities by those of the lower classes. Furthermore, a majority of the latter came from the Sahil, a distinctive geographic region noted for its ancient village civilization and the tenacity and industry of its peasant olive-tree cultivators. The Sahil gave its sons a basis for an identity other than that of the old urban elite and hence re-enforced the modernizing subculture of the lower-class university students. Indeed, when refracted in the new visions of these sons of the Sahil, regionalism stimulated a more radical nationalism than that of the old urban classes. While the old generations were content to argue legalistically for Wilsonian self-determination, the student generation led by Habib Bourguiba set out to create a new public by sustained political activity through the well-organized Neo-Destour Party.

The very power and organization of the Party, however, caused it to subordinate students as an organized force. Tunisian students, as such, played a secondary role in the Neo-Destour's twenty-year campaign against the French. UGET served political and diplomatic purposes during the first year of its existence (1953–54), when the Party was outlawed, but it was never more than a cover for the activities of its parent organization. UGET's clandestine role ended in the autumn of 1954 when negotiations were opened that led first to home rule and then to independence in 1956.

Tunisian students and former students were part of a revolutionary stratum dedicated as much to transforming Tunisian society as to gaining political concessions from France. Ironically, the indirect impetus to their dedication arose out of the success of the French educational system in instilling new values. But there were other important reasons for the Neo-Destour's success. Tunisia's old elite, discredited by compromises with French officials and economically undermined by French settlers, was already extremely vulnerable when the Party was founded in 1934. Furthermore, the French authorities tolerated the Party more than they did comparable Algerian formations, because the French economic stakes were lower in Tunisia than in richer Algeria. Periods of political repression served to legitimate rather than to liquidate the new Tunisian leadership. The decisive means of colonial emancipation were the arts of organization, polemic, debate, and negotiation — in short, the arts acquired by a French-educated elite — rather than the grenades and machine guns that leveled much of Algeria.

Algeria. Algerian students were ultimately a less significant force than their Tunisian counterparts not because the society was more "backward," as in Morocco, but because colonial rule had lasted too long and rested on bayonets. Students and graduates have fewer political opportunities in a militarized society, like that of Algeria after 1954. In fact, as early as 1937, the failure of the Blum-Violette Plan, due to settler intransigence, probably marked the end of the educated elite's dream of French assimilation and of any possibilities of a Franco-Muslim settlement short of violence.

The traditional elites were decimated and discredited by the French presence, and this disintegration of tradition deprived Algerian students of an identity or sense of national purpose. While the former student, Ferhat Abbas, chronologically of Bourguiba's generation, preached assimilation, Algerian workers in France, led by Messali Hadj, launched a more radical movement calling for independence. By the time a younger generation of university graduates was gaining control of this movement's political structure (the MTLD), the arbitrary practices of the colonial authorities had nullified moderate reforms and rendered Muslim political activity meaningless. Events again outran the intellectuals on November 1, 1954, when the secret Front of National Liberation (FLN) initiated a co-ordinated outbreak of terrorism. With the possible exception of Hocine Ait Ahmed, none of FLN's nine founders had been university students.

Nevertheless, the Algerian union of students, UGEMA, played a more significant role in the FLN's guerrilla war with France than the Tunisian or Moroccan student organizations did in their nationalist movements. The fragmentation of Algerian political and military organization meant that UGEMA, unlike UGET, enjoyed significant autonomy from its founding. At the same time, UGEMA made no secret of its solidarity with the FLN and its goals.

The young student union showed its strength by its call in May, 1956, for a general and unlimited student strike. Nearly all of the 520 Muslim students at the University of Algiers obeyed, as did most of the 1300 Algerian Muslims studying in France. UGEMA launched a brilliant campaign in France and abroad to enlist the support of international student opinion for the Algerian cause. Under the leadership of Dr. Messaoud Ait Chaalal, the Algerian student organization withstood legal dissolution by the French authorities of January 28, 1958. From exile first in Switzerland and then in Tunis, it marshaled scholarships and political support from Communist and Western countries, despite the insistence of many Western unions upon maintaining a distinction between legitimate student interest and "politics." For UGEMA, of course, the distinction made by Western groups between student syndicalism and political activity could not be considered legitimate, given the turmoil of the Algerian war.[4] The union nevertheless was usually able to keep its own autonomy vis-à-vis the FLN, and its foreign policies were distinctly to the left of those of the FLN's Provisional Government (GPRA), founded in September, 1958.

After 1958, Algerian students were scattered, due largely to UGEMA's success in procuring more than 350 scholarships in at least twenty-six countries besides France and Algeria where UGEMA had been driven underground. The union consequently became highly fragmented, despite the efforts of its leadership in exile to apply "centralism" and "very strict discipline." On the eve of independence, the FLN's Provisional Government dismissed much of UGEMA's wartime leadership in an effort to consolidate control over the organization before the eventual power struggles began. As authority collapsed in Algeria after the spectacular French withdrawal during the summer of 1962, many of UGEMA's former leaders were recruited into the country's fledgling diplomatic service. Those who, like Ait Chaalal, were too disenchanted with politics to serve Ben Bella's government also withdrew from student politics. In the end, few remained to resuscitate the organization. When, on September 5, the Fifth UGEMA Congress finally opened after several postponements, civil war was still raging just south of Algiers. Though Algeria had no effective government that might suppress student action, the students were as fragmented as their society, the various segments being mouthpieces of political factions incapable of identifying a common student interest or electing new union officers. Despite its heroic exploits during the revolution, UGEMA disintegrated at independence.

The roles of North African student organizations before independence appear, on hindsight, to have been influenced largely by four general factors: the colonial situation, the strength of traditionalism, the organizational strength of other military or political forces in the struggle for independence, and the size, prestige, and composition of the student population.

The French had the greatest vested interest in Algeria. Consequently they were more intransigent against political activism in

Algeria than in Morocco or Tunisia. French cultural, social, and economic colonial influence, too, was strongest in Algeria, somewhat milder in Tunisia, and weakest in Morocco. The colonial regimes in Algeria and Tunisia had, in a sense, sown the seeds of their own destruction and of modernizing reconstruction as well. Thus, there was a viable modernist alternative to colonial rule at the eve of independence to which a sizable group of students could lend support. Conditions were more ripe for student political participation in these countries than in Morocco. In Morocco, traditional values and social structure remained strong. At the other extreme, the extensive French influence in Algeria weakened Algerian cultural and political integrity to the extent that "assimilationism" became an obstacle to a unified independence movement.

The Algerian student union could enjoy autonomy, in part because of the fragmentation of other groups, whereas the strong and unified Neo-Destour Party actually created the Tunisian student union and kept it subordinate. The Moroccan Istiqlal Party was fairly united before independence, but there was then no student organization that it could subordinate, as in the case of Tunisia, or whose support it could enlist, as in the case of Algeria.

Moroccan students, unlike the Tunisian or Algerian, were simply too few in number and had too little prestige to become a strong organized force. Moreover, Moroccan students were not drawn, as in Algeria and Tunisia, from a variety of social classes. Thus, education did not constitute the radical restratification that it did in the two other countries, and consequently it failed to create a significant class of frustrated intellectuals whose careers were blocked by the colonial regime.

II

The Role of Students After Independence

After independence the roles of student unions were radically reversed in the three countries. Their organizational bases were transformed when indigenous universities and political structures supplanted Paris as the main focus for student activity. Ten years after independence, it appeared that only in Morocco, where students had contributed the least to national independence, could students become an "agency of historic change." Each of the three student unions reflected its country's political processes since independence.

Morocco. The activities of the Moroccan student union closely paralleled those of outside political forces opposed to the regime. Soon after its founding in 1956, UNEM became a mouthpiece for Ben Barka's radical faction in the Istiqlal Party. Ben Barka virtually ran UNEM's Third Congress, held in 1958, from behind the scenes, thereby setting the tone for UNEM's future activities. UNEM indirectly attacked the monarchy, calling its major instrument, the Royal Armed Forces, a "parade" army. (The Chief of Staff was the Crown Prince, who in 1961 became King Hassan II.) When the split within the Istiqlal was formalized in 1959 with the creation of the *Union Nationale des Forces Populaires* (UNFP), UNEM joined the rest of the Moroccan left in support of the new party. Shortly after massive arrests of the UNFP leadership in July, 1963, for an alleged "plot" against the monarchy, UNEM's Eighth Congress "declare[d] solemnly that the abolition of the regime is the necessary condition for extricating the country from the open or latent crisis which it has not ceased to suffer since independence." The calendar of the following year's events reported to UNEM's Ninth Congress boasted a total of twenty student strikes and six "occupations" of Moroccan embassies abroad.

The Moroccan government did not look kindly on the activities of the militant young student union. In 1963, a military tribunal condemned UNEM's president to death in absentia for expressing solidarity with Algeria's socialist government during the Moroccan-Algerian border war. In the autumn of 1964, the Moroccan government cut off the union's subsidies and unsuccessfully campaigned to abolish UNEM on a legal technicality. By this time, political strikes had become endemic at the University Mohammed V at Rabat, often spreading to the lesser campuses at Fez and Casablanca and into the secondary schools. Triggered by grievances of some secondary-school students and their parents, widespread rioting in Casablanca in March, 1965, shook the regime and was brutally suppressed at the cost of hundreds of lives. Soon afterward, the King granted amnesty to UNFP leaders condemned for the 1963 "plot," and he appeared, during the summer, to be preparing to collaborate with the UNFP. The kidnapping of Ben Barka on October 30, 1965, dashed all hopes of either an opening to the left or a reconciliation.

The Ministry of Education responded to a student strike held to celebrate the first anniversary of the Casablanca riots by closing the university *cité*. With the exception of the science faculty, the university was then paralyzed by striking students until vacation the following week. The government's "solution" to student agitation was to apply selectively a new law instituting universal conscription. Despite a provision for student deferments, all but one of UNEM's Executive Committee were drafted on the eve of its Eleventh Congress (July 25–27, 1966).

Ironically, the turbulence of Moroccan politics and the sharp administrative response to UNEM activities aided UNEM in developing its organizational strength during its first ten years. By the mid-sixties, UNEM had become a strong political force closely aligned with the radical activist wing of the UNFP.[5] The government occasionally consulted UNEM on educational matters, but the union was too politicized to confine itself to the role of a functionally specific interest group.

In retrospect, the Moroccan student union, unlike its Tunisian and Algerian counterparts, seems to be primarily an agency for enlisting and mobilizing radical student opinion against the regime. Still, only 27 per cent of a sample of 125 Moroccan students actually belonged to a student union.[6] Over half of the non-members, however, advocated more power for the union. Predictably, union members and, to an even greater extent, their leaders tended to be more interested in politics and more radical in their attitudes toward foreign capital, government intervention in the economic affairs of the country, and agricultural reform than non-members.

Moroccan students formed the most vociferous protest movements in North Africa, in part because the Moroccan political system was and remains a more likely target of student protest than that of Algeria or Tunisia. Behind the Moroccans' sloganistic condemnation of the "reactionary," "feudal," and despotic "personal power" of the monarch lies some realistic evaluation. Social restratification is relatively absent in Morocco, and students are unable to gain entrance into the inner political circle. The ruling class continues to consist primarily of elements of the traditional elite, together with commoners personally chosen by the King. Former students have a place in the independent regime only if they enjoy high traditional status or have caught the favor of the monarch, which they are unlikely to do. Although the King and a number of leading ministers and high Moroccan officials were once students in French universities, not one former student leader now belongs to the inner circle.

Tunisia. In Tunisia, restratification has proceeded further, and the generation gap is narrower. The process of restratification, illustrated by the victories of the Destour over more traditional political forces before independence, guaranteed that education would take precedence over family as the touchstone of both social status and political power. Though UGET was founded only three years before independence, its founders and subsequent leaders were rapidly integrated into the new ruling structure. Two general secretaries, Sayah and Chaker, became directors of the Neo-Destour's Political Bureau, an important position in any one-party state. Indeed, the fate of UGET's leadership gradually discredited it in the eyes of many students, as it became obvious that membership on UGET's executive board was a steppingstone for political careerists. Certainly the Tunisian political elite closely reflected the styles, outlook, and education of the student body. Generational struggles seemed inevitable after 1960 or so because graduates could no longer be automatically catapulted into responsible governmental positions. Nevertheless, the younger students did not represent an ideological outlook, a historical stratum, or even a socio-economic background too different from that of the Sahil peasant sons and their allies who had made good.

In striking contrast to student unionists in pluralist Morocco, those in Tunisia were stifled by the consensus elicited by the successful one-party system. UGET's essential task after independence was to maintain a constructive dialogue between the generation in power and the new student generations. The task was lightened by resemblances between the Tunisian elite and its potential critics. The Sahil, a coastal strip south of Tunis with 10 per cent of the country's population, was both the backbone of the ruling Neo-Destour and the home of more than one quarter of Tunisia's student population in 1960. Any conflict of generations in Tunisia is rooted in underlying social and intellectual similarities, rather than in vast differences. In Tunisia, there is no myth, as in Morocco, of a rising young revolutionary generation to fall back on; it arrived with independence. Tunisian revolutionary youth may feel like Miniver Cheevy, "born too late."

The Neo-Destour chose to exercise flexible control over UGET, allowing open discussion and political debate, but making sure that its political resolutions and activities were harmless to the regime. So far as is practicable, the organization is used as a channel for Party propaganda. Because of the close relationship between the two organizations before independence, the Party was able to maintain control of UGET without appearing to subvert its autonomy.

During the first few years of independence, when the Neo-Destour remained popular and the average graduate's employment prospects were brilliant, the mechanisms of control functioned smoothly. The Neo-Destour's own student federations, staffed by a loyal, capable, and authentically student leadership, co-operated harmoniously with UGET and ensured the loyalty of UGET's sections to the Executive Bureau. UGET seemed to be an effective bridge between students and politicians. It occasionally took *avant-garde* political positions (such as advocating the recognition of Communist China) which saved it from the accusation of being a Party satellite.

But this happy state of affairs could not survive the post-independence rejuvenation of the UGET rank and file. As the reliable cadres of pre-independence vintage took their diplomas and passed on into government or Party jobs, a slightly younger generation took over the organization, which was vastly expanded by the increased number of university students. The new generation had no more revolutionary battles to wage; even practical "syndical" concerns like scholarships were amply taken care of by the government. UGET was losing its mystique and acquiring a reputation as a "training ground for cadres." The more rebellious students began to look elsewhere for sources of inspiration.

Few Tunisian students actually became members of the Communist Party, either in Tunisia or in France, but many were frustrated by the Neo-Destour domination of their organization. These autonomists did not approve of one-party rule — especially when they considered that party "bourgeois." In February, 1961, a joint meeting of UGET and the Neo-Destour Youth, a tightly controlled organization of eighty thousand members, was called to protest Lumumba's assassination. At the meeting, fighting broke out between a Neo-Destour leader and some of the students, including an autonomist member of the Executive Committee. After this episode, the autonomist minority was no longer represented in UGET's Executive or the somewhat larger Administrative Committee.

The Bizerte crisis of July, 1961, momentarily resurrected Tunisian nationalism and gave UGET a cause. When in ensuing months a vigorous "socialist" policy of economic planning became the leitmotif of Tunisian politics, UGET, which had always advocated such a policy, was brought into the consultative process. The Neo-Destour thus captured the autonomists' political thunder, but UGET remained under Party control. The Neo-Destour's crackdown on autonomists — accused of being Communist, Trotskyite, "irresponsible," and "parasitic" — ruptured the delicate equilibrium theretofore maintained between the demands of Party supremacy and those of student-union autonomy. By UGET's Fourteenth Congress (August 9–14, 1966), Party control was so complete that the Neo-Destour Student Federation had become superfluous and was abolished. Though debate inside the Congress was still possible, the myth of UGET's autonomy had lost all credibility.

By toeing the Party line even to the extent of supporting Bourguiba's pro-American Vietnam policy, UGET lost the respect of many moderate Tunisian intellectuals and students who had signed critical petitions and manifestoes earlier in the year. Unprecedented student demonstrations at the end of 1966 lay bare some of the underlying antagonism toward the Party and government take-over of UGET. The demonstrations vividly testified to the students' complete loss of confidence in UGET and its leadership. According to the official diagnosis, most demonstrators were not anti-UGET, but hapless dupes of "outside agitators" — students who had recently returned from France. But even Bourguiba did not deny the substance of the problem in his New Year's Speech to the Nation:

I have been told, in fact, that certain students, a tiny minority, consider UGET to be an emanation of the Destour Socialist Party and that, by virtue of this fact, UGET takes away their liberty. But they forget that the Party consists of patriots devoted to their country and that many of them have endured sacrifices, as attested by cemeteries of martyrs throughout the country, in order for it to be possible today for thousands of youths to study and prepare to take up their elders' responsibilities tomorrow.

Thus, while invoking memories of the independence struggle when student unrest had been encouraged, Bourguiba did not disavow UGET's subordination to the Party. In a curious attempt to prove its autonomy, the Administrative Commission of UGET condemned the strike and "outside" agitators, but for the first time criticized American policy in Vietnam.

Unlike the Moroccans, Tunisians did not have an obvious target, apart from their own union, against which to protest. The left-wing opposition seemed weak and internally divided. No student organization could, as in Morocco, crystallize student opinion and guide it on a course of opposition. But student opposition outside and against UGET continued to thrive, erupting in strikes and demonstrations in 1967 and 1968.

Algeria. Despite the leveling effects of eight years of war, a pattern comparable to that in Tunisia has been evolving in Algeria. Under Boumedienne, at least to date, the former warring factions seem reconciled. Since the departure of Mahsas and Boumaza in 1966, the sovereign Council of the Revolution has contained only military officers and veterans, among whom only one is a former student, and he played no role in UGEMA. In a sense, their incorporation into the system merely neutralizes them. Those who apparently make most of Algeria's important decisions are the ministers and high officials whom Boumedienne appoints with the support of the Council, and a growing number of these, including the Minister of Education, are former leaders of UGEMA.

In the absence of an effective party, the central bureaucracy may become increasingly important. Unlike Morocco, which abounds with bureaucrats frustrated by political cross-pressures, Algeria has erected no systemic barriers against the administrative initiative of students and former students. With the consolidation of Boumedienne's power, the bureaucracy may gradually become insulated from political pressures. Thus, students are more likely to identify with the ruling class in Algeria than they are in Morocco.

Just as the FLN after 1962 lacked the mass base and cohesion of the Neo-Destour, UNEA always remained much weaker than UGET, although since FLN never enjoyed the coherent leadership of the Neo-Destour, the Party had greater difficulty controlling the students.[7] Until shortly before Ben Bella's fall, UNEA maintained a fair degree of autonomy under Houari Mouffok, a student who had attended an East German university and was a sympathizer, at least, of the outlawed Algerian Communist Party. Like the Communists, he supported Ben Bella's "socialist" policies while insisting upon the union's autonomy.

Mouffok's faction controlled the dominant Algiers section of UNEA over the opposition of a faction of FLN students and of other non-Communist groups at Algiers and abroad. Despite Ben Bella's apparent desire in the summer of 1964 to remove Mouffok, his opposition remained too divided to wrest leadership from him democratically. Had Ben Bella not been overthrown, however, it is likely that Mouffok would have lost control of the Algiers section to a growing faction of UNEA members organized by the Party.

During Mouffok's reign, UNEA does not appear to have mobilized the support or sympathies of many students, despite its militant socialist leadership. In 1964, the union claimed 2500 dues-paying members, or roughly one third of the university student body — proportionately fewer members than UGET, but more than UNEM could claim. UNEA meetings and rallies — against "counter-revolution" at home and in support of "progressive" students fighting imperialism and neocolonialism abroad — rarely drew more than three hundred students. Though it organized occasional seminars, the socialist leadership of UNEA seemed even less capable of influencing student opinion than of retaining its own autonomy. Algerian students, like the population at large, had become immune to revolutionary appeals after eight years of war followed by the spectacle of fratricidal strife within the new elite.

As in Tunisia, the students were treated too well to nourish many concrete grievances. After independence, the government went further than Tunisia's by granting a "pre-salary" to all students in good standing and then increasing the wages paid science and medical students in order to divert as many as possible into these fields. Algerian students were probably as technically and scientifically oriented as the Tunisians; more Algerians studied science than letters in 1965.

On the whole, the social composition of the Algerian student body was probably fairly similar to that of the Tunisian student body. In the first years of independence, the quality of education did not decline appreciably, and employment prospects for graduates were as favorable as they had been in the comparable early years of independence for Moroccan and Tunisian graduates. Apart from small factions of activists, students did not appear to take an active interest in politics.

When Boumedienne unexpectedly overthrew Ben Bella, however, there was a sudden upsurge of student activity. According to a correspondent of *The New York Times* who watched the students take to the street for Ben Bella, "the turn-out was not spectacular, never much more than 1000 at best, but still far above those Algiers had seen for Cuba, Vietnam, or Angola." UNEA's demand that the Council of the Revolution liberate Ben Bella was met with the arrest of three UNEA leaders. Mouffok, who went into hiding and supported the pro-Communist clandestine opposition, was finally arrested on October 7. By this time, the new regime had enlisted some of the FLN student faction on its side.

Three months later, however, a three-day general strike erupted. On January 29, 1966, a demonstration over the Ben Barka affair against the Moroccan government spontaneously changed its nature when students started yelling "liberate Mouffok," "Boumedienne to the gallows!" While the Party dissolved the Algerian section of UNEA and had ten students dismissed from the university, the union's national leadership remained silent. The dissolved section called a strike, and nearly all the students respected it. Though the Party insisted it was the work of foreigners and "counter-revolutionaries," it replaced the UNEA leadership with another equally unrepresentative group.

An unlimited strike the following month dissipated after five days when university authorities told the students that four absences from classes would disqualify them from taking examinations. The bizarre series of incidents related to these demonstrations and strikes illustrated, as the Tunisian authorities were to discover at the end of the year, that Party-controlled student unionism was not a satisfactory mechanism for eliminating student grievances. Moreover, by overreacting, the respective authorities merely magnified the spontaneous outbursts of rebelliousness. In 1967, the situation improved. "Mobilization" to pursue the war against Israel provided a rationale for inducting five thousand students into the army for six weeks. The comments of students returning to Algiers in September suggested that the army was eliciting more loyalty, or at least interest, than the Party or union ever had. Weekend drills were planned for the coming year.

Algerian students, like those in Tunisia, will probably acquire a sense of belonging to a new national elite. Only in Morocco do politically minded students usually identify with a radical counter-elite. The role of the three student unions has been influenced not only by the political and social contexts of the three countries, but also by the development of their respective universities. Impressionistically, it seems that the quality of education has been the lowest and the strains of expansion the greatest in Morocco, while the quality has been the highest and the strains the weakest in Algeria.

Spectacular changes in the composition of all three student bodies since independence have created corresponding changes in the student subculture. At the University of Algiers, where student activities have sturdy roots in the colonial heritage, the "tone" and atmosphere of student life have suddenly ceased to be European, while the heterogeneity of the new Algerian student population makes it difficult to create new traditions of autonomous student activity. The tradition of a student subculture within which a union might flourish is even less developed at Tunis and Rabat. Hence, union activities in all three countries have taken on a national rather than a distinctly student flavor. In Algeria and Tunisia, where politically active students can more easily identify with the men in power, student activism has resulted in minor outbursts of solidarity or irritation with essentially like-minded governments. In Morocco, where the "feudal" order offers something to unite against and educational grievances are added to political ones, the student union has played a more active role. It remains to be seen what its impact upon the student body may be.

III

The Political Significance of Student Unions

Does membership in the student union foster interest in politics or in radical political change? Does it serve to recruit future politicians? To what extent are other aspects of student life and social background more important than union affiliation in politicizing students?

Morocco. Our Moroccan data strongly suggests that UNEM is a principal agency for politicizing, radicalizing, and imbuing students with high expectations or hopes of a political career. Union affiliation "explained" interest in politics to a much larger extent than any other single independent variable, even when the effect of each of the others was held constant.[8] Socio-economic status was, however, more important than union membership for "explaining" radical attitudes of students. Union affiliation also "explained" more student political ambition than the other variables selected. UNEM is of extreme political significance in Moroccan student circles, though some of its shortcomings were also suggested by the data. Union membership and, in lesser degree, absence of religion are the two factors that apparently contribute the most to developing a Moroccan student's interest in politics.

The more deeply a student becomes involved in his union, the more likely he is to be interested in politics. This may either be because his union activities stimulate him politically or because the union attracts politicized students — or both. But other Moroccan university organizations are not at all associated with student politicization; indeed, it appears that members of one or more cultural, professional, or sporting associations are significantly less likely than non-members to be interested in politics. The contrast with the conventional image American sociologists have of "stable" Western pluralist societies could not be more striking. In the West, many relatively apolitical associations are supposed to attract politically interested people and help to socialize them; the "joiners" tend to be better informed and more active in politics than those who remain isolated.

It appears, however, that organizational experiences prior to entering the university significantly affect the Moroccan's interest in politics. One reason for this may be that Moroccan political parties have tried with mixed success to organize and control the various scouting and sporting associations open to secondary students. At the university level they have concentrated upon the student unions. Students who have belonged to secondary-school organizations tend, moreover, to join a university student union. The effectiveness of the Moroccan Party in eliciting student support is meager in contrast with the Tunisian situation, both at secondary-school and university levels.

While the immediate influence of the university student union, political affiliations in secondary school, and attitudes toward the university appear related to student politicization, there are also more complex underlying factors. In Morocco, the most traditional of the three North African societies, Islam, remains an inclusive way of life, the community par excellence, for most Moroccans. In traditional Islam, there is no separation of church and state, no basis for distinguishing political from religious concerns. It is therefore plausible to suppose that the student who has kept the faith of his fathers will have less interest in the profane world of modern politics. Conversely, the student who has broken or is breaking away from the traditional faith may search for a new community and seek new political commitments. The less religious a student is — as is indicated by his observance of Ramadan and daily prayers and by his own self-evaluation — the more likely he is to be interested in politics. Furthermore, the irreligious student is twice as likely as the very devout one to be a union member or leader. In fact, less religious students are more likely to be interested in politics whether they join the union or not.

To be a student in Morocco today is to belong to a privileged stratum, regardless of one's social background or career expectations. Students who come from the upper classes will not have experienced a sharp change in social status, but lower-class students will have broken with their past merely by virtue of being university students.

Moreover, the very juxtaposition of rich and poor students within the university may sharpen the latter's class-consciousness and elicit political consciousness. It seems among Moroccan students that social class is negatively correlated with interest in politics. Upper-class students seem significantly *less* interested in politics than middle- or lower-class students. The student unions do, however, seem to attract proportionately more upper-class members. While one third of all upper-class students join the union, less than one quarter of the lower- and middle-class students are members. Differences in political interests between joiners and non-joiners are greatest among the middle-class students. Possibly the concern of some students for politics is a substitute for traditional theological concerns; perhaps, too, politicization connotes a search for new, post-Islamic bases of community. But our findings also suggest that student unionism is hardly the exclusive answer; even controlling for union membership, low religious commitment appears independently to increase political interest. Union membership articulates or generates the most political concern among middle-class students, rather than among lower-class students of traditional background.

Interest in politics may also be a response from those who have made sharp breaks with their family background. The severing of religious ties seems to have this effect. The break with the past may be sharpest for those students who come from parochial towns or villages to the big university city. A simple breakdown of students from cosmopolitan cities and small towns shows no difference in interest in politics. If, however, we further divide the two groups into those who have received a traditional education (who neither speak nor read French well) and those who have received a French education, a difference in politicization appears. The poor linguists cannot share the veneer of French culture that marks Morocco's political and administrative elite; they are condemned to the second-rate Arabic sections of the university which provide fewer career opportunities.

Union membership also appears, with all other variables controlled, to be one of the two strongest predictors of "radicalism," while other organizational affiliations, either in university or secondary school, contribute almost nothing.[9] Socio-economic status, however, contributes even more to radicalism than union membership, and is quite independent of it. Since unions attract proportionately more middle- and upper-class members, there is a radical lower-class student constituency (which is also associated with rural backgrounds deprived of French culture) that UNEM has so far failed to mobilize.

The amount of exposure to the university culture does not appear to bear a strong relationship to a student's political attitudes. Nor is religious commitment, taken by itself, significantly related to student radicalism in the way that it is to interest in politics. Even controlling for exposure to French education (as inferred from a student's reading ability), religiosity does not appear to be associated with radical political attitudes. But just as lower-class students tend to be more interested in politics, they tend also to be more radical.

In fact, if we contrast the radicalism of union members and non-members within each class, the same pattern we found for interest in politics appears for radicalism. The difference in the likelihood of being radical is greater between middle-class members and non-members than between lower-class members and non-members. Thus, the student union may radicalize those students whom we might not expect, on the basis of their class origins, to be radical.. Or, conversely, middle-class radicals may, unlike their lower-class brethren, seek out an organizational vehicle for their political concerns.

Like interest in politics, radicalism is a possible response for those who have made sharp breaks with their family backgrounds or social environment. Moreover, the break with one's past, irrespective of social class, is sharpest for the student who comes from a small parochial town or village to the big university city. The small-town boy is thrice as likely as his urban classmate to display radical attitudes.

Poor linguists are twice as likely to be radical as their Gallicized comrades, but their radicalism does not seem to go beyond verbal expressions of protest. They are neither significantly more interested in politics than French speakers and readers, nor more likely to belong to a student union or to other organizations.

To what extent does membership in a student union appear not only to politicize and radicalize students, but also to produce an aspiring political counter-elite? Possibly student activists consider their union experience as training for a career in politics. The close relations between unions and opposition parties in Morocco suggest that the former could be avenues of leadership for the latter. It does not follow, however, that most aspiring student politicians are in a student union. Radical students, who are more likely than non-radicals to be union members, are also more likely than non-radicals to have political aspirations — whether or not they are union members. Not all union members are radical, nor are all radicals union members, even though union membership is the strongest single predictor of radicalism. Many non-member radicals, who are predominantly of a lower-class and parochial background, plan to join a party or trade union, but for reasons of class and style do not fit in with the predominantly middle-class and upper-class union membership. Moreover, student unions exercise less influence upon radicals than upon non-radicals. Not only does a higher proportion of lower-class students take an interest in politics and become radical, but proportionately more plan to go into politics of all sorts. Among lower-class students, it is mainly those who have been deprived of a French education who plan to become active in trade unions and parties. Though students with lower mobility expectations tend, independently of present class, to be less interested than others in politics, they also tend to be more radical and more likely to plan to become active. But neither mobility expectations nor job prospects appear directly to affect political plans. Possibly it is the student's political convictions which deter him from expecting to rise above his parents' social class.

Our survey data suggest that membership in a student union, more than any other single factor, is associated with interest in politics, radical attitudes, and future political aspirations. Although, for the purposes of analyzing our survey data, "radicalism" was defined to include the fifth of the sample displaying the most consistent left-wing attitudes and thus excluded two thirds of the union membership, it is clear from the historical record that UNEM plays a radical role in Moroccan politics. It politicizes the student and encourages his political ambitions more than any other university experience. We can also assume that students who play an active role in UNEM acquire greater political skills than those who remain aloof from the union. But our data further suggest (though better data are necessary to clarify this point) that the union does not attract and politically socialize all of the potential student activists who may revolutionize Morocco's future. UNEM does not seem to attract the lower-class, traditionally educated student of parochial small-town background who, with the government's policy of Arabization, is coming to the university in increasing numbers. Ironically, UNEM espouses hasty Arabization, but so far seems unable to absorb its uprooted products. Unless the union begins to recruit these radicals, it may find itself outflanked on the left as the new stratum finds other ways of developing political ambition and organizational skills. By absorbing them, UNEM could well set the style for a more vigorous left-wing opposition to the monarchy and infuse its political allies outside the university with new blood.

Tunisia. Although our survey data were collected before the student riots of December, 1966, it seemed pertinent to ask in light of subsequent events whether UGET was succeeding in its prime function: maintaining links of communication between students and elite, and serving as an agency of socialization, transmitting the elite's values to the future Tunisian elite.[10] Given the Tunisian political context, it makes sense to ask not whether UGET fosters or is associated with student radicalism, but whether the union contributes to the support of the ruling Neo-Destour Party.

Our data indicate that UGET is an important vehicle or channel for politically interested and ambitious students, but other factors are operative in Tunisia that are of less significance in Morocco. Contrary to our expectations, UGET does not appear to inculcate loyalty to the Party. Its primary importance lies in its training functions for future politicians. Political recruitment in Tunisia remains relatively open to students who are somewhat critical of the Party.

A student's home town and his faculty appear to be more important influences than UGET in stirring an interest in politics. As in Morocco, however, the more involved a student is in his union, the more likely he is to be interested in politics. Yet compared to the Moroccan cohorts, a higher proportion of Tunisian students outside the union, as well as a smaller proportion of leaders, express an interest in politics. Possibly they were already politicized in secondary school, to which the Destour has devoted considerably more organizational efforts than parties in Morocco. Unlike membership in a nonpolitical university organization, membership in high-school organizations of all sorts appears to contribute to a student's subsequent political interest. The student who has belonged to either the *Jeunesse Destourienne* or the *Jeunesse Scolaire,* two quasi-political organizations designed to attract the youth to the Neo-Destour Party, will be especially likely as a university student to be interested in politics and to join UGET. Significantly, too, he tends to be among the minority or university students who do not read French well. This suggests that the Party's youth organizations are especially successful among traditional sectors of high-school youth. The student's course of study has even greater effect than his extra-curricular ties, past or present, upon his interest in politics. Almost half of those who study law, a traditional steppingstone to a political career, are interested in politics, in contrast with only one quarter of those enrolled in other faculties.

Earlier influences — not only the youth organizations but also the student's regional and class background — may matter more than immediate nonacademic university experiences. One might expect students most interested in politics to come from the most politicized parts of the country — the capital, Tunis, and the Party's historic stronghold, the Sahil. These areas of the country experienced the earliest development of modern primary- and secondary-school education. But, in fact, the relatively sophisticated environments of Tunis breeds little political interest, whereas university students who come from less-developed parts of the country, where secondary-school education is a more recent phenomenon, are likely to be the most politicized. In Morocco, students from the relatively more backward parts of the country tend to be more radical but not more interested in politics than their fellow students; the reverse is true in Tunisia. While region appears more closely associated with political interest in Tunisia than in Morocco, class seems less so.

The most striking comparison between Tunisians and Moroccans concerns the impact of religion. In Morocco, nearly half of those who were not religious were interested in politics, in contrast to 9 per cent of the deeply religious. In Tunisia, 35 per cent of the non-religious and 27 per cent of the devout were interested. There are good grounds for believing that religiosity and politicization are, indeed, less interrelated in Tunisia than in Morocco. The break between traditional and modern concerns — so sharp in theocentric Moroccan society — was bridged in Tunisia by a modernizing nationalist movement, the Neo-Destour, which successfully translated religious zeal into the political concern for independence, and by an intellectual elite capable of living in two worlds and of articulating a national synthesis of modern French and traditional Tunisian values. Thus, to break with one's traditional faith is not, as in Morocco, to become lost in a new wilderness, yet keeping the faith is not inconsistent with sharing modern political concerns.

A large majority of Tunisian university students, including the most politicized, support the Neo-Destour Socialist Party without serious misgivings. More significantly, the 30 per cent of our sample that appeared unsympathetic to the Party does not appear to be more interested in politics than other students — in part, perhaps, because organizations that politicize people in single-party Tunisia also inculcate political loyalty.

Independently of all organizational ties, lower-class Tunisians still seem politically more reliable than upper-class people. They have a stronger basis for identifying with the sons of Sahil peasants who wield power, and the latter continue actively to cultivate and to rule in the interests of the masses, not the upper class. The relative significance of a student's discipline for predicting his loyalty seems more surprising; the "pure" theoretical disciplines may breed a certain intellectual detachment that inspires the students to play a Socratic role, whereas applied disciplines like law, theology, or business administration are less compatible with free, rational inquiry.

In Morocco, union membership is a powerful predictor of radicalism, whereas in Tunisia UGET seems to breed neither political conformity nor systematic opposition to the Party. It would appear that UGET, to which more than half our sample belonged, is more broadly representative of student opinion than UNEM. Its members and leaders are only slightly more likely than non-members to support the Party. Despite the close control exercised over UGET by the Party, many unionists, including some of the leaders, manage to keep their distance.

The *Jeunesse Destourienne* and the *Jeunesse Scolaire* are overwhelmingly important in inculcating Party loyalty. Thus, it would seem that the Party's decision in 1963 to expand these high-school student activities was a wise insurance policy against future political opposition from university students. In fact, the three fifths of union members who had belonged to these youth groups before entering the university are the Party's most loyal supporters. The youth groups have had their greatest impact upon Gallicized, lower-class students and upon non-Gallicized or traditional members of the upper class. Similarly, joining one or more of these groups in high school seems to have had more impact upon irreligious students — whose iconoclasm otherwise tends to reflect itself in political matters — than upon their more devout colleagues.

Within the different faculties of the university, the highest proportion of the Party's critics are in letters and science. Tunisia's educational system has perhaps been more successful in encouraging students to go into science than in politically socializing them; possibly the gap between technicians and the political bureaucracy will widen with economic and educational development.

Upper-class students, who are twice as likely to come from Tunis as elsewhere, appear significantly more disenchanted with the Party than their comrades from the lower classes. Exactly the reverse seems true in Morocco, where lower-class students are more likely to express radical attitudes connoting opposition to the regime. Differences in class outlook among students are undoubtedly related to differences in the social origins of the respective political elites. Upper-class Moroccan students tend more to identify with, or at least not to oppose, Morocco's rulers, who are also upper class. Upper-class Tunisians, on the other hand, learn from their fathers to distrust the lower-status politicians and agitators of the Neo-Destour who displaced the old *Tunisois* elite during the struggle for independence. Neo-Destour economic planning, too, hurts upper-class interests. Possibly the fathers of upper-class students have greater influence than do lower-status fathers upon the attitudes of their children; significantly fewer sons of the *bourgeoisie* belong to Neo-Destour youth groups or join UGET.

Apparently union membership has a greater impact upon the political ambitions of middle- and upper-class students than upon those of their lower-class colleagues — the latter in any case being highly interested in future political participation. Membership in UGET also appears to affect students of differing linguistic and geographical background in different ways. UGET members who speak French poorly are much more likely to have political ambitions than their non-Gallicized brethren who are not members. Membership also seems to have a greater impact upon the ambitions of rural boys than upon those of their *Tunisois* colleagues.

Curiously, Tunisian law students, who are both more likely to be interested in politics and to support the Party, are not very much more politically ambitious than students of other faculties. Nor are students who consider themselves to be "intellectuals" significantly more ambitious than vocationally or scientifically oriented students, unless they are members of UGET. This finding suggests that UGET may be especially important as an avenue of political recruitment for the self-styled "intellectuals."

Tunisian and Moroccan students differ markedly in their attitudes toward the relative importance of professional (or technical) competence and "pull" in attaining success in their work. Sixty-one per cent of all Tunisian students and only 39 per cent of Moroccan students think competence a more essential ingredient than "pull." At first glance, such attitudes appear to be unrelated to plans to go into politics, possibly because many upper-class Tunisians who are critical of the Party and place personal contacts above professional competence are not politically ambitious.

While the vast majority of Tunisian students feel that competence and not "pull" wins rewards, the minority of the Party's supporters who disagree are precisely those who plan to go into politics. In Morocco, on the other hand, the majority of students think "pull" is more important, and attitudes toward the qualities that earn career rewards are unrelated to a student's plans to go into politics.

Prospective political activists appear to be fairly evenly distributed among students of different social class and regional background. If anything, lower-class students are slightly more likely (44 per cent) to want to go into politics than middle- (42 per cent) or upper-class students (37 per cent), but the differences are very small. The same holds true for students from different geographic regions; 38 per cent of the *Tunisois* and Sahilians and 44 per cent of students from other regions plan to enter politics at the local or national level. On the other hand, deeply religious students are more likely to plan to go into politics than are non-religious students. Half of the highly religious but only a third of the non-religious students plan to become politically active. Religiosity is strongly associated with political ambitions only among students who come from Tunis. In Morocco, by contrast, the most religious students were the least likely to become politically active.

Even after ten years of increasing subordination to the Party, UGET attracts and encourages most of the politically ambitious students. It does not transform them into subservient Party hacks, nor does it, like UNEM, help to radicalize them. More than any other student experience, it seems to train the responsible political cadres constantly sought by Bourguiba and his Party. UGET's "bad" reputation as a springboard for political careers is perhaps also its major strength for the regime, in that the union continues to attract a disproportionate share of potential political talent.

Our Tunisian data have emphasized, however, that UGET is not the only organization that politicizes and socializes new student generations in this highly structured political system. In Morocco today, a modernizing elite, with forebears in the UNFP and other opposition parties, is apparently being shaped in part by UNEM. Conditions are comparable to those of Tunisia in the thirties, in that students and graduates of middle- and lower-class backgrounds are attempting to replace a decaying traditional elite.

Thus, as members of the lower classes are given increased educational opportunities, it may be possible for UNEM, in close cooperation with other political forces, to spark radical change. In Morocco, the student union politicizes, radicalizes, and instills political ambitions in its members more than any other student experience, but UNEM will have to make a concerted effort to attract the parochial, lower-class radicals into its fold if its revolutionary efforts are to be ultimately successful. The Moroccan student radicals of today come from more diverse social and cultural backgrounds than the French-educated Tunisian intellectuals of the thirties.

In countries like Tunisia or Algeria today, where political elites have broken with tradition and share an interest in rapid social change, the problems and aspirations of students become more complex. Once a social revolution has occurred — as it did gradually in Tunisia and violently in Algeria — students are no longer a self-conscious and isolated stratum with a unique interest in radical change. Student movements can no longer systematically politicize and radicalize their rank and file because there are no longer revolutions to perform, only the mundane tasks of implementing reforms. The Algerians remain disorganized, having not yet recovered from the crises of 1962 that fragmented the country's political infrastructure. But UGET suggests the roles a student movement can play in an established one-party system. It is not an exclusive organization, open only to the Party faithful, but rather a political arena that attracts large segments of potential political talent. Other experiences, especially in secondary school, seem more important in shaping a Tunisian's attitudes toward the ruling Party. Unlike the *Komsomol* or other student organizations in more rigid, ideological one-party states, UGET does not systematically indoctrinate students. Rather, allowing diversity and training the politically ambitious, the union helps the Party — though obviously not enough — to remain adaptable and responsive to the aspirations of new political generations.

The authors wish to acknowledge their gratitude for the generous support of the Institute of International Studies of the University of California, Berkeley, and the Center for International Affairs of Harvard University, and for the advice of Seymour Martin Lipset and Glaucio Soares and the research assistance of Metta Spencer. A revised and expanded version of this article appears in William J. Hanna (ed.), *Students and Politics in Africa* (forthcoming).

377

REFERENCES

1. Henry J. Benda, "Non-Western Intelligentsias as Political Elites," *Political Change in Underdeveloped Countries*, ed. J. H. Kautsky (New York, 1962), pp. 237ff.

2. By 1931–32, there were 11 Moroccans, 21 Algerians, and 119 Tunisians studying in French universities, according to a document of AEMNA cited by Monccef Dellagi in an unpublished manuscript.

3. It is difficult to find comparable figures. Helen Kitchen (ed.), *The Educated African* (New York, 1962), indicates that 261 Moroccans were studying in France in 1951-52. According to the *Statistical Yearbook for the Moroccan French Zone*, 250 Moroccans obtained the second baccalaureat, qualifying them to enter university, between 1952 and 1955. The Tunisian and Algerian figures are cited by Kitchen. According to *L'Algérie de Demain* (Paris, 1962), 589 Muslims studied at the University of Algiers in 1954–55; in an unpublished manuscript, David Ottaway claims there were 520 in May, 1956, when the French Ministry of Algeria, in *1957 Algérie*, claimed 686.

4. As the president of UGEMA explained: "It is not possible to understand the action and objectives of UGEMA unless they are placed in the framework of the national liberation struggle our people have been waging for the past six years. It is easy then to realize that all the specifically student and university problems are radically transformed by the givens of the colonial war imposed upon our people. By this fact, these problems become subordinate and contingent, yielding to the absolute imperatives dictated by the combat occurring on our soil." *IVe Congrès National de l'UGEMA* (26 July–1 August, 1960), p. 20.

5. The student union also included a strong Communist minority, among them two of the Executive Committee members drafted in 1966. The political resolution of the Eleventh Congress closely echoed the Moroccan Communist Party by calling for "unity of action" of "progressive and national forces."

6. Our Moroccan survey data have serious limitations. Of the original sample of 500, which drastically under-represented law and letters students, only 125 (25 per cent) answered the self-administered questionnaire, while 15 per cent could not be located, and the remaining 60 per cent refused to answer. The poor rate of response was due, in part, to the lack of experience of the Moroccan team that carried out the survey in the spring of 1964, and to the uneasy political atmosphere, even before the Ben Barka affair, at the university.

7. In the autumn of 1962, only seven students at the University of Algiers were members of the FLN, according to David Ottaway, whose extremely informative article on Algerian students is to be published in a volume on student movements edited by Donald Emmerson.

8. For lack of space, the numerical data have been cut from this article, though they exist in an earlier and lengthier draft to be published elsewhere. Our method for generating data substantiating the above proposition and similar ones below was that of "least squares," which estimates the independent effects of each of several variables upon a dependent variable, such as "interest in politics." For a description of this method, see Alan B. Wilson, "Analysis of Multiple Cross-Classifications in Cross-Sectional Designs," presented to the American Association for Public Opinion Research, Excelsior Springs, Missouri (May 9, 1964). Also see L. N. Hazel, "The Covariance Analysis of Multiple Classification Tables with Unequal Subclass Numbers," *Biometrics*, Vol. 11 (April, 1964), pp. 21–25; Frank Yates, "The Analysis of Multiple Classifications with Unequal Numbers in the Different Classes," *Journal of the American Statistical Association*, Vol. 29 (March, 1934), pp. 5–55. "Interest in politics" reflects high scores on the amount of time the student talked about national and international politics and his preference for being a politician rather than an academician, given that choice.

9. We designated as "radical" the 20 per cent of our sample who felt that foreign capital on the whole has bad effects, that the government should take full control of the Moroccan economy, and that economic inequalities should be reduced. These attitudes are more or less shared by the UNFP and other left-wing opposition groups.

10. Our Tunisian data are much more reliable that the Moroccan data. In the spring of 1965, when the survey was conducted, there were no political obstacles to scholarly research at the university. Moreover, an experienced sociologist of the university's Center for Economic and Social Studies and Research methodically directed the sampling and data collection. Replacements were anticipated for the many who could not be located and the 8 per cent of the original sample of 500 who refused to answer the questionnaire.

DAVID J. FINLAY

Students and Politics in Ghana

UNIVERSITY STUDENTS in Ghana, like those in other developing
nations, are an incipient elite destined to hold political power in the
future.[1] Their role in politics has, however, been unlike that of their
counterparts in many developing nations where students have been
a significant force in making or breaking governments. After independence, Ghana experienced rapid educational expansion within
an increasingly authoritarian political system. A conflict developed
after 1959 between the relatively new and elitist university system
and the government as the political regime questioned the purpose
of education and sought to destroy university autonomy. This
process is not unique to Ghana. Nevertheless, Ghana is a particularly interesting case of confrontation politics because the government, rather than the students, assumed the initiative. Thus,
Ghanaian university students — a comparatively small and homogeneous group — were both spectators and secondary participants in
the conflict growing out of competing demands of nationalism and
university autonomy.

I

Africans have viewed education both as the key to the successes
Europeans have achieved and as a primary means for African
advancement. But it was not until after World War II, when
Ghanaians began to play a major role in the government of the Gold
Coast, that rapid expansion in public education took place.[2] Since
1950, education has been one of the largest single items in the
national budget. Access to education was increased by removing
primary school fees in 1952, by introducing compulsory primary
education in 1961, and by providing scholarships for virtually all
students in the universities.[3]

There are three institutions of higher education in Ghana — the University of Ghana at Legon, the University of Science and Technology at Kumasi, and the University College of Cape Coast. Total enrollment in the three universities was 4286 for the 1965–66 academic year, and some 3410 Ghanaians were studying in other countries (1991 in the United Kingdom or the United States).

The University of Ghana, the nation's oldest and most prestigious institution, was founded in 1948 as University College of the Gold Coast upon the recommendations of the Asquith Commission in 1945.[4] By means of a special relationship, the University of London assisted University College with academic planning. Students were awarded London degrees until October, 1961, when University College assumed fully independent university status as the University of Ghana. Although the university reflects its British heritage, it is no longer merely a British institution in Africa. In recent years, it has made progress toward Africanizing the curricula and in meeting Ghana's special training needs through the creation of Schools of Administration and Medicine, and Institutes of African Studies, Statistics, and Post Basic Nursing.

The university has grown from ninety students in 1948 to slightly over two thousand today. Its student body is largely male despite an increase in the proportion of women students from 2.8 per cent in 1953–54 to 12.5 per cent in 1965–66. The small number of women students is creditable in light of the traditional emphasis on the education of sons rather than daughters and the considerable preponderance of men in secondary schools.

The faculty at the University of Ghana has been predominantly British, although the number of other nationalities represented on the faculty has increased since 1961. Africanization of the teaching staff has been gradual. Africans constituted 13 per cent of the total teaching staff in 1959–60, but 47 per cent in 1965–66. The over-all competence of the staff is difficult to judge. Although some faculty members have international reputations, others are considerably less competent and qualified. While the ratio of faculty to students has always been high, the university found it increasingly difficult to recruit expatriate faculty after 1961, when relations with the West became strained and national politics intruded into university affairs. As a result, many senior positions were left unfilled, and, in a few instances, persons were hired whose applications had previously been rejected.

Despite Ghana's progress toward realizing a system of mass education, entrance into the university is a privilege enjoyed by relatively few young people in Ghana. (Out of every 420 who start school in Ghana, one succeeds in reaching the universities.) The base of university recruitment has broadened in recent years, primarily as a result of the expansion of the entire educational system. The university is accessible to all qualified applicants through open competition, and 90 per cent of the students are provided with bursaries or scholarships.

Although the range of socio-economic backgrounds among Legon students is broad, a disproportionate number come from urban, high-income, educated families. According to Ghana's 1960 census, for example, 23.1 per cent of the population live in urban areas of five thousand or more, whereas a 1966 student sample indicates that 69.4 per cent of Legon students are from urban localities (with 27.4 per cent coming from Accra). In 1965, per-capita gross national product was estimated to be $230, and average yearly wages (in establishments employing ten or more persons) to be $664. Sixty per cent of the 302 students responding to a question about their father's income judged it to be in excess of $995 per year. Although most university students have far surpassed their parents' educational attainments, their parents have more education than the general population (76 per cent of which was classified as illiterate in the 1960 census). As a whole, Legon students are from relatively high socio-economic backgrounds, although Ghana's social stratification is closer to a "semi-open status system" than to a class hierarchy.[5]

Unbalanced enrollments among the faculties at the university have caused concern among both government and university officials. The proportion of students in the sciences and agriculture has declined steadily since 1953. In 1965–66, there were 1238 undergraduates enrolled in the faculties of arts, law, and social sciences, compared with 325 in science, agriculture, and medicine.[6]

In terms of career plans, arts, science, and agriculture students are primarily oriented toward teaching, social-science students toward government, and law students toward legal practice. Virtually all university students on scholarships are bonded to teach or work in government for a while after graduation; apart from that, career expectations reflect a growing diversity of choices, increasing demand for professionally-trained personnel, and expanding training facilities at the university. As career opportunities have widened, teaching and government — the traditional careers of educated persons — have declined slightly in popularity. Five samples taken between 1953 and 1966 show that students are increasingly interested in what they consider to be more desirable professions — law, medicine, research, university teaching, and executive and managerial positions. Correlations between age and career choice also point up changing occupational preferences. With the median age at twenty-four in the 1966 sample, 62 per cent of the students over thirty planned teaching careers, those between twenty-four and twenty-nine were split between teaching and the professions, and the largest cluster of those under twenty-three was in the professions. A student's career choice also reflects his socio-economic background. For example, in the 1966 study, the proportion of students planning teaching careers increased markedly with decreases in the degree of urban residence and the education and income of the father. Teachers seem to be recruited from lower socio-economic levels, whereas students from homes where the father has at least some secondary education and a relatively high income expect to launch careers in the "higher" professions.

Since Ghanaian students are an elite whose skills are badly needed, they have always been optimistic about their future opportunities. They are decidedly career oriented, and this orientation is paralleled by an overwhelming preoccupation with attaining a university degree, the key to mobility and success. Certain aspects of the university reinforce the students' focus on degree and career. The university staff has always insisted that Legon be a "house of study" with high academic standards. Consequently, extracurricular and political activities have been discouraged. The campus was located outside Accra, in part to minimize student involvement in politics and other "distracting" activities.

Student life at the university centers around residence halls, each of which maintains an independent system of internal government. The importance of these halls in influencing the character of the university should not be underestimated. This decentralization impeded the development of all-campus student groups, particularly during the university's early years. Nevertheless, in 1953 students organized the National Union of Gold Coast Students, a weak vehicle for student opinion. That organization was succeeded in 1958 by the National Union of Ghana Students (NUGS), which provided a link with the other universities in Ghana and with student organizations abroad. During the 1960's, student government was strengthened by more campus-wide coordination through a Student Representative Council. Organizations of the Convention People's Party (CPP) catering to students both off and on the campus existed for some time, and in 1964 the Party created the Ghana National Students' Organization as a rival to and replacement for NUGS. But Legon lacked a tradition of student activism both on the campus and in national politics, especially in its early years. Being without the deep-seated dissatisfaction with the *status quo* that often leads to political militancy, students at Legon have been inclined to accept the system.

The university has been authoritarian, at least by American standards, both in structure and in staff attitudes. Status distinctions between faculty and students (maintained originally by such rituals as high and low dining tables, separate seating in chapel, and, in Sir Eric Ashby's words, other "fripperies of British academic life"[7]) have slowly diminished over time. The faculty still regulates student conduct, however, and virtually all sanctions reside with university authorities. Dissatisfactions that have arisen at Legon have been circumscribed and fragmented by the decentralized organization of the university and its authoritarian character. While a similarly authoritarian institution in another society might provoke student activism, the strong Ghanaian tradition of deference to authority has mitigated against student hostility and protest. The sense of political efficacy has been low among Ghanaian students, and student leadership has been slow to develop. The distance between faculty and students, however, has never been so great as the gap between the university and the larger society. In their relations with each other, both the university and Ghanaian society have had difficulties communicating with, being understood by, and understanding the other.

II

After independence in 1957, Nkrumah used increasingly harsh repressive measures, including preventive detention, to whittle away the existing competitive political system and to quiet dissent. Independent organizations, such as trade unions and newspapers, were either brought within the Party structure as auxiliary organizations, neutralized, or destroyed. As a result, by 1961 the Party was virtually unchallenged in Ghana, and the University at Legon was one of the few major institutions that retained an autonomous character. Thus, conflict between the university and the CPP was perhaps inevitable, as the Party sought to mobilize the entire society within its own ideological framework.

The Party's philosophy of socialist egalitarianism conflicted sharply with the university's devotion to principles of meritocracy. But a much more important issue in the government-university confrontation concerned differing conceptions of the university. Tradition at Legon emphasized the *universalistic* nature of the university — a community of scholars pursuing knowledge in a center for learning, research, and innovation that looked beyond national considerations and loyalties. The university's conception of itself as an independent institution was reinforced by its constitution, which "guaranteed" autonomy from outside control. By contrast, the CPP viewed the university in *nationalistic* terms, stressing its obligations and responsibilities to society. The CPP claimed the university did not adequately recognize its obligations to Ghana's social needs and, more importantly, that students and faculty were hostile to the Party and, therefore, to the society. Party militants felt the university should give more attention to civic education and the training of "good" and "loyal" citizens, which — translated — meant supporters of Nkrumah and the CPP. Because the differing assumptions about the role of a university were not clearly focused, communication between the Party and Legon was difficult. Attempts by the Party to change the university and to mobilize student support were viewed by Legon as attacks on academic freedom. Conversely, in the minds of the Party stalwarts, defense of academic freedom at the university reflected a neo-colonialist mentality that had no place in the African Revolution.

Major differences in social composition and world views underlay the overt issues on which the conflict centered. In fact, the crux of conflict might be said to lodge in the mutual personal distrust each group felt for the values and life style of the other. In its early years, the top CPP leadership represented a marginal and decidedly nonintellectual sector of Ghanaian society, while the opposition parties were led largely by Ghana's educated elite and tribal leaders.[8] Although a number of well-educated men associated themselves with the CPP in later years, a certain anti-intellectualism persisted in Party attitudes and ideology. The Party argued that too many Ghanaians at Legon accepted alien values and social customs, and that Ghana needed experts to serve their own country, not intellectuals with foreign ideas.

On the other hand, the university community tended to resent the power of the semiliterates in the Party. They opposed the deification of Nkrumah as the font of wisdom and refused to take seriously the hodgepodge of ideas that passed as "Nkrumaism." The faculty wanted both the right to speak out on national issues when they wished and, at the same time, the privilege of remaining independent of all Party constraints. To the Party militants, this desire to have it both ways was academic irresponsibility in the name of academic freedom. University attitudes were incomprehensible to the Party and, therefore, considered disloyal.

Relations between the Party and the university remained cool but formally cordial until 1959 when Nkrumah delivered a speech celebrating the CPP's tenth anniversary. He accused the universities of not "pulling their weight" in national development and of being a "breeding ground for unpatriotic and anti-government elements." He then threatened:

We do not intend to sit idly by and see these institutions, which are supported by millions of pounds produced by the sweat and toil of the common people, continue to be centres of anti-government activities. We want the University College to cease being an alien institution. . . . If reforms do not come from within, we intend to impose them from outside, and no resort to the cry of academic freedom (for academic freedom does not mean academic irresponsibility) is going to restrain us from seeing that our University is a healthy Ghanaian University devoted to Ghanaian interests.

It is intolerable that we should be training people, most of whom will eventually come into Government service, who will be permeated with an anti-Government attitude, that is to say an anti-Convention People's Party attitude, for our Party forms the Government and will continue to do so for many a long day to come. How can these people serve loyally the Government and the State?[9]

The Party continued to voice similar accusations and warnings, but the first major effort toward carrying out "reforms" came as the university was ending its special relationship with the University of London. In May, 1961, a memo from Nkrumah to the university stated that "all appointments of members of the academic staff [would] automatically be terminated" when the association with the University of London ended.[10] The university community interpreted the order as a direct effort by the Party to establish political control at Legon and to dismiss staff members it considered undesirable. Although the directive was deeply resented, the appointments of one Ghanaian and five European staff members were terminated. Soon afterwards, Nkrumah appointed a number of CPP stalwarts to the governing University Council. In his first address as the University's new Chancellor, he emphasized that colonial ideas and practices would not be tolerated and that a major task of the universities would be to further "complete mental emancipation and the education of the miseducated [so] that we can achieve . . . rapid transformation."[11]

Efforts were also made to entice students into Party organizations.

> The future of Ghana depends upon the youth, and if the Party is to achieve any worthwhile results by making sure of the future national trend, then it must take positive steps to inculcate in the minds of the nation's youth the ideology of the Party. Only by this way can we envisage the continuity of our line of thought and action long after many of us are gone.[12]

Nkrumah believed that the reshaping of future Legon students could only be accomplished if new generations of students received adequate training at a much earlier state in their education. Thus, many of the "reforms" dealt only indirectly with the university. In 1960, Nkrumah dissolved the National Youth Council and established the Young Pioneer Movement, which was to inculcate youth with the ideology of Nkrumaism and to serve as a training ground for future Party members. To further ideological education, the Party somewhat unsuccessfully attempted to pressure secondary-school headmasters into organizing Young Pioneer branches in the schools and teaching Nkrumaism in the curricula. In 1961, the Kwame Nkrumah Ideological Institute was established, and all youth organizations were consolidated under the control of the Ghana Youth Authority. Other youth programs affecting university students, such as a national training scheme, were promulgated, but never got far beyond the blueprint stage.

Party attacks on the university persisted despite the initial good will that accompanied the appointment of Conor Cruise O'Brien as Vice-Chancellor in 1962. Party organizers continued their efforts to entice students into CPP Study Groups and the university CPP branch, but they succeeded only in increasing and intensifying silent hostility among the majority of students and faculty. In the fall of 1963, Nkrumah openly attacked expatriate lecturers,[13] and Party publications began a series of articles "exposing" the universities, primarily Legon. Aside from creating an aura of fear at the university, however, these harassments achieved little. Although a few students courageously complained publicly of being "cowed into silence on every issue affecting national life,"[14] most university students deftly learned to separate their public utterances from their private views.

Tensions between the Party and the university began coming to a head in 1964 as a result of confrontations over the treason trials and the referendum on the one-party state. In December, 1963, three principal defendants charged with terrorism and the 1962 Kulungugu attempt on Nkrumah's life were acquitted by a Special Court. In anger, Nkrumah dismissed the chief magistrate of the Special Court, who also happened to be Chief Justice of the Supreme Court, and shortly thereafter declared the verdict null and void using an amendment to the law of Criminal Procedure passed by the National Assembly. NUGS issued a resolution condemning Nkrumah for the dismissal and for political interference with the judiciary. That resolution was followed in January, 1964, by another, protesting the deportation orders served on six senior faculty members at Legon. A student demonstration to protest the deportations was dispersed in its early stages by club-swinging policemen, and thereafter the government closed all three universities for seventeen days, allegedly to allow students to return home to vote in the upcoming referendum on a one-party state. The students believed, however, that the shutdown was merely a ruse to intimidate and disperse university-based opposition to the referendum. Again NUGS protested, and it appeared as though a few student leaders were ready to challenge the government. Leadership from NUGS was short-lived, however, for after the referendum the Party retaliated.

The Party press charged that the universities had become "the fountainheads of reaction and fertile grounds for imperialism and neo-colonialist subversion and counterrevolution."[15] The government then arrested five student leaders, detained one prominent senior faculty member, brought others in for questioning, and warned expatriates to "bow out of the scene" if they found the situation "distasteful."[16] Yet even with the university under full attack, the fear of preventive detention deterred the faculty from rising to its own defense. Silence at Legon was broken only by O'Brien's spirited defense of academic freedom at the 1964 spring convocation. Through the pages of The Spark, the Party replied that not O'Brien, Greece in general, Socrates in particular, nor any other "spiritual talk" about academic freedom had anything to teach them about the proper role of a university.[17]

New assaults on Legon included developing Party cadre leaders at the university, establishing CPP student publications, requiring all entering students to take a two-week "orientation" course at the Ideological Institute, announcing that all scholarships would be reviewed annually on the basis of good performance and good conduct, and, with great fanfare, "inaugurating" (reconstituting) CPP branches in the universities. Students as a whole were told to "watch out for, systematically expose and vigorously combat the academic imperialism of expatriate lecturers as well as the intellectual obscurantism of some African academicians."[18] Student governments in the halls were "encouraged" to adopt one-party systems to be in harmony with the national system; student organizations such as the Marxist Forum were virtually forced to merge with the Nkrumaist Forum. Nkrumah appointed an Inspection Committee to survey all bookshops and libraries, review their book orders, check their holdings, and remove publications not reflecting Party ideology or antagonistic to its ideals. With the chartering of the Ghana National Students' Organization at a conference appropriately convened at the Ideological Institute, NUGS was dealt a last but unnecessary blow, since the organization had virtually ceased to function after the arrest of several of its leaders. One interviewed student candidly described conditions at the university after the Party campaign:

We are fed "Nkrumah" for breakfast, lunch and dinner. "Nkrumah à la mode" is not tasty and lacks essential vitamins, but it is the only food we can get, even though it gives us indigestion.

By 1965, the Party had organized an espionage system at the university using paid Party plants. At the 1965 spring convocation, O'Brien reported "with sorrow" that respect for the university's constitution and academic freedom had reached a low point.

A strange and erroneous idea has grown up that the encouragement of critical and independent thought is a colonialist or neo-colonialist scheme whereas the enforcement of intellectual conformity is anti-colonial and conducive to the freedom and unity of Africa. The reverse of this is surely true.[19]

At the expiration of his contract in July, 1965, O'Brien left Ghana. William Abraham, a Nkrumah devotee and chairman of the Inspection Committee, was made Pro-Vice Chancellor and received a new Jaguar car from Nkrumah.

The university had been brought to its knees. Yet there were indications that the Party planned more than simple control over the university. At the beginning of the 1965–66 academic year, the Ministry of Science and Higher Education transmitted to the university a report on suggestions for reform. Among the recommendations were provisions for enlarging the role of the Legon Party branch by developing Party sections in faculties and departments, giving the branch voting representation in all elected university organs, and creating the position of a full-time Party Secretary to help the Vice-Chancellor implement "progressive reforms."[20]

A CPP university was in the offing, but on February 24, 1966, Nkrumah was ousted from power through the combined efforts of Ghana's army and police, and the CPP was declared a prohibited organization. Legon immediately came to life. Students sacked the Party branch headquarters, physically beat several CPP activists, and then marched through Accra clad in academic gowns to demonstrate support for the National Liberation Council. The academic community, as a whole, spoke of the Council in the most glowing terms, for they saw themselves as prime beneficiaries of the coup.

The initial harmony between Legon and Ghana's new rulers continued in the first two years after the coup, in part because of the involvement of prominent faculty members on commissions and advisory bodies of the new regime, but also because of the new freedom in Ghana as a whole. Yet, as might be expected under a military-police regime, the government and the intellectuals had their differences. While supporting the NLC, students and faculty alike criticized the government on issues ranging from a kind of arbitrariness they found too reminiscent of the Nkrumah era to policy questions such as a contract with Abbott Laboratories to assume management of the State Pharmaceutical Corporation. When the *Legon Observer,* a biweekly forum of opinion created primarily by University of Ghana faculty, complained about the slowness with which the judiciary heard cases, twenty-nine persons associated with the journal were fined for contempt of court in January, 1968. These incidents marked the first major clash between the government and the intellectuals at a time when sentiment for return to civilian rule was growing.

III

A description of the nature of the University of Ghana and selected events in the confrontation between university and polity serves to present the context against which the role of students in Ghanaian politics must be assessed. Yet the students themselves must be considered, for their political roles are also by-products of individual levels of politicization, of ideology, and of legitimacy orientation — parameters of individual behavior intimately related to the nature of the educational and political systems in Ghana.

Politicization

Politicization refers to a continuum of individual awareness and involvement in politics and government extending from nonperception of the relevance of politics to one's own life, through perception, to active involvement. Thus, political roles may range from perceptually nonrelated to highly participant.[21] On the whole, Ghanaian students sampled in 1963 and 1966 evidenced a rather high degree of politicization at the perceptual level.[22] For example, over half characterized themselves as "actively" or "very" interested in politics, whereas only 8 per cent and 12 per cent respectively felt indifferent or not interested. About 18 per cent in both samples stated they intended to participate in politics after leaving the university; 52 per cent in 1963 and 37 per cent in 1966 said they would be candidates for public office if they had the opportunity. In addition, students exhibited considerable knowledge of public affairs. These measures of politicization indicate that students were attuned to the political world.

In light of Ghana's fluid social structure, it is not surprising that social backgrounds do not determine politicization. The most significant correlates of politicization are the faculty with which the student is associated and the degree toward which he is working. In 1966, the faculty of social sciences had the largest proportion of highly politicized students. It was followed by arts, law, science, and agriculture. The School of Administration and the Institute of African Studies included a greater proportion with low politicization scores. Students working toward B.Sc. (economics) and B.A. (honors) degrees tended to be highly politicized, in sharp contrast to students working toward certificates.[23]

Both the historical record and the survey data show that students have generally been perceptually-related nonparticipants in politics. In 1963, those who did participate were generally affiliated with the CPP, either through membership or intention to join. On the other hand, the fear of sanction and the vulnerability of those who rejected the CPP dictated acquiescent and inactive roles rather than oppositional activity. Thus, the 1963 politicization index was slanted in favor of CPP sympathizers not because they demonstrated greater perceptual politicization, but because participatory roles were open

to them. Although perceptual and activity components of politicization were in alignment in 1966, measures of actual involvement and
activity (in contrast to intended participation) were not possible
because "politics" was banned at the time of the sample.

Ideology

A high degree of consensus is the most pronounced characteristic
of the political views of Ghanaian students. Virtually all Legon
students adhere to a liberal-democratic philosophy. The slight variation among them depends upon, for example, relative emphases on
socialism or capitalism, and neutralism or alignment. The intense
left-right polarizations common among Latin American students
simply do not exist among Legon students. What differences do exist
center on social norms (means) and on particular issues rather than
on social values (ultimate ends).

This consensus on basic economic and political principles was
illustrated in 1966 by the students' attitudes toward foreign capital
and the role of government in the economy, items often used to distinguish left-right divisions. Eighty-five per cent of the responding
students felt that foreign capital brings more benefits than evils to
Ghana (6 per cent held it brought more evils than benefits). At the
extremes, 8 per cent saw only benefits and 2 per cent only evils.
Regarding the economic role of government, 78 per cent thought the
government should not only supervise the economic life of the country, but should own the basic industries. Only three students endorsed complete control of economic life by the state, and only
fifteen felt the government should abstain from all intervention.

Ideological consensus tends to reduce ideological thinking.
Political competition and debate, which might have heightened the
students' ideological consciousness, was almost nonexistent for five
years prior to the coup. Nor does it appear that ideological consciousness was intensified by disagreements with family or friends,
for most students reported high levels of agreement with others on
political issues.

Nevertheless, consensus has obviously not existed on all issues.
In 1963, attitudes toward the CPP constituted a major area of disagreement. Students' relationships to the CPP (member or non-
member) correlated with an additive index of items reflecting support or dissent from government policies and positive or negative
views of the government itself.

Table 1:
Party Classification and Index of Support or
Dissent from Government, 1963

| | Supporters* | | Dissenters* | |
Party Classification**	%	N	%	N
Party	71.4	(35)	28.6	(14)
Ambivalents	61.2	(30)	38.8	(19)
Non-Party	22.5	(18)	77.5	(62)
Totals	46.6	(83)	53.4	(95)

*No respondent received an index score unless he answered all items. Thus the "*n*" is 178 rather than 206.

**Party members are those who were currently members (45) or intended to join (14); ambivalents are non-Party members who were uncertain of their intention to join or remain outside (60); and non-Party are those non-members who were certain of their intention not to join (87).

The totals suggest a rather even distribution of student sympathies. Differences between Party and non-Party groups dealt primarily with regime evaluation, legitimacy orientations, and particular issues, such as the Preventive Detention Act. On international issues, such as coexistence and the efficacy of neutralism, Party membership made little difference, although some CPP Cold-War positions, such as support for Castro, were reflected in the responses of student Party members. On the whole, Legon students tended to view most issues pragmatically and to judge them individually and independently — quite apart from the tenets of Nkrumaism or any other ideological line, even though their political vocabulary was consistent with the language of African nationalism.

Students who professed commitment to socialism in the 1966 questionnaire included both the younger and the more highly politicized; they also tended to be from upper-income and more highly-educated families. The relationship between social-class characteristics and congruence with socialist ideology is still more pronounced. Although the vast majority of students judged their lives to be "better" or "much better" than their fathers', those who thought their lives were the "same" or "worse" were more likely to adopt a socialist ideology. The upwardly mobile and relatively less well-to-do students, who by virtue of their educational attainments are almost assured of future success, predictably have relatively conservative views toward the social and economic changes associated with socialism. Among the majority of students, politicization does not have ideological direction, other than an implicit acceptance of the fluid *status quo.*

The constant barrage of CPP propaganda before 1966 did, however, affect ideological socialization. Even after the coup, students with positive attitudes toward socialism assessed Nkrumah more favorably and were more inclined to accept the major tenets of Nkrumaism than were their nonsocialist colleagues. Yet even students who professed to be socialists had ambiguous attitudes toward social change and reform. For example, 76 per cent of the sample agreed that it is never wise to introduce changes rapidly in government and the economic order, but 47 per cent agreed that the government should introduce a program of rapid economic development even if it would result in great sacrifices for the population during the early years of its implementation.

Student commitment to democratic politics remains undetermined. In 1966, all students were looking for strong leadership, and students' political philosophies appeared, at least at the forensic level, to be mixtures of pragmatism and a welfare-state ideology.

Legitimacy Orientations

Evaluations of the political regime in power varied considerably in the two studies. In 1963, 43 per cent of the students agreed that a majority of Ghanaians supported the CPP, yet only 27 per cent thought that the government represented the will of the people. Students who were not Party members and did not intend to join were strongly negative toward the government, and even Party members showed considerable division in their evaluations of the legitimacy of Nkrumah's regime (59 per cent agreed that the CPP had majority support, and 49 per cent felt the government represented the will of the people). As Table 1 indicates, 28 per cent of the Party members dissented from government policy positions, which suggests that for some students, at least, Party membership did not necessarily mean support for CPP programs. In view of these responses, it seems fair to conclude that the CPP enjoyed only minority support at Legon. Attitudinal congruity between students and the political elite was low, yet students did not perceive themselves as "anti-government."[24] The 1966 sample produced reverse findings: 96 per cent felt the NLC had the support of the majority of Ghanaians, and 93 per cent said they personally approved of the Council's actions and policies.

Students in both samples were asked to evaluate the existing regime's record of protection of civil liberties. In 1963, 76 per cent of the sample rated the protection of civil liberties under the Nkrumah government as "fair" or "poor," and only 5 per cent considered it "excellent" or "good." Eighty-six per cent felt that freedom of the press did not exist in Ghana, and 61 per cent held negative views on the Preventive Detention Act (13 per cent were positive). Those who did hold more positive views of the regime's record on civil liberties tended to be Party members, but even their evaluations were largely negative. For example, only 29 per cent of the Party group viewed the Detention Act affirmatively. After the coup, the protection of civil liberties was rated "good" or "excellent" by 54 per cent of the sample, "satisfactory" by 31 per cent, and "fair" or "poor" by 14 per cent. Seventy-one per cent felt freedom of the press existed in Ghana.

A majority of students in both samples held negative views about politics and politicians, particularly about Ghanaian politicians. These attitudes undoubtedly reflect the students' knowledge of and experience with the Nkrumah regime. New experience that might alter student opinion of politics and politicians may come with time and the restoration of civilian government. The 1966 sample was taken too soon after the coup for any such new political experience to have modified students' attitudes. In post-coup assessments of the Nkrumah regime, 87 per cent of the students agreed that Nkrumah was a tyrant, 34 per cent that he was an able president, and 25 per cent that he was both a tyrant and an able president.

Student Activism

On the basis of past behavior, one would expect future student political activism in Ghana to center on particular issues rather than questions of broad social values, and to be fragmentary and transitory rather than extensive and sustained. Before 1964, students had voiced complaints to the government on specific issues, such as the renaming of the University in Kumasi as Kwame Nkrumah University of Science and Technology. With each successive CPP attack on the university and their own status, students directly and indirectly made their feelings known. At times, these feelings were expressed through hostility to Party representatives — even to Nkrumah himself — and at other times through sarcastic rebuttals to CPP criticisms.[25] In late 1963 and early 1964, student protests moved toward a more sweeping indictment of the CPP regime, and, at least among the active few, divisions between Party supporters and opponents sharpened. With the de-activation of NUGS, however, such activism was soon destroyed, and overt student leadership appeared to fall to the minority of CPP sympathizers.

Not all subsequent open activity was, however, the result of Party manipulation. After Ian Smith declared Rhodesia's independence, Legon students met in the halls, denounced Smith, and criticized Britain. Virtually the entire student body then demonstrated their feelings by holding a rally in Accra on November 12, 1965 — an unprecedented expression of student political opinion and that on an issue having little or nothing to do with Nkrumah. This incident was not so dramatic as student activity in Japan, India, or Indonesia, but it does indicate that Legon students were capable of expressive political activity despite their tendency to withdraw from politics during Nkrumah's reign. Some people may dismiss Ghanaian student activism during this period as minimal and ineffective, but it was responsive to CPP actions and extensive enough to effect a considerable reaction from the Party.[26]

Since the coup, student attitudes have not undergone major changes, and many student orientations still reflect Legon traditions. For example, 71 per cent of the 1966 sample felt that students should dedicate themselves solely to their studies, while only 26 per cent felt students should actively participate in politics. Ninety-three per cent of the students felt the university should be run by educators, and politicians should not tell them what to do or what to teach. Nevertheless, the coup lifted the constraints Nkrumah had placed upon the campus, and conditions now exist for the development of student activism.

One would not, however, predict such developments considering the elitist character of Legon and the high degree of congruity between campus and government in June, 1966. Moreover, the great ideological consensus and low ideological consciousness among students would not appear to be conducive to activism. Legon students, like their counterparts in many developing nations tend to be politically aware, interested, and active in sharply decreasing degrees.

Yet spirits have been high among almost all students since the coup. Their demands have been primarily confined to university matters. The Vice-Chancellor has issued warnings against student indiscipline, and on one occasion, university officials threatened to expel all students from one residence hall who did not sign a pledge to be "obedient" in the future. Since its resuscitation, NUGS has raised fundamental issues regarding student rights, arguing that "academic freedom does not exist only for the dons, but also for students."

Whether incidents that have occurred at Legon and the two sister universities are viewed as a kind of post-coup catharsis or otherwise, they, along with unrest and riots in secondary schools, may portend the rise of a new student orientation and activism that will find new avenues of expression when and if the current ban on "politics" in Ghana is lifted.

Before the February 24, 1966, *coup d'état,* Ghana's intelligentsia — including students and faculty at the University of Ghana — had become increasingly alienated from the regime of Kwame Nkrumah. The dispute over the proper social values of higher education was, in turn, exacerbated by cavalier attitudes among students and faculty and by the Party's hypersensitivity to opposition. Party "successes" in attacking the university's autonomy and redefining academic freedom were the result of forceful organizational tactics, rather than mass conversions at the university. The ousting of Nkrumah opened the way for participatory roles in politics for the Legon community, and there was a discernible shift from universalistic to nationalistic conceptions of the intellectual's responsibilities. Still unresolved, however, were the Legon students' views of the standards applicable to the conduct of political life in a modernizing society. The students, caught between the politics of absolutism and the politics of compromise, have yet to define their role in Ghana's future. In the Nkrumah period, they seemingly rejected the totalistic alternative of radical activism often found in student movements in developing nations. What future choices are made at Legon depend not only on Ghana's political milieu, but also on the nature of the students' commitment to politics.

REFERENCES

1. I should like to express my gratitude to the Hoover Institution on War, Revolution, and Peace, the Duke University Committee on International Studies, and the Office of Scientific and Scholarly Research, and the Institute of International Studies and Overseas Administration of the University of Oregon for financial assistance during various phases of research in Ghana. Thanks are owed to B. D. G. Folson of the University of Ghana, Belva Finlay, Roberta E. Koplin, C. R. Schuller, and Shirley Varmette for their cooperation and assistance.

2. Growth of Educational Institutions and Student Enrollments

	Number of Institutions		1964–	Number of Students			Percentage Increase in Number of Students	
	1950	1957	65	1950	1957	1964–65	1950–57	1957–1964–65
Primary	2,393	3,372	7,900	211,994	468,021	1,040,414	182	122
Middle	511	1,131	2,103	59,960	127,517	257,635	112	102
Secondary	56	60	90	6,162	12,119	33,071	96	173
Teacher-Training	42	76	58	2,722	9,032	15,002	231	66
Technical-Training Universities	1	2	3	108	783	2,442	625	211

On the development of education in Ghana, see the excellent study by Philip Foster, *Education and Social Change in Ghana* (Chicago, 1965).

3. According to Nkrumah's Seven Year Development Plan (1963–70), enrollments in primary, middle, and secondary schools would have doubled and the universities expanded to 25,000 by 1970. After the coup, however, the plan was abandoned. Until Ghana's financial difficulties are corrected and the acute shortage of trained teachers is eased, further dramatic expansion in education is unlikely.

4. *Report of the Commission on Higher Education in the Colonies* (London, H.M.S.O., 1945).

5. As would be expected in light of the growth of education in southern Ghana, tribes from these areas predominate at the university; only a handful of students are from the northern regions. Yet tribal composition of Legon students seems to have little political significance in comparison to other variables.

6. The University at Kumasi has not shown a relative increase in enrollments in agriculture, for example, so it does not appear that a division of labor between the two institutions accounts for the decline in science students at Legon. A partial explanation may be the relative ease and lack of expense with which large numbers of students can be absorbed into the arts and social sciences. Probably as important, however, is the long-standing tradition of respect and esteem afforded graduates of the arts, humanities, and law in Ghanaian society.

7. Eric Ashby, *Universities: British, Indian, African* (Cambridge, Mass., 1966), p. 234.

8. See Margaret G. Kelly, *The Ghanaian Intelligentsia* (Unpublished Ph.D. Dissertation, University of Chicago).

9. Kwame Nkrumah, *Speech on the Tenth Anniversary of the C.P.P.* (Accra, 1959), pp. 24–25.

10. Quoted in Adam Curle, "Nationalism and Higher Education in Ghana," *Universities Quarterly*, Vol. 16 (1961–62), p. 238.

11. Kwame Nkrumah, *Flower of Learning* (Accra, 1961), p. 11.

12. Kwame Nkrumah, *Guide to Party Action* (Accra, 1962), p. 6.

13. Kwame Nkrumah, "Speech at the Opening of the Institute of African Studies," *The Spark* (November 8, 1963).

14. Editorial, *Legonite* (Lent, 1963), p. 5.

15. Editorial, *Ghanaian Times*, February 6, 1964.

16. Editorial, *Ghanaian Times*, February 7, 1964.

17. *The Spark*, March 17, 1964.

18. This statement was made by S. G. Ikoku from the Ideological Institute at the inauguration of the Legon Party branch. *Ghanaian Times*, October 24, 1964. O'Brien later warned students that the university authorities would not tolerate students sitting in judgment or denouncing their teachers.

19. Conor Cruise O'Brien, "Vice Chancellor's Address to Congregation, 27th March, 1965," *Legonite* (Lent, 1965), p. 19.

20. A. A. Kwapong, "Vice-Chancellor's Address to Congregation, 26th March, 1966," *Legonite* (Lent, 1966), pp. 11–12.

21. Daniel Goldrich, *Sons of the Establishment* (Chicago, 1966), pp. 11–13. This conceptualization was published in greater detail in Goldrich's "Toward the Comparative Study of Politicization, with Special Reference to Latin America," *Contemporary Cultures and Societies of Latin America*, eds. Dwight B. Heath and Richard N. Adams (New York, 1965), pp. 361–378. Items used to measure politicization in the 1963 and 1966 questionnaires included: interest in politics, time spent discussing politics; intention to participate in politics; willingness to be a candidate for public office. The 1966 questionnaire also included choices among alternative roles for future political participation.

22. The 1963 data are based on a questionnaire distributed to 236 students in two political-science classes at the University of Ghana and filled out during class periods. Thirty of the questionnaires were disqualified by the respondent's nationality or unusable for other reasons. The resulting sample "n" is 206, which represents 17 per cent of all Ghanaian students at the university during the academic year 1962–63.

The 1966 data are based on two questionnaires administered simultaneously by paid research assistants to a representative sample. Eighty per cent of the distributed questionnaires were completed and returned. The total number of respondents was 376, or 20 per cent of the 1879 Ghanaian students at the university. Those responding to questions about politicization and political attitudes (asked on one of the two questionnaires) numbered 209. To test the representative quality of the survey, data were obtained on 400 students randomly selected from application forms in the

Registrar's Office. Both sets of data were checked against aggregate statistics on enrollments by faculty, age, and home residence. The survey sample compared well on these dimensions.

23. Without longitudinal data, it is difficult to determine whether the faculties served as "socializers" or as "recruiters" of students with similar levels of politicization. They may, in fact, be both. Analysis of politicization according to year in the university shows that the level of politicization tends to increase by year among arts and social-science students (a socialization function), yet those faculties also include more students who are highly politicized when they enter the university (a recruitment function).

24. When asked in 1963, "It has been suggested that students at the University are anti-government. Do you think this is true?" only 24 per cent of those sampled agreed.

25. For example, one student publication referred to CPP attacks on Legon faculty in this way: "We know our lecturers and we know what they are worth. They are worth their weight in gold just as this paper [*Ghanaian Times*] is only fit for the clearing away of a dog's vomit." Quoted in Curle, "Nationalism and Higher Education in Ghana," p. 242.

26. Others have claimed that "any casual observer will tell you that academic freedom would have been abolished completely in Ghana but for the students of our universities." L. H. Ofosu Appiah, "Authority and the Individual in Ghana's Educational System," *The Legon Observer*, Vol. 2, No. 1 (January, 1967), p. 8.

IV

LATIN AMERICA

ROBERT E. SCOTT

Student Political Activism in Latin America*

STUDENT ACTIVISM in Latin America's universities is well publicized and with good reason. During the past several years, nearly every country in the region has experienced some sort of organized student activity that disrupted or, at the least, seriously disturbed the process of higher education and not infrequently the peace of the cities in which schools were located. Newspaper headlines and magazine articles notwithstanding, the majority of such manifestations are not concerned initially with national politics. Most stem from a sense of frustration growing out of real deficiencies in educational facilities or from a feeling of insecurity that magnifies government decisions which the students see as undermining their present situation or their future hopes.

Consider just a few of the many kinds of student action which took place during 1967. Bolivian students demonstrated in January against the opening of a "Catholic" university because they feared that both the quality of the education offered by the new institution and the superior social contacts enjoyed by students who could afford a private school might reduce the value of national university training. In June, Colombian students protesting a rise in bus fares clashed with police in Cartegena and Bogotá, resulting in military occupation of the national university. In Rio de Janeiro six persons

* This paper includes some of the findings of a study role of Latin American universities in political change soon to be published by the Brookings Institution. No more than a small portion of the subject matter treated in that study is covered here, and little of the substantive data or analysis upon which the conclusions are based is offered. Generalizations beyond Peru and Mexico, which are the principal case studies of the Brookings project, reflect further investigation in Argentina, Brazil, Uruguay, Chile, and Venezuela, as well as a systematic review of the literature dealing with Latin American universities as a whole. Reproduction in any form is prohibited except on written permission of author.

were wounded during May as a result of student manifestations against Ministry of Education agreements with the United States for a study of reforms in higher education, and only two months later over a hundred students were removed from where they squatted in dormitories as a protest against crowded conditions that prevented their admittance to the University of São Paulo despite passing the entrance examinations.

The great majority of these and other student manifestations which have occurred during the past few years did not originate out of a desire to manipulate national partisan politics. Nor do my own or other studies substantiate the popular notion that all Latin American *universitarios* are highly politicized. Instead, they demonstrate rather clearly that the largest proportion of students are not political activists and do not relate strongly to any national political party. How is it, then, that university students have so widespread a reputation for political activity and, indeed, have forced governments to react so often to their political initiatives?

During 1966, for instance, many of the larger and more developed republics witnessed open clashes between government forces and students. An Ecuadorian military *junta* fell partly as a consequence of its attack upon central university students, which led to a general strike. In five other countries — Argentina, Brazil, Venezuela, Colombia, and Mexico — government troops moved against university campuses to put down activities which may have started as protests against educational policies, but ended as serious challenges to the constituted political authorities. Several other countries — Panama, Uruguay, and Nicaragua, for example — found that student involvement in public policy disputes or national elections caused severe unrest.

Events of this sort reflect the peculiar role played by the universities and their students in Latin America's rapidly changing and consequently overburdened political systems. Almost in spite of themselves, students find that they are drawn into national political life, usually in some form of confrontation politics that sets them at odds with the existing power structure. To understand why this is so, we must know more about the value system that motivates the students and about the schools in which they study. We must also know something about the political systems of the region, for students do not operate in a political vacuum. The role they play, constructive or otherwise, reflects the ability of the other social and political structures participating in the political process to meet the needs of a changing society. Despite the very obvious differences that exist among the twenty-odd republics, there are enough similarities in the educational systems and the political environments, as well as among the *universitarios* in their reactions to the world around them, to permit some generalizations about student political activism.

Latin American Universities

Taking into account national differences in level and complexity of development, the forms of university organization and curriculum content in Latin America's institutions of higher education are remarkably alike. Historically, many of the same intellectual influences were at work simultaneously in each of these countries so the schools that evolved do follow a pattern.

Originally, most universities were modeled upon Iberian prototypes, but during the nineteenth century they were strongly influenced by French thought and the example of Napoleon's Imperial University. They are divided into professional faculties (*facultades*), which are self-contained and generally have a course of study that is quite rigid. Where permitted at all, electives are kept to an absolute minimum. Until very recently, the university's principal recognized function was professional training, particularly in the traditional fields of medicine, law, and engineering. General education and culture were the responsibility of secondary or preparatory schools; teacher training was left to the normal schools. Research or public service could hardly be expected of part-time university professors whose main source of livelihood was private practice or salaried employment outside the university.

Within the past few years, however, the training and educational functions of the universities have started to expand as a result of the growing recognition of the need for post-secondary general education and for diversification of offerings into university-level education courses, business training, and other "careers" suitable for serving a more complex economy and society. At the same time, the beginnings of attempts to perform research and offer public service activities can be noted, especially in the more developed countries and particularly at the central university as opposed to provincial public institutions and private schools. These changes can be classed as part of an expanding tendency to adopt some aspects of the United States system of higher education to meet problems that seem similar to those already encountered by that country.

Clearly, none of the Latin American republics is so unaffected by change that its universities resemble those found around the turn of the century. At that time, the great majority of institutions of higher education were little more than finishing schools for the sons of the "comfortable" class. Small in numbers, aristocratic in bearing, often dilettantish in their approach to professional training, the preponderance of students came from the relatively cultured backgrounds of long-established landholding families. Most studied law or medicine, a few engineering. Many never really practiced a profession after leaving school, but devoted their time to administering their estates and pursuing eclectic intellectual interests as *pensadores,* wide-ranging social commentators who wrote in the style and spirit of the French essayists.

Neither at the university nor afterward was the traditional Latin American *universitario* deeply concerned with politics. His position was too well established to require active protection. Even the small, service-oriented middle sector of professionals who did sometimes act politically was so desirous of winning acceptance in the upper class, aping its mannerisms and way of life, that no real challenge to the established gentry was offered. When they did act politically, however, university students were accorded the status due offspring of the dominant social group.

Although the principal university-centered policy battle of this period was not couched in terms of national politics, it was a direct reaction to the social and moral norms under which government acted. Ultimately, it had an important effect upon student political views and activity. An academic power contest grew out of a humanistic revival sparked by the intellectuals' rejection of the cold-blooded social Darwinism, engendered by Comte's positivism, that so many regimes used to justify support for economic exploitation of large masses of their citizens. Given the region's Iberian cultural heritage, the humanistic upsurge became very nearly a return to scholasticism, affecting both curricular content and the intellectual approaches imparted by university education. In the long run, it influenced the *universitarios'* political style as well, for the resultant movement away from pragmatic norms freed the students from the limitations of reality just at the time when they began to discover that they had a role to play in national concerns.

A convenient date to mark the large-scale entry of university students into national politics is 1918, when the Córdoba Manifesto was adopted by Argentine young people speaking for their colleagues in schools throughout the republic. Within the next few years, students from countries all over the continent picked up the call for university reform because they were all affected by the beginnings of social and economic change and the dilatoriness of university authorities in adjusting curricula to the new conditions. Fifty years have passed, and the students still are protesting, for most of the real goals of the Córdoba movement are not yet accomplished.

In a number of countries symbolic victories have been won, with the legal, sometimes even constitutional, granting of university autonomy and the establishment of student participation in academic affairs through *cogobierno* (student membership in all university committees and governing bodies). Most older universities have added new *facultades* and a host of new institutions have been opened to accommodate a larger student body, though the total number of young people registered seldom reaches 5 per cent of the college-age youth. But formal grants of autonomy mean little to institutions still almost wholly dependent upon government for economic support, particularly where part-time teaching staff and weak administrators have neither the incentive nor the means of implementing academic independence. Similarly, the mere existence of more schools, more careers, and larger numbers of students does not necessarily mean that the larger problems of university organization or of substantive content of course material have been resolved.

In point of fact, much of the change that has occurred in most universities is piecemeal and even contradictory, so that the education available in a majority of Latin America's universities does not begin to meet today's needs. The failure is due partly to the students, with their all-too-human tendency to utilize their organizational strength to oppose upgrading of standards and tightening of requirements. But most of the blame must fall upon the national educational systems themselves, for throughout his educational career, neither course content nor the academic environment prepares a student to operate in a real world. This is true of the highly value-laden, formalistic, and non-pragmatic primary and secondary programs, which are overburdened with multiple subjects (up to twelve in a single term in some secondary schools) and generally weak on experimentation and problem-solving. It is equally true of most types of university training, which continue to reflect a kind of sterile scholasticism.

One of the complaints that led to the Córdoba Manifesto was that university professors did not fulfill their obligations, in that they frequently missed classes, did not prepare adequately for those that did meet, and failed to keep up with contemporay scholarship. Equally important, the students felt that their teachers did not relate their course materials to the realities of the world around them. These problems were due partly to the influence of the new human- ism and partly to organizational weaknesses in staff recruitment, both of which continue to the present day. Most professors who earn their living teaching must hold three or more posts to do so. The vast majority of university teachers, however, are not full-time educators, but individuals in private practice or employed by government or private organizations who offer classes in their spare time. Such an employment pattern inhibits development of academic disciplines that could encourage professional standards of preparation, teaching, and research, and almost insures that lectures will be presented from warmed-over notes or even from the original course in the subject taken by the professor when he was in school.

Absence of professional norms and lack of a professional edu- cator's career pattern mean also that university professors may feel free to carry their political preferences into the classroom, turning their lectures on almost any subject into indoctrination sessions. This sometimes happens, especially with those teachers who are most closely related to radical reform movements which otherwise find it difficult to obtain a hearing. Such instructors often devote appre- ciably more time to the *universitarios* than do their more conven- tional colleagues, who may appear at the school to present their course material and leave immediately after the class meeting. Worse still, these "Taxi Professors," as the students call them, must get back to their full-time occupations so quickly as to make virtually impossible the frequent personal contact between teacher and pupil that is so necessary as adolescents face their identity crises, especially in countries where constant and speedy change interferes with the evolution of widely accepted norms of social and political con- duct.

Dividing the universities into independent *facultades* complicates the staff-recruitment problem. If separate teachers of mathematics, chemistry, languages, biology, or any of a hundred specialties must be hired by each unit, no society would have sufficient economic or human resources to support full-time professors. But the pattern has educational and ultimately political developmental consequences as well. In a modern, complex environment neither knowledge nor the solutions to socio-economic problems segregate themselves conveniently according to the subject matter of conventional professional faculties. A few Latin American states have begun to recognize the insufficiency of the general education provided in secondary schools, and their universities now require a year or so of pre-professional training before a *universitario* enters a *facultad* like law, economics, or medicine. But even these university-level general-education curricula tend to separate students in "humanities" or "science" programs, depending upon the professional subject they intend to study. A student who has taken an inappropriate pre-professional program cannot enroll in a given faculty.

This limitation upon the exposure of young people to other modes of thought, either through formal classroom experience or through opportunities for informal interaction with students of other professional subjects, makes for over-specialization. In later life, the lawyer cannot understand the frame of reference within which the physician works, nor can the engineer conceive of a problem as a lawyer does. This makes for difficulties in their day-to-day professional relations, but much more so when they try to resolve the policy problems of an ever more diversified society. University training of this sort is hardly an adequate educational experience for the small portion of a country's inhabitants that must one day provide leadership in situations of rapid change. Even now, leading *políticos* educated in the "humanities" faculties (lawyers, schoolteachers, humanists) find it hard to organize solutions for the material problems of their country. Those from the "sciences" (physicians, engineers, architects) often act more like technocrats than political brokers representing the interests and aspirations of all their rank and file followers.

In the half century since Córdoba, student frustrations and insecurities have expanded rather than disappeared. Changes in student population add new sources of unrest, since the new student types are more insecure than the traditional *universitarios*. The wider range of university offerings suits growing social and economic diversity, but more than ever students are uncertain that they can complete their education or, if they do so, that they will be assured of acceptable employment. Larger enrollments take in a slightly higher proportion of lower-middle- and upper-lower-class youth, including some from outlying regions, and this increases the problems of confrontation concerning national integration. Having inherited much of the ascribed status of its more aristocratic forebears, the expanded student body moves into national politics with relative impunity as it struggles to resolve its educational problems and to demonstrate displeasure with the social-political system which it feels causes them.

The Córdoba reform movement and the similar activities it sparked in other parts of Latin America were the first examples of organized and continuing student pressure to influence national policy. Significantly, it combined an attempt to involve government in legislating curriculum reform with a demand for a formal statement of legal autonomy for universities. The students discovered, as have so many in a modernizing world, that they need the assistance of, as well as protection from, government. Unlike most other interest groups in the region, the university students were in an advantageous position to organize to protect what they deemed their rights. Usually they enjoyed high enough status to act safely, sufficient contact with one another to organize effectively, and adequate information to act promptly, so that they could maximize pressure on any regime that seemed indifferent to their views. The students entered the national political arena to challenge the rigidity of the university authorities and to fight for their own interests. From there it was a fairly easy step to involvement in non-university politics.

The Latin American Student Subculture

The relative ease with which university students become involved in national politics is a function of experience, which inclines them toward acceptance of some sort of political role and at the same time accentuates certain patterns of political action. Although relatively few students play a really active role in political life, except under special conditions, they all share a high expectation of having their political actions taken seriously. This was true before the Córdoba Manifesto of 1918, but it has become increasingly true since, as the dislocations of development expand the potential political functions of *universitarios* throughout Latin America. This proclivity for politics is passed from one student generation to another by a specialized student subculture.

The student value system is a product of many of the factors that make up the student's life experience, interacting to instill a broadly shared set of reactions to political stimuli. The frustrations in Latin America's academic environment and the insecurities felt by young people under the disrupting pressures of change combine with the formal authority patterns of home and schools and the highly normative content of education to inculcate a rather clearly defined set of political norms. Students tend to think in abstract, normative, and ideological terms. They seek immediate action and all-embracing solutions to socio-economic problems; they are impatient with pragmatic tests of policy suggestions, because they are suspicious that the ongoing political system that seeks them does so to avoid acting. Emotionally and in political discourse most *universitarios* are sincere democrats, but in political practice they sometimes support authoritarian movements whose ideology suggests a willingness to override the particularistic demands of established special interests in favor of a more general welfare.

Relatively few Latin American university students manifest all of these traits, but traces of them can be found in almost every member of the university population. Those students who share a higher proportion of these norms are more likely to become political activists in the sense of involvement with political movements outside the academic community. Given their marked dissatisfaction with both educational and general conditions, together with their bent toward direct action, such student activists look upon themselves as "agents of change." They tend, therefore, to be attracted to political groups that seek to dislodge the traditional power elements and restructure the political process. For their part, the challenging forces must find potential leaders who have some conception of the nation and its problems and exhibit enough of the outward characteristics of high status to treat successfully with the established elites, but who at the same time are willing to attack the *status quo*. The elements in Latin American society most likely to meet these criteria are found among the young, less committed, and frequently partially alienated intellectuals of the university environment.

Generally the minority of students who become identified with this sort of political activity do not succeed in changing the political system very much. Some accommodate themselves to the continuing pattern of politics, benefiting themselves and to an extent the interests they represent, particularly if those interests have become strong enough to pressure the older forces into compromise. Other student political activists cannot work within the existing political process, either because personality or ideology inhibits them or because the interests they lead are too weak to enforce concessions. Such student activists may become wholly alienated from the national political system. A few may end up trying to subvert it through revolutionary political parties or even attacking it physically by means of a National Liberation Movement; others may withdraw into political apathy. In later life, however, as their political experience increases, many one-time student radicals do work out some sort of adjustment with the operating political mechanisms, renewing the possibility of playing a meaningful political role.

Surprisingly few university political activists affiliate with the established political parties. Apparently the student subculture endorses the concept of students as agents of change so strongly that neither the activists nor their potential followers are attracted in any numbers to the more "respectable" parties involved in the national political process. During recent decades throughout Latin America, student federation elections show a marked pattern of support for candidates favoring challenging reform parties over those speaking for incumbent or traditional parties. Even student *políticos* representing reform political movements lose influence once their party has attained government power. This has happened to student leaders of the *aprista*-type parties in Peru, Venezuela, Costa Rica, and elsewhere; to Christian Democratic *universitarios* in various countries; to PRI supporters in Mexico; and to student politicians identified with successful personalistic reformers in a number of republics. Once a regime is in office, adolescent rebellion and normal student impatience with the *status quo* combine with the inability of any government to satisfy the rising expectations which accompany rapid change to produce an ever present nucleus of student support for opposition movements, particularly those associated with radical reform.

A majority of university young people never do become political activists, either in school or after they leave their studies. While at the university they tend to support those student leaders who fight hardest for what they conceive of as student interest — *cogobierno*, free tuition, food and housing aid, freedom to miss classes, restrictions on higher academic standards, and the like. Almost invariably the student spokesman for a challenging opposition movement can out-promise and out-perfom the representatives of the governing group. Given the average student's image of himself as an agent of change, it is no very difficult task for the university political activist to convert support for movements advocating educational improvement into acceptance of (or at least neutrality for) politically inspired demonstrations against the incumbent government and its policies. Ironically, after separation from the university, the vast majority of one-time students quickly cease acting as agents of change. Some of them function within the operating political system, but more remain passive politically. Certainly they do not provide the leadership for modernizing political mechanisms, or even an active and informed participant membership that would strengthen the hands of those few political leaders who do seek to develop national political structures adequate to the needs of a developing country.

We know that not all students participate as political activists and that of those who do some devote much more time and energy than others. The amount and nature of political activity depends upon individual personality factors, the student political style of various *facultades* and universities, the general political conditions which obtain in each country, and a host of other variables. Those demanding better course content may tend to discourage recruitment of students who must work to support themselves, or to overwhelm those who devote too much time to extracurricular politics. The very nature of the subject matter in a given curriculum may tend to attract or repel those who have an interest in politics or to cause more advanced students to view the world normatively or, on the contrary, analytically.

At first glance, socio-economic class seems like a good indicator of potential political activism, because lower-status students seem more inclined to want to challenge the *status quo* than do their more favored colleagues. More careful analysis suggests, however, that this may be as much a function of recruitment into specific faculties where political activism is more rampant as it is of the "comfort quotient." The educational experience in certain academic fields imparts a stronger sense of professionalism, with a clearer awareness of career possibilities and job opportunities, than does training in other subjects. For the most part, these professionalized faculties are older and technically oriented, with more clearly defined educational requirements for their students and more obvious career patterns for their graduates in individual, corporate, or government employment. They include medicine, engineering, and the applied sciences, and their various offshoots — agronomy, veterinary medicine, architecture, and the like. Competition both for entry and for survival in such programs is great, favoring the student from the better (usually private) secondary school, from the more intellectualized home, and from the more secure economic environment which does not require that the student work full time to support himself. Thus, a kind of built-in bias favoring the children of the advantaged sectors of society combines with a more ordered and less frustrating academic environment to produce students who are less likely to have either the time or the inclination to challenge the existing institutions.

Faculties offering less professionalized and more unstructured training are often easier to enter and not so demanding intellectually or in terms of such academic formalities as class attendance and keeping current in course work. The student with weaker preparation or one who cannot, or does not wish to, devote full time to his studies can compete here, but he is much less apt to encounter a satisfying academic experience. Most training programs of this kind are quite new to the university setting (commerce and business administration, education, social sciences, journalism, fine arts) or are older ones undergoing fundamental changes in social or economic role (philosophy, law). As yet they do not have well-established professional norms or easily identified career patterns that lead to high-status positions. The materials taught are much less technical and exact than those in the hard sciences, much more liable to subjective and normative interpretation by both professor and student. In these *facultades*, where more students are likely to be upwardly mobile, with attendant emotional and economic stresses, neither the subject matter nor its manner of presentation, much less the professional atmosphere or career expectations, seems to offer young people a sense of security in the present or hope for the future. It is scarcely surprising, under the circumstances, that activism of the radical-reform type is more common among students in these fields.

These are generalities and should be taken as such. Individual student activists can emerge from any sort of background and from study in any faculty. Fidel Castro came from a well-to-do (though not long established) family and entered the law school in Havana; Che Guevara's economic situation was not so comfortable, but he studied medicine in Buenos Aires. Both became activists while in school. On the other hand, all over the continent large numbers of students with much more reason to resent and reject the society around them remain politically passive. Clearly, individual differences are important. But this should not obscure the fact that specific conditions in certain types of faculty do make for a predisposition toward political activism among the student body.

We should recognize, too, that just as differences among individuals or among *facultades* produce variations in political style or intensity of political involvement, differences among the schools in a given country may affect the student political culture. Private universities, which usually means church-related schools, tend to maintain academic standards and to stress educational rather than political functions more easily than state-supported institutions. Students in the capital city are apt to be more politicized and sophisticated in their understanding of the policy process than those in provincial environments, no matter what type of university they attend. The particular "mix" that operates to produce the student subculture in any country can be understood only by study in depth of the local situation.

One can generalize, however, to the extent of saying that among Latin American students the educational experience reinforces the natural impatience that youth feels when it encounters the fumbling attempts of an older generation to resolve the world's problems, particularly as most young people have not yet had enough other experiences to accept the finite limitations imposed by a given situation. Both course content and style of imparting knowledge make for a maximum of memorization and a minimum of experimentation, with almost no opportunity for social analysis. This reinforces rather than counters the authoritarian outlook implanted by the broader social environment. The humanistic reaction against positivism enhances this pattern, leaving the student with little chance to "learn how to learn" about problem-solving.

At the same time, in Latin America the student's identity crisis is much more acute than in more stable countries. Within an environment undergoing rapid change, the young person has to adjust not only to an adult world, but to one in which values are constantly shifting, with the new norms always under attack by some portion of the population. Faced with such uncertainty, the student has limited opportunity to come into contact with individuals upon whom he can model his actions in unfamiliar social and political situations. Generational rebellion weakens parental effectiveness in this role, and the minimal contact available from part-time teachers reduces their potential influence.

As a consequence, unsuitable models for conduct are selected — perhaps motion-picture actors whose clever remarks and dexterous resolution of complex problems are the products of a scenarist's art; or national politicians whose real actions are so far removed from the student's immediate observation that only the vaguest and most distorted impressions are captured; or, nearer at hand, older students, including the "deans" and "fossils," as the professional political organizers who remain semipermanent students are called. Little constructive orientation to the real social and political world is available to guide the student political activist when he marches to save mankind or to assist his potential followers who must evaluate the worth of the crusade.

Should one wonder, then, that many students clutch at the kind of psychological support or instant integration offered by ideological movements such as socialism, Communism, or *aprismo,* which purport to offer a logical frame of reference within which to answer every problem? One intriguing aspect of this phenomenon is that although students, like other Latin Americans, find it easy to identify with a personalistic leader — Perón, Haya de la Torre, Fidel — they can also serve an abstract ideology like Communism or even Christian Socialism.

Although many student activists relate directly to national political movements, the student federation is their most effective mechanism for utilizing the special status students enjoy for political ends. In almost every school some sort of federation (usually composed of elected student delegates from each faculty who in turn elect a university-wide student governing council) speaks in the name of the student body. Where an institution accepts *cogobierno,* these delegates sit on official governing boards at each administrative level; at other institutions, their role may be unofficial, but potentially very influential. On educational matters, these student delegates usually perform conscientiously and constructively, frequently more so than the part-time professors who share responsibility for policy decisions. Because these student spokesmen do protect the educational interest of the non-activist majority of students in an academic world where neither government nor educational administrators and teachers always satisfy the legitimate aspirations of the *universitarios,* the politically passive members of the student body are not disposed to object very strenuously to the student activists extending their leadership to questions of national politics.

Difficulties arise, however, because of the affinity of most student leaders for those political movements that are least sympathetic to the traditional political system. To complicate the situation, because by no means all of the student activists support the same political movement, they are in constant competition to capture the student federation in order to identify the mystique of student support with their particular brand of politics. All this results in unending agitation, as each group of activists militates against authority — be it government or university — on national policy as well as educational questions, while attempting to outmaneuver its opponents. Every student-federation election becomes a national election in microcosm. Between campaigns, the activist factions wage a kind of guerrilla warfare against one another that disrupts the educational function of the university.

The University and Leadership Cadres for Nation-Building

Disruption of the university's educational function is only one of the significant consequences of political activity that results from the student subculture. Another has to do with the kind of direct political participation in which the students engage. The idea that a *universitario* has a responsibility to provide leadership as an agent of change is not novel, for throughout the world students have felt an urge to reform their society. What is new here is the degree to which the student's preconditioning toward political involvement is encouraged by a society that cannot absorb the kind of political activity the student leaders push. The question arises, why do student *políticos* find themselves playing so influential a role in Latin American politics, despite their disruptive tendencies?

It is no answer to recall that university students often are called the "conscience of the nation," a carry-over from the days when student idealism provided a kind of symbolic reassurance to the ruling sectors that someday the goals of social justice and political democracy cited by the *pensadores* would be achieved (but not quite yet, as St. Augustine would have had it). With the advent of development, a new, unexpected, and wholly unofficial function has been thrust upon Latin America's universities and their students. This "phantom" function, not generally identified as a. prime university responsibility, is that of providing leaders for nation-building.

Student involvement in the process of producing cadres of leaders is not quite the same as student activism in outside political movements, although almost every university political activist working with a challenging reform group is also very much a part of the dialogue within the academic community that seeks broadly acceptable norms around which an integrated nation might evolve. Even those students who are not usually activists in national political terms do get caught up in the discussions, the disputes, and the open interruptions of regular course work that mark the search for some common definition of the proper functions of government and the means of fulfilling those functions. In this particular context, university students can hardly avoid considering themselves as agents of change, for this is how society looks upon them.

Outside Latin America, this cadre-building function is not so strongly associated with universities because other social or political institutions are available to perform it. In a more developed country — the United States, for example — a broad consensus about the legitimacy of government and the norms which operate to regulate public activities has evolved over many years, probably centuries. These values are inculcated in the citizens through the family, reinforced by the common schools, mass media of communication, and most of the other institutions of society. Moreover, they are supported continuously by the strong ties of economic interdependence which bind such a country together. The need for leaders in the nation-building process does not arise because the nation already exists.

In the less-developed states of Africa and Asia, the history of the anticolonial struggle included a breakdown of the traditional social and economic power structures, which permits a more flexible approach to the problems of national integration. Although not all of the social institutions support norms which are receptive to change, those most likely to oppose it have been weakened. In many such countries, a single dominant political party that symbolizes the movement for national independence provides leaders who shared the experience of organizing against the colonial power and therefore also share some understandings about what the free government they sought ought to do. At the very least, they can communicate their disagreements using more or less the same political symbols. If the disagreements become too great, there is a tendency for Nasserist-style military leaders to assume the leadership role. The latter situation has obtained in the increasing number of countries where the liberation movement has been unable to convert its freedom fighters into effective post-colonial political leaders who can resolve the hard problems of development and national integration.

In all of these countries, the tasks of national integration are made easier if conditions are in sufficient flux to break down the traditional social patterns or deeply ingrained political practices. They are more difficult if tribal differences, regional competition, or other divisive elements are at work. Almost everywhere, however, some prestigious or powerful combination of social, economic, and political institutions is operating to supply leadership in the nation-building process. At the same time, in few of the ex-colonial states has the European tradition of elite higher education broken down to such an extent that large numbers of semi-educated students dissatisfied with academic life, future job opportunities, and the general political environment await an invitation to provide leadership for change. This is not to suggest that such a pattern could not emerge in either Asia or Africa, but that in most cases the combination of conditions is not yet ripe. Even in the few countries where faltering leadership and a large, discontented student body seem to presage such a possibility — in India or Indonesia, for example — class distinctions, religious differences, and regional competition act as divisive factors to weaken student initiative and to give the older politicians an extra lease on their political lives.

In most Latin American countries, the situation is quite different. As in other parts of the developing world, there is relatively little consensus about the proper functions of government, and social and economic relations are not very harmonious. Social change and economic diversification are occurring, but while change is speedy, it is not so drastic that the traditional power of the aristocracy and oligarchy has been broken, except partially in a few countries, such as Mexico, Cuba, and perhaps Bolivia. Instead, mounting pressures for popular participation in the political process, desire for greater social acceptance of the emergent modernizing middle sectors, and demands for a more equitable distribution of the benefits of economic growth clash with the recalcitrance of well-established traditional elites. Nor can the challenging elements always agree on a common set of national goals, much less upon the means through which to achieve such goals.

In the face of deep disagreements about values that reflect cultural, social, economic and political differences, some way of infusing a sense of the nation into the whole population must be discovered. At a certain stage of development, this need to inculcate a more universally shared set of norms becomes a real social necessity. If the political and social structures which deal directly with the citizens do not meet the need adequately, society is likely to work through any appropriate institution available to do so, with or without conscious decision by the policy-makers.

Neither Latin America's formal governmental units nor the informal and extra-constitutional social and political mechanisms have provided much leadership in the nation-building process. Government agencies and such older institutions as the church and the army are either dominated by traditionalists or involved in the same value conflicts as the remainder of the society. This is not to suggest that certain bureaucrats (usually technically oriented), parish priests, and military men do not see a need for national integration, but that they are usually too low in their respective hierarchies to exert much general leadership from within the system. Those who resign to work outside lose the status their former roles conferred. Even the successful businessman who translates his perception of the advantages of a national market into a conception of true political integration thinks twice before he acts to upset the *status quo* in which he has so great a stake. Most of the "mass" media also reflect the special views of region, class, or functional interests, thus inhibiting any small cry they may voice for integration of the nation.

Much the same is true of most political parties, not excluding such national-integrating, mass-oriented political movements as the so-called *aprista*-type parties or their newer Christian Democratic rivals, both of which oppose and are opposed by the traditional power elites. Even though their programs make much of integrating the "popular" classes into national life, the most active militants in such parties are members of lower-middle- or upper-lower-class factions who seek to improve their personal social-economic positions by political means and are not particularly anxious to weaken their own claims by carrying along large numbers of politically passive members of the masses. Latin America's national-integrating parties lack the recent total commitment to independent national life that marked the anticolonial struggles of Asia and Africa, giving symbolic status as nation-builders to the revolutionary party leaders and permitting them to override the traditional vested interests to some degree. The sole exception is Mexico's Revolutionary Party, which for over thirty years has provided leadership for national integration not only in the political sphere, but in most of the social and economic structures which operate in the republic.

The university is the only social institution that seems to bring together citizens from every region of the country, from the challenging middle- and upper-lower class as well as the established privileged class, from groupings representing all shades of political and social opinion. This confrontation comes just at that period in their lives when young people are most likely to question established patterns and to reject the answers provided by their elders, a tendency strengthened by the iconoclastic nature of university education. Finally, the *universitarios* are accustomed to think in terms of political participation and are accorded a high degree of status by most of their fellow citizens, but at the same time they feel discontented with both the academic and the national environment. By default as much as by acclamation then, the university students assume the role of leaders in the process of national integration.

Many Latin American universities, therefore, find themselves co-opted into a situation in which they perform a necessary sociopolitical function — providing the training ground in which cadres of leaders in the nation-building process prepare themselves. This reduces their effectiveness in satisfying the other important functions for which they were established. Their students, particularly that small portion of the student body that is most politicized, seek to forge a nation, hammering out on the anvil of political discourse a common set of values or at least a core of shared understandings about the proper role of government in shaping the destinies of man in society, economy, and polity. The vacuum resulting from a paucity of other political structures which supply leaders or implement nation-building policies encourages the students to move out of the realm of discussion into that of direct political action. Disorder results, as students struggle among themselves, engage in politically motivated strikes, riot in the streets, withdraw to the mountains to precipitate guerrilla warfare, and otherwise substitute political activism for serious study. All this plays havoc with the educational and training functions of the university. The quality of preparation deteriorates, the number of persons winning degrees drops, and the supply of adequately prepared manpower to service the needs of society dwindles.

The cause-and-effect relationship between the onset of rapid change and the growth of political activism among Latin American university students is clear. In at least one country, Mexico, there has also been a tendency toward reduced student political activity as other political mechanisms become available to perform the nation-building function and as the amount of political consensus shared by the general population grows. Here a beginning of reversal of the student role was possible because improved academic conditions and growing career opportunities for the *universitarios* gave them a greater stake in the operating political system, so much so that in 1966 a *fidelista*-inspired "reform" group decried the students' lack of revolutionary zeal. Mexico is the only state in the region where the pattern has run full circle — first student recruitment as nation-building leaders, then active involvement in the national integration process, and finally the beginnings of withdrawal from political activism. There is enough evidence of student recruitment and involvement in other countries to permit us to project the existence of a kind of three-stage cycle of Latin American student activism.

What cannot be foretold is whether in these other countries the entire cycle will take place successfully, as it has in Mexico. There, a long history of relatively slow change, joined with fundamental shifts in the political value system encouraged by the "official" Revolutionary Party, allowed the *universitarios* to move through the three stages of the activism cycle without completely disrupting the educational functions of the universities and without forcing the students into open opposition to the government. Over a period of fifty years, a system of higher education that once was a bastion of conservatism moved into the cadre-building function, producing successive generations of students who shared common experiences and who developed a similar vocabulary with which to discuss the problems of national development, even if all their goals were not identical. Simultaneously, Mexico's Revolutionary Party was evolving as an extra-constitutional mechanism for translating nationalizing norms into political reality.

Today, enough educated persons — both in and out of government — share sufficient national outlook to ease Mexico's need for university-oriented nation-building leaders. These people man the mass media, much of the educational system, key positions in both the private and public economic sectors, the government agencies, and most of the socializing and operating political mechanisms in the country. At the same time that the university's cadre-building function recedes, rapidly expanding social and economic complexity calls for more highly trained and competent manpower at the professional level. As a consequence, in Mexico's institutions of higher learning the educational and training functions have begun to reassert themselves. The cycle has moved from the transitional toward the modern stage, as national integration becomes a reality.

Entering this new stage does not mean necessarily that Mexico's students have ceased to agitate or that the educational functions became predominant overnight. The traditional student subculture called for low academic performance, and the long cadre-building phase encouraged activities that diverted the students from concentration on course work. Attempts to meet the Mexican society's demand for more effectively trained graduates by increasing the amount of preprofessional education, by raising standards in the *facultades,* and by imposing greater discipline upon both teaching staff and students led to some of the disturbances at the national university and several state schools during 1966 and 1967, as did continuing student irritation at inadequacies in educational resources, especially in the provincial schools.

Despite enormous gains over a half century, Mexico's political system is not yet fully modernized and democratized, particularly at the state and local level. It is not impossible, therefore, to encounter examples of university students still providing leadership against imposition of unpopular or unqualified candidates for public office. This occurred, for example, in the state of Sonora before the 1967 elections. Again, the 1968 pre-Olympics student demonstrations in Mexico City were a flameup of long smoldering *universitario* dislike of the closed national political system evolving under the Revolutionary party and particularly of the rather authoritarian treatment accorded young people by some government officials. Although the incident that set off the riots was unusually rough tactics applied by Federal District police and later military units against battling young people from two long-time rivals, the National University and the Politécnico, speedy consolidation of student and even some professorial reactions suggest that intellectuals increasingly believe that Mexico's politics should be more open and representative, that is, more nearly resembling the system described in the formal constitution.

These attitudes are evidenced in only a small portion of the Mexican populace, however. Significantly, unlike France a few months earlier, in Mexico the students were unable to find even temporary allies among the ranks of organized labor and peasants, whose members' political outlook is more suited to the centralized, single dominant party pattern than to an open and highly competitive political system. All this means that the government is faced with the dilemma of trying to satisfy the demands of a small but articulate group seeking greater democracy at the same time it rules a broader mass of citizens satisfied with strong central direction. The problem is not really insoluble, for to date the students have been satisfied with a degree of symbolic recognition of their demands. Despite the really vicious street battles, within a few weeks the students were back in school, and in February, 1969, when it could be done without the President losing face, the chief of police of the Federal District was allowed to resign discreetly. Compared with what they were only a decade or two ago, however, Mexico's students are much less politicized as radical activists and much more academically oriented, with the nationalizing function performed less in the university and more in other social institutions throughout the country than ever before. The same cannot be said for most of the rest of Latin America.

None of the region's university systems is in the pre-transition, "aristocratic" period, but some are not yet in the mainstream of the development process. Even where the consequences of speedy change have not accumulated to such an extent that the internal political system is in crisis and the search for leadership has forced a cadre-building function upon the schools, the example of neighboring countries has stirred the imagination of the students. In Honduras, Paraguay, and other republics where development is less evident, the *universitarios* have begun to take an interest in politics, bringing pressure on military regimes or on governments that fail to respond efficiently to the most obvious needs of the populace. As yet in such countries the students have not become a major factor in the political process, but if our thesis about the cyclical nature of the university's role in supplying leaders for national integration is correct, they soon will.

In well over half of Latin America, however, university *políticos* already are an important political force, for the pressures of society have carried the students past the stage of recruitment into that of involvement in national-policy questions. It is, of course, misleading to assume that students have equal influence, or the same sort of influence, in these countries. Amount and rate of change are important variables; so is the degree to which formal and informal structures outside the university supply leadership in the integration process or act as forces counter to it. The kinds of frustrations students feel in school and in career expectations, and the existence of a sense of alienation from the ongoing political system, must be considered.

It remains an open question whether each of these countries will pass successfully through the three stages of university cadre-building, as Mexico did. Not all have the same physical or human resources, and few have had the sort of revolutionary experience that weakens the traditional interests opposing modernization. None of the other Latin American states enjoys the luxury of time, for modern communications speed up and lump together the multifold problems terrible cost to the academic role of the university and with no foreseeable benefits to the political system. The possibilities are different for each republic. Meanwhile, however, the psychological yearning for spokesmen who can personify the national identity continues unabated, and *universitarios* answer the call.

Some of the Latin American countries are just entering the leadership-cadre-building stage, so the other functions of their universities have not yet been seriously or continuously disrupted. El Salvador, Costa Rica, and Chile probably fit this pattern. Other republics are already in the midst of serious political maladjustment problems, of which university unrest is an obvious symptom. Some states in this category seem to be making progress in evolving nation-building structures outside the university, but have a long way to go before the pressures on the cloister and its inhabitants ease. Peru, Venezuela, and perhaps Uruguay and Brazil might be examples. Other states seem to be stuck on dead center, with too many limitations on effective modernizing and institution-building to permit hope for early easing of the pressures on the university to supply leaders. Argentina, Colombia, Ecuador, Nicaragua, Guatemala, possibly Brazil, and a few others fall into this group.

Level of economic or social development does not seem to be a particularly good indicator of the amount or success of student involvement in nation-building. As José Luis de Imaz has suggested, in Argentina a fast rate of economic change and (for Latin America) an extremely high standard of social development could not counteract the effects of a static socio-political system that hindered evolution of political structures adequate to rationalize the new conditions for all sectors of society. In the Dominican Republic, with relatively weak economic development and very low indices of social growth, the same pattern of inadequate political structures emerged. In both cases, the students became very active until the traditional forces reacted to restrict their political role, after which the *universitarios* became alienated from the ongoing political system.

In assigning countries to these categories, Bolivia and Cuba seem to be cases apart, because the recentness of their revolutions does not permit one to judge the permanence of the institution-building attempts. Given the fall of Paz Estenssoro and the MNR, nation-building in Bolivia is at least temporarily sidetracked, and student agitation can be expected to grow. The 1967 instances, however, reflect frustration over immediate university needs and student insecurity with the future rather than reaction to national integration problems. In Cuba, those who do not reflect Dr. Castro's version of the nation are not allowed to participate in politics, in or out of the university. On the other hand, like all schools on the island, the universities are a principal indoctrinating mechanism for those who do accept the Cuban Revolution, and students work closely in and with the political structures enforcing the new nationalism.

Students and the Ongoing Political Process

Well-meaning as most student political activists are, their participation in national politics frequently seems counterproductive. Certainly one can see a growing tendency on the part of policy-makers, both domestic and foreign, to deplore such activity and to act against it. This is true not only of the military despot who strikes out at the challenge to his regime emanating from the university, but also of the more liberal and modernizing national leadership elements who are often a product of student political experience. Those responsible for government and foundation aid from abroad, who once saw education and participation in political life by the intellectual sectors as the best hope for constructive and evolutionary political development, are beginning to recognize that general assistance programs to universities can have unexpected political effects.

Considering the way in which student political activism diverts not only student *políticos*, but also their less-politicized university colleagues from their technical and professional studies, it is hardly surprising that responsible policy-makers react negatively. Any interruption in the orderly supply of physicians, engineers, school-teachers, or even lawyers can have serious and immediate effect upon the rate and balance of development. Yet it would be manifestly unfair to suggest that the majority of Latin America's educators and politicians reject student politics out of hand, simply because it is inconvenient. That students are engaged in a cadre-building discourse and involved in national politics does not mean automatically that the political values they espouse, the political style they adopt, or the political actions they perform are compatible with the ongoing political system or contrived to hasten the modernization of that system. On the contrary, much student political activity in Latin America today is out of phase with the contemporary needs of the society in which it takes place, harking back to an earlier, more traditional era or looking so far into the future that it has little relevance for the present.

In most republics, the economic, social, and political systems represent at least the earlier stages of modernization, with increasingly differentiated structures to perform more specialized functions, and in a number of countries the systems are far more complex. Given the nature of education and the resulting student subculture, student values and the action patterns they motivate simply have not adjusted to the new conditions, so that university activist incursions into the operating political process tend to disrupt already heavily burdened machinery.

However ineffectually the constitutional agencies work to enforce compromise for a general welfare, however inadequately ideological political movements and class- or interest-bound parties act to perform the extraconstitutional functions of aggregation, however reluctantly the old-style oligarchies accede to the more challenging new interests, day-to-day politics has become more pragmatic and problem oriented. A system for adjusting differences has evolved — one based not only on the amount of pressure the emerging interests can bring, but also on the degree to which the leaders of these challenging groups can commit their followers to assume the obligations inherent in participating in the operating political system. The student activist's approach to policy questions is very different, leaning on the emotional, the normative, the all-embracing and often simplistic solutions of abstract ideology. He does not ask what can be done, but what should be done, and insists upon doing it immediately. If his unrealistic demands upon the government are not met, he may resort to violence. He will certainly denounce the incumbent administration as abandoning the interests and needs of the masses.

It is not simply sporadic violence that bothers the policy-maker. Many of the present-day liberal leaders — Betencourt, Frei, Haya de la Torre, and the rest — began as student *políticos* who did not hesitate to resort to force to make their points. That such men did make their points to some degree has, however, altered the conditions under which politics takes place. Once the students were one of a very few organized or semi-organized groups which sought to influence politics from outside the closed circle of an oligarchy composed of landowners, incipient manufacturers, and those who benefited from co-operation with foreign-dominated extractive industries and plantation production for export (petroleum, copper, bananas, and so forth), together with their collaborators in the church, military, and government hierarchies. The university intellectuals took upon themselves the role of spokesmen and leaders for the inchoate interests of urban labor, landless *peones*, sharecroppers, and day-wage farm workers, providing a certain amount of symbolic gratification to their unwashed clientele, but relatively few immediate material benefits that might reduce the economic advantages enjoyed by the ruling elites.

Today, in the more developed countries a new set of conditions obtains. The unionized portions of the city workers, lower-range bureaucrats, small merchants, and even rural laborers in large-scale commercial agriculture are beginning to produce their own leaders. Within the traditional oligarchy, new and conflicting interests have appeared, marking the expansion of consumer-goods industries; these seek domestic markets, which require different fiscal policies than does the export trade. New, modernizing elements in the clergy and officer corps provide moral support and, to a limited extent, physical security to the challenging elements in the society and economy. A plethora of demands — for general fiscal reform, for improved social conditions, and for immediate adjustment of labor-management relations, among others — tends to overload the political systems, even if the claims are limited to representatives of interests already well enough organized to be self-sustaining politically.

The students, with their tendency to seek instant solutions to all of the country's problems, bring heavy pressure upon government to incorporate emerging, poorly-organized, and frequently not very productive elements into the competition for allocation of limited resources. Neither the students' old allies, who are now better able to fend for themselves and who fear the demands of a new order of claimants, nor the older oligarchy, who once saw university politics as a relatively harmless means of easing the clamor of rising interest groups, welcomes this kind of participation in the national political process, particularly when it may be accompanied by the activities of a National Liberation Movement supported vocally and perhaps financially and with arms by an outside power.

Interest-group and political leaders are trying to sort out the relationships among labor, management, landowners, farm workers, street-corner venders, shopkeepers, bureaucrats, and all the rest. To do so, they have begun to evolve a kind of semicorporative pattern that represents the earlier stages of modernization, with functional differentiation just beginning and the unifying structures not yet operating very smoothly. The students push mass representation in politics and all-inclusive solutions to national problems, a pattern that might suit a diffuse and unspecialized traditional society or a very modern polity with fully developed political structures to absorb and transform undifferentiated demands into workable policy

alternatives. The pattern is not suitable in the current political context of most Latin American republics.

As the number of self-sustaining interests which relate pragmatically in this corporative political process grows, the student
políticos see their long-cherished influence waning. One-time dependent groups work out a *modus vivendi* with the traditional parties, affiliate with newer groupings, or pressure the political process
without formal alliance with an organized political movement. In
almost every case, when rapid change commences, the students withdraw whatever support they may have given the traditional political
parties because to youth such parties represent specialized rather
than all-inclusive national interests. With the evolution of a corporative decision-making pattern that excludes the unorganized masses
and the student leaders who claim to represent them, not even the
older challenging, national-integrating parties can hold all their
student followers. The nucleus of such movements generally includes previously dependent popular-interest groups — organized
labor, farm workers, storekeepers — under former student politicians. Although they recognize the theoretical need for complete
national integration and social justice, and preserve a façade of
nation-building in their party platforms and slogans, the rank-and-
file members of the component units making up the older national
integrating party are not terribly eager to incorporate new participants in the political process until their own very recent gains are
fully consolidated.

To the students, this is betrayal of the abstract ideal of universalism. The politically less active students, especially those who reject
the more radical parties and violence, tend to withdraw from politics,
becoming alienated from the existing party system, which they see
as a mockery of their idealistic expectations. All too often this carries
over into later life, in terms not only of leadership in party politics,
but of responsible political participation as well. If such persons
relate to the ongoing political process at all, it is almost always
through the specialized functional interests which are its component
parts. Thus, they support a continuation of interest-group politics
rather than an expansion of national integrating movements within
the working political system.

Members of the most radical student-activist minority work outside the government system, turning more extreme in their demands
so as to attract support that can satisfy the messianic political role
they assign to themselves as *universitarios*. The national goals they

announce become more and more amorphous, and the followers they try to recruit less politicized and much less amenable to organization and discipline for a common political end. Without any real base in numbers or influence, these radical activists seek to increase their chances for success by resorting to spectacular demonstrations of power through organized violence and other indications that they reject and hold in contempt the operating political-decision-making system.

Whether or not they act with this end consciously in mind, such actions place the student radicals beyond the pale of legitimacy. In the eyes of national political leaders, liberal or otherwise, these extreme manifestations of student political values represent a subsidiary system that is attempting to destroy the more general system from which it draws nourishment. Inevitably the rulers of the system under attack turn upon the subsystem, causing the student activists to become even more alienated and the less involved students to withdraw still another step from political participation. Occupation of university campuses by troops in Caracas, Bogotá, Rio, or Buenos Aires may be a necessary step in restoring the educational function to institutions of higher learning, but unless the action is accompanied by changes in the educational system and recognition of the need for effective national integration by the political system, it is a step that will be repeated over and over again until its causes are recognized and remedied.

BIBLIOGRAPHICAL NOTE

Most of the material in this study is a product of my own investigation and interviewing, but there are other sources that can add depth to what is offered here. In this bibliography, I shall limit reference to a few of the most relevant sources available in English.

On organization of Latin America's university systems, by far the best compilation is Harold R. W. Benjamin, *Higher Education in the American Republics* (New York, 1965). It contains a few factual errors, however, and being an official publication, the formal and very often highly optimistic statements of university administrators are reported as fact. Most important, the book offers little or no critical discussion of university problems. Another study, which seems to be all criticism and little tact, is R. P. Atcon, "The Latin American University," *Die Deutsche Universitäts Zeitung* (February, 1962), pp. 7–49. The difficulty here is that the author makes a general indictment of Latin America's universities without specifying that much of what he points to may be true of a specific university, but not of all. Some of the studies prepared by and for CHEAR (Council on Higher Education in the American Republics) and by Dean George Waggonner and his associates at the University of Kansas for annual "Seminars of Higher Education in the Americas" are also valuable in the context of organization.

On the political side, the more useful studies include: K. H. Silvert and Frank Bonilla, *Education and the Social Meaning of Development: A Preliminary Statement* (New York, 1961); Daniel Goldrich, *Radical Nationalism: The Political Orientation of Panamanian Law Students* (East Lansing, Michigan, 1961); David Spencer, *Student Politics in Latin America* (Washington, D.C., 1965); Myron Glazer, "The Professional and Political Attitudes of Chilean University Students," *Student Politics*, ed. S. M. Lipset (New York, 1967), pp. 332–354; John P. Harrison, "The Confrontation with the Political University," *The Annals*, Vol. 334 (March, 1961), pp. 74–83; John P. Harrison, "Learning and Politics in Latin American Universities," *Proceedings of the Academy of Political Science*, Vol. 27, No. 4 (May, 1964), pp. 331–46; David Nasatir, "University Experience and Political Unrest of Students in Buenos Aires," *Student Politics*, pp. 318–331; Glaucio Ary Dillon Soares, "The Active Few: Student Ideological Participation in Developing Countries," *Student Politics*, pp. 124–147; K. H. Silvert, "The University Student," *Continuity and Change in Latin America*, ed. John J. Johnson (Stanford, 1964). A number of related articles on education and the educated elites also appear in S. M. Lipset and Aldo Solari (eds.), *Elites in Latin America* (New York, 1967).

MYRON GLAZER

Student Politics in a Chilean University

Luis and His Friends

LUIS, ALONG WITH one hundred other students enrolled in the School of History of the Pedagogical Institute (*Pedagogico*) in March, 1964.[1] Like the great majority of his peers, he had had little contact with political groups in secondary school, although he was aware of the struggles among the different national parties. He had even considered studying in the School of Law, the breeding ground of politicians, but feared that the entrance requirements were more difficult and the competition was keener. He also thought his lower-middle-class background would not afford him the contacts that were so useful in starting a professional practice. In the end, he decided he would have a more successful career in the teaching profession.

During his first days at the *Pedagogico*, Luis observed the spirited atmosphere in which advanced students gathered in front of the school to have long discussions, many of which derived from political agreements or differences. Luis was almost immediately beset by partisans of various political groups which handed out literature presenting their point of view or calling attention to articles in the national press. It was obvious to him that the divergent ideas were taken very seriously by the student groups in his school. These groups, student miniatures of national parties, were highly competitive.

Luis and all other first-year students were approached by the Christian Democrats, whose organization impressed him, as did their efforts in helping him with any problems in registering or getting oriented. Students of the University Leftist Movement (*Movimento Universitario Izquierdista* or MUI), who described their group as a leftist coalition including Communists, Socialists, and Independents, seemed to be less efficient in reaching incoming students. Luis was told, however, that they had a file on every history student and his political preference.

At the time Luis entered the university, the 1964 national presidential campaign had officially just begun. The candidate of the incumbent conservative coalition, the Democratic Front (*Frente Democratico*), had withdrawn in the aftermath of a defeat in a local election. There remained only the center-left Christian Democrats and the Socialist-Communist-dominated Popular Front (*Frente de Acción Popular* or FRAP) on the ballot. The two competing forces differed less in policy than in style and reputation. Their platforms were strikingly similar, especially in their general emphasis on the need for sweeping social change. Both, as opposition parties, could freely attack the incumbent regime.

The Christian Democratic Party adopted the slogan, "revolution in liberty," and stressed the need to democratize and modernize state and nation through extensive reform in all areas. It accused the FRAP of espousing a "revolution with dictatorship." The Party proposed participation by workers in industrial ownership and management, the fullest use and control of Chile's natural resources, and an end to the "power and privileges of accumulated money." Its program did not, however, advocate the nationalization of American-owned copper mines, as the FRAP's did. The FRAP claimed that Chile had too long been bled by North American copper companies whose operations were blatantly imperialistic. As long as foreign capitalists controlled the country's most vital resource, the leftist coalition bitterly predicted, Chile was doomed to remain a servant nation.

As the campaign progressed, Luis realized how difficult it was to remain neutral or aloof. The great contest stepped up the tempo of student political life and stimulated the recruitment and propaganda activities of student partisans, who worked to organize support not only in the university, but also in metropolitan Santiago.

Luis's friend Jaime was one of these ardent campaign workers. Jaime, who had been active in a political group in high school, decided, even before entering the School of History, to join the university affiliate of the same group. To Jaime, the highly politicized atmosphere of the school was a great attraction. An admirer of the FRAP candidate, Senator Salvador Allende, and strongly influenced by Fidel Castro and the Cuban Revolution, Jaime believed that student radicals had an important part to play in the modernization of his country. He reminded Luis that the Student Federation

433

(*Federacíon de Estudiantes de Chile* or FECH) had been very active in politics for over fifty years, struggling to overcome the inequalities and injustices of Chilean society. Jaime argued that the student's privileged position in Chile, a country with so many pressing problems, *obliged* him to engage in social and political action; for a student to concentrate on his studies and professional training could only be a betrayal of the suffering masses. Jaime rejected the view that student organizations should only be concerned with school issues, such as housing or financial aid. He denied that university political groups were merely party tools. He also disagreed with those who believed that students could never be politically relevant and, to illustrate his case, reminded Luis of the front-page newspaper coverage recently given a meeting held between a high government official and the leaders of FECH to discuss the nation's border dispute with Argentina. Jaime also maintained that student political work in the urban slums and rural areas could help awaken the people to their needs and rights. Urging Luis to accompany him on such a mission the following Saturday, Jaime said: "See the waste of our precious resources and tell me that Chile does not need a social revolution. Look at the poverty and try to side with those who speak of 'democracy' and moderation. Talk to our Chilean *rotos* ["broken ones"] and tell me you cannot fight our exploiting aristocracy. Don't discuss the rights of the 500,000 who live in the gracious Chile known by tourists and visitors. Speak instead of the millions who go hungry in spite of rich soil, who drown in squalor while we attend our lovely schools."

Rosa, another good friend of Luis, responded quite differently to the campus political environment. Unlike Jaime, she came from a secondary school in the northern province of Coquimbo, and the world of politics was strange to her. She realized it was difficult not to identify with a political group, but her inherent dislike of political activity was so strong that she was alienated by all the attempts to recruit her and by the political chicanery she saw going on in the school. Although she was aware of the many problems facing the teaching profession — the lack of good jobs in the cities, the poor pay, and the low prestige — she rejected political agitation as the answer. A conscientious student, she was disturbed by the chronic strikes that plagued the *Pedagogico;* good training, she thought, was most essential if she were ever to help her future students.

Luis understood the two opposing views of his friends and felt caught in the middle. He began to understand better the great rivalry between the two major groups. They seemed to have almost the same number of members and were continually battling for the sympathies and votes of the uncommitted.

Through his many conversations with other students, Luis became aware that although few actually joined the groups, about one half were strong sympathizers. As he began to spend more and more time in political conversations, he saw that in the School of History the MUI appeared slightly stronger than the Christian Democrats. This was somewhat unusual, for, both in the *Pedagogico* and in the university-wide offices, the Christian Democrats retained most of the major positions. The strength of the MUI in his school, in fact, had led a few of his classmates to identify more closely with the Christian Democrats than they ordinarily would have; some had even become members primarily for this reason. One of his friends explained: "The Marxists are very strong in this school, and since I am in sympathy with the Christian Democrats, I feel I should actively support them." The competition between the two major groups markedly increased the high degree of politicization of the school. Since each feared the other would gain an undue advantage, both tended to define all issues on the campus in highly political terms.

This situation was intensified as the presidential campaign became a widening spiral of claim and counterclaim, charge and countercharge. Under the pressure of such exchanges and because of the similarity of the two programs, partisan allegiances were personalized. Each candidate — Eduardo Frei for the Christian Democrats and Salvador Allende for the FRAP — had developed a substantial personal following over the years. Although there were some instances of personal attacks on the candidates themselves, much more energy was devoted to vilifying the supposed "real powers behind the thrones." There was a strong attempt to associate the FRAP coalition with Communist domination and to depict the Socialist Allende as a pawn whom the Communists would soon dispose of, were he elected, in order to set up their own dictatorship. Guilt by association also became a major FRAP weapon, particularly after the right-wing parties gave their support to Frei. A flood of headlines in the Communist press linked various *latifundistas* (large landowners) and "exploiters" with Frei and his party. Attempts were even made to associate the Christian Democratic candidate with Fascism and with a small Nazi group that supported him as the lesser of two evils. Not only were drastic attempts made to discredit the opposition, but also each group worked to widen the base of its own support. Ideological consistency became far less important than victory. Each national coalition attempted to build its own positive image, by portraying its opposition as representing narrow and alien interests.

As he followed the course of the campaign, Luis, like many of his peers, became increasingly aware of Chile's social and economic problems and the programs proposed to remedy them. Yet, none of the current student groups attracted him. He would have preferred a group with an independent approach and without a commitment to a national political leader. He believed that Chile needed students dedicated to solving national problems, but not overly committed to any particular party. In the relatively partisan atmosphere of the School of History, Luis's views were in the minority. In many other schools, however, a majority of the students believed that all the existing groups were too involved in *politiquería* ("dirty politics") to merit the students' support. They felt they should try to make their contribution as intelligent, unaffiliated critics of society. Many were simply uninterested in politics. Others were politically concerned, but critical of the politicians' behavior and unconvinced by the campaign rhetoric. They thought that little was to be gained through partisan action on behalf of an existing political alternative.

Luis's good friend Hector, who was studying in the School of Engineering, observed that very few students at his school had actually joined a political group and that the number of the sympathizers seemed relatively small. The School of Engineering seemed to lack the "leftist" flavor of the School of History, for the Christian Democrats controlled the elective student offices and enjoyed much more sympathy than the MUI. In both schools, a few ideologically committed activists set the tone for a large majority of sympathizers and noninvolved students. This led Luis and Hector to complain about the overpoliticization of the schools. Even many of the sympathizers of both major groups felt that the political activity had deteriorated into machinations, factionalism, and manipulations, instead of leading to serious efforts to solve university and societal problems. Generally, however, Christian Democratic and noninvolved students believed overpoliticization and *politiquería* to be more of a problem in the university than did the FRAP supporters.

As Luis's experiences in the School of History differed from those of his friends in engineering, so did they diverge from those of young Chileans entering the School of Medicine. Roberto, a first-year medical student, was well aware of the social problems of his country. This was, in fact, one of the reasons why he had decided upon a career in medicine. Yet, it was also obvious to him that his major challenge in the next few years would be to learn the basic materials in the biological sciences. Together with the majority of his classmates, he realized that becoming a good doctor had to be his primary concern.

From what other students had told him, Roberto knew that professional commitment and political interest were kept quite separate at the Medical School. The classroom was a place where medical knowledge was imparted and learned. Politics had to be put aside at the door. While other schools might be affected by strikes, the medical students had to remember that their major responsibility was to their work.

Roberto was not, however, oblivious to the political activity going on around him. He listened to many discussions in the cafeteria and read the propaganda posted in the halls. As in all other schools, when the FECH elections approached, heated arguments broke out between MUI supporters and the Christian Democrats. Roberto learned that in recent student elections his school had voted for the Christian Democrats, but that more than one class delegate and sometimes even the school's student president had come from the opposing group.

Roberto also noticed an important change in the attitudes of many medical students as they advanced through the school. They tended to become more confident of their ability to complete the required work and surer that some day they would be doctors. They grew more concerned with the broader problem of effecting change in the society, and began to think that they could make only a limited contribution through technical competence alone. As students went through the medical training program, their interest in politics sharpened, and they moved to the left. Increasingly, they found it difficult to separate the professional from the political, believing that government policy strongly affected medical progress throughout Chile.

Indeed, when asked whether it was more important to gain technical competence or to participate in attempts to bring about social change, a high percentage of student-doctors chose the latter. Students at the end of their medical or engineering training seemed the least convinced of the primary importance of their studies. Chilean students, generally, saw the intake of technical knowledge as the primary rationale of university study (Table 1). Yet as they drew closer to accepting full professional responsibilities, many became less sure that this was the best way to contribute to social progress.[2]

437

Table 1:
Preference for Student Roles: Trainee vs Activist by School and Year

	History	Engi-neering	Medi-cine	Physics	Totals	1st year	2nd–3rd years	4th–6th years
Trainee	65 (61)	72 (68)	65 (64)	67 (20)	67 (213)	82 (84)	66 (70)	55 (59)
Activist	27 (25)	24 (23)	29 (29)	17 (5)	26 (82)	15 (15)	27 (29)	35 (38)
Others°	9 (8)	3 (3)	6 (6)	17 (5)	7 (22)	4 (4)	7 (7)	10 (11)
Totals	101 (94)	99 (94)	100 (99)	101 (30)	100 (317)	101 (103)	100 (106)	100 (108)

°Includes those who did not answer and those who rejected both roles.

Student Political Partisanship: Origins and Content

Several characteristics influenced the nature and degree of a student's political involvement. Among the more outstanding factors were religion, socio-economic background, and previous political participation in secondary school. It is quite clear, for example, that those who defined themselves as practicing Catholics had a strong tendency to identify with the Christian Democratic Party and to indicate little preference for the FRAP. Conversely, students who had no religious affiliation, and who were politically involved, tended to give their support to the FRAP.

Furthermore, those who had joined political youth groups in secondary schools were much more likely to continue such involvement in the university. A number of students indicated that they had first become interested in politics through the social-action programs sponsored by the Catholic high schools.

Both inclination toward involvement and political preference were influenced by social-class background. Recruitment of children from lower-middle- and working-class families to the university tends to increase the number for whom university politics is an important concern.[3] This relationship does not, however, necessarily result from their inability to accommodate themselves to university life. More likely, politics is seen as an important means of changing an iniquitous social order and, simultaneously, as a way of gaining a place in it. In countries like Chile, student politics is an excellent way to belong to society and yet be, or believe oneself to be, engaged in its transformation.

Students from lower-middle- and working-class families supported the Christian Democrats more than they did the FRAP. This was particularly true among those who had gained admission to the schools with high social prestige, such as engineering and medicine. These students seemed to be influenced by the promise of substantial economic comfort and social recognition.

Our most important finding concerning student political affiliation is the consistency between the fathers' political views and those of their children. Of the students who said their fathers supported right-wing parties, 71 per cent were neither for the Christian Democrats nor the FRAP (Table 2). Many said they favored no political group in the forthcoming national election, but indicated in subsequent questions positive support for the incumbent conservative government of Jorge Alessandri. Sons of right-wing fathers were the single largest group implicitly or explicitly supporting the Alessandri regime.

Striking generational continuity can also be seen in the case of the FRAP and Christian Democratic supporters. Sixty-one per cent of the students whose fathers favored the FRAP had the same preference. Significantly, among those whose fathers identified with the Christian Democrats, only 4 per cent hoped for a FRAP victory; the majority (57 per cent) duplicated their fathers' political position.

Table 2:
Students' Political Preferences* by Fathers' Political Preferences

STUDENTS				FATHERS				
	Christian Democrats	Center	Right	Radical	FRAP	Independent	Unknown or Unavailable	Totals
Christian Democrats	57	33	21	21	20	10	32	32
	(41)	(1)	(9)	(12)	(10)	(1)	(27)	(101)
FRAP	4	—	7	35	61	40	13	22
	(3)	—	(3)	(20)	(30)	(4)	(11)	(71)
None or Other	39	67	71	44	18	50	55	46
	(28)	(2)	(30)	(25)	(9)	(5)	(46)	(145)
Totals	100	100	99	100	99	100	100	100
	(72)	(3)	(42)	(57)	(49)	(10)	(84)	(317)

* Students' political preference here and in Table 3 means preference for a national political group.

The children of supporters of the Radical Party represent a special case. Over the past decade, the Radical Party had lost almost all its influence among university students and had grown increasingly inept on the national scene, though it continued to maintain a tight grip over the large bureaucracy through very extensive patronage. Frequently, the children of Radical fathers rejected the Radical Party not because of its ideology, but because of its ineffectiveness. It was not inconsistent with their fathers' reformist ideology that many of these students embraced the programs of the left-wing parties. This was, no doubt, a major factor among many of the 35 per cent who supported the FRAP. Given the strong secular tradition among the Radicals, allegiance to the Christian Democrats was predictably smaller (21 per cent).

Our findings fully support a conclusion of Frank Bonilla's study of FECH leaders during the mid-1950's.[4] He noted a strong coincidence between the political affiliations of Chilean student leaders and those of their fathers.

[This coincidence helps] to explain the generally moderate tone of university politics and FECH action in this final period. The powerful psychic charge of intergenerational or parental conflict does not seem to be an important motivating factor behind the political activities of most of today's student leaders. Insofar as this works in favor of a more rational and unemotional attack on political problems, it favors the development of the technical, managerial approach associated with the "bargaining interest group" or the reformer rather than the intransigence of the agitator or revolutionary.[5]

Students reflect in their political attitudes both the current center-left trend in Chilean politics and the relatively substantial influence of their fathers. Contemporary student politics, strongly reformist in tone, enjoys considerable support in Chilean national life. The integration of student with national politics in Chile both mirrors and serves to reinforce political stability while simultaneously inhibiting independent student action.

Student Political Attitudes: A Profile

Although Chile is one of the most developed countries in Latin America, it suffers from severe agricultural problems, growing urban slums, and serious health and educational deficiencies. The difficulties of economic development are aggravated by Chile's precarious position in the international market. Most students were deeply aware of this situation, but differed in their selection of the most important factor inhibiting national development.

Respondents were asked to list what they considered the most formidable barriers to national progress. Their selections can be loosely clustered into four groups: deficiencies inherent in the character of Chilean people; the significance of personal contacts rather than competence; foreign imperialism; and an internal monopoly by an elite, requiring basic structural changes amounting to a social revolution.

Students consistently emphasized structural causes for Chile's impeded development; in fact, 44 per cent considered this the most important factor. There were no striking differences in this result by school, but entering students tended to stress these aspects less than their more advanced colleagues. Only 19 per cent of the total sample blamed the actual character of the Chilean people, while 25 per cent pointed to a still potent remnant of traditional Chilean society — the ascriptive, highly personal character of national life. These students urged a shift toward achievement as the sole criterion of personal advancement. The overwhelming majority felt that performance and competence should be the prime criteria in attaining professional success. Many were aware that the realities of the Chilean marketplace diverged greatly from this ideal, which accounts for the very large number of students who cited this as a major problem.[6]

Finally, only 8 per cent named imperialism as the major obstacle to Chile's progress.[7] The much-publicized controversy over the United States-owned copper mines would have led one to predict far greater emphasis on this factor. Attacks on imperialism were, however, associated with the extreme partisan left, and especially with the Communists, during the 1964 electoral campaign, which may have led many students to shun this choice.

The largest segment of the students fell into a center-left category. They emphasized basic structural factors as the greatest obstacle to Chilean progress, but not to the exclusion of other, less radical causes. These responses indicate that there existed a void between students' beliefs and their degree of political involvement. While many students were quite aware of the severity of national social problems, they strongly resisted the call for political action. Some students were cynical about the possibility of implementing proposed solutions. Others were suspicious of the motivations of the activists. Nonetheless, the widespread belief in the necessity of social change certainly strengthened the position of those students who saw no alternative to direct political action. Their control of major student organizations and their ideological fervor were reinforced by the political tendencies of the large majority of their fellow students. Even though this majority may have been uninvolved and in some cases, highly critical of certain aspects of student politics, they still provided the proper climate for the dominance of activist influence during a time of national political crisis. In their over-all goals, the student activists represented most of their peers.

Further evidence of the center-left tendencies of the student body came in response to a question asked of those with a stated national-party preference: "What should be the general policy of the government of your choice should it come to power?" The students divided almost evenly between those who preferred a policy of "substantial" reforms (45 per cent) and those who desired a more radical alternative of "structural" changes (43 per cent). Only 12 per cent believed "moderate" reforms would suffice.[8] By political preference, the FRAP students (65 per cent) most often proposed "structural" changes. Among the Christian Democrats, on the other hand, "substantial" reforms (52 per cent) were more frequently supported than "structural" changes (34 per cent). Thus, the students generally viewed Chile's problems as largely structural and called for changes in the social order that ranged from the substantial to the sweeping.

Students with a stated preference for a national political group were asked to recommend a course of action for their party should it fail to win power through the ballot box in the near future. Only 7 per cent advocated the use of extra-electoral means, and almost all of these students were FRAP supporters. Ninety-nine of the 101 Christian Democrats, whose party went on to win the presidential election in 1964, preferred to remain in the legal opposition in the event of a failure at the polls.

A second question testing commitment to the democratic process divided the students far more sharply. They were asked: "Do you think that any group, no matter how detrimental you believe its policies to be, should be allowed to assume office if it wins the next presidential election?" Again, a majority chose to respect the outcome of the election, but 38 per cent answered negatively or were undecided (Table 3). Although the students were not formally asked to specify which groups they would deprive of electoral victory, informal conversations showed the objectionable groups to be the Nazis and the Communists. For some students, particularly in

Table 3:
   Should Any Group That Wins Be Allowed to Take Office?
   By School and Year

	His-tory	Engi-neering	Med-icine	Phy-sics	Totals	1st year	2nd-3rd years	4th-6th years
Yes	61	56	69	57	62	57	61	66
	(57)	(53)	(68)	(17)	(195)	(59)	(65)	(71)
No	22	25	18	33	23	26	22	20
	(21)	(23)	(18)	(10)	(72)	(27)	(23)	(22)
Undecided	15	19	13	10	15	16	16	14
	(14)	(18)	(13)	(3)	(48)	(16)	(17)	(15)
Other	2	—	—	—	0	1	1	—
	(2)	—	—	—	(2)	(1)	(1)	—
Totals	100	100	100	100	100	100	100	100
	(94)	(94)	(99)	(30)	(317)	(103)	(106)	(108)

the School of Physics, the prospect of any Nazi in power was complete anathema. Some of these students were sons of Jewish refugees who had fled from Hitler. Although the Nazis were not an issue in the 1964 presidential election, Jorge Prat, an extreme right-winger associated with Fascist ideas, had been a candidate for a short time. This threat, perhaps heightened by the history of an active Nazi movement in Chile in the 1930's, did generate some fear on the part of those already sensitive to this issue.

There is little doubt, however, that the major group at issue was the Communist Party. The victory of a Communist-supported coalition (the FRAP) in the presidential election was a real and frightening possibility to some students. Many of those who felt that Chile could never recover from a "Communist-type" government were willing to exclude the Communists from their definition of democracy.

A breakdown by degree of political activity is particularly revealing in regard to a student's commitment to democracy (Table 4). The activists (69 per cent) are the most democratic, while the politically uninvolved students are both the most uncertain (28 per cent) and the least affirmative (51 per cent) in upholding the electorate's right to decide. This pattern undoubtedly reflects strong anti-Communist feelings among the politically inactive students. There were also significant differences between the FRAPists and the Christian Democrats. We had predicted that the former would have most

Table 4:

Should Any Group That Wins Be Allowed to Take Office?
By Position on Political Activity-Attitude Index and Political Preference

	Active Parti-sans[a]	Critical Sym-pathizers[b]	Non-involved[c]	Totals	Christian Democrats	FRAP	None or Other
Yes	69	62	51	62	73	63	52
	(61)	(94)	(40)	(195)	(74)	(45)	(76)
No	19	26	19	23	15	24	28
	(17)	(40)	(15)	(72)	(15)	(17)	(40)
Undecided	10	11	28	15	12	11	19
	(9)	(17)	(22)	(48)	(12)	(8)	(28)
Other	1	—	1	0	—	1	1
	(1)	—	(1)	(2)	—	(1)	(1)
Totals	99	99	99	100	100	99	100
	(88)	(151)	(78)	(317)	(101)	(71)	(145)

[a] Students who stated they were leaders in, members of, or sympathizers wholly in accord with a particular university political group.

[b] Those who sympathized with one group, but expressed strong reservations either about it or about the usefulness of any kind of political involvement, or who did not sympathize with any university group, but voiced a distinct preference for one of the national parties and voted for its campus affiliate in the student elections.

[c] Those who claimed no political affiliation, defined themselves as having no interest in politics, and showed no consistent voting pattern.

strongly defended the democratic process since they stood to lose the most by the hardening of a "military coup" mentality. On a national level, the FRAPist had attempted to expose every form of this kind of thinking. Yet, paradoxically, 11 per cent of the FRAPist students stated that they were "undecided," and 24 per cent answered negatively. The intense struggle for political power seems to have had a detrimental effect on Chilean democratic thought. The FRAP supporters apparently feared that a "reactionary" government could destroy the power which they had struggled so hard to attain. The nonaligned students would have presumably preferred a temporary limitation on democratic action rather than risk the dangers of an "extremist" government. The Christian Democrats, whose ideology precluded the use of force, resisted somewhat more successfully the expedient of denying political opponents the prerogatives which one cherished for oneself. The students' responses to the two questions on political means accurately reflected Chile's democratic political system and its simultaneous history of occasional military intervention and repressive government action.

Although the intensity and extent of student involvement vary considerably by school, three basic groups can be identified in the Chilean university: a minority of leaders and activists, a much larger group of sympathizers, and a third group, roughly equal in size to the activists, with little interest in politics. A considerable number in all three groups are concerned with the overpoliticization of the university.

The effectiveness of student political groups in asserting their power is very much affected by the nature of the learning experience in each school. Thus, political activity is limited by the difficulty of a medical student's course demands, the obligations of hospital work, and the insistence by many professors that politics be kept out of the classroom. In the School of History, on the other hand, the disadvantageous position of the student's future career as a teacher, the subject matter of the courses, and the free time resulting from limited academic requirements reinforce the attractions of politics. Our findings support the hypothesis that the greater the curricular challenge, the lower the probability of student political activity. This is especially true when political action can effect social change that will directly benefit relatively underprivileged professional groups.

Our data also lend weight to the view that the student political role is strongly influenced by the characteristics of transitional societies and their political institutions. The quality and amount of student political involvement seem to reflect the responsiveness of political institutions and the strength of the various groups representing major interests. The more rigid the institutions and the weaker the established interest groups, the greater is the students' political involvement. Students as a political force can be most effective in crisis situations. When political institutions fail or a vacuum in public leadership occurs, student leaders may suddenly find themselves enjoying national prominence and a real opportunity to influence the course of events.

In 1964, a wide variety of Chilean political parties were permitted to vie for political power without fear of repression. There was no dictatorship and no need to "mount the barricades." Major sectors of the population, including the most underprivileged, had important spokesmen at the national level. These leaders articulated the policies to which student activists responded. Disruptive action was not encouraged.[9]

Many students were active in the presidential campaign. The more astute among them were alert to the realities of political life in Chile and the shortcomings of its leaders. Should reforms — demanded by the students, promised by the politicians, and desperately needed by the people — fail to materialize, these active, dedicated students and their presently nonaligned peers may well serve as the fulcrum of future political change.[10]

Various organizations have supported this project, and I am pleased to acknowledge their generous assistance. The Inter-University Study of Labor Problems in Economic Development and the Industrial Relations Section of Princeton University provided time and facilities during the planning stage. Miss Doris McBride and other members of the Section staff always responded to requests for help. The Henry L. and Grace Doherty Foundation financed the field work, and the Center for International Studies of Princeton University supported the writing of the study materials. The work on this article has benefited directly from the generosity of the Comparative National Development Project of Harvard University and a grant from Smith College. I also extend my appreciation to Miss Marcia Alexander, Mr. Donald Emmerson, Mrs. Penina M. Glazer, Mr. Terry Lichtash, and Mr. Joel S. Migdal for their insightful criticisms of the manuscript. Our many Chilean friends have won my everlasting gratitude.

REFERENCES

1. Although Luis, Jaime, Rosa, Hector, and Roberto cannot be found among the real life students of the university, the attitudes and experiences they typify can.

   Data on Chilean students were gathered in several ways. Contemporary Chilean newspaper and journal articles, as well as scholarly and government sources, were used to secure a picture of official and popular thinking on educational problems in general and the student's role in particular. Persons well acquainted with Chilean education, including social scientists, university professors, professional practitioners, and university students, were also relied on as informants. Finally, a lengthy interview schedule, drawn up during the first few months after our arrival in Chile in September, 1963, was utilized to tap the attitudes of a representative sample of university students.

   The interview schedule covered family and educational background, professional training experiences and attitudes, political background and experiences, and political attitudes. The political questions were developed almost entirely from our observations of Chilean life and politics in 1963–64. The schedule was pretested and discussed at great length with Chileans of all political persuasions to ensure that our queries focused on those matters considered most relevant by local observers.

Student Politics in a Chilean University

The actual interviews were conducted — over half by the author and his wife, the remainder by Chilean assistants — with students in four schools of the University of Chile, the largest and most important university in the country. These schools train students in fields that are essential for national development: medicine, engineering, secondary-school (history) teaching, and physics.

Seventy-five per cent of the School of Physics' 40 students were interviewed. History had approximately 250 students; the number interviewed there was somewhat less than 40 per cent. The sample in Medicine represented about 8 per cent of 1225 students. In Engineering, with almost 1500, the sample represented around 6 per cent. All samples were stratified by year and randomly drawn. The interview schedule appears in Myron Glazer, "The Professional and Political Attitudes of Chilean University Students," S. M. Lipset (ed.), *Student Politics* (New York: Basic Books, 1967). Chile has seven state-recognized universities with a total enrollment of over twenty-five thousand students. The University of Chile accounts for almost half of this number. The bulk of the universities are concentrated in the major cities of Santiago and Valparaíso, although the University of Concepción is located well to the south. The Roman Catholic Church supports two universities whose combined enrollment consists of one fourth of the higher-education enrollment. In the past, the most important student political activity has been in Santiago, although left-wing influence has been quite strong in Concepción. A comparable study there might well find a high degree of student political involvement. An investigation at the Catholic universities, however, would probably yield findings indicative of the higher social-class background of the students and of their more conservative political views. For an overview of Chilean higher education, consult Clark C. Gill, *Education and Social Change in Chile* (Washington, D.C., 1966). Our analysis will focus on students in the Schools of History, Engineering, and Medicine. For further discussion of the School of Physics, see Myron Glazer, "Field Work in a Hostile Environment: A Chapter in the Sociology of Social Research in Chile," *Comparative Education Review*, Vol. 10 (June, 1966), pp. 367–376. Professional socialization in these schools is discussed at length in the author's article, "El proceso de socializacion profesional en cuatro carreras chilenas," *Revista Latinoamericana de Sociología*, Vol. 2 (November, 1966); pp. 333–367.

2. In the study of comparative student activity, there is a dearth of material collected over time. Since the drop-out rate is usually quite high, statements about the differences among students at different points of their training must be made with great caution. Panel studies would also be extremely useful in shedding light on the factors separating the successful from the unsuccessful degree seekers.

3. S. M. Lipset, "University Students and Politics in Underdeveloped Countries," *Student Politics*, in S. M. Lipset (ed.), *Student Politics* (New York: Basic Books, 1967), p. 29.

4. Frank Bonilla, "The Student Federation of Chile; 50 years of Political

Action," *Journal of Inter-American Studies,* Vol. 2 (July, 1960), pp. 311–334.

5. Frank Bonilla, *Students in Politics: Three Generations of Political Action in a Latin American University* (unpublished Ph.D. dissertation, Harvard University, 1959), p. 257. Major sections of this work are soon to appear in Frank Bonilla and Myron Glazer, *Students and Politics in Chile,* to be published by Basic Books.

6. For further discussion of this point, see M. Glazer, "The Professional and Political Attitudes of Chilean University Students," S. M. Lipset (ed.), *Student Politics,* pp. 335–337.

7. The nature of the question may partially explain this result. While three of the twelve problems suggested fell into the "structural" category, only one cited imperialism. Of those students who did cite imperialism, 64 per cent were in the School of History. Many contemporary students, social scientists, and politicians are obviously concerned with the extent of United States influence in Chile. The type of suspicion which many students expressed about our project was one clear indicator. See M. Glazer, "Field Work in a Hostile Environment: A Chapter in the Sociology of Social Research in Chile." For an elaboration of this theme which focuses on the problems resulting from the demise of Project Camelot and the military sponsorship of overseas research, see M. Glazer and P. M. Glazer, "Las Investigaciones Sociales y el Mundo Real: Los Chilenos y los Gringos," *Revista Latino Americana de Sociología,* Vol. 2 (July, 1968), pp. 228–249.

8. The students were asked to choose one of three alternative answers: "make mild reforms"; "make major reforms, but preserve the general structural framework of Chilean society"; and "make major structural changes in the society."

9. This was most readily evident during the general strike in March, 1964, and the rupture of diplomatic relations with Cuba in August. Both the Christian Democrats and the FRAPists were intent on maintaining order to preclude any excuse for military intervention.

10. For an expanded treatment of the Chilean student situation, see the author's article in Donald K. Emmerson (ed.), *Students and Politics in Developing Nations* (New York: Praeger, 1968), pp. 286–314.

V

HISTORICAL PERSPECTIVES

EDITH H. ALTBACH

Vanguard of Revolt:
Students and Politics
in Central Europe, 1815–1848

STUDENTS WERE AMONG the most conspicuous participants in the Revolutions of 1848. They gave strong support to the demands placed
before the absolutist rulers of the German states and the Hapsburg
Empire. Rebellions were also reported at universities in France,
Italy, and those Eastern European countries under Russian control.
Although nationalism and the counter-revolution quickly divided
what revolutionary movement remained into hostile camps, there
was truth in the French poet Lamartine's description of 1848 as "the
product of a moral ideal, of reason, logic, sentiment, and of a desire
. . . for a better order in government and society."[1] Students were a
significant, if unfulfilled and suppressed, group in the European intellectual community that articulated these hopes for a better order.

In retrospect, the historical significance of the student upheavals
of 1848 is magnified by their place as a precursor to the student
movements in the underdeveloped countries of the twentieth century. Both situations involve the critical confrontation of new political, social, and economic ideologies and institutions with the remnants of a traditional system of values.

In the new states students and university graduates are often the
sole bearers of modern development in all sectors of society, while
university students in nineteenth-century Europe were in competition with equally vital and impatient industrial and business elites
whose economic, political, and social power did not depend upon
university training.[2] In nineteenth-century Europe the universities
were remote from the centers of actual political power; in today's
developing countries, the educational institutions are a recognized
political force.

It is an often reasserted observation that youth movements arise
in times of rapid social change or crisis. During the early decades of

the nineteenth century, the German states and Austria witnessed a rapid transition from a feudalistic to an industrial economy, from a traditional to a modern university system. A substantial proportion of the student generation of 1813 had joined the military as volunteers in the Napoleonic wars; these youths returned hardened by battle, worldly wise, but filled with patriotic emotions and the desire to serve the fatherland whose freedom they had fought to save. In 1789, the year of the storming of the Bastille, young Germans were unable to go beyond verbal enthusiasm about freedom, but the generation of 1813 had participated in the war of liberation.[3] By 1819, however, authorities in some German states were wondering if the broadening and maturing influence of the war and the one-year compulsory military service for students were not partly responsible for the upsurge of political unrest among academic youth.

The movement to reform student life in style and content had been growing throughout the previous century among intellectuals, professors, and students. At the end of the eighteenth century, as many as half a dozen secret student orders in the German states had been founded to counteract the pernicious sway of the *Landsmannschaften* — student organizations catering to students from particular geographic areas. The new secret student organizations, which had intellectual links with the Free-Mason movement, sought to foster national feeling among young Germans. Government reaction to the new student groups was ambiguous. As "enlightened opponents of the traditional privileged position of the university," they were welcomed by the government; but as "bearers of liberal-democratic and (what in the divided Germany of that period was equally dangerous) either national or international ideals, they were bound to be of concern to absolutist rulers."[4]

A new type of student organization began to develop with the tacit encouragement from the governments of the German states. The most fervent supporter and esteemed leader in these student ventures was Friedrich Ludwig Jahn (1778–1852). Jahn, a pastor's son, was active in the early secret student orders around the turn of the century and had attended ten different universities. He settled in Berlin, where he had a flock of disciples to his program of "moral rearmament" and physical exercise. He remained a controversial figure throughout this period. Even his critics had to concede that his program was not without salutary effects in "shaking to their foundations the restricting formalism of school, army and government machinery."[5]

The Origins of the Student Movement — 1815–1848

Between 1815 and 1848 the student movement in Germany went through three phases, each followed by a reactionary period: the growth of the *Burschenschaft* movement from 1815 to 1819; the rise of a radical-liberal minority in the *Germania Burschenschaften* between 1827 and 1833; and the development of a "Progressive Movement" from 1839 to 1848.

The ideas generated within the student community during the previous decades found their organizational expression in the *Burschenschaft*. Amid bitter struggles with the local *Landsmannschaften*, the first *Burschenschaft* was founded in Jena on June 12, 1815. By the following year all the *Landsmannschaften* in Jena had ceased to exist, and the new *Burschenschaft* could boast three hundred members. The constitution of the Jena *Burschenschaft* is impressive in its democratic, societal orientation. The practice of some quaint ancient customs, such as the mixing of blood or saliva to symbolize brotherhood, should not obscure the modern character of these organizations.[6] The leadership was duly elected by the members, all meetings were open, and each member had equal rights and privileges. All students in Jena were eligible for membership, except *Landsmannschaft* members and Frenchmen. The only similarity with the *Landsmannschaften* was the concern over the reputation and honor of an individual. To symbolize the ideal integration of the students into society and among themselves, all members wore a common black outfit (rejecting the flamboyant uniforms popular in some student circles) and addressed one another using the familiar form *du*.

In Austria the *Burschenschaft* movement was unable to flourish under Metternich's rule, but it spread rapidly from university to university in Germany, and by 1817 it was strong enough to organize an all-German assembly, the Wartburg Festival. Convened by the Jena *Burschenschaft* ostensibly to celebrate the Jubilee year of the Reformation and to commemorate the 1813 Battle of Leipzig, the Festival gathered about five hundred representatives from the all-German and mainly Protestant *Burschenschaft* as well as many liberal professors and supporters. The Festival provided a public forum not only for the movement's ideals of freedom and nationalism, but also for the radical minority that had developed around Jahn. This group carried out a dramatic public burning of works by anti-nationalist authors. Authorities viewed the Festival, and particularly the book burning, with alarm. The Berlin authorities had grown increasingly distrustful of Friedrich Jahn's influence among the students. In April 1818, the government banned Jahn's public gymnastic events and closed the athletic field. About fifty university and high-school students who supported Jahn held a peaceful demonstration in front of Jahn's house where they sang Luther's hymn *'Ein' feste Burg ist unser Gott.'* The students then quietly dispersed, and the police were unaware of the event until rumors spread through the city the next day. The government, fearing that this was the beginning of revolutionary unrest, arrested some of the demonstrators on the strength of a law prohibiting all demonstrations.

With the memory of the Wartburg Festival still fresh, the student movement achieved added status with the founding of the General German *Burschenschaft* in 1818. Frustrated in their primary objective — the creation of a united German nation from the several states and Austria — and faced with rising repression from the authorities, the student movement had two alternatives open to it: "It could lose itself in nebulous . . . and obscure rhetoric"; or it could choose "practical political and social action."[7] There was always a tendency toward rhetoric in the movement, but the choice was made in favor of violent direct action in 1819 when student Karl Ludwig Sand assassinated the minor journalist and playwright Kotzebue. In the atmosphere of rising political expectations and dissatisfaction, Kotzebue had come to symbolize the anti-liberal and anti-nationalist forces through his articles attacking the student movement. The authorities responded to the murder by arresting all those even slightly suspected of favoring or furthering liberal or radical ideas. The Karlsbad Decisions of November, 1819, decreed that the *Burschenschaft* be dissolved. Public reaction to the murder, while not condoning the action, evidenced much support for the student movement and sympathy, even admiration, for Sand's motives. Metternich created a martyr for the student movement when Sand was hanged the following year.

This political assassination reveals much about the tendencies within the student movement. The evidence does not substantiate claims that the assassination was the act of an emotionally unbalanced boy. Sand belonged to a radical student organization in the *Burschenschaft* movement called *Die Unbedingten,* a name that refers to the group's absolute conviction as to their mission as saviours of the world. Karl Follen, who helped to found the group in Jena in 1818–19, appears to have possessed an intense charismatic personality radiating utter moral certitude and a combination of mysticism and fanaticism.[8] He believed that "everything which human reason recognizes as good, beautiful and true must be realized through moral will, immediately and without consideration . . . even if this involves the destruction of all dissenters."[9] Follen repudiated the call for lawful resistance to tyranny as "sentimental weakness." Tyrants "may be able to protect themselves from our so-called legal actions forever — they must learn to tremble before daggers."[10] Moreover, as early as 1815 a passage later deleted from the constitution of the Marburg *Burschenschaft* referred to the necessity of committing sin for the sake of a cause. And the memoirs of one of Jahn's disciples records that Jahn had defended the concept of political assassination.

But judging from other contemporary accounts, it is likely that the majority of students remained wrapped up in "nebulous and obscure rhetoric." Historian Georg Schuster concludes that "their verbose enthusiasm, their vague longing and the continual confusion of appearance and reality were hardly favorable to the development of political talent."[11] Other scholars of this period, however, detect in the students' idealism the potential for violence, seeing in Sand's choice of such a politically insignificant figure as Kotzebue both the lack of political perspective and the "ethical rigorism" prevalent among the "petit-bourgeois-proletaroid intelligentsia."[12]

During the decade following the Karlsbad Decisions, *Burschenschaft* organizations went underground. Despite a new wave of arrests and persecutions, a new General German *Burschenschaft* had been founded by 1827. The reorganized student movement at the eve of the July Revolution had undergone a number of transformations during the period of "demagogue persecution." When the political pressure subsided in Germany in the 1830's, it was discovered that the politicization had taken a radical turn and had reached a new segment of the youth. High-school groups joined the university students, and the latter consciously sought to broaden their base among depressed ranks of society.

This radicalization began in 1821 with the founding of a secret group, *Bund der Jungen*, in ten universities throughout Germany. Not surprisingly, the Follen brothers and other "red republicans," as they were known in conservative circles, gave the *Bund* guidance from exile in Switzerland. The *Bund's* political goals included nothing less than revolution leading to a united Germany under an elected representative government. Although this group was defunct by 1823, its radical political orientation had gained considerable ground by 1827 with the rise of a new trend in the *Burschenschaften*.

In Erlangen, adherents to this new trend of political liberalism formed a separate *Burschenschaft* in 1827, again with the name *Germania*. This group co-existed in rivalry with the established *Burschenschaft*, the *Arminia*. The split between *Arminia* and *Germania* groups repeated itself in many university towns. It represented the confrontation between the conservative Christian tradition (*Arminia*) within the *Burschenschaft* movement and the growing radical-liberal secular wing (*Germania*). The *Arminen* were decisively outvoted at the 1830 congress in Nuremberg, and with the advent of the July Revolution in France, the radicalization and influence of the *Germanen* increased at an accelerated pace. The *Burschenschaft* constitution, which had existed secretly since 1827, had set as the relatively moderate goal preparation for a just new state through moral, academic, and physical education. At the height of the progressive movement, the Stuttgart national congress in 1832 proclaimed the purpose of the *Burschenschaft* to be expressly "the instigation of a revolution, through which to attain the freedom and unity of Germany."[13]

The students' revolutionary fervor led them to support Polish demands for freedom and unity. In January 1832, the Polish revolutionary Dombrowski was welcomed in Jena, and in the atmosphere of rededication to their common causes, radicals among the *Germanen* proposed the formation of an academic legion to serve in the Polish revolutionary drive. In May 1832, liberal forces in Germany had the opportunity to show their new strength at the Hambach Festival. This political demonstration attracted between thirty and forty thousand people.

The last political event prior to 1848 took place the year after the Hambach Festival when a group of radical students and young intellectuals attempted a *coup* in Frankfurt am Main on April 3, 1833. This poorly planned and executed attempt to take control of the federal treasury in Frankfurt failed and reactivated the persecution of "demagogues." Some two hundred *Burschenschaft* members were convicted, and eighteen hundred arrests were made. The abortive *Putsch* was followed by a splintering of student life. Protestant and Catholic groups that were pledged to fight the anti-Christian forces usually influential in radical political circles sprang up along strict denominational lines.

The student movement responded to the new social and political situation. The Progress Movement, as it was called, appeared first in Göttingen in 1839. It began among students not organized in the existing *Burschenschaft* (usually existing secretly) and other more conservative student groups (called *Korps*). The Progress Movement proposed most significantly that students cease to cling to their old privileges and distinctions, which served only to isolate them and make them unresponsive to the needs of the people. But, as Karl Griewank has observed, "the effectiveness of the Progress Movement was in the long run hampered by the fact that its leaders generally espoused a political radicalism which only a minority of students could completely embrace."[14] Nevertheless, this movement determined to a large extent the political response of students toward the Revolutions of 1848.

The year 1848 found university and student life throughout much of Western and Central Europe in disarray. Students were divided into hostile parties, bound by old customs and traditions. The members of the student societies formed a kind of aristocracy to which the non-members were largely indifferent. The relatively new and small group of progressively-minded students constituted yet another faction, and it was this group that received strong support when the revolutionary trend started in Paris on February 22, 1848.

1848: Constitutionalism vs. Nationalism

The countries of Central and East Central Europe had long looked to France to initiate political and social changes. The Paris February Revolution, which in three days succeeded in forcing the abdication of King Louis-Philippe and the downfall of the House of Orleans, mobilized the revolutionary forces on the Continent. News of the Paris rising reached Germany by February 27, and two days later the constituent assembly in Mannheim demanded freedom of the press, open trial procedures, a civil militia, and an All-German parliament. The same day the Baden government granted the first three demands.

From the outset, the energies of the revolutionaries were divided between constitutionalism and nationalism. The student movement recognized this dual objective and seemed even to perceive vaguely the dangers of this admixture. The national revolutionaries in Germany and Austria made two fatal mistakes: They failed to place safeguards on the constitutional freedoms won in March, and they

allowed the reactionary parties to use national loyalties and preju-
dices to disintegrate the coalition of revolutionary forces.

Vienna: The Children's Crusade of the Academic Legion

Historians, with their eye for the dramatic, have meticulously
recorded the activities of the student movement as it developed in
Vienna during the Revolution of 1848. The feats of the Academic
Legion were important, if only to give a sentimental glimpse of how
intellectuals make revolution.

Students first came to the notice of the populace of the Hapsburg
capital on the morning of March 13, when they marched to the *Land-
haus* where the representatives of the Estates were meeting to discuss reforms to be proposed to the Emperor. The students hoped to
demonstrate their support of the reforms. This procession was not,
however, the students' first political act. On March 3, a petition had
been circulated among a group of students in the law faculty
demanding an end to censorship and the introduction of academic
freedom for the universities. This petition to the Estates was so
radical that few students were willing to sign it, and it was burned
to protect the signatories from government reprisals. Later, on
March 7, a gathering of students held to celebrate the end of the
Fasching Festival was transformed into a revolutionary meeting. In
a few days, these students had drafted a new petition to the Emperor
demanding freedom of press, speech, and religion, legal reforms,
improvement in the level of public education, and the introduction
of academic freedom.

In a tense, chaotic meeting at the university on March 12, the
students decided to send their petition to the Emperor through the
rector and two professors. When the students received word that the
Emperor had dismissed the student petition with the reply that he
would take the matter into consideration, the decision was made to
march to the Assembly House the next day. The students made the
radical decision to demonstrate against the advice of several professors who had gained widespread popularity among the students for
their liberal views. These professors had succeeded, despite their
small number, in stimulating and sustaining student dissatisfaction
and frustration with the government. Yet when the revolution
erupted, these liberal professors found themselves powerless; their
positions of leadership were assumed by a new group of younger
radicals who had not previously distinguished themselves politically.

The impact upon Vienna, totally unaccustomed to demonstrations of any sort, of two thousand students solemnly marching through the city was understandably great. The students who gathered at the Assembly House were without a plan or set of objectives. When the word came that the Emperor would grant only a council of Estates to discuss reforms and financial matters, the crowd grew increasingly more radical in its demands. After several hundred workers arrived from the suburbs, the frustrated crowd stormed into the Assembly House determined to state their case. In the ensuing confusion, one of the workers with experience in the Paris uprising proposed that leaders be chosen to organize their protest. A committee of twelve, composed mainly of students, was quickly "elected." Messengers and speakers were sent to keep the populace informed and to raise public morale. This provisional government was negotiating with the mayor for the mobilization of the national guard when the military opened fire on a crowd, killing five people, several of whom were students. The working class had already been won over to the side of the revolution, and the intervention of the military succeeded in winning over the bourgeoisie. By the evening of March 13, Vienna had been completely transformed. Metternich had resigned and fled the country; the military had been withdrawn and replaced by a National Guard; and the students were armed and had formed the Academic Legion. The Legion soon grew to five thousand strong; the students were joined by graduates, teachers, and even some skilled workers, artists, and clerks. This widening of its ranks left the Legion vulnerable to charges that it was being exploited and corrupted by "outside agents." The government that assumed leadership after the resignation of Metternich warned against "those demagogues who took advantage of the students' inexperience at so stormy a period."[15] The students themselves made repeated but unsuccessful attempts to restrict the membership of the Legion.

Unpacified by government promises to meet the demands for reforms, the students were the first to disobey orders to leave the city and keep order in the suburbs, where mass rioting and destruction of property had broken out among the workers. A student representative stated: "We did not take up arms only to keep order for the government but also, and indeed mainly, in order to bring the wishes of the people to fulfillment."[16] When asked what the wishes of the people were, the student replied: "a constitution." The rest of the students took up the cry and decided to remain on guard at the university. Faced with this opposition, the Emperor was forced to back down, and on March 15 he promised a constitution, freedom of the press, and a civilian army. The students were joined in their moment of victory by the very professors who had opposed their radical actions a few days earlier.

It was characteristic of the first period of the Vienna revolution, as well as other revolutions of 1848, that the students appeared as a united group. Later those who were still active in the events of the revolution were increasingly absorbed by the general political parties, which was in keeping with the progressive student movement's goal of integrating the student community into the greater society and ending the students' separate class status. The weeks following March 12–15 were ones of spontaneous feelings of brotherly love, equality, and humanity. Privileges and classes were disregarded for the time being. But Engels argues: "The Academic Legion, full of zeal for the struggle against Imperial despotism, was entirely incapable of understanding the nature of the estrangement of the two classes [middle and working], or of otherwise comprehending the necessities of the situation."[17]

Between the Revolts — Vienna: April-October, 1848

There was an obvious need for a central body to represent the will of the people, a group that had the confidence and support of the general population. Toward the end of March, the Student Committee was formed with the permission of the new government headed by Minister Pillersdorf. Through this committee the radical leaders of the revolution were able to exert their influence. For a time the Academic Legion and the Student Committee remained separate bodies. In mid-April, however, elections to the Student Committee were transferred from the university's student body to the Academic Legion. From then on, each company in the Legion elected two representatives to the Student Committee. All sessions met in the Aula — the official assembly hall of the university — and the "Aula" became synonymous for the entire revolutionary student movement. By virtue of the close bonds between the Academic Legion and the Student Committee, combining a policy-making body with an armed militia, it has been said that the academic faction was transformed into a political-military party along modern lines.[18] Furthermore, the Student Committee served as an excellent training ground for potential political leaders.

The early days of April revealed that the events had radicalized the student community. This politicization was evident in the conflict between the liberal professors and the young academics over the new press law passed by the Pillersdorf government. The radical wing's successful opposition to the law led to its repeal. Throughout April and May the students' most immediate concern was the new Austrian constitution, although they were also involved with the issue of German national unity.

The constitution proclaimed by the Imperial government on April 25 initially received enthusiastic support, but soon encountered opposition. The students began protests, and on May 5 they demanded changes in the constitution. Petitions were signed and submitted. In the midst of this wave of protests, a Political Central Committee of the National Guard was formed on May 7 with representatives from the National Guard and the students. By May 10 the Committee had framed a constitution and had a membership of two hundred. There was much governmental opposition to a political body that was also a militia. Behind-the-scenes pressure sought to force the group to disband, even after the moderates had gained control and outnumbered the more radical students. Instead of seeking to exploit the division of opinion over the constitution, the government prevailed upon the Commander of the National Guard to order the Committee to disband, and all factions rallied to the Committee's support. In an attempt to turn the moderates against the students, the government issued a false alarm, saying that the students were planning to overthrow the government. This deceit restored the solidarity of public opinion behind the students and permanently alienated the radicals. In the midst of much confusion in the city and bitterness at the university, the students sent deputations to the government demanding: a retraction of the order to disband the Central Committee; joint occupation of the important watchposts by the National Guard and the military; intervention by the military only at the request of the National Guard; and the formulation of a new electoral law. Students, ordinary citizens, and hundreds of workers marched on the Emperor's residence where the deputation was presenting its demands, and the city was transformed into a revolutionary mass. Not being absolutely sure of the loyalty of the military and outnumbered by the armed citizenry, the government had no choice but to grant all demands.

The disappearance of the Emperor and his entourage on May 17 threw Vienna into turmoil. Conflicts and open fights broke out among different factions. Many people tried to undo the democratic concessions and accused the students of willfully forcing the Emperor to flee. There was growing resentment of the powerful influence of the students, and the middle classes feared the development of a mass of revolutionary workers.

The Academic Legion, responding to the public criticism, held meetings on whether or not to disband. On the evening of May 21, it was decided not to dissolve the Legion at a meeting held at the university, a decision supported by elements within the National Guard. On May 22, the students agreed to demands that the university be closed until October. While the students also agreed to refrain from further political activity, they refused to disband until the promises of March 15 and May 15 had been met. The closing of classes effectively freed the students from all academic activity.

The radicals became stronger and stronger as the division widened between the old-liberal or constitutional tendency and the radical democratic faction. The petit bourgeoisie, the students, and the workers formed a revolutionary tribunal. The city became ever more isolated, and the peasantry lost interest in the revolution since it did not include them.

On May 25, contrary to its earlier statements, the government ordered the immediate disbanding of the Academic Legion. The military was called in, and the students and workers responded by throwing up about a hundred barricades around the university. In the face of such opposition, the government was again forced to retreat, and it retracted the order to disband the Legion.

The mistakes and miscalculations of the government served only to increase the militancy and hostility of the students, although the mass of students were not extreme radicals. Each mistake and subsequent retraction weakened the government and strengthened the students.

October Revolution in Vienna

During September the Academic Legion was able to strengthen its ties with the increasingly militant working class. A mob of workers murdered Latour, the War Minister, on October 6 after a violent encounter between the military and the Academic Legion. Complete anarchy reigned in the city. The government was powerless and indecisive; the military was demoralized; and the students were unable to control the workers as they had earlier. Significantly,

the August decision emancipating the peasants from feudal obligations to the landlords had satisfied the peasants, and they ceased to
support the revolution. Thus, the peasants never rallied to the
support of the city in the final battle that pitted the city against the
infinitely superior military power of General Windisch-Grätz. By
November 1, Vienna had fallen, all student legions had been disbanded, and all revolutionary leaders not fortunate enough to escape
were arrested and tried. By February 1849, the university had been
reopened, and the revolution was over.

Berlin

The first issue that rallied the students of Berlin concerned a
relatively minor incident during which the military mistreated a
number of people, including some students. At a meeting at the
university the students decried this infringement upon the academic
jurisdiction of the university and appealed to the rector as well as
the academic senate for protection and assistance. In an unexpected
move, the meeting sent a delegation to the government with a
demand for arms, so that the students could become a wing of the
citizens' militia. This request was denied. Open hostilities broke
out on March 18 after the military fired upon a peaceful crowd.
Student radicals rushed to the suburbs to enlist the support of some
nine hundred machine-shop workers, and the workers, armed with
iron bars, joined the students in building barricades. Paul Boerner,
a radical student leader, estimated that only one hundred of a total
student population of 1500 fought at the barricades; the rest stayed
home or spent their time making speeches or negotiating with
officials.

The King was forced to withdraw the military from the city after
hours of house-to-house fighting on March 18, and the armed
students stood guard to keep order in the city. But after the
March 18 victory, the revolutionary energies of the students seemed
spent. Radical student leaders like Boerner tried in vain to overcome
the political apathy afflicting Berlin students. Boerner spoke bitterly
of the lack of social consciousness and the preoccupation with
childish privileges and personal advancement that characterized the
student population.[19] Engels, writing of the general situation in Germany, was even harsher: "The students particularly, those 'representatives of intellect,' as they liked to call themselves, were the first
to quit their standards unless they were retained by the bestowal of

officer's rank, for which they, of course, had very seldom any qualifications."[20]

In 1848 Prussia, having recently witnessed the Silesian Weavers' uprising and the Berlin bread riots, had reached a more advanced stage of political development than had Austria. The Prussian middle classes, acutely aware of the potential power of the oppressed working class and the peasants, were ever wary of the threat of Communism. Even the Paris February revolution met with an ambiguous reception from middle-class liberals in Prussia. They realized that the Parisians had overthrown the kind of constitutional monarchy that the German revolution would seek to install. Thus, the blow dealt the revolution by Windisch-Grätz in Vienna easily paved the way for a pacific November counter-revolution in Prussia.

Other Austrian and German Universities

Events in Berlin and Vienna quickly spread to every university in the German states and the Hapsburg Empire. With the exception of Munich, the revolutionary activities of students in the smaller universities of Germany were very similar. In each city, events followed the established pattern of petitions, demonstrations, student legions, confrontations with the military, concessions from the government, counter-revolution, and return to pre-revolutionary conditions.

Munich, the capital of Bavaria, had been notably free of unrest and conflict. Even the students were allowed to have officially recognized organizations under the benevolent but inefficient rule of Ludwig I. In August 1844, there were a total of five student fraternities, corporations praised by princes, bureaucrats, citizens, and professors.

Months before the uprisings of 1848, public indignation grew in Munich over the influence a certain English-Spanish dancer had gained over the King. By March 1848, the opposition from the public, the faculty, and the students had reached such proportions that the King decided to abdicate in favor of his heir rather than meet more radical demands for a representative assembly. Before abdicating, the King granted student requests that an assembly of the Estates be convened and a student militia formed. Under the leadership of a new progressive *Burschenschaft Rhenania*, the students became the voice of the March demands and were instrumental in the King's abdication and the installation of a moderate liberal government. In the months that followed the students formed representative assemblies and a Volunteer Student Corps, composed of workers and craftsmen as well as students. While the students remained moderate, they enjoyed the trust of the workers — without, to be sure, supporting the workers' fight for higher wages and better working conditions.

Students everywhere in the Hapsburg Empire demanded similar concessions and reforms of the government. Except at Innsbruck, students shared the common demand for an armed academic legion and independent student organizations. The student legions were organized in basically the same way throughout the Empire. They were all divided according to faculty — either in corps, as in Graz, or in cohorts, as in Prague. While students in Bohemia, Rumania, Moravia, Salzburg, Graz, and other Austrian provinces joined in the movement started in Vienna, Innsbruck was conspicuous in its moderation. The Innsbruck students sent a declaration of solidarity to the Academic Legion of Vienna for their efforts in the March uprising, but they never became politically involved. They had no academic legion, and the small student military corps was serving with the Tyrolian defense forces during the crucial period from March to June.

The delegation from Prague was noticeably absent at the Wartburg Festival held in June 1848. National conflicts had come sharply into focus when the Czech majority in the Prague Student Committee voted against sending a delegation to the student conference. This controversy reveals the extent to which German nationalism worked to destroy the united front that had existed early in March among the students of various nationalities in the Hapsburg Empire. Students were dedicated, if naïve, supporters of the idea of national self-determination and cooperation among the Germans, Czechs, Hungarians, and Italians. But the outspoken nationalism of the German-speaking Austrian students brought them into an inevitable conflict with other nationality groups, especially the Czechs. Czech students in Vienna protested that the capital of the Austrian Empire had no right to consider itself solely German. In Prague the predominance of Czechs in the Academic Legion resulted in the formation of a number of German student organizations, and in Graz, the German students expelled the Slovenes from the Academic Legion when they refused to wear the German colors.

Students in Prague, unlike those in Vienna, at first pursued almost exclusively academic and norm-oriented goals rather than political objectives. A petition handed to the Prague academic senate on March 16 contained only one political demand — that of freedom of the press. The majority of the demands concerned university reform: the inclusion of the Technical Institute into the university, the formation of a student corps as part of the national guard, lectures in German and Czech (instead of in Latin), equal opportunity for faculty members of all religions, and permission for student athletic organizations and facilities. These demands were granted on March 31.

The Prague student legion did not take on a decidedly political tone until the rebellion of June 1–17. Even then, its demands did not concern the constitution, but were restricted to requests for additional arms. The military struggle against Windisch-Grätz, the same general who eventually conquered Vienna in October, reunited the student factions.

The Failure of a Revolutionary Movement

During the thirty-three years of peace from the Congress of Vienna to the Revolutions of 1848, students were able to confound the counter-revolutionary measures enforced by Metternich and his allies on three occasions — in 1817 at the Wartburg Festival, in 1833 with the abortive Frankfurt *coup*, and in 1848 with the many revolutionary academic legions. These three phases of the student movement spanned a period of economic and social change in Germany and Austria, particularly in the large urban centers of Berlin and Vienna, and of rapid evolution of the German university.

With the founding of the University of Berlin in 1810 and the tenuous establishment of German universities as centers for intellectual enquiry, intellectuals were at last given a "secure institutionalized framework" for their work.[21] With the increased governmental interest in the universities, professors were elevated from their previous dependence on princely favor or whim and attained some degree of personal and social prestige and economic security. The steady growth in wealth and importance of the middle classes in Germany after 1815 assured intellectuals and academics in particular of increased prosperity and prestige. At the same time, however, the mobility and deprivation of the professoriat's student and tutorial years and the uncertainty, heavy work load, and competitive pressures of academic life predisposed the professors toward liberalism.[22]

The motivations of the student generation of 1815 were shaped not only by the war experience, but also by the radicalizing effect of the period's economic crises. The classes affected most directly by these crises were the same ones involved in the student movement — the lower and middle classes. The leaders of the student movement were not, as has often been contended, of upper-class or noble backgrounds. Many of the most active students came from families of lower-level bureaucrats who were often downwardly mobile. The liberalism characteristic of the larger universities was, however, more a product of education than of class background. As Valentin has pointed out: "The world of the academician was, apart from most of the theologians of both churches, overwhelmingly 'liberal,' that is, humanitarian, rationalistic, yet bound to the existing scheme of things however avowedly devoted to progress."[23]

The rest of Europe looked with both fear and hope to Berlin and especially to Vienna for their response to the revolutionary movement. The differences in pace and tenor of the revolution in the two cities can in most instances be attributed to their uneven political maturity. Sensing that Vienna was a more volatile situation, many governments and revolutionaries waited to see how Austria, Europe's China, would respond.

The formation of the Academic Legion in Vienna within the space of a few days in March was a prodigious feat, because students had been forbidden any organized community life. Despite the strict ban on student societies, constant supervision, and a network of spies, however, there were nine clandestine student organizations in the *Burschenschaft* tradition. But only a Slavic student society, whose activities were restricted to an appreciation of Slavic life and culture, seems to have been under police surveillance. The nine *Burschenschaft*-styled groups were definitely revolutionary and helped to prepare a segment of the student population for the uprising. The oppressive censorship and control exercised over the universities engendered among students much hostility toward the government. In general, the relation of professor to student was similar to the officer's relation to the common soldier. The strict governmental control exercised over most faculties at the University of Vienna was a severe obstacle to the development of academic excellence and may explain, in part, the virulence with which the student movement erupted in 1848.

A comparison of the quality of education and the level of political orientation of students and faculty in the three major faculties of

Theology, Law, and Medicine reveals certain classic patterns, but also some unexpected ones. Each of these faculties prepared the graduate for a relatively well-defined position in society — as priest, lawyer or civil servant, or doctor. Recent research has determined that present-day students in professional fields tend to be less active politically, and where they do participate in politics, they tend to gravitate toward the middle-of-the-road or to the right. In the Vienna of 1848, Theology (which was at that time more nearly a "professional" faculty than it is today) and Law followed today's pattern of political non-involvement and conservatism; the Medical faculty, however, was conspicuous in its deviance from this pattern.

The Theology faculty concentrated on the training of priests and was restricted to Catholic theology since the Protestants had a separate institute. The clergy in Austria enjoyed a position of immense power, and the Theology faculty exercised self-imposed limitations on the political involvement of its members. The faculty avoided all discussion of secular matters in classes and demanded that students do likewise. Thus students predisposed toward conformity to Church and State tended to enroll in the faculty of Theology; others were often forced into Theology because of financial or intellectual limitations. Once there, deadly clerical seminars, Church duties, and restrictions on extra-curricular life further constrained them to a narrow outlook.

Since the authorities regarded the Faculty of Medicine as being politically harmless, it enjoyed a measure of academic freedom. Of the three faculties, only Medicine had a constitution and relative independence in faculty appointments and curriculum. The Medical faculty was furthered by several monarchs in Austria and was one of the best in Europe, attracting a large international student enrollment and an excellent faculty with many young liberal professors. The period of internship at the city's hospitals afforded students and faculty the opportunity to work closely together and to develop an academic community life. Together they witnessed the worst social conditions in Vienna's hospitals. The living quarters of the medical students were the scene of many clandestine student meetings, held ostensibly for purposes of entertainment but in reality having a markedly political character.[24] Two of these secret groups, the *Arminia* and *Liberalia*, sponsored the petition movement that crystalized the will of the people on March 13.

The Polytechnic Institute of Vienna, encompassing the fields of Mathematics, the Natural Sciences, and Technology, also held a privileged position by virtue of the non-political nature of its curriculum. Although the Institute did not have its own constitution, the situation of the students and faculty at the Polytechnic Institute was comparable to that of the Medical Faculty.

The social class origins of the students at Vienna were not so solidly middle class as one might expect. In 1845–48 the largest single group of students there was drawn from families of shopkeepers and artisans.[25] In contrast, about half of the students at the University of Berlin came from families of higher officials, clergy, professionals, and military officers. The Viennese upper classes did not attend the university, but were tutored privately or attended the prestigious military officer training school. Severe government travel restrictions prevented Austrian students from studying at foreign universities.

The students, coming as they did from families of factory managers, merchants, handicraft workers, and sometimes peasants, were acutely aware of the injustices and growing hardship of these social groups. Although there had been steady, if not spectacular, economic growth during the first half of the nineteenth century, certain segments of society were in severe financial straits in 1848. The development of factory-based industries attracted many peasants and unskilled workers to the city, but by 1847 inflation had compelled the industrialists, already plagued by shrinking markets and competition from England, to reduce the number of their employees. Even with these cutbacks the factory-based industries forced many artisans and handicraft workers into the ranks of the unemployed. By 1848, one hundred thousand people were unemployed in Vienna. Bad harvests throughout Europe and a severe housing shortage in Vienna compounded the crisis. Between 1818 and 1846 Vienna's population grew from 240,000 to 407,000, while housing increased by only 11 per cent. The suburbs had to accommodate the overflow, and by 1846 they housed six-sevenths of Vienna's population.[26]

Forty per cent of the students in Vienna were classified as "paupers" and relieved of all tuition charges, although they still had to find room and board for themselves. Students thus released from tuition because of economic hardship came from all classes and backgrounds: sons of factory owners, civil servants, and professional people were represented as well as those of merchants, workers, and peasants.[27] But the majority of Vienna's students came from the provinces or from foreign countries and were forced to find housing in the suburbs, mostly in the homes of workers and artisans, who were the driving force behind the revolution. These provincial students were, therefore, well prepared for their role as mediator between the middle-class liberal democrats of the city and the radical workers and artisans of the suburbs. Organized activity among the provincial students took the form of regional groups — Silesian student groups, Moravian student groups, and so forth.

Although one would expect a university education to have improved the social and economic prospects of these students, this was not the case. The goal of many Viennese university students was the civil service over which the wealthy families of the nobility and the upper-middle class exercised a monopoly, leaving free only the lower echelons. Professional opportunities in the field of law were not much better. Only a limited number of practicing lawyers were permitted in each province, and the influence of feudal-based guilds was still strong. (The universities in Prussia, however, seem to have enjoyed higher status as providing legitimate training for responsible civil-service positions.)

The teaching profession was an equally restricted field. A graduate wishing to enter the teaching profession at the university level had to pass a series of examinations and be considered by numerous administrative bodies before being assigned as an assistant to a full professor. He would then serve as the subordinate of that professor until the latter's retirement or death. The only other avenue to university teaching was the arduous and insecure position of a *Privatdozent* at the university. In this capacity the individual did not receive a salary, but was paid by the students which he could attract; furthermore, he had no assurance of ever being accepted as a regular faculty member. Professors in Austria held a very subordinate position in society, supervised and harassed by bureaucrats, the church, and the government.

The professional opportunities connected with the various disciplines are reflected in the composition of the students in each faculty. Because of the selective and competitive nature of the field of law, the majority of the law students at Vienna were sons of officials and the lower nobility — those classes most likely to be conservative or reactionary in political outlook.[28] This was also the case at the University of Berlin.[29] The student body at Vienna as well as at Berlin considered the law section of the Academic Legion reactionary. The Medical Faculty, probably the largest at the university, attracted a much more diverse student body. The profession was rapidly expanding and provided professional opportunities for social and economic advancement not possible in other disciplines. Interestingly, many Jews, barred from the civil service and tolerated only in literary and scientific fields, turned to medicine and sought to overcome the obstacles placed in their way.[30] These students were quick to support the demands for political and social reform and have been referred to as the "leavening of the democratic revolution."[31] Jews were among the most depressed classes in the society economically. While most students were able to find some financial stability by tutoring part-time, even this was denied the Jewish students. In due course the opponents of the revolution began to associate the radical nature of student politics with the influence of the Jewish members of the academic and intellectual circles. It is more likely that Jews became active only after the beginning of the revolution, when Jewish intellectuals and students did distinguish themselves as leaders, speakers, and writers. Engels refers to a group of Austrian Jews who, as writers, developed a "roaring trade" publishing books outside Austria and then smuggling them into the country where they were eagerly read among liberal circles.[32]

The Revolutions of 1848 were intellectual revolutions. Liberal intellectuals and democratic or republican students were able to articulate and mobilize the discontent and demands of the relatively unorganized working classes. Aided by the mass support of the workers, the middle classes forced political reforms on their governments. But in the final outcome little remained of the radical demands of the working classes and the left-wing democrats and republicans. As Namier has commented: "The working classes touched it off, and the middle classes cashed in on it."[33] Each of the Revolutions of 1848 began to lose its limited character when the workers came to distrust the motives of the intellectuals and the middle classes grew to fear the increasing militancy of the working classes.

In Austria, German nationalism served temporarily as a uniting force in the early stages of the revolution. But the early sentiments of brotherhood and cooperation of all nationalities that had characterized the student movement in Vienna and other parts of Austria soon disappeared. Similarly, the students of Berlin, in the flush of victory after the March struggles, temporarily turned their energies to supporting Polish demands for national recognition, but later reverted to more narrowly nationalistic aims.

After the monarchies were restored to power in Berlin and Vienna in the fall of 1848, students were, for the most part, content to return to a more orderly life at the expense of further political activity. In some student circles, politics even gained a bad connotation and a norm-orientation replaced the previously strong value-orientation of the student movement. There was a general regression from the gains of the revolution, with the exception of those won by the peasantry. Some of the demands for university reform were, however, granted during the 1860's and 1870's. In Austria, the focal point of the revolutionary struggle, the student movement produced lasting results. In Prague, for instance, a Reading and Discussion Society of German Students was founded in November 1848 as the central union of German students in that city. This organization remained the gathering point for German academicians until May 1892, when the *Germania* was founded as the result of a split in the movement caused by the growing Anti-Semitism.

The student organizations of 1848, which played so important a role in the social and political revolutionary movements, were a completely different phenomenon from the romantic German youth movement of the early-twentieth century. The German youth movement of the early 1900's was dedicated to a "youth ideology" that set youth up as a distinct social group with a completely negative attitude to existing patterns of authority and with a notable lack of political involvement; the student movement of 1848 sought to mobilize and organize the academic youth as an educated and socially responsible agent for political change. The democratic ideology embraced by the students of 1848 was expressed in the constitutions of their organizations and in their support for the workers; the romantic youth ideology of the 1900–1933 period led the youth instead to seek the authority of a charismatic leader with whom they could identify and around whom they could base their separate community life.[34]

REFERENCES

1. Lewis Namier, *1848: The Revolution of the Intellectuals* (New York, 1964), p. 2.

2. Seymour Martin Lipset, "University Students and Politics in Underdeveloped Countries," *Student Politics*, ed. S. M. Lipset (New York, 1967), p. 1.

3. Hans H. Gerth, *Die sozialgeschichtliche Lage der bürgerlichen Intelligenz um die Wende des 18. Jahrhunderts* (Berlin, 1935), p. 68.

4. *Ibid.*, p. 12.

5. *Ibid.*, p. 67.

6. Gerth, *Die sozialgeschichtliche Lage*, p. 63.

7. Carl Brinkmann, *"Der Nationalismus und die deutschen Universitäten in Zeitalter der deutschen Erhebung,"* *Sitzungsberichte der Heidelberger Academie der Wissenschaften Philosophisch-historische Klasse*, 32 (1931), p. 8.

8. Karl Follen was born in 1795 in Giessen, the same year as Sand. In 1819, Follen was a *Privatdozent* in Law at Jena, where Sand was presumably a student. Several years prior to this, in 1817, the Follens had founded a radical *Burschenschaft* in Giessen, called derogatorily *Die Schwarzen* (the Blacks) by members of *Landsmannschaften*. This group soon was suspected, probably with good reason, of being a secret organization with revolutionary tendencies. This hindered its growth.

9. Georg Schuster, *Die geheimen Gesellschaften, Verbindungen und Orden* (Leipzig, 1906), Vol. 2, p. 331.

10. Gerth, *Die sozialgeschichtliche Lage*, p. 74.

11. Schuster, *Die geheimen Gesellschaften*, p. 306.

12. Gerth, *Die sozialgeschichtliche Lage*, p. 78.

13. Karl Griewank, *Deutsche Studenten und Universitäten in der Revolution von 1848* (Weimar, 1949), p. 12.

14. *Ibid.*, p. 18.

15. Baron Franz von Pillersdorf, *Austria in 1848 and 1849. The Political Movement in Austria* (London, 1850), p. 86.

16. Maximilian Bach, *Geschichte der Wiener Revolution im Jahre 1848* (Vienna, 1898), p. 81.

17. Friedrich Engels, *Revolution and Counter Revolution* (London, 1952), p. 80.

18. Rolland Ray Lutz, Jr., "The Aula and the Vienna Radical Movement of 1848" (unpublished Ph.D. Dissertation, Cornell University, 1956), p. 75.

19. Paul Boerner, *Erinnerungen eines Revolutionärs* (Leipzig, 1920), p. 95.

20. Engels, *Revolution and Counter Revolution*, p. 123.

21. Joseph Ben-David and Avraham Zloczower, "Universities and Academic Systems in Modern Societies," *European Journal of Sociology*, 3 (1962), p. 61.

22. Gerth, *Die sozialgeschichtliche Lage*, p. 39.

23. Veit Valentin, *1848. Chapters of German History*, trans. Ethel Talbot Scheffauer (Hamden, Conn., 1965), p. 266.

24. Heinrich Reschauer, *Das Jahr 1848. Geschichte der Wiener Revolution* (Vienna, 1872), p. 68.

25. *Ibid.*, p. 76.

26. Lutz, "The Aula and the Vienna Radical Movement of 1848," p. 48. Berlin at this period is both similar to and different from Vienna. Valentin offers the following description of Berlin: "From 1815 to 1847, the population of Berlin had risen from 180,000 to over 400,000 — as many as Vienna, but less than London, Paris, Constantinople and St. Petersburg. It was the home of a small class of merchants and tradespeople who were steadily growing richer and more prosperous, but burdened more and more heavily by the terrible poverty among the masses. The number of inhabitants rose by 30 per cent from 1841–50, but the expenses of the poor-box by 63 per cent. Looking after the poor swallowed up nearly 40 per cent of the city's budget. Over 6,000 peoples received alms in the course of a year." (*1848. Chapters of German History*, p. 54.) Prussia was, of course, no welfare state. In 1842 Berlin spent 200,000 *Taler* on the Winter Garden, 150,000 on the opera and the ballet, 10,000 on the music director's salary, while a thousand rural schoolteachers had an annual income of less than 20 *Taler* per year in 1840. (See Hermann Meyer, *1848. Studien zur Geschichte der deutschen Revolution* [Darmstadt, 1949], p. 37.)

27. Lutz, "The Aula and the Vienna Radical Movement of 1848," p. 51.

28. Anton Füster, *Memoiren* (Frankfurt am Main, 1850), p. 191.

29. Max Lenz, *Geschichte der Königlichen Friedrich-Wilhelms Universität zu Berlin* (Halle, 1910), Vol. 1, p. 404.

30. Later, in the 1880's, there was consternation in Vienna over the "Jewish influence" in the medical field. The faculty had 48 per cent Jewish students and many Jewish professors in 1893. Hugo Gold, *Geschichte der Juden in Wien* (Tel-Aviv, 1966), p. 30.

31. Ernst Fischer, *Österreich 1848* (Vienna, 1946), p. 47.

32. Engels, *Revolution and Counter Revolution*, p. 38.

33. Namier, *1848. The Revolution of the Intellectuals*, p. 6.

34. S. N. Eisenstadt, *From Generation to Generation* (New York, 1964), p. 112.

RICHARD CORNELL

Youthful Radicalism and the Formation
of Communist Youth Organizations:
A Historical Precedent

THE CURRENT ACTIVISM among the younger generation in Europe,
East and West, has emerged after a long period of generally "peaceful coexistence" between the generations. Although many observers
view this radicalism among the younger generation as a new and
unique phenomenon, there are precedents in recent history for active
involvement of youth in political affairs. The examples of Hungary
and Poland in 1956 are evident, as are the protest and political
involvement provoked by the Depression years and the rise of Hitler.
What is less evident is the importance of youthful activism and
radicalism a half century ago during and after World War I.

But the vehicle or agent of discontent in these earlier times was
the political youth organization, whereas today the arena of youthful
unrest is the university and the student organization. In the earlier
period, some students were activists, but they did not play a major
role either as leaders or followers. Not only were there fewer students compared to present times, but they came from a more restricted social base. Furthermore, these students apparently did not
question so seriously or so deeply the educational and professional
commitments required of them as does the student generation of
today. Nevertheless, discontented or alienated sons of "bourgeois
intellectuals" with considerable education did enter the socialist
youth organizations and in some cases provided the leadership of
the movement for a period.

More importantly, in this earlier period the ideologically-inspired
political movements had their first great impact on youth and students. Youth movements associated with and inspired by the developing Marxist socialist movements had been in the process of
formation in Europe even before the turn of the century, and they
reached their high point in size and influence during World War I

and the postwar years. They were able to do so by providing, in a revolutionary era, those radical and revolutionary slogans and programs most likely to rally the deep discontent of an angry, impatient younger generation. Thus, the socialist youth organizations, whose membership was drawn primarily from young workers, provided the leadership for the extensive youthful activism in the years 1914–21. For the first time, organization, ideological rationalization, and political purpose were provided on a large scale to traditional youthful dissatisfaction.

The manner in which the socialist youth movements developed had important consequences for the growth of radicalism among the younger generation a half century ago. Complementing initiatives from the socialist parties were spontaneous efforts of young workers and intellectuals to form their own organizations. The result of this self-assertion was a variegated pattern of national socialist youth movements, differing as to internal organization, focus of activities, and degree of involvement in political matters. Many of the youth organizations arose essentially from a pacifist reaction to the militarism and imperialism of the times. Pacifism and anti-militarism coincided with attitudes in the parties and led to mutual support between youth and adult at the outset.

Yet there were other motivations behind the independent formation of youth organizations. Some groups, while they engaged in anti-military propaganda, were primarily the product of the economic and social dissatisfaction of young workers and apprentices, although this factor was not absent from the more anti-militarist oriented youth organizations. The stimulus to organization came from the deplorable working conditions and a concern with improving the economic position of the young worker and raising his living standards.

The movement toward organization led to independent organizations for a variety of reasons, the most important being the rejection by the youth themselves of the "spiritual tutelage of the older generation, no matter whether well- or ill-intended." The "tutelage" was rejected whether it was in the form of a master exploiting an apprentice, a foreman exploiting a young worker in the shop or factory, or an adult socialist leader guiding or leading the young socialists. A conflict of generations thus emerged at the outset of the socialist youth movement.

The most active among the young socialists played upon the psychological disposition of their fellows and called for separation from the adult organization and adult guidance and control. The search for individual identity and "their own way" led those who joined the socialist youth organizations to struggle continuously to preserve the independent existence of their organization. Thus, from an early date most of the socialist youth organizations developed a tradition of independence in organizational structure, but, more significantly, also in decision-making and the determination of policy.

This inherent tendency toward the formation and maintenance of independent organizations was subsequently accentuated by the growing philosophical and ideological differences within the socialist movement. As socialists sought to persuade workers and intellectuals of the necessity to accept socialist doctrine, they turned also to the youth in an effort to provide them with a "socialist" education. The efforts of the socialist parties to limit the activities of the youth groups primarily to non-political work later became a major point of dispute between the factions within the international socialist movement, as well as between the youth and the party leaderships.

This dispute resulted from differing conceptions of what constituted a "socialist" education. Believing that socialism could be achieved through the reform of capitalist society from within, the reformists or revisionists on the Right saw no need for the direct participation of the masses in the efforts to overthrow capitalist society — and still less for radical activities among the youth. The younger generation was to be gathered together and imbued with the socialist *Weltanschauung*, but political decisions were to be the concern of the party. For the democratic socialists of the Right, political action meant first and foremost voting and parliamentary maneuvering. And as the youth were not yet of voting age, their activities acquired a political character only in the sense that the socialist *Weltanschauung* had a clearly political basis.

The revolutionaries within the socialist movement remained convinced that the evils of capitalist society could be eliminated only by the overthrow of that society and its institutions. All elements of the working class, including the youth, were to be mobilized for this end. Thus, active participation in the "revolutionary struggle" was to be an essential element in the socialist education of the younger generation. The revolutionaries, however, were divided into the uncompromisingly activist revolutionaries on the Left (such as Lenin) who thought in the traditional Marxist terms of violent confrontations, and those who remained Marxists, but to whom revolution meant any change that took the capitalists out of power and put the proletariat in power. This latter group, which came to be known as the Center, were pacifist, basically democratic in terms of relations within the parties, and reluctant to resort to violence.

Where a sizable minority within the socialist movement repudiated the dominant trend toward relating Marxism more meaningfully to reality and remained "revolutionary" Marxists, the younger generation of socialists increasingly came to reject the "revisionist" or "reformist" solutions in favor of more radical ones. With certain notable exceptions, the dispute grew in the years before World War I to be a question of revolutionary youth versus reformist party. The more radical, revolutionary, and vehemently anti-militarist elements in the socialist parties turned to the independent youth organizations as sources of support. In return, the youth organizations usually encouraged and aided the radical minorities within the socialist parties. For their part, the leadership of the reform socialist (Right socialist, Majority socialist) party sought with mixed, but essentially limited success to control the youth organizations and bring them under party supervision. As the socialist youth organizations developed before World War I, the role they were to play in the movement to overthrow or reform capitalism increasingly came to be a major issue in dispute between the youth and the dominant elements within the parties. To what degree were the youth to become involved in political questions, especially in the anti-militarist struggle of the socialists?

Militarism and colonialism were of the greatest importance to both young and old in the international socialist movement, especially from the turn of the century through World War I. Not only were the international congresses occupied with these problems, but there was a continual debate within each national socialist movement. Socialism and anti-militarism came together for a number of reasons: the idealistic pacifism of many of those attracted to socialism; the doctrinal association of capitalism and bourgeois society with conflict, exploitation, and the use of violence; the belief that the observable militarism of the era was a product of and support for capitalist society; and more practical reasons such as the tension and threat to peace from the colonial rivalries of European powers and the fears of some more nationalist socialists that war would worsen the relative position of their own state.

By 1907 and the international socialist congress in Stuttgart, anti-militarism had become the predominant issue within the movement. Thus, the main debate at Stuttgart was on the question of militarism and war — on methods of anti-militarism. A division, corresponding more broadly to the debate on revolution versus reform, had developed within the movement and was reflected in the discussions. Those who supported agitation among the troops, insurrection, and a general strike to prevent war, or use of an outbreak of hostilities as the occasion for class struggle, were opposed by those who were either unwilling to resort to such violent measures in principle or felt that these methods were tactically self-defeating in light of the strength of the dominant bourgeois governments.

The first international youth conference convened immediately after the conferences of the parties. The young socialists responded eagerly to the urgings of the German revolutionary and anti-militarist socialist Karl Liebknecht to accept as a moral obligation the active struggle against war and militarism in the sense of the decisions of the congress of the Second International. The youth also decided to play a political role, contrary to the intent of the socialist parties. Dominated by the reform socialists, the socialist parties viewed the youth organizations as merely "recruiting schools" for the party — structures in which young workers and students could be gathered and imbued with the Marxist point of view before they entered the party as adults. As the Left within the socialist movement and its calls to action found an increasingly receptive audience among the younger generation, the question of whether or not the youth organizations were to become involved generally in political affairs became the primary point of dispute between youth and party in the socialist movement in the years prior to World War I.

The youth delegates had founded, with party encouragement, an International Union of Socialist Youth Organizations (IUSYO) at Stuttgart. From its inception in 1907 until the outbreak of World War I, the IUSYO remained a loose association of socialist youth organizations. Any international activities that did exist were carefully limited by the reformist leaders of the Second International. But within the member organizations there was much ferment. The independent youth organizations were rapidly drifting away, politically and ideologically, from the prevailing opinion within the parties, and strong currents of opposition were also developing in those youth organizations that, although organizationally independent, were clearly under party control.

Thus in the years before World War I there was a strong movement within the new socialist youth international to transform the organization into a more unified and politically active institution.

As a result of the radicalization of the socialist youth during World War I, the socialist youth organizations had not only developed a tradition of independence in organization by the end of the war, but had become deeply involved in political and factional questions.

The end of the war brought great opportunities for expansion of political activity among the youth in the formerly belligerent countries. In Germany and Austria, revolutions overthrew autocratic regimes that had inhibited or prohibited political activity among the youth. During the war the movement existed primarily in the neutral countries, but after November, 1918, the focus of attention shifted to Germany, France, Russia, and the new countries formed from the old Austro-Hungarian empire. The large socialist youth organizations in these countries began to resume their traditional organizational and educational activities. The supporters of the various factions in the socialist movement formed new organizations of young workers and students, with the more radical elements having the greatest success. But all socialist youth organizations experienced a rapid rise in membership as war tasks ended and attention turned to domestic political, economic, and social problems. The rapidly growing youth movement was the scene of great political controversy, and the factional disputes, which had been only barely contained during the war, broke out in full force.

The political climate in Europe at the end of the war was one of growing radicalism. Most of the socialist youth organizations which had been members of the socialist youth international during the war had moved gradually toward the Left. They supported the Bolsheviks in Russia, the call for a Third International to replace the moribund and discredited Second International, and a policy of revolution in order to win power for socialism in the individual countries.

Because of the growth of youth movements as important political forces, all of the factions in the international socialist movement were active among the young workers and students, seeking to take them out of politics or to use them to factional advantage. War-weariness, great economic privation, the discrediting of the capitalist system in many young people's minds as a result of the war, the unleashing of nationalist antagonisms, an endemic political tension, a general upheaval of previously accepted social standards, the appeal of the new Bolshevik regime in Russia, and the inherent ease with which younger people accept, indeed demand, change all contributed in turning many young workers, former soldiers, and students to the more revolutionary socialist organizations. Countering these forces toward the Left were "bourgeois" traditions, the desire for peace and an end to conflict, and the appeals of the leaders of reform socialism. In the postwar years these various diverging forces exerted considerable pull on the young workers and students. For a while, the radical ideas were clearly the strongest, but in the end the reform views prevailed.

The high point of youthful radicalism was the transformation of most of the socialist youth organizations into Communist youth organizations during 1919 and 1920. In November, 1919, the IUSYO was reconstituted as the Communist Youth International, as under the initiative of both the Bolsheviks in Russia and the pro-Bolshevik forces among the socialist youth in Western Europe; representatives of most of the member organizations of the IUSYO met in Berlin. The purpose of the meeting was to bring about the formal union of the youth international with the fledgling Communist International formed in March. Excluded from participation were those socialist youth organizations, either former members of the IUSYO or newly formed groups that were associated with either the Right or the Center in the socialist parties. These included the important Austrian youth organization, as well as the minority Right and Center organizations in Germany. In France, Czechoslovakia, and Finland struggles were still going on for control of the youth organization, but in all cases the Left eventually won.

The revolutionary line of the Bolshevik functionaries who were trying to breathe life into the Comintern at this time was adopted by the Berlin Congress. Thus, from the outset the new Communist Youth International, containing an overwhelming majority of the socialist youth organizations in Europe, actively supported the revolutionary Bolshevik position within the national socialist parties. The main task was to carry on extensive propaganda work. The young Communists, it was argued, could play a decisive role in the efforts to win over the masses — a necessary prerequisite for acquiring power.

The mood of the Berlin Congress reflected the view that the success of the Bolsheviks in Russia, the unrest in the other countries of Europe in the aftermath of the war, and the sharpening of the struggle between the social classes would lead to a general European revolution bringing the proletariat to power. The young workers were to carry out in the working-class organizations those tasks that most corresponded to their psychological disposition — revolutionary propaganda inside the armies, revolutionary and illegal agitation, and the preparation and staging of demonstrations. Through these tasks, the youth would be in the front ranks of all revolutionary meetings and actions of the working class. As had been the case in Finland, Russia, Lithuania, and Germany, the youth would provide the cadres of the Red Army. The youth would supply, as a result of "education through action," the most important source of recruits for the Communist parties as they marched to power. To aid in bringing the political, economic, and social tensions in Europe to a revolutionary breaking point, the program of the new Communist Youth International and its constituent youth organizations was to include: further incitement of the revolution; efforts to shatter the bourgeois state; the erection of the dictatorship of the proletariat; and then the building of the Communist society.

Within the Left — the new Communist parties, and the youth organizations — there were those who criticized this general line for not being radical enough. Supporters of the "Left opposition" within the Communist movement or the "ultra-Left," which was especially strong in Germany, argued against using parliamentary methods and for a boycott of the reformist-controlled trade unions. This opposition developed during 1919, after an attempt at revolution by the newly-formed Communist Party of Germany (KPD) failed in January. The new party leaders were accused by many of passivity and failure to promote "the revolution" vigorously. The critics of the leadership included Communists whose orthodox Marxist ideological framework made it inconceivable for them to adopt anything other than a clearly revolutionary policy of agitation and uprisings at all times; those who simply overestimated the existing unrest, tension, and possibilities for revolution; and the considerable number of anarchists and syndicalists who had joined the Communist movement after the war. The latter, while supporting the Communist activities designed to precipitate "the revolution," tended to bring their traditional anti-parliamentary views with them.

The "ultra-Left" was strongly represented among the youth, and at the Berlin Congress proposals for more direct revolutionary activities were advanced. It was argued that the efforts of the capitalist governments to reconstruct the economies of their countries and thus to reassert capitalist domination over their countries should be obstructed by direct action (general strike). The "ultra-Left" thought that the Communist movement ought to conduct "the most deliberate, the most aggressive revolutionary activity in order to eradicate capitalism, in order to demolish the capitalist state." These far more optimistic and aggressive views were opposed by those who argued that the revolutionary movement could only be discredited and the bourgeoisie strengthened by revolutionary action at a time when it had limited prospects for success.

For its first year and a half, the Communist Youth International followed an unclear and uneasy policy sympathetic to the revolutionary enthusiasm of the "ultra-Left," but at the same time it tried to reconcile these forces with the Comintern in the interest of unity. The manifesto issued by the Berlin Congress was a general call to revolution, with the specific policies left vague. "It is the historic task of our generation, young comrades," said the manifesto, "to realize the world revolution and to begin the erection of a communist society."

The decisions at Berlin put the organized socialist youth movement, encompassing the most disaffected and activist among the younger generation, clearly behind the Bolsheviks in Russia and represented a clear break with the other tendencies or factions.

Discontent, however, was not limited to the new Communist youth organizations. The disputes within the socialist youth movements, as within the parties, was not in terms of, for, or against the *status quo*. The question in dispute was how to effect the changes, and what was to be erected in place of the old bourgeois society. The Right and Center had their supporters within the socialist youth, although they remained in a minority. Even among the church-affiliated and other bourgeois youth, there was a widespread questioning of those values and institutions that were held to have been responsible for the war. But as the war receded into the past and reconstruction was begun, radicalism among the youth, at least in its activist forms, diminished, and the size and influence of the Communist youth organizations fell correspondingly.

For the most part, the successes and failures of the Communist youth movement in 1919 and 1920 can be attributed to the same factors that influenced the Communist movement as a whole. The years after World War I saw great changes in the social, political, and economic patterns of Europe. Old institutions, such as the monarchy in Germany and Austria, were abandoned and secure replacements were sought. New nation-states were being created in many cases, and the new political patterns meant a sudden change of allegiances or loyalties. Pacifism and dismay at the horrors of the war led to disillusionment with, or rejection of, the system that had permitted it all to happen. This upheaval was most marked in Germany, for not only was it the defeated major power, but it experienced a full-scale revolution. The nationalist and militarist forces on the political (as differentiated from the socialist) Right represented in 1919 and 1920 a distinct threat to the gains of the German revolution of 1918. This threat — plus the unwillingness of any of the Right, or reform, socialists to go beyond the already-won gains (the creation of a republic) — turned most of the more active and even many of the moderate workers and supporters of socialism to the Left in frustration.

The unrest throughout Europe after the war was in great measure the result of difficult economic conditions. It took considerable time for the European countries — neutrals as well as belligerents — to recover from the physical and moral devastation of the war and revive their economies. A further factor encouraging support for the Left socialists was the example of the Bolshevik Revolution. Dazzled by the promise or hope of ending wars and economic misery, many were able to overlook the avowed and growing anti-democratic nature of the new Bolshevik regime. An emotional affinity between many socialists and the Bolsheviks remained despite disappointments over the direction that the new regime in Russia was taking.

Thus, in the immediate postwar years most of the youthful idealism and pent-up frustration was channeled into the new Communist movement. The Communist youth, especially in France, Germany, Britain, and Scandinavia, worked to hinder the production and transportation of munitions to Poland during the Russo-Polish War in 1920. After the fall of 1919, the new German Communist party recruited its most active workers from among the German Communist youth and often used the youth organization to conduct propaganda where the local party groups were part of the opposition to Comintern policies. In Sweden and Denmark, the youth organizations provided the majority of the members of the Left-Socialist (Communist) parties; in Norway the youth organization took the lead in developing Communist influence within party and trade-union circles. In France and Czechoslovakia, the youth organizations accepted the program of the Communist Youth International considerably before the socialist parties decided to join the Comintern and become Communist parties. In Switzerland, the youth organization was the backbone of the new Communist party, and in both Belgium and Spain the youth organization actually became the Communist party. In Italy, the Communist-dominated socialist youth organization supported, and often led, all efforts to carry out the Twenty-One Conditions for admission to the Comintern within the Italian socialist party. The youth organizations could play this important role as "vanguard" of the Communist movement because of their independence, their increasing involvement in political affairs during the war, and their radicalism. These organizations provided a highly useful tool for the new Comintern leaders in their attempts to win control of the working masses in the various European countries.

By the latter part of 1920, the Communist Youth International had succeeded in developing a life of its own as the largest, most politically active, and influential youth organization in Europe. With few exceptions, its major constituent members were the most representative organization of the young workers in their countries. At this time, however, the latent political differences between the youth and the adults began to break the surface of unity.

The Communist youth movement in Western Europe maintained its independence from the positions sponsored by the Comintern and the Russian leaders, in part, because the leaders of the Russian youth organization (Komsomol) had not been able to assert control over the Communist youth movement outside Soviet Russia before early 1921.

At the founding congress in Berlin, the Komsomol representative had not been able to win acceptance for the program drafted in Moscow without several major modifications concerning the relationship between the Communist parties and youth organizations, the revolutionary anti-militarism program, and participation in parliament and the trade union. After Berlin, the Komsomol — formed in October 1918 — was too busy with its own problems to pay much attention to the West European movement. The military and political situation made communication extremely difficult, and the leadership of the CYI in Berlin, supported by the German Communist youth organization, continued to govern the West European Communist youth movement. For the most part, the leadership represented the mood of the member organizations. If anything, the leadership was more willing to compromise its sympathies in order to promote Comintern views and maintain unity in the movement.

At this time, the national Communist youth organizations went their own way. A highly developed sense of national feeling existed, although there was acceptance of the need for unity and discipline within the Communist movement.

After the Russo-Polish War and the Civil War, communications between Russia and Western Europe were facilitated, and the Komsomol, acting on behalf of the Russian party and the Comintern leadership, began to devote considerably more time to the affairs of the international Communist youth movement.

The disciplining effort initiated by the Comintern through the Russian youth organization expressed a fundamental cleavage on basic principles. One of the major threads in this controversy concerned the character of the Communist youth organizations. In the fall of 1920, the rapid rise of the trade unions and other economic mass organizations of the workers, usually under the influence or control of the Right-socialists (social-democrats), forced the Communists to decide what tactics to employ with regard to these groups. Of greatest importance for the Communist youth were the youth sections formed by the large and influential reformist trade unions. The question of organizational form was whether the Communist youth organizations should work among the broad masses of young workers or only among the most radical youth. If the latter possibility were chosen, should a separate organization, apart from the youth organization and concerned solely with the economic interests of the mass of young workers, be created?

The discussion in the CYI at this time was to a degree a later manifestation of the controversy within the Russian Komsomol during 1919 and 1920 over the desirability of having the youth organization become a mass organization. The faction in the Komsomol opposed to making the Komsomol into a mass organization believed that the Communist youth were the "vanguard of the revolution" and, as such, had to remain "pure." The masses of the young workers would be organized outside the Komsomol, but under the Komsomol's influence. The opposition faction struggled to retain independence for the youth organization because they feared that power might become overly concentrated in the new Soviet state. The opposition arose in no small measure from a desire to give the young workers the means — an independent youth organization — by which they could protect their own interests, without relying on the "good will" of the State. The issue was decided against the opposition in mid-1919 when the Komsomol Central Committee issued the call for the Komsomol to become a mass organization.

Similar arguments and concerns were behind the opposition of the European communist youth to the efforts to impose the Russian solution on the CYI and its member organizations.

Communist Youth Organizations: A Historical Precedent

At this time, the young Communists in Europe sought primarily to carry through Lenin's policy of polarizing the socialist movement and gathering all "true" socialists into the Communist parties and youth organizations. If the Communist youth organizations were to become mass organizations, they would, of course, have to win the masses of young workers to their side. In order to do so, the opposition argued, the Communist youth organizations would have to make the same "opportunist" promises of better economic conditions and working arrangements that the reformist trade unions were making. Such promises, it was contended, would fill the young workers with hopes that the Communists could not fulfill during the capitalist period and the masses would then turn away from the Communists. The opposition concluded that as long as the capitalist system remained, the Communist youth groups would have to remain "pure" organizations of disciplined and dedicated revolutionaries.

At the founding congress in Berlin, the Bolshevik view of complete unity and centralization had been pressed by the representative of the Comintern and the Russian Komsomol. After a lively debate, this concept carried the day insofar as the relations between the Comintern and the CYI were concerned — the youth international was to be subordinated to, and not a "sister" organization of, the Comintern. The youth organizations were obligated to follow either the political program of "that party or fraction in their country which is a member of the Third International," or the political program of the Comintern. In any event, the organizational independence of the youth organization was recognized.

The right to decide when and where to hold meetings and what to discuss was implicit in the notion of organizational independence held by the Communist youth in Western Europe at this time. The Communist youth leaders did not contemplate in any way that the Comintern executive or the Central Committee of the national Communist party would eventually decide the time, place, and agenda for CYI youth organization meetings. Following the Berlin Congress, the supporters of centralization complained that some Communist youth groups (particularly the Swiss) were making independence from the party an end in itself rather than a means to carry on the fight for the Bolshevik position against "unclear" (Centrist) parties.

The issue of independence for the youth organizations arose during 1920 in the context of the conflict with the Centrists over control of the socialist youth organizations, acceptance of the Twenty-One Conditions, and adherence to the CYI. The pro-Bolshevik forces of the Left naturally wanted the youth organizations to be free from control by those party leaderships of the Right or Center so that they could support the Left within the party. The Centrists had supported the involvement of youth in political affairs before and during the war, but by 1920 political involvement had come to mean intrusion of the youth in the party in favor of unconditional acceptance of the Bolshevik view of "proletarian internationalism," something which the Centrist youth were unwilling to do, and the Centrist elements in the party unwilling to permit.

After the struggle with the Centrists for control of the socialist youth organizations had ended, the demand that the youth have autonomy of political judgment was reasserted by the Communist youth organizations when the Bolshevik-led Comintern sought to subordinate the youth organizations. After the second Congress of the Comintern in Moscow in the summer of 1920, representatives of the CYI leadership, several youth organizations, and the Comintern leadership agreed that the youth organization should have considerable autonomy in implementing policy, but that it was to accept the program of the party as its own and work within the scope of the political directives of the party. Lenin, increasingly extending his notions of centralization within the movement to the developing international organizations and the other Communist parties, initiated the steps by which the Russian party was to exercise complete control over the Communist movement.

The decisions at Moscow stimulated a discussion in the national Communist youth organization that was almost unanimous in its support of full independence for the youth. The youth of the "ultra-Left" in the Communist movement were particularly vociferous in their arguments for independence for the youth organizations. When the party was a "really revolutionary party," it was argued, it would naturally exercise a healthy influence upon the youth. Thus, not only was there no need for a close organizational tie to the party, there was a positive necessity for the youth to keep their independence so as to prevent a "slipping" Communist party from diluting the revolutionary spirit of the youth. Subordination of the Communist youth to the recognized Communist party would have meant, for the "ultra-Left" youth, that there could be no support for the only "real" Communists — those of the "ultra-Left" who by now were outside the party.

The Swiss gave voice to an argument that was often heard in the discussion over political autonomy for the youth — that the differences between the Russian and the West European situations called for differences in the relations between the parties and the youth organizations. The subordination and discipline of the youth were necessary in Russia, said the Swiss, first because of the Intervention and Civil War and later in order to mobilize the resources of the country for the construction of the new Soviet society. Such a relationship, however, was *not* necessary or desirable between parties and youth organizations in Western Europe. Willi Münzenberg, the leading figure in the transformation of the socialist youth movement during and after the war and later Secretary of the CYI, reiterated this theme. In this he was reflecting not only the views of the leadership of the Communist Youth International, but also the preponderant sentiment within the youth organizations. Münzenberg continually sought to reconcile the need for central direction and firm discipline in the Communist movement (especially at a time of anticipated revolutionary expansion) with the desire to avoid its becoming merely an instrument of Russian policy.

In the spring of 1921, when the debate on the role of the youth organizations within the broader Communist movement was at its height, the Communist Youth International attempted to hold its second Congress in Germany. The Congress was to be a gathering of the entire "revolutionary proletarian youth," thus including the "ultra-Left" and syndicalists as well as the anarchists. Believing in the necessity and possibility of direct revolutionary action, most of the West European Communist youth supported the "theory of the [revolutionary] offensive," put forward by a leading Comintern functionary and former leader of the Hungarian Soviet, Bela Kun, as well as by the leaders of the German Communist party.

The Russian Komsomol, beginning to assert itself in the youth international, did not want a broad congress that would provide more support for the advocates of independence and the "theory of the [revolutionary] offensive," — both positions the Russian party and thus the Komsomol rejected.

Despite Russian disapproval, the Communist Youth International leadership and member organizations went ahead and convened a meeting of almost all member organizations in early April, 1921. The Russians were the only notable missing member. Expressing support for the "theory of the [revolutionary] offensive," the meeting gave clear evidence of the preponderant, if not unanimous, sentiment among Communist youth, even in the face of a bitter defeat in Germany. Upon the issuance of peremptory instructions by the Comintern from Moscow, however, the meeting was ended and the proceedings held in abeyance until the summer, when the officially recognized second Congress took place in Moscow after the third Comintern Congress.

In the spring of 1921, the Russian party imposed the first moves designed to tighten discipline in the party as the New Economic Policy was introduced into the country. Defeats in the movement to spread the revolution led Lenin to impose the so-called "retreat policy" on the Comintern and the other Communist organizations at the third Comintern Congress in June and July, 1921. This new line called for a withdrawal from militant, provocative tactics and for an attempt to win broader support from the mass of workers.

Over considerable opposition, the new policy was extended to the youth at the second CYI Congress, which followed that of the Comintern. If the Bolsheviks were to control the international Communist movement effectively, they had to make sure that the international Communist movement was tightly centralized. Firm discipline had to be exerted from the top of the hierarchy to the bottom. More important, perhaps, for the Communist youth movement was the Russian insistence that the traditional independence of the youth from the parties be buried.

Having struggled so hard to win or maintain independence from the reformist or non-Bolshevik revolutionary socialist parties, and being wary of the less radical right-wing within the Communist parties and the Comintern, the West European Communist youth leaders fought the efforts of the Russian Komsomol and the Comintern to control them by tying the youth organizations firmly to the parties. This struggle was destined to be futile. Authority, prestige, and money were located in Moscow, and the full weight of Lenin, Trotsky, Zinoviev, Bukharin, and the other leading figures in the Russian party was brought to bear on the youth delegates. In the interest of maintaining unity, the CYI leaders accepted the "retreat policy" and a new statute that committed the youth organization to political subordination.

The force of tradition, however, was too strong for the Congress decisions to be carried out immediately. The "leftism" of the Communist youth and the disagreement with the new "retreat policy" of the Comintern remained within the national youth organizations for some time after the second Congress. But from this time the fortunes of the Communist youth organizations began to wane. The movement's initial successes were not consolidated or developed. In a short period, the membership of the youth organizations fell off drastically, as they moved from the most radical fringe of the Comintern to its most active supporters. As the nineteen-twenties wore on, the disillusionment even among the more committed young workers and students grew.

The intensity of youthful radicalism and activism, of "commitment" and "involvement" in political and social issues, during the war and the early postwar period was the result of specific circumstances. The Bolshevik Revolution, the conditions in Europe after the war, the ideological and moral conflict of the era — all served to enflame the younger generation. They had a vision of a better society and were promised a role of leadership in achieving, or at least *actively* working toward, that goal. The Bolshevik Revolution and the efforts of the new regime to build the "new socialist society" served as an inspiration to many. The formation of Communist parties and youth organizations provided a means by which many youth thought that the Russian experience could be repeated within their society.

For source citation and bibliographic information, see Richard Cornell, "The Origins and Development of the Communist Youth International: 1914–1924" (Doctoral dissertation, Columbia University, 1965).

VI

FUTURE POSSIBILITIES

SEYMOUR MARTIN LIPSET

The Possible Effects of Student
Activism on International Politics

ANYONE WHO ATTEMPTS to interpret the revival of student activism in recent years must face the fact that he is dealing with a worldwide phenomenon. Wherever one looks — at stagnant underdeveloped countries like Indonesia, at rapidly expanding, economically successful ones like Japan, at right-wing dictatorships like Spain, at Communist systems such as Czechoslovakia and Poland, and at such Western democracies as Germany, France, Italy, and the United States — one finds aggressive student movements that challenge their governments for not living up to different sets of social ideals.

These movements all appear to have in common confrontation with authority and some exhibit a readiness to take to the streets if necessary. And far from being in contradiction to the environment of student life, it can be argued, these manifestations are often acutely a product of it. Many suggested explanations have been specific to their time and place. Germans have pointed to the decline in institutionalized opposition following the Great Coalition of the two big political parties, or the coming of age of a student generation who are the grandchildren of the Nazi generation, hence able to directly attack the German past without talking about the behavior of their own parents. The French and Italians have credited student unrest to the inability of a highly traditionalist, almost feudal university structure to adapt to the needs of a rapidly expanding system. The London School of Economics, the center of British student protest, blew up against the appointment of a Director who was (falsely) charged with having been involved in sponsoring segregated institutions in Rhodesia, as Edward Shils points out. The Berkeley revolt was a reaction to administrative measures that seemingly restricted the political freedoms of civil rights activists. But given the widespread character of student activism, the special circumstances of the university system in a particular country or the nature of the initiating event can have been no more than aggravating factors. The sparks set off fires that were ready to go off.

Some have suggested that student tension reflects the lack of student participation in the affairs of the university, that some aspect of student power would reduce the potential for strong confrontation tactics, that if students felt they could communicate effectively to university authorities, they would limit the expression of their demands to legitimate conventional channels. While there can be little doubt that this position has some validity, one must also point out that the one university in Germany in which students have been represented on the Senate and other organs, the Free University of Berlin, is the Berkeley of West Germany. It is the school in which the greatest and most aggressive student movement was organized, and the German student movement in general stems from the Berlin protests. At the University of Urbino in Italy, which had established co-government in the Faculty of Economics in 1966, the student protesters objected in 1968 to joint student-faculty organs on the grounds that these institutions were a form of co-optation, a means by which they were involved in responsibility for the activities of the university. They demanded the right to go back to a pattern of negotiations between student representatives and the university. In 1968–69, the New Left student groups in France and Japan refused to take part in elections to co-government institutions on similar grounds. Similarly, co-government in many Latin American countries has not made for a cooperative or institutionally responsible student movement. Many analysts of the Latin American university have, in fact, argued that the political representatives of the students tend to be institutionally irresponsible — for example, by bringing politics into faculty appointments and often resisting efforts to improve the institution academically.

The view that student protest is causally related to large size and bureaucratization, to impersonality, lack of contact with professors, is also probably valid to some degree, yet it provides an insufficient explanation. Studies of attitudes of American students, for example, do show that in large state universities students are more dissatisfied with the quality of their education and student life than those at small private ones, but this is not the whole story. A survey of the attitudes of students at the major first-rate large state universities, such as Berkeley in California, Madison in Wisconsin, or Ann Arbor in Michigan — leading centers of activism — indicate approval, on the whole, toward the quality of their education. These schools receive many transfers from first-rate small private schools. Berkeley studies at the time of the protest showed *no* relationship between attitudes toward the school as an educational institution and involvement in the movement. On the other hand, a number of private small elite U.S. institutions, such as Reed, Brandeis, Antioch, Oberlin, Swarthmore, Haverford, and Chicago, have been strongholds of political activism, at times including resistance to the school administration itself.

A recent study by Alexander Astin, which collected questionnaire data from samples of over 30,000 students in 246 institutions in 1966 and 1967, sheds strong doubts on the hypotheses that relate American activism to characteristics of different types of universities or administration policies. He found "high correlations between student input characteristics [personal traits] and each of the three protest items [participation in demonstrations against racial discrimination, the Vietnam war, or university administration policies]," but the almost total absence of any correlations with aspects of the university environment, after controls for student trait inputs. In other words, Astin's comprehensive analysis suggests that the differences between universities that are demonstration prone and those that are not are a function of variations in the backgrounds of the students who attend them, rather than of aspects of university environment, structure, or policies.

In citing these data, it is not suggested that the viewpoints are wrong that attempt to relate specific cases of student unrest to such things as actual structural grievances, bad political rules, inadequate channels of communication, bureaucracy and impersonality, lack of involvement in the decision-making process, or inadequate instruction. They are not, but these internal sources of grievance cannot come close to accounting for the presence of large numbers of political activists, and they certainly do not explain the current spread of the outbreaks.

Essentially the sources of political activism *among* students must be found in politics, in the factors associated with different types of politics. The explanations for more political activism at one time rather than another must also be found on a political level, in the sources of variations in political response.

Students as a stratum are more responsive to political trends, to changes in mood, to opportunities for action, than almost any other group in the population, except possibly intellectuals. As a result, students have played a major role in stimulating unrest and fostering change in many countries.

Although it may be argued that student activism is the result rather than the cause of social discontent, it is important to recognize that student groups, once activated, have played a major role in mobilizing public opinion behind the causes and ideologies fostered by them. Social unrest causes student unrest, but once students and intellectuals start expressing their disquiet, they have been in many ways the vanguard of revolution.

They are among the most articulate segments of society and therefore are able to communicate their opinions to other segments. Thus, in Czarist Russia, student groups organized workers and peasants against the regime. The first members of many revolutionary parties were recruited from student movements in many countries. In Communist Poland and Czechoslovakia, student movements supported by intellectuals initiated the process that led to a break in the totalitarian regimes. In the Soviet Union today, these groups constitute the principal source of opposition. In the United States, the campus-based anti-war movement has been responsible for the eventual growth of large-scale opposition to the Vietnam war. Senator Eugene McCarthy's election campaign, which was heavily influential in Lyndon Johnson's withdrawal as a candidate for re-election, would have been impossible without widespread student participation and organization. In West Germany, the "extra-parliamentary" student opposition has initiated a process of extremist conflict on the Left and Right that might lead to a break-up of the Great Coalition.

In general, then, one should learn to expect a sharp increase in student activism in a society where, for a variety of reasons, accepted political and social values are being questioned, in times particularly when events are testing the viability of a regime and policy failures seem to question the legitimacy of social and economic arrangements and institutions. And mere observation shows that in societies where rapid change, instability, or weak legitimacy of political institutions is endemic, there is what looks like almost constant turmoil among students.

The Past Directions of Student Politics

From a historical point of view, it would be erroneous to suggest that student political activism has had a consistent orientation. In large measure, student and other youth groups tend to differ from adult political organizations by their emphasis on what Max Weber has called "the ethic of absolute ends," as contrasted with "the ethic of responsibility." Youth tend to take the values that they have been taught in absolute ways and hold up existing institutions to criticism because they do not meet the pure ideals of the social system or of the subgroup of which the youth are a part. The notion of ethic of responsibility involves concern for the consequences of action and the recognition that it may be necessary to compromise with one's values in order to achieve whatever good is possible in the situation. Recognition of a need to compromise, to take up an ethic of responsibility, presumably is associated with increased age and experience, which inures individuals to the fact that there are conflicting values and role demands.

Absolute ends or values can take any form. They may be the values of a church, a political party, a large society, or another specific segment. Where there is some degree of consensus about the larger values of a national system or the subgroup, one may expect to find many youth questioning why there is deviation between these values and the practice of the society. Thus, in Communist society, many young people and particularly students have raised questions about the discrepancy between the agreed-on ideals of Communism, such as equality and freedom, and the actual practice of the system. Similarly, in the United States, there is considerable consensus about the value of equality with respect to race relations, and youth here have questioned the discrepancy between this ideal and the actual practice of the society.

The limited evidence on student political behavior in Europe during the nineteenth century suggests that the politicized students, on the whole, supported the Left position of the time. As Martinotti has pointed out, they were in favor of nationalism when that was an issue, as in Italy, or of increased democracy and freedom. To a considerable degree, the political struggles were also linked to a conflict between traditional religion and its claim to dictate in the areas of science and anticlerical liberalism. Scholars and students concerned with science, including medical students, were on the Left because of their opposition to the church's resistance to modern science. In Eastern Europe, intellectuals and students tended to look upon their countries as backward as compared to the advanced cultures of the West, particularly the French, and one found the phenomenon of radical students denigrating the elites of their own society for being culturally backward. This meant, among other things, that students were found among the major activists in all the revolutionary movements, and that many of the revolutionary leaders were first recruited to their political activity as students.

There is some variation among nations as to whether student activity was identified with the Left or the Right, which is associated with the issue of whether nationalism was considered a leftist or rightist phenomenon in given countries. In Germany where nationalism was identified with Bismarck and the Prussian monarchy after 1870, nationalism became a conservative trait. And, as might be expected, many German intellectuals and students were nationalist and right wing. In the Latin Catholic countries, the split between clerical and anticlerical elements, referred to earlier, meant that those young people and intellectuals who were identified with religion were conservative. They often formed the shock troops of right-wing conservatism, being more idealistic about their conservatism than were the older people.

More recently we find evidence of sharp divergencies in the political orientations of students. Following World War I, the Italian Fascist movement had a strong appeal to many students in Italian universities that was presumably based on its theme of the proletarian defeated nation. The anthem of the Fascist Party was *Giovenezza*, "Youth." The leadership of the party was extremely young, and many of the leaders were in their twenties when they came to power. Of course, the Left also had some student support. There is no evidence to differentiate the sources of the appeal at that time. As Shils has indicated, Fascist and right-wing groups had considerable backing in various European universities during the 1930's. In Germany, the Nazis were extremely strong in the technical universities — that is, in the engineering and science schools — but they also had a great deal of strength in the universities oriented more toward the liberal arts. This was particularly true of the more provincial ones, such as Kiel. There were strong Fascist student groups in other parts of Europe as well. Seemingly, the student right-wing extremists were recruited from right-wing elements in the population.

In the underdeveloped and colonial countries during the 1930's there were links between student activism and Fascist or Nazi appeals. The Fascist-Nazi ideology was directed internationally against British, American, French, and Dutch imperialism. Nazi Germany was the aggressive anti-*status quo* nation. The Nazis were ready to fund groups opposed to their international enemies, and various groups in certain countries in Latin America, in the Arab world, and to some extent in the Asian colonies of Britain with considerable student support were willing to take help from the Axis and to identify their nationalist ideology as pro-Fascist. The pro-Fascist movements in these countries differed considerably from those in Europe itself, since they were more totally revolutionary, seeking to overthrow either the ruling colonial power or the existing elites of the society. These pro-Fascist youth groups met with resistance from various left-wing ones, which had also considerable strength in many underdeveloped countries. The right- and left-wing groupings, however, shared a common antipathy to foreign control.

Protest Since World War II
in the Third and Communist Worlds

The rise of student protest movements since World War II has been more extensive and more important than in earlier periods. These contemporary movements .have a great deal in common with respect to tactics and political style. Student culture is a highly communicable one, its mood and mode translating readily from one center to another, one country to another. Yet it would be a mistake to try to interpret the seeming phenomenon of a worldwide student revolt as a response to common social conditions or as an effort to secure a common objective. The sources of student protest must be differentiated among different types of societies: underdeveloped systems, authoritarian regimes (mainly Communist), and the developed democratic societies.

In various underdeveloped countries and new states of the Third World, the sources of intellectual and student protest may be found in the wide gap that exists between the social outlook of the educated younger part of the population and the more traditional less-educated older age groups. The gap between the social and political expectations engendered within universities and the reality of underdeveloped societies motivates students and intellectuals to accept ideologies that define the *status quo* as unacceptable and to seek drastic institutional changes so as to foster modernization — that is, the values of the "advanced" societies. This gap is reinforced by the logic of the university, which imposes values of achievement and competitive standards of merit that are frequently in conflict with the traditional, particularistic values both of the controlling elite and the population at large. Thus, the intellectuals and students of eastern Europe in the nineteenth century rejected the institutions of their own societies as backward compared to those of France and Britain. Chinese "returned students" in the early years of this century favored the overthrow of the backward Manchu dynasty so as to catch up to the West.

Although the principal source of ideological tensions within such societies involves the conflict between "modern" and "traditional" values — a conflict largely linked to differences in education and age — such differences are often tied to positions on international issues. In much of the underdeveloped world, the opposition to existing domestic elites and social-cultural-economic systems for being involved in and responsible for national backwardness is accompanied by support for the Communist model as an example of a successful effort to break through the restrictions on development and modernization. Since the existing social system is often allied internationally with the United States, the student opposition movements tend to associate the symbols of the United States, capitalism, and the free world with the conservative elites of their own society. Opposition to domestic traditionalism and liberalism becomes translated into support for some form of leftism that, in international terms, means opposition to the United States. Hence, leftist student activism in most of the underdeveloped world is, in large measure, a force against any alignment with the United States. It is, however, not necessarily a force for support of the Soviet Union.

The leftist student groups differ considerably from country to country, and in recent years there has been an increasing growth of "third force" revolutionary organizations that are both anti-American and anti-Soviet. Some tend to be Maoist, others identify in a loose way with Trotskyism, and a few are explicitly anarchist. There is an increasing tendency to take over a variant of what has come to be known as the New Left ideology — that is, opposition to all power groups. But regardless of the differences among the leftists, there can be little question that the United States is the focus of their hostility in international terms. This opposition has become intensified with the escalation of the Vietnam war since 1964. In large measure, opposition to American intervention in Vietnam has become the predominant political issue of many of the left-wing groups.

One major variation among the different underdeveloped countries relates to the image and role of the governing power, whether it is viewed as leftist or not. Two outstanding examples of this phenomenon occurred in Indonesia under Sukarno and in Ghana under Nkhrumah. In both of these countries led by pro-Communist leaders, the students took a position in opposition to the regime and argued in favor of increased liberty within the universities and within political life generally. Their advocacy of greater freedom and their criticism of various actions of the regime led them to foster the ideologies of democracy and certain kinds of liberalism. In a sense, the general proposition may be advanced that the most activist student groups tend to be opposed to the existing regime and, consequently, take on a political ideology in opposition to it. The situation in the various Communist countries is, of course, a case in point. Where student activism has developed in Communist societies, it criticizes the existing regime as being oppressive and opposes its international orientation. To some degree in Eastern Europe, the oppositionist students have favored withdrawal from the Warsaw Pact, have shown signs of being pro-Western, and in the last year have treated Communist-Israeli relations as a symbolic issue. The protesting students in Poland and Czechoslovakia have been strongly in favor of Israel.

The sources of the tensions between the regime and the university and intellectual life that are conducive to student activism in Communist countries are somewhat different from those in the Third World. As in the underdeveloped countries, there is an inherent gap between certain norms that are an aspect of university and intellectual life — namely, academic and intellectual freedom — and the structure of society. Intellectual and scientific life requires freedom. Simply to mouth party truths, or to limit the problems that one studies or the conclusions one reaches to those authorized by the regime places a basic strain on intellectual activity. Lenin and the Bolsheviks, of course, distrusted intellectuals precisely for this reason. It is antithetical for an intellectual to be simply a publicist or spokesman for a given system. Intellectuals place a premium on originality as a source of status, and originality means rejecting the verities of the present and past. Hence those involved in the world of the intellect, whether inside or outside of the university, are predisposed to resist authority on such issues — a strain that becomes manifest during periods of crises. One of the most dramatic examples of the strength of such values among intellectuals and students under Communism surfaced during the brief "hundred flowers bloom" period in China in 1956. The relaxation of controls by the Maoist regime produced a sudden outburst of critical speeches and statements on the country's campuses. The government was denounced for inhibiting free speech, research, and teaching and for maintaining an absolutist state. Many of these criticisms pointed to Titoist Yugoslavia as an example of a Communist state that supposedly allowed freedom and followed an independent policy with respect to the Soviet Union. The students of Yugoslavia, in turn, demonstrated strongly in the Spring of 1968 against the existence of sharp income differentials and the violations of political freedom in their effort to show their independence of authority. And ironically, the Chinese Communist ideologists hailed the opposition to inequality of income voiced by the Yugoslav students as evidence of the viability of Communists equalitarian beliefs in the very center of revisionism.

Improvements — that is, a relaxation of controls — often serve to stimulate increased criticism of the system among those who take the values of freedom seriously. For new generations of eastern European (or Spanish) university students, the fact that there is more freedom than in Stalin's day, or than three years ago, is an ineffective argument. They only know that the present system is not free, that the present rulers are repressive even if they happen to be men who pressed for more freedom a few years earlier. Thus, once the issue of freedom is joined in authoritarian states, we may expect students and intellectuals to fight to drop the existing restrictions. This struggle can lead either to greater liberalization or to a return to absolutist controls, as events in Poland and Czechoslovakia have unfortunately demonstrated.

Student Protest in the Developed
Democracies — The United States and Europe

On the basis of the analyses of the sources of intellectual and student protest in the Third and Communist worlds, it would seem that radical student activism should occur less frequently and be less prevalent in the developed democracies of Europe and the English-speaking states. Since modern industrial societies are largely characterized by their support for a universalistic ethic of merit, of freedom, and of scientific and intellectual creativity and originality, there should be diminished tension between the values of the intellectual world and the larger society. This would be true even recognizing that the universities still place a greater emphasis on egalitarianism and the free competition of ideas than do other institutions. The current wave of student unrest in the United States arose as a response to the one issue — race relations — in which the United States has retained an aspect of pre-modern traditional caste values basically at odds with the norms of a democratic industrial society. Anti-imperialism — that is, opposition to colonial rule — is another example of student identification with the explicit values of democratic society against its own practices. Previous to the emergence of American student protest, the largest upheaval in the Western world was occasioned by French student support for the FLN in the Algerian war. The protest against the Algerian war involved many thousands of students, who engaged in fairly drastic measures to sabotage the war effort.

Although the recent student protest has been directed against much of the adult world, including the faculty, it is important to note that a significant section of the faculty in many countries has been quite sympathetic. Indeed, some have themselves been leading "activists." This is not so paradoxical as it may seem to some. At all the major centers of Western student protest — Berkeley, Berlin, the London School of Economics, and Nanterre — some senior faculty members and many younger ones played a significant role in stimulating or supporting student protest.

Changes in the backgrounds and opinions of the rapidly growing numbers of university faculty have undoubtedly been as marked as, if less noticed than, those of the students. During the 1930's, the Depression and the struggle against Fascism motivated many faculty to join in the fight for social reform or the preservation of democracy. In Europe, the impact of Fascism and the experience of Nazi occupation led most intellectuals to reject conservative dogmas and tendencies and to identify with liberal or leftist ideologies. The sanctions that had existed in some countries against the employment of leftists in universities broke down. Although the pattern has varied considerably from country to country, there can be little doubt that a significant number with strong Left or liberal views finally moved onto the campuses. This was particularly noticeable among the younger faculty who had come of political age during the Depression or the anti-Fascist struggles.

The shift to the Left in the opinions of the faculty — and of other intellectuals as well — is, of course, not simply explained by the changing composition of the stratum. It also reflects a heightened resentment among humanistically inclined, "general" intellectuals toward the increased emphasis on intellectual technology and expertise, toward the decline of the status of diffuse intellectualism in the social and political arena.

The differentiation of social science knowledge into distinct fields of technical expertise has sharply undermined the role of the humanist intellectual who has traditionally claimed the right to comment on and influence public policy. This phenomenon may be seen most strikingly in economics. Economists now contend that many of the decisions about economic policy require technical knowledge beyond the competence of the informed layman. And as the other social sciences have extended their spheres of competence and have become more systematically empirical and quantitative, they also question the ability of laymen to understand the factors that affect educational achievement, child-rearing practices, international relations, and the like.

Increasingly, the expert tells the general intellectual that the particular matters under discussion are simply too complicated, too technical, for them to be influenced through advocacy of relatively uncomplicated solutions associated with a particular ideological bent. Those who seek to reform society in some specific way find themselves up against arguments supposedly derivative from specialized scholarly knowledge. And commitment to the increasing importance of social science and specialization reinforces the ideology of the "end of ideology" — the position that ideologically dictated positions are basically irrelevant. This argument was strongly put forward by John F. Kennedy in a speech at Yale in the Spring of 1963.

These trends have contributed to the rise among intellectuals and students on the Left of a kind of "intellectual *Poujadisme*," a backlash opposition to systematic and quantitative social science, to large scale social research, to the conception of the utility of efforts at value-free objective scholarship in policy relevant fields. Many intellectuals react to the emphasis on social science and the concomitant belief in gradualism, expertise, and planning with a populist stress on the virtues of direct action against evil institutions and practices. They argue that the involvement of the university in policy matters inherently corrupts the values of pure scholarship and intellectual freedom.

Studies of the sources of leftist activities within universities indicate, as we have seen, that the humanities and softer social sciences contribute disproportionately. (Parenthetically, it should also be mentioned that those scholars who are in the theoretical or pure mathematical disciplines also tend to support the Left. Mathematicians, statisticians, theoretical physicists, molecular biologists, and the like seemingly are disposed to attack going complex social systems for not working efficiently, according to the logic of an abstract moral model.)

The intellectual *Poujadist* reaction is, of course, related to a much older and continuing source of conflict between intellectuals and the power structure: the tension between the patron or consumer and the intellectuals. A conservative or rightist critic views democracy as a mass society in which intellectual elites are pressed to conform to the low taste of the public, and a leftist sees the source of the corruption in the power held by those who buy and distribute intellectual products — that is, business or government. The conservative critique has in recent years been absorbed in many countries into the left-wing one. The view that there is an inherent conflict between the values of intellectuals and those of the market place has sustained an anti-capitalist ideology among many humanistically inclined intellectuals and has affected students preparing for such pursuits.

The general discussion of some of the bases of tensions between intellectuals, students, and the social systems of the developed democracies does not, of course, explain why after two decades of relative inactivity and acquiescence, a New Left student and intellectual opposition should have arisen in many Western countries. To understand this phenomenon, it is necessary to emphasize the effects of the changing international picture, in addition to the factors discussed earlier by Shils and others.

Roughly speaking, from 1940 until some time after the Hungarian Revolution of 1956, the Western world was subject to considerable concern about the expansionist tendencies of totalitarian regimes — first the Fascist ones and later the Communist states. Concentration on resistance to these expansionist societies had two ideological consequences. First, it became necessary to defend the virtues of democratic systems against totalitarian critiques, both of the Fascist and Communist varieties. This necessity put a heavy premium on intellectual justifications of the virtues of the society and defined serious criticism as contributing to the enemy. Second, it led to a general acceptance of the worth of some form of collective security and international cooperation as the means of resisting totalitarian expansion.

These developments contributed to a decline in ideological controversy within the democratic camp in Western Europe. The celebrated discussion and formulation of a concept of "the end of ideology" emerged from an important symbolic event — a large meeting in Milan, sponsored by the Congress for Cultural Freedom in September, 1955. At this meeting, intellectuals from all political camps of the democratic world, ranging from left-wing socialists to conservatives, seemed to reach a real consensus directed against Communism. The anti-Communist consensus led to a deprecation of the cleavages among the different groups in the West. Many who wrote about the end of ideology during the next year or so were present at this conference and were struck by the degree of ideological consensus.

From 1956 on, however, much of the political rationale for domestic consensus based on international anti-Communism began to disappear. The emergence of visible tensions within the Communist world, the opposition that surfaced in Russia after Khrushchev's speech about Stalinism, and the protest movements in Poland, Hungary, and other Communist states, sharply reduced the image of a threatening monolithic totalitarian Communism. Communism, in fact, was liberalizing, was subject to internal divisions, and was not unified internationally. The split with China illustrated the extent to which international Communism had ceased being a system defined by the concept of Stalinism. And, conversely, within the Communist world itself the idea of capitalist encirclement, that the Soviet Union or other Communist states might be attacked from without, declined considerably.

These changes in the image of the opposition social system resulted in an increasing generation gap on both sides. The generation of Western leaders whose political orientations had been formed during the international conflicts with Fascism and Stalinism continued to see a commitment to collective security as a basic prerequisite for a peaceful world. For the generations coming of age after the Hungarian Revolution and perhaps even more importantly after the building of the Berlin Wall in 1961, the assumptions about totalitarian society and its expansionist and war-making potential did not correspond to the reality that they witnessed.

The differences particularly affected reactions to the Vietnam war. From the point of view of the older generations who dominate policy in the United States and other countries, Vietnam may be regarded as the latest battle or event in a twenty-year war that began in 1948 or earlier. The newer generations, however, refused to accept the view that Communism is inherently expansionist. Clearly Hanoi and the Viet Cong are not puppets of a unified Communist world movement.

Since the idea of an imperialist Communist enemy was no longer viable, there was no longer any need to inhibit criticism of the evils, social inequities, or bad policies of one's own society. The international strains that had contributed to a decline in sharp domestic criticism by intellectuals and students began to disappear.

In a sense, during the 1960's the Western world has returned to a more "normal" or peaceful social environment, in which the main focus of intellectual and student politics has been able to return to the domestic scène. The domestic system, including the educational system itself, is criticized for not living up to the ideals fostered by the society. The rise of a critical intelligentsia and a New Left student body in the West is one reflection of the change.

The current political scene increasingly resembles that which existed before World War I. In that earlier age, the mood of liberals and progressives about social change was generally optimistic. Even though the socialist movements campaigned against the possibility of international war, there was no real expectation that the prolonged period of peace, economic growth, and the expansion of democracy dating from the 1870's would end. Rather, as the economic situation improved, the Left, socialist, anarchist, and progressive forces continued to grow, and intellectuals criticized their domestic systems for various internal inequities and inequalities. The first student socialist movements in the United States, Germany, and France date from the period 1900 to 1914.

It may also be worth noting in this connection that students and intellectuals were involved in highly visible activist opposition movements in the underdeveloped countries, particularly in Latin America and parts of Asia, during the 1950's, before the emergence of major university-based opposition movements in the developed states. Anti-Communism and Cold War ideologies were much weaker in these poorer states. Hence, they were less subject to ideological constraints on their propensities to attack the *status quo* in society or university.

The Content of Student Activism

The growth in student opposition during the 1960's is, in large measure, identified with a left-wing critique of the social-welfare planning state in the Western democracies. The available data on the backgrounds of student activists in a number of countries suggest that many activists, particularly the leaders, are the children of relatively affluent, liberal left-wing parents. They have been reared in progressive households to accept the ideology of equality, democracy, helping the poor, and the like. Their parents represent a generation that was pushed to the Left by the events of the Depression and the anti-Fascist conflict. Right-wing radical critiques of the existing society have to a certain extent been outmoded by the discrediting of Fascist doctrines and the reduction of extreme movements on the Right to forms of *Poujadisme* based in the outlying and declining provincial areas of different societies. The politicized university students have the values of modern egalitarian democracy. The small minority of them that is impelled to be activist has concentrated the fire of its attack on domestic ills.

This domestic concentration, however, has resulted in a criticism of international collective-security, anti-Communist alignments as outmoded and unjustified. The New Left is sympathetic to movements in other countries seeking social change in an egalitarian direction — which means, in the underdeveloped world, Communist or pro-Communist movements of the Castro, Viet-Cong, Maoist varieties. Since the United States can obviously be identified as a force seeking to maintain the *status quo* in the underdeveloped countries, as well as a source of support for the conservative social system of their own country, the Student Left is inherently and sharply anti-American and against the American alliances. It simply does not accept the underlying theses that justify such alliances as NATO and SEATO or the opposition to revolutionary pro-Communist movements.

The Vietnam war with direct armed conflict and intervention by the United States has, of course, exacerbated the extent of the opposition to the U.S. The common theme justifying alliances among the Student Left in different countries has been opposition to American foreign policy. This fact, however, should not lead us to underestimate the extent to which these movements are primarily domestically oriented or directed against local power structures, the universities, the political parties, and the culture. These are the revolts of activist youth against the older generation in power in their own country. They have the effect, however, of also being a revolt against the system of international alliances and against America's role in the world.

In the Eastern bloc countries, of course, as noted earlier, these revolts are directed to some considerable degree against the system of alliances among the Communist countries. There the alliance is also a power system through which the Soviet Union keeps control over other countries. But basically politicized youth on both sides of the Iron Curtain are seeking to reform or revolutionize their own societies, and they are opposing the main power to which their country is linked, seeing this as a source of support for the *status quo* at home and abroad. In short, precisely because the Cold War has declined, and the basis for the system of alliances is no longer so strong as it once was, a new international youth movement has been possible.

The movement of the 1960's differs in a number of significant ways from earlier student movements. As compared to the previous ones, it has almost no relationship to adult organizations. Student and leftist youth groups before World War I or during the interwar period before World War II were to a large extent the youth or student affiliates of adult political parties. They usually were more extreme in their ideology than the adult organizations, but essentially they thought that social change in their country was to be achieved through the adult party coming into power or increasing its influence. This meant that the primary tasks of the youth group were to recruit support and train leaders for the adult organization and also to provide the mass base for demonstrations. Insofar as the adult groups were involved in parliamentary activities and tactics, the student groups were as well.

This pattern may still be seen today in the activities of the young Communists in various countries — that is, the youth or student sections of the pro-Russian Communist parties. In the West and in many underdeveloped countries, the pro-Russian Communists tend, where possible, to rely on the use of parliamentary and pressure-group tactics. Their student groups also follow the same procedures, essentially the traditional legal methods of demonstrating, striking, picketing, and the like.

Most of the non-Communist left-wing student movements in the underdeveloped states of Latin America and Asia also retain an instrumental orientation toward social change in their own country. They believe in the possibility of progressive social change through policies designed to foster economic development, education, land reform, and political democracy. To achieve these objectives, they favor placing a new adult group in power. Similarly, the student activists in Eastern Europe are concerned with concrete reforms, usually of a political nature.

The Student Left of the Western democracies, however, is in a post-reformist phase. The New Left youth groups reject almost all political parties. For them, the political parties of the Left, both Socialist and Communist, are parties of the parliamentary establishment. They identify these groups as supporters of the domestic or foreign — Russian — *status quo*. They see no adult organizations that are genuinely revolutionary or resistant to the major trends of the society that they oppose. Hence, there is now an international revolutionary movement of students and youth that expresses in almost unadulterated form the ethic of absolute ends. These youths are almost completely uninhibited and uncontrolled, since they have no relations to the parties and organizations that have some sort of interest in adhering to the rules of the game and accept the need for compromise. Their politics is often expressive rather than instrumental. The New Left groups also have no clear concept of any road to power, of a way of effecting major social change. They are ready and willing to use tactics that violate the normal democratic game.

The story of how they developed the confrontation tactics of civil disobedience in the current period, of course, derives directly from American experience. The American student movement first emerged out of the civil rights activities in the South. And the southern movement formulated the tactics of sit-ins and other forms of civil disobedience as the only way to resist the coercive, illegal tactics of the southern white segregationists who controlled the police and the courts. These tactics of sit-ins and civil disobedience spread to the North and have been used effectively, particularly in battles within universities. Since Berkeley in 1964 they have diffused throughout Europe and other parts of the world.

Such tactics used by students are particularly effective since there are strong norms operative in most cultures against the use of violence or strong force against students, as Shils and I pointed out in the first section. The idea of university autonomy — that the police should not come on a campus, that students should not be arrested for deviant behavior — is very strong. Efforts to break up the student demonstrations, no matter how illegal, by the use of force, almost invariably lead the more moderate segments of the university community, both students and faculty alike, to join the student protesters against the police and have the effect of radicalizing them. Recognition that protest which brings about police repression increases support for the radical position has exacerbated the willingness of the Student Left to use such tactics. These methods are clearly potent.

The significance of the growth of student activism is also enhanced by the enormous increase in the numbers attending universities and the equivalents of junior colleges in various countries. The statistics of growth in countries like Italy, France, Germany, Britain, and the United States are fantastic. This growth has had at least two different important consequences. First, it has meant that the absolute number of students has become much greater than it once was and that a relatively small percentage of the total student body, either on a given campus or nationally, can more readily become a major force in absolute numbers than ever before. In brief, this growth means that, even without a relative increase in the proportion of students committed to a Left or activist position, the possibilities to wage impressive protests have increased.

Second, the increase in numbers of students has in many countries led to a deterioration in their position in terms of the type of education they receive, their status in the society, and their expectation level after graduation. Many countries have expanded the numbers of students, particularly in the humanities and social sciences, without increasing the size of the faculty or, in some countries, living accommodations or libraries. Hence many students are subject to a much greater degree of impersonality, to less attention from faculty. Their generalized sense of insecurity, which inherently flows from their marginal position between dependence on parental family and future independent position, is greater than ever before. Students increasingly lack a clear-cut sense of their personal future, of what kind of job will be available to them after they graduate. To attend university is no longer an elite activity. There is a greater objective basis for student discontent about their situation as students. At the same time, it is easier than ever to mount large demonstrations. The increasing pressures for university reform reinforce the sources of concern for social reform.

Assuming a continuation of present trends, both international and domestic, it may also be assumed that the phenomenon of student activism is not a temporary one, although it should have peaks and declines. Specific issues that enable the activist minority to mobilize strength outside their own ranks will result in increases in the movement, but such support will largely drift away as specific issues disappear or lose salience.

One example of this phenomenon was the opposition to the Algerian war in France. This opposition involved tens of thousands of students. The movement was very much like the one in the United States today against the Vietnam war. Once the war ended in 1962, however, the mass support for the French student movement almost totally collapsed. It simply disappeared on many campuses. This event, of course, cannot be separated from the general decline of political activity that occurred under DeGaulle in the same period, but it does indicate the way in which changing political events can affect the movement. We are not necessarily dealing with a secular pattern.

A somewhat similar development occurred in Britain in the late 1950's. The concept of a New Left arose in Britain at this time, seemingly as a reaction against both the Labour and Communist parties. The New Left youth and student movement that emerged in many of the universities was largely concerned with cultural critiques of the larger society rather than with demonstrations, although many of its members were also involved in the Campaign for Nuclear Disarmament. The subsequent electoral victory of the Labour Party under Harold Wilson, who was then identified as a left-wing Labourite, sharply reduced the appeal of the British New Left, and it declined during the first few years of Labour rule. It has since regained strength, in some part fostered by the impression that the Wilson Labour government is a failure, that it is conservative in practice.

Nineteen sixty-eight seems to be a new benchmark in the strength of the student groups. The most important event was the May revolt in France. But the German student movement also engaged in widespread, relatively violent demonstrations during Easter week and has become a fairly potent movement. Many Italian universities were closed down by prolonged strikes during the Spring; and the issues of university reform and the power of the student movement have become important in Italy. In Belgium, the students at Louvain University, up in arms about the language issue, played a major role in bringing down the Belgian government. In Eastern Europe, also, student protest has been important in Poland, Czechoslovakia, and Yugoslavia. In Africa, there were major demonstrations in seventeen countries.

The Short-Term Effects of Student Activism

What will be the effect of this growing wave of student protest on the politics of the respective countries? The answer clearly is not a simple one. On one hand, the growing student movement is pressing the moderate Left and the Communists further to the Left, to be more militant in order to secure the support of the students. Many adult radicals have begun to identify with the student movement, and this, too, presses on the parties on the Left. Many student demonstrations

have been interpreted as reflecting the existence of genuine grievances, and various efforts are made to appease these concerns, particularly by university reform and occasionally other kinds of social
reform.

On the other hand, the irresponsibility of the student movements
— their willingness to rely on extra-parliamentary, illegal methods,
their proclamation that their goal is the revolutionary overthrow of
society, their resort to street violence — may also create a backlash
among the more moderate, conservative, and established parts of the
electorate. In France, the student revolt has had one obvious political consequence; it has given France its first majority party government in history, one which is right-wing. The continued massive student demonstrations in Japan seemingly helped the conservative
Liberal Democrats increase their vc'e in the 1968 upper house elections there. Thus, it may be argued that student demonstrations
strengthen the conservatives within the body politic, that they help
place conservatives in power or increase their majority. Such con-
tentions also have been made about California politics and U.S. politics generally. The Berkeley disturbances were credited with having
played an important role in electing Ronald Reagan in California.

The picture, of course, is not clear-cut, even in electoral terms.
In Italy, the 1968 elections did not produce a movement to the Right;
if there was any change, it was a slight shift to the Left. On the
whole, however, the Italian case seems to be the exception. The
general effect of extra-parliamentary youth politics is to strengthen
the Right, at least in the short run.

The strengthening of the Right, therefore, may actually have the
effect of contributing to strengthening the foreign alliances with the
United States. Since the conservative parties, France apart, are the
more pro-American, collective-security oriented ones, this paradoxically could have the opposite effect on what the students themselves
are striving for internationally. This outcome, however, is not a
necessary one.

The dominant political groups in various countries are concerned
with maintaining domestic tranquillity. Consequently, they should
be interested in reducing the size of opposition student movements
and will try to avoid giving the activists any justification for engaging
in violence against the government. Many politicians see foreign
policy issues as a major source of annoyance for their students.
Chancellor Kiesinger has explicitly credited the Vietnam war with
responsibility for the growth of a violent German student movement

and for the alienation of many German youth. Whether he is right or wrong is irrelevant; what is important is that he sees it this way. In Japan, which witnessed a strong New Left-type student movement before the phenomenon occurred in the United States and Western Europe, student opposition to international alliances with the United States, while not upsetting them, has had the effect of reducing the public commitment of the Japanese politicians to such alliances. The U.S. has withdrawn forces to avoid student protests.

In evaluating the cost to the nation or to the government and the political forces of a given international policy, those currently in power must count as one of these costs an increase in street opposition to the government, a decline in respect for law and order. Should the other forces pressing for maintenance of the alliance weaken, one may assume that the rise of a student movement will become a force for isolationism. If a politician must choose between internationalism and isolationism and if he feels that the international consequences of the choice have become less important, he may opt for the isolationist course to gain domestic tranquillity, to maintain law and order, to reduce emotional opposition.

The continuation of the Vietnam war has, of course, made international relations a major source of emotional tension. For those opposed to the war, any alliance with the United States may be perceived as an alliance with murderers, with those who are killing a small country. In the absence of the war, the issue of whether a given country remains part of NATO or has a mutual security treaty with the United States still may remain an important issue for debate and controversy, but presumably will not provoke so intense a set of reactions.

Generation Differences — The Long-Term Effects

In the long run, the most important effect of the current wave of student activism on foreign policy may reflect the outcomes of differences in outlook toward politics among different age groups or generations. The experiences that have sustained a strong commitment to the Western alliances are an outgrowth of the struggles against Fascism and Stalinism. As noted earlier, Munich, the Hitler-Stalin Pact, the 1948 Czech Coup, the Korean War, and the Hungarian Revolution are all ancient history to the generations that have come of age during the 1960's. Adults often find it hard to understand the extent to which relatively recent events simply are not salient to a given group of youth if they occurred before the youths reached political and intellectual consciousness.

A major consideration of the consequences of political events on a society requires the specification of the role of political generations. Many analysts of politics and cultural styles have stressed the extent to which the concept of the generation must be used as an independent analytical one. The thesis underlying this type of analysis indicates that people tend to form a defined frame of reference in late adolescence or early youth within which they fit subsequent experiences. Thus, the first formative political experiences are most important.

A number of scholars have attempted to trace through the participation of different generations in the politics of various nations. They have pointed to the way that people who came of age during the Great Depression have continued to react to issues of unemployment, economic security, and the like. The Depression youth are much more likely to be concerned about the welfare state than earlier and subsequent generations. Similarly, as noted earlier, many who were concerned in their youth with foreign-policy issues stemming from Fascist or Communist expansionism have continued to react along such lines to more recent issues. It is easy to visualize how such processes operate. A small increase in the current unemployment rate will shock someone who has experienced the Depression, while it might not even be noticed by someone who has not. The Soviet Union's military action in Czechoslovakia will concern those who remember the Czech Coup or the Hungarian Revolution as a major experience of their political youth much more than those who did not. A generation may also be somewhat more conservative or leftist than preceding or later ones because of the climate of politics when it first came to political consciousness. Presumably the generation who came to consciousness in the United States during the 1950's is more conservative than subsequent ones. The events that surround the entry of a generation into politics may continue to have their impact on national life for many decades after these events are forgotten as topics of political discussion.

In foreign-policy terms, the United States apparently created an isolationist generation out of the events of World War I and the immediate years thereafter. This generation as it grew older, remembering the way it had been "fooled" in World War I, resisted steps toward intervention during the 1930's. Conversely, however, the young people of the latter 1930's and early 1940's learned that isolationism and neutralism had led to the rise of Fascism and World War II. They presumably have shown up as a much more interventionist group.

To a considerable extent, the contemporary political leaders of the United States and many other Western countries are people who came to political consciousness at a time when foreign-policy issues involving the containment of Fascism or Communism were most salient. This generation of political leaders and their supporters did not need much convincing to react militantly to Communist threats. In this connection, it may be important to point out that the U.S. government did not feel it necessary to justify the decisions concerning Vietnam taken by Presidents Eisenhower, Kennedy, and Johnson, by exposing the domestic inequities of North Vietnam regime, its use of force against its own people, or of the terror tactics of the Viet-Cong.

This policy was dictated, in part, by the desire of each Administration to keep the U.S. role in Vietnam as limited as necessary to prevent a Communist takeover in the south, to restrain the pressure of the "hawks" who sought to escalate the war, and thus to reduce the risk of its widening far beyond the borders of Vietnam. But the reluctance to undertake any significant propaganda campaign in support of the war also reflected in some part the feeling of those older men in charge of our information policy that there was no need for elaborate justifications of efforts to prevent a Communist takeover of another country. All Americans, they thought, recognized that Communism is an evil social system, and hence they could be expected to back this latest episode in the struggle to contain it.

The internal conflict that developed in the U.S. over the war illustrates the phenomenon of the generation gap as well as any event that can be presented. For the new generations of college students, the past evils of Stalinism have little relevance to the immediate present. European Communism can no longer be identified with Stalinist oppression, with the slaughter of the innocents, or with monolithic absolutist power.

Thus, different generations have reacted to a different sense of the nature of and the political potential of Communism. Though those who have dictated American policy in the past decade have been aware of the changes in the Communist system as much as the younger people, there can be little doubt that the variations in the reactions of the generations reflect the fact that the older know from personal experience the potential for evil in Communism, while the younger ones only know it as words in the history books. It is perhaps inevitable that they should react quite differently to arguments concerning the need to resist a Communist movement in another country.

The same situation, of course, exists in other countries. It is perhaps most strikingly illustrated in Berlin where, until the Berlin Wall, there was considerable support for strong anti-Communist policies among all groups in the city, including the students. The Free University of Berlin, in fact, was founded by refugees from Communism. But the Berlin Wall was more successful than those who planned it could have expected. They built it in order to prevent people from leaving East Germany. But by so doing, they destroyed the past relationship to, and function of, West Berlin for East Germany. West Berliners, including students, no longer talk to people who have fled Communism. For the Berlin youth, Communism exists in a society with which they have little contact, while they see many things wrong with the society in which they live. And the student movement of West Berlin, once primarily concerned with the East, is now mainly interested in changing the society of West Berlin and West Germany.

Recognition that there are generational differences in outlook is not simply relevant to an analysis of any given contemporary scene. The most important thing about generations is that they persist. Thus, any effort to evaluate the consequences of the present political revival of student militancy must include a consideration of its potential impact on future events. Some years ago, a privately sponsored Japanese opinion study of the attitudes and political beliefs of younger members of the Japanese business executive stratum, those under forty, revealed that the majority of such executives voted for the Japanese Socialist Party — that is, the pro-Marxist, relatively radical party. Seemingly, the majority of Japanese youth who go to university, particularly in the better ones, become supporters of some brand of Marxism or socialism. This remains true even after most of them go to work for bureaucratic industry or government, climbing ladders that can take them fairly high in the Japanese elite.

The Japanese data, however, indicate that although most Japanese young radicals become more moderate in their opinions and their actions as they get older, many of those who become business executives remain on the Left politically, adhering to various doctrines of socialism and, in the Japanese context, anti-Americanism. Assuming that this study is accurate, it suggests that Japan may be moving into a period in which it will have an elite which does not believe in the system it operates. This more radical elite may not do anything to change the system, but its beliefs may affect the way it reacts to radical pressure from other groups, as well as its view of new issues as they occur.

In a history of Czarist Russia, written in 1910, Bernard Pares devoted about two hundred pages to the political activities of the intellectuals and students of the Czarist empire. He discussed in great detail the radical and anti-regime position of the students. Pares then stated, however, that these activities did not mean much, since the students went to work for the bureaucracy or entered other sections of the elite and thus became supporters of the system after they were graduated. There is little data on what former Russian radical students did in later years, but clearly there is a good possibility that there is some relationship between the radicalism of the Russian students and the weakness of the elite in 1917.

Currently in the United States, a more radicalized student generation is gradually moving into the lower and sometimes even the upper rungs of important parts of the society. For example, in the university, in journalism, in other aspects of the communications industry, and in various government agencies, observers have noted that the youthful members of the staffs tend to be much more radical in their reaction to the functions of the organization and of society at large than are the older hands. As in Japan, it is probable that many of them retain important parts of the opinions which they formed as students. Despite the coercive pressures on them to conform which come from participation in the bureaucracy, many aspects of their environment will continue to support their youthful opinions. It is likely, therefore, that the current generation of radical university students will continue to affect the larger body politic in many countries ten, twenty, or even thirty years from now. Their elites will contain a much larger proportion of liberals or leftists than they now do. They will also include many whose image of the United States and its role in the world will be quite different from that of earlier generations.

As another illustration of this process, it may be noted again that some analysts of the contemporary American university scene have argued that one of the factors contributing to increased student activism today is the presence on university faculties of many whose political attitudes were formed during the New Deal experience, the Depression, or the struggle against Fascism. University faculties, as indicated earlier, are much more liberal or even leftist than they ever have been in the past. It is noticeable that a visibly significant number of senior faculty members of American universities today are individuals who took part in student movements or liberal and radical politics during the thirties and early forties. Research studies suggest that the current generation of student activists are literally the children of people who were active in radical movements in the earlier period. Kenneth Keniston has spoken of "the Red diaper babies." In a sense, these studies indicate that generations sometimes may even appear twice, first in their own right and then through their influence over their children who are given a set of ideals that they try to activate, ideals that stem back to the conditions of their parents' formative political years.

This discussion of the impact of the early political experience of youth on their subsequent behavior as adults is not designed to challenge the assumption that people adjust their beliefs as they mature, get involved in complex experiences, and take on assorted responsibilities. Clearly the idea that youth adhere to an ethic of absolute ends, while older generations adhere to the ethic of responsibility, would appear to be valid. The conflict of the generations is not simply or even primarily a conflict among generations that have had different formative experiences; it is also a conflict between the young and the older. Nevertheless, one must recognize the existence of specific generations that have different long-term impacts. The concept of the generation, therefore, is valuable not only for historians seeking to explain what happened, but for anyone seeking to predict what will happen.

No society should find it remarkable that a segment of its student population should be involved in activist student politics that is directed militantly against the *status quo*. It can be strongly argued, as C. Wright Mills did, that students are the one group who will continue to supply recruits for such causes, even when no other stratum is available. A completely inactive student body is a much more curious phenomenon historically than one which is involved to some degree in activism. Any efforts to analyze the future of politics, whether on the domestic or international scene, will ignore the students at the peril of being in error.

NOTES ON CONTRIBUTORS

ERIK ALLARDT, born in 1925, is professor of sociology at the University of Helsinki. He is the author of *Social struktur och politisk aktivitet* (Social Structure and Political Activity; 1956), *Drinking Norms and Drinking Habits* (1957), and *Sociologi,* a textbook in Finnish and Swedish.

EDITH H. ALTBACH, born in 1941, has been research assistant with the Comparative Universities Project at the Center for International Affairs of Harvard University.

PHILIP G. ALTBACH, born in 1941, is associate professor of Educational Policy Studies and Indian Studies at the University of Wisconsin. He is the author of *Student Politics in Bombay* (1968) and a *Select Bibliography on Students, Politics, and Higher Education* (1967); Mr. Altbach also edited *Turmoil and Transition: Higher Education and Student Politics in India* (1968).

RICHARD CORNELL, born in 1927, is associate professor of political science at York University, Toronto, Ontario. He is the author of *Youth and Communism: An Historical Analysis of International Communist Youth Movements* (1965).

GARY R. FIELD, born in 1934, is associate professor of political science at San Fernando Valley State College.

A. BELDEN FIELDS, born in 1937, is assistant professor in the Department of Political Science at the University of Illinois.

DAVID J. FINLAY, born in 1934, is a post-doctoral fellow at the Western Behavioral Sciences Institute and assistant professor at the University of Oregon. He is the co-author of *Enemies of Politics* (1967).

MYRON GLAZER, born in 1934, is associate professor of sociology and anthropology at Smith College. He is the co-author of *Student Politics in Chile* and *The Research Process,* both of which will be published in early 1970.

A. H. HALSEY, born in 1923, is head of the Department of Social and Administrative Studies at the University of Oxford and a Professional

Fellow of Nuffield College, Oxford. He is the editor of *Education, Economy, and Society* (1961) and author of *Power in Cooperatives* (1965) and *The British Academics* (forthcoming).

ARLIE R. HOCHSCHILD, born in 1940, is acting instructor in the Department of Sociology and a postgraduate research analyst in the Department of Education at the University of California, Berkeley.

JOHN ISRAEL, born in 1935, is associate professor of history at the University of Virginia. He is the author of *Student Nationalism in China, 1927–37* (1966).

SEYMOUR MARTIN LIPSET, born in 1922, is professor of government and social relations at Harvard University. He is the author of *Revolution and Counter-Revolution* (1968), *The First New Nation: The United States in Historical and Comparative Perspective* (1963), *Political Man: The Social Bases of Power* (1960), and *Agrarian Socialism* (1950). He is the editor of *Students and Politics* (1967).

STEPHEN MARKS, born in 1945, is a postgraduate fellow at New College, Oxford University. Mr. Marks was formerly on the executive committee of the National Association of Labour Student Organizations.

GUIDO MARTINOTTI, born in 1938, is professor of sociology in the Faculty of Architecture at the University of Milan. He is the author of *Gli Studenti Universitari* (Padua, 1969) and vice-secretary of the International Sociological Association.

CLEMENT H. MOORE, born in 1937, is assistant professor of political science at the University of California, Berkeley. He is the author of *Tunisia Since Independence: The Dynamics of One-Party Government* (1965), and co-author of *Tunisia: The Politics of Modernization* (1964).

RICHARD E. PETERSON, born in 1931, is a research psychologist and acting chairman of the Higher Education Research Group in the Developmental Research Division of the Educational Testing Service. He is the author of *The Scope of Organized Student Protest* (1966).

FRANK A. PINNER, born in 1914, is professor of political science at Michigan State University. He is the senior author of *Old Age and Political Behavior* (1959). Mr. Pinner is also the author of "The Crisis of the State Universities: Analysis and Remedies," in *The American College* (1962), ed. Nevitt Sanford; and "Parental Overprotection and Political Distrust," *The Annals of the American Academy of Political Science*, Vol. 361 (Sept., 1965).

LESLIE L. ROOS, JR., born in 1940, is a Ford Foundation Faculty Research Fellow on the faculty of Northwestern University as assistant professor of political science.

NORALOU P. ROOS, born in 1942, is assistant professor of organizational behavior in the School of Management at Northwestern.

Notes on Contributors

ROBERT E. SCOTT, born in 1923, is professor of political science at the University of Illinois. He is the author of *Mexican Government in Transition* (1959).

EDWARD SHILS, born in 1911, is professor of sociology and social thought at the University of Chicago and Fellow of King's College, Cambridge University. His books include *The Present State of American Sociology* (1948) and *The Intellectual Between Tradition and Modernity: the Indian Situation* (1961). Mr. Shils is also editor of *Minerva*, a quarterly review of the relations of science, learning, and policy.

MICHIYA SHIMBORI, born in 1921, is associate professor of sociology of education and Vice-Dean of Students at Hiroshima University. He is the author of *Nihon no Daigaku-Kyoju Shijo* (Academic Marketplace in Japan; 1965), *Gakureki* (School Career; 1966), and *Durkheim Kenkyu* (Study of Emile Durkheim; 1966).

JOSEF SILVERSTEIN, born in 1922, is professor of political science at Rutgers University. He is the editor of *Southeast Asia During World War II* (1966). Mr. Silverstein was Visiting Fulbright Lecturer in the Department of History at the University of Malaya in 1968–69.

RICHARD F. TOMASSON, born in 1928, is associate professor and chairman of the Department of Sociology at the University of New Mexico. He is the author of *Swedish Society* (forthcoming). His translation of and introduction to *The Swedish Social Democrats*, by Herbert Tingsten, is in press.

BIBLIOGRAPHY

I. GENERAL

Abernethy, David, and Coombe, Trevor. "Education and Politics in Developing Countries," *Harvard Educational Review*, 35 (Summer, 1965), 287–302.

Altbach, Philip G. *Students, Politics, and Higher Education: A Select Bibliography.* Cambridge, Mass.: Harvard University Center for International Affairs, 1967.

Coleman, James S. *Education and Political Development.* Princeton: Princeton University Press, 1965.

Cornell, Richard. *Youth and Communism.* New York: Walker, 1965.

Douglass, R. Bruce (ed.). *Reflections on Protest.* Richmond: John Knox Press, 1967.

Eisenstadt, Shmuel. *From Generation to Generation.* Glencoe: Free Press, 1956.

Emmerson, Donald (ed.). *Students and Politics in Developing Countries.* New York: Praeger, 1968.

Erikson, Erik H. (ed.). *The Challenge of Youth.* Garden City: Doubleday, 1965.

Friedmann, John. "Intellectuals in Developing Societies," *Kyklos*, 13 (1960), 513–544.

Hajda, Jan. "Alienation and Integration of Student Intellectuals," *American Sociological Review*, 26 (May, 1961), 758–777.

Lipset, S. M. (ed.). *Student Politics.* New York: Basic Books, 1967.

Matza, David. "Position and Behavior Patterns of Youth." In Robert E. L. Faris (ed.). *Handbook of Modern Sociology.* Chicago: Rand McNally, 1964, 191–215.

McIntyre, William. "Student Movements," *Editorial Research Reports*, 2 (1957), 913–929.

Musgrove, F. *Youth and the Social Order.* London: Routledge & Kegan Paul, 1964.

Shah, A. B. (ed.). *Education, Scientific Policy, and Developing Countries.* Bombay: Manaktalas, 1967.

Shils, Edward. "The Intellectuals in the Political Development of the New States," *World Politics*, 12 (April, 1960), 329–368.

II. INTERNATIONAL STUDENT AFFAIRS

Altbach, Philip G. "The International Student Movement: An Analysis," *Journal of Contemporary History*, forthcoming.

Clews, John. "Communism's 'Fourth Lever': The Youth and Student Fronts," *Problems of Communism*, 5 (November-December, 1956), 39–45.

Institute for International Youth Affairs. *The Youth Fronts, 1946–1966.* New York: Institute for International Youth Affairs, 1966.

"The International Youth Movement," *Youth and Freedom*, 5 (1962), 1–8.

Schleimann, Jorgen. "The Organization Man: The Life and Work of Willi Münzenberg," *Survey*, 55 (April, 1965), 64–91.

Stern, Sol. "CIA: NSA: A Short Account of International Student Politics and the Cold War," *Ramparts*, 5 (March, 1967), 29–39.

Van Maanen, Gert. *The International Student Movement.* The Hague: Interdoc, 1966.

III. AFRICA

Craig, A. J. M. "Egyptian Students," *Middle East Journal*, 7 (Summer, 1953), 293–299.

Curle, Adam. "Nationalism and Higher Education in Ghana," *Universities Quarterly*, 16 (June, 1962), 229–242.

DuBois, Victor. *The Student-Government Conflict in the Ivory Coast.* New York: American Universities Field Staff, 1965.

Emmerson, Donald. "African Student Organizations," *Africa Report*, 10 (May, 1965), 6–22.

Glickman, Julius (ed.). *African Student Affairs.* Washington, D.C.: U.S. National Student Association, 1965.

Goldthorpe, J. E. *An African Elite: Makerere College Students, 1922–1960.* Nairobi: Oxford University Press, 1965.

Hanna, William John. "Students." In James S. Coleman and Carl G. Rosberg, Jr. (eds.) *Political Parties and National Integration in Tropical Africa.* Berkeley: University of California Press, 1964, 413–443.

Marvick, Dwaine. "African University Students: A Presumptive Elite." In James S. Coleman (ed.), *Education and Political Development.* Princeton: Princeton University Press, 1965, 463–498.

Moore, Clement. "The Case of the Students," *Tunisia Since Independence.* Berkeley: University of California Press, 1965, 175–181.

Smythe, Hugh, and Smythe, Mabel. *The New Nigerian Elite.* Stanford: Stanford University Press, 1960.

IV. ASIA

Altbach, Philip G. "Japanese Students and Japanese Politics," *Comparative Education Review*, 7 (October, 1963), 181–188.

Altbach, Philip G. *Student Politics in Bombay.* Bombay and New York: Asia Publishing House, 1968.

Altbach, Philip G. (ed.). *Turmoil and Transition: Higher Education and Student Politics in India.* New York: Basic Books, 1969.

Battistini, L. H. *Postwar Student Struggle in Japan.* Tokyo: Tuttle, 1956.

Chow Tse-Tung. *The May Fourth Movement.* Cambridge, Mass.: Harvard University Press, 1960.

Cormack, Margaret. *She Who Rides a Peacock: Indian Students and Social Change.* Bombay: Asia Publishing House, 1961.

Doolin, Dennis J. *Communist China: The Politics of Student Opposition.* Stanford: Hoover Institution on War, Revolution, and Peace, 1964.

Douglas, William A. "Korean Students and Politics," *Asian Survey,* 3 (December, 1963), 584–595.

Fischer, Joseph. "The University Student in South and Southeast Asia," *Minerva,* 2 (Autumn, 1963), 39–53.

Goldman, Rene. "Peking University Today," *China Quarterly,* No. 7 (July-September, 1961), 101–111.

Israel, John. *Student Nationalism in China, 1927–1937.* Stanford: Stanford University Press, 1966.

Israel, John. "Kuomintang Policy and Student Politics, 1927–1937." In Albert Feuerwerker, Rhoads Murphy, and Mary C. Wright (eds.). *Approaches to Modern Chinese History.* Berkeley: University of California Press, 1967.

Koyama Kenichi. "The Zengakuren," *New Politics,* 1 (November, 1962), 124–135.

Lyman, Princeton M. "Students and Politics in Indonesia and Korea," *Pacific Affairs,* 38 (Fall, Winter, 1965–66), 582–593.

Marr, David. "Political Attitudes and Activities of Young Urban Intellectuals in South Vietnam," *Asian Survey,* 6 (May, 1966), 249–263.

Pieris, Ralph. "Universities, Politics, and Public Opinion in Ceylon," *Minerva,* 2 (Summer, 1964), 435–454.

Scalapino, Robert. "Prelude to Marxism: The Chinese Student Movement in Japan." In Albert Feuerwerker, Rhoads Murphy, and Mary Wright (eds.). *Approaches to Modern Chinese History.* Berkeley: University of California Press, 1967.

Shils, Edward. *The Intellectual Between Tradition and Modernity: The Indian Situation.* The Hague: Mouton, 1961.

Shimbori, Michiya. "Comparison Between Pre- and Post-War Student Movements in Japan," *Sociology of Education,* 37 (Fall, 1963), 60–70.

Shimbori, Michiya. "Zengakuren: A Japanese Case Study of a Student Political Movement," *Sociology of Education,* 37 (Spring, 1964), 229–253.

Silcock, T. H. *Southeast Asian University.* Durham: Duke University Press, 1964.

Silverstein, Josef, and Wohl, Julian. "University Students and Politics in Burma," *Pacific Affairs,* 37 (Spring, 1964), 50–65.

Spector, S. "Students and Politics in Singapore," *Far East Survey,* 25 (May, 1956), 65–73.

Useem, John, and Useem, Ruth. *The Western Educated Man in India.* New York: Dryden Press, 1955.

Wang, Y. C. *Chinese Intellectuals and the West.* Chapel Hill: University of North Carolina Press, 1966.

Bibliography

Wohl, Julian, and Silverstein. Josef. "The Burmese University Student: An Approach to Personality and Subculture," *Public Opinion Quarterly*, 30 (Summer, 1966), 237–248.

Wurfel, David. "The Violent and the Voiceless in Japanese Politics," *Contemporary Japan*, 26 (November, 1960), 663–694.

V. EUROPE

Bair, Jake. "The Spanish Student Movement," *Studies on the Left*, 5 (Summer, 1965), 3–20.

Bourdieu, Pierre, and Passeron, Jean-Claude. *Les héritiers: les étudiants, et la culture*. Paris: Éditions de Minuit, 1965.

Brewster, Ben, and Cockburn, Alexander. "Revolt at the LSE," *New Left Review*, 43 (May-June, 1967), 11–26.

Burg, David. "Observations on Soviet University Students," *Daedalus*, 89 (Summer, 1960), 520–540.

Fournière, Michel De La, and Borella, François. *Le Syndicalisme étudiant*. Paris: Éditions de Seuil, 1957.

Galvin, Enrique Tierno. "Student Opposition in Spain," *Government and Opposition*, 1 (May-August, 1966), 467–486.

Gaudez, Pierre. *Les étudiants*. Paris: Éditions Julliard, 1961.

Griewank, Karl. *Deutsche Studenten und Universitäten in der Revolution von 1848*. Weimar: Herman Bohlaus Nachfolger, 1949.

Habermas, J., *et al*. *Student und Politik: Eine soziologische Untersuchung zum politischen Bewusstsein Frankfurter Studenten*. Berlin: Hermann Luchterhand Verlag, 1961.

Hammer, Darrell. "Among Students in Moscow: An Outsider's Report," *Problems of Communism*, 13 (July-August, 1964), 11–18.

Kassof, Allan. *The Soviet Youth Program*. Cambridge, Mass.: Harvard University Press, 1965.

Kiss, Gabor. *Die gesellschaftpolitische Rolle der Studentbewegung in vorrevolutionaren Russland*. Munich: Georg Heller Verlag, 1963.

Kravetz, Marc. "Naissance d'un syndicalisme étudiant," *Les Temps Modernes*, No. 213 (February, 1964), 1447–1475.

Laqueur, Walter. *Young Germany*. New York: Basic Books, 1962.

Nitsch, Wolfgang, *et al*. *Hochschule in der Demokratie*. Berlin: Luchterhand, 1965.

Nowak, Stefan. "Factors Determining Egalitarianism of Warsaw Students," *American Sociological Review*, 25 (April, 1960), 219–231.

Nowak, Stefan. "Social Attitudes of Warsaw Students," *Polish Sociological Bulletin*, 1/2 (January-June, 1962), 91–103.

Pinner, Frank A. "Student Trade Unionism in France, Belgium, and Holland," *Sociology of Education*, 37 (Spring, 1964), 1–23.

Pross, Harry. *Jugend Eros Politik*. Bern: Scherz Verlag, 1964.

Schelsky, Helmut. *Die skeptische Generation*. Düsseldorf: Eugen Diedrichs Verlag, 1957.

Thoenes, Piet. "The Provos of Holland," *Nation*, 204 (April 17, 1967), pp. 494–497.

VI. Latin America

Albornoz, Orlando (ed.), *Estudiantes y Política en las Americas.* Caracas: *Publicaciones del Instituto Societas,* 1968.
Albornoz, Orlando. "Student Opposition in Latin America," *Government and Opposition,* 2 (October, 1966-January, 1967).
Bakke, E. Wight. "Students on the March: The Cases of Mexico and Colombia," *Sociology of Education,* 37, Spring (1964).
Bonilla, Frank, and Glazer, Myron. *Student Politics in Chile.* New York: Basic Books, 1969.
Federacion Universitaria de Buenos Aires. *La Reforma Universitaria, 1918-1958.* Buenos Aires: 1959.
International Student Conference. *University Reform in Latin America.* Leiden: International Student Conference Research and Information Commission, 1960.
Lipset, S. M., and Solari, Aldo (eds.). *Elites in Latin America.* New York: Oxford University Press, 1967.
Mazo, Gabriel Del. *Participacion de los estudiantes en el gobierno de las universidades.* La Plata: Edicion del Central, Estudiants de Derecho, 1942.
Osvaldo Inglese, Juan, Yegros, Doria, and Carlos L. *Universidad y estudiantes.* Buenos Aires: Ediciones Libera, 1965.
Rotblat, Miguel. "The Latin American Student Movement," *New University Thought,* 1 (Summer, 1961), 29-36.
Silvert, Kalman. "The University Student." In John Johnson (ed.). *Continuity and Change in Latin America.* Palo Alto: Stanford University Press, 1964, 206-226.
Spencer, David (ed.). *Student Politics in Latin America.* Philadelphia: U.S. National Student Association, 1965.
Walter, Richard. *Student Politics in Argentina.* New York: Basic Books, 1968.

VII. United States

Altbach, Philip G. *Students, Politics, and Higher Education in the United States: A Bibliography.* Cambridge, Mass.: Harvard Center for International Affairs, 1968.
Cohen, Mitchell, and Hale, Dennis (eds.). *The New Student Left: An Anthology.* Boston: Beacon Press, 1967.
Draper, Hal. *Berkeley: The New Student Revolt.* New York: Grove Press, 1965.
Draper, Hal. "The Student Movement of the Thirties: A Political History." In Rita Somon (ed.). *As We Saw the Thirties.* Urbana, Ill.: University of Illinois Press, 1967, 151-189.
Glazer, Nathan. "Student Politics in A Democratic Society," *American Scholar,* 36 (Spring, 1967), 202-217.
Horowitz, David. *Student: The Political Activities of Berkeley Students.* New York: Ballantine, 1962.

Howe, Irving. "New Styles in Leftism," *Dissent*, 12 (Summer, 1965), 295–323.

Jacobs, Paul, and Landau, Saul (eds.). *The New Radicals*. New York: Vintage, 1966.

Katz, Joseph (ed.). *No Time for Youth*. San Francisco: Jossey-Bass, 1968.

Keniston, Kenneth. *The Young Radicals: Notes on Committed Youth*. New York: Harcourt, Brace, 1968.

Lipset, S. M. "Student Opposition in the United States," *Government and Opposition*, 1 (April, 1966), 351–374.

Lipset, S. M., and Wolin, S. S. (eds.). *The Berkeley Student Revolt*. Garden City: Anchor Books, 1965.

Lipset, S. M., and Altbach, Philip G. "Student Politics and Higher Education in the United States." In S. M. Lipset (ed.). *Student Politics*. New York: Basic Books, 1967, 199–252.

Miller, Michael, and Gilmore, Susan (eds.). *Revolution at Berkeley*. New York: Dell, 1965.

Newfield, Jack. *A Prophetic Minority*. New York: Ballantine, 1967.

O'Brien, James. "The New Left's Early Years," *Radical America*, 2 (May-June, 1968), 1–25.

Peterson, Richard E. *The Scope of Organized Student Protest in 1964–5*. Princeton: Educational Testing Service, 1966.

Sampson, Edward E. (ed.). "Stirrings out of Apathy: Student Activism and the Decade of Protest," *Journal of Social Issues*, 23 (July, 1967), 1–139.

Schiff, Lawrence. "The Obedient Rebels: A Study of College Conversions to Conservatism," *Journal of Social Issues*, 20 (October, 1964), 74–96.

Wechsler, James. *Revolt on the Campus*. New York: Colvici, Friede, 1935.

Zinn, Howard. *SNCC: The New Abolitionists*. Boston: Beacon Press, 1964.

INDEX